T0134819

Integrated Series in Information Systems

Series Editors
Ramesh Sharda
Oklahoma State University, Stillwater, OK, USA

Stefan Voß
University of Hamburg, Hamburg, Germany

Integrated Series in Information Systems (IS2) aims to publish scholarly work in a book series. The series will strive to publish work in the technical as well as the organizational side of the field. This series will contain three sub-series including: monographs, handbooks, and edited volumes. The Expository and Research Monographs as well as the Integrative Handbooks sections will focus on the state-of-the-art of application domains and/or reference disciplines, as related to information systems. In a parallel effort – recognizing that some of the cutting edge research in IS will be coming from doctoral research – selected dissertations may also be published in the monograph section of the series. The Annals of Information Systems will be a journal of leading-edge research topics in IS.

Proposals are invited for a book to be published under one of the sub series. Publish your dissertation or write a monograph or an integrative handbook. Edit a book in your research area. If you are organizing a conference, develop a refereed collection of chapters based on the conference. This series will focus on high quality scholarly publications, and you will benefit from Springer's international network for promotion of your authored/edited book.

If you are interested in developing a book, please contact the series editors at the email addresses below or visit the Springer website at http://www.springer.com/west/home/authors for more information.

Stefan Voß, Universität Hamburg, Chair, Institut für Wirtschaftsinformatik, Germany, email: stefan.voss@uni-hamburg.de;

Ramesh Sharda, Conoco Chair and Regents Professor of Management Science and Information Systems, Oklahoma State University, USA, email: sharda@okstate.edu

More information about this series at http://www.springer.com/series/6157

Jason Papathanasiou • Pascale Zaraté
Jorge Freire de Sousa
Editors

EURO Working Group on DSS

A Tour of the DSS Developments
Over the Last 30 Years

 Springer

Editors
Jason Papathanasiou
Department of Business Administration
University of Macedonia
Thessaloniki, Greece

Pascale Zaraté 🆔
University Toulouse 1 Capitole - IRIT
Toulouse University
Toulouse, France

Jorge Freire de Sousa
Faculty of Engineering
University of Porto
Porto, Portugal

ISSN 1571-0270   ISSN 2197-7968   (electronic)
Integrated Series in Information Systems
ISBN 978-3-030-70379-0   ISBN 978-3-030-70377-6   (eBook)
https://doi.org/10.1007/978-3-030-70377-6

This Springer imprint is published by the registered company Springer Nature Switzerland AG
The registered company address is: Gewerbestrasse 11, 6330 Cham, Switzerland

Preface

The EWG-DSS (EURO Working Group on Decision Support Systems, https://ewgdss.wordpress.com/) is one of the most active EURO (www.euro-online.org) official working groups. It has a history that spans more than 30 years since the group commemorated the 30th anniversary of the EmC-ICDSST 2019 event hosted at the UMA University of Madeira from May 27th to May 29th, 2019 in Madeira Island, Portugal. Indeed, the event celebrated the three decades of a very energetic and fruitful working group created as a direct product of the ESI VI—EURO Summer Institute on DSS, in the same Madeira Island in the distant May of 1989.

The group was founded during that memorable EURO Summer Institute on DSS organized by Prof. Jean-Pierre Brans and Prof. José Paixão, among others. A diverse group of 24 young and eager researchers coming from 16 different nationalities participated; most of them are still present in the field today. They are lively and prolific members of the group (many of them being authors in this volume), and they are enthusiastically working on areas related to OR and, more specifically, Decision Support Systems.

Since then, the group has grown to more than 300 members from different nationalities and backgrounds and has organized many events such as workshops, seminars, and conferences across Europe. The group is governed and promoted by a coordination board and focuses on establishing a platform for encouraging state-of-the-art high-quality research and collaboration work within the international DSS community; that mainly means networking activities, journal publications, and research projects. The development of innovative models and tools and sharing of ideas was and still is one of the main objectives of the group.

This volume includes the insights and experiences of well-known researchers in the DSS field. We are delighted by the fact that some of them (as well as two of the editors of this volume) are from the original group of young researchers that created the EWG-DSS. Their experiences and insights over the last 30 years offer a deep understanding of the discipline and its future trends; thus, the chapters provide a sophisticated and in-detail overview of the achievements and sometimes of the failures during this period. The editors are grateful to the authors for the collaboration and effort they have invested in this book. They are also grateful to the reviewers and the publisher for sharing our vision and realizing this endeavor into a wonderful book.

We are looking forward to the next 30 years!

Thessaloniki, Greece	Jason Papathanasiou
Toulouse, France	Pascale Zarate
Porto, Portugal	Jorge Freire de Sousa

Contents

Decision Support Systems: Historical Innovations and Modern Technology Challenges 1
Christer Carlsson and Pirkko Walden

Thirty Years of Decision Support: A Bibliometric View 15
Peter B. Keenan

Two Grand Challenges for DSS Evolution 33
David Paradice

30 Years of the EWG-DSS Through the Lens of the Collab-Net Project 51
Isabelle Linden, Jean Gomes Turet, Fatima Dargam, Shaofeng Liu, Rita A. Ribeiro, Pascale Zaraté, and Ana Paula Cabral Seixas Costa

Decision Support in the Era of Social Media and User-Generated Content 79
Kathrin Kirchner, Marek Opuszko, and Sven Gehrke

The Evolution of Decision Support Systems for Agriculture: A Bibliometric Network Approach 97
Dimitris Kremmydas, Alvertos Konstantinis, and Stelios Rozakis

30 Years Business Intelligence: From Data Analytics to Big Data 115
Isabelle Linden

A Systematic Literature Review of Knowledge Mobilisation and Its Support for Business Decisions Over Two Decades (1999–2019) 129
Shaofeng Liu, Ali Ibraheem Alkhuraiji, and Abdullah Alkraiji

Social Responsibility of Algorithms: An Overview 153
Alexis Tsoukias

Negotiation Support: Trends and Problems 167
Rudolf Vetschera

**From Data and Models to Decision Support Systems: Lessons
and Advice for the Future** 191
Marko Bohanec

**DSS for Multicriteria Preference Modeling with Partial
Information and Its Modulation with Behavioral Studies** 213
Adiel Teixeira de Almeida, Eduarda Asfora Frej, and Lucia Reis Peixoto
Roselli

**From Radical Movement to Organizational Mainstream:
A Behavioral Economics Perspective on DSS History** 239
David Arnott and Shijia Gao

The History and Future of PROMETHEE 259
Bertrand Mareschal and Georgios Tsaples

On the Impact of Big Data Analytics in Decision-Making Processes 273
Fatima Dargam, Shaofeng Liu, and Rita A. Ribeiro

The Evolution of DSS in the Pig Industry and Future Perspectives 299
Lluís M. Plà-Aragonès

**Game-Based Learning and Decision-Making for Urban
Sustainability: A Case of System Dynamics Simulations** 325
Stefano Armenia, Federico Barnabè, and Alessandro Pompei

**Advanced Rule-Based Approaches in Customer Satisfaction
Analysis: Recent Development and Future Prospects of fsQCA** 345
Evangelia Krassadaki, Evangelos Grigoroudis, and Constantin Zopounidis

**Use of Multicriteria Analysis for Enchancing Sustainable Urban
Mobility Planning and Decision-Making** 379
Maria Morfoulaki and Jason Papathanasiou

Index 399

Decision Support Systems: Historical Innovations and Modern Technology Challenges

Christer Carlsson and Pirkko Walden

Abstract Managerial tasks carry latent needs for *support to do a better job*; classical DSS had at its core the approach *to support, not replace*. We worked out a DSS called *Woodstrat* for strategic planning and management and could verify—in full-scale implementation—the DSS characteristics Sprague worked out and most of the DSS benefits Keen had found. We also found that a relevant and useful DSS could help "self-confident professionals" to back away from predictions on future demand and competition that could not find support in facts. The digital disruption of the 2010s brought big data and the need for decision-making in almost real time. It also introduced analytics and faster, more effective algorithms developed in computational intelligence. The road map for DSS for the 2020s points to digital coaching systems that adapt to the cognitive levels of the users.

Keywords Classical DSS · Modern DSS · Computational intelligence

1 Introduction

The ICDSST 2019 offered a possibility to look at 40 years of DSS history, the innovations that DSS introduced and the successes these innovations brought. There have also been expectations on successes and breakthroughs that did not happen, and DSS promoters were too enthusiastic in some cases in promising improvements in productivity and profitability. Nevertheless, the DSS brought some innovations that have stood the test of time and have returned—again and again—only changing shape to new forms as DSS technology has developed.

We have some history ourselves with DSS—the first IFPS-based DSS projects were started in Finland in 1985 and a research group that later formed the IAMSR was the driving force. The first DSS applications built on the original Fortran-based

C. Carlsson (✉) · P. Walden
Institute for Advanced Management Systems Research, Abo Akademi University, Turku, Finland
e-mail: christer.carlsson@abo.fi; pirkko.walden@abo.fi

© Springer Nature Switzerland AG 2021
J. Papathanasiou et al. (eds.), *EURO Working Group on DSS*, Integrated Series in Information Systems, https://doi.org/10.1007/978-3-030-70377-6_1

IFPS mainframe version and were challenging to design and build, to run as decision support tools and to get models, algorithms, and solutions close enough to real-world problem-solving for them to give valid and relevant support to the users (cf. [1–3]).

The first DSS conference was the DSS-81 in Atlanta, Georgia sponsored by Execucom Systems Corporation, the developer of the IFPS software system. Gerald R. Wagner, then President of Execucom, and Peter G. W. Keen initiated this conference and more or less defined the agenda for the development and use of DSS. Peter Keen had a keynote address—"Decision Support Systems—Lessons for the 80s"—and Ralph H. Sprague gave a tutorial on Decision Support Systems in which he defined all the key elements of a viable DSS. Several papers pointed out technology challenges that then triggered development efforts for successive versions of the IFPS (and competing software).

Most of the early authors note the Gorry and Scott Morton [4] paper ("A Framework for Management Information Systems") in Sloan Management Review in 1971 as the starting point for DSS. The paper builds on Scott Morton's doctoral thesis [5] at Harvard Business School in 1971 that outlined "management decision systems." The Sprague [6] paper ("Framework for the Development of Decision Support Systems") in MIS Quarterly in 1980 then summarized all the essential elements for the design, development, implementation, and use of decision support systems.

The keynote of Peter Keen and the tutorial of Ralph Sprague at DSS-81 summarize the key innovations that decided the emergence and the success of decision support systems. We need to note the context in the early 1980s: Data Processing (DP) dominated how managers and corporations viewed the use of computers for management. The focus was on cost-effectiveness and productivity, the systems were dominantly run on mainframe computers (then dominated by IBM), the dominating software were Cobol and Fortran, information systems were large, complex and inflexible, and investment costs were high. The agenda presented by the DSS pioneers did not in many cases get friendly responses; in some cases, reactions were outright hostile [7].

DSS builders focused on the users' priorities, they developed systems linked to key business activities and they viewed the quality of a system from the value it gives to the users rather than the level of (advanced) technology applied.

DSS reflects demand economics: service, fast delivery, ease of use, benefit focused more than cost, imprecision allowed for timely delivery, and user control.

Early case studies by Keen [8] showed a number of benefits identified by DSS users: (a) increase in the number of alternatives examined; (b) better understanding of the business; (c) fast response to unexpected situations; (d) ability to carry out ad hoc analysis; (e) new insights and learning; (f) improved communication; (g) improved management control; (h) cost savings; (i) better decisions; (j) more effective team work; (k) time savings; (l) making better use of data. These and similar benefits still appear in the literature, even if the underlying DSS technology has changed several times and the technology gets a different label than DSS [9, 10].

Managerial tasks are not routine and the latent needs they create are for "support to do a better job," which is an informal DSS credo.

The DSS architecture builds on mainly three components: (a) a dialogue manager/interface between the user and functional routines; (b) a data manager; (c) functional routines. This approach is a distinctive technology contribution of DSS.

The philosophical, attitudinal core of Decision Support is "support, not replace." It is impossible to support individuals if we do not know what they do, how they think, what doing a "better job" means to them, and what they need to have (cf. Keen [11], p. 190). In the 1970s and 1980s, the prevailing management science paradigm (cf. [12]) developed a "black box" approach to better decisions. In case human cognitive ability was not enough optimization algorithms took over (replaced, if we like) and offered the best possible solution. The algorithms were quite often beyond the knowledge and skills of the users who sometimes did not see why optimal solutions would be the best possible in any given problem situation. The DSS addressed this problem and promoted problem-solving that built on managers' intuitive understanding and experience of how to solve problems. The reasoning was simple—there is no need to "sell" solutions if managers (the problem owners) run the problem solving process with some support from computer-based technology.

Sprague [13] found it more useful to collect the "characteristics" of DSS than to try formal definitions or to distill some common understanding from actual use cases. He collected the following "characteristics" from several authors [13]: (a) DSS aim at the less well-structured, underspecified problems of upper level management; (b) DSS combine the use of models or analytic techniques with traditional data access and retrieval functions; (c) DSS focus on features which make them easy to use by non-computer people in an interactive mode, and (d) DSS emphasize flexibility and adaptability to accommodate changes in the environment and the decision-making approach of the user.

A distinctive feature of the early descriptions of DSS is that it should support all phases of decision-making. Sprague [6] connects this to Simon [14]: intelligence (environment search for decision needs), design (inventing, developing, and analyzing action alternatives) and choice (selecting a particular action from available alternatives).

A final distinguishing feature of DSS is the iterative design [13]. The typical four steps of an information systems development process—analysis, design, construction, and implementation—combine in a single step, which repeats iteratively. A typical process starts with the manager and the DSS builder agreeing on a small but significant sub-problem, designing support functions needed for decision-making and collecting experience of the functionality. Then another sub-problem is tackled with the same approach and when the decisions are sufficiently good, the two DSS modules are connected to allow the solutions to be integrated. Then the process continues over n sub-problems and m modules until we have a full DSS construct. The integration of sub-problem solutions tends to offer challenges [2].

The rest of the paper will address the key issues of DSS from two perspectives: experience gained from actual work with DSS to test the benefits and characteristics of DSS that Keen and Sprague outlined. Secondly, we will find out if the core ideas of DSS are still relevant with the technology and the decision-making contexts of the 2010s and 2020s. In section *two*, we will work through experience gained from a DSS developed and used for strategic planning and management. Section *three*, works out some key principles on decision-making. In section *four*, we will introduce analytics and the requirements of a digital economy. Section *five*, outlines some promising design principles for the DSS of the 2020s.

2   DSS for Strategic Management: The *Woodstrat*

We were working with 11 strategic business units (SBU) in a forest industry corporation to help them make their annual strategic planning process both more detailed and faster with computer support. The timeline was the mid-1990s and the support technology we used is now outdated. Even the strategic business units have merged, split, and reorganized several times. The corporation has adapted to changing customer needs and markets, to new and advanced production technology, and to new competitors. Nevertheless, we have found that the experience we gained offers a useful illustration of the DSS visions we collected from the early pioneers and the Transactions of DSS-81. It turned out that even with the rather rudimentary technology we applied (compared with the possibilities now offered) we could support strategic decisions that SBU managers made for their real-world operations.

At the time, there was some debate about strategic planning vs. strategic management [15] and the SBU-managers wanted to form a joint understanding with us. Thus, we agreed that *strategic management* is the process through which a company for a chosen planning period (a) defines its operational context, (b) outlines and decides upon its strategic goals and long-term objectives, (c) explores and decides upon its strengths, weaknesses, opportunities, and threats, (d) formulates its sustainable competitive advantages, and (e) develops a program of actions. The actions exploit its competitive advantages and ensure profitability, financial balance, adaptability to sudden changes, and a sound development of its capital structure. This lengthy joint understanding changed a number of times until the SBU-managers agreed that it makes sense to them and their own SBUs. We learned that this is a crucial step for the development of support technology—unless the users have sufficient understanding of the process we are going to support the possibilities for success will be rather slim.

As the conceptual framework was in place the decision support technology should provide a platform to deal with practical issues. Sufficient and reliable data on markets and competitors needs first to be stored in usable form for the strategic planning (previously corporate planners sent out macro-level reports that were mostly irrelevant for the SBUs). SBU-managers had experience of strengths and weaknesses of key competitors but needed tools to work out their insight and build data for strategic planning. It turned out that SBU-managers also had good perceptions of their own competitive advantages relative to their competitors and their own competitive positions in key market segments. Again, they needed tools to work out their insight as data for strategic planning. The final step, connecting competitive, and market positions with productivity and profitability for an SBU and then with a financial position and capital structure offered more challenges and the help from support tools was very welcome.

In the mid 1990s, the Mintzberg ideal for strategic management stressed the notion of an *emerging strategy*, which (simply stated) built on continuous dialogue among senior managers about present and future markets, competitors, and relative competitive positions that would decide strategic positions, return on assets and shareholder value [15]. The dialogue would converge to consensus on future directions through a viable conceptual framework that Mintzberg offered and that would guide the managers to find a joint understanding of the emerging strategy.

Mintzberg did not believe in computer support for senior managers and he quite emphatically stated that computers have no place in strategic management [16]. We need to remember that the context for Mintzberg's position built on the (mainframe) computer technology of the 1970s and that senior managers did not operate computers at that time. Nevertheless, his conclusions on the role of computers—still widely quoted in the 1990s—was wrong. Eden [17] demonstrated with his *Decision Explorer* that computer support is very useful for cognitive mapping that the software is manageable for (senior) managers and that computer support is instrumental for a Mintzberg dialogue on future directions.

In the work on *Woodstrat,* we got inspiration from Eden's systems constructs and then applied some new principles for *hyperknowledge* that Chang, Holsapple, and Whinston had introduced [18]. A decision takes form through navigation in a universe of concepts. Some of the concepts are descriptive, some are procedural, and some are context-dependent, abstract goal formulation, and motivation concepts that serve as instruments to forge a joint value and goal system. The hyperknowledge process will interlink the concepts to allow the impact of changes in one concept to be worked out in another concept (cf. Fig. 1—interlinking shown with blue, green, and red lines). For the *Woodstrat* the interdependences represented the internal logic of an SBU business context.

Figure 1 shows the overall structure of the *Woodstrat* and the strategy formation process.

The *Woodstrat* took form through a series of prototypes (cf. the iterative DSS building approach). The first versions used an *LISP*-based expert system shell, which proved too inflexible for the internal logic of the business context. The next series of prototypes used *Toolbook* to introduce the hyperknowledge constructs. This platform was too hard to implement for managers who are not skilled software users. The full-scale system took form as a hybrid system in *Visual Basic* in which we rewrote the *LISP* and *Toolbook* constructs as objects. The *Visual Basic* offered graphical user interfaces, multiple-document interfaces, object linking and embedding, dynamic data exchange, effective graphics and custom controls with procedures from dynamic-link libraries. We built in *what* if- and *goal* seeking features that had proved very useful in IFPS. These features are now available—even if most users do not even realize it—in *Microsoft Excel*, in further developed and advanced forms.

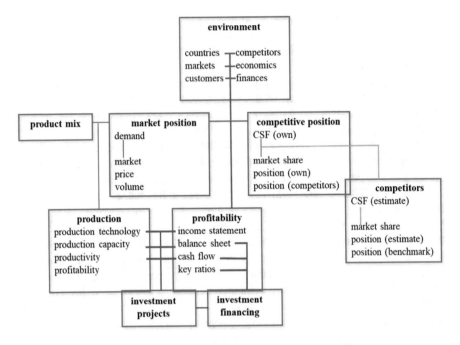

Fig. 1 The *Woodstrat* decision support system for strategic management [2]

The *Woodstrat* supported the strategy formation process of an SBU; we designed and built versions of the DSS for 11 SBUs with the help of 40 senior managers who worked on the annual strategic planning of the division. The Senior VP of the division was project champion, as he wanted to mobilize the experience, insight, and intuitive strategic knowledge of his managers, something that he had found that the standard corporate planning process did not capture.

An SBU operates in several countries, with well-defined product groups and specified customer segments. Markets and segments differ for different product groups, and their importance varies over the planning period. The strategic market positions (MP) are determined hierarchically: segments are defined for each product group and product groups are selected for each country; for each segment demand and price development estimates are made and consolidated to product group and country levels. The weighted average of growth and price development estimates update the estimated *net sales* line in the income statement through functional links.

We built rather an extensive database of country-specific economic indicators and related forecasts as part of *Woodstrat* to which we added market and segment specific forecasts on the development of price and demand levels. It turned out that this helped the SBU-managers to anchor and calibrate their assessments of growth and price developments. This offered a base of facts for the strategic visions.

The competitive positions (CP) are activated with logical links from the same base of facts as the MP, and the MP and CP are worked out in parallel. The CP builds on critical success factors (CSF), which are SBU-specific and worked out in a series of seminars with the SBU-managers. The CSF are calibrated with relative changes to the previous year and changes to the CP. This process changes and adapts visions of the MP when evaluated against the CSF and the relative strength of the competitors.

Three selected competitors were evaluated on the same CSF in a benchmarking workshop with each SBU. Effort and time were spent to identify "good" competitors, i.e., competitors that had managed to take away good customers and have an impact on the MP. CSF and CP averages were determined for the competitors; the relative differences in CP were calculated and used to assess the relative strategic CP for the SBU. The CP estimates were linked to the MP and used to calculate an estimated development in volumes and prices; here, we had built in a function for the SBU-managers to override the estimates with their own estimates on volumes and prices. The principle was that the managers' active customer relationships should decide the MP.

We used graphs to summarize relative competitive positions, the expected market development and total sales. This again proved to be useful as the SBU-managers wanted to get graphical overviews but had learned in previous years that the corporate planners could produce that for them "only with considerable difficulty."

The production position (PRO) estimates productivity as a consequence of the MP and the CP. *Production sold* is determined and transferred from the growth and price development specified in the MP. *Productivity* is determined from several factors—labor, raw material, electricity, steam, and technology. The module has functions for *profitability* and *capacity limits*. The cost factors of the income statement update the productivity factors with knowledge-based links. The productivity and profitability measures are numerical functions of the CSF and the visions implemented in the MP and CP.

There is an SBU Report activated from the summary level of the MP module with MP data and raw material costs. In the report, there is a projected income statement, linked with a balance sheet, a statement of funds and a report on key ratios. The modules update each other through knowledge-based links that follow proper accounting principles. The main key ratio followed by the forest industry is the return on net assets (RONA). We added a *what if* type of graphical RONA simulation to the report which allowed SBU-managers to find critical sales or operating cost levels for reaching target levels of the RONA. A major benefit of the linked modules is that an SBU-manager can work out several MP and CP scenarios and quickly find out how reasonable they are in terms of the division's RONA targets. The linked modules were also major time savers.

A *Woodstrat* feature the SBU-managers much wanted allowed them to work with investment plans interlinked with financing plans and further linked to *net sales, cash flows,* and *key ratios*. This allowed them to demonstrate and motivate the impact and consequences of the investments they wanted the corporation to accept and fund. The existing corporate policy routinely rejected investment proposals without any changes to revenues; now the SBU-managers could demonstrate the impact on *net sales, cash flows,* and *key ratios* if an investment proposal is not approved (to the surprise of corporate planners who were not used to fact-based arguments and negotiations).

We included a *Memo* module to allow the SBU-managers to keep track of their assumptions, knowledge points, and motivations for market and competitor estimates. Several factors were not well known and registered in the *Memo* for follow-up studies; a number of questions and ideas went to sales offices in Europe for verification and collection of more and better data. We were able to collect and analyze the *Memo* material from the 40 SBU-managers, which gave rather unique insight in the strategy formation process that the DSS guided and supported. Mintzberg [15] would probably not have agreed, but we noted that the DSS helped managers to formulate strategic visions for the business context.

We carried out systematic follow-up studies with the SBU-managers to find functions that needed improvement and links that at some point would produce invalid outcomes. We also collected some positive evaluations: *"the system guides the user to focus on important issues which eliminates unnecessary work."* Also, *"compared with my old way I worked more thoroughly and used more time than before."* On the DSS, *"the DSS captured us—the drawback was that we concentrated too much on details in the MP and CP."* Finally, *"the planning process became real teamwork."*

An evaluation of the *Woodstrat* experience shows that strategic planning and management fulfills (a) in Sprague's list of DSS "characteristics" [6, 13]. The support system works with interlinked modules (models with algorithms and hyperknowledge links) that use *Visual Basic* dynamic data exchange for data access and retrieval (cf. (b)). The SBU-managers worked interactively with us on the *Woodstrat* design, implementation, and use, which resulted in functionality suited to non-computer people (cf. (c)). The support system design aimed at an adaptive platform that supports strategic planning for the next 3–5 years (cf. (d)). The follow-up studies with the SBU-managers verified that the benefits that Keen [8] had collected could be verified also for *Woodstrat*. We identified (a)–(b), (d)–(g), (i)–(l).

3   Support for Decision-Making

We will now change context from the history of DSS to the 2010–2020s and the challenges of the growing digital economy. Decision support systems have decision-making at their core, and we propose that this core will be the same also in the digital economy. Decision support has to tackle the fast growth of big data, which invites proposals that things will be more complex and difficult in the 2020s than in the 1970s. Streaming big data now appears to make algorithms and modelling impractical as the huge amounts of data will take too much time to process, which again will make decision-making too slow. Fast decision-making in almost real-time is a necessity in the digital economy ("the fast eat the slow" as the slogan goes). Kahneman [19] shows that fast decision-making in many/most cases will produce bad decisions; a good credo for the DSS to follow is—"if there is time to make bad decisions, there should be time to make good or better decisions."

Zeleny [12] wrote a classical contribution to decision-making. First, with a single attribute or objective or utility function there is no decision-making involved, the decision is implicit in the measurement and becomes explicit in the search for a best value. With multiple criteria (attributes, objectives) or value functions, we get actual decision-making. As a human process—also when guided by DSS—decision-making is dynamic and composed of partial decisions in pre-decision, decision, and post-decision stages. The three stages require support from different kinds of data sources, data, information (knowledge), modelling tools, and experiments, which all should be part of the DSS constructs (still consistent with Sprague [13] and Simon [14]: intelligence, design, choice).

Kahneman [19] offers numerous examples of how limitations to human cognitive ability create bias when we want to address future uncertainties. In the *Woodstrat* cases, we had to build foresight to guide business decisions for 3–5 years into the future. SBU-managers had to understand customers, markets, competitors, and future economic and financial scenarios in order to find reasonable and valid estimates of demand, prices, and market shares (the actual process was a bit more detailed and complex). Then managers face what Kahneman [19] calls *vivid outcomes*. Probability estimates of future outcomes are sensitive to how much detail we know and use. Probability estimates become too optimistic with positive details or too pessimistic with negative details. Probability estimates are subjective and may give very wrong impressions of the future. In contrast, DSS offers a factual database and tools for objective estimates. Many strategic planning scenarios turned out to be far off the mark in the SBU's before the *Woodstrat*.

Kahneman [19] raises a sensitive issue—"when can you trust a self-confident professional who claims to have an intuition." SBU-managers are professionals; they have been working with their products, customers, competitors, and markets for years. It is a difficult process to challenge their intuition on future development of key strategic factors. These include demand, possibly competitive prices, relative market and competitive positions, raw material and operative costs. They also include uncertain facts about future economic scenarios for the countries in which they operate. Kahneman [19] simply states that it is wrong to blame anybody for inaccurate forecasts in an unpredictable world. It turned out that *Woodstrat* helped the professionals to test, adjust, and correct their initial intuitive forecasts without drama.

4 Decision Support for the 2020s

In a recent report called *"Competing in 2020: Winners and Losers in the Digital Economy"* [20] Harvard Business Review worked out the impact digitalization will have in a few key industrial sectors. The method was a multinational survey aimed at senior managers, executives, and board members; 783 respondents completed the survey; all of them indicated that they are digital decision-makers or influencers. The key industries covered were manufacturing or resources, financial services, and technology, mainly organizations with more than 10,000 employees.

Among the respondents 16% stated that their companies are *digital* (most products/operations depend on digital technology), 23% that they are *non-digital* (few if any products/operations depend on digital technology), and 61% that they are *hybrid* (some products/operations depend on digital technology).

The business world changes taking place are "the digital disruption" and "the digital revolution." The contention is that digitalization will have significant impact on both the structure and the operations of the business world, on the business models and on how companies cope with increasing competition, slimmer margins for productivity and profitability and growing requirements for effective planning, problem-solving and decision-making. Digitalization is of course bringing opportunities: the two most significant are enhanced customer relationships that allows to work out (and charge for) individual value adding in ways that have not been possible before and value chain integration that offers control of markets and rapid market changes with much better tools.

The report found a significant performance gap between digital leaders ("*digitals*") and the rest (called "*non-digitals*"). It shows that 84% of the digitals use big data and analytics, but only 34% of the non-digitals; 51% of the digitals use cognitive computing/AI, but only 7% of the non-digitals. Another significant difference—the digitals have data science and data engineering on staff (62%), the non-digitals much fewer (20%); all professionals working for the digitals have the ability to work with and make sense of data and analytics (76%), not that common for the non-digitals (30%). The conclusion is that a strong analytics capability is key to digital business—companies that want to compete in the digital economy will have to invest in analytics people, processes, and technology. The message is—curiously enough—the same we learned from Keen [11] and Sprague [13] almost 40 years ago but the context (digitalization) and the modelling methods (analytics) are now very different; how different we will find out.

In their policy statement for the new *Journal of Business Analytics* Delen and Ram [21] show in a word cloud analysis (Fig. 2) that big data—analytics—(text) mining over the last decade started to appear as related concepts in journals and conference publications. This is not surprising as digitalization produces fast growing sets of big data, and it is now evident that analytics offers useful tools to cope with big data.

Delen and Ram [21] also offer an overview of the evolution of (business) analytics that shows it as growing out of the DSS movement in the 1970s (Fig. 3).

Business analytics has three functional orientations: descriptive, predictive, and prescriptive; INFORMS has the same specification of analytics—descriptive ~ business intelligence, predictive, and prescriptive ~ advanced analytics. DSS literature usually lists the functions specified [7] (cf. also [22]):

Fig. 2 Analytics and Big Data [21]

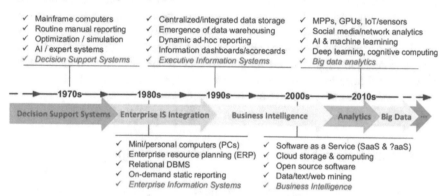

Fig. 3 A historical view to the evolution of analytics terminology [21]

1. *Descriptive*—business reporting, dashboards, scorecards, data warehousing
2. *Predictive*—data mining, text mining, web/media mining, machine learning
3. *Prescriptive*—optimization, simulation, algorithms, network science

The classifications are not precise and exhaustive, e.g., machine learning methods and simulation models appear in descriptive modelling.

Visions similar to Delen and Ram of the possible developments of DSS methods and applications appeared earlier, which anchors business analytics as part of the decades-long traditions. In *Past, Present, and Future of Decision Support Technology* [23], in a special issue of the DSS journal [24] published in 2002, the starting point was Keen's agenda for DSS entering the 1990s [7], and the aim was to work out the most promising research areas based on new technology. Keen (in 1987) wanted DSS developers to apply analytic models and methods for a more prescriptive view of how to make decisions that are more effective (he also wanted focus on "decisions that matter"). Keen encouraged DSS developers to exploit software tools and AI to make DSS move towards semi-expert systems. We followed up on Keen's proposals in [7] and worked out the following agenda:

1. Identify areas where tools can transform qualitative insight and uncertain and incomplete data into useful knowledge
2. Use intelligent systems and methods for prescriptive, more effective decision-making
3. Exploit advanced software tools to improve the productivity of decision and working time
4. Assist and guide DSS practitioners for effective decision-making

These guidelines are general and open-ended, but they still make sense and are useful in the present business context of digitization and big data. A key difference between 2002 and 2018 [21] is the portfolio of tools we have for building decision support. The algorithms belong to the computational intelligence family, are faster, more powerful, and can handle (very) big data. The user support is adaptive and interactive, and it will evolve with the cognitive ability of the user. The platforms build on smartphones, tablets, laptops, and powerful desktops to provide users with real-time decision support wherever they are and whenever they need it. The users, however, still need to provide the cognitive ability, the experience, the intelligence and the insight to make effective and better decisions.

5   Computational Intelligence in Decision Support

The digital economy and the big data challenges appear to disqualify the classical algorithmic methods (cf. [10])—optimal problem-solving is nice but useless if it cannot meet the hectic pace of the digital economy. Classical algorithms cannot process big data in reasonable time—or even not at all. Some of these claims are fallacies—it is not necessary to process big data at all if we first use classical statistical methods (such as *principal component analysis*) to find the smaller subsets of factors that are relevant and actually influence the problems we need to solve [10]. The classical algorithms are again relevant for the smaller subsets.

In case we actually have to work with big data, it appears that we should look to *computational intelligence* algorithms, which offer to be much faster than polynomial methods [25]: neural networks, support vector machines, genetic algorithms, genetic programming, swarm intelligence, software agents, and soft computing. There is a drawback, users need to have some fairly advanced mathematical and software skills to operate computational intelligence.

There is a central challenge in digitization; the human users of advanced automated systems are the weak links (cf. [9]). Large, automated systems rely on advanced algorithms and large complex computational systems; it is not self-evident that human system users have the knowledge and/or the skills to manage the systems and to operate them to produce a competitive RONA.

System users have diverse backgrounds and different levels of experience. Some users understand everything and master the systems in a short time; then they will start to contribute to development. On the other hand, some users are slow to learn and/or are not motivated; it will take time for them to reach even minimal acceptable levels.

The D2I joint industry and university research program [9] proposed that we build on human and system joint intelligence for digitization, that we use fast, automatic algorithms for large, well-structured datasets, and combine this with knowledge mobilized from seasoned context experts. In order to make it work, human systems users need context relevant advice (in real time, with real data and information) that is adapted to their cognitive abilities and background knowledge (i.e., advice they can understand and use). *This could be the mission statement for the DSS of the 2020s.*

The *digital coaching systems* got started a few years ago [26] as an answer to the demand on human operators to master advanced automated systems in complex and very large industrial process systems. Digital coaching will work with data that is collected from digital devices, instruments, tools, monitoring systems, sensor systems, software systems, data and knowledge bases, data warehouses, etc. and then processed to be usable for the digital systems that will guide and support users.

Digital coaching requires that we master the transition from data to information, and on to knowledge, also known as *digital fusion*. Data fusion collects and harmonizes data from a variety of sources with different formats and labels. Information fusion uses analytics to build syntheses of data to describe, explain, and predict key features for problem-solving and decision-making. Knowledge fusion uses ontology to build and formalize insight from data and information fusion as a basis for computational intelligence methods, AI, machine learning, soft computing, approximate reasoning, etc. The early versions of DSS hinted at the need for what we now call digital fusion [9, 10]) but lacked the necessary software tools. They are now available and appear to be on a path towards becoming both more intelligent and effective.

The DSS of 2020s will quite possibly be digital coaching systems that will guide users in the digital economy over smartphones, tablets, laptops, terminals to cloud services, and new digital support devices that will appear as part of the environment.

References

1. Walden, P., & Carlsson, C. (1994). Strategic management with a hyperknowledge support system. In *Proceedings of the twenty-seventh annual Hawaii international conference on system sciences* (Vol. III). Los Alamitos: IEEE Computer Society Press.
2. Carlsson, C., & Walden, P. (1997). Cognitive maps and a hyperknowledge support system in strategic management. *Group Decision and Negotiation, 6*(1), 7–36.
3. Walden, P., & Carlsson, C. (1995). More effective strategic management with hyperknowledge: Case Woodstrat. In J. Darzentas, J. S. Darzentas, & T. Spyrou (Eds.), *Perspectives on DSS* (pp. 139–156). Mitilini: University of the Aegean.

4. Gorry, G. A., & Scott Morton, M. S. (1971). A framework for management information systems. *Sloan Management Review, 13*(1), 55–70.
5. Scott Morton, M. S. (1971). *Management decision systems: Computer-based support for decision making*. Cambridge, MA: Division of Research, Harvard University.
6. Sprague, R. H. (1980). Framework for the development of decision support systems. *MIS Quarterly, 4*(4), 1–26.
7. Keen, P. G. W. (1987). Decision support systems: The next decade. *Decision Support Systems, 3*(3), 253–265.
8. Keen, P. G. W. (1981). Information systems and organizational change. *Communications of the ACM, 24*(1), 24–33.
9. Carlsson, C. (2018). Analytics mobilized with digital coaching, Intelligent Systems in Accounting. *Finance and Management, 25*(1), 3–17.
10. Carlsson, C. (2018). Decision analytics—Key to digitalization. *Information Sciences, 460–461*(12), 424–438.
11. Keen, P. G. W. (1981). Decision support systems—lessons for the 80's. In D. Young & P. G. W. Keen (Eds.), *DSS-81 Transactions* (pp. 187–192). Georgia: Atlanta.
12. Zeleny, M. (1982). *Multiple criteria decision making*. New York: McGraw-Hill.
13. Sprague, R. H. (1981). Decision support systems: A tutorial. In D. Young & P. G. W. Keen (Eds.), *DSS-81 Transactions* (pp. 193–203). Georgia: Atlanta.
14. Simon, H. A. (1980). Cognitive science: The new science of the artificial. *Cognitive Science, 4*(1), 33–46.
15. Mintzberg, H. (1994). *The rise and fall of strategic planning*. Prentice-Hall: Penguin.
16. Mintzberg, H. (1978). Patterns in strategy formation. *Management Science, 24*(9), 934–948.
17. Eden, C. (1993). Strategy development and implementation—cognitive mapping for group support. In J. Hendry & G. Johnson (Eds.), *Strategic thinking: Leadership and the management of change*. New York: Wiley.
18. Chang, A.-M., Holsapple, C. W., & Whinston, A. B. (1993). Model management issues and directions. *Decision Support Systems, 9*(1), 19–37.
19. Kahneman, D. (2011). *Thinking, fast and slow*. London: Penguin Books.
20. Competing in 2020: Winners and Losers In The Digital Economy. (2017). A Harvard Business Review Analytic Services Report, April 25, 2017.
21. Delen, D., & Ram, S. (2018). Research challenges and opportunities in business analytics. *Journal of Business Analytics, 1*(1), 2–12.
22. Arnott, D., & Pervan, G. (2008). Eight key issues for the decision support systems discipline. *Decision Support Systems, 44*(3), 657–672.
23. Shim, J. P., Warkentin, M., Courtney, F., Power, D. J., Sharda, R., & Carlsson, C. (2002). Past, present, and future of decision support technology. *Decision Support Systems, 33*(2), 111–126.
24. Carlsson, C., & Turban, E. (2002). DSS: Directions for the next decade. *Decision Support Systems, 33*(2), 105–110.
25. Kordon, A. K. (2010). *Applying computational intelligence*. Berlin: Springer.
26. Fern, A., Natarajan, S., Judah, K., & Tadepalli, P. (2014). A decision-theoretic model of assistance. *Journal of Artificial Intelligence Research, 49*, 71–104.

Thirty Years of Decision Support: A Bibliometric View

Peter B. Keenan

Abstract This chapter uses a bibliometric approach to examine the growth of and changes in the Decision Support Systems (DSS) field over the 30 years from 1990 to 2019. Bibliographic databases such as Web of Science (WOS) provide valuable information on academic disciplines as they contain both the articles published and the articles cited. The changing disciplinary balance in the DSS field is indicated by the topics of the articles published, and the disciplinary categorisation of the journals where they are published. The citation links of these papers illustrate the intellectual influences on the DSS field. Network analysis of the bibliographic network allows the identification of key papers, authors, and journals. We identify important papers and concepts within the period and identify when these concepts subsequently became less important.

Keywords Bibliographic analysis · Decision support · Decision support systems · Scientometrics · Web of science

1 Introduction

Decision support systems (DSS) have their origin in the 1960s in attempts to use information technology (IT) to assist with decision-making [1]. The DSS field is generally regarded as having been founded by the work of Gorry and Scott-Morton [2], who argued that existing IT primarily focused on structured decisions and that there should a distinct class of system known as DSS for semi-structured and unstructured decisions. In the 1970s and 1980s, the DSS field became a recognised one, with research groups being formed and new conferences beginning [3]. One method of characterising an academic field is to use scientometric techniques that allow the examination of aggregate trends in academic publications represented

P. B. Keenan (✉)
UCD School of Business, University College Dublin, Dublin, Ireland
e-mail: Peter.Keenan@ucd.ie

© Springer Nature Switzerland AG 2021
J. Papathanasiou et al. (eds.), *EURO Working Group on DSS*, Integrated Series in Information Systems, https://doi.org/10.1007/978-3-030-70377-6_2

in computerised bibliographic databases. These techniques include the analysis of quantitative data such as publication counts or citation counts. Citations can be viewed as forming a graph of links between citing authors, cited authors, citing texts, and cited texts and network analysis techniques can be used on that graph.

Scientometric investigation has greatly increased in recent years owing to the increased availability of bibliographic databases, the introduction of new software to visualise and analyse bibliographic data [4], and the improved capacity of modern desktop computers to analyse large datasets. Modern software allows the summarisation of datasets through techniques like keyword analysis, techniques which are increasingly necessary as the increasing number of papers is beyond the capacity of one reader. One of the most comprehensive bibliographic databases is the Web of Science (WOS) maintained by Clarivate Analytics (previously Thomson Reuters), formerly known as the Web of Knowledge. This database records articles from 1898 to the present drawn from a wide range of disciplines and identifies the publications cited by those articles. In mid-2020, WOS covers over 34,000 journals and has almost 1.9 billion cited references from over 171 million citing records (http://wokinfo.com).

In this study, we aim to use the WOS to examine the DSS field as represented by publications and their citations for the three decades from 1990 to 2019. In searching for such papers, we search the titles, abstracts, and keywords in WOS for the search terms "decision support systems", "decision support software", and "decision support tool" and the combination (DSS and "decision support"). We have only included journal articles, as the WOS indexing of book chapters and conference proceedings is less consistent than that of journals. Nevertheless, citations from journal articles to book chapters and conference proceedings are included. Our search would not find articles describing systems that do not use this terminology but whose operation could reasonably be characterised as DSS, while it did find some systems that might not be characterised as a DSS by a manual assessment, despite these articles describing themselves as DSS. At an earlier stage of DSS, when the number of papers was fewer, manual assessment of the entire literature was feasible [5], but the larger volume of articles makes this approach infeasible today. However, this research aims to form an aggregate picture of the field and the inclusion or absence of a small proportion of systems should not materially affect its conclusions. Our search on WOS returned 14,330 records from 2822 journals. After processing, we had 12,387 usable articles with 324,163 cited references.

There has been continuous growth in the number of papers in WOS identified by these search parameters (Fig. 1), and there are also a smaller number of book chapters and conference papers not included in this analysis. The growth in the number of articles was facilitated by new journals; for instance, the journal *Decision Support Systems* and the journal *Expert Systems and Applications* both started in 1991 and have become important across the DSS field since then, and other journals started which publish DSS articles in particular disciplines.

The structure of citations can be analysed using a classification of subject disciplines. There are two approaches to this; databases such as WOS use their own distinct classification schemes, while an alternative bibliographic alternative

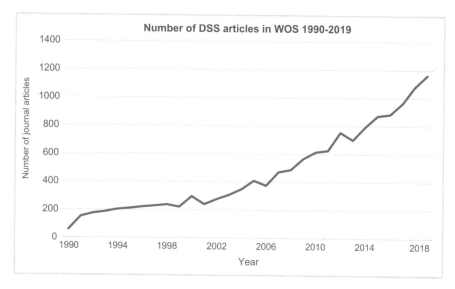

Fig. 1 Number of DSS journal articles in Web of Science 1990–2019

is to use a clustering algorithm to group the disciplines based on the strength of their citation links. WOS introduced ISI Subject Categories, now known as Web of Science Categories (SC), as proxies of scientific fields defined above the level of individual journals. Consequently, when examining changes in the disciplinary structure of a field any changes in the proportions of papers or citations for a particular SC would illustrate the trends in that discipline. Note that journals may be categorised in several SCs. For instance, the Decision Support Systems journal is in five categories: Operations Research and Management Science, Computer Science, Information Systems, Computer Science, Artificial Intelligence, AI, Robotics and Automatic Control, and Computer Science. While this overlap presents some problems, analysis of these categories is still informative for aggregate datasets where there are significant numbers of papers involved and which would be difficult to understand by other approaches [6]. WOS has further introduced a newer classification scheme known as Research Areas (RAs) which are somewhat larger categories, and these also provide insight, although they are not yet as widely used for bibliographic analysis as the SC classification.

In Table 1, Operations Research/Management Science (OR/MS) is the most important SC for DSS over the period, and Computer Science categories show a similar level of growth. However, there has been a marked increase in the number of papers in categories such as Environmental Science, Water Resources, and Environmental Engineering.

The interpretation and aggregate analysis of journal databases is facilitated by standard visualisations of the subject space and the clustering of disciplines. One useful approach is developed by Leydesdorff, with various collaborators.

Table 1 Number of DSS articles in most important WOS subject codes 1990–2019

WOS Category	1990– 1999	2000– 2009s	2010– 2019	1990– 2019	% Change 1990s–2010s (%)
Operations Research/Management Science	527	731	992	2250	88
Environmental Sciences	151	470	1117	1738	640
Computer Science Artificial Intelligence	259	577	898	1734	247
Computer Science Interdisciplinary Applications	338	499	808	1645	139
Computer Science Information Systems	371	428	605	1404	63
Management	332	285	350	967	5
Water Resources	71	284	593	948	735
Engineering Civil	75	296	529	900	605
Medical Informatics	147	196	519	862	253
Engineering Industrial	205	202	393	800	92
Engineering Electrical Electronic	71	194	489	754	589
Engineering Environmental	65	252	423	740	551

This visually maps all scientific disciplines by reference to their citation patterns, allowing specific disciplines to be plotted on the same background map.

Such visualisations can use data from WOS on journals or subject categories. Keenan [7] plotted the DSS field using a journal visualisation based on Leydesdorff et al. [8]. Figure 2 shows a visualisation of the subject distribution of DSS articles, this is based on a 2015 update of earlier approaches (see http://www.leydesdorff.net/wc15/). This visualisation uses the Vosviewer software [9, 10] using a disciplinary layout reflecting the analysis of all WOS publications by Leydesdorff et al. [11] and used by Carley et al. [12] to plot different research portfolios.

In addition to categories, WOS provides a higher level aggregation in its Research Area (RA) classification, Table 2 shows the changes in the proportions of DSS articles in RA groupings through the three decades. In this classification, there are no DSS articles in the Arts and Humanities grouping, while most of the papers are in the Technology group. This group includes the three most important WOS RAs relating to DSS; Engineering, Computer Science, and OR/MS.

These proportions also show the same trend of an increase in the importance of DSS papers in the environmental and medical areas, which are grouped into Life Sciences and Biomedicine in Table 2. This includes both environmental RAs; (Environmental Sciences and Ecology, Agriculture) and medical areas (Medical Informatics, Health Care Sciences). The most important RA within the Physical Sciences top-level grouping is Water Resources, which is also related to the

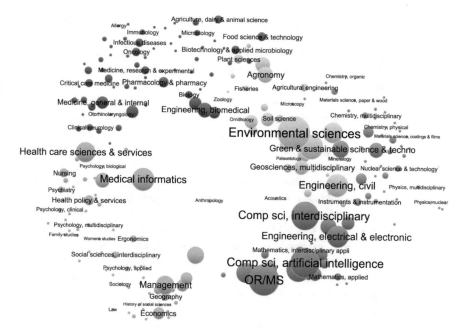

Fig. 2 Visualisation in Vosviewer of WOS subject areas for DSS articles 2010–2019

Table 2 Proportions of DSS articles in WOS Research Area groupings

WOS discipline grouping	1990–1999 (%)	2000–2009 (%)	2010–2019 (%)
Arts and Humanities	0.0	0.0	0.0
Life Sciences and Biomedicine	21.7	25.8	32.0
Physical Sciences	5.1	8.3	9.5
Social Sciences	11.3	6.1	4.1

environment and which had eight times as many papers in the 2010–2019 decade as in the 1990–1999 decade.

2 Bibliographic Analysis

Bibliographics uses mathematical graphs based on citation links as the basis of analysis and bibliographic software can produce such graphs from downloaded data such as our WOS dataset. In bibliographic networks, each document (paper, journal, author) is represented by a node, and the citations from that publication are represented as links on the network. These networks provide both a visual representation of a field and facilitate the automated analysis of that field [13]. Bibliographic analysis is now a subset of the broader field of social network analysis, which has become an important area of research in recent years, as the widespread use of social networks have made much more data available [14].

A basic citation network is a mathematical graph where each node represents a citing document, and each directed link represents a citation from the current document to an earlier cited document. A simple cited reference search on WOS will show all the publications which cite an earlier publication. Bibliographic coupling looks at the citations of a paper and groups the documents which cited that earlier paper. Co-citation coupling [15] looks at all of the references cited by a document and forms an undirected co-citation network linking documents that are cited together. Co-citation coupling looks back from a document to the citations that it contains, which presumably represent the academic influences on the article. Two documents are said to be co-cited (Fig. 3) when they are both cited by a third document, if they are cited together multiple times then they have a stronger relationship. In a co-citation network, the link weights represent the number of times that two documents were jointly cited. These links and link weights can be used to identify research clusters formed from strongly connected document groups. Earlier papers can be clustered because of their common citation by later publications, revealing a commonality in earlier concurrent papers which was not necessarily apparent at the time of their publication. Co-citation coupling can also identify intersections between different disciplines, as documents may include citations from both disciplines.

The document co-citation analysis (DCA) approach was built on the methods pioneered by Small [16, 17] and is widely used to analyse individual papers DCA may include links between all documents cited by articles of interest. As each paper may cite from 20 to 50 citations, this approach can produce large networks which are

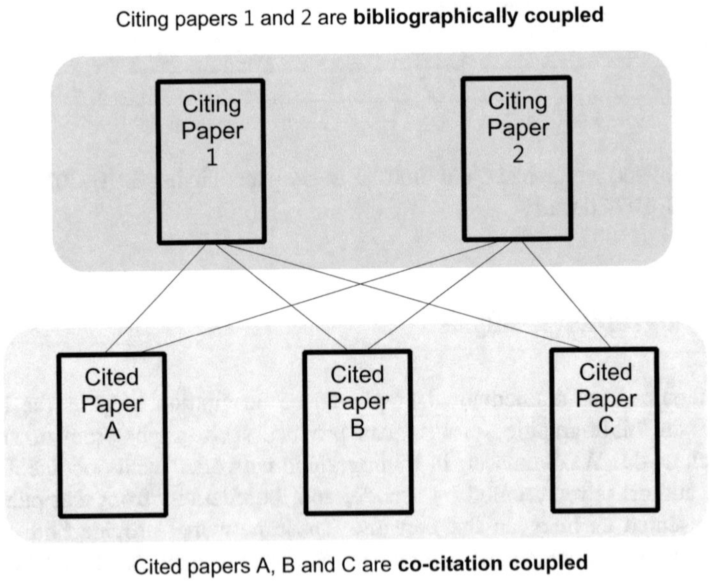

Citing papers 1 and 2 are **bibliographically coupled**

Cited papers A, B and C are **co-citation coupled**

Fig. 3 Bibliographic and co-citation coupling

difficult to process. Consequently, DCA bibliographic analysis frequently reduces the size of the network by excluding documents with a small number of citations and with low levels of co-citation.

In this research, we used the CRExplorer software [18, 19] to clean the data by removing references without dates and to identify similar references. This software allows the merging of citations where there are small differences in the reference. For instance, where the number of initials of an author is different or there is a slightly different abbreviation for a journal. Although this software eliminated some of the data issues, some errors likely remain, especially with older references. This would have the effect of reducing the citation counts of some papers. However, as we are concerned with the aggregate picture, we believe that a useful analysis can still be obtained although some data errors still exist. We used the Vosviewer software [9, 10] to build DCA and keyword networks and to visualise the network and we used the efficient Pajek network software [20] to perform network analysis and to identify key papers in the network.

Social network analysis builds on ideas originating with Freeman [21] and now plays an important role in bibliographic analysis [22]. These techniques are now routinely included in citation analysis software tools (Moral-Muñoz et al. [4]). "Betweenness centrality" is a measure of how often a node is located on the shortest path between other nodes in the network. In a bibliographic analysis, a node is a journal, a book, or a paper. A node with high betweenness is located on multiple shortest paths and can be characterised as linking two groups in the network. In general, nodes with many citations and with higher betweenness scores represent papers, authors, or journals which play an important role in connecting different parts of the network. If g_{jk} is defined as the number of geodesic paths between j and k, and g_{jik} is the number of these geodesics that pass through i, then node i's betweenness centrality is defined as

$$\sum_j \sum_k \frac{g_{jik}}{g_{jk}} \quad i \neq j \neq k$$

"Closeness centrality" is a measure of the distance of a node from all other nodes in the network, this too is usually normalised. $C_c(n_i)$ is the closeness centrality of node i where $d(n_i, n_j)$ is the distance between two vertices in the network.

$$C_C(n_i) = \sum_{j=1}^{g} \left[\frac{1}{d(n_i, n_j)} \right]$$

Centrality measures have been used in social network analysis and to some extent in citation analysis. Wang et al. [23] used co-citation networks and centrality measures to characterise the cloud computing literature and emphasised the importance of betweenness. Lin et al. [24] analysed the public risk governance literature using betweenness centrality. Keenan and Jankowski [25] used centrality measures to identify key journals and papers in Spatial Decision Support Systems (SDSS). Argoubi, Ammari, and Masri [26] used these techniques to examine the literature on OR/MS research in Africa. Leydesdorff, Wagner, and Bornmann [27] considered betweenness as an approach to measuring the interdisciplinary of journals. Research continues on the appropriate measure to use in different situations [28].

We used the Vosviewer software [9, 10] to build and visualise the publication co-citation network. To reduce the size of the network for network calculations, we excluded papers with few citations. This exclusion may marginally change the absolute value of the calculations but should not affect the rank of well-cited papers. We used the Pajek network software, which is an efficient network tool, to calculate betweenness and closeness centrality values.

Vosviewer also allows term co-occurrence analysis of text found in titles or abstracts [9]. In this analysis, we removed keywords associated with the search terms, as these were inevitably found in the article abstracts. Consequently, keyword phrases such as "Decision Support System" or "DSS" do not appear in the results, we also removed the generic terms "information" "information technology" and "computers" from the analysis. We also removed publisher names and words like "copyright" from the analysis as these do not relate to the academic content of the article.

3   DSS Published in 1990–1999

Figure 4 shows a visualisation using Vosviewer for the top 50 keywords for DSS articles in the period 1990–1999. This software both clusters and positions the keywords based on their co-occurrence in the titles and abstracts of papers.

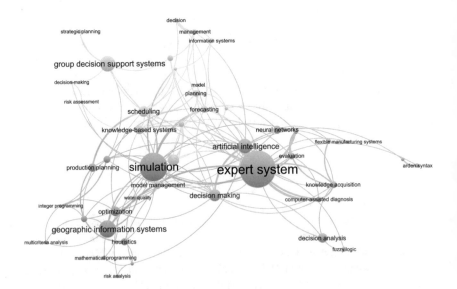

Fig. 4 Vosviewer co-occurrence network for keywords of DSS articles in the period 1990–1999

The cluster on the bottom left contains Geographic Information Systems (GIS), Simulation, and terms related to Multicriteria Analysis (MCA) and the Analytical Hierarchy Process (AHP). The cluster on the top left contains Group Decision Support Systems (GDSS) and terms related to modelling. The cluster on the right has several keywords related to artificial intelligence and expert systems. The comparative separation between strategic analysis and computer-assisted diagnosis illustrated that even at this stage there were distinct bodies of DSS research on quite different themes.

We can analyse DSS journals by looking at both citing papers and the papers they cited (Table 3). The journal *Decision Support Systems*, established in 1991, quickly became the main outlet for DSS papers. However, the European Journal of Operational Research had the most citations. The relationship between citing and cited journals reflects that DSS papers often cite modelling techniques or decision theory. We see the agriculture and medical fields represented in the top ten journals cited, showing that these fields were already becoming important to DSS.

We can identify the influences on the DSS field by looking at the papers cited by DSS papers. Figure 5 shows a visualisation in Vosviewer of the co-citation network of the 45 most cited papers by DSS articles in the period 1990–1999. One limitation of WOS is that it only stores the first author of a paper and so the visualisation labels only the first author. The visualisation shows two clusters, the smaller cluster on the right representing GDSS while that on the left contains the well-known foundational DSS literature.

These papers can also be assessed by the number of citations and by their position in the co-citation network, which can be calculated using closeness and betweenness centrality, shown in Table 4. On all measures, the most important papers influencing DSS research in the 1990s were Sprague and Carlson [29] and Keen and Scott-Morton [30]. Closeness centrality relates to the centrality within the field and these papers are positioned centrally in the visualisation reflecting their higher centrality values. Bonczek et al. [32] and Alter [38] are also widely recognised pioneers in the DSS field. Keeney and Raiffa [35] and Saaty [33] did foundational work in MCA.

Table 3 Top journals cited by DSS papers in the period 1990–1999

	Cited	Citing
European Journal of Operational Research	3228	89
Decision Support Systems	3025	143
Organisation Science	1511	3
Decision Sciences	1143	28
Agricultural Systems	986	28
Interfaces	963	47
International Journal of Production Economics	808	21
Information and Management	753	40
MIS Quarterly	664	4
Journal of the American Medical Informatics Association	624	42

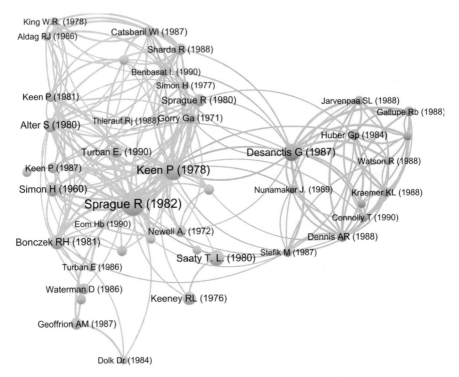

Fig. 5 Co-citation network in Vosviewer of the most important papers 1990–1999

Table 4 Centrality measures for papers cited by DSS articles 1990–1999

Cited Paper	Number of Citations	Closeness	Betweenness
Sprague and Carlson [29]	122	0.53122	0.14016
Keen and Scott-Morton [30]	88	0.51509	0.08388
Simon [31]	43	0.47382	0.03106
Bonczek et al. [32]	44	0.47354	0.02507
Saaty [33]	51	0.4721	0.04925
Desanctis and Gallupe [34]	61	0.46995	0.02836
Keeney and Raiffa [35]	37	0.46938	0.04203
Newell and Simon [36]	28	0.46726	0.02652
Mintzberg et al. [37]	22	0.4653	0.01375
Alter [38]	41	0.46468	0.02044

Desanctis and Gallupe [34] is the most cited GDSS paper. Simon [31], Newell and Simon [36], and Mintzberg et al. [37] are important works in decision-making.

This analysis of cited literature shows that the DSS field in the 1990s was still very much based on its traditional roots in management decision-making theory and the seminal work of business school-based researchers. GDSS and MCA were important areas at that time, as also noted by other studies, Eom [39] found the contributing disciplines of DSS to be multiple criteria decision-making, cognitive science, organisation science, artificial intelligence, group decision-making, and systems science.

4 DSS Published in 2000–2009

The middle decade of our period of study saw the development of systems that had taken advantage of earlier technical developments that facilitated DSS [40]. These developments included inexpensive personal computers and laptops of sufficient power to do useful work, the universal use of graphic user interfaces (GUIs), and the development of the World Wide Web. These technical developments made computerised decision support accessible to larger number of users and by this time there was a larger number of decision-makers who were computer literate and who appreciated the potential of the technology.

In this period, Shim et al. [41] was an important paper reflecting on the progress of DSS. This chapter resulted from several prominent DSS researchers meeting at a panel at the 30th Decision Sciences Institute Annual Meeting in New Orleans in 1999. The authors noted the technical changes since the early days of DSS and discussed Data warehouses, OLAP, data mining, and web-based DSS. They also noted that the increased use of networks facilitated the use of collaborative DSS.

This period also saw the emergence of new journals, which represented the extension of modelling and computer use to new domains. For instance, the journal *Environmental Modelling and Software* started in 1997 and became a significant outlet for DSS papers in that domain while the *Journal of the American Medical Informatics Association* started in 1994 and subsequently published many DSS related articles in the medical domain.

Figure 6 shows the co-occurrence network of the top 46 keywords for DSS articles in the period 2000–2009. The keyword with the highest occurrence is GIS, including its variants like geographical information systems. This reflects the increasingly widespread use of SDSS facilitated by cheaper powerful computers and the increasing availability of spatial datasets [25]. In the figure, GIS is grouped on the lower left of the visualisation with areas of DSS application which use spatial techniques, like water resources and climate change. Other frequently occurring keywords relate to modelling and modelling techniques; simulation, neural networks, expert systems, optimisation, modelling, genetic algorithms, fuzzy logic, AHP, and fuzzy sets. Clinical decision support systems (CDSS) are positioned close to expert systems, reflecting their frequent use of that approach. Unlike the earlier period, in this decade GDSS is now a relatively infrequently mentioned keyword and one that does not often occur with other frequent keywords. This visualisation clearly shows that spatial and medical DSS applications had already become important subfields, somewhat separate from each other and from the more traditional DSS areas of application.

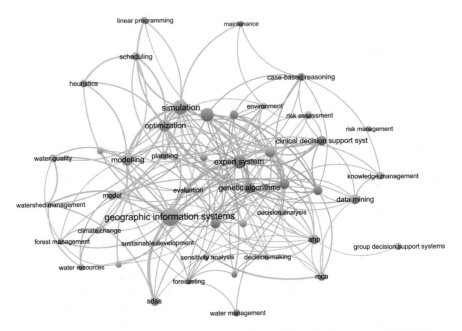

Fig. 6 Vosviewer co-occurrence network for keywords of DSS articles in the period 2000–2009

Table 5 shows the number of citing and cited articles in the top ten journals for DSS articles in the period 2000–2009. The Decision Support Systems journal and Expert Systems with Applications journal are central to the DSS field, publishing many articles and being widely cited. The European Journal of Operational Research is widely cited and modelling techniques drawn from articles there are used in a variety of DSS areas of application, not just traditional ones [42]. We see significant numbers of publications and citation to journals in the environmental and medical fields, reflecting the growth of these fields relative to traditional business school and engineering domains, as reflected in Tables 1 and 2 above.

If we look citations from DSS articles in the period 2000–2009 (Table 6), we see that Saaty [33] is both the most cited paper and the one with the highest value for both closeness and betweenness centrality in the DSS field, with Zadeh [43] playing a similarly important role. Sprague and Carlson [29] and Keen and Scott-Morton [30] are still influential in this decade, especially in its first half, but Shim et al. [41] had become the most important paper from within the DSS field and Turban's textbook was often cited (various editions). The importance of Goldberg [44] and Holland [45] reflected the growth of genetic algorithms as a modelling technique. Davis [46] is a widely cited paper on the adoption of information technology. Densham [47] is a seminal paper on SDSS and represents the increased importance of GIS-based DSS.

Table 5 Top journals cited by DSS papers in the period 2000–2009

Journal	Cited	Citing
European Journal of Operational Research	1793	97
Decision Support Systems	1495	161
Management Science	897	2
Agricultural Systems	636	44
JAMA Journal of The American Medical Association	596	3
Water Resources	556	24
Journal of The American Medical Informatics Association	551	42
Environmental Modelling Software	525	96
International Journal of Production Economics	506	32
Operations Research	501	7
International Journal of Production Research	482	30
Expert Systems with Applications	478	132

Table 6 Centrality measures for papers cited by DSS articles 2000–2009

Paper	Citations	Closeness	Betweenness
Saaty [33]	146	0.50419	0.09084
Shim et al. [41]	49	0.49599	0.04743
Zadeh [43]	103	0.49340	0.07928
Keen and Scott-Morton [30]	35	0.47695	0.02511
Goldberg [44]	59	0.46944	0.03952
Sprague and Carlson [29]	52	0.46891	0.02666
Keeney and Raiffa [35]	64	0.46833	0.03383
Davis [46]	32	0.46518	0.02206
Holland [45]	40	0.45210	0.02046
Turban [56]	30	0.45009	0.01277
Densham [47]	26	0.44834	0.01015

5 DSS Published in 2010–2019

Figure 7 shows the keyword co-occurrence network for DSS articles in the period 2010–2019, the most frequent keyword is CDSS. In this visualisation, CDSS is grouped on the right-hand side with related areas of application like primary care and with modelling techniques like machine learning and neural networks that are especially important in the medical domain. The cluster on the top left includes GIS, the second most common keyword, and SDSS and multicriteria-based approaches. The cluster on the bottom left mainly contains modelling techniques, the most common of which are simulation and optimisation. This visualisation also reflects the growth of spatial and medical DSS as important subfields.

Table 7 shows the main journals cited by DSS articles in the decade 2010–2019. The Decision Support Systems journal and the Expert Systems with Applications journal are central to the field, with many widely cited DSS articles published in

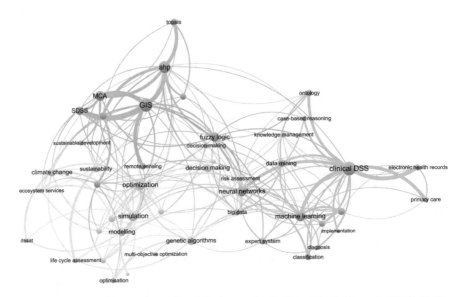

Fig. 7 Vosviewer co-occurrence network for keywords of DSS articles in the period 2010–2019

Table 7 Top journals cited by DSS papers in the period 2010–2019

	Cited	Citing
European Journal of Operational Research	5230	50
Expert Systems with Applications	4301	237
Decision Support Systems	3113	177
Environmental Modelling and Software	2412	87
International Journal of Production Economics	1964	37
Journal of The American Medical Informatics Association	1737	47
Journal of Cleaner Production	1675	104
JAMA Journal of The American Medical Association	1532	5
International Journal of Production Research	1507	70
Journal of Environmental Management	1410	63

these outlets. The European Journal of Operational Research is widely cited and modelling techniques there are cited in a variety of domains, not just traditional ones [42]. There are several journals which are both widely cited and which publish a substantial number of papers, representing the environmental, production, and medical domains.

Table 8 shows the key papers in this period, the papers by Zadeh [43] and Saaty [33] continue to play a central role in the citation of DSS articles. This reflects that a large proportion of DSS articles are concerned with MCA approaches. Breiman [48] is a widely cited machine learning approach, while Jang [49] is a widely cited fuzzy logic paper. Shim et al. [41], Power [51], and Power and Sharda [50] are influential articles from within the DSS field. Mysiak et al. [52] is an important paper

Table 8 Centrality measures for papers cited by DSS articles 2010–2019

	Citations	Closeness	Betweenness
Zadeh [43]	264	0.56079	0.09064
Saaty [33].	290	0.55071	0.06989
Shim et al. [41]	87	0.5202	0.03165
Breiman [48]	108	0.5005	0.02403
Davis [46]	56	0.496	0.02078
Jang [49]	51	0.494	0.01067
Power and Sharda [50]	45	0.49293	0.01259
Power [51]	42	0.49173	0.01097
Mysiak et al. [52]	51	0.48843	0.00753
Garg [53]	210	0.48791	0.04753

in environmental DSS, while Garg et al. [53] is an influential review of the CDSS field. Some important papers have a lower score for closeness centrality as they tend to be cited only within their own cluster, but the relatively high betweenness centrality value for Garg et al. [53] shows its value in connecting papers in the medical DSS area.

6   Conclusion

This research has used bibliographic techniques to examine the aggregate nature of the DSS field over the 30 years from 1990 to 2019. We have divided this period into three decades and the change between these decades illustrates the changing nature of the DSS field. The first decade still had a predominance of articles concerned with the business and engineering disciplines where early DSS was most common and still largely referred to the widely known seminal papers of the 1970s and 1980s. In the second decade, starting in 2000, we saw new technologies such as the Internet and GIS become more important and these extended the range of DSS areas of application. The environmental area became more important and journals in that area started publishing significant numbers of DSS papers. A range of modelling approaches from OR/MS and Computer Science were joined by distinctive environmental models. The final decade from 2010 to 2019 sees the growth in environmental applications continue, together with an increasing number of medical applications.

This picture is a fragmented one. In earlier decades, there were frequent citations of a core body of well-known DSS literature. However, as each sub-field built up more research, it continued to cite modelling examples from core OR/MS and Computer Science papers but increasingly tended to discuss decision support by reference to its own domain. Notably, earlier DSS papers frequently cited work on DSS from within the core Information Systems field, but this is less and less common over time. The major IS journals have largely sought to leave DSS research behind as if it is a solved problem of no further interest and they haven't shown much interest in the new areas of application. While Shim et al. [41] was an influential attempt to bring together issues in the DSS field, there has not been a similarly influential paper since then. There are very limited connections from the newer DSS domains to the traditional groupings of DSS researchers. This fragmentation has long existed, and Arnott and Pervan [54, 55] noted the conservative nature of DSS research and the slow dissemination of new decision theories in the field. This fragmentation makes it likely that new methodologies and approaches will be slow to disseminate and consequently some "reinvention of the wheel" could occur. Greater cross-fertilisation between the business school-based DSS communities and the newer SDSS and CDSS groupings would be to everyone's benefit.

References

1. Power, D. J., Heavin, C., & Keenan, P. (2019). Decision systems redux. *Journal of Decision Systems, 28*(1), 1–18. https://doi.org/10.1080/12460125.2019.1631683.
2. Gorry, A., & Scott-Morton, M. (1971). A framework for information systems. *Sloan Management Review, 13*(1), 56–79.
3. Csáki, C., Meredith, R., O'Donnell, P., & Adam, F. (2016). Understanding the scientific contribution of an international community of researchers: The case of the IFIP WG 8.3 Conferences on DSS (1982–2014). *Journal of Decision Systems, 25*(sup1), 198–215.
4. Moral-Muñoz, J. A., Herrera-Viedma, E., Santisteban-Espejo, A., & Cobo, M. J. (2020). Software tools for conducting bibliometric analysis in science: An up-to-date review. *El profesional de la información (EPI), 29*, 1.
5. Eom, S., Lee, S., & Kim, J. (1993). The intellectual structure of decision support systems (1971-1989). *Decision Support Systems, 10*(1), 19–35.
6. Leydesdorff, L., & Rafols, I. (2009). A global map of science based on the ISI subject categories. *Journal of the Association for Information Science and Technology, 60*(2), 348–362.
7. Keenan, P. (2016). Changes in DSS disciplines in the Web of Science. *Journal of Decision Systems, 25*(Sup1), 542–549.
8. Leydesdorff, L., Rafols, I., & Chen, C. (2013). Interactive overlays of journals and the measurement of interdisciplinarity on the basis of aggregated journal–journal citations. *Journal of the American Society for Information Science and Technology, 64*(12), 2573–2586.
9. van Eck, N. J., & Waltman, L. (2010). Software survey: VOSviewer, a computer program for bibliometric mapping. *Scientometrics, 84*(2), 523–538.
10. van Eck, N. J., & Waltman, L. (2017). Citation-based clustering of publications using CitNetExplorer and VOSviewer. *Scientometrics, 111*(2), 1053–1070. https://doi.org/10.1007/s11192-017-2300-7.
11. Leydesdorff, L., Carley, S., & Rafols, I. (2013). Global maps of science based on the new Web-of-Science categories. *Scientometrics, 94*(2), 589–593.
12. Carley, S., Porter, A. L., Rafols, I., & Leydesdorff, L. (2017). Visualization of disciplinary profiles: Enhanced science overlay maps. *Journal of Data and Information Science, 2*(3), 68–111.
13. de Solla Price, D. J. (1965). Networks of scientific papers. *Science, 149*(3683), 510–515.
14. Kurt, Y., & Kurt, M. (2020). Social network analysis in international business research: An assessment of the current state of play and future research directions. *International Business Review, 29*(2), 101633. https://doi.org/10.1016/j.ibusrev.2019.101633.
15. Small, H. (1973). Co-citation in the scientific literature: A new measure of the relationship between two documents. *Journal of the American Society for Information Science, 24*(4), 265–269.

16. Small, H. (1980). Co-citation context analysis and the structure of paradigms. *Journal of Documentation, 36*(3), 183–196.
17. Small, H. (1999). Visualizing science by citation mapping. *Journal of the Association for Information Science and Technology, 50*(9), 799.
18. Thor, A., Bornmann, L., Marx, W., & Mutz, R. (2018). Identifying single influential publications in a research field: New analysis opportunities of the CRExplorer. *Scientometrics, 116*(1), 591–608. https://doi.org/10.1007/s11192-018-2733-7.
19. Thor, A., Marx, W., Leydesdorff, L., & Bornmann, L. (2016). Introducing CitedReferencesExplorer (CRExplorer): A program for reference publication year spectroscopy with cited references standardization. *Journal of Informetrics, 10*(2), 503–515.
20. Mrvar, A., & Batagelj, V. (2016). Analysis and visualization of large networks with program package Pajek. *Complex Adaptive Systems Modeling, 4*(1), 6.
21. Freeman, L. C. (1978). Centrality in social networks conceptual clarification. *Social Networks, 1*(3), 215–239.
22. Leydesdorff, L. (2007). Betweenness centrality as an indicator of the interdisciplinarity of scientific journals. *Journal of the Association for Information Science and Technology, 58*(9), 1303–1319.
23. Wang, N., Liang, H., Jia, Y., Ge, S., Xue, Y., & Wang, Z. (2016). Cloud computing research in the IS discipline: A citation/co-citation analysis. *Decision Support Systems, 86*, 35–47.
24. Lin, X., Zhang, H., Wu, H., & Cui, D. (2020). Mapping the knowledge development and frontier areas of public risk governance research. *International Journal of Disaster Risk Reduction, 43*, 101365. https://doi.org/10.1016/j.ijdrr.2019.101365.
25. Keenan, P. B., & Jankowski, P. (2019). Spatial decision support systems: Three decades on. *Decision Support Systems, 116*, 64–76. https://doi.org/10.1016/j.dss.2018.10.010.
26. Argoubi, M., Ammari, E., & Masri, H. (2020). A scientometric analysis of operations research and management science research in Africa. *Operational Research Forthcoming.* https://doi.org/10.1007/s12351-020-00555-9.
27. Leydesdorff, L., Wagner, C. S., & Bornmann, L. (2019). Interdisciplinarity as diversity in citation patterns among journals: Rao-Stirling diversity, relative variety, and the Gini coefficient. *Journal of Informetrics, 13*(1), 255–269. https://doi.org/10.1016/j.joi.2018.12.006.
28. Waheed, W., Imran, M., Raza, B., Malik, A. K., & Khattak, H. A. (2019). A hybrid approach toward research paper recommendation using centrality measures and author ranking. *IEEE Access, 7*, 33145–33158. https://doi.org/10.1109/ACCESS.2019.2900520.
29. Sprague, R. H., & Carlson, E. D. (1982). *Building effective decision support systems.* Englewood Cliffs, NJ: Prentice Hall International.
30. Keen, P. G. W., & Scott-Morton, M. S. (1978). *Decision support systems: An organizational perspective. Addison-Wesley series on decision support.* Reading, MA: Addison-Wesley.
31. Simon, H. A. (1960). *The new science of management decision.* New York: Harper & Brothers.
32. Bonczek, R. H., Holsapple, C. W., & Whinston, A. B. (1981). Foundations of decision support systems. In *Operations research and industrial engineering.* Orlando: Academic Press.
33. Saaty, T. L. (1980). *The analytic hierarchy process: Planning, priority setting, resources allocation.* New York: McGraw.
34. Desanctis, G., & Gallupe, R. B. (1987). A foundation for the study of group decision support systems. *Management Science, 33*(5), 589–609.
35. Keeney, R. L., & Raiffa, H. (1976). *Decision with multiple objectives.* New York: Wiley.
36. Newell, A., & Simon, H. A. (1972). *Human problem solving, vol 104. vol 9.* Englewood Cliffs, NJ: Prentice-Hall.
37. Mintzberg, H., Raisinghani, D., & Theoret, A. (1976). The structure of "unstructured" decision processes. *Administrative Science Quarterly, 21*, 246–275.
38. Alter, S. (1980). *Decision support systems: Current practice and continuing challenges.* Reading, USA: Addison-Wesley.
39. Eom, S. B. (1998). The intellectual development and structure of decision support systems (1991–1995). *Omega, 26*(5), 639–657.
40. Power, D. J., & Kaparthi, S. (1998). The changing technological context of decision support systems. In D. Berkeley, G. Widmeyer, P. Brézillion, & V. Rajkovic (Eds.), *Context sensitive decision support systems* (pp. 41–54). London: Chapman Hall.

41. Shim, J. P., Warkentin, M., Courtney, J. F., Power, D. J., Sharda, R., & Carlsson, C. (2002). Past, present, and future of decision support technology. *Decision Support Systems, 33*(2), 111–126.

42. Keenan, P. (2020). Bibliographic analysis of operations research citation in the environmental domain. *International Journal of Decision Support System Technology (IJDSST), 12*(2), 67–79. https://doi.org/10.4018/IJDSST.2020040104.

43. Zadeh, L. A. (1965). Fuzzy sets. *Information and Control, 8*(3), 338–353.

44. Goldberg, D. E. (1989). *Genetic algorithms in search, optimization, and machine learning.* Reading, MA: Addison-Wesley.

45. Holland, J. H. (1975). *Adaptation in natural and artificial systems.* Ann Arbor, MI: University of Michigan Press.

46. Davis, F. D. (1989). Perceived usefulness, perceived ease of use, and user acceptance of information technology. *MIS Quarterly, 13*(3), 319–340. https://doi.org/10.2307/249008.

47. Densham, P. J. (1991). Spatial decision support systems. In D. J. Maguire, M. F. Goodchild, & D. W. Rhind (Eds.), *Geographical information systems, Volume 1: Principles* (Vol. 1, pp. 403–412). Harlow, Essex: Longman Scientific & Technical.

48. Breiman, L. (2001). Random forests. *Machine Learning, 45*(1), 5–32.

49. Jang, J.-S. (1993). ANFIS: Adaptive-network-based fuzzy inference system. *IEEE Transactions on Systems, Man, and Cybernetics, 23*(3), 665–685.

50. Power, D. J., & Sharda, R. (2007). Model-driven decision support systems: Concepts and research directions. *Decision Support Systems, 43*(3), 1044–1061.

51. Power, D. J. (2002). *Decision support systems: Concepts and resources for managers.* Westport, Conn., USA: Quorum Books.

52. Mysiak, J., Giupponi, C., & Rosato, P. (2005). Towards the development of a decision support system for water resource management. *Environmental Modelling & Software, 20*(2), 203–214.

53. Garg, A. X., Adhikari, N. K. J., McDonald, H., Rosas-Arellano, M. P., Devereaux, P. J., Beyene, J., Sam, J., & Haynes, R. B. (2005). Effects of computerized clinical decision support systems on practitioner performance and patient outcomes a systematic review. *JAMA, 293*(10), 1223–1238. https://doi.org/10.1001/jama.293.10.1223.

54. Arnott, D., & Pervan, G. (2005). A critical analysis of decision support systems research. *Journal of Information Technology, 20*(2), 67–87.

55. Arnott, D., & Pervan, G. (2008). Eight key issues for the decision support systems discipline. *Decision Support Systems, 44*(3), 657–672.

56. Turban, E. (1995). Decision support and expert systems: Management support systems. Englewood Cliffs: Prentice Hall.

Two Grand Challenges for DSS Evolution

David Paradice

Abstract A review of Decision Support Systems (DSS) research shows technology and DSS evolve in a synchronized fashion. As new technological tools are introduced, researchers leverage the tools to expand the capabilities of DSS. However, advances in DSS are often piecemeal, lacking synergies that could come from adopting a grand challenge. The future will exhibit a similar pattern of technological advances, with analytics and artificial intelligence being two technologies that can be expected to impact DSS design. Analytics and artificial intelligence are broad technologies that have the potential to make significant impacts on decision support. For DSS to have a meaningful impact on decision-making processes, DSS must get "smarter." DSS can get smarter by having greater understanding the contexts in which they operate. Two grand challenges are proposed: expanding the model of context implicit in all DSS and implementing a model of shared context understanding for networks of DSS. Each grand challenge provides opportunities for DSS researchers in many specialty areas to contribute, while also moving the discipline forward in a significant way.

Keywords Analytics · Artificial intelligence · Grand challenge · Decision context · DSS design · Collaborative AI · Cynefin concept · Philosophical basis of DSS

1 Introduction

Throughout the history of Decision Support Systems (DSS), there have been periodic calls for some type of review on the status of the concept. In the 1980s, there was some debate about whether DSS was a subarea of Management Information Systems (MIS) or vice versa [1, 2]. In the early 2000s, a call was made to expand

D. Paradice (✉)
Raymond J. Harbert College of Business, Auburn University, Auburn, AL, USA
e-mail: dparadice@auburn.edu

© Springer Nature Switzerland AG 2021
J. Papathanasiou et al. (eds.), *EURO Working Group on DSS*, Integrated Series in Information Systems, https://doi.org/10.1007/978-3-030-70377-6_3

the boundaries of DSS [3]. In 2014, a response to some concern about the future of DSS declared the discipline "alive and well" [4].

An advantage that we have today is that we have several decades of prior work that can be evaluated. When I look at that work, two issues emerge. First, the DSS discipline builds in concert with advances in technological tools. Advances in the capabilities of DSS are well synchronized with advances in the capabilities of the technical tools at hand. Second, the DSS discipline has lacked explicitly declared grand challenges. The lack of explicit grand challenges hampers the discipline's ability to make a transformative impact on decision-making processes.

This chapter will unfold as follows. The next section will review the evolution of DSS and tool technologies to illustrate how the DSS concept has evolved as various technologies have evolved. The subsequent section identifies two technologies— analytics and artificial intelligence—that I believe are the next ones to have a major influence on DSS evolution. Unlike previous DSS eras, these two technologies are not new technologies to DSS researchers. However, our processing capabilities for each are vastly different from what they were several decades ago, so the section explores how these technologies will be valuable in advancing the DSS discipline.

The technologies alone do not drive DSS evolution. The technologies allow DSS to evolve in ways that expand decision-making capabilities. With that in mind, I discuss how a specific design philosophy guides DSS development and the role of context in decision-making processes. This is followed by a deeper examination of context as a construct to be modeled in DSS. That section is then followed by a brief section that defines a grand challenge for DSS researchers, which is followed by concluding remarks.

2   DSS Evolution

Arnott and Pervan [5] analyzed DSS research and described the field in terms of different DSS categories. They embedded a timeline in their analysis, which roughly corresponds to the various evolutions of DSS. Prior to the 1970s, they identify the influences on the DSS movement as transaction processing and reporting systems (coming from more general computer-based information systems), optimization and simulation models (coming from operations research/management science), and behavioral decision theory. As the DSS concept developed in the 1970s, emphasis was on the design of the reporting systems and data access systems. The issue at that time was that managers needed more timely information and that the batch-oriented systems of the day were not responsive to the needs of managers due to the dynamic nature of the business environment.

The 1970s were the age of personal DSS, with the term DSS first appearing in a paper by Gorry and Scott-Morton [6]. Leveraging computer technology to support managerial decision-making was the goal. Computer systems configured on "minicomputers" that did not require large, environmentally controlled rooms (e.g., DEC VAX systems) emerged during this decade. Conceptually, the computing environment was still similar to the mainframe environment with "dumb" terminals connected to a central computing processor. The smaller size of the main processing units, the ability to operate them in nonspecialized environments (as long as the environment was not too hot and the air around them was clean), and especially the reduced purchase expense made minicomputer systems attractive to departments within organizations as a way to provide computer support to specific groups. Specialized DSS could be developed for these groups, with individual, computer-based decision-making needs being met in a timely and dynamic manner for the first time.

Arnott and Pervan's analysis focused on the evolution of research in DSS, so they do not discuss the development of small, personal computers that occurred during this time. Engineering and technically oriented hobbyists were building their own personal computers during this decade. The Altair 8800 was one of the first computers available in the mid-1970s, being sold via mail order. It could be programmed in BASIC or FORTRAN, giving individuals a platform for writing programs to meet their personal needs. The Apple II, the Commodore PET 2001, and the TRS-80 followed in the late 1970s, driving innovation to produce reliable, inexpensive, personal computing environments. A critical software application, VisiCalc spreadsheet software, was also developed for the Apple II in the late 1970s.

This parallel development of technology and the DSS concept is important, for the two forces work together to accelerate the development of each individually. IBM's announcement in the early 1980s that it would market a personal computing machine, the IBM-PC, was widely seen as evidence that IBM believed desktop computing systems were legitimate business computing environments. Although initial installations of IBM-PCs in corporate environments did little more than replace the dumb terminals with the new PC, the desktop computing capability would soon be leveraged within corporations through the incorporation of spreadsheet software by workers wanting to develop quantitative analyses. Word processing software was developed to handle document construction and database software was developed to handle data processing needs. The corporate world realized the advantages of a possessing a desktop computing platform to perform calculations for applications as routine as budgeting to as complex as electric power plant maintenance [7]. However, work is rarely performed entirely by individuals in organizations. It is typically performed by groups, and this reality drove the next generation of DSS evolution.

Arnott and Pervan identify group DSS (GDSS) emerging as an extension of personal DSS in the early 1980s, being influenced by research in social psychology in general and group behavior and processes more specifically. The recognition that work occurs in groups, combined with a need to provide a file sharing capability that was at the heart of mainframe systems that were being replaced by smaller computing devices, drove innovation into network developments. In 1983, Novell, Inc. launched NetWare, a network operating system used to run various services on personal computers.

The 1980s also witnessed advances in data management and general processing that led to relational database systems being viable corporate data management environments. The ability to manage, and especially to relate, data from across an organization gave impetus to the executive information systems concept. At this point, "DSS" was fading as a name for systems that provide decision support, reflecting perhaps the ubiquity of the idea that computer-based information is used throughout corporate decision-making. Although online analytical processing (OLAP) technically began in the 1970s, it took off as a corporate computing necessity in the early 1990s as advances in OLAP, executive information systems, and dimensional modeling began to get folded into data warehousing concepts. The 1990s also saw negotiation support systems emerge as a special class of group DSS, being driven by innovations in the underlying network technology that supported group DSS and work in negotiation theory.

The evolution of the programming environments during this time also cannot be overlooked. During this period, significant programming languages and concepts were evolving. COBOL, BASIC, and FORTRAN were soon just choices among a host of languages. Some, such as ALGOL, PASCAL, and PL/1, were designed to be modular, maintainable, and able to support computational tasks in any domain, be it science, engineering, or business. Others, such as LISP, APL, and PROLOG, were designed to be specifically used in more focused applications in domains like artificial intelligence. As a result, a new genre of DSS, identified by Arnott and Pervan as intelligent DSS, evolved.

The convergence of local area network technology, database management, and programming language advances provided technical capabilities needed by decision-makers, but it did not ensure that the decisions being made were good decisions. Arnott and Pervan identify the influence of developments in artificial intelligence and expert systems in this period that led to the intelligent DSS concept that was developed throughout the 1980s and into the 1990s. Individual and organizational learning [8] began to be a focus, as support for decision-making transitioned to improving individual decision-making in specific situations and organizational decision-making more generally. Simultaneously, an emphasis on knowledge management and organizational learning [9] began.

This review describes how DSS research has been successful at integrating new technology to advance DSS capabilities. But most of these advances have been piecemeal in nature and lacking in their ability to gain synergies through coordinated and shared research efforts. Research is an inherently cumulative activity, in that studies build on earlier work to create new knowledge. But coordinated efforts focused on big goals can have transformative impacts. Computer science, for example, has had big goals such as natural language processing, handwriting recognition, and commonsense reasoning that have been pursued by researchers across the world. When big goals like these are the focus, the smaller steps needed to achieve them are recognized as valuable and they are shared more readily. The focus shifts from theory-building to theorizing, an activity that the DSS discipline has not recognized as being as valuable as theory development.

The DSS discipline has, however, had some organized efforts focused on big goals. For example, in the mid-1980s, IBM announced 20, one million-dollar grants that would be awarded to universities to support research. The University of Arizona won one of these awards and, recognizing that most decision-making processes in complex environments involved groups of decision-makers, used the money to construct an environment to study decision support for groups. Studies emerged from this laboratory that advanced our understanding of how groups function and how they could be supported with technology [10].

A second example is summarized in Paradice et al. [11]. They document a period of 30 years in which research was focused on a goal to implement a DSS for general managerial problem formulation. Originally begun at Texas Tech University, this stream of research was pursued by multiple generations of researchers at many universities. It began with a goal of supporting a single manager confronting a problem situation and ultimately evolved into studies of how to integrate a range of technological tools and philosophical concepts of knowledge inquiry into the foundations of DSS.

The relationship between technology tool development and the development of DSS at a macro level is implicit in Arnott and Prevan's work. A similar symbiotic development of tools and design can be seen at a micro level in the Arizona group DSS work and the general managerial problem formulation work. Additionally, these research programs illustrate how tool development combined with a specific design goal can focus effort and lead to success. In looking at the future, it seems reasonable then to think in terms of what technologies are likely to be integrated into DSS and what type of big goal might guide the field's development.

3   Two Technologies: Analytics and Artificial Intelligence

Two broad technologies that will be integral in DSS are analytic methods and the use of artificial intelligence (AI). Neither is new to DSS. Analytics in DSS can be traced back to the earliest conceptions of DSS and researchers were looking for ways to incorporate "intelligence" into systems that would support decision-making processes well before the term DSS was created. However, what we know now about each area and the tools we now have for integrating these technologies into a DSS have evolved significantly in the last 40 years.

In the realm of analytics, the descriptive, predictive, and prescriptive categories of analytical analysis provide a complementary way of conceiving DSS. Descriptive analytics are used to describe what has happened in an environment. Predictive analytics are used to forecast what could happen in an environment. Prescriptive analytics are used to help determine what should happen in an environment. Decision support is enhanced by each of these types of analysis, but the context of each is different. Context will be a concept/construct that will require greater consideration and development in the DSS of the future. Context is considered in greater detail later in this paper.

With respect to AI, recent developments in adaptive learning and collaborative AI have significant implications for DSS. DSS are becoming simultaneously ubiquitous and invisible in our lives when we think of the "smart" devices in our homes and automobiles that we implicitly rely upon for decision-making support. There is a need to significantly broaden what type of system is included under the umbrella term of DSS in order to adequately identify the potential impact of our field. Advances in robotics are such that robotic systems are becoming a type of DSS for police work. Nanotechnology in smart pills mean a physician's DSS might be ingestible.

The frontier in technology tool development must be how we integrate artificial intelligence into DSS. However, the nature of AI requires that we re-envision DSS in terms of what AI allows us to do. Our goal should not be to do better what we have done before. Our goal should be to imagine (and build) DSS that supports decision-making in new ways through the integration of AI. According to one executive interviewed by Ransbotham et al. [12], one company has not found a situation where AI could not be used to automate or semi-automate an existing process in some way.

DSS has typically been approached from a mindset of distilling structure from a class of problems so that the structure can be used to guide a user to a decision choice within that problem class. The common characteristics of problems in a class of problems are used to build a model that can support future decision-making in the same problem class context. We can take as an example DSS for supporting tax decisions. A typical approach models the tax provisions that are applicable in a decision-making situation and produces one or more scenarios that reflect different decision choices. However, the "best" decision may be one that is a new interpretation of the tax provisions; one that is not typically applied or has not ever been applied. The most valuable accountants, lawyers, doctors, and other professionals are those who can draw on their expertise to design new solutions. The expert that we once turned to can be an AI-augmented DSS in the future. It may be time for us to enhance our general underlying focus of unstructured/semi-structured/structured problems with an additional consideration of what parts of the problems may include non-automatable/semi-automatable/automatable tasks. DSS research needs to explore the characteristics of decision-making contexts in ways that support decision-making for a unique decision case as well as in ways that support common decision-making needs in a class of decisions. DSS should support a decision that needs to be made for a specific patient, client, or customer by incorporating the specific and perhaps novel contextual situation of that patient, client, or customer.

The notion of collaborative AI, where a user/decision-maker works with an AI system, is already being developed [13] and yet it is difficult to find any reference to DSS in that literature. However, one can find implications of the DSS philosophy within this literature. Human–technology collaboration has always been at the heart of DSS. DSS has always been conceived as *supporting* decision-making, not replacing it. Wilson and Daugherty state that the AI "technology's larger impact will be in complementing and augmenting human capabilities, not replacing them." What could be more compatible with DSS? In their analysis, they find that firms "achieve the most significant performance improvements when humans and machines work together." We have an opportunity to influence AI-based man-machine collaboration through our work in DSS. An argument can be made that AI has been driving DSS for 40 years. The development of knowledge-based systems, learning systems, intelligent systems, and so forth all have their roots in attempts to integrate more intelligence (however defined) into DSS. As has always been true for DSS, the value proposition we have is that we design systems to work with decision-makers. DSS has never sought to replace human judgment with technology.

Wilson and Daugherty [13] identify new roles for humans that will result from collaborative AI environments, and many of them can be adapted to the DSS environment. There will be new roles for the DSS designer and developer. There will also be many new job roles that are related to DSS. An example is the person who will ensure a learning DSS is generating feasible alternatives. While self-learning capabilities are being developed in the technology, humans who "teach" DSS systems are needed. Humans will be needed to validate system learning. We already see this work in the role of humans who validate various predictive models and machine learning models. Humans will determine what needs to be learned.

In the short run, humans are needed to explain the output of AI enhanced DSS. Today, these humans are often called "consultants," but we should work toward a time when a DSS is able to explain not only the results of an analysis but also all the underlying assumptions and factors influencing the analysis. The system must be able to explain "why" a DSS recommendation is reasonable, justifiable, and valid. An area of research can be determining what will be needed to build systems that perform this explanation. The decision-making context will be an important factor in explanation.

During development, we should not think of errors made by DSS with AI learning capabilities as we do the errors made by a small child when learning. Many students in our college classes make errors attempting to extrapolate concepts in the classroom to novel or more complex cases. Humans will be needed to supervise the DSS as it learns, guiding the DSS to add appropriate concepts, use cases, and decision rules to its capabilities. This human role will also be needed to ensure that the DSS continues to function for its original purpose or evolves (in some sense) into providing adequate decision support in a problem domain. But how should the DSS evolve? What is an appropriate domain into which a given DSS should evolve? These are questions of an ethical nature. Prior research has explored how system designers embed their personal ethics into systems [14], and we should revive that work in the evolution of DSS. As systems become more autonomous, the human role in guiding the ethical development of the self-learning system becomes increasingly important and necessary.

Ransbotham et al. [12] note that firms that lead in the utilization of AI "enable their organizations to *consume* as much as to produce AI" (their emphasis, page 2). They emphasize that a strategic focus for AI development and use is critical for positive returns for the organization. That is, "tying a strategy for AI to the company's overall strategy" is a factor that distinguishes companies that have had successful AI experiences from those that have not (page 6). The successful companies find "areas in which the strategy needs support" and then find a way to support it. Machine learning will enable users to gain insights that were not possible under traditional DSS approaches. Traditional DSS were model based, and while

the concept of learning DSS has been discussed in the research literature, the advent
of machine learning techniques makes a learning DSS truly feasible. The ability to
learn allows DSS to enter into strategic decision-making support for the first time in
the history of the concept.

DSS has traditionally looked for ways to support existing decision-making
processes without envisioning new (related) processes or expanding the scope of the
business to utilize new processes. DSS researchers must explore how AI-based DSS
can define new business processes. Ransbotham et al. [12] relate a story in which a
German bank leveraged AI to refine its loan application assessment process to allow
potential loan applicants to know whether their application would be accepted or
rejected. In the German system, a rejected loan application has a negative impact
on a German citizen's credit rating. By providing a service to applicants before they
apply, the bank builds goodwill and reaches those who may not have applied without
this safety net for rejection. The bank has essentially provided an AI-augmented loan
application DSS to potential loan applicants. The more traditional approach would
have focused on providing decision support to current bank customers, not potential
bank customers.

Business processes need to be re-imagined considering how to leverage the AI
enhanced DSS. Where the traditional DSS concept has not redefined the decision-
maker's task, the AI enhanced DSS creates an opportunity for a decision-maker's
task to evolve into one that incorporates more creative aspects of the work.
Continuing the tax scenario from earlier, perhaps the design of the DSS for tax
support can lead to a situation where the user searches for the unique interpretation
(in the short run). In the long run, the system could "understand" that context
determines which situations call for a routinely good decision and which ones call
for a uniquely different, yet also good, decision.

4   Design Philosophy

The idea that DSS operate in semi-structured problem spaces has always been
somewhat problematic. What is semi-structured for one user may be unstructured
for another user and structured for a third. Thus, the line of demarcation for where
a DSS should be operating has always been somewhat fluid. Regardless of the
perceived structure of the problem domain, AI enhanced DSS should allow users
to operate in domains which they perceive to lack structure or allow the user to
search out the unique problem characteristics on their way to the unique and good
decision. Again, this is not a new idea for DSS researchers.

The general model for problem formulation specified in Paradice and Courtney
[15] assumed managerial decision-makers perceived the business environment as
semi-structured. It placed a manager's experiential knowledge at the center of
a decision-making situation but provided tools to support the decision-making
process. As managers hypothesized the structure of business problems, the system
would draw on data from the corporate database, analyze the data with various

analytical tools, apply rules from a knowledge base, and present assessments of the hypothesized relationships to the user.

The system contained two additional components for decision support that were unique at the time. One was a "discovery module" that was intended to assist a manager in discovering important information in the business environment automatically. The discovery module was intended to be a solution to the problem of managers having limited information processing capabilities compared to the size, complexity, and dynamic information environment of the corporation. Simply put, the discovery module would assist the manager in knowing as much as possible about the business environment by automating the process of forming hypotheses to be tested.

The system also contained a "rejection base." This DSS component was intended to be a reservoir for hypotheses that failed to be confirmed by the system. The rejection base concept evolved to support the scenario in which a manager hypothesizes a relationship among business constructs and uses the system to test the hypothesis, but the system is unable to confirm the hypothesis as correct. That the manager found the hypothesis worthy to test was considered an indication that the hypothesis should be retained for future use by the system. The system was designed on the premise that the context in which the hypothesis was tested should be recognized as dynamic. In a complex and dynamic business environment, conditions could change over time that would render the hypothesis confirmable later.

For example, suppose a manager hypothesizes that an increase in incentive pay to a sales force will result in increased sales volume. In some cases, this hypothesis is likely to be confirmed, while in others it will not be. In fact, within a sales force, the hypothesis may be confirmed for some members of the sales team and not for others. In this simple example, one explanation could be the perception of the individual salesperson of his/her work/life balance. The salesperson who is content may be less likely to work to increase sales. Perhaps the trade-off for this person is working harder for an increase that will not perceptibly improve her life. On the other hand, the salesperson who desires more income as a means to change her economic situation, or the person who sees an increase in discretionary income as leading to a more enjoyable overall quality of life, may respond to the increased incentive pay with a corresponding increase in sales productivity. This example illustrates how the context of the hypothesis impacts its confirmation.

The discovery module was intended to support learning. Billman [16] investigated three approaches to automate a discovery process. She adapted work by Einhorn and Hogarth [17] which implements "a causal inferencing model of the way people evaluate the potential strength of a causal relationship between two models" (p. 25) [18]. This approach, however, was embedded in a static causal map created from a manager's understanding of a business environment. As such, it did not support automated learning by the system. Success in creating a DSS that learns becomes much more likely if the DSS can take data from the environment in real time and update itself, a capability that can be envisioned using machine learning.

What we see in Paradice and Courtney's model, which was unrecognized at the time, is that context plays a critical role in the knowledge created by the system. Humphreys and Brezillon [19] have discussed context in decision-making and DSS has long recognized that decision contexts have stakeholders (c.f., [20]). The Cambridge Dictionary defines context as the situation within which something exists or happens, and that can help explain it [21]. Fakude [22] refers to context as the "communal condition of an environment" and refers to it as a "process which involves the evaluation of information that will have an effect of the probability of success regarding the communication process." However, developing context as a construct for DSS will require that we understand how context affects meaning across the spectrum of DSS use, from the user interface to the decision model.

5   Context

DeVito [23] identifies four types of context. Any or all of them may be relevant to a given situation. Physical context refers to the tangible environment. Communication changes, and things have different meanings, given our physical environment. Cultural context refers to values, beliefs, lifestyles, and behaviors. Cultural factors can influence one's assessment of whether something is right or wrong. Social-psychological context involves group norms. How and what is communicated between people in an office differs from communication at a sporting event. Temporal context is the positioning of a message within a sequence of conversational events.

We know, for example, that a word can mean different things in different sentences. For example, the word "log" means one thing in the sentence "The grey fox jumped over the log" and something different in the sentence, "The captain's log contained a curious entry." Indeed, a single sentence may be interpreted in multiple ways, as demonstrated by the interpretations of the sentence "Time flies like an arrow." One interpretation takes "time" to be the passage of time and suggests that it moves quickly, as an arrow does. Another interpretation is a command, to time small insects in a manner similar to the way one would time (one assumes, the flight of) an arrow. A third interpretation references an insect known as a "time fly" and suggests that these insects have an affinity for arrows. There are other interpretations.

In the simple word example, we can determine the meaning of "log" from other cues in the sentence. This example relies on the other parts of the sentence to help the reader (or listener) derive meaning. It is an anaphoric reference. In the more ambiguous sentence, we must have some context to determine the meaning of the sentence. We draw on the situational aspects of the sentence to derive its meaning.

This will not be a trivial problem to address, as can be found by examining the AI literature for natural language understanding. However, not all DSS need to be capable of natural language understanding to provide benefits to users, so we need not attempt to solve the problem of natural language understanding. What we need to do is better understand the notion of context.

For example, consider a situation in which a person must make a drive to a destination. The decision situation is simply "what time should the person begin the drive?" For this example, let us assume our smartphone's calendar application has DSS capability. If we have the destination included in our calendar event, the calendar application can use the smartphone's GPS capability to determine our current location, use a map application to determine the distance between our current location and the destination, and suggest a time to begin the drive. If our map application can also access traffic information and provide it to the calendar application, it may suggest an earlier departure time or a different route. If our smartphone has a weather application that the calendar application can access, that information may also impact the suggested departure time. Time of day may be an important factor, as traffic may fluctuate depending on the time of day.

These are likely to be obvious factors that we would want considered. Suppose we have riders to take with us. Without that information, the decision support could be less accurate, depending on how we expect them to rendezvous with us. The information about other passengers might be in the calendar app. Or, it could be partially derived from text messages or email. Suppose the reason for the travel is exceptionally important, such that being late has significant negative consequences. The importance might be detected from other sources (text messages, email, telephonic conversation content). Depending on the user's comfort with risk, the calendar application might want to adjust the suggested departure time. Changing other appointments on the calendar may also be advisable, depending on their characteristics.

Two things are evident from this example. First, the various apps involved must have a common way of representing information, or there must be a translation capability among them and the calendar application, for it to process the data. Second, the level of capability that the calendar application will exhibit depends on its understanding of the context of the decision situation; a context that grows progressively more complicated to model as situational factors are added. This is a simple example. Decision-making situations can be much more complicated than this. For example, triage decisions in disaster situations involve considerations far more difficult to model than this calendar application example. Decisions in active shooter situations are complicated. Decisions made by deployed military decision-makers can involve conflicting or ambiguous environmental cues to process [24]. During military action, the environment in which decisions must be made could be chaotic.

Snowden and Boone [25] present the Cynefin (pronounced ku-*nev*-in) concept as a way to consider environmental context in decision-making situations. They describe five categories of decision-making contexts: simple, complicated, complex, chaotic, and disorder for describing the nature of the relationship between cause and effect. In this approach, simple contexts are understood by decision-makers and primarily require decision-makers to categorize issues and respond to them. Problems in these contexts typically have a correct response. Problems in complicated contexts may have multiple correct responses. Complicated contexts are the "domain of experts." Decision-making in these contexts requires analysis before response. Complex contexts are characterized by problems having at least one correct response, but that response may be difficult to identify. In these environments, a decision-maker needs to probe the environment to gain understanding, then respond. To clarify, the environment of a complicated context may contain many components, but an expert understands how the components interact and influence each other. In a complex environment, the components of the environment may be identified, but knowledge of the nature of their interactions contains uncertainty. Snowden and Boone use the examples of a Ferrari as a complicated context and the Brazilian rainforest as a complex context. A chaotic context is one in which the nature of the relationships between cause and effect are unknown "because they shift constantly." In this environment, a decision-maker "must first *act* to establish order" (their emphasis). A disordered context occurs when a decision-maker cannot determine which of the prior four contexts exists. Regardless of the decision-making context, knowledge is necessary to act.

One outcome of the goal to develop a DSS for managerial problem formulation described in Paradice et al. [11] was the identification of the critical role of philosophical concepts in knowledge management. These studies initially incorporated Churchman's [26] work on inquiring systems which described five processes for inquiry based in the philosophical writings of Leibniz, Locke, Kant, Hegel, and Singer. Churchman believed these philosophical bases differed in their ability to handle inquiry in complex environments.

Briefly, a Leibnizian inquirer is grounded in notions of formal logic. It requires a logical foundation of axioms and a means for deducing new knowledge from them. A Lockean inquirer is model based. It is characterized by a single model of an environment and relies on the correctness of the model in deducing new knowledge. A Kantian inquirer works with multiple models of a decision environment. It fits data to models to determine which model performs best and creates new knowledge based on the model fit results. A Hegelian inquirer is grounded in dialectic processing. This inquirer relies on a debate between a thesis and an antithesis. An "objective observer" creates new knowledge through a synthesis of the best assumptions of each perspective into a new thesis. A Singerian inquirer relies on conflict to create new knowledge. The Singerian premise is that learning occurs only when there is disagreement in a situation. When there is no disagreement, A Singerian approach introduces something new into a situation to create disagreement. Later work in the effort to embed philosophical concepts in decision support examined other philosophies as bases for new knowledge creation. Parrish [27], for example, introduced the notion of a Weickian "sensemaking" inquirer. Sensemaking relies heavily on context, as context shapes how people act and how they interpret events. It is a social construction, reflecting the social context discussed earlier. People extract cues from a situation context to determine what information to process and what explanations are acceptable [28].

Table 1 shows how these concepts can be combined to guide DSS design and use.

Table 1 Process, technology, and philosophy combinations for different contexts

Context	Process	Processing	Analytics	Philosophy
Simple	Categorize	Traditional Processing	Descriptive	Leibnizian, Lockean
Complicated	Analyze	Traditional DSS	Descriptive and Predictive	Kantian
Complex	Probe and Sense	AI-augmented DSS with vetted knowledge	Descriptive, Predictive, and Prescriptive	Hegelian, Weickian
Chaotic	Act and Sense	AI-augmented DSS with ML emphasis	Descriptive	Singerian, Weickian
Disorder	Assume chaotic			

In the simple context, the decision-maker knows what to do once the situation is properly categorized. Traditional processing, which may be a transaction processing system rather than a DSS, is employed. To the extent analytics are needed, descriptive analytics are sufficient because the goal is simply to recognize the appropriate category for the situation. Once categorized, the decision process follows standard operating procedures. The Leibnizian approach fits well with an "if x is true, then do y" type of response. The Lockean approach allows a more sophisticated model to be used to guide the response.

Analysis is needed in the complicated context. This is the domain of traditional DSS. Analytic processing involves descriptive analytics to gather data and predictive analytics to support scenario analysis. The Kantian approach works well in this situation, allowing multiple models to be evaluated to determine which one has the best "fit" to the decision situation.

The complex context is one in which a correct solution exists, but it is unknown. Here DSS augmented with AI capabilities could be effective. Descriptive and predictive analytics are needed to play the same roles they played in the complicated context, but now prescriptive analytics will be needed to answer the question of what should be done. Snowden and Boone describe the complex context as the realm of unknown unknowns. They believe, however, that a path forward for a decision-maker can emerge if the decision-maker patiently conducts experiments that are safe to fail and allows the path forward to present itself. Implicit in this approach is that the decision-maker learns from the experiments. Hodges [29] demonstrated a dialectic process could be implemented in software. Updating his approach to incorporate current machine learning techniques would create an opportunity for a decision-maker to serve as an objective observer in the Hegelian inquiring approach. Supplementing this with Weick's notions of sensemaking creates an opportunity to transform the context from complex to complicated.

6 Two Grand Challenges for DSS

Grand challenges seek to make drastic changes to a field [30]. Grand challenges are characterized by multiple research efforts that unfold over time, typically involving researchers from different disciplines who combine their expertise and perspectives to tackle a difficult problem. During a grand challenge, new processes, procedures, and technologies may be developed. Researchers are willing to invest in grand challenge participation because they feel a successful outcome will significantly impact their discipline and their personal careers. Despite the benefits of pursuing grand challenges, the DSS discipline as a field has not defined one. They have been pursued only by co-located groups of researchers focused on a specific goal.

Consequently, two grand challenges are proposed:

1. Develop a general model of context that a DSS can use to provide nuanced decision support based on the context of the decision environment.
2. Develop a general model of context that supports networks of DSS so that the synthesized support of the individual DSS provides better support for decisions than any individual DSS could provide.

Context affects meaning [31], and the future of DSS will be determined by the extent to which DSS are able to consider the context of decision situations, both singularly and in a network of DSS. Because context impacts meaning, the model of context must be developed in a consistent manner from the user interface through the model of the decision situation. The DSS discipline would benefit by taking on the grand challenge of modeling problem context across the continuum of its applicability: from the micro-uses of context to create more effective user interfaces to the macro-uses of context to provide support in problem domains. The DSS discipline should also work on the grand challenge of networking DSS, using a shared context in which specialized DSS contribute knowledge in a coordinated fashion to provide support in a more general decision-making environment.

Specific types of research projects occur in grand challenges [11]. Prelude projects are projects that lead to the grand challenge definition. Since DSS operate in specific problem domains, they already have initial concepts of context built into them. Any prior research that developed a DSS could be a prelude project in this grand challenge because a natural next step is to explicitly focus on enhanced modeling of that DSS's decision context. Once identified, foundation projects are executed to develop the concepts and tools needed to achieve the grand challenge. These projects will fall into two categories. One category will be the development of the design philosophy for the DSS. Projects in this category will be focused on answering questions such as "How should context be utilized by a DSS in this domain?" and "How should context (as a construct) be modeled?" The second category will be the development of the technological tools needed to answer the questions that emerge in the first category. Progress in each of these categories will unfold in a synchronized fashion, with design philosophy driving tool development and tool development refining design philosophy. As the research matures, realization projects will be executed to determine whether the grand challenge has been achieved.

The earlier example regarding support for a decision on when to leave for an appointment can provide an example of the work to pursue. For the first grand challenge identified above, the calendar application context includes the date of the event, the time of the event, the location of the event, the decision-maker's current location, and other constructs that immediately impact the decision about when to leave. Following the example provided earlier, the context expands to include additional riders, the weather, and the importance of the meeting. Foundation projects would focus on how the context of the "when to leave" decision is modeled.

For the second grand challenge identified above, the foundation projects would investigate how elements of the context model developed in response to the first grand challenge could be distributed across multiple DSS. In this case, the calendar application has a context, the message application has a context, and the weather application has a context. The applications also have a shared context of some kind that allows them to recognize either when one of them needs information from another one or when one of them has knowledge that another application would benefit from having. In both grand challenges, one should expect a focus on the technological tools in some foundational projects and a focus on the DSS design in others. Finally, realization projects would be executed when researchers believed their foundational projects were achieving successes that warrant a realistic test of the DSS.

7 Conclusion

The history of DSS research shows technology and DSS evolve in a synchronized fashion. As new technological tools are introduced, researchers leverage the tools to expand the capabilities of DSS. The future will exhibit a similar pattern, with analytics and artificial intelligence being two tools that can be expected to impact DSS design. Our discipline has not, however, recognized this synchronicity to its advantage. Researchers generally focus on topics of interest that are not always part of a larger goal.

Analytics and artificial intelligence are broad technologies that have the potential to make significant impacts on decision support, and a piecemeal approach to integrating them into DSS will certainly result in some progress. However, for DSS to have a meaningful impact on decision-making processes, DSS must get "smarter." DSS can get smarter by having greater understanding of the contexts in which they operate. The two grand challenges proposed here provide opportunities for DSS researchers in many specialty areas to contribute, while also moving the discipline forward in a significant way.

References

1. Blanning, R. W. (1983). What is Happening in DSS? *Interfaces, 13*(5), 71–80.
2. Naylor, T. H. (1982). Decision support systems or whatever happened to M.I.S.? *Interfaces, 12*(4), 92–94.
3. Paradice, D. B. (2007). Expanding the boundaries of DSS. *Decision Support Systems, 43*, 1549–1552.
4. Hosack, B., Hall, D., Paradice, D. B., & Courtney, J. F. (2012). A look toward the future: Decision support systems research is alive and well. *Journal of the Association for Information Systems, 13*, 315–340.
5. Arnott, D., & Pervan, G. (2005). A critical analysis of decision support research. *Journal of Information Technology, 20*, 67–87. https://doi.org/10.1057/palgrave.jit.2000035.
6. Gorry, G. A., & Scott-Morton, M. S. (1971). A framework for management information systems. *Sloan Management Review, 13*, 55–70.
7. Taylor, L. L., Lee, S. T., Sustman, J. E., Ganz, G. L., & Maschoff, D. C. (1981). A screening model for utility strategic planning. *IEEE Transactions on Power Apparatus and Systems, PAS-100*(8), 4093–4103. https://doi.org/10.1109/TPAS.1981.317004.
8. Courtney, J. F., Croasdell, D. T., & Paradice, D. B. (1998). Inquiring organizations. *Australian Journal of Information Systems, 6*(1), 3–14.
9. Hall, D. J., & Paradice, D. B. (2005). Philosophical foundations for a learning-oriented knowledge management system for decision support. *Decision Support Systems, 39*(3), 445–461.
10. Nunamaker, J. F., Jr., Briggs, R. O., Mittleman, D. D., Vogel, D. R., & Pierre, B. A. (1996). Lessons from a dozen years of group support systems research: A discussion of lab and field findings. *Journal of Management Information Systems, 13*(3), 163–207. https://doi.org/10.1080/07421222.1996.11518138.
11. Paradice, D. B., Parrish, J. L., & Richardson, S. (2019). Grand challenge pursuits: Insights from a Multi-year DSR project stream. *Communications of the Association for Information Systems, 2019*, 45. https://doi.org/10.17705/1CAIS.04519.
12. Ransbotham, S., Khodabandeh, S., Fehling, R., LaFountain, B., & Krion, D. (2019). Winning with AI. In *MIT Sloan management review*. Boston: Boston Consulting Group.
13. Wilson, H. J., & Daugherty, P. R. (2018). *Collaborative intelligence: Humans and AI are joining forces*. Harvard: Harvard Business Review.
14. Hirschheim, R., Lyytinen, K., & Myers, M. D. (2011). Special Issue on the Kleinian approach to information system research—Forward (Guest Editorial). *European Journal of Information Systems, 20*, 418–421.
15. Paradice, D. B., & Courtney, J. F. (1987). Causal and non-causal relationships and dynamic model construction in a managerial advisory system. *Journal of Management Information Systems, 3*(4), 39–53.
16. Billman, B. H. (1989). *Automated discovery of causal relationships in managerial problem domains*. College Station, TX, USA: Dissertation, Texas A&M University.
17. Einhorn, H. J., & Hogarth, R. M. (1986). Judging probable cause. *Psychological Bulletin, 99*(1), 3–19.
18. Billman, B. H., & Courtney, J. F. (1993). Automated discovery in managerial problem formulation: Formation of causal hypotheses for cognitive mapping. *Decision Sciences, 24*(1), 23–41.
19. Humphreys, P., & Brezillon, P. (2002). Combining rich and restricted language in multimedia: Enriching context for innovative decisions. In F. Adam, P. Brezillon, P. Humphreys, & J. C. Pomerol (Eds.), *Decision making and decision support in the internet age* (pp. 695–708). Cork: Oaktree Press.
20. Mason, R. O. (1969). A dialectical approach to strategic planning. *Management Science, 15*, B403–B414.

21. Cambridge University Press. (2020). Retrieved from https://dictionary.cambridge.org/us/dictionary/english/context.
22. Fakude, N. Y. (2019). *The importance of understanding context in communication.* Retrieved from https://medium.com/@ntsikayezwefakude/the-importance-of-understanding-context-in-communication-3f921f1b5b24.
23. DeVito, J. A. (2005). *Essentials of human communication* (3rd ed.). Boston: Pearson Education, Inc..
24. Powell, G. M., Matheus, C. J., Kokar, M. M., & Lorenz, D. (2006). *Understanding the role of context in the interpretation of complex battlespace intelligence.* Fort Monmouth, NJ, USA: Army Research, Development, and Engineering Command, CERDEC, Intelligence and Information Warfare Directorate (I2WD). https://doi.org/10.1109/ICIF.2006.301719.
25. Snowden, D. J., & Boone, M. E. (2007). A leader's framework for decision making. *Harvard Business Review, 85*(11), 68–76.
26. Churchman, C. W. (1971). *The design of inquiring systems: Basic concepts of systems and organizations.* New York: Basic Books.
27. Parrish, J. L. (2008). *Sensemaking and information systems: Toward a Weickian inquiring system.* Orlando, FL, USA: Dissertation. University of Central Florida.
28. Weick, K. (1995). *Sensemaking in Organizations.* London: Sage.
29. Hodges, W. S. (1992). *Dialectron: A prototypical dialectic engine for the support of strategic planning and strategic decision-making (vols. I and II).* College Station, TX, USA: Dissertation. Texas A&M University.
30. Winter, S. J., & Butler, B. S. (2011). Creating bigger problems: Grand challenges as boundary objects and the legitimacy of the information systems field. *Journal of Information Technology, 26*(2), 99–108.
31. Doyle, T. F. (2007). *The role of context in meaning and understanding.* Germany: Dissertation, University of Potsdam.

30 Years of the EWG-DSS Through the Lens of the Collab-Net Project

Isabelle Linden ⓘ, Jean Gomes Turet ⓘ, Fatima Dargam ⓘ, Shaofeng Liu ⓘ, Rita A. Ribeiro ⓘ, Pascale Zaraté ⓘ, and Ana Paula Cabral Seixas Costa ⓘ

Abstract Originally founded by 24 participants of the ESI VI-EURO Summer Institute on DSS, in Madeira in 1989, the EURO Working Group on Decision Support Systems (EWG-DSS) is now considered as one of the most stable and active groups of EURO and a reference on DSS in Europe and Worldwide. The EWG-DSS membership has continuously grown since its creation. The group currently counts with over 250 registered members, 340 members in LinkedIn, and 174 Twitter followers. Besides organizing annual scientific events and publications, the EWG-DSS leads a long-term research project on the analysis of its research activity, the Collab-Net project that is currently at its version 5. This chapter aims to explore the life of the group along the 30 last years of its existence through the optics of the Collab-Net project, its outcomes and its analysis.

Keywords DSS · EWG-DSS · Collab-Net · Research collaboration · Social network analysis

I. Linden (✉)
Namur Digital Institute (NADI), University of Namur, Namur, Belgium
e-mail: isabelle.linden@unamur.be

J. G. Turet · A. P. C. S. Costa
Universidade Federal de Pernambuco, Recife, PE, Brazil

F. Dargam
SimTech Simulation Technology, Graz, Austria
e-mail: F.Dargam@SimTechnology.com

S. Liu
University of Plymouth, Plymouth, UK
e-mail: shaofeng.liu@plymouth.ac.uk

R. A. Ribeiro
UNINOVA, CA3, Caparica, Portugal
e-mail: rar@uninova.pt

P. Zaraté
University Toulouse 1 Capitole - IRIT, Toulouse University, Toulouse, France
e-mail: Pascale.Zarate@ut-capitole.fr

© Springer Nature Switzerland AG 2021
J. Papathanasiou et al. (eds.), *EURO Working Group on DSS*, Integrated Series in Information Systems, https://doi.org/10.1007/978-3-030-70377-6_4

1   30 Years of History

The EURO Working Group of Decision Support Systems (EWG-DSS) was created as a product of the ESI VI—EURO Summer Institute on DSS, in the Madeira Island, Portugal, in May 1989 [1]. This summer institute was organized by Prof. Jean-Pierre Brans and Prof. José Paixão, among others; and the participants were 24 young researchers of 16 different nationalities, being 22 from Europe, 1 from the USA and 1 from Brazil. The EWG-DSS is now considered as one of the most stable and active groups among the EURO Working Groups. The interest from the DSS community in the EWG-DSS together with its membership has continuously grown since its creation in 1989. The group currently counts with over 397 members from 46 countries, as well as 340 members in its LinkedIn Group, and 174 Twitter followers.

The main purpose of the EWG-DSS is to promote and encourage state-of-the-art high-quality research and collaboration work within the DSS community. Other aims of the EWG-DSS are to:

Encourage the exchange of information among practitioners, end-users, and researchers in the area of Decision Systems.

Enforce the networking among the DSS communities available and facilitate activities that are essential for the start-up of international cooperation research and projects.

Facilitate professional academic and industrial opportunities for its members.

Favour the development of innovative models, methods, and tools in the field Decision Support and related areas.

Actively promote the interest on Decision Systems in the scientific community by organizing dedicated workshops, seminars, mini-conferences, and conference streams in major conferences, as well as editing books and special issues in relevant scientific journals.

This chapter reports on the dynamic activity of the group and related members along its 30 years of existence. To reach its aims, the EWG-DSS leads a set of scientific events and publications that are presented in Sect. 2. Since 2002, the EWG-DSS also edits an annual newsletter [2], which updates its members about the activities of the year and promotes the work of its DSS community, with projects and publications presentations for instance. The EWG-DSS also offers annually special support to young researchers through its EWG-DSS Award, attributed since 2011. Besides organizing scientific events and promoting knowledge dissemination activities, the group leads a long-term research project on the analysis of its research activity, the Collab-Net project, whose history is presented in Sect. 3. The current architecture of the platform associated to the project is described in Sect. 3. Then, Sect. 4 analyses the data collected through the platform and provides rich insight on the life of the group, while Sect. 5 describes the future plan development steps related to the Collab-Net Platform. Finally, Sect. 6 draws conclusions and expresses acknowledgement to the group members and to the students that contributed to the technical developments and analysis at one or another stage of the Collab-Net project.

In addition to the historical testimony and specific contributions that will be of particular interest to the members of the group, the authors aim, through this testimony, to offer a source of inspiration for the life of other international scientific communities. Indeed, both the tools and methods of analysis and the practices implemented and tools developed to support the life of the group form a rich heritage that they are happy to share here.

2 Events and Publications

After 17 informal technical meetings of the EWG-DSS, formal workshops, with published proceedings, were initiated in 2005 in Graz, as well as formal organization of DSS streams in EURO and IFORS conferences in 2007. Since 2015, the annual workshop organized by the EWG-DSS has turned into a conference: the International Conference on Decision Support System Technology (ICDSST). Table 1 presents the complete list of the events (co-)organized by the EWG-DSS from 2005 to 2019, including their related publications in Journal Special Issues and details of the generated contributions, like: number of published full papers, short papers, extended abstracts, and posters.

In particular, the 30th anniversary edition of the EmC-ICDSST 2019, which happened in the format of a EURO Mini-Conference (https://icdsst2019.wordpress.com/) in Madeira, aimed at recapitulating the developments of the Decision Support Systems area in the last 30 years, as well as enforcing the trends and new technologies in use, in order to establish a consensus about the appropriate steps to be taken in future DSS research work.

Besides the proceedings of each of the above-mentioned events, a number of Special Issues of Journals and Books have been (co-)edited by EWG-DSS board members (they are listed in Appendix, Table 5). As it can be noticed in Table 1, the decision to turn the EWG-DSS annual scientific events into international conferences has shown to be an incredible powerful tool to enhance the number of publications and collaboration work among the EWG-DSS members.

Figure 1 presents the publications resulting of the EWG-DSS organized events, along the time span 2005–2019 and classified by their types. It is worth noting that year 2014 involves a significant number of full papers in the LNBIP book edited as proceedings of the Joint International Conference of the INFORMS GDN Section and the EURO Working Group on DSS, Toulouse, June 10th–13th, 2014. Similarly, 2015 involves the publication of two LNBIP books including a high number of full papers. Those two Springer LNBIP books included on the one hand, the volume 221 involving selected papers issued from 2014 EWG-DSS workshop in Toulouse and EWG-DSS track at IFORS 2014 in Barcelona; and, on the other hand, the volume 216, edited as pre-proceedings of full papers presented at the new born International

Table 1 Events (co-)organized by EWG-DSS

Place-Year	Full title	Related publications	#FP	#SP	#AP
Dublin (Ireland) 2019	EURO XXX, DSS Streams at Euro 2019, Dublin, Ireland, 23–28th June 2019				11
Madeira (Portugal) 2019	Emc-EWG-DSS International Conference on Decision Support System Technology, 27–29th May 2019		11	30	4
Valencia (Spain) 2018	EURO XXIX: DSS Streams at EURO 2018, Valencia, Spain, 8–11th July 2018.				8
Heraklion (Crete) ICDSST 2018	EWG-DSS 2018 International Conference on Decision Support System Technology, (and Promethee Days), 22–25 May, 2018, Heraklion, Crete.	SI24, SI25, SI26	15	38 (+17)	5
Quebec (Canada) 2017	IFORS 2017: DSS Stream at the 21st Conference of the IFORS Quebec, Canada—17–21 July 2017.				19
Namur (Belgium) ICDSST 2017:ᵃ	EWG-DSS 2017 Third International Conference on Decision Support System Technology, 29–31 May 2017, Namur, Belgium	SI22, SI23	13	19	10
Poznan (Poland) 2016	EURO XXVIII, DSS Stream at EURO-2016 in Poznan, July 3–6, 2016. EWG-DSS Stream on Decision Support System				11
Plymouth (UK) ICDSST 2016	EWG-DSS 2016 Second International Conference on Decision Support System Technology, 23–25 May 2016, Plymouth, UK	SI20, SI21	15	22	2
Glasgow 2015	EURO XXVII, July 12–15 EWG-DSS Stream on Decision Support System				15
Belgrade (Serbia) ICDSST 2015	EWG-DSS 2015 First International Conference on Decision Support System Technology, 27–29 May 2015, Belgrade, Serbia	SI17, SI18, SI19	9	40	4
Barcelona (Spain) 2014	20th Conference of the IFORS, EWG-DSS Stream on Decision Support Systems—Barcelona, Spain—July 13–18, 2014	SI17, SI18, SI19			20
Toulouse (France) 2014	Joint International Conference of the INFORMS GDN Section and the EURO Working Group on DSS, Toulouse, June 10th–13th, 2014 Special Focus: Group Decision Making and Web 3.0	SI15, SI16	31	12	5
Graz (Austria) 2013	EURO Mini-Conference on "Collaborative Decision Making Systems in Economics, Complex Societal and Environmental Applications"				14

Location/Year	Event	SIXX	#FP	#SP	#AP
Thessaloniki (Greece) 2013	EWG-DSS Thessaloniki-2013 Workshop on "Exploring New Directions for Decisions in the Internet Age", May 29–31, 2013.	SI14	27		
Rome (Italy) 2013	2013: EWG-DSS DSS Stream on the EURO-INFORMS—Rome—1–4 July 2013	SI14			16
Vilnius (Lithuania) 2012	EURO XXV—2012 EWG-DSS Stream on Decision Support Systems—Vilnius, Lithuania—July 8–11th, 2012	SI12, SI13			13
Liverpool (UK) 2012	EWG-DSS Liverpool-2012 Workshop on "Decision Support Systems & Operations Management Trends and Solutions in Industries". April 12–13, 2012	SI11	42		
Paris (France) 2011	EWG-DSS/DASIG Paris-2011 Joint-Workshop. "EWG-DSS Stream on Collaborative Decision Making". November 30th, 2011	SI10	13		
London (UK) 2011	EWG-DSS London-2011 Workshop on "Decision Systems". June 23–24, 2011	SI9, SI10	39		
Lisbon (Portugal) 2010	EURO XXIV—2010 EWG-DSS Stream on Decision Support Systems—Lisbon, Portugal—July 11–14, 2010	SI8		7	
Bonn (Germany) 2009	EURO XXIII—2009 EWG-DSS Stream on Decision Support Systems—Bonn, Germany, July 5–8, 2009			14	
Toulouse (France) 2008	IFIP TC8/WG8.3 International Conference on Collaborative Decision Making (CDM'08) Manufacture des Tabacs, Toulouse, France, July 1st–4th 2008	SI6	41		
Prague (Czech Republic) 2007	EURO XXII—2007 EWG-DSS Stream on Decision Support Systems—Prague, Czech Republic, July 8–11, 2007				16
Reykjavick (Iceland) 2006	EURO XXI—2006 EWGD-DSS Stream on Decision Support Systems—Reykjavick Iceland, July 2–5, 2006			22	
London (UK) 2006:	Joint workshop of SIG-DSS and the EURO working Group on DSS, June 28, 2006		8		
Graz (Austria) 2005	Joint Workshop on Decision Support Systems, Experimental Economics & e-Participation, June 5th–7th, 2005	SI3, SI4		23	

Related publication "SIXX" numbers refer to the Special Issues listed in Table 5 in the Appendix. #FP number of full papers, #SP number of short papers, #AP number of abstracts and posters

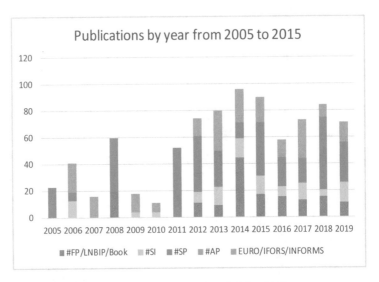

Fig. 1 Number of EWG-DSS publications by year from 2005 to 2019

Conference on Decision Support System Technology, whose first edition was held in Belgrade, Serbia in 2015.

At the time of writing this paper, more publications are already under preparation, among which special issues following ICDSST 2019 as well as publications associated with ICDSST 2020.

3   Collab-Net: The History of the Project

Following its community dynamic activity in research, the EWG-DSS board was quickly interested in finding proper means "to analyse and unfold collaboration relationships among the EWG-DSS members on one hand, and also to encourage new research and academic cooperation on the other". This was the birth of the Collab-Net project [3].

Literature on network analysis enhances that affiliation networks are highly reliable. Scientific collaboration networks are typical social networks with vertices representing scientists and edges representing collaborations among them [4]. Tangible and well-documented forms of collaboration among scientists include co-authorship and co-citation [5, 6]. Inspired by these results, since 2008, the EWG-DSS Coordination Board has been undertaking the network analysis project, defining a publication co-authorship network structure among its associate researchers.

The EWG-DSS Collaboration Academic Social Network Project (Collab-Net) targets mainly to disseminate research being conducted by members of the group.

Its development counts with efforts of the Coordination Board team and with the support of some associate researchers and their students.

The project was first presented at the ISMICK conference in Brazil, in 2008 [3]. It has been the subject of multiple communications [7–11], publications [12–16], and technical reports [17, 18]. This section presents the Collab-Net project and how it has evolved into a platform, which is now known as Collab-Net V.5.

3.1 First Versions of the Project

First versions of the Collab-Net project have tackled the structure for providing collaboration analysis among the members of EWG-DSS group and other external researchers. The first version [3, 7, 8, 12, 13] is illustrated in Fig. 2. At that early stage in the EWG-DSS live, one can observe that most members were isolated nodes, which means that they did not have any co-authors inside the EWG-DSS group. We also observe that few key researchers were acting as collaboration pivot (e.g. A49). A significant evolution of these aspects is observed with the following studies.

For this first version, all the affiliated members of the EWG-DSS group were requested by the coordination board to submit relevant information, concerning their publications since 1989, stating for each of them the main areas of research, apart from the co-authorship and edition details. Therefore, the acquisition process of this information was extremely time consuming to be completed since it was provided

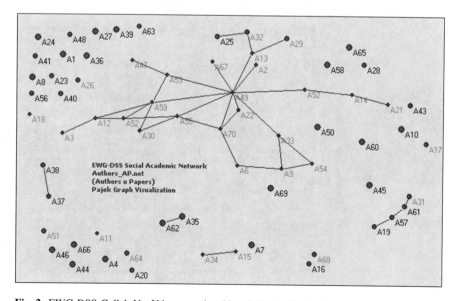

Fig. 2 EWG-DSS-Collab-Net V.1—co-authorship relation in Version 1

manually under the responsibility of the relative members. Furthermore, lack of data and imprecise information could hinder both extraction and transformation process.

The second version of the Collab-Net project [9, 14, 17] extends the original implementation of Version 1. However, Collab-Net Version 2 had significant evolutions on the methodology, model of the publication relationship structure, ontology structure model, and on its collaboration relationship structure. A hybrid methodology was proposed to the input data collection (manual and automatic), using web mining of electronic databases to automatically detect relationships of members and collect such information. Besides, a refined model of the publication relationship structure has also been proposed, taking into account "author title journal/conference-multiple keywords-multiple topics". Other improvements were related to an ontology-based data structure model and to a more refined model of the collaborative relationship structure, illustrated in Fig. 3.

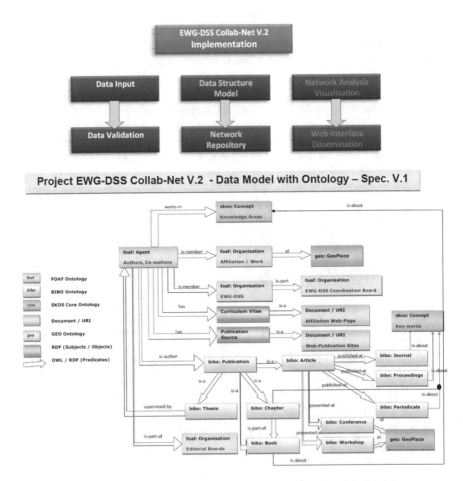

Fig. 3 EWG-DSS-Collab-Net V.2 Implementation Concept & Data/Ontology Model

All advances in the Version 2 aimed to perform collaboration trend analysis, showing co-authorships and co-citations to further illustrate the dynamics of EWG-DSS publications overtime. Furthermore, Collab-Net Version 2 planned to promote continued new research and collaboration among the academic members of the group and to attract new members for further fruitful collaboration. Nonetheless, the development of a Web application was essential to the success of those objectives, supporting data collection automatically based on the new publication relationship structure and aggregating the other features proposed by that version of the Collab-Net project.

3.2   Collab-Net V3

Collab-Net Version 3 was developed to face the data collection issue of previous versions. Version 3 [10, 11] brought the following new features to the project: the automation of data collection via Google Scholar database publication, an interactive environment to support members search by name or knowledge area, tools for export the collected data, and a local database for the collected data. Such improvements were the first steps of development of web-based platform that could aggregate several databases and all features required in Version 2.

Simultaneously, the proposed platform aimed to enable the affiliated members to investigate the publication relationship of the collaborative interaction among papers authors within a publication database. This feature was performed in an automatic way by the selecting either one or more affiliated members to be analysed. All data about the selected members were collected from the Google Scholar database, imported to the local database and could be exported as Excel format for further post-processing (Fig. 4).

After Collab-Net V3, the specification of the next development improvements composed the version 4, which by the time of the deployment was named already Collab-Net Version 5.

3.3   The Current Collab-Net V5

Aiming at avoiding local deployment of the application, Version 5 of the Collab-Net platform [11, 16] was developed as a Web application available to run through any web browser. Including the same features as the previous version, Collab-Net V5 improved the process of data extraction, bringing a more user-friendly design that allowed the user to export the collected data into csv files; and offered node-link representation of the co-authorship graph and subgraphs. The architecture of V5 is presented in Fig. 5.

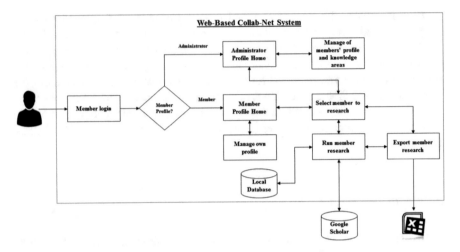

Fig. 4 Web-based Collab-Net V3

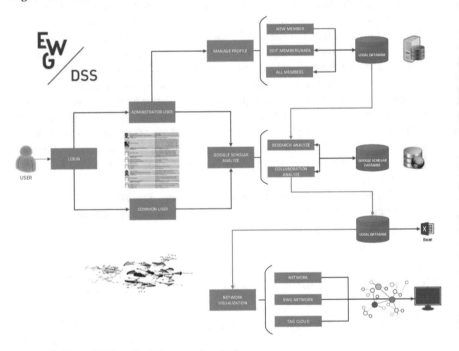

Fig. 5 Web-based Collab-Net V5 system flow [16]

This new version provides more resources to analyse the relationships between members and the identification of potential partners, contributing to encourage new research and academic cooperation.

4 Network Analyses

The context of Collab-Net project offered the opportunity to identify many of the published work from EWG-DSS members, based on the co-authorship network and the topic analysis. The various network analyses carried out in the project are summarized, respectively, in Sects. 4.1 and 4.2.

Aiming to complete these contributions by results on the 30 years of life of the EWG-DSS, a new data collection process was enforced, preserving the choices of the current Collab-Net platform, with the data being extracted from Google Scholar. This process is presented in Sect. 4.3. Then, the current state of the network is analysed in Sect. 4.4 and the publication collaboration evolution from 1989 to 2019 is studied in Sect. 4.4.

4.1 Summary of Previous Studies on Network Analysis

Previous analyses were conducted on two data sets. The first data set was composed of 1350 papers published by 70 of the EWG-DSS members between 1989 and 2008. This data set marks a milestone for the 20 years of existence of the EWG-DSS. Publications were collected by an email campaign, in plain text format.

As illustrated by Fig. 2, the first analyses [13] revealed a network with 35 isolated nodes, 6 nodes in 3 pairs, a group of 4 co-authors, and a giant component of 25 members. In this major component, Pascale Zaraté (represented in the figure by the node A49), the board chair, appeared to act as a real connector among the members.

Likewise, considering the network formed by all the 782 authors appearing in the data set, [9] completed the global analysis with a local analysis, the study of centralities. The major component of this network involves 527 authors connected by 2505 links (details of the graph metric are given in Fig. 6. The analysis of degree centrality, betweenness centrality and eigenvector centrality enhanced again, that board members (Pascale Zaraté, Rita Ribeiro, and Fatima Dargam) and founding members were strong cohesive agents in the group and so fully played their key role in the group.

Another study of the network [15] focused more specifically on the publications issued from EWG-DSS events between 2003 and 2012. This second data set consists in a more limited set of 218 abstracts and papers involving 417 authors, but presents the positive aspect of being exhaustive. The resulting co-authorship network is illustrated in Fig. 7. Besides the small components, the network presents four components involving 10–20 authors. A single big component (the major component of the network) involves 53 (13%) authors.

Complementarily to the global network analysis, a study of local properties was drawn on the same data set. It focused on three centrality measures: (a) the *degree centrality* (related to the number of connections) offers a proxy of the capacity of a node to acquire every kind of information that passes through the network, (b)

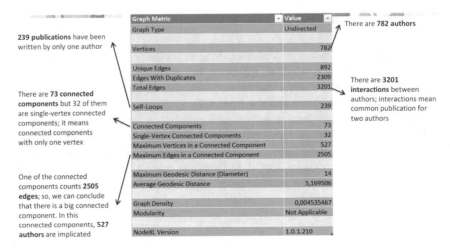

Fig. 6 Description of the metrics applied to the network analysis [9]

the *closeness centrality* (proportion of shortest paths going through a given node) quantifies the facility to interact rapidly or not with other actors of the network, and (c) the *eigenvector centrality* (that takes into account the neighbours' strength) reflects the ability of a given node to be strongly connected with core nodes. The centralities (degree, betweenness, and eigenvector) analyses realized confirm the leadership role of committee members already enhanced in previous publications.

4.2 Summary of Previous Study on Topics Analysis

Every member enjoys a full scientific freedom in his research agenda, the EWG-DSS has never aspired to influence the topics choices of its members. The topic analysis aims to understand their positioning and interests in order to offer them an appropriate support.

The 1350 papers mentioned in the previous subsection were associated with 34 topics (one per paper), as shown in Fig. 8. This revealed [13] that the most popular areas of research within the publications of the group members were: Decision Support System (150 papers), Operation Research (140), Information Systems (105), Information and Telecommunication Technologies (95), and Multi Criteria Decision Aiding (90).

In the same study [13], the analysis of the co-topic relationship among the authors (where two authors are connected if they both have a paper associated with the same topic) reveals that this relation connects the board chair with 51 of the 70 authors in the network.

The work done in [15] performed a topic analysis of the second data set, on the basis of the author-defined keywords associated to the publications. An application

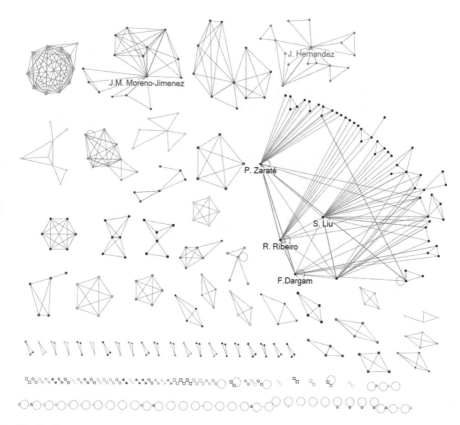

Fig. 7 Co-authorship network in EWG-DSS events

of the Louvain method [19] allowed to specify the search of the publication topics, by enhancing five axes:

- Axis 1: DSS, Decision-making, Network, Data-Mining, Simulation, Optimization, Fuzzy, Supply chain, Performance, Decision support, Case study, and Risk.
- Axis 2: Collaboration, Collaborative decision-making, System science, Multiagent system, MDA, ERP.
- Axis 3: MCDA, Group decision, Multicriteria decision-making, Decisionmaking process, Preference, AHP, Sustainability.
- Axis 4: Information, Uncertainty, Statistics, Bayesian, e-management, software engineering.
- Axis 5: Knowledge management, Production, Model.

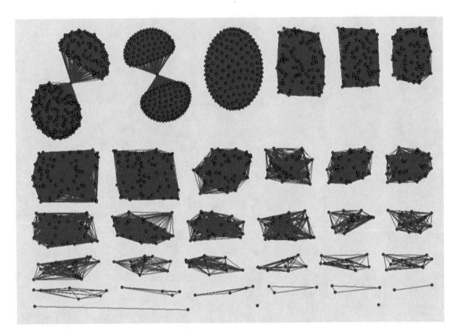

Fig. 8 Visualization of the co-topic relationship among papers represented in PAJEK, with separate components [13]

4.3 Data Collection and Preparation for the 30 Years Analysis

Following the analysis of the previous data collection, and a mailing campaign, a list of 132 authors out of the 250 EWG-DSS Members have been identified on Google Scholar. The disambiguation is done on the basis of the personal knowledge of the board members and introduced in the data collection process using the unique Google Scholar ID. However, most of the currently scientifically active members of the group are involved among the 132 identified authors. Among the missing ones, we observe mainly the following aspects: (a) members among the oldest ones, probably not willing to engage in new social network application; (b) young researchers and Ph.D. students, for whom we really want to push them to create and open their profiles; and (c) members from the industry, having lower engagement in scientific publications.

The data collection process has been performed using the Publish or Perish software [20]. The last data collection was run on February the 14th 2020. The data collection was limited to 1000 publication/author. This limit is reached by 2 of the 132 authors, namely: Adiel Teixeira de Ameida (2599) and José M. Merigo Lindahl (3000).

The data base involves 132 authors, 16,319 Publications and 17,181 Author-Publication Associations. Among the collected papers 1492 do not have a publication year (a cursory check enhances that most of them provide duplicates or

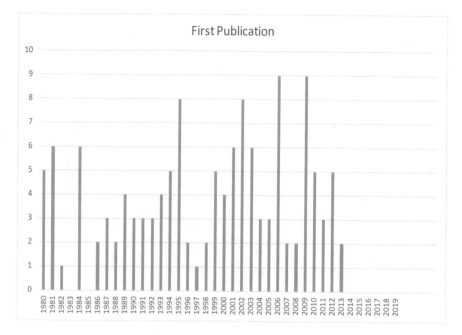

Fig. 9 Number of authors having their first publication each year

incorrect data), 11 have a year ≤1940, 120 have a year <1980, and 57 have 2020 as year. Only the remaining 14,650, published between 1980 and 2019 are preserved for the analysis presented here.

The evolution of the size of the community is reflected by the number of new authors by year. It is presented in Fig. 9. It is interesting to note that there are no authors, whose first publication appeared after 2015. This could be the result of the combination of various phenomena. Indeed, on the one hand, data updating in Google Scholar suffers some delay, on the other hand, young researchers do not worry about their Google profile before completing their Ph.D.

4.4 Authorship Evolution

The parallel evolution of the numbers of authors, publications, and the number of publications per author is presented in Fig. 10. The evolution of the yearly publication number is growing exponentially. This growth is the consequence of two combined phenomena: the inclusion of new members and the productivity increase of members. The last five years, one observes a stabilization of number of authors as well as decreases in both publication numbers and ration publications/author. This is probably more the reflect of the incompleteness of data than a phenomenon in the community.

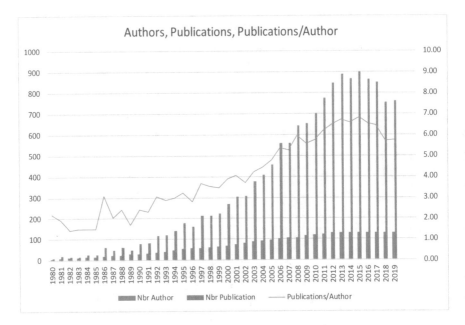

Fig. 10 Yearly number of authors, publications, and publications/author

Table 2 Yearly number of authors, publications, and publications/author

Year	Authors Nbr	Publications Nbr	Publications/Author
1989	29	49	1,69
1999	65	225	3,46
2009	117	653	5,58
2019	132	759	5,75

To get a quantitative view on the evolution, Table 2 presents the numbers every 10 years since the foundation of EWG-DSS. Let us observe, that for the two first decades, the number of authors doubled every 10 years, combined with a significant augmentation of the productivity, this leads to the explosion of yearly publications number.

4.5 Co-Authorship Network in 2019

The network of 132 authors connected by the 14,650 publications, extracted as described in Sect. 4.3, provides a network of 132 vertices, connected by 444 symmetric oriented edges with associated weights ranging from 1 to 981. These involve 132 self-loops and 156 bidirectional edges.

The co-authorship network is composed of 56 connected components, among which the major components involve 68 authors. The other connected components

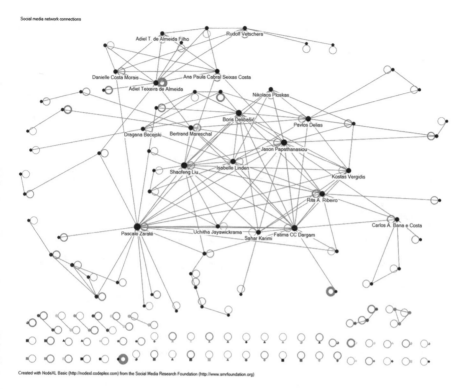

Fig. 11 Graph of the EWG-DSS co-authorship network as in 2019

are: 47 single vertex components (isolated authors), 6 components involving 2 vertices (pairs of co-authors), and 2 components involving 3 vertices. This network is illustrated in Fig. 11 by a node-link diagram where names are associated with the 20 authors having the highest degrees in the network.

4.6   Co-Authorship Network 30 Years Evolution

The evolution of the number of authors (Vertices in the graph), collaboration relations (Edges in the graph), number of connected components, number of isolated authors (Single Vertex Connected Components), and the number of authors in the giant component (Maximum vertices in a Connected Component) are summarized in Fig. 12. It is interesting to observe that until 2009 the numbers evolve in a linear way. The number of collaborations begins a smooth increase between 2002 and 2009. Suddenly in 2009, the number of collaborations skyrocketed. This correspond to a new dynamism in EWG-DSS, the will to turn the group into a true community is materialized by annual organization of specific event, followed by the edition

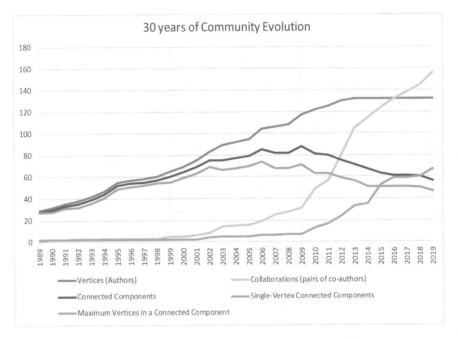

Fig. 12 EWG-DSS co-authorship network parameters evolution (1989–2019)

of journal special issues. This dynamic policy is really followed by relationships increase.

It is also interesting to observe in Fig. 12 the relative evolution of the various curves with respect to the size of the network (number of vertices/authors). Indeed, we can observe the following:

– The number of collaborations (pairs of co-authors) significantly increases even when the number of members stabilized. This suggests that the group really acts as a broker-platform among its members.
– The increase of the giant component (maximum vertices in a connected component) enhances that people do not only join the group to gain visibility but are really committed to the group.
– Since 2009, the number of connected components, in particular the number of single vertex connected components has been decreasing. This indicates that members of the group are more and more directly and indirectly connected in publications co-authorships.

The key players, as revealed by their metrics of: degree, betweenness centrality, and eigenvector centrality, are presented in Table 3 (w.r.t. 2009) and in Table 4 (w.r.t. 2019). Since 2009, the EWG-DSS coordination board's policy is also characterized by a policy of openness and inclusion: new members progressively join the board. And they become active members and group cohesive agents. As we can see the

Table 3 Top 10 centralities in 2009

2009	Betwn. Centrality	Degree	EV Centrality
Pascale Zaraté	12,000	7	0,257
Adiel Teixeira de Almeida	6,000	6	0,000
Rita A. Ribeiro	5,000	5	0,195
Zohar Laslo	1,000	4	0,000
Christer Carlsson	1,000	4	0,000
Sanja Petrovic	1,000	4	0,000
Carlos A. Bana e Costa	0,000	4	0,000
João Carlos Lourenço	0,000	4	0,000
João O. Soares	0,000	4	0,000
Fatima CC Dargam	0,000	4	0,174

Table 4 Top 10 centralities in 2019

2019					
Betweeness Centrality		Degree		EV Centrality	
Pascale Zaraté	890,389	Pascale Zaraté	22	Shaofeng Liu	0,068
Shaofeng Liu	362,099	Bertrand Mareschal	18	Fatima CC Dargam	0,067
Jason Papathanasiou	300,227	Jason Papathanasiou	17	Jason Papathanasiou	0,067
Fatima CC Dargam	286,852	Fatima CC Dargam	17	Pascale Zaraté	0,065
Boris Delibašić	265,421	Shaofeng Liu	16	Boris Delibašić	0,062
Isabelle Linden	248,000	Manuel Díaz	13	Rita A. Ribeiro	0,056
Rita A. Ribeiro	244,600	Adiel Teixeira de Almeida	13	Isabelle Linden	0,055
Adiel Teixeira de Almeida	214,500	Frederic Adam	12	Kostas Vergidis	0,051
Pavlos Delias	213,528	Boris Delibašić	12	Sahar Karimi	0,047
Kostas Vergidis	191,000	Carlos A. Bana e Costa	11	Pavlos Delias	0,035

founding board members (Pascale Zaraté, F. Dargam, and Rita R. Ribeiro) are joined in the 2019 table by the added subsequent board members Shaofeng Liu, Jason Papthanasiou, Isabelle Linden, Boris Delibasic, and Pavlos Delias.

5 The Future of Collab-Net: A DSS for Research Consortium Building

At the time of writing this chapter, V6 of the Collab-Net Platform is under specification. Starting from the observation that many advanced topics require huge sets of competences and transdisciplinary approach. The new version of the platform aims to support research and innovation project leaders in their identification of potential partners within the EWG-DSS [21].

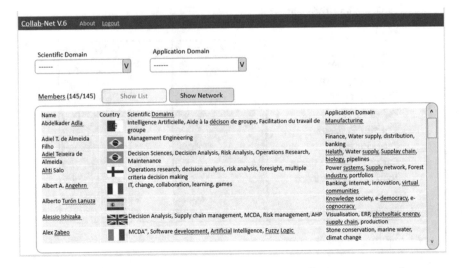

Fig. 13 Prototype Collab-Net DSS interface

5.1   The New Functionalities

Figure 13 presents the interface of the new functionalities of V6. The system presents (a) the lists of members (with their nationality, scientific domains, and application domains), (b) the (drop-down) list of application domains, and (c) the (drop-down) list of scientific domains. Note that the button "show the list" is currently activated and the "Show Network" is enabled.

This interface offers several interactions. As expected, selection of a specific scientific domain and/or an application domain will restrict the list to the members having interest in the specified domain(s). The "show network" and the "show list" buttons allow to swap from the list of the members to the node-link representation of the members network, where the links denote the co-authorship relation (and back to the list view). Moreover, pointing a member's name with the mouse, opens a pop-up with his related information and double clicking opens his Google Scholar profile in a new tab.

Figure 14 presents a prototype view of the interface where the "MCDA" scientific domain has been selected, the "show network" button is currently activated and the mouse points to the node representing the member/author Ana Paula Cabral.

The data collection of this platform follows a process similar to the one described in Sect. 4.3.

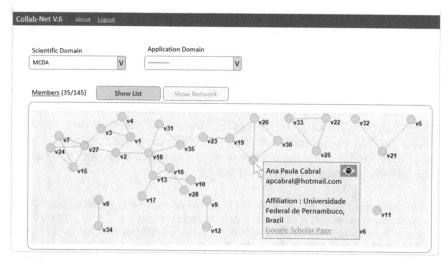

Fig. 14 Prototype Collab-Net DSS with "MCDA" scientific domain selection

5.2 Future Works in Collab-Net

The above description mentioned the notion of scientific domains and application domains. Scientific domains will be retrieved based on the topics declared by members in their Google Scholar profile. This data collection is already done; however, these topics are user-defined outside any typology. A matching has to be defined among them and a more standardized list, as for example this used in [12, 13]. This is a topic for further exploration on the project.

Regarding the application domains, a typology has to be selected. We plan to use text mining technique on the list of publication, in order to associate the relevant domains with each of the members of the group. Reports on future developments in this direction will be made available as soon as results are obtained solving this issue.

6 Conclusion

This chapter aimed to reflect the life of the EWG-DSS along the last 30 years and to show the impact of the research collaboration analysis in enhancing its contribution within the Decision Support System Scientific Community. Moreover, it presented the Collab-Net project and the analyses of the collected data relative to EWG-DSS publications and co-authorships.

That look in the rear mirror revealed a truly dynamic group, with a coordination board that plays a key connecting role with all its active members. At the time which the founding members are considering to leave the EWG-DSS Coordination Board for the Advisory Board of the group, one can underline and appreciate the concern they had to integrate new members in the long term, aiming at the continuation of the right pace of the group highly qualified management with equally high-level motivation. The deep integration observed in our analysis brings sound and positive expected impacts for the group's future. Similarly, the planned projects (including Collab-Net V6) and research activities (ICDSST next editions, planned special issues, etc.) praise many more prosperous and dynamic years for the Decision Support System community with the EWG-DSS.

Acknowledgements This chapter would not have been possible without contributions from all the developers to the project at all stages. Rahma Bouaziz who was a student at IRIT-University Toulouse III, developed the first analysis of the Collab-Net Project as described in [12]. David Dardenne, a master student at the University of Namur, studied the network in his master thesis [22] and ran the first centralities study involved in [9]. Mélanie Motte, a researcher at the University of Namur, conducted the analysis of 10 years of publications of the group, whose work is published in [15]. Jadielson Moura, a Ph.D. student at Federal University of Pernambuco, developed the V3 Platform as presented in [10, 11]. All of their work is highly appreciated!

A.1 Appendix

Table A.1 Special issues of journal (co-)edited by board members of EWG-DSS

	Journal Issue	Editors, Title	Source events	# papers
SI26	International Journal of Information and Decision Sciences, InderScience	G. Aifantopoulou, Jesus Gonzalez-Feliu, B. Delibasic	ICDSST 2018	To appear
SI25	Kybernetes, Emerald, To appear	Stefano Armenia, Georgios Tsaples, Jason Papathanasiou, Promoting Sustainable Decision-Making	ICDSST 2018	To appear
SI24	International Journal of Decision Support Systems Technologies, IGI Global, 12(2)	Ana Paula Cabral	ICDSST 2018	2
SI23	Operation Research: and international Journal, Springer, 19(4), 2019	Corentin Burnay, Fatima Dargam, Pascale Zaraté, Special Issue on Data Visualisation for Decision-Making: An Important Issue	ICDSST 2017	10
SI22	International Journal of Decision Support Systems Technologies, IGI Global, 11(1), 2019	Nikolaos Ploskas, Pavlos Delias, Isabelle Linden, Special Issue on Decision Support System Technology	ICDSST 2017	5
SI21	Industrial Management and Data Systems, Emerald, 117(7), 2017	Shaofeng Liu, Boris Delibasic, Lynne Butel, Xue Han, Sustainable knowledge-based decision support systems (KB-DSS) for business performance improvement in real industrial environment	ICDSST 2016	12
SI20	International Journal of Decision Support Systems Technologies, IGI Global, 9(4), 2017	Jason Papathanasiou, Festus Oderant, Uchita Jayawickrama, Special Issue on Decision Support Systems for Sustainable Applications	ICDSST 2016	4
SI19	International Journal of Information and Decision Sciences, InderScience, 10(1), 2018	I. Linden, J. Papathanasiou, M. Bohanec, Special Issue on Analytics for Decision Making	ICDSST 2015 EURO 2015	5
SI18	International Journal of Decision Support Systems Technologies, IGI Global, 8(2), 2016	B. Delibasic, S. Liu, N. Ploskas Challenges in Business Information Processing	ICDSST 2015 EURO 2015	4
SI17	International Journal of Decision Support Systems Technologies, IGI Global, 8(1), 2016	B. Delibasic, S. Liu, N. Ploskas Business Data Analytics and Management	ICDSST 2015 EURO 2015	4

(continued)

Table A.1 (continued)

	Journal Issue	Editors, Title	Source events	# papers
SI16	*EURO Journal on Decision Processes*, Springer, 3(3–4), 2015	Pascale Zaraté, Fatima Dargam	GDN 2014	6
SI15	*Journal of Decision Systems*, Taylor & Francis, 24(2), 2015	Isabelle Linden, Jason Papathanasiou and Shaofeng Liu, *Integrated Decision Support Systems*	GDN 2014 IFORS 2014	6
SI14	*Journal of Decision Systems* Taylor & Francis, 23(3), 2014	Shaofeng Liu, Pascale Zaraté, Rita Ribeiro, *Knowledge-based Decision Systems*	EWG-DSS 2013 Workshop Thessaloniki, Euro 2013	8
SI13	*International Journal of Decision Support Systems Technologies*, IGI Global, 5(2), 2013	Fatima Dargam, Shaofeng Liu, Isabelle Linden, *Modelling Decision Systems for Critical Applications*	EURO 2012	4
SI12	*International Journal of Decision Support Systems Technologies*, IGI Global, 5(3), 2013	Fatima Dargam, Shaofeng Liu, Isabelle Linden, *Prediction, Simulation and Optimization Methods for Decision Making*	EURO 2012	4
SI11	*Production Planning & Control Journal*, 25(8), 2014	Jorge E. Hernández, Andrew C. Lyons, Pascale Zarate & Fatima Dargam *Collaborative Decision-Making Trends and Solutions for Industries*	EWG=DSS Liverpool-2012 Workshop	6
SI10	*International Journal of Decision Support Systems Technologies*, IGI Global, 4(2–3), 2012	Fatima Dargam; Boris Delibasic; Jorge E. Hernández; Shaofeng Liu, *Special Issue on Networking Decision Making and Negotiation* (Part1and 2)	EWG-DSS London-2011, EWG-DSS/DASIG Paris-2011 Workshops	8
SI9	*International Journal of Information and Decision Sciences*, InderScience, 5(3), 2013	J.Papathanasiou, S. Liu and P. Zaraté, *Special Issue on Collaborative Decision Making*	EWG=DSS workshop in London2011	6
SI8	*International Journal of Decision Support Systems Technologies*, IGI Global, 2(4), 2010	F. Dargam and P. Zaraté	EURO 2009	4
SI7	*International Journal of Decision Support Systems Technologies*, IGI Global, 1(4)	A. Respicio and P. Zaraté, *Technologies for Collaborative Decision Making*	CDM08	4

SI6	Group Decision and Negotiation, Springer, 20(1), Jan. 2011	J. Pino and P. Zaraté	CDM08	6
SI5	European Journal of Operational Research, Elsevier, 195(3), 2009	P. Zaraté (Ed). Formal tools and methodologies for DSS	CIDMDS Conference 2006	4
SI4	Journal of Decision Systems, Hermès Science Publications, 15,(2–3) Sept. 2006	Fatima Dargam,Pascale Zaraté (Ed). Decision Support Systems: Méthodologies and Application	Joint-Workshop Graz 2005	7
SI3	Central European Journal of Operations Research, Springer-Verlag, 14(4), Dec. 2006	Fatima Dargam, António Rodrigues (Ed). Special Issue on "Methods and Strategies for Decision and Management Problems"	Joint-Workshop Graz 2005	6
SI2	European Journal of Operational Research, Elsevier, 145(2), mars 2003	Rita Ribeiro,Antonio Rodriguez,Pascale Zaraté (Ed). Decision Support Systems: Current Research	Meetings in Toulouse and Cascais	18
SI1	Journal of Decision Systems, Hermès, 12(3–4), 2003	Pascale Zaraté (Ed). Decision Support Systems: from theory to practice	Mini-Euro Conference	10

Table A.2 Books Edited by board members of EWG-DSS

Book Title	Editors	Publisher
Decision Support Systems IX—Cognitive Decision Support Systems & Technologies	Jose-Maria Moreno, Isabelle Linden, Fatima Dargam, Uchitha Jayawickrama	Springer LNBIP 384, 2020
Decision Support Systems VIII—Sustainable Data-Driven and Evidence-Based Decision Support	Fatima Dargam, Pavlos Delias, Isabelle Linden, and Bertrand Mareschal	Springer LNBIP 313, 2018
Decision Support Systems VII—Data, Information and Knowledge Visualization in Decision Support Systems	Isabelle Linden, Shaofeng Liu, and Christian Colot	Springer LNBIP 282, 2017
Decision Support Systems VI—Addressing Sustainability and Societal Challenges	Shaofeng Liu, Boris Delibasic, and Festus Oderanti	Springer LNBIP 250, 2016
Decision Support Systems V—Big Data Analytics for Decision Making	Boris Delibasic, Jorge Hernandez, Jason Papathanasiou, Fatima Dargam, Pascale Zarate, Rita Ribeiro, Shaofeng Liu, and Isabelle Linden	Springer LNBIP 216, 2015
Decision Support Systems IV—Information and Knowledge Management in Decision Processes	Isabelle Linden, Shaofeng Liu, Fatima Dargam, and Jorge Hernandez	Springer LNBIP 221, 2015
Decision Support Systems III—Impact of Decision Support Systems for Global Environments	F. Dargam, J.E. Hernández, P. Zaraté, S. Liu, R. Ribeiro, B. Delibasic, J. Papathanasiou	Springer LNBIP 184, 2014
Group Decision and Negotiation. A Process-Oriented View	Pascale Zaraté, Gregory Kersten, Jorge E. Hernandez	Spinger LNBIP 180, 2014
Decision Support Systems II—Recent Developments Applied to DSS Network Environments	J.E. Hernández, S. Liu, B. Delibasic, P. Zaraté, F. Dargam, R. Ribeiro	Springer LNBIP 164, 2013
Collaboration in Real Environments	J. Hernández, P- Zaraté, F. Dargam, R. Ribeiro, B. Delibasic and S. Liu	Springer LNBIP 121, 2012.
Collaborative Decision Making: Perspectives and Challenges	Pascale Zaraté, Jean Pierre Belaud, Guy Camilleri, Franck Ravat	IOS Press Publisher, 2008

References

1. EWG-DSS. Home page. Retrieved March 23, 2020, from https://ewgdss.wordpress.com/about/history/.
2. EWG-DSS. Newsletters. Retrieved from https://ewgdss.wordpress.com/newsletters/.
3. Dargam, F., Ribeiro, R., & Zaraté, P. (2008). A Collaboration Network for the EURO Working Group on DSS. In *International Symposium on the Management of Industrial and Corporate Knowledge*. Rio de Janeiro: Niteroi.
4. Shi, Q., Xu, B., Xu, X., Xiao, Y., Wang, W., & Wang, H. (2011). Diversity of social ties in scientific collaboration networks. *Physica A, 390*, 4627–4635.
5. Newman, M. E. J. (2001). Scientific collaboration networks. II. Shortest paths, weighted networks, and centrality. *Physical Review E, 64*, 016132.

6. Newman, M. E. J. (2001). Scientific collaboration networks. I. Network construction and fundamental result. *Physical Review E, 64*, 016131.
7. Dargam, F., Ribeiro, R., & Zaraté, P. (2009). Towards a collaboration network for the EURO Working Group on DSS (Advances of the Project). In *Proceedings of the 23rd European Conference on Operational Research*. Bonn: EURO XXIII.
8. Dargam, F., Ribeiro, R., & Zaraté, P. (2010). How does the EURO Working Group on DSS interact? A social academic network analysis 1998–2008. In *Proceedings of the 24th European Conference on Operational Research*. Lisbon: EURO XXIV.
9. Dardenne, D., Dargam, F., Linden, I., Liu, S., Ribeiro, R., Sun, W., & Zaraté, P. (2012). Extending the Analysis of the EURO Working Group on DSS Research Collaboration Network (EWG-DSS Collab-Net V2). In *Proceedings of the 25th European Conference on Operational Research*. Vilnius, Lithuania: EURO XXV.
10. Moura, J., Cabral Seixas Costa, A. P., Dargam, F., Linden, I., & Zaraté, P. (2016). Collab-Net on line: An online platform for DSS-research collaboration in EWG-DSS. In *Poster In International Conference on Decision Support System Technology*. Plymouth: Royaume-Uni.
11. Turet, J., Moura, J., Cabral, A. P., Dargam, F., Zaraté, P., & Linden, I. (2018). DSS Research Collaboration in the EWG-DSS. In *Poster In International Conference on Decision Support System Technology*. Grèce: Heraklion.
12. Bouaziz, R., Simas, T., Dargam, F., Ribeiro, R., & Zaraté, P. (2010). A Social-Academic Network Analysis of the EURO Working Group on DSS. *International Journal of Decision Support Systems Technologies, 2*(4), 13–36.
13. Dargam, F., Ribeiro, R., & Zaraté, P. (2011). Networking the EWG-DSS: How do we proceed now? (Short Paper). In F. Dargam, J. Hernández, S. Liu, R. Ribeiro, & P. Zaraté (Eds.), *Proceedings of the EWG-DSS London-2011 Workshop on Decision Systems, IRIT, Report IRIT/RR–2011-14-FR*. Toulouse: Université Paul Sabatier.
14. Dargam, F., Linden, I., Liu, S., Ribeiro, R., & Zaraté, P. (2013). The development roadmap of the EWG-DSS collab-net project: A Social Network Perspective of DSS Research Collaboration in Europe. In J. E. Hernández, S. Liu, B. Delibašić, P. Zaraté, F. Dargam, & R. Ribeiro (Eds.), *Decision Support Systems II—Recent Developments Applied to DSS Network Environments. Lecture Notes in Business Information Processing, vol.164* (pp. 1–18). Berlin, Heidelberg: Springer.
15. Linden, I., & Motte, M. (2014). A reflection of the EWG-DSS's life through the application of SNA techniques to its publications. In D. P. Zaraté, G. Camilleri, D. Kamissoko, & F. Amblard (Eds.), *Proceedings of the Joint International Conference of the INFORMS GDN Section and the EURO Working Group on DSS* (pp. 158–167). Toulouse: Toulouse University.
16. Turet, J., Moura, J., Cabral Seixas Costa, A. P., Dargam, F., Zaraté, P., & Linden, I. (2019). An on-line platform for supporting DSS-research collaboration (EWG-DSS Collab-Net Version 5). In P. S. Abreu Freitas, F. Dargam, R. Ribeiro, J. M. Moreno Jimenez, & J. Papathanasiou (Eds.), *EmC-ICDSST 2019 5th International Conference on Decision Support System Technology: Decision Support Systems: Main Developments & Future Trends* (pp. 186–192). Toulouse: Toulouse University.
17. Dargam, F., Ribeiro, R., Zarate, P., & Liu, S. (2013). *A social network perspective of DSS research collaboration in Europe. IRIT, Research Report IRIT/RR–2013-27-FR*. Toulouse: Université Paul Sabatier.
18. Moura, J., Cabral Seixas Costa, A. P., Dargam, F., Linden, I., & Zaraté, P. (2016). *Collab-net version 3*. Toulouse, France: Technical Report, IRIT/RR–2016–06—FR.
19. Blondel, V. D., Guillaume, J.-L., Lambiotte, R., & Lefebvre, E. (2008). Fast unfolding of communities in large networks. *Journal of Statistical Mechanics: Theory and Experiment, 10*, P1000.
20. Publish or Perish Software. Homepage. Retrieved January 02, 2020, from https://harzing.com/resources/publish-or-perish.

21. Linden, I., Turet, J. G., Cabral Seixtas Costa, A.-P., Dargam, F., & Zaraté, P. (2020). *Collab-Net as a DSS for the Identification of Potential Partners and the Creation of Research Consortia*. Zaragoza: ICDSST 2020 6th International Conference on Decision Support System Technology.
22. Dardenne, D. (2012). Analyse de Réseaux Sociaux: Propositions pour des Etudes de Cas. Mémoire de Master en Ingenieur de Gestion. University of Namur, Faculté des Sciences Economiques. *Sociales et de Gestion, 2012*, 2011–2012; (in French).

Decision Support in the Era of Social Media and User-Generated Content

Kathrin Kirchner, Marek Opuszko, and Sven Gehrke

Abstract Social media and the huge amount of user-generated content offer new possibilities for decision-making in companies, as more data can be acquired easily without extra cost. However, a larger database does not automatically lead to better decisions, and volume, variety, and veracity of data from different sources are often overwhelming and challenging. This chapter provides two cases where we used big social data as basis for decision-making. The first case describes the incorporation of extracted information from social media to decision-making models. The second case focuses on the veracity challenges of social media data. By relying on these two cases, we derive guidelines for tackling the veracity of social media data and provide insights how decision-making can be influenced positively and negatively by social media and user-generated content. With the guidelines, it can be determined how much big social data has an influence on quality and rigor in the decision-making process.

Keywords Social media · User-generated content · Decision support · Big data · Veracity · Multi-criteria decision-making

1 Introduction

Making the right decisions has always been a core component of all business activities. The fundamental components of the decision-making process are data, information, and knowledge. For a long time, decision-makers were dependent on information from a few carefully selected sources. In particular, the process of obtaining information was associated with high costs and efforts. In many cases,

K. Kirchner (✉)
Technical University of Denmark, Kgs. Lyngby, Denmark
e-mail: kakir@dtu.dk

M. Opuszko · S. Gehrke
Friedrich Schiller University, Jena, Germany
e-mail: marek.opuszko@uni-jena.de; sven.gehrke@uni-jena.de

© Springer Nature Switzerland AG 2021
J. Papathanasiou et al. (eds.), *EURO Working Group on DSS*, Integrated Series in Information Systems, https://doi.org/10.1007/978-3-030-70377-6_5

it was even impossible to obtain relevant information at all. This situation has changed dramatically in recent years and the emergence of huge online networks and the increasing availability of ever more user-generated data is nothing less than a revolution.

Social media is one of the biggest sources for a variety of big data generated from users, e.g., on public platforms like Facebook, YouTube, Twitter or LinkedIn, or organization-internal platforms. People are enthusiastic to share, interact, and collaborate via these platforms with other users.

Nevertheless, using such social media data for decision-making can be challenging—data have to be carefully selected among the huge amount of available data, and their quality, credibility, and objectivity might be questionable. Furthermore, the question arises if we can use existing decision-making methods. Maybe it is necessary to develop new decision support methods that are able to cope with this specific type and amount of data.

This chapter aims to provide insights on the impact of social media and user-generated content on decision-making. After discussing related work, we present two case studies that illustrate the challenges in using user-generated social media data for decision-making. Finally, we derive recommendations for the identified challenges.

2 Related Work

Information systems in general and decision support systems in particular support individual, group, and organizational decision-making processes. In the last years, social media platforms like social networks (e.g., Facebook, LinkedIn, Yammer) or microblogs (e.g., Twitter) provide opportunities to share knowledge, create new ideas, express opinions, or even integrate employees, business partners, and customers in decision-making processes [1]. These social media platforms also deliver data that can be used as a basis for a data-based decision-making [2].

Data from social platforms can be analyzed on three different levels: (1) interpretation of the whole network, (2) interpretation of groups and components (socio-centered), and (3) interpretation of individual positions (ego-centered) [3]. The analysis of data from social platforms can thus provide a basis for decisions on different levels. The elements for a multi-criteria decision-making can be obtained from social media data. For instance, an analysis of key terms used in a discussion can help to analyze alternatives to solve a problem. Determining the number of times a concept or alternative is mentioned helps to derive preferences for decision alternatives. By analyzing different opinions and sentiments in discussions about a certain topic, group positions about this topic can be estimated.

Social media data play a role, e.g., in social media marketing and consumers' decision-making based on word-of-mouth [4, 5]. In a study among internet users, social media was even influential for 40% of respondents for their decision-making regarding travel, and 74% rely on reviews posted by others [6]. Social media data also play a role in emergency cases, where real-time information can be used by both authorities and citizens for making safer decisions [7].

Every minute, users produce new content on social media—with every click, like, share, and contribution in different formats. In 2019, more than 500,000 tweets or 4.5 million YouTube videos were posted per minute worldwide [8], which can be named social big data. The term social big data comprises the domains of big data and social media [9].

This huge amount of available data provides new possibilities for analysis and decision-making. The promises of the Big Data age are indeed great: more data, more information, and more knowledge. However, there is no guarantee that more data will automatically result in better decisions. Many researchers therefore point out the challenges in dealing with Big Data [10], especially regarding the so-called information paradox, according to which decision-makers are thirsty for knowledge but drown in information [11]. This is especially true for data generated by users in social media. However, companies are looking for ways to harness the power of this data to improve their decision-making.

Big data is characterized by 3 V: Volume, Velocity, and Variety [12]. Later, three more V were added: Value, Variability, and Veracity [13].

In the context of data analytics in social media, volume, velocity (the high speed of data transfers) and variety (different types of structured and unstructured data) can be critical in big data projects. However, they can be handled by taking samples and using an intelligent experimental design [9]. Furthermore, data frameworks like Apache Hadoop [14] and Spark [15] or algorithms based on MapReduce [16] allow the handling of big amounts of data for decision-making.

In the literature, and from our experiences, veracity is the most critical characteristic of big social data and requires the biggest effort to handle it. Veracity refers to the correctness and accuracy of data as well as to privacy and legal concerns. Lukoianova and Rubin [17] propose the following main subcategories for veracity: Credibility/Implausibility, Deception/Truthfulness, and Objectivity/Subjectivity. Credibility (i.e., believability) is the perceived quality of simultaneously evaluated trustworthiness and expertise. Deception is connected with the verification of the writer's intention to create a truthful impression in the readers' mind, which is also connected with the credibility of the writer. Objectivity refers to the fact that a message can be objective (fully supported or proven) or subjective knowledge (unsupported or weakly supported).

In the following, we will discuss challenges in using social media data for decision-making based on two own cases. The first case studies the decision-making based on a variety of social media data and the second case studies the veracity of this data.

3   Case 1: Incorporating Different Social Media Data into the Decision-Making Process

The introduction of a new software, e.g., an e-commerce software, is a big challenge for many companies. If the software affects many business areas, it is a strategic decision with sometimes far-reaching consequences [18], as the example of the disastrous ERP implementation of MillerCoors shows [19]. For this reason, great attention is paid to the procurement decision. If we divide the procurement process into four phases as described in [20, 21], the analysis and acquisition, in addition to operation and implementation, comprise 50% of the entire process.

The decision-making process can typically be illustrated as shown in Fig. 1. Starting point is the problem definition, in our case the selection of an (enterprise) e-commerce software. In the following, we will mainly limit ourselves to the phases of selecting possible sources of knowledge and evaluating the alternatives since this is where the use of information from social media can come into play.

To illustrate the process within this case study, we assume that five Open Source e-commerce platforms are available, from which an alternative should be chosen at the end of the decision process. These five options are among the most used Open Source e-commerce platforms according to builtwith.com: Magento, Prestashop, OpenCart, VirtueMart, and WooCommerce.

Companies want to avoid introducing software that becomes obsolete or outdated after a few years and then has to be replaced by another software product at great expense. Since very high switching costs can arise, especially with integrated software, an incorrect decision can have disastrous consequences. In addition, the usually strong network effects of software products play a role [22]. For instance, based on total cost of ownership, a high distribution of software might reflect future stability and longevity. Furthermore, the probability of finding trained personnel is also higher if the software is widely distributed and even represents a quasi-industry standard, as is the case with Microsoft Office, for example [23, 24]. On the other hand, network effects can lead to a lock-in and dependence on a single provider. It is precisely this scenario where information from social media and user-generated content can help to examine these questions more closely. This is especially true due to the real-time aspect of social media.

The choice of adequate knowledge sources is of course dependent on the way the subsequent evaluation is carried out. The type of evaluation and thus the problem

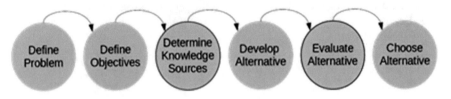

Fig. 1 Decision-making process

definition is often adapted to available data sources. The criteria for evaluating software alternatives are numerous and range from functional aspects such as the functional scope of a software, economic effects such as depreciation, network effects, or possible lock-ins to a holistic cost consideration that goes far beyond the directly attributable acquisition costs. For example, Benlian and Hess [25] describe seven criteria for evaluating software alternatives for the purchase of an office suite:

- Functionality
- Reliability
- Cost
- Ease of use
- Ease of customization
- Ease of implementation
- Software support

The evaluation of the functionality of a software is usually of less difficulty. Since features are implemented directly in the development of the software, they can be determined relatively easily [26]. For this purpose, numerous services and websites exist that compare and rank the functional aspects of software products. For example, the Google search for "comparison e-commerce platform" delivers about 77,200,000 search hits (as of 15 March 2020).

However, it is much more difficult to assess fuzzy criteria such as reliability, costs, and sustainability. This is all the more difficult if the manufacturer is not a software development company, but a community that produces open source software (OSS) on a decentralized basis [20, 27]. Especially when estimating costs, serious errors can quickly occur if only directly attributable costs such as pure procurement costs are used. For a long time, there have been methods for a holistic assessment of the investment costs. The total cost of ownership (TCO) approach allows costs to be recorded and evaluated in full. This is particularly important in the procurement of digital goods that are subject to network effects. Here, the recording of all cost types represents a major challenge. Since the main purpose of this case study is to demonstrate the use of data from social media for decision support, we will focus on reliability, costs, and support.

In many business decisions, costs play a significant, if not the most significant, role alongside the benefits of a product. For this reason, special attention will be paid to the decision dimension of costs. In addition to pure acquisition costs, all cost types that arise during the entire life cycle of the product have to be considered. In the context of a product purchase decision such as that of an e-commerce platform, these are the costs of pre-selection, acquisition, use, care, maintenance, backup, and many more. Therefore, costs can be extremely diverse in nature and decision-makers have to collect and evaluate them within the decision-making process.

This becomes more serious if open source products are among the alternatives for software procurement. OSS has long since reached a level of maturity that makes its use in an enterprise environment possible [27]. In the past, however, the focus has usually been on the criteria for purchasing proprietary software [28]. Only recently has the criteria for the selection of OSS been examined more closely [25]. This is of great importance because OSS promises cost reduction through obtaining a free copy, yet the majority of the total costs of ownership will arise elsewhere, for instance in staff costs. In addition, global communities can dissolve at any time, so there is no guarantee of support or bug fixes [29]. These risks and costs have to be factored into the purchase decision, and the communities must be adequately assessed. In the context of OSS and TCO assessment, other cost factors are as follows:

- Distribution of the software platform
- Insufficient level of knowledge of the users
- Insufficient maturity of the platform
- Lack of community support/activity
- Poor knowledge base
- Lack of available skilled workers

In order to weigh up influencing factors and reach a decision in a structured manner, a wide variety of methods can be used. A well-known procedure is the analytic hierarchy process (AHP) [30, 31]. In this decision support procedure for complex decisions, data is collected, compared, weighted, and processed in several phases until a decision is reached. In the absence of historical data or studies, the data can also be derived from the assessment of experts [32, 33] or user studies [25]. Within the AHP, the criteria matrix can be supplemented by information from social media and enters the decision matrix of an AHP or a cost-utility analysis as further criteria. The advantage is that the process of decision support remains unaffected and can be carried out as before. Figure 2 shows a snapshot of a possible AHP structure with goal, criteria, and alternatives for the present case study.

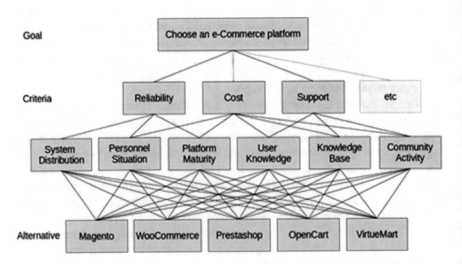

Fig. 2 Exemplary structure of the AHP

In the present case, we focus on the criteria of reliability, cost and support, and subsequential criteria identified based on a TCO approach. The next step is to determine how the criteria can be evaluated. The question arises which indicators exists to measure and assess the criteria and which sources of knowledge can be used to measure these criteria. In a first step, indicators are identified which may reflect the questions or the criteria. For example, the distribution of the software platform can be approximated by the search interest on search engines over time. Other indicators are the number of live systems that use a particular shop system. It becomes clear that these indicators are context dependent and can vary greatly for each decision problem. Therefore, the skill and experience of the decision-maker is required. Once all indicators are defined, the search for possible data sources begins. For example, services such as Google Trends can be used to record online search interest. The number of live systems are shown on websites such as builtwith.com that use a search engine not unlike crawler to search websites worldwide for information about the software used. An interesting question, especially with OSS, is the evaluation of the activity of the community and thus the sustainability of the platform. Here, possible indicators are the general activity of the community, which can be determined by the intensity of communication in message boards and forums.

For this purpose, the online forum Stackoverflow, an internet platform aimed at software developers, is suitable. On this platform, users and developers can exchange information, ask questions, and get answers. The intensity of the number of questions and answers can therefore provide information about the general activity of a community. Furthermore, the quota of help can also be determined by analyzing the answers.

Table 1 shows indicators assigned to the criteria and possible sources of knowledge where relevant information can be found. These too must be collected and structured within the decision-making process and must be context dependent. Fortunately, today there are possible sources of knowledge for almost every question. These results can then act as supplementary information from social media and enter the decision matrix of an AHP or a cost-utility analysis as further criteria. The advantage is that the process of decision support remains unaffected and can be carried out as usual. For reasons of clarity and space limitations, we will limit ourselves to describing the bold indicators and knowledge sources in Table 1 in this case study.

3.1 Results: Distribution of the Systems

Figure 3 shows the search interest of the five alternatives over the last 4 years in the form of search queries to the search engine Google. A decrease in the overall search frequency can be clearly seen. Above all, the longstanding top-ranked shop system Magento is clearly losing interest in searches suggesting that interest is declining and which points to an increasing sustainability risk. If the trend continues and Magento loses interest and distribution in the future, there is a risk of costs

Table 1 Criteria, indicators, and knowledge sources as basis for decision support

Criteria	Indicator	Knowledge source
Distribution of the system	**Online Searches**, Downloads, **Live Websites**	**Google**, Bing, **builtwith.com**
Level of knowledge of the users	Members	LinkedIn, XING, Stackoverflow
Maturity of the development	Release Status	Platform Website, GitHub, SourceForge
Community support/activity	**Tutorials, Videos**, Threads, Questions, Answers, Bugfixes, Release History	**YouTube, Stackoverflow**, Twitter
Knowledge base	Forums, **Tutorials, Courses**	**Udemy, YouTube**, Stackoverflow
Available skilled workers	Employment Service Platforms	LinkedIn, XING, Stackoverflow

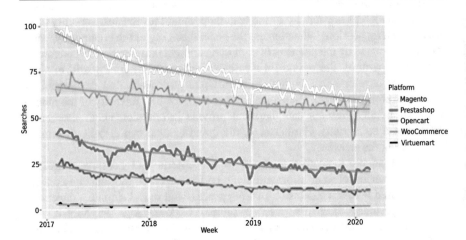

Fig. 3 Search for the five alternatives over the last 4 years in Google search engine

associated with a changeover to another system in the future. In contrast to Magento, the WooCommerce system in particular is showing a constant high level of search interest.

What also becomes clear in the diagram is a generally declining interest in on-premise systems. This also represents a high-cost risk for the future, as cloud-based e-commerce platforms may be the means of choice in the future. However, in the present scenario we assume that a self-hosted solution is a prerequisite, due to the higher flexibility and customizability.

Another key figure is the number of systems installed worldwide. Table 2 illustrates the wide range in terms of the distribution of installed systems. WooCommerce shows with almost four million live websites an absolute top position. This can be associated with a high spread of knowledge about how to use the system. It is

Table 2 Distribution of e-Commerce platforms

Platform	Live websites[a]	6 Month trend	Points	Relative
Magento	190,731	Falling	2	0.05
WooCommerce	**3,876,748**	**Rising**	**5**	**1.00**
Prestashop	250,603	Rising	3	0.06
VirtueMart	56,768	Falling	1	0.01
OpenCart	337,025	Stagnating	4	0.09

[a] According to builtwith.com (accessed 2020-03-02)

Table 3 Indicators on stackoverflow.com

Platform	Threads	Answers per question	Average votes per question	Points	Relative
Magento	**37,666**	**1.37**	**1.09**	**5**	**1.00**
WooCommerce	22,641	1.01	0.8	4	0.60
Prestashop	4835	1.22	0.51	2	0.13
VirtueMart	723	1.14	0.42	1	0.02
OpenCart	5026	1.22	0.49	3	0.13

in turn is a cost factor in the operation of such a system as well as for the recruitment of suitable specialist personnel. The last two columns "Points" and "Relative" show a simple ranking with points and a rating based on the percentage relative to the best result. These values are exemplary evaluations and can be used later in a cost-utility matrix or AHP to evaluate the alternatives.

Table 3 shows an example of the results of the ratios on Stackoverflow. Here, the number of threads, responses, and ratings of the contributions to the respective e-commerce platform were measured. Points and relative points are also listed here as an example of evaluation.

The diagram of the course of the aggregated response frequencies in Fig. 4 illustrates this graphically. It also shows the decreasing response frequency for many e-commerce platforms except WooCommerce. Magento shows the highest overall number of questions and answers, which is displayed in Table 3. However, the graph in Fig. 4 shows a clear trend change in recent months.

Table 4 shows the measured key figures in the area of knowledge base and community support in terms of online courses and tutorials on the platforms Udemy and YouTube. Here, too, a diverse picture emerges. WooCommerce, for example, shows a very large view interest on YouTube with almost 12 million views in comparison with VirtueMart with a view count of 52,184. The data from YouTube was collected via YouTube's own API. For the information from Udemy, a web crawler was used. The evaluation of points and relative points would be analogous to the evaluations of the previous key figures.

Once all criteria are collected, the evaluations of all key figures can be performed. Table 5 shows the ranking points that could be also transformed into relative points (like in Table 3). The results can be used as a basis or component for a utility-cost matrix or AHP and are only shown here as an example. Above all, it is the task of

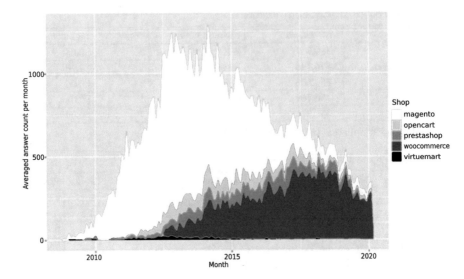

Fig. 4 Aggregated answer count per thread on Stackoverflow

Table 4 Knowledge base and community support indicators on Udemy and YouTube

Platform	Udemy topics	Udemy search results	Tutorial Videos on YouTube	Tutorial views on YouTube
Magento	48	81	562	3,204,093
WooCommerce	**78**	**725**	**570**	**11,929,255**
Prestashop	31	65	550	1,988,160
VirtueMart	0	4	73	52,184
OpenCart	19	54	479	1,979,464

Table 5 Assigned points to e-Commerce Platform

	Live Websites	Stackoverflow			Udemy		YouTube		Total
Magento	2	5	5	5	4	4	4	4	33
WooCommerce	**5**	**4**	**1**	**4**	**5**	**5**	**5**	**5**	**34**
Prestashop	3	2	4	3	3	3	3	3	24
VirtueMart	1	1	2	1	1	1	1	1	9
OpenCart	4	3	4	2	2	2	2	3	22

the decision-maker to weight the individual criteria, such as number of tutorials on Udemy, or number of threads on Stackoverflow.

This case study clearly shows how characteristics and information from different social media can be incorporated into decision support. When the data is carefully selected and aggregated, well-known decision algorithms like AHP can be easily applied without any adaptations to social big data.

4   Case 2: Tackling Veracity in Big Social Media Data

In the past, classic in-house databases and OLAP systems were the primary sources for decision support in companies. With the emergence of Web 2.0 and social media, a comprehensive range of data and information is available for decision support. This includes all resources on the web, from classic websites to discussion boards and social networks; a heterogeneous pool of information has emerged.

In the past, analysts often had to develop their own crawlers to extract information from websites. Even though this is a frequently used procedure, it is still fraught with a number of hurdles and shortcomings. Many websites are characterized by the fact that data is stored in a weakly structured manner. Additionally, websites are subject to frequent changes, e.g., in format and style sheet, which makes a permanent adaptation of the web crawler necessary. According to Glez-Peña et al. [34], the Web scraping process comprises several tasks: Site access through HTTP, HTML Parsing, and Output building.

Especially the parsing of HTML is a big challenge for automated crawlers, which is mainly due to the often low-structural strength of HTML. Although many libraries exist for parsing web pages such as Curl, Scrapy, BeautifulSoup, crawlers are considered weak software due to their vulnerability to changes in the web pages.

Because of the hurdles described above, classical data sources were preferred over the use of web crawlers. An alternative to extracting content from web pages are standardized interfaces. Recently, numerous Application Programming Interfaces (API) have become accessible, especially on the World Wide Web. These interfaces offer a structured and well-defined programming interface to access information on the corresponding platform [35]. Leading social media services like Twitter, Google, or Facebook operate well-defined interfaces in the form of an API. The advantage of APIs is the uniform interface and the strong structuring of the data. Disadvantages are the sometimes-limited access to data, quotas, and limits as well as the dependence to single providers. In general, data sources can be classified according to their structure (Fig. 5). APIs usually have the highest level of structuring, which makes data processing the easiest. Traditional HTML web pages are often unstructured and require a large amount of data preparation. In addition, other sources exist, e.g., databases, wikis, which differ in their structure, according to whether they are operated in-house and allow direct access or are public. This should be taken into account during planning and implementation.

4.1   Analyzing Data from a Social Network

For an educational institution, it is interesting to analyze professional qualifications that people in companies possess. The results help to understand, which types of skills are needed and whether general or very specific qualifications are important.

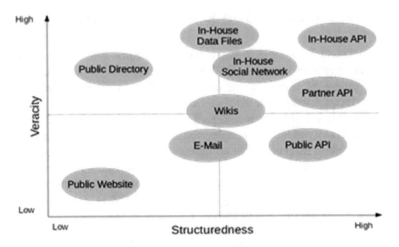

Fig. 5 Structuredness-veracity matrix of social media sources

This can influence decisions in study programs or courses in order to qualify students for the workplaces.

In this case study, we analyzed data from a career-oriented social network in order to identify and investigate distributions of professional qualifications. The aim was to find out whether—besides of the classical generalists and specialist—other types of qualifications can be found with unsupervised learning, and whether these can be found in specific types of companies [36]. Unsupervised learning is a type of machine learning that finds previously undetected patterns in data when class labels are not already known and training data from the past is not available. The data is thus grouped according to similarities and differences between the data.

Profile data was extracted in this case study from the career-oriented network. In a first step, we investigated the collected samples in order to assess whether the samples are representative. The selected social media platform returns only a limited amount of samples per data request, in this case, 200. By a systematic modification of the query, we could collect 7000 data samples. It remained unclear with which criteria the platform selected these samples. Maybe the data was chosen randomly, or the newest, oldest, or most active profiles were selected. Social networks do not provide transparency of how their filtering mechanism decides what data is selected from the social data stream. The selection algorithm can be furthermore biased by the so-called filter bubble, where the user is trapped inside the limited boundaries of his/her interests and cannot be exposed to any surprising, new, and desirable information [37]. The profile selection could therefore be also influenced by the available information of the person who extracted the data (IP-address, own profile . . .).

Based on the data analysis only, it could not be validated how the algorithm selected the data. The only way to validate is indirectly by analyzing the distribution of the qualification types and comparing it to the expected distribution.

4.2   *Veracity Challenges*

The second step was the classification of qualifications among the collected samples. It turned out, that they were written in different languages: German, English, Chinese, or several languages were used in the same profile. Classic methods of natural language processing (NLP) could be used only in a limited way because tokens (smaller parts of a text like words) especially in English and German can overlap and the learned model would get very inefficient. A learned model is the outcome of a machine-learning algorithm like rules, numbers, or data structures. Such a model was learned on data and can be later applied to new data.

In the investigated data, some qualification information contained writing errors, or skills were written in different ways (e.g., names of software with shortcut or long name or version number). As a solution to this problem, we manually created dictionaries with synonyms. In addition, we also manually created stop words. A stop word is a commonly used word (like "the", "in") that is removed before the application of an algorithm because it increases the amount of effort for the algorithm while providing only minimal benefit for the outcome. However, we were aware that parts of the information could be lost by removing these stop words later in the analysis.

Regarding the veracity, and especially the objectivity of the qualification information, we have to distinguish between the perspective of the creator and the reader of this information. In the investigated career-oriented network, we can assume sufficient objectivity of the information because via network connections (contacts) of the profile owner, a person is not anonymous anymore and would therefore not provide wrong information. However, the depth and quality of the given qualifications are subjective. If two people write "SQL" as a qualification, then the perspective, focus, and depth of this knowledge can differ between a database expert and someone who is just able to write simple SQL queries. The information reader can also read and understand such a qualification in a different way.

Another question was, whether we can investigate the development of qualifications over the time. This was impossible because the data samples contained only the current state of the profiles. Neither the timestamp of the last profile update nor the time when a specific information was added to the profile could be investigated. A longitudinal analysis would require a regular repetition of the data collection, which requires a bigger effort. Additionally, changes would only be visible at the time of the collection of new data, and some changes from the past would be still lost.

It was also difficult to analyze the company affiliation because profile owners used different ways of writing their company name in the free-text field. We could identify the following patterns:

- *Different granularity*: The company names are different depending on using the name of a holding (e.g., Siemens) or the name of the subsidiary (e.g., Siemens Healthineers).

- *Different timeline*: Company names were written down when the person was working there once (e.g., Siemens Medical Services) or the new name was used (e.g., Siemens Healthineers).
- *Different conventions*: The name was either written using the official registered name (e.g., Siemens Medical Solutions), or the officially used shortcut (e.g., SMS) or an industry-specific name (e.g., SMED).

We found similar problems in all the free-text data fields of a profile. This leads to a problem if the profile data has to be connected with other data sources (to achieve a bigger variety). Thus, we were not able to connect the carrier network data automatically with other data from company portals in order to see whether certain qualifications are especially needed in certain types of companies.

From the case study, we can conclude that social media data can be used as a basis for decision-making, but the veracity is a challenge. Every additional data source adds to a higher data variety and thus to more problems with veracity that can be only partly, and maybe only manually, fixed.

5   Conclusions from the Case Studies

The chapter approaches how data produced by users on social media can be the basis for decision-making. Social media with its user-generated content provides new possibilities for decision-making through a huge amount of different types of interesting data from different sources. However, some challenges have to be addressed.

The first case described decision-making based on a variety of social media data. This case showed how different data from social media and websites can provide novel, sometimes even contradictory information that were not available before and provide a good basis for decisions. Existing procedures for decision-making such as value analyses or AHP will not be changed by the inclusion of social media data, but additional criteria will become part of the analysis. Nevertheless, we should view the weighting of the individual criteria critically. Furthermore, it is difficult to find a holistic approach due to the sheer number of possible sources. Since social media provide user-generated content, special attention should be always paid to the veracity of the data.

In the second case study, our focus was therefore especially on the veracity. Based on our analysis, we propose the following guidelines in order to tackle the veracity of big social data:

1. Check if the results from the collected social media data (or of a randomly selected subset of this data) can be verified by the results from additional data sources or alternative analytics.
2. Check if it is necessary to create a platform-specific dictionary including stop words. Evaluate how the usage of such a dictionary will influence results.

3. During data understanding and data preparation, several platform-specific assumptions were made. Think about how these assumptions influence your results in terms of precision, recall, and specificity and how this can be measured.
4. Determine when the information was created. Does the platform allow the creator to manipulate timestamps or can invalid information be corrected or removed?
5. Verify if all information readers can understand the information equally. If not, assess the range of individual subjectivity.

With the help of these guidelines, it can be determined how much big social data has an influence on quality and rigor in the decision-making process. All cleansing approaches are associated with a loss of samples, which can easily melt the impressive data set to 10–50%. Overall, the tradeoff between accuracy of the result and sample size should always be estimated.

References

1. Kirchner, K., & Razmerita, L. (2019). Managing the digital knowledge work with the social media business value compass. In *Proceedings of the 52nd Hawaii International Conference on System Sciences* (pp. 6438–6447). New York: APA.
2. Power, D. J., & Phillips-Wren, G. (2011). Impact of social media and Web 2.0 on decision-making. *Journal of Decision Systems, 20*, 249–261. https://doi.org/10.3166/jds.20.249-261.
3. Freire, M., Antunes, F., & Paulo Costa, J. (2015). Exploring social network analysis techniques on decision support. In *Proceedings of the 2nd European Conference on Social Media ECSM* (Vol. 2015, pp. 165–173).
4. Keegan, B. J., & Rowley, J. (2017). Evaluation and decision making in social media marketing. *Management Decision, 55*, 15–31.
5. Wang, J. C., & Chang, C. H. (2013). How online social ties and product-related risks influence purchase intentions: A Facebook experiment. *Electronic Commerce Research and Applications, 12*, 337–346. https://doi.org/10.1016/j.elerap.2013.03.003.
6. DiStaso, M., & McCorkindale, T. (2017). *The science of influence: How social media affects decision-making in the healthcare, travel, retail, and financial industries.* Report retrieved from https://instituteforpr.org/science-influence-social-media-affects-decision-making-healthcare-travel-retail-financial-industries/
7. Conrado, S. P., Neville, K., Woodworth, S., & O'Riordan, S. (2016). Managing social media uncertainty to support the decision making process during emergencies. *Journal of Decision Systems, 25*, 171–181. https://doi.org/10.1080/12460125.2016.1187396.
8. Martin, N. (2019). How much data is collected every minute of the day. In: *Forbes.* Retrieved April 30, 2020, from https://www.forbes.com/sites/nicolemartin1/2019/08/07/how-much-data-is-collected-every-minute-of-the-day/#72daa1c33d66.
9. Bello-Orgaz, G., Jung, J. J., & Camacho, D. (2016). Social big data: Recent achievements and new challenges. *Information Fusion, 28*, 45–59. https://doi.org/10.1016/j.inffus.2015.08.005.
10. Labrinidis, A., & Jagadish, H. V. (2012). Challenges and opportunities with big data. *Proceedings of VLDB Endow, 5*, 2032–2033. https://doi.org/10.14778/2367502.2367572.
11. Orman, L. V. (2015). Information paradox: Drowning in information, starving for knowledge. *IEEE Technology Society, 2015*, 63–73.
12. McAfee, A., & Brynjolfsson, E. (2012). Big data: The management revolution. *Harvard Business Review, 90*, 60–68.
13. Gandomi, A., & Haider, M. (2015). Beyond the hype: Big data concepts, methods, and analytics. *International Journal of Information Management, 35*, 137–144. https://doi.org/10.1016/j.ijinfomgt.2014.10.007.

14. White, T. (2015). *Hadoop: The definitive guide* (4th ed.). Newton: O'Reilly Media.
15. Zaharia, M., Chowdhury, M., Franklin, M. J., & Shenker, S. (2010). Spark: Cluster computing with working sets. In: *Proceedings of the 2nd USENIX conference on Hot topics in cloud computing*. pp. 1–7.
16. Dean, J., & Ghemawat, S. (2008). MapReduce: Simplified data processing on large clusters. *Communications of the ACM, 51,* 107–113. https://doi.org/10.1145/1327452.1327492.
17. Lukoianova, T., & Rubin, V. (2013). Veracity roadmap: Is big data objective, truthful and credible? *Advanced Classification Reseasrch Online, 24,* 4–15. https://doi.org/10.7152/acro.v24i1.14671.
18. Umble, E. J., Haft, R. R., & Umble, M. M. (2003). Enterprise resource planning: Implementation procedures and critical success factors. *European Journal of Operational Research, 146,* 241–257. https://doi.org/10.1016/S0377-2217(02)00547-7.
19. Beardwood, J. P., & Millar, P. (2019). Failed ERP implementation case study of MillerCoors v HCL. *Computer Law Review International, 20,* 136–142.
20. Larsen, M. H., Holck, J., & Pedersen, M. K. (2004). *The challenges of open source software in IT adoption: Enterprise architecture versus total cost of ownership.* IRIS'27, 2–20.
21. Jansen, A., Müller, C., Prümper, J., & Stein, B. (2005). Software-Einführung in KMU-(kein) Platz für Benutzerbeteiligung?-Eine qualitative Bestandaufnahme. In: *Berichtband des dritten Workshops des German Chapters der Usability Professionals Association e.V.* pp. 108–114.
22. Gallaugher, J. M., & Wang, Y. M. (2002). Understanding network effects in software markets: Evidence from Web server pricing. *Management Information Systems Quarterly, 26,* 303–327.
23. Katz, M. L., & Shapiro, C. (1994). Systems competition and network effects. *The Journal of Economic Perspectives, 8,* 93–115. https://doi.org/10.1257/jep.8.2.93.
24. Liebowitz, S., & Margolis, S. (2001). Network effects and the Microsoft case. In *Dynamic competition and public policy: Technology, innovation, and antitrust issues* (pp. 160–192). Cambridge: Cambridge University Press.
25. Benlian, A., & Hess, T. (2011). Comparing the relative importance of evaluation criteria in proprietary and open-source enterprise application software selection—a conjoint study of ERP and Office systems. *Information Systems Journal, 21,* 503–525. https://doi.org/10.1111/j.1365-2575.2010.00357.x.
26. Huang, Z., & Benyoucef, M. (2013). From e-commerce to social commerce: A close look at design features. *Electronic Commerce Research and Applications, 12,* 246–259. https://doi.org/10.1016/j.elerap.2012.12.003.
27. Fitzgerald, B. (2006). The transformation of open source software. *Management Information Systems Quarterly, 30,* 587–598. https://doi.org/10.2307/25148740.
28. Jadhav, A. S., & Sonar, R. M. (2009). Evaluating and selecting software packages: A review. *Information and Software Technology, 51,* 555–563.
29. Krivoruchko, J. (2007). The use of open source software in enterprise distributed computing environments: A decision-making framework for OSS selection and planning. In *IFIP International Conference on Open Source Systems* (pp. 277–282). Boston, MA: Springer.
30. Saaty, T. L. (1990). How to make a decision: The analytic hierarchy process. *European Journal of Operational Research, 48,* 9–26.
31. Vaidya, O. S., & Kumar, S. (2006). Analytic hierarchy process: An overview of applications. *European Journal of Operational Research, 169,* 1–29. https://doi.org/10.1016/j.ejor.2004.04.028.
32. Tung, Y. A. (1998). Time complexity and consistency issues in using the AHP for making group decisions. *Journal of Multi-Criteria Decision Analysis, 7,* 144–154. https://doi.org/10.1002/(SICI)1099-1360(199805)7:3<144::AID-MCDA180>3.0.CO;2-4.
33. Ulbricht, S., Opuszko, M., Ruhland, J., & Thrum, M. (2017). Towards an analysis and evaluation framework for in-memory-based use cases. In: *The twelfth international multiconference on computing in the global information technology.* pp. 22–27.
34. Glez-Peña, D., Lourenço, A., López-Fernández, H., et al. (2014). Web scraping technologies in an API world. *Briefings in Bioinformatics, 15,* 788–797. https://doi.org/10.1093/bib/bbt026.

35. Dig, D., & Johnson, R. (2006). How do APIs evolve? A story of refactoring. *Journal of Software Maintenance and Evolution: Research and Practice, 18*, 83–107. https://doi.org/10.1002/smr.328.
36. Gehrke, S., Wenige, L., & Ruhland, J. (2019). Feasibility study of analysis of senior IT Management Skills/Qualifications in Social Networks. In: *ECSM 2019 6th European Conference on Social Media.* pp. 324–333.
37. Nagulendra, S., & Vassileva, J. (2013). Providing awareness, understanding and control of personalized stream filtering in a P2P social network. In *Collaboration and Technology. CRIWG 2013. Lecture Notes in Computer Science* (pp. 61–76). Berlin, Heidelberg: Springer.

The Evolution of Decision Support Systems for Agriculture: A Bibliometric Network Approach

Dimitris Kremmydas, Alvertos Konstantinis, and Stelios Rozakis

Abstract We use the Scopus database and naïve Bayes text classification to identify almost a thousand and a half DSS papers targeting problems in agriculture during the last three decades. We then use bibliometric network analysis to establish the chronological trends regarding the methodologies, the technologies, the topics, and their interrelation. We also provide insights into the evolution of international research and academic community cooperation and specialization.

Keywords DSS · Agriculture · Naïve Bayes · Network analysis

1 Introduction

Decision Support Systems (DSS) are human–computer systems that assist stakeholders to make effective decisions. This usually involves the presentation of data from heterogeneous sources in a more intuitive way, and quite often, scientific models that use them in order to provide further insights [1]. In the agricultural domain, the term appears in the late 1980s and the number of publications follows an increasing trend. The applications cover diverse topics, for example, water management, environmental modeling, climate change, crop protection, farm management, agricultural policy, and precision agriculture [2, 3].

DSS have facilitated the exchange and transfer of knowledge between the scientific community and the stakeholders or practitioners [4, 5]. However, this exchange is not trouble-free, and the DSS performance depends on several factors.

D. Kremmydas (✉)
Department of Agricultural Economics and Rural Development, Agricultural University of Athens, Athens, Greece

European Commission, Joint Research Centre, Seville, Spain
e-mail: Dimitrios.KREMMYDAS@ec.europa.eu

A. Konstantinis · S. Rozakis
School of Environmental Engineering, Technical University of Crete, Crete, Greece

© Springer Nature Switzerland AG 2021
J. Papathanasiou et al. (eds.), *EURO Working Group on DSS*, Integrated Series in Information Systems, https://doi.org/10.1007/978-3-030-70377-6_6

The literature mentions quite a few. For example, the degree of user-centered design, the quality of the human–computer interface, the skills of the end-users, etc. [6–8]. Thus, due to the unequal performance of the DSSs developed by the research community, the scene is not homogeneous.

The purpose of this chapter is to outline and discuss the trends of the last 30 years regarding the methodologies, the technologies, and the application domains of DSS in agriculture and their interrelation. We also aim to provide insights into the evolution of the international research and academic community cooperation and highlight any specialization that has emerged. The contribution is twofold. Firstly, we identify a vast amount of literature related to DSS in agriculture that can be further used by other researches for more focused reviews. Secondly, we facilitate the discussion opened in this volume, about the assessment of what has occurred during the last three decades and what can be the implications for the future of the field.

To accomplish those objectives, we resort to a bibliometric approach. The published literature is a reliable measure of the research trends and can thus be used to sketch the evolution of any discipline. However, in order to utilize the information found in the bibliographic databases, we need to resolve two issues.

The first relates to the fact that the term "DSS" refers at the same time to the research domain of "decision support systems" and the implementation of a "decision support system" to other science domains. Thus, a search with the keyword "DSS," returns publications of both kinds. Yet, we are interested in the latter group of publications, and thus we need a way to filter them efficiently. The second issue relates to the fact that agriculture is a relatively large, heterogeneous, and interdisciplinary scientific domain. So a search with the keyword "agriculture," returns but a portion of the actual documents in the field since many of them will include keywords not containing the root "agricult*." On the other hand, it is not possible to enumerate all keywords relevant to the domain. Thus, we need an efficient way to identify the literature related to agriculture.

We overcome the difficulty of efficiently identifying the relevant literature by starting from a broad query that contains "DSS" in the title. This query returns 6000 documents. Then, we narrow down the candidate publications by utilizing a naïve Bayes text classification algorithm, as this method has been used for similar tasks in the past [9, 10].

Then, in order to identify the evolution of the literature and their interrelations, we utilize a network analysis approach. We use the VOSviewer tool [11] to construct two bibliometric networks, one with the author keywords and one with countries. For the first type, we use the co-occurrence analysis in which the proximity of the keywords in the network is determined by "the number of documents in which they occur together" [12]. For the countries' network, we use the co-authorship analysis according to which the spatial relation of the country affiliations in the network is determined by the degree of collaboration for producing research.

The aforementioned networks allow us to identify how the scientific community combined different terms, and not only which key terms that the authors were most interested in during different periods but also how the transnational scientific collaboration evolved.

2 Methodology

2.1 Naïve Bayes Text Classification

Naïve Bayes is a simple machine learning technique widely used for text classification with satisfying accuracy [13–15].

The core idea of the naïve Bayes classifier is that we update our prior belief on the probability that a document belongs to a class using the likelihood of the set of words of this document given the class. We estimate the likelihood of using a set of explicitly classified documents (training set). We can utilize either the presence or absence of words using a binomial Bayes classifier or we can use their frequencies and apply a multinomial naive Bayes.

In mathematical terms, we express the naïve Bayes as

$$P\left(\text{class}_j | \textbf{words}_i\right) = \frac{P\left(\textbf{words}_i | \text{class}_j\right) \bullet P\left(\text{class}_j\right)}{P\left(\textbf{words}_i\right)}$$

Where

- class_j are the classes we want to classify the documents into. In our case, we have two classes: the *valid* class, for agriculture domain-related documents; and the *invalid* class for non-agriculture domain-related documents.
- $\textbf{words}_i$ are the words of document-i.
- $P(\text{class}_j)$ is the prior probability of class-j. In our case, we used the frequency of the documents of the training set that belong to the agricultural domain.
- $P(\textbf{words}_i)$ is the probability of a certain bag of words to appear.
- $P(\textbf{words}_i | \text{class}_j)$ is the likelihood of observing a certain bag of words for class-j. In naïve Bayes, we assume the conditional independence of the words of the documents. That is, the probability of each word appearing in a document does not depend from the other words of the document. This is a naïve assumption and the reason that the method is called *naive*. Anyhow, given this assumption, we are allowed to estimate this likelihood easily as $P(\textbf{words}_i | \text{class}_j) = P(\text{word}_{i,\,1} | \text{class}_j) \bullet P(\text{word}_{i,\,2} | \text{class}_j) \bullet \cdots \bullet P(\text{word}_{i,\,n} | \text{class}_j)$
- $P(\text{class}_j | \textbf{words}_i)$ is the posterior probability, i.e., the probability of the document-i belonging to class-j given its words. We compute the posterior probability of a document for all classes and classify the document to the class that has the higher one.

In order to prepare the data for the classifier, several preprocessing steps are essential [16–18]. Primarily, the documents must be broken down into the set

Table 1 Document feature matrix, as shown from the quanteda R package [19]

Document-feature matrix of: 6 documents, 1637 features (98.3% sparse), and 6 docvars

docs	object	knowledg	Features enhanc	abil	maker	task	provid
2-s2.0-0025505218	1	1	1	1	1	2	2
2-s2.0-0038176956	2	0	0	0	0	0	0
2-s2.0-0025700733	0	0	0	0	0	0	0
2-s2.0-0025444756	0	0	0	0	0	0	0
2-s2.0-0025431677	0	0	0	0	0	1	0
2-s2.0-7044990132	0	0	1	0	0	0	0
[reached max_nfeat ... 1627 more features]							

of individual words (tokenization). Tokens can also include consecutive word combinations (n-grams). For example, the sentence "I read many books" will include the 1-g tokens {"I," "read," "many," "books"} and the 2-g tokens {"I read," "read many," "many books"}. After tokenization, the words that provide little information are removed (at minimum, the so-called stopwords, e.g., "a," "and," and "if"). Letters can be converted to lower case and punctuation or numbers are removed if they do not convey information. Finally, most often, the words are transformed into their root form, e.g., the words "ability" or "abilities" were converted to "abil" (this process is called *stemming*).

The preprocessing step will result in a *document feature matrix* (DFM) structure. A DFM is a matrix where documents are in the rows and their containing words (their features) in the columns and the values are the frequency of each word for each document. In the example below (Table 1), we give an excerpt of a DFM of the abstracts we downloaded from SCOPUS. Each row is a different paper abstract, each column is a word detected and the numerical values of the table show the frequency of each word in each abstract. In Table 1, in the first row, the abstract of the first publication (id=2-s2.0-0025505218) contains the words "object" one time, "knowledge" one time, "enhanc" one time, etc. In the second row, the second document (id=2-s2-0.-0038176956) contains the word "object" two times, the word "knowledg" zero times, etc.

2.2 Bibliometric Network Analysis

The basic concept behind network analysis is that the construction of a network allows the exploration of complex and multi-factorial subjects or fields by the visualization of their interconnections with nodes and vertices. Its combination with bibliometric analysis is termed bibliometric network analysis.

Initially, the bibliometric analysis was limited to extracting mostly descriptive statistical indices to evaluate the progress of the academic research, based on the creation of simple productivity indicators of the authors or countries. Gradually, more complex indexes were introduced which allowed the researchers to be able to identify the emergence of new multi- and trans-disciplinary fields.

Nowadays, with more advanced visualization techniques available, the most contemporary statistical indices can be implemented in a mapping procedure of the networks of the scientific literature. In this chapter, we have used the visualization of similarities (VOS) developed by Van Eck and Waltman [11]. There, the mapping is combined with clustering methods to transcend the two-dimensional constraint of the former [11]. There is a sufficient amount of relevant literature in which the reader can get familiar with the VOS technique implemented in different scientific fields [20–22]. Although the VOS technique is, in principle, similar to the multidimensional scaling technique [23]; it is more visual-oriented as it is a distance-based mapping tool, which implies that the distance in which the nodes-terms are placed in the network, represents their relative relatedness which is defined by the method of analysis we have chosen.

Our choice for the VOS technique was based on four (4) central criteria [24]. At first, it is a broadly used technique. Secondly, it is accepted as a reliable mapping technique. Thirdly, the VOS viewer tool is user friendly and; fourthly, it is an open source software. The four pre-mentioned factors increase both the accessibility and the repeatability of the results and thus, increase the validity of the present study.

3 Identification of the Relevant Literature

As already mentioned, we are interested in publications that (1) are focused on the implementation side of a Decision Support System and (2) respond to a problem in the agricultural domain.

We selected publications that complied with the first criterion by requiring the terms *decision support system*, *decision support systems*, or *dss* to be explicitly included in their title. Since the title of a publication signals the focal subject of the chapter, this requirement excludes all publications where DSS is incidental. This, although does not separate DSS-domain papers from DSS-implementation papers, must include the vast majority of papers that focus on presenting a DSS.

The following query in the SCOPUS database returns 13,747 documents.[1]

(TITLE ("DECISION SUPPORT SYSTEMS") OR TITLE ("DECISION SUPPORT SYSTEM") OR TITLE ("DSS")) AND PUBYEAR > 1989
13,747 documents

To distinguish only the documents related to the agricultural/environmental domain, we initially remove items classified by the SCOPUS database to profoundly

---

[1]The same query on the title or abstracts or the keywords, returns 111,569 documents.

irrelevant fields (e.g., Medicine, Psychology). The refined SCOPUS query returns 9779 documents.[23] Furthermore, since we use the abstract and the keywords to facilitate our analysis, we also exclude the items that are missing either the abstract or the keywords and thus conclude to 6725 documents.

(TITLE ("DECISION SUPPORT SYSTEMS") OR TITLE ("DECISION SUPPORT SYSTEM") OR TITLE ("DSS")) AND PUBYEAR > 1989 AND (EXCLUDE (SUBJAREA, "MEDI") OR EXCLUDE (SUBJAREA, "BIOC") OR EXCLUDE (SUBJAREA, "HEAL") OR EXCLUDE (SUBJAREA, "ARTS") OR EXCLUDE (SUBJAREA, "PSYC") OR EXCLUDE (SUBJAREA, "PHYS") OR EXCLUDE (SUBJAREA, "MATE") OR EXCLUDE (SUBJAREA, "IMMU") OR EXCLUDE (SUBJAREA, "PHAR") OR EXCLUDE (SUBJAREA, "CENG") OR EXCLUDE (SUBJAREA, "NURS") OR EXCLUDE (SUBJAREA, "CHEM") OR EXCLUDE (SUBJAREA, "NEUR") OR EXCLUDE (SUBJAREA, "DENT"))

9779 documents in the query/6725 documents with metadata on both abstract and author keywords

---

Due to the high number of documents, the use of a semi-automated method for identifying the documents related to the agriculture domain is beneficial. Thus, we use the *Naive Bayes* classifier to accelerate the filtering of the publications.[4] The algorithm will be applied to the title, the abstract, and the author keywords of the 6725 documents.

The first step is to estimate the probability of a random document of the 6725 documents being related to agriculture. This will be the prior for the naïve Bayes. In order to do so, we randomly selected 1689 documents and manually inspected and classified them as either "related to agriculture" or "not related to agriculture".[5] We found that 18.85% of the sample (352 documents) was related to agriculture while the rest did not. The prior probability of the naïve Bayes is thus set to 0.1885.

Then, based on the above-classified sample (i.e., each paper classified as "related to agriculture" or "not related to agriculture"), we computed the likelihood for each word of the abstracts to appear on each of the classes ("related to agriculture"; "not

---

[2]The excluded subjects were: Medicine; Biochemistry, Genetics and Molecular Biology; Health Professions; Arts and Humanities; Psychology; Physics and Astronomy; Materials Science; Immunology and Microbiology; Pharmacology; Toxicology and Pharmaceutics; Chemical Engineering; Nursing; Chemistry; Neuroscience; Dentistry.

[3]The included subjects were: Computer Science; Engineering; Environmental Science; Business, Management, and Accounting; Decision Sciences; Social Sciences; Agricultural and Biological Sciences; Earth and Planetary Sciences; Energy; Economics, Econometrics, and Finance; Multidisciplinary; Veterinary.

[4]For processing the text and applying the naïve Bayes, we used the *quanteda* R package [19].

[5]We opted for randomly inspecting 1689 documents (25% of the 6725) for two reasons: (a) the higher the number, the most accurate the estimator of the prior; (b) on the other hand, we want to minimize the effort of manually classifying documents; inspecting abstracts and other metadata for 1689 documents is a reasonable effort for an extended literature review.

related to agriculture"). We also compute the probability of observing each word (the frequency a word appears in the corpus of documents).

Next, using the above information, we ran three naïve Bayes classifiers for the remaining non-classified documents (5036 out of 6725); one for titles, one for abstracts, and one for author keywords.[6] Thus, it was possible that a document is classified as "related to agriculture" based on the abstract, but not based on the title. In order to consolidate our findings, we used the following rules:

1. We classify a document as "related to agriculture" if the result of the naïve Bayes is "related to agriculture" in the following cases: in all three fields, i.e., title, abstract, keyword (rule 1.1); or in both title and abstract (rule 1.2); or solely in title (rule 1.3); or only in abstract (rule 1.4). The number of documents classified under these rules is given below:

Classified as	Rule 1.1: Title AND Abstract, AND Keyword	Rule 1.2: Title AND Abstract	Rule 1.3: Title	Rule 1.4: Abstract
"related to agriculture"	509	121	166	384

2. If a document is classified in all three fields (title, abstract, keyword) as "not related to agriculture," then we classify it as "not related to agriculture".

Classified as	Rule 2.1: Title AND Abstract, AND Keyword
"not related to agriculture"	3552

3. The remaining documents are classified as "unknown class".

Classified as	Rule 2.1: Title AND Abstract, AND Keyword
"unknown class"	115

Based on the above results, we manually inspected all documents classified as "related to agriculture" due to rule 1 and all documents classified as "unknown class." We also did a random sampling manual inspection on the "not related to agriculture" documents derived from rule 2. The results are presented in Table 2.

The results of the classification are presented in more detail in the next section.

---

[6]We did so because the information load may differ for each of the above document properties and those three document properties are of different nature and cannot be concatenated.

Table 2 Naive Bayes results

	Rule 1				Rule 2	Rule 3	
Initial naïve Bayes classification:	1.1: Title AND Abstract, AND Keyword	1.2: Title AND Abstract	1.3: Title	1.4: Abstract	Title AND Abstract, AND Keyword	Remaining documents	Already classified manually for the training set
Manual classify-cation "related to agriculture"	498	97	75	288	1	3	352
"not related to agriculture"	11	24	91	96	3551	112	1337
Accuracy of rule	97.8%	80.1%	45.1%	75%	99.2%[a]	–	–

[a]Notes: For this estimation, since we reviewed manually a sample of 120 documents of this category, the accuracy was calculated as the number of correct guesses (119) to the sample size

4 Results

4.1 Naïve Bayes Classification

The distribution of the identified documents in time is shown in Fig. 1 and in Table 3. We observe that there is a steady increase in the absolute number of publications, especially for journal papers. It is also interesting that 95% of the journals has published five or fewer papers in total in the 1990–2019 period and 75% of the journals have published 2 or fewer papers in the same period. Two journals seem to publish papers in the field regularly (Table 4).

In Fig. 2, we also provide the *word cloud* per 5-year period of the most frequent words in the identified publications' abstracts. The size of the word in each group denotes its frequency.

The metadata (titles, abstracts, and author keywords) of the initial data set, the results of the training manual classification, the results of the naïve Bayes, and the final classification are provided in the "01.naive_bayes_results.xlsx" file of the supplementary material.

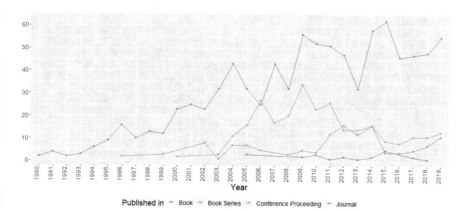

Fig. 1 Evolution of DSS publications for agriculture, 1990–2019 (source: identified papers according to Sect. 2)

Table 3 Number of DSS for agriculture publications for 5-year periods

Period	Books	Book Series	Conference Proceeding	Journal
1990/1994	0	0	0	17
1995/1999	0	5	0	60
2000/2004	0	16	16	146
2005/2009	5	20	114	188
2010/2014	9	60	93	240
2015/2019	8	31	52	258

Table 4 Number of identified publications in most frequent journals

Journal	1990–1999	2000–2009	2010–2019
Computers and Electronics in Agriculture	25	27	30
Environmental Modelling and Software	4	38	25
Agricultural Systems	2	11	6
Transactions of the Chinese Society of Agricultural Engineering	0	18	3
Water Resources Management	0	8	9

Fig. 2 Word cloud of author-keywords quinquennially

4.2   Bibliographic Network Analysis

Using the metadata of the identified "DSS in agriculture" publications, we constructed two sets of networks.[7]

The first network contains the relationships of the selected papers according to the author keywords. We have constructed two such networks, one for 2000–2009 and one for 2010–2019 (Figs. 2 and 3). The nodes of the network represent author keywords. The size of the node indicates the number of occurrences of this keyword in our data set (i.e., in how many papers it appears). If there is an arc connecting two nodes, it means that those two keywords appeared in the same paper at least once. The width of the arc's line is a measure of the frequency those two keywords appear together in papers (more thick line, more times the keywords appear together). The distance between two nodes is a sign of their *relatedness*. The relatedness of two nodes is determined by the number of times the two keywords occur together, considering the relatedness of all other nodes that are connected with them. Thus, while the weight of the arc is a direct sign of the number of co-appearances in papers, the relatedness is a more holistic measure that displays the relation of the

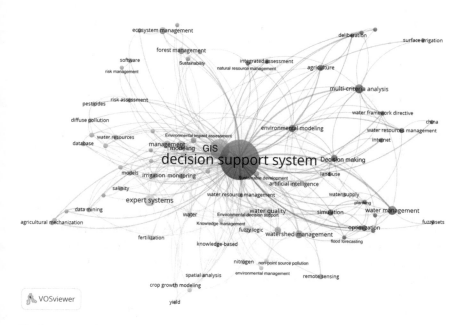

Fig. 3   Network for the decade 1999–2008

---

[7]Certain quantitative properties of those networks (degree, betweenness, and closeness centrality) are provided in the supplementary material.

Table 5 Relative frequency of selected keywords

Period	1990/94 (%)	1995/99 (%)	2000/04 (%)	2005/09 (%)	2010/14 (%)	2015/19 (%)
GIS "*gis*","*geog*inf*"	11.8	29.2	26.3	29.1	28.3	18.9
Machine Learning "*mach*learn", "*neural*", "*genet*algo*", "big*data*"	0.0	3.1	2.8	2.1	2.5	7.4
Mobile technologies "*mobil*", "pda*", "android","*wsn*"	0.0	0.0	0.0	2.1	2.7	7.1

two nodes without ignoring the big picture. Finally, the colors of the nodes are a cluster of keywords that form "sub-networks" within the principal network.

The second network contains the countries, based on the papers' affiliations, for the 2000–2009 and 2010–2019 periods (Figs. 5 and 6). The nodes are the individual countries and the arcs and the relatedness refer to the volume of co-authoring between countries. We have chosen this type of analysis as we believe, in principle, that the higher the number of co-authored documents between two countries, the higher the collaboration and the scientific proximity between them is.

5 Discussion

In both 1999/2008 and 2009/2019 author-keyword networks, the position of GIS is very central. That reveals that the initiation and the evolution of DSS are very much connected to GIS technologies. This could be attributed to the fact that spatial dimension is integral to agriculture, whether on the farm or on the policy level. Thus, the perspective of the GIS technologies naturally fitted into the agricultural decision-making framework. In turn, the rise in the availability of spatial data and the user-friendliness of the GIS interface resulted in the central position of this technology in the DSS in agriculture. If we look at the relative frequency of the GIS-related terms, it seems that the relative frequency in journal papers decline in the last 5 years (Table 5). In contrast, the share of emerging technologies, like machine learning and mobile networks is increasing. However, as shown from the network and is confirmed quantitatively by network metrics (see supplementary material), is that its central role is maintained.

The apparent changes of the last decade are the decrease in the frequency and the centrality of the 'expert systems" and the appearance of the terms "climate change" and "precision agriculture" in a relatively central place. Also water-related keywords, like "watershed management" or "water," decrease in centrality in the new decade, possibly because they are not anymore examined isolated but rather

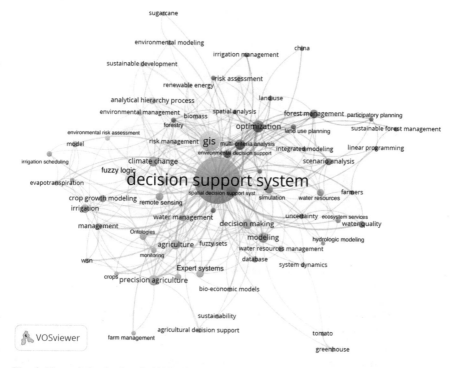

Fig. 4 Network for the decade 2009–2019

under the "climate change" perspective. Regarding the methodologies, "simulation" and "multicriteria analysis" are becoming more central.

Regarding the clusters of the author-keywords network, we observe the following: In the 1999/2008 period (Fig. 3), there are two apparent clusters. The red cluster contains topics related to water management and environment, having the multicriteria methods at its center, while simulation, optimization, and integrated assessment are part of it. The yellow cluster is related to the topics of "water," "fertilization," "nitrogen," and "yield," and the "expert systems" methodology/technology. The existence of two clusters, containing both a water-related topic can be attributed to the fact that the second cluster targets the farm level while the second a more generic level (resources in general). This indicates that a different focus level affects the methodologies used. This becomes more apparent in the author-keyword of the second decade (Fig. 4). The green cluster is a farm level-related cluster, with many "management" keywords and with technologies like sensor networks (wsn) and precision agriculture.

In general, for both decades, there does not seem to be a very clear separation of keyword clusters. If this was the case, one would observe distinct groups of keywords, without nodes of one cluster positioned inside another cluster. This can be attributed to either the need for multidisciplinary solutions to actual decision-making problems.

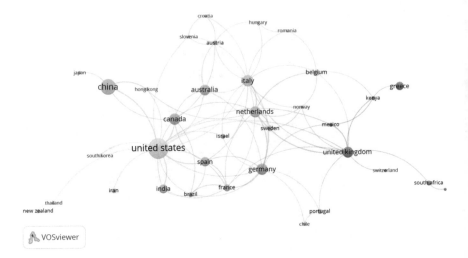

Fig. 5 Country Network for the decade 1999–2008

Regarding the country co-authorship networks (Figs. 5 and 6), there are significant changes between the two decades. In the 1999/2008 period, the Netherlands take a central position, which means that authors of that country seem to have the most connections with authors of other countries. The United States, China, and the United Kingdom, although relatively significant in terms of publications, lie in more isolated locations of the network. This structure changes completely in the current decade (2010–2019). The group of European countries with dense connections between them emerges. European countries that in the previous decade were far from the other European countries (e.g., Greece, Austria), in the current one become part of this European network.

6 Conclusions

We have used a naïve Bayes text classification algorithm to identify around 1600 agricultural DSS papers. We then have constructed the author keywords co-occurrence network and the co-authorship network for countries, one for each of the 1999/2008 and 2009/2019 periods. The methodology applied accelerated the review process and accurately identified the relevant literature. It can be easily extended to other bibliographic databases (Google Scholar, Web of Science) and can be used to efficiently identify the literature of other subjects too.

We have found that the Geographical Information System technology has a central position in the discipline for both decades. New terms appear and take a central position in the current decade's network, like "climate change" and "precision agriculture." However, in all author-keyword networks, there are

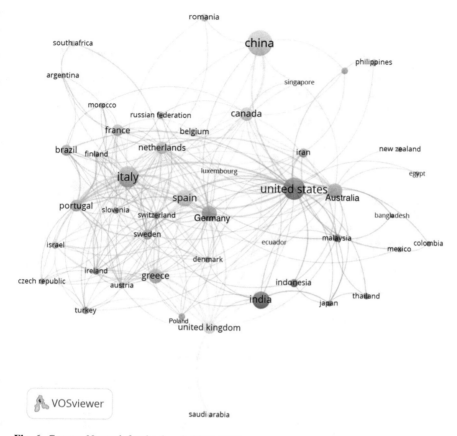

Fig. 6 Country Network for the decade 2009–2019

no clear clusters, probably denoting the need for multidisciplinary solutions to actual decision-making problems. Regarding the evolution of the discipline in the country's dimension, the European countries emerge as a distinct group with dense connections between its members.

Regarding the future trends, DSS literature is increasingly connected to the new technological advances of mobile applications, machine learning, and the internet of things. DSS have a great potential for bringing these technologies in the farm. However, the concern of low intake from end-users of the DSS applications in agriculture remains and more research is required regarding the user-centered design of DSS [7].

References

1. Airinei, D., & Homocianu, D. (2009). DSS vs. business intelligence. *Revista Economica*, 2009, Available at SSRN: https://ssrn.com/abstract=2381821.
2. Manos, B. D., Ciani, A., Bournaris, T., Vassiliadou, I., & Papathanasiou, J. (2004). A taxonomy survey of decision support systems in agriculture. *Agricultural Economics Review, 5*, 80–94.
3. Sun, Y. Y., & Shen, S. H. (2019). Research progress in application of crop growth models. *Chinese Journal of Agrometeorology, 40*(7), 444–459.
4. Zasada, I., Piorr, A., Novo, P., Villanueva, A. J., & Valánszki, I. (2017). What do we know about decision support systems for landscape and environmental management? A review and expert survey within EU research projects. *Environmental Modelling and Software, 98*. 63–74. https://doi.org/10.1016/j.envsoft.2017.09.012.
5. Zhai, Z., Martínez, J. F., Beltran, V., & Martínez, N. L. (2020). Decision support systems for agriculture 4.0: Survey and challenges. *Computers and Electronics in Agriculture, 170*, 105256.
6. Gutiérrez, F., Htun, N. N., Schlenz, F., Kasimati, A., & Verbert, K. (2019). A review of visualisations in agricultural decision support systems: An HCI perspective. *Computers and Electronics in Agriculture, 163*, 104844.
7. Rose, D. C., Parker, C., Fodey, J., Park, C., Sutherland, W. J., & Dicks, L. V. (2018). Involving stakeholders in agricultural decision support systems: Improving user-centred design. *International Journal of Agricultural Management, 6*(3–4), 80–89.
8. Rose, D. C., Sutherland, W. J., Parker, C., Lobley, M., Winter, M., Morris, C., et al. (2016). Decision support tools for agriculture: Towards effective design and delivery. *Agricultural Systems, 149*, 165–174.
9. Adeva, J. G., Atxa, J. P., Carrillo, M. U., & Zengotitabengoa, E. A. (2014). Automatic text classification to support systematic reviews in medicine. *Expert Systems with Applications, 41*(4), 1498–1508.
10. Gulo, C. A., Rúbio, T. R., Tabassum, S., & Prado, S. G. (2015). Mining scientific articles powered by machine learning techniques. In *2015 Imperial College Computing Student Workshop (ICCSW 2015)*. Schloss: Dagstuhl-Leibniz-Zentrum fuer Informatik.
11. Van Eck, N. J., & Waltman, L. (2010). Software survey: VOSviewer, a computer program for bibliometric mapping. *Scientometrics, 84*(2), 523–538.
12. Van Eck, N. J., & Waltman, L. (2013). VOSviewer manual. *Leiden: Univeristeit Leiden, 1*(1), 1–53.
13. Hartmann, J., Huppertz, J., Schamp, C., & Heitmann, M. (2019). Comparing automated text classification methods. *International Journal of Research in Marketing, 36*(1), 20–38.
14. Manning, C. D., Raghavan, P., & Schütze, H. (2008). *Introduction to information retrieval. Online Edition* (p. 258). Cambridge: Cambridge University Press. ISBN: 0521865719.
15. Pranckevičius, T., & Marcinkevičius, V. (2017). Comparison of naive bayes, random forest, decision tree, support vector machines, and logistic regression classifiers for text reviews classification. *Baltic Journal of Modern Computing, 5*(2), 221.
16. Chen, J., Huang, H., Tian, S., & Qu, Y. (2009). Feature selection for text classification with Naïve Bayes. *Expert Systems with Applications, 36*(3), 5432–5435.
17. Raschka, S. (2014). Naive bayes and text classification i-introduction and theory. arXiv preprint arXiv:1410.5329.
18. Schneider, K. M. (2005, February). Techniques for improving the performance of naive bayes for text classification. In *International conference on intelligent text processing and computational linguistics* (pp. 682–693). Berlin, Heidelberg: Springer.
19. Benoit, K., Watanabe, K., Wang, H., Nulty, P., Obeng, A., Müller, S., & Matsuo, A. (2018). quanteda: An R package for the quantitative analysis of textual data. *Journal of Open Source Software, 3*(30), 774. https://doi.org/10.21105/joss.00774, https://quanteda.io.

20. Cancino, C., Merigó, J. M., Coronado, F., Dessouky, Y., & Dessouky, M. (2017). Forty years of Computers & Industrial Engineering: A bibliometric analysis. *Computers & Industrial Engineering, 113*, 614–629.
21. Sweileh, W. M., Al-Jabi, S. W., AbuTaha, A. S., Sa'ed, H. Z., Anayah, F. M., & Sawalha, A. F. (2017). Bibliometric analysis of worldwide scientific literature in mobile-health: 2006–2016. *BMC Medical Informatics and Decision Making, 17*(1), 72.
22. Van Eck, N. J., & Waltman, L. (2011). Text mining and visualization using VOSviewer. arXiv preprint arXiv:1109.2058.
23. Borg, I., & Groenen, P. J. (2005). *Modern multidimensional scaling: Theory and applications.* Berlin: Springer Science & Business Media.
24. Konstantinis, A., Rozakis, S., Maria, E. A., & Shu, K. (2018). A definition of bioeconomy through bibliometric networks of the scientific literature. *AgBioforum, 21*(2), 64–85.

30 Years Business Intelligence: From Data Analytics to Big Data

Isabelle Linden (iD)

Abstract At the crossing of disciplines as Information Systems, Management, Decision Support Systems, Data Mining, and Data Visualization, Business Intelligence (BI) is understood in very different ways by the multiple concerned actors. This chapter aims to offer to all of them an integrated view on multiple perspectives. To this end, it first proposes a standard Business Intelligence approach. Then, it describes the main technical challenges addressed in the literature with a particular focus on those risen by the emergence of Big Data.

Keywords Business intelligence · Big data · Decision support systems

1 A Brief History of Business Intelligence

Since men have been involved in production and trade activities, and probably more critically since the industrial revolution, there have always been people to analyse their performance and question their optimization. Statistics and later data mining offered powerful tools to support this type of quest.

The 1980s and 1990s saw the explosion of computerization in organizations. Many data and information previously processed by hand on paper were digitized. Digital data sources multiplied not only in administration but also at the very heart of production chains and processes.

At the same time, processors gained in power, memories in capacity, and algorithms in efficiency. Such convergence has offered analysts unprecedented processing capabilities. They have extremely wide fields of exploration to investigate. But often, the dream becomes a nightmare when it comes to supporting top management and analysing issues that cut across their organization. Indeed, analyses require then access to information disseminated in various and varied

I. Linden (✉)
FOCUS Research Group, NADI institute, University of Namur, Namur, Belgium
e-mail: isabelle.linden@unamur.be

© Springer Nature Switzerland AG 2021
J. Papathanasiou et al. (eds.), *EURO Working Group on DSS*, Integrated Series in Information Systems, https://doi.org/10.1007/978-3-030-70377-6_7

systems. Moreover, data sources are not only multiple but also heterogeneous in their formats and structures.

Specific architectures and platforms emerged in the 1990s to address these challenges and offer efficient support to decision-maker, namely Business Intelligence platforms. Nowadays, the expression "Business Intelligence" is widely spread, and anyone has a more or less precise idea of what it covers. However, it involves many aspects from most technical ones to very strategic management-oriented ones and many authors are tempted to reduce the domain to one or the other perspective. Conversely, industries tend to widen the scope by including analytics, typically, Gartner 2018 report on the domain is entitled "Magic Quadrant for Analytics and Business Intelligence Platforms" [1].

In Chen et al. [2], the authors propose the following definition of Business Intelligence and Analytics (BI&A):

> "[...] BI&A, [...] is often referred to as the techniques, technologies, systems, practices, methodologies, and applications that analyze critical business data to help an enterprise better understand its business and market and make timely business decisions. In addition to the underlying data processing and analytical technologies, BI&A includes business-centric practices and methodologies [...]."

Indeed, a BI platform is conceived to provide access to specific information required by managers in their decision-making process. Consequently, it would be a nonsense to imagine that a BI platform could be developed independently of a deep knowledge of the specific business to which it is dedicated and its strategy. A BI platform as to be seen as one of the technical bricks into the complete wall of the specific business performance management of the concerned company.

In this chapter, we focus our purpose to technical aspect. However, regarding managerial perspective, we would refer the interested readers to the broad literature on Key Performance Indicators (KPI, see for example Parmenter [3]), scorecards [4–6], and Business Performance Management (BPM, see for example Neely [7], Neely et al. [8]).

From a user perspective, a BI platform appears as framework providing access to a variety of tools among which one commonly find (a selection among): interactive dashboards, reports, OLAP query tools, data mining tools, alerts, . . .

But the specific value of a BI platform lies not so much in the tools offered to users (some of which have existed since long before BI was mentioned) as in the information to which it gives access. Indeed, one of the main challenges of BI is to give users access to information across the organization by allowing them to query a single source while the data needed to build this information is disseminated in multiple sources with heterogeneous structures and riddled with semantic and quality problems. This while avoiding disrupting the behaviour of the operational system.

To achieved this magic, the common reference architecture is structured as illustrated in Fig. 1. On the right are the users, at the different levels of the organization, who access the relevant applications according to their function. On the left side, the multiple heterogeneous data sources both within and outside the

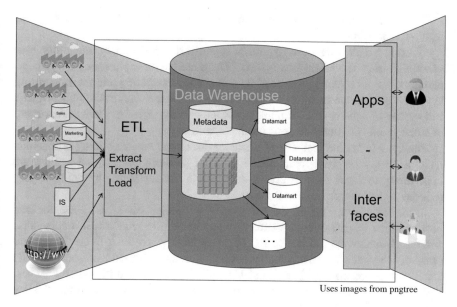

Uses images from pngtree

Fig. 1 Standard business intelligence architecture

organization are illustrated. In between is the BI platform, the various components of which will be discussed below.

For now, let us underline a few essential aspects expected from such an implementation. As a first specificity, observe that the data flow is one way from operational systems to the analytical system. This is also described as isolation of both world. Combined with adequate data extraction planning, this system splitting implements the requirement that, regardless of the analysis workload, the operational system should not be disrupted.

Downstream of the data ow, all the applications offered to users consult a single source: the data warehouse. Ignoring here the various implementation possibilities (which are discussed below), note that the data warehouse offers a single view of all the retained information, a property generally required under the expression "single truth".

Although they may look like traditional databases, the uses of data warehouses have a set of specificities with respect to operational data bases that impact their design:

- Data warehouses do not support update and delete operations, but only inserts (usually batch at night or week-end) and read
- Queries on data warehouses commonly address wide set of data (in lines and columns)
- Numbers of users and queries are less limited
- For huge queries, acceptable response time is higher

These characteristics gave leads to multidimensional modelling preferably over relational modelling.

Offering a data warehouse requires a sophisticated preliminary integration task denoted Extract-Transform-Load (ETL). These are the three phases of a very complex process of collecting the data, then cleaning, integrating and (re-)formatting before loading in the data warehouse. Depending on the size, availability, variety, and quality of sources, ETL's implementation can be carried out in a wide variety of architectures relying or not on specific data storage.

Finally, it is to note that, even for mature disciplines as data mining or machine learning, being involved interaction with a BI platform offer to the analyst the opportunity to focus their effort on their specific added value, by being largely relieved of data pre-processing issues.

In the rest of the chapter, we aim to offer a double view on BI. First, looking back over the last 30 years, we offer an overview of the standard BI architecture, and the dominant approaches to BI. In a second step, we look to the future and draw an overview of the main challenges BI has to face. Section 2 presents the data warehouse approaches of Inmon and Kimball. Despite their different approaches, they are almost unanimously considered as the fathers of data warehouses, the key component at the heart of standard BI architectures.

Then, Sect. 3 extends the technical purpose to the global architecture of BI platforms and presents a typology that organizes their heterogeneity. Turning to the development methodology, Sect. 4 addresses a few BI engineering aspects. After these Sects. 2–4 drawing the state-of-the-art basic BI platform knowledge, Sect. 5 sketches out the main challenges addressed by current scientific literature on BI and Sect. 6 discusses these specifically risen by Big Data.

More than an exhaustive survey of the domain, this chapter aims to offer a pedagogical introduction to the domain, so together with references collected through a standard literature review process, some others more connected to industry or less cited ones are introduced in order to provide a complete structured view on the domain.

2 Inmon and Kimball's Approaches of Data Warehouses

Unanimously mentioned as the fathers of data warehouses in both industrial and scientific literature, Inmon and Kimball do not, however, propose completely the same approach.

Inmon defines a data warehouse as "a subject-oriented, integrated, non-volatile, and time-variant collection of data in support of management's decisions" [9]. His approach is commonly qualified as "top-down". He conceives the data warehouse as a single centralized information repository for the entire company at a low level of granularity. The main purpose is to offer a view on data being (i) single truth, (ii) enterprise wide, and (iii) persistent. The implementation of a data warehouse in this perspective is a relational database. Deduced from the data warehouse a set of departmental data marts are then built to address efficiently the specific needs for reporting and analytics and OLAP queries.

Adopting an approach often consider as more pragmatic, Kimball defines a data warehouse as "a copy of transaction data specifically structured for query and analysis" [10]. His focus relies mainly in the ability to provide efficiently an answer to the actual questions of business management. Kimball builds one by one multidimensional data marts. Their consistency is guaranteed by "conformed dimensions" which ensure the unicity of a global logical schema as data warehouse.

Beside these two references approaches, a wide variety of implementations and implementations process emerged from the diversity of businesses specificities and projects environments. Extending the scope, the following section presents different BI platform architectures.

3   Global Architecture Typology

Data warehouses are recognized as key components of BI infrastructure. To be implemented actually and effectively implemented, they need to be integrated into a complete BI infrastructure.

As mentioned above, data warehouses offer a solution to data access, reconciliation, and quality problems. To reach that goal, and feed a data warehouse, a significant job has to be done by a commonly called Extract-Transform-Load (ETL) Process.

Downstream of the data warehouse, a whole set of applications with different levels of interactivity are grafted: from predefined reports to interactive dashboards, involving OLAP querying tools or even complete data mining suites.

Each company has its specific IT environment, data sources complexity, heterogeneity, diversity, and update frequencies vary significantly from one business to another. Correlatedly, a variety of architectures can be observed in BI platform architecture implementations. Golfarelli and Rizzi [11] organize a typology following the number of physical data layers.

The single-layer architecture involves no other data storage than the operational data sources. There is no physical data warehouse but a "data warehouse-like" conceptual model which serves as a middleware to access the data sources.

This kind of solutions fail to meet the recommended isolation between operational and analytical application and most of the advantages of an actual data warehouse implementation. However, it makes sense to consider such an architecture if the number of data sources is limited, their structures simple and their quality good and if, in addition, the number of analytical queries is relatively low.

In two layers' architectures, a data warehouse layer is actually implemented. It stores integrated data provided by the ETL process. Its physical implementation involves either an integrated data warehouse, or a set of conformed data marts, or both of them. These architectures are probably the most common in textbooks and offer both the single truth (integration) and the no disruption of operational system qualities commonly expected from BI platforms.

There are situations, in particular when ETL is highly sophisticated, or original data source access very constrained, where ETL process requires a specific data storage. A third layer, reconciled data layer is then added. This layer materialized (partially) reconciled source data, not yet fully formatted (integrated, cleaned, or whatever required pre-treatment) to be integrated in the data warehouse.

4   BI Engineering

Introduction of BI through the architecture could give the illusion that BI platforms are built in a fully bottom-up approach. This would be a false idea. Indeed, even more critically than for any IT system, BI platforms require a strong strategy/IT alignment [12]. To ensure that the proposed solution meets business needs, a V-shaped approach can be used, as illustrated in Fig. 2. In the downward phase, the business question is translated step by step in an information, and a data question. Then, when useful data is retrieved, in the ascending phase of the process, data is gradually aggregated in information and then in knowledge to answer the business question and be integrated as decisions and actions in the managerial process.

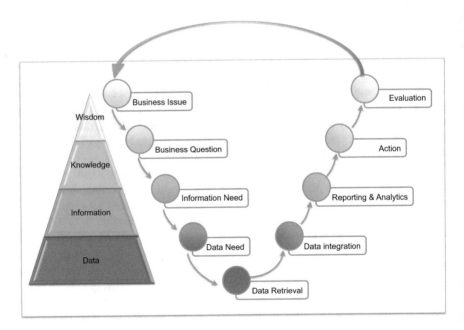

Fig. 2 V-shaped BI approach

However, the infrastructure is not developed business question by business question, but a global solution is designed to address wide sets of parametrical requests. This requires strong methodologies. Discussing all the full project management alternatives would bring us deep in the general project management literature and far out of the allowed length for this paper (interested reader can refer to [13]). Let us focus here on the data warehouse design.

A broad part of industrial literature addresses the data warehouse design at the logical level, starting with a dimensional model as a star or a snowflake schema. This approach can be compared with a data base design that would start at the logical level, designing a relational schema. If this approach can be efficient for small or standard situation, the IT engineering literature has evidenced the need for a preliminary conceptual design drawing entity-relationship schema for example. No language has yet emerged as a standard, the scientific literature involves several propositions to address conceptual data warehouse modelling.

Among them, let us mention Golfarelli and Rizzi [11] and Vaisman and Zimányi [14]. They both propose similar design processes. The first steps, led in parallel, consist, on the one hand, in data sources analysis (bottom-up) and, on the other hand, in requirements analysis (top-down). Then the design goes through conceptual, logical, and physical phases. At the conceptual level, Golfarelli and Rizzi [11] propose a language called Dimensional Fact Model (DFM), and Vaisman and Zimányi [14], a language called MultiDim. Both involves the ability to define facts, dimensions, and hierarchies with sophisticated structures.

5 Big Data Challenges

Big Data is one of these buzz words commonly used with a poor and limited understanding. Specifically, beside volume problems, Big Data covers a wide variety of challenges risen by a new generation of data types and sources. Since the emergence Web 2.0, business data has been supplemented by user generated content on social media platforms, integrating semi-structured textual data, pictures and videos. Even more remarkably, e-commerce platforms and multiple apps offer data sources that do not require manual encoding. These sources are constantly multiplying with the omnipresence of mobile devices and will not stop exploding with the deployment of the Internet of Things increasing significantly the volume of spatio-temporal data and frequencies of collection. Let us address them here following the seminal 3 V's classification: Volume, Velocity, and Variety [15].

5.1 Volume

In the first time of Big Data, some actors have sometimes been tempted to use the term Big Data in an abusive way as a rebranding of traditional data mining and analytical approaches. However, all business areas are now affected by the multiplication of source and Business Intelligence actors can no longer ignore volume challenges. In particular, e-commerce, digital businesses, international companies as well as public administrations can no longer be satisfied with the support provided by standard technologies.

At the physical level, Business Intelligence can benefit from the recent Big Data architectures and tools [16]: Hadoop, GFS, Chukwa, Map-reduce, NoSQL, HBase, Cassandra. Chen and Zhang [17] propose a broad overview of the Big Data techniques and technologies addressing the volume challenges at the levels of data capture and storage, data transmission, data curation, data analysis, and data visualization.

Beside the implementation of BI platform on Big Data architecture, specific data warehouse designs aim to target high volume capacity, large data sets while preserving adaptability. One significant attempt in this perspective lies in Data Vault [18] and Conceptual Data Vault [19].

5.2 Velocity

The second "V" of Big Data leads to Velocity. Two challenges are covered by this single word. On the one hand, the velocity of production of large and complex data, as for example streams of images, requires specific real-time pre-processing to be stored in a manageable space and format. On the other hand, systems are expected to provide real-time information. Basic architecture, as described above, are not conceived to offer hard real-time access to data, solutions can be developed integrating approaches such as those of Business Activity Monitoring (BAM) [20]. For many businesses, the constraint is (a bit) more flexible. Approaches are the called "almost-real time" or "Just in time" [21, 22]. Applications can be found in domains as airlines companies [23], supply chain analytics [24] or on production lines with the industry 4.0.

5.3 Varity

Variety is probably not the least of the challenges involved in Big Data management. Indeed, while businesses are now well doing with standard relational data, Big Data integrates a large set of diversity in data sources formats. Thinking only to the social web, one finds unstructured texts, photos, videos, graphs (models for networks), geographic information to mention only the most obvious one. Each of these formats brings a set of methods and application domains: text mining, natural language processing (NLP), sentiment analysis, opinion mining, multilingual analysis, network analysis. Integration of this information in data warehouses and the analytics tools in BI platform requires new models.

Mobile devices generate large sets of context aware and spatio-temporal data [25]. Specific storage and design methods have been proposed to deal with these in data warehouses [26].

With regard to texts, multidimensional models for OLAP queries on textual documents have been proposed [27], as well as specific tools for semi-structured text, as XML document [28], or on the basis of text metadata or extracted information as keywords [29], topic analysis [30], or context [31, 32]. Complementarily, specific visualization and interaction for texts are still an ongoing challenge [33].

6   Other Challenges

Beside the integration of Big Data challenges, Business Intelligence scientific literature addresses many other challenges, this last section before conclusion aims to present two of them that will complete our survey of the fields: the domains addressed by BI and its methodologies.

6.1   *Specific Domain*

Business Intelligence enters all business domains, for many of them this requires specific models development or systems adaptation as well as the identification and use of levers specific to the business domain.

Non-surprisingly, one finds among the domain-specific studies: market intelligence [34], magazine distribution [35], banking [36], resource allocation [37], production management [38], security and risk management [39], operational risk management with real-time business intelligence food traceability [40].

Health data and health management are well developed. Specifically, let us mention Electronic Health Record [41], radiology [42], health institution management [43, 44], public health management [45], and propositions for a BI implementation framework in healthcare [46].

A last trend to mention proposes a BI system to support decisions about use and evolution of a BI system: BI4BI [47].

6.2   *Methodology*

The huge literature on Information Systems design and implementation methodologies provides a solid background for Business Intelligence Platform development. However, specificities of analytical perspective give rise to the development of specific design and implementation strategies [48] as well as specific requirements and goals elicitation methods for the BI platform [49], one specific component as its data mining tools [50, 51], or the data warehouse [52]. Users are also involved to assess the usability of the proposed BI solution [53].

Self-service BI is a recent trend, highly implies users not only clients but elevates them to the rank of co-developers giving (some of) them the ability to develop and integrate their own requests [54, 55], Alpar & Schulz [56].

Given the complexity of the systems, the number and diversity of data sources, the sophistication of integration, there is a high risk for BI platform of lack of flexibility and adaptability. An important literature addresses the challenge of agile development of BI platforms [57–62].

7 Conclusion

This chapter first proposes a standard Business Intelligence approach. It then describes the main technical challenges addressed in the literature with a particular focus on those risen by the emergence of Big Data.

The Managerial challenges is another aspect of BI which cannot be dissociated of technics in a BI project, Van-Hau [63] explores how business value can be obtained from BI Systems, he summarizes the state of the art in a framework for business value creation from BI that integrates findings. Among the proposals for a complementary research agenda, he identifies: probabilistic models linked necessary condition from BI investments to BI assets to BI impacts; focus on team, industry, and societal levels as well as multi-level studies.

This chapter neither addresses security and GDPR aspects which are crosscutting issues across all IT platforms, but which probably require special attention in systems that are developed to provide information in an easy-to-understand business-oriented fashion.

Employment agencies and job markets never stop underlying the need for competencies in BI, analytics, and Big Data. More and more degrees, in diverse faculties, involve analytical skills. Profiles able to manage the design and develop BI platform can only be developed through a transdisciplinary approach including math, data mining, IT, and business perspectives. We hope that this chapter will fruitfully contribute to this kind of training by offering to students and researchers in these disciplines an introduction to the issues and challenges of Business Intelligence.

References

1. Howson, C., Sallam, R., Richardson, J., Tapadinhas, J., Idoine, C. & Woodward, A. (2018). *Magic quadrant for analytics and business intelligence platforms, Technical report.*
2. Chen, H., Chiang, R. H. L., & Storey, V. C. (2012). Business intelligence and analytics: From big data to big impact. *MIS Quarterly, 36*(4), 1165–1188. Retrieved from http://dl.acm.org/citation.cfm?id=2481674.2481683.

3. Parmenter, D. (2015). *Key performance indicators: Developing, implementing, and using winning KPIs, 3rd edn.* New York: Wiley. Retrieved from https://books.google.be/books?id=MSWsBwAAQBAJ.

4. Kaplan, R., & Norton. (2001). *The strategy-focused organization: How balanced scorecard companies thrive in the new business environment, the strategy-focused organization: How balanced scorecard companies thrive in the new business environment.* Boston: Harvard Business School Press.

5. Kaplan, R., & Norton, D. (2004). *Strategy maps: Converting intangible assets into tangible outcomes.* Baston: Harvard Business School Press. Retrieved from https://books.google.be/books?id=vCnhFu52rosC.

6. Kaplan, R. S., & Norton, D. P. (1996). *The Balanced Scorecard: Translating strategy into action.* Boston: Harvard Business School Press.

7. Neely, A. (2007). *Business performance measurement: Unifying theory and integrating practice.* London: Cambridge University Press. Retrieved from https://books.google.be/books?id=EnFsx6svfL8C.

8. Neely, A., Books, I., & Austin, R. (2002). *Business performance measurement: Theory and practice.* London: Cambridge University Press. Retrieved from https://books.google.be/books?id=1KIEoQYx5ewC.

9. Inmon, W. H. (1992). *Building the data warehouse.* New York, NY, USA: John Wiley & Sons, Inc..

10. Kimball, R. (1996). *The data warehouse toolkit: Practical techniques for building dimensional data warehouses.* New York: Wiley. Retrieved from https://books.google.be/books?id=8IMpAQAAMAAJ.

11. Golfarelli, M., & Rizzi, S. (2009). *Data warehouse design: Modern principles and methodologies, 1 edn.* New York, NY, USA: McGraw-Hill, Inc..

12. Villamarín García, J., & Díaz Pinzón, B. (2017). Key success factors to business intelligence solution implementation. *Journal of Intelligence Studies in Business, 7*(1), 46–69.

13. Moss, L. (2003). *Business intelligence roadmap: The complete project lifecycle for decision-support applications.*

14. Vaisman, A., & Zimányi, E. (2014). *Data warehouse systems: Design and implementation.* Heidelberg: Springer.

15. Gandomi, A., & Haider, M. (2015). Beyond the hype: Big data concepts, methods, and analytics. *International Journal of Information Management, 35*(2), 137–144. Retrieved from http://www.sciencedirect.com/science/article/pii/S0268401214001066.

16. Chen, M., Mao, S., & Liu, Y. (2014). Big data: A survey. *Mobile Networks and Applications, 19*(2), 171–209. https://doi.org/10.1007/s11036-013-0489-0.

17. Chen, C. P., & Zhang, C.-Y. (2014). Data-intensive applications, challenges, techniques and technologies: A survey on big data. *Information Sciences, 275,* 314–347. Retrieved from http://www.sciencedirect.com/science/article/pii/S0020025514000346.

18. Linstedt, D., & Olschimke, M. (2015). *Building a scalable data warehouse with data vault 2.0, 1st edn.* San Francisco, CA, USA: Morgan Kaufmann Publishers Inc..

19. Jovanovic, V. & Bojicic, I. (2012), Conceptual data vault model, in *Proceedings of the Southern Association for Information Systems Conference, Atlanta, GA, USA March 23rd–24th, 2012,* pp. 131–136.

20. Golfarelli, M., Rizzi, S., Risorgimento, V., Cella, I., & Matteotti, V. (2004). Beyond data warehousing: What's next in business intelligence, in Proceedings of the 7th ACM international workshop on Data warehousing and OLAP. *DOLAP, 4,* 1–6.

21. Azvine, B., Cui, Z., & Nauck, D. D. (2005). Towards real-time business intelligence. *BT Technology Journal, 23*(3), 214–225. https://doi.org/10.1007/s10550-005-0043-0.

22. Panian, Z. (2009), Just-in-time business intelligence and real-time decisioning, in *AIC'09 Proceedings of the 9th WSEAS international conference on applied informatics and communications,* pp. 106–111.

23. Anderson-Lehman, R., Watson, H. J., Wixom, B., & Hoffer, J. A. (2004). Continental airlines ies high with real-time business intelligence. *MIS Quarterly Executive, 3,* 1.

24. Sahay, B., & Ranjan, J. (2008). Real time business intelligence in supply chain analytics. *Information Management and Computer Security, 16*(1), 28–48.
25. Colot, C., Linden, I., & Baecke, P. (2016). A survey on mobile data uses. *International Journal of Decision Support System Technologies, 8*(2), 29–49.
26. Malinowski, E., & Zimányi, E. (2008). *Advanced data warehouse design: From conventional to spatial and temporal applications (Data-centric systems and applications), 1 edn.* New York: Springer Publishing Company, Incorporated.
27. Tseng, F. S. C., & Chou, A. Y. H. (2006). The concept of document warehousing for multi-dimensional modeling of textual-based business intelligence. *Decision Support Systems, 42*(2), 727–744. https://doi.org/10.1016/j.dss.2005.02.011.
28. Pujolle, G., Ravat, F., Teste, O., Tournier, R., & Zuruh, G. (2011). Multidimensional database design from document-centric xml documents. In A. Cuzzocrea & U. Dayal (Eds.), *Data warehousing and knowledge discovery* (pp. 51–65). Berlin, Heidelberg: Springer.
29. Ravat, F., Teste, O., Tournier, R., & Zuruh, G. (2008). Top keyword: An aggregation function for textual document OLAP. In I.-Y. Song, J. Eder, & T. M. Nguyen (Eds.), *Data warehousing and knowledge discovery* (pp. 55–64). Berlin, Heidelberg: Springer.
30. Zhang, D., Zhai, C., Han, J., Srivastava, A., & Oza, N. (2009). Topic modeling for OLAP on multidimensional text databases: Topic cube and its applications. *Statistical Analysis and Data Mining: The ASA Data Science Journal, 2*(5–6), 378–395. https://doi.org/10.1002/sam.10059.
31. Oukid, L., Benblidia, N., Bentayeb, F., Asfari, O., & Boussaid, O. (2015). Contextualized text OLAP based on information retrieval. *International Journal of Data Warehousing and Mining, 11*, 1–21.
32. Oukid, L., Boussaid, O., Benblidia, N., & Bentayeb, F. (2016). TLabel: A new OLAP aggregation operator in text cubes. *International Journal of Data Warehousing and Mining, 12*(4), 54–74. Retrieved from https://hal.archives-ouvertes.fr/hal-01484335.
33. Clarinval, A., Linden, I., Wallemacq, A., & Dumas, B. (2018). *Evoq: A visualization tool to support structural analysis of text documents in Proceedings of the 2018 ACM Symposium on Document Engineering.* New York, NY, USA: ACM Press.
34. Stone, M. D., & Woodcock, N. D. (2014). Interactive, direct and digital marketing: A future that depends on better use of business intelligence. *Journal of Research in Interactive Marketing, 8*(1), 4–17.
35. McBride, N. (2014). Business intelligence in magazine distribution. *International Journal of Information Management, 34*(1), 58–62. Retrieved from http://www.sciencedirect.com/science/article/pii/S0268401213001163.
36. Moro, S., Cortez, P., & Rita, P. (2015). Business intelligence in banking: A literature analysis from 2002 to 2013 using text mining and latent Dirichlet allocation. *Expert Systems with Applications, 42*(3), 1314–1324. Retrieved from http://www.sciencedirect.com/science/article/pii/S0957417414005636.
37. Linden, I. (2014). Proposals for the integration of interactive dashboards in business process monitoring to support resources allocation decisions. *Journal of Decision Systems, 23*(3), 318–332.
38. Linden, I., Liu, S., Moizer, J., Subramaniam, P. & Leat, M. (2010), Decision support for erp-based production management: A business intelligence perspective, in *Proceedings of the 15th IFIP WG8.3 International Conference on Decision Support Systems.*
39. Azvine, B., Cui, Z., Majeed, B., & Spott, M. (2007). Operational risk management with real-time business intelligence. *BT Technology Journal, 25*(1), 154–167. https://doi.org/10.1007/s10550-007-0017-5.
40. Gianni, M., Gotzamani, K., & Linden, I. (2016). How a bi-wise responsible integrated management system may support food traceability. *International Journal on Decision Support System Technology, 8*(2), 1–17. https://doi.org/10.4018/IJDSST.2016040101.
41. Bonney, W. (2013). Applicability of business intelligence in electronic health record. *Procedia - Social and Behavioral Sciences, 73*, 257–262. Retrieved from http://www.sciencedirect.com/science/article/pii/S1877042813003431.

42. Cook, T. S. & Nagy, P. (2014), Business intelligence for the radiologist: Making your data work for you, *Journal of the American College of Radiology.*
43. Barone, D., Topaloglou, T., & Mylopoulos, J. (2012). Business intelligence modelling in action: A hospital case study. In J. Ralyté, X. Franch, S. Brinkkemper, & S. Wrycza (Eds.), *Advanced information systems engineering* (pp. 502–517). Berlin, Heidelberg: Springer.
44. Mettler, T., & Vimarlund, V. (2009). Understanding business intelligence in the context of healthcare. *Health Informatics Journal, 15*(3), 254–264. https://doi.org/10.1177/1460458209337446.
45. Rivest, S., Bédard, Y., Proulx, M.-J., Nadeau, M., Hubert, F., & Pastor, J. (2005). SOLAP technology: Merging business intelligence with geospatial technology for interactive spatio-temporal exploration and analysis of data. *ISPRS Journal of Photogrammetry and Remote Sensing, 60*(1), 17–33. Retrieved from http://www.sciencedirect.com/science/article/pii/S0924271605000614.
46. Foshay, N., & Kuziemsky, C. (2014). Towards an implementation framework for business intelligence in healthcare. *International Journal of Information Management, 34*(1), 20–27. https://doi.org/10.1016/j.ijinfomgt.2013.09.003.
47. Brichni, M., Dupuy-Chessa, S., Gzara, L., Mandran, N., & Jeannet, C. (2017). BI4BI: A continuous evaluation system for business intelligence systems. *Expert Systems with Applications, 76*(C), 97–112. https://doi.org/10.1016/j.eswa.2017.01.018.
48. Gangadharan, G. R., & Swami, S. N. (2004). Business intelligence systems: Design and implementation strategies. *26th International Conference on Information Technology Interfaces, 1*, 139–144.
49. Burnay, C., Jureta, I., Linden, I. & Faulkner, S. (2014), A framework for the operationalization of monitoring in business intelligence requirements engineering, *Software and Systems Modeling.*
50. Britos, P., Dieste, O., & García-Martínez, R. (2008). Requirements elicitation in data mining for business intelligence projects. In D. Avison, G. M. Kasper, B. Pernici, I. Ramos, & D. Roode (Eds.), *Advances in information systems research, education and practice* (pp. 139–150). Boston, MA: Springer US.
51. Olszak, C. M., & Ziemba, E. (2007). Approach to building and implementing business intelligence systems. *Interdisciplinary Journal of Information, Knowledge, and Management, 2*, 135–148.
52. Giorgini, P., Rizzi, S., & Garzetti, M. (2005). Goal-oriented requirement analysis for data warehouse design. In *Proceedings of the 8th ACM International Workshop on Data Warehousing and OLAP, DOLAP 05* (pp. 47–56). New York, NY, USA: ACM. https://doi.org/10.1145/1097002.1097011.
53. Jooste, C., van Biljon, J., & Mentz, J. (2014). Usability evaluation for business intelligence applications: A user support perspective. *South African Computer Journal, 53*, 198. Retrieved from http://sacj.cs.uct.ac.za/index.php/sacj/article/view/198.
54. Abelló, A., Darmont, J., Etcheverry, L., Golfarelli, M., Mazòn, J.-N., Naumann, F., Pedersen, T., Rizzi, S. B., Trujillo, J., Vassiliadis, P., & Vossen, G. (2013). Fusion cubes: Towards self-service business intelligence. *International Journal of Data Warehousing and Mining (IJDWM), 9*, 23.
55. Schlesinger, P. A., & Rahman, N. (2016). Self-service business intelligence resulting in disruptive technology. *Journal of Computer Information Systems, 56*(1), 11–21. https://doi.org/10.1080/08874417.2015.11645796.
56. Alpar, P., & Schulz, M. (2016). Self-service business intelligence. *Business & Information Systems Engineering, 58*(2), 151–155. https://doi.org/10.1007/s12599-016-0424-6.
57. Collier, K. W. (2011). *Agile analytics: A value-driven approach to business intelligence and data warehousing, 1st edn.* Boston: Addison-Wesley Professional.
58. Dasgupta, S. & Vankayala, V. K. (2007), Developing real time business intelligence systems the agile way, in *2007 1st Annual IEEE Systems Conference*, pp. 1–7.
59. Krawatzeck, R., Dinter, B. & Thi, D. A. P. (2015), How to make business intelligence agile: The agile bi actions catalog, in *2015 48th Hawaii International Conference on System Sciences*, pp. 4762–4771.

60. Larson, D., & Chang, V. (2016). A review and future direction of agile, business intelligence, analytics and data science. *International Journal of Information Management, 36*(5), 700–710. Retrieved from http://www.sciencedirect.com/science/article/pii/S026840121630233X.
61. Muntean, M. (2013). Agile BI—the future of BI. *Informatica Economica Journal, 3,* 114–124.
62. Sadegh Sangari, M., & Razmi, J. (2015). Business intelligence competence, agile capabilities, and agile performance in supply chain an empirical study. *The International Journal of Logistics Management, 26,* 1.
63. Van-Hau, T. (2017). Getting value from business intelligence systems: A review and research agenda. *Decision Support Systems, 93,* 111–124.

A Systematic Literature Review of Knowledge Mobilisation and Its Support for Business Decisions Over Two Decades (1999–2019)

Shaofeng Liu (iD), Ali Ibraheem Alkhuraiji, and Abdullah Alkraiji

Abstract The importance of knowledge and knowledge management (KM) has been widely recognised, from the context of individuals, groups, organisations to the economy. KM has greatly evolved over the last few decades in terms of its processes, life cycles, boundary-spanning mechanisms and facilitating technologies. Knowledge mobilisation, as one of the key stages of the KM process and life cycle, holds the key to the success of organisations' learning and innovation activities, especially in the context of crossing knowledge boundaries to support business decisions. This chapter provides a systematic literature review (SLR) of knowledge mobilisation and its support to business decision-making. The SLR process used includes five well-structured, transparent stages. Key findings from the SLR reveal some important trends of the topic along four key themes of knowledge mobilisation: knowledge boundaries, boundary-spanning mechanisms, facilitating ICT technologies and support for business applications. All these trends will certainly provide insights into future research in knowledge mobilisation and its potential use to improve business decisions.

Keywords Knowledge mobilisation · Business decisions · Systematic literature review · Descriptive analysis · Thematic analysis · Knowledge boundary · Boundary-spanning mechanisms

S. Liu (✉)
University of Plymouth, Plymouth, UK
e-mail: shaofeng.liu@plymouth.ac.uk

A. I. Alkhuraiji
Ministry of Interior, Riyadh, Saudi Arabia

A. Alkraiji
King Fahd Security College, ICT Department, Riyadh, Saudi Arabia

© Springer Nature Switzerland AG 2021
J. Papathanasiou et al. (eds.), *EURO Working Group on DSS*, Integrated Series in Information Systems, https://doi.org/10.1007/978-3-030-70377-6_8

1 Introduction

The importance of knowledge has been highlighted at the individual, organisation, and economy levels by a series of well-known expressions, including "knowledge is power", "knowledge-based view (KBV)", and "knowledge economy". It is widely believed that individuals with more knowledge tend to have more decision power hence more influence on others. At the organisational level, KBV emphasises that knowledge, rather than physical resources, is the business asset that gives organisations unique, long-lasting competitive advantage [1, 2]. The term "knowledge economy" emerged to address that the whole economy is driven by knowledge intangibles rather than physical capital, natural resources, or low-skilled labour [3]. Because of the well-recognised importance of knowledge, knowledge management (KM) has become one of the most attractive areas over the last few decades. Even though the term KM started to enter popular usage in late 1980s such as at conferences, most scholars agree that mid-1990s saw KM turning into a distinctive discipline and a field of practice, when experienced a big surge of systematic studies presented through dedicated international conferences and published books. During the period, various definitions of KM were proposed and debated. Spurred by the extremely active research and discussion on KM, devoted international journals were born to publish KM work, including reputable Journal of Knowledge Management which was launched in 1997 and Journal of Knowledge Management Practice in 1999.

Effective KM requires clearly defined and well-structured processes that can provide disciplinary guidance to practice, hence a huge number of KM process models have been proposed over time. A review by Heisig [4] analysed 160 KM process frameworks with a wide range of activities being included and different terms being used sometimes representing similar activities. Liu [1] recently studied different KM activities and classified them into four main stages of a KM process, as illustrated in Fig. 1: knowledge building stage, knowledge holding stage, knowledge mobilisation stage, and knowledge utilisation stage. Three of the four stages—knowledge building, holding, and utilisation—are self-explanatory and easy to understand. Knowledge building stage includes activities happening at the early stage of a KM process, such as knowledge creation, capture, and acquisition. In this stage, usually the amount of knowledge increases through the knowledge

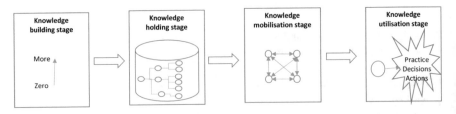

Fig. 1 The four-stage process framework for KM [1]

activities. Knowledge holding is about keeping knowledge for later utilisation. In this stage, the volume of knowledge may or may not increase; however, it is likely that knowledge will be sorted, structured, or indexed for easy retrieval. Knowledge utilisation is the last stage in a KM process where knowledge is used or may be reused.

The knowledge mobilisation is a novel stage in [1] compared with previous KM process models. Previously, terms such as knowledge share, transfer, exchange, dissemination, diffusion, and flow are often used. However, Liu [1] argues that for knowledge to be effectively mobilised in organisations and value chains, especially in crossing knowledge boundary situations, significant efforts are often required from both sides involved in the knowledge activities or even third parties. To highlight the proactive efforts from both sides and third parties, knowledge mobilisation is used to represent the KM stage that close cognitive gaps between knowledge senders and receivers. In [1], a detailed discussion of knowledge mobilisation is provided. Besides the knowledge senders' willingness and eagerness of donating knowledge, knowledge receivers are required to collect and absorb the knowledge, reflect on and learn from the knowledge. Important conditions for the knowledge mobilisation to take place efficiently include trust and mutual respect between the knowledge senders and receivers. In addition, enablers such as knowledge space are also crucial. Because of this high complexity and novelty of the concept, this chapter is dedicated to knowledge mobilisation.

A number of review papers on KM are available in the literature. Majority of the reviews are on the broad KM such as KM frameworks [4], KM approaches [5], KM measurement [6], and KM life cycles [7]. A few reviews have discussed one single specific aspect that may impact on knowledge mobilisation, for example, learning organisation [8], triple loop learning [9], community of practice [10], and knowledge networks [11]. However, there is no review paper that has focused on providing a comprehensive analysis of knowledge mobilisation, especially taking a systematic literature review approach to synthesising all aspects of knowledge mobilisation in the last two decades. This chapter aims to fill in the gap by providing an overall picture of the topic and eliciting the most common themes addressed in the literature about knowledge mobilisation.

The next section defines the SLR process adapted for this study in detail. Then, Sects. 3 and 4 present descriptive analysis and thematic analysis, respectively. Finally, conclusions are drawn in Sect. 5.

2 Review Method: SLR

Systematic Literature Review (SLR) has been selected as the research method for this study because it is well suited with our aim to understand the trends of knowledge mobilisation over the last two decades and detect any gaps for future research. SLR is a structured, transparent, and valuable method that allows to integrate work from various sources to provide an overall picture of a particular

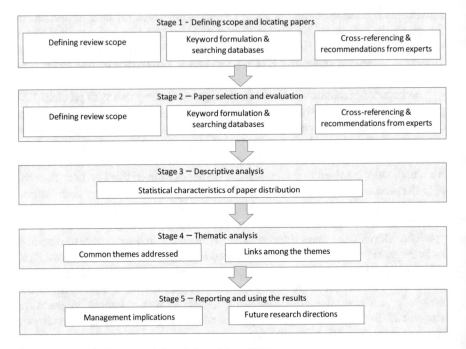

Fig. 2 Five-stage SLR methodology (adapted from [12])

topic [12]. Compared with traditional literature review, SLR is advantageous in that it reduces bias and subjectivity because in SLR criteria for paper inclusion/exclusion and for quality assessment are explicitly defined to guide the review process. In order to provide consistency, this study adapted a five-stage process originally defined by Denyer and Tranfield [13] and later used by Melacini et al. [12] in the context of supply and distribution networks. Figure 2 shows the SLR process customised for this research.

- Stage 1 defining the review scope and locating papers: keywords and search strings, databases, cross-referencing, and expert recommendations.
- Stage 2 paper selection and evaluation: paper inclusion/exclusion criteria, elimination of duplications, and paper quality assessment criteria.
- Stage 3 descriptive analysis: statistical characteristics of paper distribution in terms of publications, geographical areas, subject disciplines, research methods used, etc.
- Stage 4 thematic analysis: common themes across the papers.
- Stage 5 reporting the results: implication for management practice and recommendation for future research.

The scope of this study is a narrower area under the umbrella of knowledge management. It is the overlap among a number of topic areas: knowledge mobilisation, boundary-crossing knowledge activities, and business decision-making. In order to obtain a comprehensive collection of core contributions pertinent to the research

Table 1 Keywords and their variations defined

Keyword groups	Variations
Knowledge mobilisation	Knowledge mobilisation, knowledge share (or sharing), knowledge transfer, knowledge flow, knowledge chain, knowledge exchange, knowledge dissemination, knowledge diffusion, knowledge integration
Boundary-crossing knowledge activities	Boundary-spanning, crossing boundaries, inter-organisational, community of practice
Business decisions	Decisions, decision-making, business applications

Table 2 Selected databases and brief information of them

Database	Brief information
Business Source Complete (EBSCO)	Full-text access to more than 2800 scholarly business publications including over 900 peer-reviewed journals. Also includes book content, conference proceedings, country, industry, and market reports
Science Direct	Journals published by Elsevier with a strong focus on social, scientific, technical, and medical literature
Scopus	Journal indexing and abstracting database with citation metrics from Elsevier. It covers international research output in the fields of science, technology, medicine, social sciences, and arts and humanities (with a growing coverage of book chapters)
Web of Science	Major research database of the world's top science and technology journals and conference proceedings with some additional social sciences, arts, and humanities coverage

scope, three groups of keywords and their variants have been defined, as shown in Table 1. Boolean operators such as AND and OR are used to combine the keywords to form search strings.

In order to keep in line with the scope of the study, in the meantime to reduce bias, four scientific databases are chosen to conduct literature search: Business Source Complete (EBSCO), Science Direct, Scopus, and Web of Science. Brief information about these databases is provided in Table 2 to show the suitability of selection.

Besides database searching, cross-referencing is also used in order to include potential papers that had not been selected from the above-mentioned four databases. Furthermore, as suggested by Melacini et al. [12], papers recommended by experts are included in the analysis as well.

At the stage of paper selection and evaluation, the main purpose is to distinguish between relevant and irrelevant articles. A list of inclusion and exclusion criteria including quality assessment have been used for paper selection and evaluation, as shown in Table 3.

We first searched the databases using the search strings. Our search resulted in a preliminary return of 562 contributions. Because of the great number of returns from the search, this study decides to focus on journal articles while contributions in other types such as books, conference proceedings, and short

Table 3 Inclusion/exclusion and quality assessment criteria

Criteria	Inclusion	Exclusion
Availability	Full-text articles	Parts of the original texts (e.g., abstracts, selected sections, or bibliographical references)
Quality of articles	Articles with solid theoretical foundation, well-defined methodology, reliable data	Conceptual paper without systematic framework developed, empirical paper with insufficient or unreliable data, any paper without clear methodology
Peer review	Peer-reviewed papers	Not peer-reviewed papers
Relevance	High relevance	Low relevance
Language	English	Articles not in English

Fig. 3 The selection/evaluation process to obtain the final collection of 103 papers

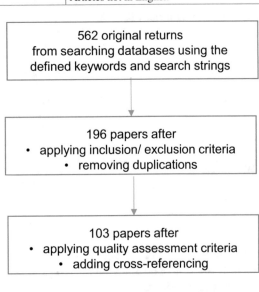

communications were dropped. Next, through scanning of abstracts, introductions, and conclusions, we were able to implement the inclusion/exclusion criteria to distinguish between high and low relevance of the papers. To ensure the rigour of this SLR process and reduce subjective bias, each paper was scanned independently by two researchers. In particular, this study excludes papers with a mere marketing purpose and papers where "knowledge mobilisation", "boundary-crossing", and "business decision-making" were only a secondary concern. Subsequently, 196 papers remain in the process. Finally, the papers were read in their entirety, again by two researchers independently, using the quality assessment criteria. Furthermore, by cross-referencing all the citations and discussing with experts in the field, a number of potential contributions that might otherwise have been missed, a final collection of 103 papers were selected for analysis. The two-stage paper selection and evaluation process is shown in Fig. 3. The results of the analysis are presented in the following two sections, firstly descriptive analysis and then thematic analysis.

3   Descriptive Analysis and Findings

All 103 papers in the final collection were analysed in-depth to draw descriptive analysis findings according to a number of characteristics, including year of publication, journal titles, geographic distribution, methods used, and key themes addressed. Table 4 summaries the key features of each paper. These papers are organised in chronological order to show how research on knowledge mobilisation evolves over time.

As can be seen from the Table 4, the 103 articles included in the analysis are published between 1999 and 2019. If we split the 20 years into four periods, the number of publications from each period of 5 years differs significantly, as shown in Fig. 4. Period one (1999–2004) has 11 papers, period two (2005–2009) has 18 papers, period three (2010–2014) has 29 papers, and period four (2015–2019) has 45 papers. The numbers demonstrate a steady growth of publications along the years. Almost three quarters of the articles are published during the last decade (2010–2019).

In terms of publishing platforms, two journals clearly stand out. The one comes first is Journal of Knowledge Management (JKM). More than one third of the articles (i.e. 38 out of the 103) are published in JKM. This is not surprising as JKM is the earliest journal established to disseminate research in KM area. The journal has the second highest number of papers is Learning Organisation which has nine papers. Other articles are widely scattered over 50 different journals which is a good thing because it means that knowledge mobilisation is a topic that is of wide interest of journal editors and publishers. It also demonstrates the great importance of the topic.

The wide interest of the topic is also reflected in the geographic distribution of the authors who led the publications. The top three countries with the highest number of publications are the USA with 22 articles, the UK with 17 and China with 12. Figure 5 illustrates the distribution of the 103 articles according to geographic areas. Overall, Europe (45%), North America (26%), and Asia (22%) are the three big areas contributed to the research publications. Another pattern that can be observed from the Table 3 is that up to early 2000s, the authors are highly concentrated in the USA and Western Europe. In the second decade (2010–2019), the authors are more widely distributed around the world. However, the number of publications from Africa is still very low (in fact 1) compared with other areas and there is no publication from South America included in the final collection for analysis.

Another interesting aspect we have analysed is the research methods used by the articles. Among the 103 papers, there are 11 review papers and 12 conceptual papers. The remaining 82 papers are empirical studies with support from primary data. The top two data collection methods have been used for empirical research are questionnaire survey (37%) and case study (26%), followed by interview with 11%. Other methods include observation, focus group, modelling, and virtual experiment. Percentage of the methods used is shown in Fig. 6.

Table 4 Overview of key features of the final collection of papers

No.	Refs.	Journal	Country	Form of k. mobilisation	Method used	Themes addressed A	B	C	D
1.	[14]	Journal of Knowledge Management	USA	k. diffusion	Citation analysis				x
2.	[15]	Academy of Management Review	USA	Organisational learning	Conceptual	x	x		
3.	[16]	Journal of Knowledge Management	Belgium	Organisational learning	Conceptual				x
4.	[17]	Expert Systems Research and Applications	USA	Lessons learned	System review			x	
5.	[18]	Organization Science	USA	k. integration	Observation	x	x		
6.	[19]	Journal of Leadership and Organization Studies	USA	k. sharing	Case study		x		
7.	[20]	Organization Science	USA	Community sharing	Observation, interview	x	x		
8.	[21]	Organization Science	USA	k. transfer, translation, and transformation	Case study	x	x		x
9.	[22]	Management Science	USA	k. transfer	Questionnaire survey	x	x		
10.	[23]	Journal of Knowledge Management	Korea	KM	Questionnaire survey	x		x	
11.	[24]	Journal of Knowledge Management	UK	KM	Conceptual	x			
12.	[25]	Academy of Management Journal	USA	k. sharing	Questionnaire survey		x		
13.	[26]	European Journal of Innovation Management	Finland	k. sharing	Conceptual	x			
14.	[27]	MIS Quarterly	USA	k. boundaries	Case study	x			
15.	[28]	Journal of Knowledge Management	USA	Sharing best practice	Case study	x	x		
16.	[29]	IEEE Transactions on Engineering Management	USA	k. integration	Questionnaire survey	x	x		x
17.	[30]	Journal of Management Information Systems	USA	KM	Case study	x			
18.	[31]	The Learning Organization	Netherlands	k. sharing	Questionnaire survey	x			x
19.	[32]	The Learning Organization	Spain	Learning	Questionnaire survey	x	x		x
20.	[8]	The Learning Organization	Australia	Learning	Literature review	x			
21.	[33]	Journal of Knowledge Management	Bahrain	k. sharing	Survey, interview	x	x		
22.	[34]	Journal of Information Sciences	China	k. sharing	Questionnaire survey	x	x		
23.	[35]	Journal of Knowledge Management	France	k. transfer	Case study	x			x
24.	[36]	Tourism Management				x	x		

No.	Ref	Journal	Country	Knowledge concept	Method					
25.	[37]	Journal of Knowledge Management	Lebanon	k. transformation	Conceptual		x			
26.	[38]	Strategic Management Journal	USA	k. transfer	Questionnaire survey	x				x
27.	[39]	Journal of International Business Studies	Netherlands	k. sharing	Questionnaire survey	x				x
28.	[4]	Journal of Knowledge Management	UK	KM frameworks	Literature review	x	x			
29.	[40]	International Journal of Information Management	China	k. sharing	Questionnaire survey		x	x		
30.	[41]	Journal of Knowledge Management	Canada	KM	Literature review	x				
31.	[42]	Journal of Knowledge Management	USA	k. sharing	Questionnaire survey	x				
32.	[43]	R and D Management	Ireland	k. flow	Case study			x		
33.	[44]	Academy of Management Review	USA	Organisational learning	Conceptual	x	x			
34.	[45]	Journal of Knowledge Management	Korea	Community of practice	Questionnaire survey		x			
35.	[46]	Journal of Knowledge Management	Norway	k. communities	Questionnaire survey	x	x			x
36.	[47]	Journal of Knowledge Management	Spain	Organisational learning	Questionnaire survey	x	x			
37.	[48]	Journal of Knowledge Management	UK	k. networking	Case study	x				
38.	[49]	Systems Research and Behavioural Science	China	k. transfer	Virtual experiment		x			
39.	[9]	Management Learning	UK	Triple loop learning	Literature review	x	x			
40.	[50]	Knowledge and Process Management	Netherlands	k. sharing	Case study	x	x			
41.	[51]	Journal of Knowledge Management	Australia	k. sharing	Questionnaire survey	x				
42.	[52]	Journal of Knowledge Management	Germany	k. ecology	Conceptual			x		
43.	[53]	Management Decision	Spain	k. boundaries	Conceptual	x	x			
44.	[54]	Decision Support Systems	China	k. transfer	Questionnaire survey	x	x	x		x
45.	[55]	Journal of Management	France	k. networks	Literature review		x			
46.	[56]	The Learning Organization	USA	k. sharing	Questionnaire survey	x	x			
47.	[57]	Project Management Journal	Finland	k. networks	Conceptual	x	x			x
48.	[58]	International Journal of Production Research	UK	k. networks	Conceptual		x			
49.	[59]	Advances in Developing Human Resources	USA	Learning organisation	Case study	x	x			
50.	[60]	Journal of Knowledge Management	France	k. transfer	Simulation			x		

(continued)

Table 4 (continued)

No.	Refs.	Journal	Country	Form of k. mobilisation	Method used	Themes addressed			
						A	B	C	D
51.	[61]	Managing Service Quality: an International Journal	UK	k. dissemination	Interview	x			
52.	[62]	International Journal of Production Research	UK	k. chain	Case study				x
53.	[6]	Journal of Knowledge Management	Ireland	k. measurement	Literaturereview		x		
54.	[63]	Journal of Decision Systems	UK	k. networks	Modelling		x	x	
55.	[64]	Journal of Knowledge Management	Korea	k. flow	Case study	x			x
56.	[65]	Production Planning and Control	UK	k. chain	Case study		x		x
57.	[66]	Journal of Knowledge Management	India	k. flow	Literature review	x			
58.	[67]	Journal of Knowledge Management	UK	k. mobilisation	Case study			x	
59.	[68]	Electronic Journal of Knowledge Management	Canada	k. sharing	Questionnaire survey	x	x		
60.	[69]	Journal of Enterprise Information Management	Malaysia	k. integration	Questionnaire survey		x		
61.	[70]	Journal of Knowledge Management	France	k. transfer	Literature review		x		
62.	[71]	The Learning Organization	Hungary	Learning and k. transfer	Interview			x	
63.	[72]	The Learning Organization	USA	Organisational learning	Questionnaire survey	x	x		x
64.	[10]	Journal of Knowledge Management	Saudi Arabia	Community of practice	Literaturereview	x	x		
65.	[73]	Action Learning: Research and Practice	Ireland	Organisational learning	conceptual	x			x
66.	[74]	Journal of Business Research	UK	Knowledge mobilisation	Interview		x	x	
67.	[75]	Journal of Knowledge Management	Finland	Community of practice	Case study	x	x	x	x
68.	[76]	Journal of Knowledge Management	Netherlands	k. sharing	Questionnaire survey	x			
69.	[77]	Journal of Knowledge Management	Oman	k. sharing	Interview		x		x
70.	[7]	Electronic Journal of Knowledge Management	South Africa	KM life cycle	Literature review				
71.	[78]	Research Policy	UK	k. networks	Questionnaire survey		x		x
72.	[79]	Knowledge Management Research and Practice	China	k. sharing	Case study	x			x

#	Ref	Journal	Country	Topic	Method							
73.	[80]	International Journal of Decision Support System Technology	UK	k. mobilisation	Case study					x	x	
73.	[80]	International Journal of Decision Support System Technology	UK	k. mobilisation	Case study				x	x	x	
74.	[81]	Journal of Knowledge Management	Italy	k. integration	Questionnaire survey	x					x	
75.	[82]	Journal of Knowledge Management	Canada	Lessons learnt	Interview	x	x		x	x	x	
76.	[83]	Journal of Knowledge Management	China	k. protection	Questionnaire survey	x				x	x	
77.	[84]	Enterprise Information Systems	USA	k. sharing	Questionnaire survey	x	x	x	x	x	x	
78.	[85]	International Journal of Project Management	UK	k. sharing	Questionnaire survey							x
79.	[86]	Journal of Knowledge Management	New Zealand	Triple loop learning	modelling				x			
80.	[87]	Journal of Knowledge Management	China	KM	Case study, interview			x	x	x		x
81.	[88]	Journal of Enterprise Information Management	China	k. sharing	Questionnaire survey	x		x	x			
82.	[89]	Journal of Knowledge Management	UK	KM	Case study			x	x	x		x
83.	[90]	Journal of Product Innovation Management	China	k. transfer	Questionnaire survey	x			x	x		
84.	[91]	Benchmarking: An International Journal	India	k. flow	Questionnaire survey				x	x		x
85.	[92]	Journal of Decision systems	UK	k. mobilisation	modelling			x	x	x		
86.	[93]	The Learning Organization	Norway	k. sharing	Interview		x	x	x	x	x	
87.	[94]	The Learning Organization	Norway	Triple loop learning	Conceptual	x	x			x		
88.	[95]	The Learning Organization	USA	Learning organisation	Interview	x	x			x	x	
89.	[96]	Journal of Knowledge Management	Hungary	k. sharing	Questionnaire survey	x	x			x		
90.	[97]	Journal of Organizational Change Management	Indonesia	k. sharing	Questionnaire survey	x					x	
91.	[98]	Journal of Knowledge Management	USA	k. sharing	Questionnaire survey		x			x	x	
92.	[99]	Technological Forecasting and Social Change	Italy	k. flow	Questionnaire survey				x			
93.	[100]	Journal of Knowledge Management	Iran	k. sharing	Questionnaire survey		x					
94.	[11]	Journal of Business Research	China	k. integration	Questionnaire survey		x					
95.	[101]	International Journal of Operations and Production Management	Netherlands	k. flow	Case study	x	x			x		x

(continued)

Table 4 (continued)

No.	Refs.	Journal	Country	Form of k. mobilisation	Method used	Themes addressed			
						A	B	C	D
96.	[102]	Computers in Industry	UK	k. chain	Case study		x	x	x
97.	[103]	Production Planning and Control	UK	k. sharing	Interview	x	x	x	x
98.	[104]	Benchmarking: An International Journal	UAE	Organisational learning	Questionnaire survey	x		x	
99.	[105]	Journal of Knowledge Management	Korea	organisational learning	Questionnaire survey		x		x
100.	[106]	Journal of Business Research	UK	k. sharing	Questionnaire survey	x	x		x
101.	[107]	Advanced Engineering Informatics	China	k. sharing	Case study		x		x
102.	[108]	Information and Management	USA	k. dissemination	Focus group		x	x	
103..	[109]	International Journal of Production Economics	Romania	k. dissemination	Case study		x		x

Note: Theme A—Knowledge boundary types, Theme B—Boundary-spanning mechanisms, Theme C—Advanced ICT technologies facilitating knowledge mobilisation, Theme D—Business decision applications

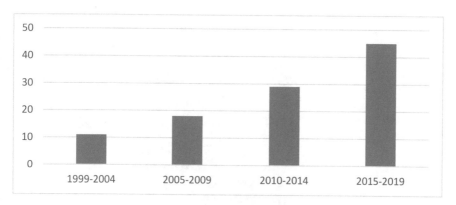

Fig. 4 Growing number of publications by time period

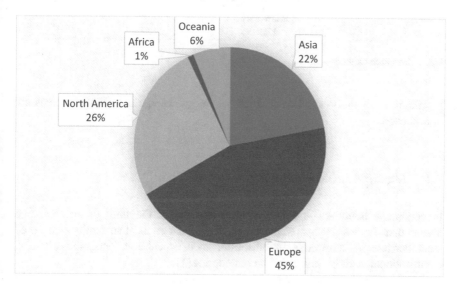

Fig. 5 Geographic distribution of the articles

4 Thematic Analysis and Findings

On the far right hand side of Table 4, key themes emerged from the SLR process are presented. Links between each of the paper and relevant themes are marked with "x", representing evidence of the theme from the particular paper. The four key themes are:

- Theme a: boundary types that might erect barriers to knowledge mobilisation
- Theme b: boundary-spanning mechanisms
- Theme c: ICT technologies facilitating knowledge mobilisation crossing boundaries

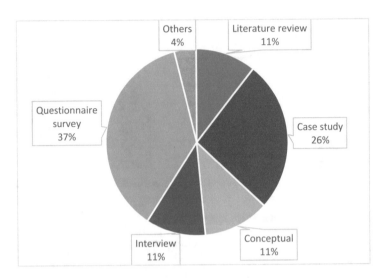

Fig. 6 Research methods used

- Theme d: Business application areas where knowledge mobilisation issues are addressed

4.1 Theme A: Knowledge Boundaries

In general, a boundary is a demarcation that makes the limit of an area or a border that divides groups. Many types of boundaries exist in reality that could erect barriers to knowledge mobilisation, such as cultural, geographic, social, organisational, activity, and resource boundaries [1].

Organisational culture is one of the most common boundaries identified in the literature for knowledge mobilisation [47, 79, 83, 84, 88, 97, 104]. Culture is a very complex type of boundary which could consist of many different factors, such as interpersonal trust [31, 42, 56, 76], commitment from staff [51], rewards and resistance [95].

Organisation structure also plays an important role in defining the relationships between staff, such as knowledge provider reputation and recipient reputation [28]. These factors in turn provide possibilities of generating obstacles to knowledge sharing [66], let alone privacy concerns crossing country borders [35]. Lack of resources such as insufficient time and money often hinder knowledge movement and learning activities [51, 95]. In many organisations, lack of leadership [65, 69, 88, 95] and top management support [83] are critical failure factors to knowledge mobilisation initiatives and programmes.

Power boundary or political boundary or pragmatic boundary has been recognised as a boundary that is very difficult to cross [93, 94]. This type of boundary occurs when people have very different interests in the business and knowledge activities, ultimately resulting in conflicts among the participating actors and bodies. In order to resolve the conflicts, different actors and bodies need to be willing and prepared to negotiate and compromise. Otherwise, common interests cannot be reached and knowledge mobilisation is hardly possible [18, 21].

Syntactic and semantic boundaries are usually discussed together. Syntactic boundary is considered relatively easy to cross because people involved share a common logic, a set of values and worldview [18, 53]. For example, a common lexicon can be developed for knowledge transfer crossing a syntactic boundary. This is especially the case in most traditional technology-based knowledge systems where explicit knowledge is mobilised. Comparatively, semantic boundary is where people have different understanding and interpretation of the same knowledge. It is important that people can develop an understanding of and sensitivity to other people's understandings and interpretations if semantic boundary is to be crossed [53]. The emphasis is usually put on knowledge translation and the development of common meanings to address interpretive differences [1].

To understand the key characteristics of these different types of knowledge boundaries is the foundation to develop appropriate mechanisms to successfully cross the boundaries, which is the focus of the next theme.

4.2 Theme B: Boundary-Crossing Mechanisms

A great number of mechanisms have been discussed in literature to cross various types of knowledge boundaries. These mechanisms can be classified into four main categories: boundary objects such as knowledge networks, boundary spanners such as knowledge brokers, boundary practice, and knowledge motivation systems [1, 53, 84].

Boundary objects are the most fundamental boundary-spanning mechanisms that refer to physical, abstract, or mental entities and artefacts enabling knowledge mobilisation [26, 53]. Knowledge networks are among the most widely used boundary objects consisting of knowledge nodes and relationships among the knowledge nodes. The relationships are the linkages among the nodes, representing not only knowledge combination possibilities and capabilities but also knowledge flow channels through which knowledge diffuses and flows [1]. Knowledge networks can be in the form of social networks [11, 25, 52, 60, 64, 77, 78, 100, 108] or technology networks [57, 74, 95, 107]. A clear advantage of using knowledge networks is social interaction and social learning [39, 40]. A typical example of such social learning is the popular concept of community of practice [45, 50, 61, 75]. To develop successful knowledge networks, knowledge taxonomy and ontology play a key role in terms of their implementation [6].

A second boundary-spanning mechanism highlighted in literature is boundary spanners [18, 53]. They are human agents who frame and translate knowledge from one domain to another in an effort to promote knowledge mobilisation. Human agents are good at using languages to articulate and using their cognitive power to enable the movement of knowledge; hence, this mechanism is believed to be effective in mobilising both explicit and tacit knowledge. Research also indicates that the position or standing of human agents in a knowledge network is an important factor to impact on the effectiveness of knowledge mobilisation [1]. There have been many different types of human agents all playing the boundary spanners' role, including gatekeeper, knowledge brokers [43, 70, 96], knowledge mentors and taxonomists [67].

By boundary practice it means that human agents engage in collective activities and learn from each other in order to overcome barriers to knowledge mobilisation, in simple words, learning by doing things together [53]. Because of the social learning effect, the outcome from boundary practice is not just sharing knowledge, but also improving existing knowledge and generating new knowledge [1]. Compared with boundary objects and boundary spanners, boundary practice particularly suits for the mobilisation of tacit knowledge. Boundary practice is also a relatively new concept, which provides a direction for future research.

The fourth category of boundary-spanning mechanism commonly acknowledged in literature is motivation systems, for example, organisational reward systems [19], incentives [84], motivational factors such as reciprocal benefits, knowledge self-efficacy, and enjoyment in helping others. Research finds that these factors were significantly associated with employee's knowledge sharing attitudes and intentions [34].

The above boundary-spanning mechanisms were mostly explored in an isolated manner at the early stages when these mechanisms were proposed. However, more recent publications advocate for the combinatory use of the mechanisms for better effectiveness of knowledge mobilisation activities [1, 84]. Even though these mechanisms sufficiently distinct from each other, they are actually mutually interdependent. It can be considered that the four types of boundary-spanning mechanisms provide four complementary perspectives of a knowledge mobilisation process. Boundary spanners provide an actor perspective, that is, "who" is making the knowledge mobilisation activities happen. Boundary objects represent the artefact perspective, that is, what boundary spanners need to use to mobilise knowledge. Thirdly, boundary practice provides an activity perspective, that is, by doing what. Finally, motivation systems provide a reward perspective, that is, why do people want to mobilise knowledge. If only people's effort and investment in knowledge mobilisation is rewarded, can the knowledge activities be maintained over time, which may develop into a culture that can foster knowledge mobilisation and learning long term [1].

4.3   Theme C: Advanced ICT Technologies Facilitating Knowledge Mobilisation

There is no doubt that ICT technologies have been playing a crucial role in removing boundaries for communication and knowledge activities, hence have been considered as an enabler for knowledge mobilisation. There has been a massive amount of literature which has already discussed in great detail of ICT support for knowledge management and learning in general [63, 75, 84, 85, 104]. This section will focus on three state-of-the-art ICT technologies and examine how they facilitate knowledge mobilisation. These are Internet of Things (IoT), Big Data Analytics (BDA), and enterprise systems.

IoT refers to an emerging paradigm consisting of a continuum of uniquely addressable objects communicating with each other to form a worldwide dynamic network [1]. IoT is rapidly gaining momentum, bringing millions of devices and objects into a connected world. This interconnected network uses disruptive digital technologies to influence business daily operations as well as long-term strategies, in order to increase the technologies' efficiency and innovativeness in the current knowledge economy [89]. Literature has concluded that IoT has three clear orientations. Firstly, IoT is things-oriented, which focus on the "objects" and on finding a paradigm that is able to identify and integrate the objects. Secondly, IoT is internet-oriented, of which the focus is on the networking paradigm and on the exploitation of internet protocols to establish an efficient connection between the objects. Thirdly, IoT is semantic-oriented, aiming to use semantic technologies describing objects and to manage a massive amount of data provided by the increasing number of objects [1, 43, 99]. The adoption of IoT technologies is accelerating benefited from a number of technological factors, including fast decline in the costs of objects such as sensors and actuators, an increasing ability of connecting the sensors and actuators, and the ability to analyse huge amount of data, for example, by using Big Data Analytics [89].

Big Data is one of most popular terms in today's knowledge economy. The capture and analysis of Big Data can generate new knowledge and business intelligence which has great value in supporting business decision-making. Big Data is typically represented by 5Vs: volume, variety, velocity, veracity, and value [87]. Volume refers to the enormous size of the data. Variety means that data exist in various forms, mostly in not structured and usable way. Velocity indicates the huge pace data are generated and flow, which could be well beyond the analytical capabilities of most traditional database software tools. Veracity refers to the fact that data may contain noise, be incomplete or out of date, which could affect the quality and usefulness of the data. Value extracted from hidden data is a source of competitive advantage. Value is often linked to an organisation's ability to make better business decisions [1]. It is widely accepted that the real business value of Big Data is not in the data themselves but rather in the knowledge discovered through Big Data Analytics (BDA). BDA is a complex, multi-stage process, consisting of data acquisition, information extraction and cleansing, data integration, modelling and analysis, and interpretation and deployment [86]. One of the biggest challenges identified in BDA is a lack of vision, which usually leads to data being collected but not analysed, hence researchers have recommended that organisations should put business objectives in the centre of Big Data activities and programmes [86, 87].

Lastly, enterprise systems such as ERP systems have been playing a key role for the mobilisation of explicit knowledge all the time [69]. Enterprise systems integrate data across departments and functional work units through a unified software programme structured around an organisation-wide database, which is a great way to facilitate knowledge mobilisation [108]. In comparison with traditional enterprise systems such as MIS (Management Information Systems), the major difference of ERP lies in its power to provide integrated and streamlined internal information to synergise work in the supply chain for businesses to create new competitive advantages [54]. For example, Sasidharan [108] investigated the incorporation of domain expertise of knowledge sources and knowledge flow intensity by reconceptualising knowledge networks in the implementation of ERP systems. Based on evidence from empirical data collected from UK industries, Jayawickrama et al. [103] found that ERP systems have positive impact on knowledge transfer and retention of knowledge.

4.4   Theme D: Business Decision Applications

Literature has discussed the application of knowledge mobilisation to support business decision-making in all major industries and sectors. They range from semiconductor industry [14] to automotive industry [75, 79, 101], from public sector [93] such as education [97] to parking service in transportation [89], from healthcare [73] to pharmaceutical companies [22], and from oil and gas industry [87] to agri-food industry [80]. Knowledge mobilisation in project management also attracted a lot of attention [48, 57, 82, 85].

Among the collection of 103 articles analysed, manufacturing is one of the most researched industry. Literature not only discusses knowledge mobilisation and its support for business decisions in general manufacturing [16, 98], but also in international manufacturing MNCs [39, 81, 109] and manufacturing supply chains [65, 91]. In close association with manufacturing, there have been great amount of literature exploring the mobilisation of knowledge for design decisions [57, 107], for new product development decisions [25], for R&D decisions [38, 79, 90], and for innovation decisions [26].

5   Conclusions

This chapter provides a comprehensive analysis of over a hundred of publications on knowledge mobilisation over two decades, that is, from 1999 to 2019. A systematic literature review comprising five standardised stages is employed. Key contributions of the chapter lie in three aspects. Firstly, this is the first systematic review on the topic of knowledge mobilisation, even though review on general knowledge management has been existent. Secondly, the descriptive analysis findings revealed a number of trends in terms of articles' publication year, publishing platforms (journals), geographic distribution of the publications and research methods used. Thirdly, the thematic analysis discovered four main themes: types of knowledge boundaries, boundary-spanning mechanisms, advanced ICT technologies facilitating knowledge mobilisation, and the main application areas. These findings provide insights into future research directions and potential management implications in terms of mobilising knowledge to achieve better business decisions.

Acknowledgements The work reported in this chapter has benefited from the RUC-APS project funded by European Commission under the Horizon 2020 Programme (H2020-MSCA-RISE Award No. 691249).

References

1. Liu, S. (2020). *Knowledge management: An interdisciplinary approach for business decisions.* London, New York and New Delhi: Kogan Page.
2. Mbhalati, O. J. (2012). The genesis of the knowledge-based view. *Journal of Knowledge Management Practice, 13*, 2.
3. Ceruti, M., Williams, A., Bedford, D., Ceruti, M., Williams, A., & Bedford, D. (2019). *Building knowledge capacity for a knowledge economy, in book: Translating knowledge management visions into strategies (Working methods for knowledge management)* (pp. 3–21). Bingley: Emerald Publishing Limited.
4. Heisig, P. (2009). Harmonisation of knowledge management – comparing 160 KM frameworks around the globe. *Journal of Knowledge Management, 13*(4), 4–31.
5. Lloria, M. B. (2008). A review of the main approaches to knowledge management. *Knowledge Management Research and Practice, 6*, 77–89.
6. Ragab, M. A. F., & Arisha, A. (2013). Knowledge management and measurement: A critical review. *Journal of Knowledge Management, 17*(6), 873–901.
7. Shongwe, M. (2016). An analysis of knowledge management lifecycle frameworks: Towards a unified framework. *The Electronic Journal of Knowledge Management, 14*(3), 140–153.
8. Thomas, K., & Allen, S. (2006). The learning organization: A meta-analysis of themes in literature. *The Learning Organization, 13*(2), 123–139.
9. Tosey, P., Visser, M., & Saunders, M. N. K. (2011). The origins and conceptualizations of 'triple-loop' learning: A critical review. *Management Learning, 43*(3), 291–307.
10. Aljuwaiber, A. (2016). Communities of practice as an initiative for knowledge sharing in business organizations: A literature review. *Journal of Knowledge Management, 20*, 731–748.
11. Wang, M. C., Chen, P. C., & Fang, S. C. (2018). A critical view of knowledge networks and innovation performance: The mediation role of firm's knowledge integration capability. *Journal of Business Research, 88*, 222–233.
12. Melacini, M., Perotti, S., Racini, M., & Tappia, E. (2018). E-fulfilment and distribution in omni-channel retailing: A systematic literature review. *International Journal of Physical Distribution and Logistics Management, 48*(4), 391–414.
13. Denyer, D., & Tranfield, D. (2009). Chapter 39: Producing a systematic review. In D. Buchanan & A. Bryman (Eds.), *The Sage handbook of organizational research methods* (pp. 671–689). London: Sage Publicationsn Ltd..

14. Appleyard, M. M., & Kalsow, G. A. (1999). Knowledge diffusion in the semiconductor industry. *Journal of Knowledge Management, 3*(4), 288–295.
15. Crossan, M., Lane, H. W., & White, R. E. (1999). An organizational learning framework: From intuition to institution. *The Academy of Management Review, 24*(3), 522–537.
16. Selen, W. (2000). Knowledge management in resource-based competitive environments: A roadmap for building learning organizations. *Journal of Knowledge Management, 4*(6), 346–353.
17. Weber, R., Aha, D. W., & Becerra-Fernandez, I. (2001). Intelligent lessons learned systems. *Expert Systems Research and Applications, 20*(1), 17–34.
18. Carlile, P. (2002). A pragmatic view of knowledge and boundaries: Boundary objects in new product development. *Organization Science, 14*(4), 442–455.
19. Bartol, K. M., & Srivastava, A. (2002). Encouraging knowledge sharing: The role of organizational reward systems. *Journal of Leadership and Organizational Studies, 9*(1), 64–76.
20. Bechky, B. A. (2003). Sharing meaning across occupational communities: The transformation of understanding on a production floor. *Organization Science, 14*(3), 312–330.
21. Carlile, P. (2004). Transferring, translating and transforming: An integrative framework for managing knowledge across boundaries. *Organization Science, 15*(5), 555–568.
22. Levin, D. Z., & Cross, R. (2004). The strengths of weak ties you can trust: The mediating role of trust in effective knowledge transfer. *Management Science, 50*(11), 1477–1490.
23. Park, H., Ribiere, V., & Schulte, J. W. D. (2004). Critical attributes of organizational culture that promote knowledge management technology implementation success. *Journal of Knowledge Management, 8*(3), 106–117.
24. Yew, K. W., & Aspinwall, E. (2004). Characterising knowledge management in the small business environment. *Journal of Knowledge Management, 8*(3), 44–61.
25. Hansen, M. T., Mors, M. L., & Lovas, B. (2005). Knowledge sharing in organizations: Multiple networks, multiple phases. *Academy of Management Journal, 48*, 776–793.
26. Koskinen, K. U. (2005). Metaphoric boundary objects as co-ordinating mechanisms in the knowledge sharing of innovation processes. *European Journal of Innovation Management, 8*(3), 323.
27. Levina, N., & Vaast, E. (2005). The emergence of boundary spanning competence in practice: Implications for implementation and use of information systems. *MIS Quarterly, 29*(2), 335–363.
28. Lucas, L. (2005). The impact of trust and reputation on the transfer of best practices. *Journal of Knowledge Management, 9*(4), 87–101.
29. Sabherwal, R., & Becerra-Fernandez, I. (2005). Integrating specific knowledge: Insights from Kennedy Space Centre. *IEEE Transactions on Engineering Management, 52*(3), 301–315.
30. Alavi, M., Kayworth, T. R., & Leidner, D. E. (2005–2006). An empirical examination of the influence of organizational culture on knowledge management practices. *Journal of Management Information Systems, 22*(3), 191–224.
31. Bakker, M., Leenders, R. T. A. J., Gabbay, S. M., Kratzer, J., & Engelen, J. M. L. V. (2006). Is trust really social capital? Knowledge sharing in product development projects. *The Learning Organization, 13*(6), 594–605.
32. Prieto, I. M., & Revilla, E. (2006). Learning capability and business performance: A non-financial and financial assessment. *The Learning Organization, 13*(2), 299–331.
33. Al-Alawi, A. I., Al-Marzooqi, N. Y., & Mohammed, Y. F. (2007). Organizational culture and knowledge sharing: Critical success factors. *Journal of Knowledge Management, 11*(2), 22–42.
34. Lin, H. F. (2007). Effects of intrinsic and extrinsic motivation on employee knowledge sharing intentions. *Journal of Information Science, 33*(2), 135–149.
35. Perrin, A., Rolland, N., & Stanley, T. (2007). Achieving best practices transfer across countries. *Journal of Knowledge Management, 11*(3), 156–166.
36. Yang, J. T. (2007). Knowledge sharing: Investigate appropriate leadership roles and collaborative culture. *Tourism Management, 28*(2), 530–543.

37. Feghali, T., & El-Den, J. (2008). Knowledge transformation among virtually co-operating group members. *Journal of Knowledge Management, 12*(1), 92–105.
38. Kachra, A., & White, R. E. (2008). Know-how transfer: The role of social, economic/competitive and firm boundary factors. *Strategic Management Journal, 29*, 425–445.
39. Noorderhaven, N., & Harzing, A. (2009). Knowledge sharing and social interaction within MNEs. *Journal of International Business Studies, 40*(5), 719–741.
40. Yang, S. C., & Farn, C. K. (2009). Social capital, behavioural control and tacit knowledge sharing—a multi-informant design. *International Journal of Information Management, 29*(3), 210–218.
41. Choo, C. W. A., & Ivarenga Neto, R. C. D. (2010). Beyond the Ba: Managing Enabling Contexts in Knowledge Organizations. *Journal of Knowledge Management, 14*(4), 592–610.
42. Holste, J. S., & Fields, D. (2010). Trust and tacit knowledge sharing and use. *Journal of Knowledge Management, 14*(1), 128–140.
43. Whelan, E., Teigland, R., Donnellan, B., & Golden, W. (2010). How Internet technologies impact information flows in R&D: Reconsidering the technological gatekeeper. *R and D Management, 40*(4), 400–413.
44. Crossan, M. M., Maurer, C. C., & White, R. E. (2011). Reflections on the 2009 AMR decade award: Do we have a theory of organizational learning? *Academy of Management Review, 36*(3), 446–460.
45. Jeon, S., Kim, Y. G., & Koh, J. (2011). An integrative model for knowledge sharing in communities of practice. *Journal of Knowledge Management, 15*(2), 251–269.
46. Nesheim, T., Olsen, K. M., & Tobiassen, A. E. (2011). Knowledge communities in matrix-like organizations: Managing knowledge towards application. *Journal of Knowledge Management, 15*(5), 836–850.
47. Sanz-Valle, R., Naranjo-Valencia, J. C., Jimenez-Jimenez, D., & Perez-Caballero, L. (2011). Linking organizational learning with technical innovation and organizational culture. *Journal of Knowledge Management, 15*(6), 997–1015.
48. Swart, J., & Harvey, P. (2011). Identifying knowledge boundaries: The case of networked projects. *Journal of Knowledge Management, 15*(5), 703–721.
49. Tang, F. (2011). Knowledge transfer in intra-organization networks. *Systems Research and Behavioural Science, 28*(3), 270–282.
50. Verburg, R. M., & Andriessen, E. J. H. (2011). A typology of knowledge sharing networks in practice. *Knowledge and Process Management, 18*(1), 34–44.
51. Casimir, G., Lee, K., & Loon, M. (2012). Knowledge sharing: Influences of trust, commitment and cost. *Journal of Knowledge Management, 16*(5), 740–753.
52. Chatti, M. A. (2012). Knowledge management: A personal knowledge network perspective. *Journal of Knowledge Management, 16*(5), 829–844.
53. Hawkins, M. A., & Rezazade, M. H. (2012). Knowledge boundary spanning process: Synthesizing four spanning mechanisms. *Management Decision, 50*(10), 1800–1815.
54. Hung, W. H., Ho, C. F., Jou, J., & Kung, K. H. (2012). Relationship bonding for a better knowledge transfer climate: An ERP implementation research. *Decision Support Systems, 52*(2), 406–414.
55. Phelps, C., Heidl, R., & Wadhwa, A. (2012). Knowledge, networks and knowledge networks: A review and research agenda. *Journal of Management, 38*(4), 1115–1166.
56. Swift, P. E., & Hwang, A. (2012). The impact of affective and cognitive trust on knowledge sharing and organizational learning. *The Learning Organization, 20*(1), 20–37.
57. Alin, P., Lorio, J., & Taylor, J. (2013). Digital boundary objects as negotiation facilitators: Spanning boundaries in virtual engineering project networks. *Project Management Journal, 44*(3), 48–63.
58. Choudhary, A. K., Harding, J. A., Koh, S. C. L., Camarinha-Matos, L. M., & Tiwari, M. K. (2013). Knowledge management and supporting tools for collaborative networked organizations. *International Journal of Production Research, 51*(7), 1953–1957.
59. Dirani, K. (2013). Does theory travel? Dimensions of the learning organization culture relevant to the Lebanese culture. *Advances in Developing Human Resources, 15*(2), 177–192.

60. Guechtouli, W., Rouchier, J., & Orillard, M. (2013). Structuring knowledge transfer from experts to newcomers. *Journal of Knowledge Management, 17*(1), 47–68.
61. Lages, C. R., Simoes, C. M. N., Fisk, R. P., & Kunz, W. H. (2013). Knowledge dissemination in the global service marketing community. *Managing Service Quality: An International Journal, 23*(4), 272–290.
62. Liu, S., Leat, M., Moizer, J., Megicks, P., & Kasturiratne, D. (2013). A decision-focused knowledge management framework to support collaborative decision making for lean supply chain management. *International Journal of Production Research, 51*(7), 2123–2137.
63. Alkuraiji, A., Liu, S., Oderanti, F., Annansingh, F., & Pan, J. (2014). Knowledge network modelling to support decision-making for strategic intervention in IT project-oriented change management. *Journal of Decision Systems, 23*(3), 285–302.
64. Kim, Y. G., Hau, Y. S., Song, S., & Ghim, G. H. (2014). Trailing organizational knowledge paths through social network lens: Integrating the multiple industry cases. *Journal of Knowledge Management, 18*(1), 38–51.
65. Liu, S., Moizer, J., Megicks, P., Kasturiratne, D., & Jayawickrama, U. (2014). A knowledge chain management framework for global supply chain integration decisions. *Production Planning and Control, 25*(8), 639–649.
66. Sudhindrea, S., Ganesh, L. S., & Arshinder, K. (2014). Classification of supply chain knowledge: A morphological approach. *Journal of Knowledge Management, 18*(4), 812–823.
67. Venkitachalam, K., & Bosua, B. (2014). Roles enabling the mobilization of organizational knowledge. *Journal of Knowledge Management, 18*(2), 396–410.
68. Evans, M. M., Wensley, A. K. P., & Frissen, I. (2015). The mediating effects of trustworthiness on social-cognitive factors and knowledge sharing in a large professional service firm. *Electronic Journal of Knowledge Management, 13*(3), 240–254.
69. Ghazali, R., Ahmad, M. N., & Zakaria, N. H. (2015). The mediating role of knowledge integration in effect of leadership styles on enterprise systems success: The post-implementation stage. *Journal of Enterprise Information Management, 28*(4), 531–555.
70. Hass, A. (2015). Crowding at the frontier: Boundary spanners, gatekeepers and knowledge brokers. *Journal of Knowledge Management, 19*(5), 1029–1047.
71. Hortovanyi, L., & Ferincz, A. (2015). The impact of ICT on learning on-the-job. *The Learning Organization, 22*(1), 2–13.
72. Zhou, W., Hu, H., & Shi, X. (2015). Does organizational learning lead to higher firm performance? An investigation of Chinese listing companies. *The Learning Organization, 22*(5), 271–288.
73. Doyle, L., Kelliher, F., & Harrington, D. (2016). How multi-levels of individual and team learning interact in a public healthcare organization: A conceptual framework. *Action Learning: Research and Practice, 13*(1), 10–22.
74. Alkhuraiji, A., Liu, S., Oderanti, F., & Megicks, P. (2016). New structured knowledge network for strategic decision making in IT innovative and implementable projects. *Journal of Business Research, 69*(5), 1534–1538.
75. Pohjola, I., & Puusa, A. (2016). Group dynamics and the role of ICT in the life cycle analysis of community of practice of practice-based product development: A case study. *Journal of Knowledge Management, 20*(3), 465–483.
76. Rutten, W., Blaas-Franken, J., & Martin, H. (2016). The impact of (low) trust on knowledge sharing. *Journal of Knowledge Management, 20*(2), 199–214.
77. Saifi, S. A., Dillon, S., & McQueen, R. (2016). The relationship between face to face social networks and knowledge sharing: An exploratory study of manufacturing firms. *Journal of Knowledge Management, 20*(2), 308–326.
78. Brennecke, J., & Rank, O. (2017). The firm's knowledge network and the transfer of advice among corporate inventors – a multilevel network study. *Research Policy, 46*, 768–783.
79. Chang, W. J., Liao, S. H., & Wu, T. T. (2017). Relationships among organizational culture, knowledge sharing and innovation capacity. *Knowledge Management Research and Practice, 15*, 471–490.

80. Chen, H., Liu, S., & Oderanti, F. (2017). A knowledge network and mobilization framework for lean supply chain decisions in agri-food industry. *International Journal of Decision Support System Technology, 9*(4), 37–48.
81. Ferraris, A., Santoro, G., & Dezi, L. (2017). How MNC's subsidiaries may improve their innovative performance? The role of external sources and knowledge management capabilities. *Journal of Knowledge Management, 21*(3), 540–552.
82. Herbst, A. S. (2017). Capturing knowledge from lessons learned at the work package level in project engineering teams. *Journal of Knowledge Management, 21*(4), 765–778.
83. Lee, J., Min, J., & Lee, H. (2017). Setting a knowledge boundary across teams: Knowledge protection regulation for inter-team co-ordination and team performance. *Journal of Knowledge Management, 21*(2), 254–274.
84. Lyu, H., & Zhang, Z. (2017). Incentives of knowledge sharing: Impact of organizational culture and information technology. *Enterprise Information Systems, 11*(9), 1416–1435.
85. McClory, S., Read, M., & Labib, A. (2017). Conceptualising the lessons-learned process in project management: Towards a triple-loop learning framework. *International Journal of Project Management, 35*, 1322–1335.
86. Pauleen, D. J., & Wang, Y. C. (2017). Does big data mean big knowledge? KM perspectives on big data and analytics. *Journal of Knowledge Management, 21*(1), 1–6.
87. Sumbal, M. S., Tsui, E. T., & See-to, E. W. K. (2017). Interrelationship between big data and knowledge management: An exploratory study in the oil and gas sector. *Journal of Knowledge Management, 21*(1), 180–196.
88. Tseng, S. M. (2017). Investigating the moderating effects of organizational culture and leadership style on I—adoption and knowledge sharing intention. *Journal of Enterprise Information Management, 30*(4), 583–604.
89. Uden, L., & He, W. (2017). How the Internet of Things can help knowledge management: A case study from the automotive domain. *Journal of Knowledge Management, 21*(1), 57–70.
90. Wang, T., Libaers, D., & Park, H. D. (2017). The paradox of openness: How product and patenting experience affect R&D sourcing in China? *Journal of Product Innovation Management, 34*(3), 250–268.
91. Bhosale, V. A., Kant, R., & Shankar, R. (2018). Investigating the impact of knowledge flow enablers on SC performance in Indian manufacturing organizations. *Benchmarking: An International Journal, 25*(2), 426–439.
92. Boshkoska, B. M., Liu, S., & Chen, H. (2018). Towards a knowledge management framework for crossing knowledge boundaries in agricultural value chain. *Journal of Decision Systems, 27*(s1), 88–97.
93. Filstad, C., Simeonova, B., & Visser, M. (2018). Crossing power and knowledge boundaries in learning and knowledge sharing: The role of ESM. *The Learning Organization, 25*(3), 159–168.
94. Flood, R. L., & Romm, N. R. A. (2018). A systemic approach to processes of power in learning organizations: Part 1—literature, theory and methodology of triple loop learning. *The Learning Organization, 25*(4), 260–272.
95. Haight, V. D., & Marquardt, M. J. (2018). How chief learning officers build learning organizations. *The Learning Organization, 25*(5), 331–343.
96. Keszey, T. (2018). Boundary spanners' knowledge sharing for innovation success in turbulent times. *Journal of Knowledge Management, 22*(5), 1061–1081.
97. Nugroho, M. A. (2018). The effects of collaborative cultures and knowledge sharing on organizational learning. *Journal of Organizational Change Management, 31*(5), 1138–1152.
98. Park, S., & Kim, E. J. (2018). Fostering organizational learning through leadership and knowledge sharing. *Journal of Knowledge Management, 22*(6), 1408–1423.
99. Santoro, G., Vrontis, D., Thrassou, A., & Dezi, L. (2018). The Internet of Things: Building a knowledge management system for open innovation and knowledge management capacity. *Technological Forecasting and Social Change, 136*, 347–354.
100. Sedighi, M., Lukosh, S., Brazier, F., Hamedi, M., & van Beers, C. (2018). Multi-level knowledge sharing: The role of perceived benefits in different visibility levels of knowledge exchange. *Journal of Knowledge Management, 22*(6), 1264–1287.

101. Wilhelm, M., & Dolfsma, W. (2018). Managing knowledge boundaries for open innovation—lessons from the automotive industry. *International Journal of Operations & Production Management, 38*(1), 230–248.
102. Boshkoska, B. M., Liu, S., Zhao, G., Che, H., Fernandez, A., Gamboa, S., del Pino, M., Zarate, P., & Hernandez, J. (2019). A Decision support system for evaluation of the knowledge sharing crossing boundaries in agri-food value chains. *Computers in Industry, 110*, 64–80.
103. Jayawickrama, U., Liu, S., Hudson-Smith, M., Akhtar, P., & Al-Bashir, M. D. (2019). Knowledge retention in ERP implementations: The context of UK SMEs. *Production Planning and Control, 30*(10–12), 1032–1047.
104. Kassem, R., Ajmal, M., Gunasekaran, A., & Helo, P. (2019). Assessing the impact of organizational culture on achieving business excellence with a moderating role of ICT: An SEM approach. *Benchmarking: An International Journal, 26*(1), 117–146.
105. Oh, S. Y. (2019). Effects of organizational learning on performance: The moderating roles of trust in leaders and organizational justice. *Journal of Knowledge Management, 23*(2), 313–331.
106. Oyemomi, O., Liu, S., Neaga, I., Chen, H., & Nakpodia, F. (2019). How cultural impact on knowledge sharing contributes to organizational performance: Using the fsQCA approach. *Journal of Business Research, 94*, 313–319.
107. Peng, G., Wang, H., Zhang, H., & Zhang, K. (2019). A hypernetwork-based approach to collaborative retrieval and reasoning of engineering design knowledge. *Advanced Engineering Informatics, 42*, 100956.
108. Sasidharan, S. (2019). Reconceptualising knowledge networks for enterprise systems implementation: Incorporating domain expertise of knowledge sources and knowledge flow intensity. *Information and Management, 56*(3), 364–476.
109. Szasz, L., Racz, B. G., Scherrer, M., & Deflorin, P. (2019). Disseminative capabilities and manufacturing plant roles in the knowledge network of MNCs. *International Journal of Production Economics, 208*, 294–304.

Social Responsibility of Algorithms: An Overview

Alexis Tsoukias

Abstract Should we be concerned by the massive use of devices and algorithms which automatically handle an increasing number of everyday activities within our societies? This chapter makes a short overview of the scientific investigation around this topic, showing that the development, existence and use of such autonomous artefacts are much older than the recent interest in machine learning monopolised artificial intelligence. We then categorise the impact of using such artefacts to the whole process of data collection, structuring, manipulation as well as in recommendation and decision making. The suggested framework allows to identify a number of challenges for the whole community of decision analysts, both researchers and practitioners.

Keywords Automated decisions · Automated decision support · Algorithmic decision making

1 Motivations

There is increasing concern around us about the impact of using automatic devices making decisions for several aspects of our life, including credit scoring, admissions to universities, pricing of goods, recommender systems, up to automatic vehicles or predictive justice (see [2, 24, 26]). However, the use of algorithms in order to automatise decision making is not recent [13]; actually algorithms exist even before computer science became the industry we know. We can summarise the situation today under the following observations:

- We are creating and using autonomous artefacts with increasing decision autonomy.
- We have autonomous artefacts with increasing learning capacities.

A. Tsoukias (✉)
CNRS-LAMSADE, PSL, Universite Paris Dauphine, Paris, France
e-mail: tsoukias@lamsade.dauphine.fr

© Springer Nature Switzerland AG 2021
J. Papathanasiou et al. (eds.), *EURO Working Group on DSS*, Integrated Series in Information Systems, https://doi.org/10.1007/978-3-030-70377-6_9

- There is evidence of biased decisions, of counterintuitive decisions, of inappropriate use of personal and sensible data, of unforeseen consequences, when such devices are largely adopted and used.[1]
- Software editing and data services are concentrated to few industrial players.

The aim of this chapter is to clarify a number of issues which affect both researchers and practitioners interested in decision support (decision analysts). It turns out that many of the concerns we are discussing today already existed in the literature (see, for instance, [52]) and are less "new" and "urgent" from what they appear to be. On the other hand, the extension today of designing, testing and actually using autonomous artefacts represents a real challenge for the community of decision analysts. The chapter aims at identifying which are these challenges and how can we appropriately handle them.

The chapter is structured as follows. In Sect. 2, we make a brief survey of the literature with no pretention to be exhaustive, essentially in order to identify the principal trends. Section 2 introduces the principal concepts through which we can establish a common framework. Section 3 presents two brief examples which help understanding the topics discussed in the previous section. Finally, Sect. 4 summarises the challenges we have in front of us the next years.

2   Historical Background

History

The literature about decision support systems dates back to the 1970s: see the seminal paper [18] and the two well-known books Keen [25], Sprague and Carlson [47]. This literature builds upon already existing research and practice with "management information systems" (see [32]). The idea is simple: exploit the information existing and circulating within an organisation in order to improve decision making under different types of requirements (see also the interesting discussion in [27]).

In more recent days, the same idea came alone under the concept of "analytics" (or business analytics or business intelligence; see [12]). The "new" idea is to extend the use of data in order to support decision making creating and assessing massive databases (more or less open), thanks to a large increase of computing capacity. However, the application of these ideas remains bounded at supporting "human decision makers" within organisations, the scope of "analytics" being to produce suitable information for decision makers.

A relatively innovative idea has been instead to increase the decision capacity of "autonomous artefacts" in order to improve the overall performance of complex

---

[1]The best known controversy is the "COMPASS" case: https://www.propublica.org/article/machine-bias-risk-assessments-in-criminal-sentencing

systems. However, once again, automatising decisions is not a totally new idea; we can see how this evolved through the following topics:

- Automatically conducted vehicles have been designed since a century ago: automatic pilots for aircrafts date at the beginning of the twentieth century (see [1] or [48]). Automatically controlled devices and robots exist since the middle of the twentieth century [22, 50] and represent today a very important scientific and industrial area.
- Multi-agent systems started being designed in the 1980s (see [44] or [53]) allowing software agents to perform with increasing decision autonomy.
- Recommender systems appeared soon after as software platforms where consumers could be automatically guided among huge catalogs of goods and being advised about their choices matching their preferences with product features and the behaviour of similar consumers (see [3] or [42]).
- Blockchains introduced the possibility to decentralise trust construction procedures through distributed cryptography on the web (see [34, 35]).

As can be noted, the idea of increasing the decision capacity of autonomous artefacts already has several decades of development, including commercial and industrial applications of large scale (virtually any aircraft today is automatically driven and most e-commerce platforms include a recommender system). There have been though two breakthroughs:

- The increasing availability and accessibility to data (of any type and quality, including personal and sensible ones)
- The massive expansion of "deep learning algorithms" allowing high level correlations among data with excellent accuracy and predictive capacity (for a presentation, see [17], while for an interesting discussion about correlation and causality, see [37]).

Such developments fuelled a literature about the impact and the consequences of automated decision making. This literature has been essentially focussed around three areas:

1. **Fairness**. Since the seminal paper [14], there have been several tentatives in order to establish a general definition of "fairness" for decisions taken by algorithms. This notion of fairness assumes the existence of "protected" groups within the society, which are potentially threatened by biased algorithmic decision making processes (see also [21, 28]). However, such "protected groups" are only recognised within certain countries, and it soon appeared that there are several formal and substantial difficulties in establishing a model of general validity (see [15]).
2. **Accountability and explicability**. Not independent from the fairness issue, there has been the discussion about the accountability of algorithms (see [8, 51]). The issue here is the possibility to provide convincing explanations on why an algorithm would end taking a certain type of decisions (possibly unfair, biased or counterintuitive). The topic includes explicability of data mining and machine

learning algorithms (see [20]) with specific emphasis to the case where the algorithms behave as black boxes with unpredictable behaviour (such as deep neural networks).
3. **Ethics**. Finally, there has been discussion about the ethical dimension of automated decision making. The issue arises essentially in the case of automatically conducted and/or unmanned vehicles and devices which may need to take decisions with high ethical impacts (such as impacting human life: see [5, 39]). The topic, however, has gone beyond this specific area questioning the possibility and/or opportunity to endow algorithms with ethical principles (see, for instance, [19]).

The result of such discussions has been the creation of new scientific communities, possibly interdisciplinary ones, the largest for the moment being the ACM-FAccT series of conferences (see https://facctconference.org/index.html).

3 What Is the Problem?

The survey presented in the previous section, far from being exhaustive, highlights the fast growth of an area of scientific investigation, but also of public concern. In reality, there exist several different problems which both scientific papers and press and blogs tend to put together under different "titles" basically sharing a number of keywords: artificial intelligence, data protection, algorithmic transparency, etc. (see [29, 36]). Most of them tend to raise concerns of the general public of how such technologies could impact our life. It pays, however, to clarify a number of issues starting with establishing precisely the object of scientific investigation.

From our perspective, this object is the *design, implementation and systematic use of autonomous artefacts with enhanced decision capacity*. In the following, we are going to analyse which are the different problems this object includes.

In conducting our analysis, we will adopt an industrial production perspective because we are talking about the evolution of an industry whose raw material is data. Under such a perspective, we are going to focus upon the raw material itself (the data), the transformation process (the algorithms), the implementation (the software), the outcome and the impact to the society. However, before analysing the components of this industrial process, we may analyse a number of fundamental topics.

3.1 Fundamentals

The first fundamental topic to remember is that automation is not a straightforward perspective, but a choice. There are plenty of examples around us of processes which are not automated and nobody thinks to automatise them. If automation is a choice, then there is somebody who makes the choice and there should be reasons for which this choice has been done. Automation for certain types of production has been decided by the industry and their management essentially in order to increase profits (although several times quality of the products has been used as a reason). Automation of other industrial processes has been decided for safety purposes or in order to alleviate workers from unhealthy or dangerous activities. If automatising a decision process is a choice, we should always ask ourselves who decides to automatise, for which reasons and who is going to pay the cost of it. If the process to automatise concerns the public (such as college admissions or predictive justice), there is a matter of democracy and citizens' participation to such decisions.

The second fundamental topic to remember is that decisions imply responsibility and responsibility implies liability for the consequences of any decision. Each time we consider automatising a decision process, we should always ask ourselves who is liable for the decisions taken by the autonomous artefact we create. In the flying industry, this issue has been long time solved: liable are the airlines who use aircrafts with automatic pilots and there is a chain of responsibilities, certifications and training in order to keep such liability clear. The liability issue does not concern solely the principle but also the practical aspect: be sure that responsibilities can be traced, recognised and affected to those who could be liable. Automatising a decision process means that we have a clear idea of how the liability issue is going to be considered.

The third fundamental topic concerns the fact that algorithms can mirror how our societies are, but cannot change them. It is clearly annoying to discover through what an algorithm learns that our societies are unfair, discriminate minorities, behave aggressively and in other terms are politically incorrect. But these are the societies as our democracies shaped them. If we do not like them, there are democratic paths for changing our societies, but algorithms will always mirror what our societies actually are. We cannot introduce innovation in society just designing innovative algorithms.

3.2   The Raw Material

The raw material of the type of processes we are concerned is data. Data are collected, stored, retrieved and manipulated, and each single step of these processes could have an impact upon the whole decision process to automatise. There are two basic topics to consider as far as the use (term resuming all the above steps) of data is concerned.

The first topic concerns the rights an individual (a citizen) and/or a group have upon certain data. Data (of any type) do not belong specifically to somebody, and for certain types of data, we could consider them as "commons". However, we can have certain rights upon certain data, and as soon as these rights are established, we can consider whether these can be traded. However, trading rights implies establishing clear contracts. The problem today is that there is an absolute information asymmetry (see [30]) between each single citizen and his rights on the one side and the data industry on the other side. Besides, there is a value scaling about data availability: the value of the rights I have upon my personal data alone is an extremely small fraction of the value of owing the rights of millions of individuals.

The second topic concerns the certification of the data used within automated decision processes. Biased data will result in biased outcomes. Noisy data will result in bad quality outcome. Corrupted data will result in unverifiable outcomes. There is necessity to certify the whole pipeline of collecting, storing and retrieving data used for any automated decision process (see [9]).

3.3   The Outcome

First of all, we need to make an important distinction. Autonomous artefacts can provide two types of outcomes: "decisions" and "recommendations". For this purpose, we may define a decision as an *irreversible allocation of resources to tasks or actions*. In the first case is the artefact that makes such an allocation which results in some action being undertaken, while in the second case the artefact only makes a recommendation (generally to a human agent) which "decides".

From a practical point of view, there are very few autonomous artefacts which actually have full decision autonomy, and generally this concerns "low level" actions in automatic controlled devices (such as in self-conducted vehicles). Most of the automated decision processes concern in reality artefacts which suggest a certain action to be undertaken. It can be the case of credit scoring, of predictive justice scores, college admissions, job candidates screening, etc. However, this "final decision freedom" of the human agent is far from being a warranty about the controllability of the final outcome. Most automatically formulated recommendations are rarely contested and usually are followed by the human decision makers, which essentially explains why such *suggestions* are regularly considered as *decisions*. In the following, we will focus on automated "recommendation" processes, since these are the most frequent (and complex).

A first issue to consider is the fact that the result of information manipulation is never straightforward: there is no (and will never exist) universal procedure through which we can obtain from raw data a synthesis. Data manipulation ought being *meaningful* (see [43]), *useful* (see [6]) and *legitimate* (see [49]), these requirements still allow for plenty of different procedures. It is a matter of choice for the designers and users.

The second issue, following from the previous one, is that we may desire adding further properties to the outcome: we may desire having a recommendation which is *fair, unbiased, neutral, etc.* The fact is that there is no unique definition to such concepts. Both economists in mechanism design theory [23, 31] and computer scientists more recently [15] realised that there are several different ways to define notions such as "fairness", each corresponding to different hypotheses about the society, the inequalities within the society and the ways to prevent or to correct them. This means we need to establish both the requirement of a feature to meet and a formal definition for each requirement and how to test it.

Establishing which requirements the recommendations need to meet is a matter of choice. The third issue is to know who decides which requirements an outcome of a given autonomous artefact has to be satisfied. Several of such requirements might be inconsistent one with respect to another. Somebody (who?) has to make a choice resulting in satisfying a certain property and thus failing to satisfying another one. Under such a perspective, it is important when designing an autonomous artefact to know which properties/requirements/axioms an automated recommendation procedure satisfies and which not. This is rarely the case today (the reader can check that no recommender systems specify how notes are aggregated among users and products and thus nobody knows which properties are satisfied by such procedures).

What happens in case the autonomous artefact is "data driven": in other terms, the outcome depends essentially upon the data feeding process, but the data manipulation is unknown (as happens for many black-box automated procedures)? The fourth issue related to the quality of the outcome concerns the "hidden values" embedded within many autonomous artefacts. Decisions and recommendations are never based directly on raw data. Between these and any decision, there are "preferences" or "values" which allow to compute a "choice" (or whatever else a decision or a recommendation may mean; see [10]). Preferences and values are always subjective and represent an individual or a society of individuals. If an autonomous artefact is able to make a decision or to compute a recommendation, it means that somebody embedded within the artefact his/her preferences. And these are independent from how the artefact turns to learn out from the data feeding it. It turns out that is of paramount importance to know how values are actually embedded in any of such systems and/or how these are learned (see [16]).

3.4 The Process

It is often the case that not only the outcome of a process matters but also the process itself. This is both the case for automated decisions and automated recommendations. The former might need to be explained, justified, tested and proven to be "correct" in case of accidents, misbehaviour, unforeseeable consequences, etc. The latter might need to be trusted, defended, argued, recused, might need to be convincing, trustworthy, understandable, etc. In all such cases, we need to check whether the autonomous artefact is *accountable*. However, there are several different levels of *accountability*:

1. Given an algorithm or to be more precise a bundle of algorithms setting an automatic decision procedure, can we trace precisely what these algorithms do?

2. Provided that we can trace the execution of the algorithms, can we provide "explanations" (interpretable, understandable, usable) to any type of stakeholder about the choices done and the obtained results?
3. Provided we can trace and explain the behaviour of an algorithm, can we provide the "ultimate reasons" for which the algorithm/automatic device made a precise decision or recommendation? If it is the case, can we replicate the decision providing the same input?
4. Supposing the algorithm cannot guarantee replicability (for instance, in case the algorithm learns each time is executed, we cannot guarantee that for a given input the output will remain the same), what type of explanations/justifications/reasons would be considered satisfying in case of a dispute?

Besides the above-introduced aspects of accountability, there are also long-term consequences to take into account when a certain type of autonomous artefact is largely used in the real world. How should we define accountability for the long-term impact of e-commerce platforms using recommender systems (using certain types of algorithms) for promoting their business?

3.5   The Implementation

Autonomous artefacts are essentially software. Certainly in the case of robots and other autonomous devices, there are physical parts which are equally important, but the essential of what we are talking is software. Indeed, algorithms and procedures not necessarily are implemented in software, but we are concerned with the ones who actually are used under form of computer programs.

The first issue to consider is the formal verification that a given software implementation of a bundle of algorithms endowing an autonomous artefact actually does what these algorithms are expected to do. This is far from being self-evident, and the more complex the artefact is, the more difficult the verification becomes.

The second issue concerns security. Any software implementation can be attacked and/or manipulated. We can certainly choose safer, redundant and highly protected implementations (as the stakes of the artefact scope increase; see the case of e-voting), but this comes at a price which needs to be commensurable to the benefits and the value of the automation.

The third issue concerns the use of open-source software. While this apparently could be inconsistent with straight security requirements, open-source software remains the ultimate possibility to analyse why an autonomous artefact actually acts as observed. While security issues can easily be handled even when using open-source code, being able to check the code through collective intelligence processes remains a fundamental warranty for most accountability issues.

3.6 The Impact to Society

Introducing a drug to a living system has expected and unexpected consequences. It is exactly for this reason that new drugs before being cleared and allowed to be used are extensively tested under rigid protocols, are permanently checked and submitted to scrutiny and possibly can be retired from commerce. Usually there is an independent authority which takes care of this process. We are going to use this "metaphor" (introducing a new drug to a living system) in order to consider the long-term impact of introducing an autonomous artefact in handling some aspect of our everyday life.

Should we demand a certification for the whole process (raw material, outcome, process and implementation) before allowing to release an autonomous artefact in the society? Should we create an independent agency or authority for this purpose? While many of the known unknowns can be handled through appropriate design and preliminary testing, the only way to discover the unknown unknowns is to do extensive testing and monitoring.

The use of autonomous artefacts for some types of business implies modifying the business model of the enterprise and/or the organisation introducing this "innovation". The issue is whether stakeholders, consumers or users are aware of the consequences such a modification will introduce upon the goods and services delivered by that type of business. Organisational studies are plenty of innovation failure cases [41] for businesses, organisations and markets, because the process was poorly designed, not understood, not fitting the expectations, undesired, etc., and this includes the choices about automatising decisions and processes.

The industry of automated decisions and recommendations is dominated by few big players, both with respect to the collection, storage, retrieval and use of data and services and with respect to software editing and engineering. Monopolies never benefited consumers, and this case will not be an exception. This market, as many others, needs regulations, and these need to be global.

If we need to audit autonomous artefacts and monitor their long-term impact and if we need to establish global rules for this market, we need to bear in mind that the life cycle of these products can be short (even very short) compared to the length of audits and regulations. It might make sense to be innovative as far as the timing of regulation is concerned if we do not want to miss any real opportunity to control.

4   Examples

The following examples are voluntarily not among the typical ones used within the artificial intelligence literature just in order to show that several issues discussed in this chapter are far beyond the AI challenges.

4.1 Automatic Pricing

Automatic pricing became popular since the late 1970s because of the innovation introduced by American Airlines: yield management. The simple idea consists in adjusting prices and seats offered on commercial flights following the demand prediction and possible capacity of the airline (see [46]). Today is a regular practice, not only for the airlines industry: many retailers practice automatic pricing in order to optimise revenue management. That said, we can make a number of observations:

1. Implementing the automatisation of this activity has been a choice, both for profit maximisation purposes and for gaining competitive advantages for the first runners. It is less obvious whether this resulted in better and less cheap services for the customers. In any case, it was not a choice of the users who can find exactly the same product at several, significantly different, prices (see [33]).
2. There exist several different economic models helping to compute automatically prices, depending upon the type of product, the type of the market and the hypotheses about the consumers' behaviour (see [11]). It is actually unknown whether the choice of any among such models has been discussed before using them.
3. We know instead that adopting a precise model of pricing, considering the density of the competition (on the retailers market), can lead to unforeseen consequences, as in the famous "Stapler" case,[2] where the same object (a stapler) was sold at different prices in different neighbours. The use of competition density resulted in discounting the object in the "rich neighbours" (high density) and selling it at full price in the "poor neighbours" (low density). Not necessarily this was the policy and will of the retailer.
4. Automatic pricing strongly depends upon the quality and timing of the necessary data feeding the economic and decision models of yield management. However, there is no warranty that the data pipeline for any of the retailers adopting such tools is reliable and trustworthy. This is all the more important in case part of the data feed a black-box learning procedure for which we may have no convincing justifications available. On the other hand, the liability for any "wrong" decision remains internal to the retailer who will just have to absorb the consequences in their business.
5. Automatic pricing modified how the travel industry is organised and influenced how people travel and organise their leisure time. In other terms, it had a huge impact upon the whole society (as often happens when industries introduce new products or services). On the other hand, what is the long-term impact of such new patterns of mobility and leisure time consumption? Are these sustainable at a long run? Nobody ever discussed that, when yield management models and algorithms have been introduced (more than 40 years ago).

---

[2]https://www.wsj.com/articles/SB10001424127887323777204578189391813881534

4.2   Voting

Voting is not an automatic decision procedure or at least is not perceived as such. However, the reader will note that when we adopt the term voting, we implicitly consider voting procedures (algorithms) which "compute" a "winner" of an electoral contest. There exist several such algorithms, and generally they may yield totally different results even when the preferences of the voting society are clear. The fact is that we (the society) need to make choices of which among such algorithms should be used and possibly we (the society) have to trust that the result is legitimate. For a presentation of electoral systems, see [40], while a theoretical investigation about social choice theory can be found in [4] or in [45]. For an interesting survey about such methods being considered under a computational aspect, see [7]. Once again, we make a number of observations:

1. We vote in order to elect representatives, presidents, committees, chairs, etc., and this is done for legitimating governing. However, "electing" is not the only way to appoint representatives, committees, chairs etc. Our societies (after centuries of struggles) decided to use such procedures (which might result in less efficient decision procedures, but certainly more legitimated). We vote because we want to.
2. As already mentioned, there exist many different voting procedures and algorithms computing the winner(s). It is well known that it does not exist and it will never exist an universal procedure, because even simple "democratic" requirements are inconsistent among them and cannot be satisfied simultaneously. This means we need to choose one. In doing that, it pays knowing which requirements are satisfied and which not, and this has been the scope of large part of the social choice theory literature.
3. Different voting procedures promote different views about our societies, the ways to govern the society and about citizens' participation (see [38]). Moreover, each of such systems needs to make choices on how "fair representation" should be interpreted (proportionality among citizens, among regions and among ethnic groups are typical topics which are typically impossible to satisfy all together). These are political choices which need to be discussed as such and not as technical problems.
4. Electronic vote is increasingly popular but has been tested to be easily hacked, corrupted and manipulated, while manual procedures are far more complicated to alter (at least under usual democratic institutions operating). As already noted previously, the software version of an algorithm does not coincide with the algorithm itself.

5 Conclusion

Let us try to summarise our overview. Does it make any sense to talk about the *social responsibility of algorithms*? Technically speaking, no, since algorithms cannot be liable for what they compute. Designers, clients demanding for algorithms, software editors can be considered responsible (and thus liable), but not the algorithms. On the other hand, the use of algorithms in order to improve our decision making is older that computer science itself and the demand for extending their use, for creating further autonomous artefacts with decision capacity is never lasting.

As decision analysts, we share part of the responsibility of how such autonomous artefacts are shaped, designed, implemented and used in the real world. Under such a perspective, we should pay attention and further develop our theoretical research as well as our reflection about our practices around the following topics:

- Characterising algorithms and procedures through the properties they satisfy or do not satisfy
- Remembering that each time we choose a precise procedure in order to solve a given decision problem, this is rarely a straightforward choice, but one among many options, and as such needs to be justified and considered for its impact beyond that precise problem
- Characterising and specifying the data to be used by algorithms, reflecting the three basic requirements: meaningfulness, usefulness and legitimacy
- Analysing how our methods, procedures and protocols are used and adopted within real organisations and within our societies

Algorithms and formal models will never stop being used in order to improve how decisions are taken both by humans and machines. It is upon the designers to define what improvement means and for whom. This is our social responsibility.

Acknowledgments This document follows discussions which took place during the two workshops about this topic in Paris, December 2017 and 2019 (www.lamsade.dauphine.fr/sra), and I am indebted to the participants for their contributions. Although several ideas are due to these discussions, I remain the sole responsible for this essay.

References

1. Åström, K., & Murray, R. (2008). *Feedback Systems: An Introduction for Scientists and Engineers*. Princeton: Princeton University Press.
2. Abu-Elyounes, D. (2020). Contextual fairness: A legal and policy analysis of algorithmic fairness. *Journal of Law, Technology and Policy, 2020*, 1–54.
3. Aggarwal, C. (2016). *Recommender Systems: The Textbook*. Berlin: Springer.
4. Arrow, K. (1951). *Social Choice and Individual Values* (2nd ed., 1963). New York: Wiley.
5. Bonnefon, J., Shariff, A., & Rahwan, I. (2016). The social dilemma of autonomous vehicles. *Science, 352*(6293), 1573–1576.

6. Bouyssou, D., Marchant, T., Pirlot, M., Perny, P., Tsoukiàs, A., & Vincke, P. (2000). *Evaluation and Decision Models: A Critical Perspective*. Dordrecht: Kluwer Academic.
7. Brandt, F., Conitzer, V., Endriss, U., Lang, J., & Procaccia, A. (2016). *Handbook of Computational Social Choice*. Cambridge: Cambridge University Press.
8. Casteluccia, C., & Le Métayer, D. (2019). *Understanding Algorithmic Decision Making: Opportunities and Challenges*. (EPRS Study, 104pp). Brussels: European Parliament.
9. Christophides, V., Efthymiou, V., Palpanas, T., Papadakis, G., & Stefanidis, K. (2020). End-to-end entity resolution for big data: A survey. Technical report, ARXIV. https://arxiv.org/pdf/1905.06397.pdf
10. Colorni, A., & Tsoukiàs, A. (2013). What is a decision problem? Preliminary statements. In *Proceedings of ADT 2013* (LNAI 8176, pp. 139–153). Berlin: Springer.
11. Cross, R. (1997). *Revenue Management: Hard-Core Tactics for Market Domination*. New York: Broadway Books.
12. Davenport, T., & Harris, J. (2007). *Competing on Analytics: The New Science of Winning*. Harvard: Harvard Business School Press.
13. Davenport, T., & Harris, J. G. (2005). Automated decision making comes of age. *MIT Sloan Management Review, 46*, 11.
14. Dwork, C., Hardt, M., Pitassi, T., Reingold, O., & Zemel, R. (2012). Fairness through awareness. In *Proceedings of ITCS'12* (pp. 214–226).
15. Friedler, S., Scheidegger, C., & Venkatasubramanian, S. (2016). On the (im)possibility of fairness. Technical report, CoRR abs/1609.07236.
16. Fürnkranz, J., & Hüllermeier, E. (2010). *Preference Learning*. Berlin: Springer.
17. Goodfellow, I., Bengio, Y., & Courville, A. (2016). *Deep Learning*. Boston: MIT Press.
18. Gory, G., & Scott-Morton, M. S. (1971). A framework for management information systems. *MIT Sloan Management Review, 13*, 55–70.
19. Greene, J., Rossi, F., Tasioulas, J., Venable, K., & Williams, B. (2016). Embedding ethical principles in collective decision support systems. In *Proceedings of the AAAI 2016* (pp. 4147–4151).
20. Guidotti, R., Monreale, A., Ruggieri, S., Turini, F., Giannotti, F., & Pedreschi, D. (2018). A survey of methods for explaining black box models. *ACM Computing Surveys (CSUR), 51*(5), 93. https://doi.org/10.1145/3236009.
21. Hajian, S., & Domingo-Ferrer, J. (2013). A methodology for direct and indirect discrimination prevention in data mining. *IEEE Transactions on Knowledge and Data Engineering, 25*, 1445–1459.
22. Hunt, V. (1985). *Smart Robots: A Handbook of Intelligent Robotic Systems*. London: Chapman and Hall.
23. Hurwicz, L., & Reiter, S. (2006). *Designing Economic Mechanisms*. Cambridge: Cambridge University Press.
24. Keats Citron, D. (2008). Technological due process. *Washington University Law Review, 85*, 1249–1313.
25. Keen, P., & Scott-Morton, M. (1978). *Decision Support Systems: An Organizational Perspective*. Reading: Addison Wesley.
26. Kroll, J., Huey, J., Barocas, S., Felten, E., Reidenberg, J., Robinson, D., & Yu, H. (2017). Accountable algorithms. *University of Pennsylvania Law Review, 165*, 633–705.
27. Landry, M., Pascot, D., & Briolat, D. (1983). Can DSS evolve without changing our view of the concept of problem? *Decision Support Systems, 1*, 25–36.
28. Lepri, B., Oliver, N., Letouzé, E., Pentland, A., & Vinck, P. (2018). Fair, transparent, and accountable algorithmic decision-making processes. *Philosophy and Technology, 31*, 611–627.
29. Lepri, B., Staiano, J., Sangokoya, D., Letouzé, E., & Oliver, N. (2017). The tyranny of data? The bright and dark sides of data-driven decision-making for social good. In T. Cerquitelli, D. Quercia, & F. Pasquale (Eds.), *Transparent Data Mining for Big and Small Data* (Studies in Big Data, Vol. 32, pp. 3–24). Cham: Springer.
30. Mas-Colell, A., Whinston, M., & Green, J. (1995). *Microeconomic Theory*. New York: Oxford University Press.

31. Maskin, E. (2008). How to implement social goals mechanism design. *American Economic Review, 98,* 567–576.
32. Mason, R., & Mitroff, I. (1973). A program for research on management information systems. *Management Science, 19,* 475–487.
33. Mauri, A. (2007). Yield management and perception of fairness in the hotel business. *International Review of Economics, 54,* 284–293.
34. Nakamoto, S. (2008). Bitcoin: A peer-to-peer electronic cash system. Technical report, bitcoin.org.
35. Narayanan, A., Bonneau, J., Felten, E., Miller, A., & Goldfeder, S. (2016). *Bitcoin and Cryptocurrency Technologies: A Comprehensive Introduction.* Princeton: Princeton University Press.
36. O'Neil, C. (2016). *Weapons of Math Destruction: How Big Data Increases Inequality and Threatens Democracy.* New York: Crown.
37. Pearl, J. (2009). *Causality.* Cambridge: Cambridge University Press.
38. Rae, D. (1971). *The Political Consequences of Electoral Laws.* Yale: Yale University Press.
39. Rahwan, I. (2020). Society-in-the-loop: programming the algorithmic social contract. *Ethics and Information Technology, 20,* 5–14.
40. Reynolds, A., Reill, B., & Ellis, A. (2005). *Electoral System Design. The New International IDEA Handbook.* Stockholm: IDEA
41. Rhaiem, K., & Amara, N. (2019). Learning from innovation failures: A systematic review of the literature and research agenda. *Review of Managerial Science.* In press. https://doi.org/10.1007/s11846-019-00339-2.
42. Ricci, F., Rokach, L., Shapira, B., & Kantor, P. (2011). *Recommender Systems Handbook.* Berlin: Springer.
43. Roberts, F. (1979). *Measurement Theory, with Applications to Decision Making, Utility and the Social Sciences.* Boston: Addison-Wesley.
44. Russel, S., & Norvig, P. (1995). *Artificial Intelligence: A Modern Approach.* New York: Prentice Hall.
45. Sen, A. (1986). Social choice theory. In K. Arrow & M. Intriligator (Eds.), *Handbook of Mathematical Economics* (Vol. 3, pp. 1073–1181). Amsterdam: North-Holland.
46. Smith, B., Leimkuhler, J., & Darrow, R. (1992). Yield management at American Airlines. *Journal on Applied Analytics, 22,* 8–31.
47. Sprague, R., & Carlson, E. (1982). *Building Effective Decision Support Systems.* Englewood Cliffs: Prentice Hall.
48. Stevens, B., & Lewis, F. (1992). *Aircraft Control and Simulation.* New York: Wiley.
49. Tsoukiàs, A. (2007). On the concept of decision aiding process. *Annals of Operations Research, 154,* 3–27.
50. Wiener, N. (1948). *Cybernetics.* Cambridge: MIT Press.
51. Wieringa, M. (2020). What to account for when accounting for algorithms: A systematic literature review on algorithmic accountability. In *Proceedings of FAT 2020* (pp. 1–18).
52. Winograd, T., & Flores, F. (1986). *Understanding Computers and Cognition.* Norwood: Ablex.
53. Wooldridge, M. (2002). *An Introduction to Multi-Agent Systems.* New York: Wiley.

Negotiation Support: Trends and Problems

Rudolf Vetschera

Abstract Early approaches to negotiation support viewed negotiations mainly from a decision perspective and extended decision support systems by a communication component that allowed negotiators to exchange highly structured offers. In this chapter, we argue, based on a comprehensive survey of negotiation research of the last decades, that negotiation processes are more complex and involve multiple dimensions of substantive issues, communication, and emotions. We review the development of empirical research on negotiations along these three dimensions and explore possibilities for a comprehensive support of negotiation processes. Finally, we discuss the necessity to consider these dimensions not only in isolation but also their interactions. A successful negotiation support system would need to guide users through the complex interactions of all dimensions.

Keywords Negotiation processes · Offers · Communication · Emotions · Negotiation support systems · Economic outcomes · Relational outcomes

1 Introduction

When reading an early paper on negotiation support systems (NSS) such as [58, 86], one would have probably been convinced that the breakthrough of NSS was just around the corner and that 30 years later practically all negotiations would be conducted using such systems. Obviously, this is not the case today. To understand why these early ideas about negotiation support were not successful, it is necessary to consider not only developments in the field of decision support systems and NSS. Research on negotiations and negotiation processes has also made considerable progress in the last decades and has led to a much clearer understanding of what is needed to support negotiators.

R. Vetschera (✉)
Department of Business Decisions and Analytics, University of Vienna, Vienna, Austria
e-mail: rudolf.vetschera@univie.ac.at

© Springer Nature Switzerland AG 2021
J. Papathanasiou et al. (eds.), *EURO Working Group on DSS*, Integrated Series in Information Systems, https://doi.org/10.1007/978-3-030-70377-6_10

The goal of this chapter is to review the current state of knowledge on negotiation processes and to relate these insights to the design of NSS. A thorough understanding of the different dimensions of negotiation processes is important to identify all the areas in which negotiators need support. Furthermore, it is necessary to understand how characteristics of negotiation processes influence the outcome of negotiations so that interventions by a support system lead to desired rather than undesirable changes in the process and outcomes. Empirical research on negotiations has uncovered many such relationships that can inform the developers of support systems.

Negotiation processes are complex phenomena. In the following section, we will argue that they have multiple dimensions and can be analyzed from different perspectives, and provide a first overview of these perspectives. The following section will then discuss these dimensions in detail. In the concluding sections, we present approaches to integrate the different dimensions and provide an outlook on possible future research.

2 Dimensions of Negotiation Processes

Before developing a system to support negotiators, one has to clarify what a "better" outcome of a negotiation actually means. Negotiations are collective decision processes in which a decision (other than the status quo) is only reached when all parties to the negotiation agree on it [72]. However, the fact that a negotiation ended in agreement is only one possible definition of success of a negotiation. It is also necessary to consider the benefits that this agreement provides. Since negotiations are collective decision processes, each party could benefit in a different way from an agreement. A negotiation support system can support either a single party to the negotiation or all parties simultaneously. In the first case, the relevant goal is the outcome of the supported party. In the latter case, global criteria like overall efficiency and fairness become important. Efficiency and fairness can be measured in different ways. Efficiency is often interpreted as Pareto efficiency (i.e., an agreement is efficient if it is not possible to improve the situation of one party without harming another party) or as the sum of individual outcomes (utilities) [120]. Fairness criteria in negotiations might refer to various aspects of justice such as distributional justice (considering the allocation of outcomes) or procedural justice (the fairness of the process) [28].

All these concepts assume that the outcome of a negotiation is clearly defined. However, the "outcome" is an ambiguous concept. Most (business) negotiations obviously have an economic outcome, but negotiations have many more outcome dimensions. An agreement typically provides a plan for actions to be undertaken by both parties. Thus, the negotiation is often followed by an implementation phase, in which the parties have to work together to implement the agreement. The quality of the relationship between parties after the negotiation is therefore another important negotiation outcome [24, 48, 108].

During a negotiation, the parties thus not only allocate (economic) outcomes but also create a relationship between them. Creating a relationship requires communication. Very early concepts of NSS thus already established that a negotiation support system needs to contain a decision support component, which helps parties in evaluating different allocations, and a communication component [66, 86]. However, communication at that time was mainly interpreted as an exchange of offers describing proposed values of the negotiation issues in quantitative terms. The main task of communication was seen to overcome distances between parties in time and space [11]. A Decision Support System (DSS) would then map these offers onto a formal representation of the decision maker's preferences [12] to support negotiators in evaluating complex offers, frequently using methods from multicriteria decision making [56, 75].

At roughly the same time, negotiation researchers coming from the fields of communication research and social psychology began to develop a much more differentiated view of communication in negotiations [123, 136] by studying properties of communication processes that lead to collaboration and agreements. Classification systems were developed [98] to distinguish different functions that communication acts can have during a negotiation.

These classifications refer to explicit acts of communication, such as distinct messages that negotiators send via electronic channels in an NSS. However, communication in negotiation also takes more implicit forms. In face-to-face negotiations, emotions might be transmitted between negotiators, for example, via their body language. Even pure textual messages in electronic communication can transmit emotions [51]. The role of emotions in negotiations has also been studied intensively in the last decades [50, 128].

Negotiation processes therefore take place at several different levels, which are represented in the ICE (issues-communication-emotions) framework of negotiations [36] shown in Fig. 1.

The model distinguishes between three dimensions of the negotiation process: a substantive dimension, which deals with the issues to be resolved in the negotiation; a communication dimension, which represents the explicit communication acts; and an emotional dimension, which is implicitly transmitted during the negotiation. In the following section, we will consider these three dimensions individually and discuss insights from (empirical) negotiation research on each dimension as well as approaches to support negotiators in their behavior in each dimension.

3 Process Models and Support

3.1 Substantive Level

The substantive dimension is concerned with the specific issues to be resolved during the negotiation. Negotiation processes can proceed in different ways [132].

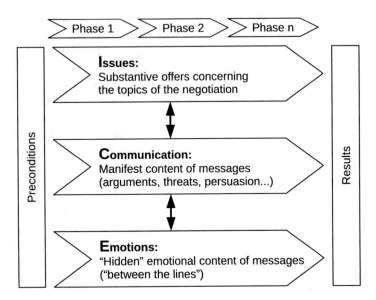

Fig. 1 ICE framework of negotiation processes [36]

The most common form is concession-based processes, in which the parties start at their most favorable positions and then gradually make concessions to move closer to an agreement. Alternatively, the process can consist of mutual improvements. Both parties start at a solution which is not favorable to either of them (such as the status quo) and search for changes that would improve the situation for both sides. Since this process utilizes only one proposal, it is sometimes referred to as a "single negotiation text" (SNT) approach [29, 30, 78, 104].

In a concession-based negotiation, each party at a given step of the negotiation has to decide among three possible alternatives:

1. Accept the other party's offer, thereby ending the negotiation in agreement.
2. Continue the negotiation with a counteroffer.
3. Terminate the negotiation in disagreement.

A counteroffer typically involves a concession, so the new offer is worse for that party than its previous offer, and better for the other party. However, a party could also insist on the previous position or even try to improve its outcome. Furthermore, one party must make a first offer. Thus, at the beginning of the negotiation process, both parties have to decide whether to wait for the opponent or make an initial offer and what that offer should be.

The level of the initial offer has been the subject of considerable empirical research, starting already in the 1960s [22]. Research on face-to-face negotiations [93, 129] as well as electronic negotiations [61, 131] indicates that negotiators who make tougher initial offers ultimately achieve better outcomes. One possible explanation for this relationship is the anchoring bias [38]. The initial offer forms an anchor, which the other party unconsciously uses when selecting the counteroffer. Furthermore, comparatively soft initial offers could be interpreted as a sign of weakness and lead to tougher counteroffers from the opponent [61].

The initial offer is typically followed by a sequence of alternating offers and counteroffers. If parties start at positions favorable to them, an agreement can only be reached if concessions are made. The importance of concessions is clearly demonstrated in empirical research [37]. Negotiations differ not only in whether concessions are made at all but also in the timing and size of concessions. Concession behavior in negotiations can be characterized by a concession curve, which represents the output (utility) level a negotiator claims over time. If the concession curve has a concave shape, the negotiator initially makes only small concessions and moves to substantial concessions only near the end of a negotiation. Such a concession curve therefore represents a distributive, tough bargaining style. In contrast, a convex concession curve in which a negotiator makes large concessions early on corresponds to an integrative bargaining style. Thus, the speed of concessions can be used as a measure of a negotiator's toughness [122]. Shapes of concession curves were used in empirical study to classify negotiators [16, 70, 96], and empirical results confirm that integrative negotiations are more likely to end in agreement. Concessions are also evaluated differently by the opponent depending on when they are made [79].

The concept of a concession curve implicitly assumes that concessions can easily be evaluated by the opponent. This assumption is not problematic if the two parties bargain over a single issue, for which they have opposing preferences (like buyer and seller bargaining only about the price). Then, it is clear that whatever one party concedes, the other party gains. However, the utility gains or losses which the two parties associate with the same change might still be different, so what one party views as a large concession could still be only a small gain for the other party. The situation becomes more difficult in multi-issue negotiations, where a move that leads to a utility loss of one party might also cause a loss in utility to the other party. In multi-issue negotiations, one can therefore define different types of bargaining steps, depending on whether a party improves or worsens its position in different issues [37], or how the step affects the utility of both sides [54].

Negotiation support systems can support negotiators in this process in different ways. Obviously, a negotiator should accept the opponent's offer if he or she would be willing to make a counteroffer that is worse than the opponent's offer currently on the table. NSS therefore need to support negotiators in evaluating and comparing offers. This feature becomes particularly important in multi-issue negotiations, where each offer is a package resolving different issues. Thus, early approaches to negotiation support already involved methods of multi-attribute decision making [57, 65, 113]. Consequently, early negotiation support systems such as Negotiation Assistant [105], Inspire [64], or Negoisst [110] contained modules to elicit multi-attribute value functions and applied these functions to evaluate offers. Models of the opponent's preferences that can be inferred from offers made by the opponent can be used to determine concession size from the opponent's perspective [9, 10].

Most NSS use an additive utility model to represent a negotiator's preferences. Different methods are used to elicit these functions [8], and some variants allow for incomplete specification of parameters [23] or use fuzzy sets to represent uncertainty [92, 140]. Many other methods of multicriteria analysis have also been proposed to represent negotiator preferences such as the AHP [89], reference point methods [7], the weighted Tchebychev method [13], or TOPSIS [106]. Other models used outranking methods such as PROMETHEE [31] or ELECTRE [135]. Surveys of the methods used are provided in [71, 118, 130].

To provide effective decision support, the system needs to present information to users in a useful and easily understandable way. So far, information presentation has only rarely been addressed in the NSS literature. Existing NSS such as Inspire [64] or Negoisst [110] typically employ standard graph formats such as line charts to represent the development of the parties' positions over time. Since these systems treat preference information as confidential information of each side, all offers are evaluated from the perspective of the negotiator who receives that information, and information that also represents the opponent's preferences is provided only after an agreement has been reached. There is only scarce literature about the effects of such representations. Gettinger and Koeszegi [41] discuss different graph types from a theoretical perspective, and [43] provide empirical evidence about their impact. At a more general level, [117] discuss the benefits of visualizations to create a common understanding of the problem.

Tools such as preference models and visualization of preferences enable negotiators to evaluate offers but do not actively provide advice on which offers to make. A more active approach would require prescriptive models of the negotiation process, which are still lacking. Formal bargaining models of game theory such as the model by [107] or the Zeuthen-Hicks model [5, 52] are based on far-reaching assumptions on the rationality and the information of players, which limit their usefulness for decision support. More application-oriented models were developed for negotiations involving autonomous software agents.

Three main approaches for concession making by autonomous software agents were developed in literature [32]:

(i)   Time-dependent concessions
(ii) Resource-dependent concessions
(iii) Concessions depending on the opponent's behavior

Time-dependent concessions refer to the concept of a concession curve, which represents the utility a negotiator claims over time. In resource-dependent concession making, the negotiator adjusts his or her demand according to the resources left. Concessions which depend on the opponent's behavior typically reflect the concept of reciprocity [47, 101], i.e., responding to a large concession from the opponent also with a large concession. These approaches can also be combined to create complex offer strategies [32].

Several empirical studies tested whether such concession functions are an adequate model of actual negotiation processes. Nastase [96] as well as [16] used concession curves ex post to classify behavior as distributive or integrative and found clear relationships between shapes of concession curves and the outcomes of negotiations. However, these analyses were conducted ex post, so these models cannot be used to support a negotiator during an ongoing negotiation (e.g., to identify the strategy employed by the opponent). Agrawal and Chari [2] developed a support system that estimates concession curves during an ongoing negotiation to infer the reservation value of the opponent, which is a useful information to support the focal negotiator's concession behavior.

Prediction of the opponent's offer and concession behavior can also be based on other tools. Carbonneau et al. [15] and Lee and Ou-Yang [82] used neural networks to predict offers made by the opponent and achieved good accuracy in predicting offers of human negotiators [15] and simulated data [82]. Such predictions can then form the basis of reciprocal counteroffers.

In purely automatic negotiations between software agents, many different concession strategies were proposed [e.g., 80]. In contrast, only a few systems support human negotiators in formulating their offers. eAgora [20] is an NSS which contains a software agent to assist users. This agent has two functions: it can evaluate and criticize offers that the supported negotiator receives or intends to make, and it generates suggestions for offers. In the latter mode, it uses fuzzy rules to determine an appropriate amount of concession and then generates offers that would implement the desired change. In multi-issue negotiations, several offers could lead to the same or similar utility levels. For example, the same decrease in utility could be achieved by a large concession in a less important issue, by a small concession in an important issue, or by a mixture of the two.

Another approach to support negotiators in concession making is the AC-AT (analytical concession-advising technology) model by [134]. This model assumes that a system knows the utility functions of both parties. It generates proposals for offers that fulfill three principles:

(i) *True concessions:* A concession should lead to a decrease in the focal negotiator's utility.
(ii) *Reciprocity:* A concession should match a previous concession of the opponent so that the opponent gains at least as much in utility in the concession made by the focal negotiator as the opponent has given up in his or her previous concession.
(iii) *Value creation:* The opponent's gain in utility should exceed the loss in utility incurred by the focal negotiator.

The conditions of true concession and value creation define a cone in utility space in which offers are located, and the condition of reciprocity defines a minimum step size of concessions. The user can control the process by specifying an acceptable range of trade-offs how much own utility the user is willing to give up to increase the opponent's utility by one unit. This trade-off can be adjusted during the negotiation, allowing the negotiator to follow different bargaining strategies over time. The system also maps utility values to values of the issues using a mixed integer programming model. A prototype of this method was implemented as an add-on to the negotiation support system Negoisst [110].

These models use preference models based on utility functions. Other systems model negotiation processes and concession making via different approaches. In particular, several systems such as Family_winner [4], Negoplan [68, 69], or ProCON [84, 85] used rule-based and logic models to represent goal hierarchies. However, these systems were not intended to guide a negotiator through a negotiation process with several offers and therefore cannot be considered to provide process support.

The assumption that a system knows about both parties' preferences might seem problematic during an ongoing negotiation. Even if the system is trusted not to reveal confidential preference information, parties still might fear that their opponent is able to "reverse engineer" the preferences from the offers. However, revealing this information (perhaps also only indirectly) is less problematic once the negotiation is completed. Several NSS such as Inspire [64] or Negotiation Assistant [105] therefore contain a post-settlement phase. In this phase, the system checks whether an agreement reached by the negotiators is Pareto-optimal and if possible proposes efficient agreements that dominate the agreement reached by the negotiators. Although accepting such a dominating agreement would be beneficial to both sides, empirical research indicates that negotiators are often reluctant to enter a post-negotiation phase at all [67] or do not agree on one of the dominating solutions [40].

A very different model of negotiations is the concept of a "single negotiation text" [104], which is frequently used in international political negotiations. The main stage of this process is the mutual improvement of the single proposal on the table. However, indicating a direction of potential improvement requires knowledge about the preferences of all parties. If a party suggests such an improvement, it also reveals information of its preferences. Furthermore, a Pareto improvement might imply a large improvement for one party, and a small or even no improvement for the other party, raising fairness concerns. Several approaches have been developed in literature to address the issues of incomplete preference information and fairness [29, 30]. These approaches try to find directions of mutual improvement based on the utility functions of the two parties. Other approaches [7, 77, 78] use aspiration-based models to represent the preferences of the parties.

By definition, approaches using a single negotiation text consider only one possible agreement at any given point in time. This differentiates these approaches from concession-based approaches, in which the two offers from both sides are simultaneously on the table. A recent generalization of the SNT approach is negotiation by veto [34], in which the parties successively rule out entire sets of possible agreements by increasing aspiration levels and thereby approach the efficient frontier.

3.2 Communication Dimension

The early literature on NSS already emphasized that an NSS needs to contain both a decision support component and a communication component [86]. However, the main task of the communication component was seen to bridge the distance between users in space and time [56]. However, the fact that negotiators communicate via an electronic medium rather than face-to-face might change the negotiation process significantly.

Negotiations have two types of outcomes: a substantive outcome, which is represented by the agreement concluded between negotiators, and a relational outcome, which describes the relationship that the negotiators have built during the negotiation [108]. This relationship is important for several reasons. First, the quality of the relationship directly influences behavior during the negotiation. Rapport and mutual understanding between negotiators leads to revealing more information, and this increases the likelihood of reaching an agreement and the joint benefit that negotiators can achieve [94]. Second, implementation of an agreement in many cases requires some joint effort by the parties. The quality of the relationship might influence the success of the implementation phase.

Early research on communication in electronic negotiations frequently studied negotiations conducted via e-mail rather than via a dedicated NSS. Researchers found considerable differences in personal rapport between negotiators compared to face-to-face negotiations [119]. These differences lead to different patterns of coordination between negotiators, less information exchange, and a decline in mutual adjustment. In particular, negotiators using electronic media performed less relationship-oriented communication, which [95] refer to as "schmoozing." This "schmoozing" is an important factor for reaching integrative, win-win agreements. This negative effect of electronic communication could be overcome if negotiators in electronic negotiations consciously shared more personal information to establish a closer relationship [94].

Research on electronic communication in negotiations identified several other biases, which negatively influence outcomes. Negotiators using e-mail often failed to recognize that they are in a situation of asynchronous communication and expect others to respond immediately. A delayed response is attributed to purposeful destructive behavior of the opponent (the "sinister attribution" bias). However, negotiators using electronic communication media might also deliberately display negative emotions and exhibit socially unconstrained behavior [62, 119]; these two phenomena were labeled "squeaky wheel" and "burning bridges" bias. Furthermore, negotiators communicating via electronic media are less able to identify deception by their counterparts [45].

Electronic communication can take many different forms, and negotiators might employ very different tactics when using different media. Negotiators can communicate just via text messages, but electronic media also offer the possibilities to include audio or video communication, which has been shown to improve negotiation outcomes [137]. A deeper understanding of the effects of electronic communication on negotiation requires both a typology of different media and a classification of communication acts in negotiations.

The media richness theory by Daft and Lengel [25, 26] provides a useful framework for classifying communication media. It distinguishes media of different richness according to four criteria: (i) the speed of feedback (instant or delayed feedback); (ii) the multiplicity of cues (such as voice, body gesture, or physical presence) that a medium provides; (iii) the language variety, i.e., the possibility of expressing facts in different ways (e.g., natural language vs. numbers); and (iv) the personal focus, whether the medium allows to address recipients individually.

According to media richness theory, rich media are particularly useful in situations characterized by uncertainty (i.e., a lack of factual knowledge) and equivocality (i.e., the possibility of multiple, different interpretations of the same information). Since negotiations exhibit these properties, this theory predicts that rich media (such as face-to-face meetings) are more suitable for negotiations than, e.g., text messages. Building on media richness theory, several researchers have studied the impact of electronic communication on negotiations using even more differentiated criteria. Hatta et al. [53] considered the characteristics of exitability and correctability. Electronic media make it easier for participants to exit a negotiation (by simply not replying to messages) and to reflect on and edit a message before sending it. A concept similar to correctability was also used by [103], who studied the different impacts of synchronous (chat) and asynchronous (e-mail) electronic media on negotiations. Both authors argue that having time to carefully consider and possibly revise messages is beneficial to negotiations. Thus, negotiations conducted via an asynchronous medium such as e-mail lead to "cooler" behavior than negotiations in which parties respond immediately (and thus sometimes unreflectedly).

An analysis of communication behavior in (electronic) negotiations also requires a classification of communication acts. Several classification schemes for negotiations were developed in literature. Olekalns et al. [98] distinguish between different functions of communication (information vs. action) and different orientations (integrative vs. distributive) a negotiator might have. Distributive action refers to all statements that a negotiator makes to claim value, while integrative action aims at creating value by finding win-win situations. Similarly, distributive information strengthens the negotiator's position, while integrative information supports value creation and logrolling by, for example, providing information about preferences. Another classification scheme for communication acts was developed by [94], who distinguish, among others, between information seeking and information sharing statements, arguments, goal statements, offers, relationship statements, procedural statements, and statements displaying emotions.

The use of these different types of communication acts is influenced by the medium used for a negotiation and in turn influences the outcomes of negotiations. A comprehensive survey of the impact of media on process and outcome variables is provided by [39]. These empirical results can inform negotiation support in several ways. First, they can be used to assist negotiators in selecting the best media to use. Not all negotiations involve the same level or type of conflict, such as functional conflicts, in which parties mainly disagree on ways to achieve a common goal, or dysfunctional conflicts, in which parties see each other as adversaries. Different media have different effects in these types of conflict [21]. A support system could advise negotiators on the type of media that is most appropriate for their particular type of conflict.

These types of support could be provided before an actual negotiation begins and mainly would automate checklists that are available in a similar form in the practical negotiation literature. To take a more active role during a negotiation, an NSS needs prescriptive models of "optimal" negotiation processes, and diagnostic tools to evaluate the current status of the negotiation, which then can be compared to the prescriptive model to correct deviations.

Empirical research on communication in negotiations has developed phase models, which describe how the use of different communication acts changes over time during a negotiation, for example, the three-phase model of [55] or the four-phase model of [1]. These models consider the share of different types of communication acts (such as claiming or creating value) over time in a negotiation. Empirical research [35, 46] has shown that these patterns differ significantly between negotiations that end in agreement and failed negotiations, in particular with respect to creating and claiming value. In failed negotiations, the fraction of value claiming activities increases constantly over time, while it decreases in successful negotiations. The converse holds for value creation. If a support system is able to identify such trends, it can inform negotiators about the danger that their negotiation might fail and advise them to change their behavior. Statistical analysis of coded data on negotiation behavior can be used to infer effect sizes of situational characteristics and behavior on outcomes or to predict future behavior from previous patterns [27]. In particular, time series analysis can be performed even on data from a single case (after several rounds), enabling the system to provide support in an ongoing negotiation [27].

To perform this situational diagnosis, the actual messages sent via an electronic system must be mapped to different categories of communication acts defined by theory, such as claiming or creating value. The support system thus needs to "know" which type of communication act a negotiator performs with a given statement, while negotiators communicate in natural language. To a certain extent, this problem can be overcome by semantic enrichment of the communication environment. The NSS Negoisst [110, 111] allows users to classify the messages they send into various types such as question, answer, or offer [112]. Each of these message types has a defined semantic meaning, which also specifies its effect on the substantive dimension of the negotiation. For example, offers are binding, while information provided in the question and answer categories does not become part of the agreement, if one is found at all. However, classification of messages by the parties themselves is obviously limited to certain categories of information; it is unlikely that parties would, e.g., be willing to classify their utterings as "threats."

Text mining could provide a solution to this problem. Sokolova and Szpakowicz [115, 116] used text mining methods to identify communication differences between negotiations that reach an agreement and failed negotiations and were able to achieve a recall (i.e., a correct identification of positive examples) of over 80%. Nastase et al. [97] compared the results of an automatic classification of messages sent in an NSS into classes such as persuasion or affective statements to the classification by human coders and also achieved quite high rates of accuracy, depending on the type of messages. In particular, substantive and affective messages could be distinguished well. Thus, it seems possible that in the long run, an automated recognition of communication patterns could be part of an NSS that warns negotiators when detecting communication patterns that are likely to lead to a failure of the negotiation.

3.3   Emotional Level

Although the early literature on NSS focused mainly on the substantive dimension of the negotiation process, some early authors already recognized the importance of emotions for NSS [e.g., 33]. Emotions have both intra- and interpersonal effects on the behavior of negotiators [50, 87]. Intrapersonal effects refer to the influence of one's own emotions on the behavior of a negotiator, and interpersonal effects to the influence that emotions of one side have on behavior of the other party. The relative strength of intra- and interpersonal effects depends, among others, on the power of a negotiator [100].

Research on emotions in negotiations initially focused on intrapersonal effects. Emotions have an influence on decision making, and therefore it is plausible that the behavior of a negotiator such as concession making is influenced by the negotiator's emotions. This line of research [17, 18] showed that negotiators experiencing positive emotions typically are more cooperative and make larger concessions than negotiators having negative emotions.

More recently, interpersonal effects came into the focus of research. Negative emotions such as anger frequently result in larger concessions from the opponent [127], in particular if the opponent is in a weaker position [114]. Negotiators who communicated in a "warm" and polite way achieved lower economic outcomes [59]. In contrast, [74] found that negotiators who strategically displayed positive emotions were able to extract larger concessions from their opponents.

The effect of emotions depends on situational factors such as time pressure. Surprisingly, emotions such as anger have a stronger effect when negotiators have more time to reflect on their opponent's behavior and are under less pressure to close the negotiation [128]. The EASI (emotions as social information) model by [126] explains the different effects of emotions by distinguishing between affective vs. inferential processing of observed emotions. In affective processing, the negotiator reacts to the perceived emotions of the opponent with an emotional response. This might lead to emotional contagion, for example, a negotiator observing an angry opponent might become angry him- or herself. In inferential processing, the negotiator consciously interprets the opponent's emotions. For example, anger can be interpreted as an indication that the opponent is close to the limits of acceptable outcomes. Therefore, the negotiator facing an angry opponent might respond by making larger concessions to avoid an impasse. Whether affective or inferential processing takes place depends, among others, on situational factors such as time pressure. This could result in a side effect of substantive decision support: if the use of a decision support tool reduces the cognitive load on negotiators, this frees cognitive resources, which then can be used for inferential processing of emotional clues [50]. A broad survey of different effects of emotions on negotiator behavior is given by [99].

Negotiation support systems typically provide text-based communication channels for the negotiators. Compared to face-to-face negotiations, these communication channels are less rich [26]. This raises the question whether emotions can be transmitted and detected across such channels at all. Obviously, negotiators can explicitly refer to their emotional state by statements such as "I am angry about your offer." Such explicit references to emotions occur very rarely in text-based communication [51]. However, messages can be formulated in different ways, which convey different emotions. Empirical research [49, 51] has shown that, e.g., messages about trade-off offers (indicating a concession in one issue and a demand in another issue) contain a clear emotional value.

Any analysis of the emotional dimension of negotiations requires methods to measure and quantify the emotional content of such messages. Emotions can be conceptualized in two different ways: either as discrete emotions such as anger, joy, regret, etc., or in dimensional models, which represent emotional states in two- or three-dimensional coordinate systems. While early studies often used discrete typologies of emotions (and studied, e.g., the impact of anger on concessions), studies that try to infer emotional content from text messages frequently apply a dimensional model of emotions. Frequently used dimensions are the valence of an emotion (positive vs. negative), the level of arousal (intensity), other vs. self-orientation, or submission vs. dominance [49, 51].

Initial studies on the effect of emotions in negotiations such as those on the impact of anger on concessions [17, 18, 127] considered the entire negotiation as the unit of analysis, which [51] refer to as macro-level analysis. For negotiation support, it is necessary to consider emotional patterns over time that could influence the success of a negotiation. Considering different phases of a negotiation in a meso-level analysis shows clear patterns. Most negotiations start with positive emotions but turn to a more negative state in the middle phase. In failed negotiations, this leads to a downward spiral with even more negative emotions in the third phase, while in successful negotiations, the parties manage to return to a positive emotional state [51]. Similar differences can also be observed at the micro level, e.g., in the fairness of offers that negotiators make in response to certain emotions [49].

To provide support with respect to emotions, an NSS must be able to correctly identify the emotional state of negotiators. Most empirical studies on emotions in negotiations used human coders to either directly classify (discrete) emotions or extract dimensional models from ratings via multidimensional scaling [e.g., 51]. Text mining methods have been used successfully to determine the broad emotional content of messages in other contexts such as Facebook postings [76] or the "warmth" of messages sent during a negotiation [59]. Similar tools might also be successful in providing a dimensional classification of emotions in NSS. In contrast, recent studies have indicated that the classification of emotions in text messages using a discrete model does not deliver consistent results even between human coders [81], and there is also no correspondence between the classification of human coders and algorithms.

Since emotions are a rather recent topic in negotiation research, existing NSS mostly do not yet take emotions into account. Some experimental systems added the possibility for users to indicate their emotions in messages via emoticons [42] or by selecting facial expressions [138]. The system by Yuasa et al. [138] also calculated transition probabilities between emotional states but does not include a support component. A similar approach is taken in a system for automated mediation by [139], where participants select actions of figures in a comic representation of a conflict to play out different developments. The actions and messages from which the players can choose are evaluated ex ante according to their emotional content, and the system monitors and guides the parties through different phases of the conflict. The system is intended to educate parties about peaceful solution of conflicts. There are also some attempts to include emotions into the decision models of negotiation agents [e.g., 91], but these systems also do not include any methods to measure the actual emotions of human participants.

A very comprehensive concept of affective NSS was developed by [6]. They use a phase model of negotiations to identify possible functions of an affective NSS in each phase. In their concept, an affective NSS should have the ability to identify the short-term emotions and long-term moods of parties, warn them of emotional developments that would endanger the negotiations, and also advise them in the strategic use of displayed emotions. However, as these authors admit, the technology to actually implement these functions is not yet available.

Gimpel et al. [44] propose a rather different approach. They suggest to measure emotions of negotiators using psychophysical indicators like heart rate and to provide immediate feedback of this data to the negotiators. This information could then be used to reflect on one's own emotional state; to suggest to take a break; or to warn about dangerous developments. They also consider such measurements as useful tools in training to improve the capabilities of negotiators to regulate their emotions. While this approach seems to be quite far-fetched, the increasing popularity of self-monitoring devices such as smart watches indicates that such tools might become acceptable for users.

4 Integrated Perspective

So far, research on negotiations has mostly considered the three dimensions of the ICE framework separately. However, there are a few studies that connect at least two of the dimensions, so the negotiation literature already provides some insights into relationships between these dimensions.

The two dimensions of substantive offers and communication are integral parts of a negotiation process. Several researchers have considered the mutual influences of these two dimensions. In decision making, the fact that different ways of communicating (identical) information can lead to different decisions is often associated with framing biases [124, 125]. For example, if the outcomes of a risky situation are presented as gains, decision makers tend to act in a more risk-averse manner than when the same outcomes are presented as losses. Decision biases such as gain-loss framing and their effect on negotiations are also considered in the negotiation literature [3, 14, 19]. Negotiators in a gain frame behave more risk averse and make more concessions to avoid the risk of failure.

Other types of frames are specific to negotiations, and empirical studies have analyzed their impact on the negotiators' decision making and substantive behavior such as concession making. Trötschel et al. [121] considered the effect of procedural framing. A negotiation problem can be presented to a negotiator either as distributing a resource that the negotiator initially holds or as distributing the opponent's resources. For example, a buyer-seller negotiation could be presented either as allocating the object of the deal (which initially belongs to the seller) or as an allocation of money (which initially belongs to the buyer). Negotiators who frame the problem as a distribution of their own resources make less concessions than negotiators who frame the problem as one of distributing the opponent's resources.

While the concept of framing thus links communication to the substantive dimension of negotiations, creation and manipulation of frames is rarely considered as an explicit type of communication act. A major function of communication in negotiations is to provide arguments for demanding concessions. Although this view directly links communication and substantive behavior, there are only few studies that consider it explicitly. Maaravi et al. [90] studied whether arguments that accompany the initial offer have a positive or negative effect. According to their study, the effect depends on how easy it is to find counterarguments. If arguments supporting an initial offer are easy to counter, that might lead to a tougher counteroffer. On the other hand, if arguments are hard to contradict, they might improve the outcome for the negotiator using them. The role of arguments in electronic negotiations was also studied by [88], who compared their effect in different communication media such as instant messaging and e-mail. They found that when a medium such as instant messages encourages communication at a fast pace, providing complex arguments might overwhelm the opponent and lead to better outcomes for the negotiator who thereby dominates the conversation. In contrast, the effects of dominating the conversation are alleviated if the medium proceeds at a slower pace, which allows each party to reflect more on the arguments.

For research that originated from the perspective of framing biases, it is natural to consider communication as a factor that affects (and sometimes impedes) decision making. Effects in the opposite direction, how substantive behavior influences communication, are studied only rarely. One interesting approach, which is highly relevant for the development of NSS, was followed by [73, 109]. They both argue that if an NSS provides decision support, the system will free cognitive resources of the negotiator, which then can be used to focus on the communication process. However, contrary to expectations, [73] found that negotiators supported by a system that offers DSS capabilities exchange less task-oriented messages and exhibit less tactical behavior. Similarly, [109] found a stronger focus on relationship building (rather than economic goals), but also less concessions, when negotiators use a DSS.

In negotiations performed via electronic media, emotions manifest themselves mainly through communication. Only few studies explicitly considered emotions and communication as two different variables and studied the relationship between these variables. It is often argued that electronic media lead to more uninhibited communication such as flaming, and this behavior is even more likely when parties are angry [62]. However, [62] introduced an important distinction concerning emotions in negotiations. In a negotiation, anger (and consequently flaming) could be directed against the person of the opponent, or against the situation, such as the current offers on the table. Considering communication acts at a finer level of granularity, [87] noted that anger leads to more distributive positional statements and less integrative behavior such as logrolling. A similar effect of negative emotions on value claiming was found by [51].

More research dealt with the impact of emotions on substantive behavior such as concessions. Early studies on emotions such as [127] already noticed that anger causes the opponent to make larger concessions, in particular if the angry negotiator him- or herself makes only small concessions. Similar to the effects of emotions on communication, one has to distinguish between emotions that are directed at the opponent or at the situation [83]. Anger leads to higher concessions from the opponent if it is directed against the offer, while disappointment leads to more concessions if it refers to the person. This effect is moderated by the media used and is stronger for audio communication compared to text messages [60].

Not only negative emotions such as anger or disappointment affect negotiator behavior, but also positive emotions. [60] found a positive effect of positive emotions on the opponent's concessions. In contrast to the effects of negative emotions, this effect seems to be independent of the media type [63]. Positive emotions increase concessions and also lead to fairer and more balanced offers from the opponent [49]. Another factor that seems to moderate the effect of emotions on concessions is power. Powerful negotiators are better able to claim value by showing anger than less powerful negotiators. In contrast, value creation increased when any negotiator in a dyad was angry, irrespective of power.

The relationship between emotions and negotiator behavior is thus a very complex one. Both positive and negative emotions as well as the negotiator's own and the opponent's emotions have an impact on substantive behavior. The situation becomes even more complex when the dynamics of negotiations are taken into account. As [114] have shown, negotiators who behave inconsistently and rapidly move between positive and negative emotions obtain even larger concessions than negotiators who consistently exhibit the same (positive or negative) emotion.

The relationships between all three dimensions of the ICE model were explicitly studied in [36]. This study analyzed the relationship between dimensions across several negotiation phases using the SIPA model of [133]. In contrast to other studies, this study did not find a significant relationship between emotions and substantive behavior. However, significant correlations between communication and emotions were found. The valence of emotions (along the dimension of positive and negative emotions) is positively correlated with the value creating communication and negatively related to value claiming in all phases of a negotiation.

5   Conclusions and Research Topics

Over the past decades, negotiation research has made considerable progress in demonstrating and to a certain extent understanding the complexity of negotiation processes. Negotiations are more than just an exchange of structured offers and substantive arguments explaining them. Given this complexity and the variety of dimensions along which negotiation processes take place, it is not surprising that early attempts at NSS, which only considered the exchange of highly stylized offers, were not successful and research on NSS has obtained little practical relevance [102].

Even though considerable progress has been made, several building blocks for a comprehensive support of negotiations are still missing. Many of the relationships identified in empirical negotiation research are dependent on a multitude of moderating variables such as power, culture, personal characteristics of negotiators, and many more. All these factors need to be included in a coherent framework in order to be able to provide the specific support that a particular negotiator in a given situation would require.

Successful interventions in the process of negotiations require not only a clear understanding of the process and the interdependence of all its variables, but also a prescriptive model of a successful negotiation process. Such models are still missing to a large extent. Empirical research so far has identified some properties of processes that lead to a successful negotiation (e.g., that the emotions return to a positive valence at later stages of the negotiations), but these elements are not yet integrated into an overall model of an "ideal" negotiation process. A prescriptive process model should not only consider each dimension of the negotiation process individually but also their interactions. The effects of coherence (or a lack thereof) on negotiation outcomes are still an open question. For example, it is not clear whether comparatively large concessions at the substantive level are more or less effective if they are accompanied by integrative or distributive communication behavior.

A negotiation process takes place in different, interacting dimensions, and it also generates different types of outcomes. Existing NSS follow the tradition of DSS and focus mainly on quantifiable, economic outcomes. Negotiations also have relationship outcomes, which eventually also might lead to economic effects in the implementation phase, and many negotiation tactics have opposite effects on these two outcome dimensions. A comprehensive negotiation support system should enable users to identify possible trade-offs between outcome dimensions and assist them in striking the optimal balance.

Thus, there are many conceptual issues in the development of NSS that need to be resolved by close cooperation between (empirical) research in negotiations and the developers of such systems. On the one hand, existing empirical research on negotiations can inform the development of NSS and future research could explicitly consider questions that are of importance for the development of negotiation support systems. On the other hand, technological developments can help negotiation research to obtain new insights. Innovative methods of text mining and machine learning can help to automate many of the encoding tasks that are now performed manually in researching communication and emotions in negotiations. Even technologies developed for health monitoring could be used for the latter purpose.

While the original idea of negotiation support systems has been developed more than 30 years ago, the intersection between the two fields of negotiation research and decision support has been smaller than it could have been. It is time for both fields to take a closer look at the progress the other field has made in the past decades and to identify new topics for fruitful collaboration.

References

1. Adair, W., & Brett, J. (2005). The negotiation dance: Time, culture, and behavioral sequences in negotiation. *Organization Science, 16*(1), 33–51.
2. Agrawal, M., & Chari, K. (2020). Negotiation behaviors in agent-based negotiation support systems. *International Journal of Intelligent Information Technologies, 5*(1), 1–23.
3. Bazerman, M. H., & Neale, M. A. (1983). Heuristics in negotiation: Limits to effective dispute resolution. In M. H. Bazerman & R. J. Lewicki (Eds.), *Negotiating in Organizations* (pp. 51–67). Beverly Hills: Sage.
4. Bellucci, E., & Zeleznikow, J. (2001). Representations of decision-making support in negotiation. *Journal of Decision Systems, 10*(3–4), 449–479.
5. Bishop, R. L. (1964). A Zeuthen-Hicks theory of bargaining. *Econometrica, 32*, 410–417.
6. Broekens, J., Jonker, C., & Meyer, J.-J. (2010). Affective negotiation support systems. *Journal of Ambient Intelligence and Smart Environments, 2*(2), 121–144.
7. Bronisz, P., Krus, L., & Wierzbicki, A. P. (1988). Towards interactive solutions in a bargaining problem. In A. Lewandowski & A. Wierzbicki (Eds.), *Aspiration Based Decision Support Systems* (pp. 251–268). Berlin: Springer.
8. Brzostowski, J., & Wachowicz, T. (2014). Negomanage: A system for supporting bilateral negotiations. *Group Decision and Negotiation, 23*(3), 463–496.
9. Buffett, S., Comeau, L., Spencer, B., & Fleming, M. W. (2006). Detecting opponent concessions in multi-issue automated negotiation. *ICEC06* (pp. 11–18)
10. Buffett, S., & Spencer, B. (2007). A Bayesian classifier for learning opponents' preferences in multi-object automated negotiation. *Electronic Commerce Research and Applications, 6*, 274–284.
11. Bui, T. X., & Jarke, M. (1986). Communications design for Co-oP: A group decision support system. *ACM Transactions on Office Information Systems, 4*, 81–103.
12. Bui, T. X., & Shakun, M. F. (1996). Negotiation processes, evolutionary systems design, and NEGOTIATOR. *Group Decision and Negotiation, 5*(4), 339–353.

13. Cakravastia, A,. & Nakamura, N. (2002). Model for negotiating the price and due date for a single order with multiple suppliers in a make-to-order environment. *International Journal of Production Research, 40*(14), 3425–3440.
14. Caputo, A. (2013). A literature review of cognitive biases in negotiation processes. *International Journal of Conflict Management, 24*(4), 374–398.
15. Carbonneau, R. A., Kersten, G. E., & Vahidov, R. M. (2010). Pairwise issue modeling for negotiation counteroffer prediction using neural networks. *Decision Support Systems, 50*(2), 449–459.
16. Carbonneau, R. A., & Vahidov, R. M. (2014). A utility concession curve data fitting model for quantitative analysis of negotiation styles. *Expert Systems with Applications, 41*(9), 4035–4042.
17. Carnevale, P. J. (2008). Positive affect and decision frame in negotiation. *Group Decision and Negotiation, 17*, 51–63.
18. Carnevale, P. J., & Isen, A. M. (1986). The influence of positive affect and visual access on the discovery of integrative solutions in bilateral negotiation. *Organizational Behavior and Human Decision Processes, 37*(1), 1–13.
19. Chang, L., Cheng, M., & Trotman, K. T. (2008). The effect of framing and negotiation partner's objective on judgments about negotiated transfer prices. *Accounting, Organizations and Society, 33*, 704–717.
20. Chen, E., Vahidov, R., & Kersten, G. E. (2005). Agent-supported negotiations in the e-marketplace. *International Journal of Electronic Business, 3*(1):28–49.
21. Chen, I. S., & Tseng, F.-T. (2016). The relevance of communication media in conflict contexts and their effectiveness: A negotiation experiment. *Computers in Human Behavior, 59*(Supplement C), 134–141.
22. Chertkoff, J. M., & Conley, M. (1967). Opening offer and frequency of concession as bargaining strategies. *Journal of Personality & Social Psychology, 7*(2), 181–185.
23. Climaco, J. N., & Dias, L. C. (2006). An approach to support negotiation processes with imprecise information multicriteria additive models. *Group Decision and Negotiation, 15*, 171–184.
24. Curhan, J., Elfenbein, H., & Kilduff, G. (2009). Getting off on the right foot: Subjective value versus economic value in predicting longitudinal job outcomes from job offer negotiations. *Journal of Applied Psychology, 94*(2), 524–534.
25. Daft, R. L., Lengel, R., & Trevino, L. (1987). Message equivocality, media selection, and manager performance: Implications for information systems. *Management Information System Quarterly, 11*, 354–366.
26. Daft, R. L., & Lengel, R. H. (1986). Organizational information requirements, media richness and structural design. *Management Science, 32*(5), 554–571.
27. Druckman, D. (1993). Statistical analysis for negotiation support. *Theory and Decision, 34*(3), 215–233.
28. Druckman, D., & Wagner, L. M. (2016). Justice and negotiation. *Annual Review of Psychology, 67*(1), 387–413.
29. Ehtamo, H., & Hämäläinen, R. P. (2001). Interactive multiple-criteria methods for reaching Pareto optimal agreements in negotiations. *Group Decision and Negotiation, 10*(6), 475–491.
30. Ehtamo, H., Verkama, M., & Hämäläinen, R. P. (1999). How to select fair improving directions in a negotiation model over continuous issues. *IEEE Transactions on Systems, Man, and Cybernetics – Part C: Applications and Reviews, 29*(1), 26–33.
31. Espinasse, B., Picolet, G., & Chouraqui, E. (1997). Negotiation support systems: A multi-criteria and multi-agent approach. *European Journal of Operational Research, 103*, 389–409.
32. Faratin, P., Sierra, C., & Jennings, N. R. (1998). Negotiation decision functions for autonomous agents. *Robotics and Autonomous Systems, 24*, 159–182.
33. Faure, G. O., Le Dong, V., & Shakun, M. F. (1990). Social-emotional aspects of negotiation. *European Journal of Operational Research, 46*, 177–180.
34. Filzmoser, M., & Gettinger, J. R. (2019). Offer and veto: An experimental comparison of two negotiation procedures. *EURO Journal on Decision Processes, 7*(1), 83–99.

35. Filzmoser, M., Hippmann, P., & Vetschera, R. (2014). Multidimensional analysis of negotiation processes. In P. Zaraté, G. Camilleri, D. Kamassoko, & F. Ambalard (Eds.), *Proceedings, Group Decision and Negotiation 2014* (pp. 8–15).
36. Filzmoser, M., Hippmann, P., & Vetschera, R. (2016). Analyzing the multiple dimensions of negotiation processes. *Group Decision and Negotiation, 25*, 1169–1188.
37. Filzmoser, M., & Vetschera, R. (2008). A classification of bargaining steps and their impact on negotiation outcomes. *Group Decision and Negotiation, 17*(5), 421–443.
38. Galinsky, A. D., & Mussweiler, T. (2001). First offers as anchors: The role of perspective-taking and negotiator focus. *Journal of Personality and Social Psychology, 81*(4), 657–669.
39. Geiger, I. (2020). From letter to Twitter: A systematic review of communication media in negotiation. *Group Decision and Negotiation, 29*(2), 207–250.
40. Gettinger, J., Filzmoser, M., & Koeszegi, S. T. (2016). Why can't we settle again? Analysis of factors that influence agreement prospects in the post-settlement phase. *Journal of Business Economics, 86*(4), 413–440.
41. Gettinger, J., & Koeszegi, S. T. (2014). Far from eye, far from heart: Analysis of graphical decision aids in electronic negotiation support. *Group Decision and Negotiation, 23*(4), 787–817.
42. Gettinger, J., & Koeszegi, S. T. (2015). More than words: The effect of emoticons in electronic negotiations. In B. Kamiński, G. E. Kersten, & T. Szapiro (Eds.), *Outlooks and Insights on Group Decision and Negotiation* (pp. 289–305). Cham: Springer International Publishing.
43. Gettinger, J., Koeszegi, S. T., & Schoop, M. (2012). Shall we dance?—The effect of information presentations on negotiation processes and outcomes. *Decision Support Systems, 53*(1), 161–174.
44. Gimpel, H., Adam, M., Philipp, P. T., & Teubner, T. (2013). Emotion regulation in management: Harnessing the potential of NeuroIS tools. In *ECIS 2013 Research in Progress.*
45. Giordano, G. A., Stoner, J. S., Brouer, R. L., & George, J. F. (2007). The influences of deception and computer-mediation on dyadic negotiations. *Journal of Computer-Mediated Communication, 12*(2), 362–383.
46. Goering, E. M. (1997). Integration versus distribution in contract negotiations: An interaction analysis of strategy use. *The Journal of Business Communication, 34*(4), 383–400.
47. Gouldner, A. W. (1960). The norm of reciprocity: A preliminary statement. *American Sociological Review, 25*(2), 161–178.
48. Greenhalgh, L., & Chapman, D. (1998). Negotiator relationships: Construct measurement, and demonstration of their impact on the process and outcomes of negotiation. *Group Decision and Negotiation, 7*(6), 465–489.
49. Griessmair, M. (2017). Ups and downs: Emotional dynamics in negotiations and their effects on (in)equity. *Group Decision and Negotiation, 26*(6), 1061–1090.
50. Griessmair, M., Hippmann, P., & Gettinger, J. (2015). Emotions in e-negotiations. In B. Martinovsky (Ed.), *Emotion in Group Decision and Negotiation* (pp. 101–135). Dordrecht: Springer.
51. Griessmair, M., & Koeszegi, S. (2009). Exploring the cognitive-emotional fugue in electronic negotiations. *Group Decision and Negotiation, 18*(3), 213–234.
52. Harsanyi, J. C. (1956). Approaches to the bargaining problem before and after the theory of games: A critical discussion of Zeuthen's, Hicks', and Nash's theories. *Econometrica, 24*(2), 144–157.
53. Hatta, T., Ohbuchi, K., & Fukuno, M. (2007). An experimental study on the effects of exitability and correctability on electronic negotiation. *Negotiation Journal, 23*, 283–305.
54. Hindriks, K., Jonker, C. M., & Tykhonov, D. (2007). Negotiation dynamics: Analysis, concession tactics, and outcomes. In T. Y. T. Lin, J. M. Bradshaw, M. Klusch, C. Zhang, A. Broder, & H. Ho (Eds.), *Proceedings of the 2007 IEEE/WIC/ACM International Conference on Intelligent Agent Technology* (pp. 427–433). Washington: IEEE Computer Society.
55. Holmes, M. E. (1992). Phase structures in negotiation. In L. L. Putnam & M. E. Roloff (Eds.), *Communication and negotiation* (pp. 83–105). Newbury Park: Sage.

56. Jarke, M. (1986). Knowledge sharing and negotiation support in multiperson decision support systems. *Decision Support Systems, 2*(1), 93–102.
57. Jarke, M., Jelassi, M. T., & Shakun, M. F. (1987). Mediator: Towards a negotiation support system. *European Journal of Operational Research, 31*(3), 314–334.
58. Jelassi, M. T., & Foroughi, A. (1989). Negotiation support system: An overview of design issues and existing software. *Decision Support Systems, 5*(2), 167–181.
59. Jeong, M., Minson, J., Yeomans, M., & Gino, F. (2019). Communicating with warmth in distributive negotiations is surprisingly counterproductive. *Management Science, 65*(12), 5813–5837.
60. Johnson, N. A., & Cooper, R. B. (2009a). Media, affect, concession, and agreement in negotiation: IM versus telephone. *Decision Support Systems, 46*, 673–684.
61. Johnson, N. A., & Cooper, R. B. (2009b). Power and concession in computer-mediated negotiations: An examination of first offers. *MIS Quarterly, 33*(1), 147–170.
62. Johnson, N. A., Cooper, R. B., & Chin, W. W. (2009). Anger and flaming in computer-mediated negotiation among strangers. *Decision Support Systems, 46*, 660–672.
63. Johnson, N. A., Cooper, R. B., & Holowczak, R. D. (2016). The impact of media on how positive, negative, and neutral communicated affect influence unilateral concessions during negotiations. *European Journal of Information Systems, 25*(5), 391–410.
64. Kersten, G., & Noronha, S. (1999). WWW-based negotiation support: Design, implementation, and use. *Decision Support Systems, 25*(2), 135–154.
65. Kersten, G., & Szapiro, T. (1986). Generalized approach to modeling negotiations. *European Journal of Operational Research, 26*, 142–149.
66. Kersten, G. E., & Lai, H. (2007). Negotiation support and e-negotiation systems: An overview. *Group Decision and Negotiation, 16*(6), 553–586.
67. Kersten, G. E., & Mallory, G. R. (1999). Rational inefficient compromises in negotiations. *Journal of Multi-criteria Decision Analysis, 8*(2), 106–111.
68. Kersten, G. E., Michalowski, W., Matwin, S., & Szpakowicz, S. (1988). Representing the negotiation process with a rule-based formalism. *Theory and Decision, 25*(3), 225–257.
69. Kersten, G. E., Michalowski, W., Szpakowicz, S., & Koperczak, Z. (1991). Restructurable representations of negotiation. *Management Science, 37*(10), 1269–1290.
70. Kersten, G. E., Vahidov, R., & Gimon, D. (2013). Concession-making in multi-attribute auctions and multi-bilateral negotiations: Theory and experiments. *Electronic Commerce Research and Applications, 12*, 166–180.
71. Kilgour, D. M., Chen, Y., & Hipel, K. W. (2010). Multiple criteria approaches to group decision and negotiation. In M. Ehrgott, J. Figueira, & S. Greco (Eds.), *Trends in Multiple Criteria Decision Analysis* (pp. 317–338). Berlin: Springer.
72. Kilgour, D. M., & Eden, C. (2010). Introduction to the handbook of group decision and negotiation. In D. M. Kilgour & C. Eden (Eds.), *Handbook of Group Decision and Negotiation* (pp. 1–7). Dordrecht: Springer.
73. Koeszegi, S., Srnka, K., & Pesendorfer, E.-M. (2006). Electronic negotiations – a comparison of different support systems. *Die Betriebswirtschaft, 66*(4), 441–463.
74. Kopelman, S., Rosette, A. S., & Thompson, L. (2006). The three faces of Eve: Strategic displays of positive, negative, and neutral emotions in negotiations. *Organizational Behavior and Human Decision Processes, 99*, 81–101.
75. Korhonen, P., Moskowitz, H., Wallenius, J., & Zionts, S. (1986). An interactive approach to multiple criteria optimization with multiple decision-makers. *Naval Research Logistics Quarterly, 33*, 589–602.
76. Kramer, A. D. I., Guillory, J. E., & Hancock, J. T. (2014). Experimental evidence of massive-scale emotional contagion through social networks. *Proceedings of the National Academy of Sciences, 111*(24), 8788–8790.
77. Kruś, L. (2015). Supporting cooperative decisions with a multicriteria generalization of the Nash solution. In M. Núñez, N. T. Nguyen, D. Camacho, & B. Trawiński (Eds.), *Computational Collective Intelligence* (pp. 193–202). Cham: Springer International Publishing.

78. Kuula, M., & Stam, A. (2008). A win–win method for multi-party negotiation support. *International Transactions in Operational Research, 15*(6), 717–737.
79. Kwon, S., & Weingart, L. R. (2004). Unilateral concessions from the other party: Concession behavior, attributions, and negotiation judgments. *Journal of Applied Psychology, 89*(2), 263–278.
80. Lai, G., & Sycara, K. (2009). A generic framework for automated multi-attribute negotiation. *Group Decision and Negotiation, 18*, 169–187.
81. Laubert, C., & Parlamis, J. (2019). Are you angry (happy, sad) or aren't you? Emotion detection difficulty in email negotiation. *Group Decision and Negotiation, 28*(2), 377–413.
82. Lee, C. C., & Ou-Yang, C. (2009). A neural networks approach for forecasting the supplier's bid prices in supplier selection negotiation process. *Expert Systems with Applications, 36*(2, Part 2), 2961–2970.
83. Lelieveld, G.-J., Van Dijk, E., Van Beest, I., Steinel, W., & Van Kleef, G. A. (2011). Disappointed in you, angry about your offer: Distinct negative emotions induce concessions via different mechanisms. *Journal of Experimental Social Psychology, 47*(3), 635–641.
84. Lempp, F. (2016). A logic-based model for resolving conflicts. *International Journal of Conflict Management, 27*(1), 116–139.
85. Lempp, F. (2017). A software implementation and case study application of Lempp's propositional model of conflict resolution. *International Journal of Conflict Management, 28*(5), 563–591.
86. Lim, L.-H., & Benbasat, I. (1992). A theoretical perspective of negotiation support systems. *Journal of Management Information Systems, 9*(3), 27–44.
87. Liu, M. (2009). The intrapersonal and interpersonal effects of anger on negotiation strategies: A cross-cultural investigation. *Human Communication Research, 35*, 148–169.
88. Loewenstein, J., Morris, M. W., Chakravarti, A., Thompson, L., & Kopelman, S. (2005). At a loss for words: Dominating the conversation and the outcome in negotiation as a function of intricate arguments and communication media. *Organizational Behavior and Human Decision Processes, 98*(1), 28–38.
89. Lootsma, F. (1989). Conflict resolution via pairwise comparison of concessions. *European Journal of Operational Research, 40*, 109–116.
90. Maaravi, Y., Ganzach, Y., & Pazy, A. (2011). Negotiation as a form of persuasion: Arguments in first offers. *Journal of Personality and Social Psychology, 101*(2), 245–255.
91. Marreiros, G., Santos, R., Ramos, C., & Neves, J. (2010). Context-aware emotion-based model for group decision making. *IEEE Intelligent Systems, 25*(2), 31–39.
92. Meng, B., & Fu, W. (2004). A negotiation model based on fuzzy multiple criteria decision making method. In *Fourth International Conference on Computer and Information Technology (CIT'04)*.
93. Min, H., LaTour, M. S., & Jones, M. A. (1995). Negotiation outcomes: The impact of the initial offer, time, gender, and team size. *International Journal of Purchasing and Materials Management, 31*(4), 19–24.
94. Moore, D. A., Kurtzberg, T. R., Thompson, L. L., & Morris, M. W. (1999). Long and short routes to success in electronically mediated negotiations: Group affiliations and good vibrations. *Organizational Behavior and Human Decision Processes, 77*(1), 22–43.
95. Morris, M., Nadler, J., Kurtzberg, T., & Thompson, L. (2002). Schmooze or lose: Social friction and lubrication in e-mail negotiations. *Group Dynamics: Theory, Research, and Practice, 6*(1), 89.
96. Nastase, V. (2006). Concession curve analysis for Inspire negotiations. *Group Decision and Negotiation, 15*, 185–193.
97. Nastase, V., Koeszegi, S., & Szpakowicz, S. (2007). Content analysis through the machine learning mill. *Group Decision and Negotiation, 16*(4), 335–346.
98. Olekalns, M., Brett, J. M., & Weingart, L. R. (2003). Phases, transitions and interruptions: Modeling processes in multi-party negotiations. *International Journal of Conflict Management, 14*(3/4), 191–211.

99. Olekalns, M., & Druckman, D. (2014). With feeling: How emotions shape negotiation. *Negotiation Journal, 30*(4), 455–478.
100. Overbeck, J. R., Neale, M. A., & Govan, C. L. (2010). I feel, therefore you act: Intrapersonal and interpersonal effects of emotion on negotiation as a function of social power. *Organizational Behavior and Human Decision Processes, 112*, 126–139.
101. Parks, C. D., & Komorita, S. S. (1998). Reciprocity research and its implications for the negotiation process. *International Negotiation, 3*, 151–169.
102. Pervan, G. P., & Arnott, D. (2014). Issues and strategies for group and negotiation support systems research. *International Journal of Decision Support System Technology (IJDSST), 6*(4), 49–66.
103. Pesendorfer, E.-M., & Koeszegi, S. (2006). Hot versus cool behavioural styles in electronic negotiations: The impact of communication mode. *Group Decision and Negotiation, 15*, 141–155.
104. Raiffa, H. (1982). *The Art and Science of Negotiation.* Cambridge, MA/London: Belknap.
105. Rangaswamy, A., & Shell, G. (1997). Using computers to realize joint gains in negotiations: Toward an "Electronic bargaining table". *Management Science, 43*(8), 1147–1163.
106. Roszkowska, E., & Wachowicz, T. (2015). Application of fuzzy TOPSIS to scoring the negotiation offers in ill-structured negotiation problems. *European Journal of Operational Research, 242*(3), 920–932.
107. Rubinstein, A. (1982). Perfect equilibrium in a bargaining model. *Econometrica, 50*(1), 97–109.
108. Savage, G. T., Blair, J. D., & Sorenson, R. L. (1989). Consider both relationships and substance when negotiating strategically. *The Academy of Management Executive, 3*(1), 37–48.
109. Schoop, M., Amelsvoort, M., Gettinger, J., Koerner, M., Koeszegi, S., & van der Wijst, P. (2014). The interplay of communication and decisions in electronic negotiations: Communicative decisions or decisive communication? *Group Decision and Negotiation, 23*(2), 167–192.
110. Schoop, M., Jertila, A., & List, T. (2003). Negoisst: A negotiation support system for electronic business-to-business negotiations in e-commerce. *Data and Knowledge Engineering, 47*(3), 371–401.
111. Schoop, M., Köhne, F., & Staskiewicz, D. (2004). An integrated decision and communication perspective on electronic negotiation support systems. *Journal of Decision Systems, 13*(4), 375–398.
112. Schoop, M., & Quix, C. (2001). Doc.com: A framework for effective negotiation support in electronic marketplaces. *Computer Networks, 37*(2), 153–170.
113. Seo, F. (1985). Multiattribute utility analysis and collective choice: A methodological review. In Y. Y. Haimes, & V. Chankong (Eds.), *Decision Making with Multiple Objectives* (pp. 170–189). Berlin: Springer.
114. Sinaceur, M., & Tiedens, L. Z. (2006). Get mad and get more than even: When and why anger expression is effective in negotiations. *Journal of Experimental Social Psychology, 42*(3), 314–322.
115. Sokolova, M., & Szpakowicz, S. (2005). Analysis and classification of strategies in electronic negotiations. In B. Kégl, & G. Lapalme (Eds.), *Advances in Artificial Intelligence* (pp. 145–157). Berlin/Heidelberg: Springer.
116. Sokolova, M., & Szpakowicz, S. (2007). Strategies and language trends in learning success and failure of negotiation. *Group Decision and Negotiation, 16*, 469–484.
117. Swaab, R. I., Postmes, T., Neijens, P., Kiers, M. H., & Dumay, A. C. (2002). Multiparty negotiation support: The role of visualization's influence on the development of shared mental models. *Journal of Management Information Systems, 19*(1), 129–150.
118. Teich, J., Wallenius, H., & Wallenius, J. (1994). Advances in negotiation science. *Transactions on Operational Research, 6*, 55–94.
119. Thompson, L., & Nadler, J. (2002). Negotiating via information technology: Theory and application. *Journal of Social Studies, 58*(1), 109–124.

120. Tripp, T. M., & Sondak, H. (1992). An evaluation of dependent variables in experimental negotiation studies: Impasse rates and Pareto efficiency. *Organizational Behavior and Human Decision Processes, 51*, 273–295.

121. Trötschel, R., Loschelder, D. D., Höhne, B. P., & Majer, J. M. (2015). Procedural frames in negotiations: How offering my resources versus requesting yours impacts perception, behavior, and outcomes. *Journal of Personality and Social Psychology, 108*(3), 417–435.

122. Tutzauer, F. (1993). Toughness in integrative bargaining. *Journal of Communication, 43*(1), 46–62.

123. Tutzauer, F., & Roloff, M. E. (1988). Communication processes leading to integrative agreements – three paths to joint benefits. *Communication Research, 15*(4), 360–380.

124. Tversky, A., & Kahneman, D. (1974). Judgement under uncertainty: Heuristics and biases. *Science, 185*, 1124–1131.

125. Tversky, A., & Kahneman, D. (1986). Rational choice and the framing of decisions. *Journal of Business, 59*(4), 251–278.

126. van Kleef, G. A. (2009). How emotions regulate social life: The emotions as social information (EASI) model. *Current Directions in Psychological Science, 18*(3), 184–188.

127. van Kleef, G. A., De Dreu, C. K. W., & Manstead, A. S. R. (2004a). The interpersonal effects of anger and happiness in negotiations. *Journal of Personality and Social Psychology, 86*(1), 57–76.

128. van Kleef, G. A., De Dreu, C. K. W., & Manstead, A. S. R. (2004b). The interpersonal effects of emotions in negotiations: A motivated information processing approach. *Journal of Personality and Social Psychology, 87*(4), 510–528.

129. van Poucke, D., & Buelens, M. (2002). Predicting the outcome of a two-party price negotiation: Contribution of reservation price, aspiration price and opening offer. *Journal of Economic Psychology, 23*(1), 67–76.

130. Vetschera, R. (1990). Group decision and negotiation support – A methodological survey. *OR Spektrum, 12*(2), 67–77.

131. Vetschera, R. (2007). Preference structures and negotiator behavior in electronic negotiations. *Decision Support Systems, 44*(1), 135–146.

132. Vetschera, R. (2013). Negotiation processes: An integrated perspective. *Euro Journal on Decision Processes, 1*(1–2), 135–164.

133. Vetschera, R., & Filzmoser, M. (2012). Standardized interpolated path analysis of offer processes in e-negotiations. *International Conference on Electronic Commerce ICEC 2012* (pp. 134–140).

134. Vetschera, R., Filzmoser, M., & Mitterhofer, R. (2014). An analytical approach to offer generation in concession-based negotiation processes. *Group Decision and Negotiation, 23*, 71–99.

135. Wachowicz, T. (2010). Decision support in software supported negotiations. *Journal of Business Economics and Management, 11*(4), 576–597.

136. Womack, D. F. (1990). Communication and negotiation. In D. O'Hair & G. L. Kreps (Eds.), *Applied Communication Theory and Research* (pp. 77–101). Hillsdale: Lawrence Erlbaum.

137. Yuan, Y., Head, M., & Du, M. (2003). The effects of multimedia communication on web-based negotiation. *Group Decision and Negotiation, 12*(2), 89–109.

138. Yuasa, M., Yasumura, Y., & Nitta, K. (2001). A negotiation support tool using emotional factors. In *Proceedings Joint 9th IFSA World Congress and 20th NAFIPS International Conference (Cat. No. 01TH8569)* (Vol. 5, pp. 2906–2911).

139. Zancanaro, M., Stock, O., Schiavo, G., Cappelletti, A., Gehrmann, S., Canetti, D., Shaked, O., Fachter, S., Yifat, R., Mimran, R., & Weiss, P. L. T. (2020). Evaluating an automated mediator for joint narratives in a conflict situation. *Behaviour & Information Technology, 39*(9), 1022–1037.

140. Zandi, F., & Tavana, M. (2012). A fuzzy e-negotiation support system for inter-firm collaborative product development. *International Journal of Computer Integrated Manufacturing, 25*(8), 671–688.

From Data and Models to Decision Support Systems: Lessons and Advice for the Future

Marko Bohanec

Abstract Model-based Decision Support Systems (DSSs) employ various types of models, such as statistical, optimization, simulation, or rule-based. Models are used to assess and analyze the given decision situation, and on this basis advise the decision-maker. Generally, the DSS development process involves three steps: (1) model development, (2) implementing the model(s) in a DSS, and (3) using the DSS. In this chapter, we focus on two model development approaches: Data Mining and Expert Modeling. We advocate for combing the two in order to get better models and better DSSs in general. We illustrate some points and potential pitfalls using an example of the PD_manager DSS, which is aimed at supporting medication change decisions in the management of Parkinson's disease. Based on the experience from PD_manager and some other DSS development projects, we propose the so-called 5C requirements for better DSS models: correctness, completeness, consistency, comprehensibility, and convenience. Finally, we summarize the lessons learned and give advice to DSS developers and researchers.

Keywords Decision support system · Model-based DSS · Model development · Decision model · Data mining · Machine learning · Expert modeling · 5C Requirements · Method DEX · Decision trees

M. Bohanec (✉)
Department of Knowledge Technologies, Jožef Stefan Institute, Ljubljana, Slovenia

University of Nova, Gorica, Slovenia
e-mail: marko.bohanec@ijs.si

© Springer Nature Switzerland AG 2021
J. Papathanasiou et al. (eds.), *EURO Working Group on DSS*, Integrated Series in Information Systems, https://doi.org/10.1007/978-3-030-70377-6_11

1 Introduction

During the last 20 years, the author of this chapter was involved in a number of European projects[1] whose goal was, among others, to develop some kind of a *decision support system* (DSS). The projects were diverse and addressed different decision problems. There was a series of four projects (called ECOGEN, SIGMEA, Co-Extra, and DECATHLON) concerned with agricultural food production and supply chains involving genetically modified crops. More recently, there were two projects (PD_manager and HeartMan) aimed at supporting the management of chronic diseases: the Parkinson's disease and congestive heart failure, respectively. The remaining projects addressed data mining and decision support for business competitiveness (Sol-Eu-Net) and financial decision-making (FIRST).

In all these projects, we employed the concept of *model-based* (or *model-driven*) DSS [1]. Such DSSs employ various types of models, such as statistical, optimization, simulation, or rule-based. Models are used to assess and analyze the given decision situation, and on this basis advise the decision-maker. In most of the mentioned projects, we developed models using the method DEX [2, 3]. DEX (Decision EXpert) is a multi-criteria decision modeling method that represents decision criteria in a form of hierarchically structured qualitative attributes. Decision problem requirements and decision-maker's preferences are represented by decision rules. The development of DEX models is supported by free software DEXi [4].

In the above-mentioned projects, we often combined DEX with *Machine Learning* and *Data Mining* methods, which are capable of developing decision models from data, for instance, from examples of past decisions or from results of simulations.

In this chapter, we investigate three critical steps of DSS development using the model-based approach. The first step is *developing* a model or multiple models, which eventually become "the heart" of the DSS that governs its decision-analytic tasks. There are numerous requirements that have to be fulfilled so that the model development is feasible and that the obtained model is "fit for purpose" for the considered decision problem. But there is also the second step, which is often overlooked, particularly in research literature: *implementing* and *embedding* the model in the DSS, thus making the DSS "useful for the user(s)." The model itself does not make a DSS, it only constitutes one of its parts. In the third stage, the implemented DSS is put in operation to be used by one or more end-users.

In this chapter, we highlight the possible pitfalls of and requirements for these three stages, present lessons learnt and formulate advice for DSS model developers and researchers. But before going there, we first define some basic terms and concepts and introduce an illustrative use-case.

---

[1] Please see http://kt.ijs.si/MarkoBohanec/mare.html for more information about these projects.

2 Basic Definitions and Concepts

2.1 Decision Support Systems

Power [1] defines a *decision support system* as:

> an interactive computer-based system or subsystem intended to help decision makers use communications technologies, data, documents, knowledge, and/or models to identify and solve problems, complete decision process tasks, and make decisions. Decision support system is a general term for any computer application that enhances a person or group's ability to make decisions.

This definition raises two points, important for the aim of this chapter. First, it mentions *decision-makers*, who use technologies to accomplish their decision-making tasks. This indicates that DSSs are concerned with *human decision-making*. DSSs are not supposed to make decision on their own, but rather to *support* their *users* (e.g., managers, experts, patients) by providing *useful* information to them, and possibly supporting an *active user-initiated exploration* of relevant information, possible *solutions,* and expected *consequences* of decisions. So, whenever developing a DSS, we should always consider the DSS' *users* and their needs.

There are classes of DSSs aimed at finding or generating some kind of a "best decision," usually according to some criteria and by means of data analysis, search, simulation, or optimization. Even in these cases we consider such solutions only as *suggestions*, which are presented to the user for further deliberation. It is the DSS user who is expected to make the final decision and bear its consequences. In this understanding, DSSs are different from *decision systems* or *automation systems*, which are concerned with *machine decision-making* and make decisions on their own. Such systems are often associated with Artificial Intelligence (AI) and involve machines such as robots, space probes, and autonomous vehicles.

The second important aspect of the above definition is that it mentions the main approaches and technologies that are commonly used by the DSSs. These are further elaborated in the expanded framework for specifying and classifying DSS ([1], p. 37); the framework defines five main DSS types, which are driven by: communications, data, documents, knowledge, and models. In this chapter, we focus on *model-driven* and *knowledge-driven* DSS. We also consider *data*, but not from the viewpoint of data-driven DSS (which typically present data to the user and facilitate data analysis tasks), but rather as a source for developing models to be used in model-driven DSS.

2.2 Model-Driven, Knowledge-Driven, and Model-Based DSS

According to Power [1], a *model-driven* DSS provides access to and manipulation of a quantitative model, which is typically used for tasks such as "what-if" analysis, creating and managing scenarios, goal seeking, and value elicitation. A *knowledge-*

driven DSS suggests or recommends actions to targeted users; other terms used for this purpose include advisory systems, consultation systems, suggestion systems, knowledge-based systems, recommender systems, rule-based DSS, and management expert systems ([1], p. 45). Knowledge-driven DSS are often associated with AI, as they involve concepts, developed in that discipline, such as expert systems, rule-based systems, and machine learning.

The model-driven and knowledge-driven DSS are often difficult to tell apart. The reason is that both types contain one or more *models*, either quantitative or qualitative, simulation or optimization, etc. Each model represents some aspect of reality, relevant for the addressed decision problem. Human *knowledge* is required in order to develop and run the model, regardless of its type. Thus, many DSSs can be simultaneously categorized as model-driven and knowledge-driven. To alleviate the dilemma, we prefer using the term *model-based* DSS, in the sense which includes both types.

2.3   *Model and Model Development*

Model is a term with many meanings. Here, we take the viewpoint of *business analytics* [5] and define *model* as an abstraction of a real problem, which tries to capture its essence and key features. A model is developed to represent the decision problem, facilitate logical analysis, and prescribe a recommended course of action. In Decision Analysis, the most common model types are decision trees, Markov models, Bayesian models, Bayesian networks, influence diagrams, and multi-criteria models.

There are several possible ways of developing a decision model for a DSS. Probably, the easiest case is when the model has already been developed, for instance, when available in the literature or via internet. We can say from experience that such cases are extremely rare and, even if some model has been already developed, it has to be substantially adapted for the problem at hand. In most cases, it is thus necessary to develop the model from the scratch. There are two prevailing approaches:

1. From *data*, using some statistical [6], machine learning and/or data mining method [7] (Fig. 1);
2. By *expert modeling*, i.e., "hand-crafting" the models in collaboration of decision-maker and experts (and possibly using some suitable model development tools) (Fig. 2).

Nowadays, in the times of abundant data and powerful data analysis algorithms, the first approach is usually preferred (Fig. 1). The idea is to employ a data base of events or decisions that had occurred in the past. This data is investigated for possible patterns or regularities, and one or more models are developed that (1) describe those regularities and can (2) make future predictions, suggestions, or decisions in new situations. Typical model representations include decision trees,

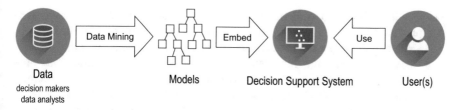

Fig. 1 Development of DSS models from data

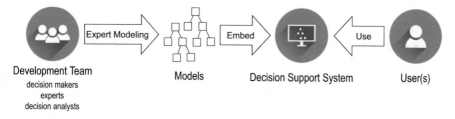

Fig. 2 Development of DSS models by expert modeling

decision rules, association rules, Bayesian models, support vector machines, or neural networks. In principle, this approach promises an automated development of models, which is quick, efficient, and requires as little as possible human involvement. As part of this promise, it is also often believed that such models can be easily and painlessly *embedded* in the final DSS.

The *expert modeling* approach (Fig. 2) is more traditional. It originates in Expert Systems, where, according to Kidd [8], "building an expert system involves eliciting, analyzing, and interpreting the knowledge that a human expert uses when solving problems." Here, we use the term in a wider sense: manually developing *any* type of a model suitable for solving a given decision-making task; this includes decision trees, multi-criteria models, Bayesian networks, and other types of models. The process usually involves a team of decision-makers, decision owners, decision analysts, experts, and/or stakeholders, who define the decision problem, formulate decision alternatives, and think about criteria and possible consequences of decisions. In doing that, they may consult the literature, perform statistical analyses, and use various tools for formulating decision models.

Embedding a model into a DSS (Figs. 1 and 2) involves some computer implementation of the model, but often requires additional activities, such as connecting the model with a database, providing a user interface for accessing the model, and implementing decision-analytic techniques to utilize the model (e.g., "what-if" or sensitivity analysis).

One may notice that the right-hand parts of Figs. 1 and 2 are identical. In both cases, once appropriate models have been developed, they are embedded in the DSS and put in service for the DSS user. In practice, however, there are subtle differences between the two, due to using models of different types and characteristics, such as completeness and comprehensibility; these are discussed in more detail in Sect. 4.

Our standpoint regarding the two model development approaches is that they are two sides of the same coin and should be combined whenever possible. There are many ways in which one branch can support the other [9]. For instance, data mining can be applied to formulate a first draft of a model, which is then enhanced through expert modeling. Or, alternatively, an expert model can be constructed from various "chunks" obtained by data or statistical analysis.

3 Example: PD_manager DSS on Medication Change

In this section, we illustrate the above concepts with examples from a real-world healthcare project *PD_manager*. The purpose of this illustration is threefold:

- To illustrate the model-based DSS development and some model development techniques
- To highlight possible problems with developing models from data
- To provide arguments in favor of combining the data- and expert-based modeling.

PD_manager [10] was an EU Horizon 2020 project, aimed at developing an innovative, mobile-health, patient-centric platform for the management of Parkinson's disease [11]. Patients are monitored using commercial wrist and insole sensors together with a smartphone to monitor and estimate their motor (e.g., tremor, dyskinesia, bradykinesia), and non-motor (e.g., cognition and mood) symptoms. This data is used by clinicians to monitor and assess the patient's state and make therapy decisions.

A part of the platform is concerned with *medication change* [12]. When the disease progresses and new symptoms emerge, it is essential to perpetually assess the patient's situation and identify the need for changing the medication plan. With this in mind, we developed a DSS [13] aimed at suggesting whether or not to change medication (i.e., a *"yes-no"* suggestion) based on the following data about an individual patient:

- *Motor symptoms*: bradykinesia, tremor, gait, dyskinesia, and on/off fluctuations
- *Non-motor symptoms*: daytime sleepiness, cognitive disorder, impulsivity, depression, hallucinations
- *Epidemiologic data*: patient's age, employment status, disease duration, and whether or not the patient is living alone.

Additional requirements for the DSS [13] included the need to explain and justify the suggestions and to achieve properties such as robustness, completeness, consistency, transparency, accuracy, and validity.

The original idea was to develop the decision model exclusively by data mining. There is a well-known database, called PPMI (Parkinson Progression Marker Initiative) [14], which contains an extensive collection of datasets describing

VISIT	Motor symptoms					Non-motor symptoms					Epidem. data		Class
	bradykinesia	tremor	gait	dyskinesia	on/off fluct.	daytime sleep.	cog.disorder	impulsivity	depression	hallucinations	age	dis. durat.	Change
1	problematic	problematic	normal	normal	normal	problematic	normal	normal	normal	normal	older	short	no
2	problematic	problematic	normal	normal	normal	problematic	normal	normal	normal	normal	older	short	no
3	problematic	problematic	normal	normal	normal	problematic	normal	normal	normal	normal	older	short	no
4	problematic	problematic	normal	normal	normal	normal	normal	normal	normal	normal	older	short	no
5	problematic	problematic	normal	normal	normal	normal	normal	problematic	normal	normal	older	short	yes
...			...		...		...	...	...	...	...	...	...
1027	normal	problematic	normal	normal	normal	problematic	normal	problematic	normal	normal	younger	short	no

Fig. 3 Data for machine learning of "yes-no" medication change models

different aspects of PD patients' daily living, including records of actual physicians' decisions regarding medication change. For our purpose, we extracted those records from the PPMI and prepared the data table, partly shown in Fig. 3. In total, the table contains data about 1027 visits of 362 patients. Each cell in the table contains a single verbal value, such as *normal* or *problematic*, indicating the severity of the corresponding symptom. The rightmost column contains the class attribute *Change*, which indicates whether or not medication has been changed after the corresponding patient's visit in a hospital. The possible values of *Change* are *no* or *yes*.

The distribution of *Change* classes is 654 *no*'s and 373 *yes*'s. Thus, the majority class is *no* and the *a-priori* classification accuracy of the dataset is $654/1027 = 0.6368 = 63.68\%$. The *a-priori* accuracy is the accuracy which would have been achieved by blindly saying *no* at any patient's visit. The *a-priori* accuracy is an important threshold for measuring the quality of decision models, either those developed by data mining or "hand-crafted" by expert modeling. In principle, a good model is expected to outperform the *a-priori* accuracy.

We run a number of machine learning algorithms on this dataset, using:

- Different data mining platforms: Orange [15], Weka [7], and ClowdFlows [16]
- Different data mining algorithms: decision trees (J48, C4.5), rule learner (JRip, CN2), Naïve Bayes, and Support Vector Machine (SVM)
- Using different attribute subsets

Results were disappointing. The classification accuracy of the models was mainly in the range from 62% to 64%; the differences were small and insignificant, and very few models exceeded the *a-priori* accuracy by a small margin. A more detailed look at those models that facilitated a deeper "open-box" insight into their contents revealed some disturbing problems. An example of such a model, i.e., a decision tree produced by Orange, is shown in Fig. 4.

At the first sight, the decision tree in Fig. 4 appears fine. One can easily follow the branches, beginning from the root at the top, checking conditions in the internal nodes of the tree, and eventually finding themselves in one of the terminal nodes, which indicate the *yes* or *no* decision. This tree was accepted very well when shown to medical professionals; they generally found it easy to understand and use. The terms used in the tree sounded familiar to them and they recognized some familiar rules. For instance, on the very left side of the tree there is a node requesting to change medication if the patient is depressed. In other words, the model is comprehensible; it makes sense to the users and captures medical knowledge.

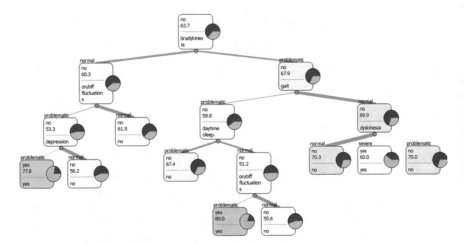

Fig. 4 A decision tree: classification model for suggesting medication change

A more detailed look, however, reveals some problematic issues:

1. The model is *incomplete* as it ignores some symptoms. Comparing Figs. 3 and 4, one can note that several attributes are left out from the model: tremor, cognitive disorder, hallucinations, and duration of the disease. Whenever we asked physicians about the importance of these symptoms, they responded that they were important and should not have been overlooked.
2. It is even more evident that only a few combinations of attributes are tested in the paths of the trees. For instance, dyskinesia, which is one of the most important indicators for medication change, appears only once in the tree in Fig. 4, where it is associated with *problematic* bradykinesia and *normal* gait. But what about other situations, such as *problematic* gait or *normal* bradykinesia?
3. It is somewhat less evident that the tree is also *inconsistent* and does not obey the *principle of dominance*: the more severe the symptoms, the more imperative the change. For example, check the intermediate subtree in Fig. 4, which is bound to *problematic* bradykinesia and *problematic* gait. According to the subtree, a patient having normal daytime sleepiness, but problematic on/off fluctuations, would be suggested to change the therapy. But what about a patient whose both symptoms are problematic, that is, the patient's situation is worse? The tree would recommend *no*, which seems inconsistent and inappropriate.

Furthermore, the classification accuracy of this decision tree is low, 61.25%, which is below the a-priori accuracy The low accuracy is not necessarily the fault of the machine learning method or using decision trees themselves, but may indicate that the underlying data is so varied or incomplete that better accuracy could not be achieved at all. Low classification accuracy achieved with other methods seemed to corroborate this hypothesis.

Faced with decision models of low quality, it was deemed necessary to try a different approach, expert modeling: asking medical experts to formulate their rules for medication change, based on their medical expertise and experience. The approach was made possible by a number of medical experts collaborating in the PD_manager project [13]. We employed the method DEX [2, 3].

DEX is a qualitative multi-criteria decision analysis method; DEX models have a hierarchical structure, which represents a decomposition of some decision problem into smaller, less complex sub-problems. The hierarchy is formulated in terms of attributes and decision rules. A DEX model has the following characteristics:

- All attributes are discrete (nominal, ordinal, qualitative).
- Each attribute has an associated value scale that consists of words, such as {"low," "medium," "high"} or {"no," "yes"}. The values may, but need not, be preferentially ordered, i.e., from "bad" values on the left to "good" values on the right of the scale.
- Attributes form a hierarchical structure, i.e., a directed acyclic graph or, most commonly, a tree.
- Aggregation is defined in terms of decision rules, grouped in decision tables.
- Decision rules, while being formulated, are checked for completeness and consistency.
- All elements of a model are acquired interactively, using software DEXi, from experts (i.e., no data mining is involved).

For a detailed description of the DEX modeling process and results, the reader is referred to [13]. Here, we illustrate the approach by showing one of the resulting models (Fig. 5) and summarizing the findings.

The left side of Fig. 5 shows the structure of the model. On the very left, there are the 13 input attributes used in the assessment. The first five ones represent motor

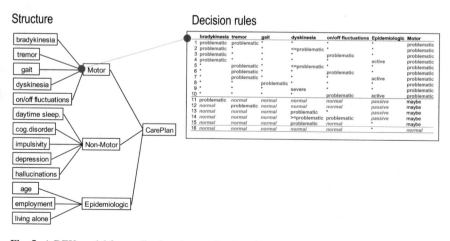

Fig. 5 A DEX model for medication change, developed by an expert neurologist

symptoms and are grouped in the *Motor* subtree. Similarly, the next groups of five and three attributes compose the subtrees *Non-Motor* and *Epidemiologic*, respectively. The three main subtrees are aggregated into the overall *CarePlan* suggestion. Each of the internal nodes has an associated decision table; Fig. 5 shows the table associated with *Motor* symptoms. Each row identifies a combination of symptoms (together with epidemiologic assessment) that indicate a "normal," "problematic," or potentially problematic ("maybe") state of motor symptoms. The asterisk "*" indicates any value. Since *dyskinesia* uses a three-valued scale {"severe," "problematic," "normal"}, the notations ">=*problematic*" and "<=*problematic*" indicate the value sets {"*problematic*," "*normal*"} and {"*severe*," "*problematic*"}, respectively.

Interpreting the table, one can easily see that rules 1–10 indicate situations that generally require medication change according to motor symptoms. In most cases, they involve a combination of two *problematic* symptoms, except rule 9, which indicates that a "*severe*" *dyskinesia* alone is a sufficient reason for change. Rules 11–15 indicate combinations of *problematic* and *normal* symptoms, which are difficult to judge and generally require considering other factors (such as non-motor symptoms in the other part of the model) or obtaining more information about the patient's state. Rule 16 indicates a "*normal*" situation without any motor symptoms.

This model has a number of desired properties. It is (provably) *complete* in the sense that it does consider all input attributes and does provide a final yes-no suggestion for any combination of input attributes' values. Similarly to decision trees, it is also comprehensible and makes medical sense. In spite of these favorable properties, the model achieves very low classification accuracy, measured on the PPMI data: only 46.28%. Similar accuracy, ranging from 36.32% to 52.50%, was achieved with other expert-developed models [13]. This came as a huge surprise. We identified several possible reasons for that, from a high variability and inconsistency of decisions captured in the PPMI, to the fundamental difference between *normative* knowledge, which is captured in DEX models, and *descriptive*, real-life performance, which is reflected in the PPMI dataset and corresponding models. For the PD_manager DSS, the normative aspect was considered more relevant and, consequently, DEX models more relevant for embedding into the DSS.

Later, we also compared the performance of the DEX model with physicians, whose decisions on selected patient cases were captured by a questionnaire. The results were substantially better: there was about 80% match between the models' and physicians' answers [13]. This provided another strong argument for including this model in the DSS.

As an interesting digression, let us also show a DEX model that was not developed by a medical expert, but rather by a decision analyst (the author of this chapter), who has only very elementary medical knowledge. Again, the PPMI dataset was used as the information source. Using the same model structure as in Fig. 5, decision rules were developed using the method as sketched in [17]: looking at statistical properties of the dataset and observing conditional probabilities, decision rules were gradually "hand-crafted" so that they match the data as closely as possible, simultaneously obeying the principle of dominance.

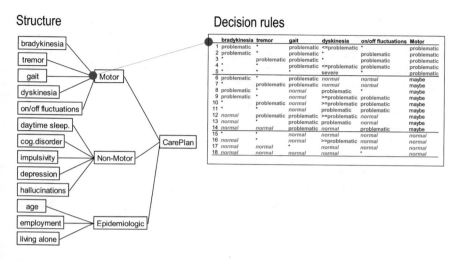

Fig. 6 A DEX model, developed by a decision analyst from the PPMI data

The result of this experiment is shown in Fig. 6. In terms of classification accuracy, which is 61.11%, this model performs slightly worse, but comparable to other models developed by machine learning algorithms from data. Being a DEX model, it is guaranteed to be complete, consistent, and transparent. However, its decision rules appear very messy, and their correctness from the medical point is questionable, to put it mildly. In comparison with Fig. 5, the decision table is larger and less regular. There are rules (e.g., rule 16) that contradict expert's rules (rule 10 in Fig. 5). Particularly problematic are rules 6–14, which involve combinations of serious motor symptoms, but lead to indecision (indicated by the class "maybe").

This digression illustrates two points:

- Relatively good DEX models can be developed from data even by non-experts, preserving the desired properties (completeness and consistency), and achieving comparable classification performance to machine learning algorithms
- Classification accuracy, measured on some dataset, is not the only relevant property and can be even misleading. While it is important, other properties must be taken into account as well.

4 The "5C Requirements" for DSS Models

The above example shows that models obtained by Data Mining are often insufficient or inappropriate for Decision Support. Despite their accuracy, they may be illogical, incomplete, violate the principle of dominance and contradict domain knowledge. Consequently, the approach may not work as anticipated and has to be combined with other approaches, such as expert modeling.

Models are key components of model-based DSS, but developing a model is only one step in the development of a DSS and bringing it to the user. This process should mind the users, their needs, and requirements of the considered decision process.

Having this in mind, we formulated five requirements for models to be used in DSSs. We call them the "5C requirements":

- *Correctness*: Providing correct (valid, right) information, focused on the decision problem
- *Completeness*: Considering all relevant aspects of the decision problem and providing answers for all possible inputs
- *Consistency*: Logical and preferential consistency
- *Comprehensibility* of provided information for the user
- *Convenience*: Easily accessible, timely information, appropriate for the task and the user

4.1 Correctness

The *correctness* requirement confronts the developed model with the decision task to be supported by the model. The main questions are: Does the model provide "the right" information to help the user in solving the problem? Is the information valid and in accordance with both domain knowledge and competences or expectations of the user? Does the model answer the right questions? Does the model facilitate key operations required by the task, such as "what-if" analysis and justification of the decision?

In Data Mining, there are many quantitative measures available for assessing the quality of models: classification accuracy (as shown in the example above), area under ROC, precision, F-measure, relative standard error, etc. They are usually measured on a fraction of data that was not used for learning (the training set), but left out for quality assessment (the testing set). These measures are important in determining the model quality and providing information for choosing the right model. However, the problem is that they look "backwards," from the model to the input data source that was used in the process (see Fig. 1). They do not really address the quality of the model in the "forward" sense, i.e., with respect to the decision problem. There is abundant literature about developing models from data, where only quantitative measures for judging the quality of models are taken into account, and the search for a best model is reduced to a competition between various machine learning algorithms. It is not uncommon to find papers in which authors, after developing a model from data, claim they "have developed a DSS." Yet they hardly ever ask themselves whether or not their models can be really implemented in a DSS, do they answer the right questions and satisfy the user's requirements.

In our experience, decision models developed from data usually solve only a part of the decision problem. In the above PD_manager example, the decision tree had missing features and incomplete rules. Also, the model answered only the "yes-no" question about the patient's medication change. There are many other questions that interest the physician, for instance *how* to change the therapy, e.g., by changing one medication with another or increasing the dosage of the current one? *Why* changing the medication, what are the medical reasons? *What* are the consequences of the change, and *what if* the new therapy turns out ineffective?

In some other projects, we were faced with a situation where only a part of the DSS model could have been developed from data, and the remaining part had to be completed by experts. For instance, in the DSS called SMAC Advisor [18], we addressed the decision problem of how to achieve coexistence between genetically modified and conventional maize when grown on fields located close to each other. Using data and results of deep simulation models, we were able to determine decision rules only with respect to gene interchange due to cross-pollination. For other aspects, such as gene interchange through seeds and sharing harvesting machinery, only expert knowledge was available at that time.

Assessing the model correctness with respect to the decision problem is much harder than measuring its statistical properties on data. This is still a largely open question. Nevertheless, this question should be kept in mind in every model-based DSS development process and not avoided because it is difficult.

4.2 Completeness

The *completeness* of DSS models refers to considering all relevant aspects of the decision problem and providing answers for all possible inputs.

In the PD_manager example, the decision tree was shown to exclude attributes representing symptoms that were considered important by medical experts. Some attributes did not appear in the tree at all, while some others were missing in specific contexts of individual tree branches. In machine learning, not including all attributes in a model is normal and may occur for a variety of reasons, from incomplete data that does not cover all relevant (or borderline) cases, to inconsistencies in the data that cause the elimination of unreliable data (e.g., decision tree pruning). But even if this is normal or even justified by statistical evidence, one should always ask: are all the relevant attributes really incorporated in the model and affect the right parts of the model?

Completeness in terms of providing answers for all possible inputs is closely related to *robustness*: does the model provide an answer to all possible values of its input attributes? In other words, none of the inputs provided by the DSS user or obtained from some dataset should remain unhandled by the model. We also stand on the point that, in the spirit of expert systems, the model should be able to provide some appropriate answer even in the case of missing or uncertain input values. We should add that "I don't know" (such as "maybe" in Fig. 5) is a perfectly acceptable answer; however, it should be made as a deliberate suggestion rather than coming as a surprise because something has been excluded from the model.

Completeness is rarely addressed explicitly in Data Mining. Fortunately, there are many model types that are generally complete, decision trees included. But there are other types of models, such as rule-based, which may not be complete. Thus, the issue is that for possibly incomplete models, one should explicitly assess and ensure their completeness before embedding them in a DSS. This is why completeness is regularly assessed in connection with DEX models, which are essentially rule-based, as an important property of the approach.

4.3 Consistency

In dictionaries, *consistency* is defined as:

> "the quality of always behaving or performing in a similar way, or of always happening in a similar way" (Cambridge Dictionary)
>
> "agreement or harmony of parts or features to one another or a whole," "ability to be asserted together without contradiction," "harmony of conduct or practice with profession" (Merriam-Webster)
>
> "agreement; harmony; logical connection" (Your Dictionary)

In the DSS context, we are particularly interested in logical and preferential consistency of models [19]. In Decision Theory, a formal framework for making logical choices in the face of uncertainty [20], one of the fundamental approaches is to represent decision-maker's preferences with preference relations [21]. For example, assuming two alternatives, A and B, we may define the weak preference relation "$\preccurlyeq$" so that $A \preccurlyeq B$ means "A is not preferred to B." In order to keep some preference-modeling model "rational," it has to satisfy a number of conditions, such as *transitivity*:

$$\forall A, B, C : A \preccurlyeq B \wedge B \preccurlyeq C \Rightarrow A \preccurlyeq C.$$

One of the fundamental concepts in Multi-Criteria Decision Analysis (MCDA) [22] is the *principle of dominance*. Given two alternatives, A and B, let us assume that they are represented by ordered sets of values that correspond to multiple attributes $X = \{X_1, X_2, \ldots, X_n\}$:

$$A = \langle a_1, a_2, \ldots, a_n \rangle, a_i \in X_i, i = 1, 2, \ldots, n.$$

$$B = \langle b_1, b_2, \ldots, b_n \rangle, b_i \in X_i, i = 1, 2, \ldots, n$$

Then, A *dominates* B if A is at least as good as B on all attributes

$$a_i \succcurlyeq b_i, i = 1, 2, \ldots, n$$

and is strictly better on at least one attribute:

$$\exists k \in \{1, 2, \ldots, n\} : a_k \succ b_k.$$

Dominance is the main principle that guides the ranking of decision alternatives [23]. An important branch of MCDA, called Dominance-Based Rough Set Analysis (DRSA) [24] employs the principle of dominance to develop rule-based models. Value functions that obey the principle of dominance are monotone, that is, they are increasing in the direction of their arguments. This helps in learning preference models from data [25]. Dominance is also important in verbal decision analysis [26]. In DEX [17], dominance is employed in order to reduce the number of possible values assigned to individual decision rules and guide the user while developing the model. By default, the monotonicity of produced decision tables is checked, thus keeping models consistent with respect to dominance.

Unfortunately, the importance of dominance is not as prominent in Data Mining. Most of the popular data mining suites, such as Weka or Orange, generally disregard the concepts of preferences and preference orders. Consequently, they generally produce models that violate the principle of dominance, such as the decision tree in Fig. 4. Actually, algorithms for developing monotone models already exist, such as for developing decision trees [27–29] or rule sets [30–32]. The problem is that these algorithms are somewhat less known and unavailable in popular software suites.

4.4 Comprehensibility

Comprehensibility in modeling refers to the ability of the DSS developers and users to understand relevant aspects of and information provided by the DSS model. Comprehensibility requires *transparent* models, also called "open-box," "white-box," or "glass-box" models, which allow both developers and users to look inside the model, examine its components and ultimately understand their meaning. This is in contrast with "black-box" models whose operation may be traced, but hardly interpreted in terms of domain knowledge. Comprehensibility is closely related to *interpretability*, which refers to the ability and easiness of interpreting information produced by the model performing decision-analytic tasks, such as evaluation of alternatives and sensitivity analysis.

In expert modeling, comprehensibility is almost granted, as the models are produced by human developers who are assumed to understand the corresponding methods. In the early days of Machine Learning [33], comprehensibility was considered one of the two modeling objectives, together with predictive accuracy. Symbolic models are favored to statistical ones because of their better comprehensibility. This is why in DSS projects, such as PD_manager, we strongly prefer symbolic models, such as decision trees and decision rules, even at the expense of accuracy.

Over the last two or three decades, developments in Data Mining tended to favor the predictive accuracy and statistical, "black-box" models [34]. The mainstream

Data Mining development went just the opposite to what is needed for DSS modeling.

Fortunately, this trend seems to be changing. A recent European Commission initiative for "trustworthy AI" raises a number of challenges, such as [35]:

> Transparency: This requirement is closely linked with the principle of explicability and encompasses transparency of elements relevant to an AI system: the data, the system and the business models.
>   Explanation methods: For a system to be trustworthy, we must be able to understand why it behaved a certain way and why it provided a given interpretation.
>   "Human agency: Users should be able to make informed autonomous decisions regarding AI systems. They should be given the knowledge and tools to comprehend and interact with AI systems to a satisfactory degree [. . .].

In response to these challenges, the number of publications on comprehensibility seems to be growing, addressing the comprehensibility of specific model types, such as decision trees [36] or inductive logic programs [34], methods for explaining "black-box" models [37], creating trustworthy models [38], and formulating comprehensibility frameworks of modeling [39].

4.5 Convenience

The *convenience* requirement refers to providing easily accessible and timely information that is appropriate for the task and adapted to the user. It is included in this list in order not to forget about the DSS developers and users, and their needs. Convenience is important in all three stages of DSS modeling (see Figs. 1 and 2): developing the model, embedding (implementing) it in a DSS, and using the DSS. All stages are expected to be supported by appropriate methods and software tools, which are easily accessible and convenient to use. General-purpose and free software is particularly welcome. The final DSS implementation, for instance, in a form of a mobile or web application, should be easily accessible, too, and should speak in the language of the user, emphasizing the role of user interfaces.

The Data Mining area has a long tradition of providing excellent general-purpose software tools.[2] There are data mining software suites, such as the already mentioned Weka, Orange, and ClowdFlows, which provide dozens of data mining algorithms and employ data mining workflows to combine multiple methods in developing decision models for the particular modeling task. There are also software libraries for various programming languages, such as R and Python, which support both model development and embedding into a DSS.

---

[2] See, for example, https://www.softwaretestinghelp.com/data-mining-tools/.

In the area of Expert Modeling and MCDA, the situation is not as good. Decision modeling tools are available,[3] but they appear very fragmented. Most of them support only one or a small collection of methods, which were developed by the same research team as the software (DEXi is no exception to this). There are also commercial software tools, which typically implement only the most popular MCDA methods, such as the Analytical Hierarchy Process (AHP); implementations of methods that might be more appropriate for specific tasks are difficult to find. Different tools use different data and model representations and are thus notoriously difficult to combine. There are many MCDA methods and model types that do not provide any support for embedding them in a DSS, which effectively excludes them from serious DSS development.

We are aware of only one active MCDA attempt that went in a similar direction as data mining suites: Decision Deck.[4] This project provides collaboratively developed Open Source software tools to support the MCDA process. Among others, it provides *diviz*, software for designing, executing, and sharing MCDA methods, algorithms and experiments [40], and *XMCDA*, a standardized XML recommendation for representing MCDA components and facilitating software interoperability [41]. Even though Decision Deck is targeted at practitioners, teachers, and researchers, it appears more focused on researchers and their experimenting with various methods. To use it effectively requires a strong technical and theoretical background [42]. Despite the XMCDA standard, the porting of developed models to other environments, such as DSS, is still largely unsupported.

5 Conclusions and Take-Home Messages

Decision Support Systems are here to stay. Originating in 1960s, DSS is a mature discipline that provides stable and well-understood decision support methods and tools. The DSS will, of course, adapt to new technologies and ever increasing needs to support more and more complex decisions.

Data Mining and Expert Modeling are two sides of the same coin. In this chapter, we advocated in favor of bringing them together to build better DSSs.

In model-based DSS development, always mind the user. Generally, there are three types of users involved in the process: model developers (e.g., decision-makers, experts, decision analysts, stakeholders), model implementers (software developers), and DSS users (individual or corporate decision-makers, stakeholders, "ordinary" users such as patients). Model-based DSS development methods should acknowledge and take care of all these categories.

---

[3] https://www.capterra.com/decision-support-software/,   http://kt.ijs.si/MarkoBohanec/dss.html, https://www.mcdmsociety.org/content/software-related-mcdm.

[4] https://www.decision-deck.org/project/.

Decision Support puts special requirements on models (the "5C requirements"): correctness, completeness, consistency, comprehensibility, and convenience. Every model-based DSS development should carefully consider these requirements and try to depart from the "black-box," accuracy-first approaches that currently prevail in Data Mining.

The "naïve" Data Mining → Decision Support schema rarely works really well and may require human (expert) intervention. In our opinion, expertise should be employed whenever it exists at a sufficient level to solve the given problem.

Expert Modeling comes at a price. Nowadays, data is abundant and data mining tools are widely available for anyone. Expertise is not as abundant as data. Experts are generally difficult to work with, they speak they own domain-specific language, they are expensive and seldom available. Nevertheless, overcoming these obstacles may turn out essential for the decision problems and substantially improving the quality and trustworthiness of DSS models.

Despite our emphasis on expert modeling, Data Mining is and remains an indispensable tool whenever data about past decisions is available. It alleviates understanding the problem domain, identifying common problem-solving patterns, and ultimately developing a working DSS model. We just say that models, submitted to expert verification and validation, might turn out better.

In spite of the excellent Decision Deck initiative, the Expert Modeling and Decision Modeling disciplines are still in desperate need of high-quality, general-purpose, multiple-method, dataflow-based, and free-to-use modeling software. The MCDA modeling should become easier, and more methods suitable for solving diverse decision support tasks should be made available. Model and data interchange should be encouraged and supported by widely accepted standards.

On the other side, despite that Data Mining already provides excellent software suites, these generally lack features that are essential in DSS modeling: considering preferentially ordered features and classes, fulfilling the dominance principle and ensuring the monotonicity of models, measuring and improving the comprehensibility of models, and measuring and ensuring their completeness. Also, Data Mining and Decision Support researchers should work together to develop better methods of verification and validation of models with respect to the end-user's problem. All these issues provide great future challenges for researchers, developers, and scholars.

Acknowledgments The author acknowledges the financial support from the Slovenian Research Agency, research core funding P2-0103. The PD_manager project was funded within the EU Framework Programme for Research and Innovation Horizon 2020, under grant number 643706. Data used in the preparation of this article were obtained from the Parkinson's Progression Markers Initiative (PPMI) database (www.ppmi-info.org/data). For up-to-date information on the study, visit www.ppmi-info.org. PPMI—a public–private partnership—is funded by the Michael J. Fox Foundation for Parkinson's Research and funding partners, including Abbvie, Allergan, Amathus, Avid, Biogen, BioLegend, Bristol-Myers Squibb, Celgene, Jenali, GE Healthcare, Genentech, GlaxoSmithKline, Janssen Neuroscience, Lilly, Lundbeck, Merck, MSD, Pfizer, Piramal, Prevail, Roche, Sanofy Genzyme, Servier, Takeda, Teva, UCB, Verily, and Voyager.

References

1. Power, D. J. (2013). *Decision support, analytics, and business intelligence* (2nd ed.). New York: Business Expert Press.
2. Bohanec, M., Rajkovič, V., Bratko, I., Zupan, B., & Žnidaršič, M. (2013). DEX methodology: Three decades of qualitative multi-attribute modelling. *Informatica, 37*, 49–54.
3. Trdin, N., & Bohanec, M. (2018). Extending the multi-criteria decision making method DEX with numeric attributes, value distributions and relational models. *Central European Journal of Operations Research, 26*, 1–41.
4. Bohanec, M. (2020). *DEXi: Program for multi-attribute decision making, user's manual, version 5.04. IJS Report DP-13100*. Ljubljana: Jožef Stefan Institute. Software retrieved from: http://kt.ijs.si/MarkoBohanec/dexi.html.
5. Albright, S. C., & Winston, W. L. (2016). *Business analytics: data analysis & decision making* (6th ed.). Boston: Cengage Learning.
6. Hastie, T., Tibshirani, R., & Friedman, J. (2016). *The elements of statistical learning: Data mining, inference, and prediction* (2nd ed.). Berlin: Springer Series in Statistics.
7. Witten, I. H., Frank, E., Hall, M. A., & Pal, C. J. (2017). *Data mining: Practical machine learning tools and techniques* (4th ed.). Amsterdam: Elsevier.
8. Kidd, A. (1987). *Knowledge acquisition for expert systems: A practical handbook. University Series in Mathematics*. New York: Springer.
9. Lavrač, N., & Bohanec, M. (2003). *Integration of data mining and decision support. Data mining and decision support: Integration and collaboration* (pp. 37–48). Boston: Kluwer Academic Publishers.
10. PD_manager. (2015–2018): *mHealth platform for Parkinson's disease management*. EU Horizon 2020 Project H2020-PHC-643706. Retrieved from http://www.parkinson-manager.eu/
11. Tsiouris, K. M., Gatsios, D., Rigas, G., Miljković, D., Koroušić-Seljak, B., Bohanec, M., Arredondo, M. T., Antonini, A., Konitsiotis, S., Koutsouris, D. D., & Fotiadis, D. I. (2017). PD_manager: An mHealth platform for Parkinson's disease patient management. *Healthcare Technology Letters, 4*(3), 102–108.
12. Mileva Boshkoska, B., Miljković, D., Valmarska, A., Gatsios, D., Rigas, G., Konitsiotis, S., Tsiouris, K. M., Fotiadis, D., & Bohanec, M. (2020). Decision support for medication change of Parkinson's Disease Patients. *Computer Methods and Programs in Biomedicine, 196*, 105552.
13. Bohanec, M., Miljković, D., Valmarska, A., Mileva Boshkoska, B., Gasparoli, E., Gentile, G., Koutsikos, K., Marcante, A., Antonini, A., Gatsios, D., Rigas, F., Fotiadis, D. I., Tsiouris, K. M., & Konitsiotis, S. (2018). A decision support system for Parkinson disease management: Expert models for suggesting medication change. *Journal of Decision Systems, 27*, 164–172.
14. PPMI. (2011). Parkinson progression marker initiative: The Parkinson progression marker initiative. *Progress in Neurobiology, 95*(4), 629–635.
15. Demšar, J., Curk, T., Erjavec, A., Gorup, Č., Hočevar, T., Milutinovič, M., Možina, M., Polajnar, M., Toplak, M., Starič, A., Stajdohar, M., Umek, L., Žagar, L., Žbontar, J., Žitnik, M., & Zupan, B. (2013). Orange: Data mining toolbox in Python. *Journal of Machine Learning Research, 14*(1), 2349–2353.
16. Kranjc, J., Orač, R., Podpečan, V., Lavrač, N., & Robnik-Šikonja, M. (2017). ClowdFlows: Online workflows for distributed big data mining. *Future Generation Computer Systems, 68*, 38–58.
17. Bohanec, M., & Delibašić, B. (2015). Data-mining and expert models for predicting injury risk in ski resorts. In *Decision support systems V—Big data analytics for decision making. First International Conference ICDSST 2015* (pp. 46–60). Berlin: Springer.
18. Bohanec, M., Messéan, A., Angevin, F., & Žnidaršič, M. (2006). *SMAC advisor: A decision-support tool on coexistence of genetically-modified and conventional maize* (pp. 9–12). Ljubljana: Proc. Information Society IS 2006.

19. García-Lapresta, J. L., & Montero, J. (2006). Consistency in preference modelling. In B. Bouchon-Meunier, G. Coletti, & R. Yager (Eds.), *Modern information processing: From theory to applications* (pp. 87–97). Amsterdam: Elsevier.
20. Parmigiani, G., & Inoue, L. Y. T. (2009). *Decision theory: Principles and approaches.* Chicester: Wiley.
21. Steele, K., & Stefánsson, H. O. (2016). Decision theory. In Z. N. Zalta (Ed.), *The Stanford Encyclopedia of Philosophy (Winter 2016).* Stanford: Stanford University.
22. Greco, S., Ehrgott, M., & Figueira, J. (2016). *Multi criteria decision analysis: State of the art surveys.* New York: Springer Verlag.
23. Kadziński, M., Słowiński, R., & Szeląg, M. (2016). Dominance-based rough set approach to multiple criteria ranking with sorting-specific preference information. In S. Matwin & J. Mielniczuk (Eds.), *Challenges in computational statistics and data mining* (pp. 155–171). New York: Springer.
24. Greco, S., Matarazzo, B., & Slowinski, R. (2002). Rough sets methodology for sorting problems in presence of multiple attributes and criteria. *European Journal of Operational Research, 138*(2), 247–259.
25. Denat, T., & Öztürk, M. (2017). Dominance based monte carlo algorithm for preference elicitation in the multi-criteria sorting problem: Some performance tests. In J. Rothe (Ed.), *Algorithmic decision theory* (Lecture Notes in Computer Science) (Vol. 10576). Cham: Springer.
26. Moshkovich, H. M., & Mechitov, A. I. (2013). Verbal decision analysis: Foundations and trends. *Adv. Decis. Sci., 2013,* 1–9.
27. Ben-David, A. (1995). Monotonicity maintenance in information-theoretic machine learning algorithms. *Machine Learning, 19*(1), 29–43.
28. Cao-Van, K., & De Baets, B. (2003). Growing decision trees in an ordinal setting. *International Journal of Intelligent Systems, 18*(7), 733–750.
29. Potharst, R., & Feelders, A. J. (2002). Classification trees for problems with monotonicity constraints. *ACM SIGKDD Explorations Newsletter, 4*(1), 1.
30. Błaszczyński, J., Słowiński, R., & Szeląg, M. (2011). Sequential covering rule induction algorithm for variable consistency rough set approaches. *Information Sciences, 181*(5), 987–1002.
31. Kotłowski, W., & Słowiński, R. (2014). Rule learning with monotonicity constraints. In *Proceedings of the 26th Annual International Conference on Machine Learning* (Vol. 2009, pp. 537–544). New York: ACM.
32. Moshkovich, H. M., Mechitov, A. I., & Olson, D. L. (2002). Rule induction in data mining: Effect of ordinal scales. *Expert Systems with Applications, 22*(4), 303–311.
33. Michie, D., & Bratko, I. (1986). *Expert systems: Automating knowledge acquisition.* Boston: Addison-Wesley.
34. Muggleton, S. H., Schmid, U., Zeller, C., Tamaddoni-Nezhad, A., & Besold, T. (2018). Ultra-strong machine learning: Comprehensibility of programs learned with ILP. *Machine Learning, 107*(7), 1119–11140.
35. AI HLEG. (2019). *Ethics guidelines for trustworthy AI. High-level expert group on artificial intelligence.* Brussels: European Commission. Retrieved from https://ec.europa.eu/futurium/en/ai-alliance-consultation.
36. Piltaver, R., Luštrek, M., Gams, M., & Martinčić-Ipšić, S. (2016). What makes classification trees comprehensible? *Expert Systems with Applications, 62,* 333–346.
37. Guidotti, R., Monreale, A., Ruggieri, S., Turini, F., Giannotti, F., & Pedreschi, D. (2018). A survey of methods for explaining black box models. *ACM Computing Surveys, 51*(5), 1–42.
38. Felici, M. (2012). How to trust: A model for trust decision making. *International Journal of Adaptive, Resilient and Autonomic Systems, 3*(3), 20–34.
39. Gleicher, M. (2016). A framework for considering comprehensibility in modeling. *Big Data, 4*(2), 75–88.
40. Meyer, P., & Bigaret, S. (2012). Diviz: A software for modeling, processing and sharing algorithmic workflows in MCDA. *Intelligent Decision Technologies, 6*(4), 283–296.

41. Bigaret, S., & Meyer, P. (2015). XMCDA: An XML-based encoding standard for MCDA data. In R. Bisdorff, L. C. Dias, P. Meyer, V. Mousseau, & M. Pirlot (Eds.), *Evaluation and decision models with multiple criteria: Case studies* (pp. 591–617). Berlin, Heidelberg: Springer.
42. Ishizaka, A., & Nemery, P. (2013). *Multi-criteria decision analysis: Methods and software*. Chichester: Wiley.

DSS for Multicriteria Preference Modeling with Partial Information and Its Modulation with Behavioral Studies

Adiel Teixeira de Almeida, Eduarda Asfora Frej, and Lucia Reis Peixoto Roselli

Abstract This paper discusses the trends for building DSS (Decision Support Systems) for Multicriteria Preference Modeling by using partial information to be obtained from DMs (Decision-makers). Also, it discusses the use of results from behavioral studies, including those that take a Decision Neuroscience approach, in order to modulate changes in the decision process and in the design of a DSS. The preference modeling is considered from two different perspectives: elicitation by decomposition and elicitation by holistic evaluations. This chapter focuses on a DSS that deals with Multicriteria Preference Modeling in the scope of MAVT (Multiattribute Value Theory) and describes the evolution of these DSSs in recent years. Finally, the trends in the decision aiding process using this kind of DSS for Preference Modeling with partial information is illustrated with the DSS for the FITradeoff method. The trends in the flexibility of this DSS is one of the features explored. It is shown how to combine two different paradigms for preference modeling: decomposition and holistic evaluations. Also, this chapter demonstrates how results from neuroscience experiments can be used to prompt the analyst to have insights when talking with and advising decision-makers (DMs) and how to improve the design of the DSS, both for the choice and the ranking problematic.

Keywords Preference modeling · Partial information · Elicitation by decomposition · Holistic evaluation · Behavioral decision making · Decision neuroscience

A. T. de Almeida (✉) · E. A. Frej · L. R. P. Roselli
CDSID—Center for Decision Systems and Information Development, Universidade Federal de Pernambuco, Recife, PE, Brazil
e-mail: almeida@cdsid.org.br; eafrej@cdsid.org.br; lrpr@cdsid.org.br

© Springer Nature Switzerland AG 2021
J. Papathanasiou et al. (eds.), *EURO Working Group on DSS*, Integrated Series in Information Systems, https://doi.org/10.1007/978-3-030-70377-6_12

213

1 Introduction

Practical problems in organizations inherently involve multiple and conflicting objectives that should be appropriately considered. Several Multicriteria Decision-Making/Aiding (MCDM/A) methods have been developed in the literature over recent years. MCDM/A methods can be classified according to the DM's rationality, depending on the way in which he/she behaves regarding compensation among criteria. When a DM is willing to allow a lower performance in some criterion to be compensated for a better performance in another criterion, a compensatory rationality is present in such a DM's preference structure, and therefore he/she may be willing to consider tradeoffs among the multiple criteria involved in the process [1]. Additive aggregation methods are a particular case of compensatory methods, and they require the DM to establish scaling constants for each criterion in order to define the substitution rates among them [2]. Since these parameters do not reflect only the level of importance of the criteria, the elicitation should be conducted based on a structured procedure that takes into account the ranges of consequences in each criterion, which is a challenging step in MCDM/A due to DMs having difficulty in providing the level of precise information required [3, 4].

Therefore, in order to address such a challenge, several partial information methods have been developed in the literature, i.e., methods that require less and easier information from DMs. These methods indeed improve the applicability of MCDM/A techniques to practical problems thus narrowing the gap between theoretical research in MCDM/A and practical applications. However, in order to try to make such methods more attractive for use in practical problems, what needs to be done is to develop practical tools by means of which the method is operated, such as a Decision Support System (DSS), which should be easy to use and have a user-friendly interface for users and analysts.

In this chapter, we discuss how to approach the decision process in Decision Support Systems, and we highlight also how decision neuroscience tools can be useful for prompting the analyst to have insights that will assist him/her to discuss issues with and advise DMs during the decision-making process and to improve the design of DSSs. The particular case of the FITradeoff DSS is analyzed. It operationalizes the Flexible and Interactive Tradeoff method. The investigation of particular features of FITradeoff brings us to another discussion regarding two main paradigms in preference modeling: elicitation by decomposition and holistic evaluation. We discuss how the FITradeoff method combines both approaches in its structure, and how this can cause both the analyst and users to have insights during the preference modeling process.

This chapter is structured as follows. Section 2 presents a background on MCDM/A methods for preference modeling that work based on partial information about DMs' preferences. Section 3 describes the DSS of the FITradeoff method and its main features. Section 4 discusses the two different perspectives of conducting the preference modeling process: elicitation by decomposition and holistic evaluation. Section 5 presents a perspective on how neuroscience decision tools can help to design DSSs and aid the decision process. Finally, some conclusions and final remarks are presented in Sect. 5.

2   DSS for Multicriteria Preference Modeling with the Use of Partial Information

Multicriteria decision-making problems involve a preference modeling step in order to gather the DM's preference structure so as to make the appropriate evaluation among criteria. Within the scope of the Multiattribute Value Theory (MAVT—[2]), alternatives receive a score which is built based on an aggregation function of the criteria. Therefore, the global value of each alternative is calculated according to Eq. (1).

$$v\left(a_j\right) = \sum\nolimits_{i=1}^{n} k_i v_i \left(x_{ij}\right) \tag{1}$$

In Eq. (1), k_i is the scaling constant of criterion i, and $v_i(x_{ij})$ is the value of the performance of alternative j in criterion i, normalized on a 0–1 scale. The main concern about preferences modeling in additive models is about establishing the values of the scaling constants of the criteria k_i, since these parameters do not represent only a measure of importance, but they also reflect issues related to the range of consequences in each criterion scale [2, 3].

To elicit these parameters however traditional methods require too much information from the DM, since this is cognitively hard to provide, and therefore inconsistencies occur during the process [4, 5]. In this context, plenty of methods have been developed in the literature with the aim of facilitating the elicitation process for DMs—these are the so-called partial information methods. These methods received this name because of the nature and amount of information that DMs give. These methods are able to build a recommendation for the DM without a precise specification of the criteria weights; only partial/incomplete/imprecise information about these parameters is given. De Almeida et al. [1] proposed a framework that describes the different ways that partial information methods and DSSs work. These authors divided them into three main categories: preference statements, forms of partial information, and a synthesis step. This framework is illustrated in Fig. 1.

In Fig. 1, the first category is about the way in which the DM gives preference statements. This category is divided into three subcategories. The first subcategory separates structured elicitation processes from nonstructured elicitation processes. Methods with a structured process are those that have a formal elicitation procedure on which it is based, such as the tradeoff procedure [2] or the swing procedure [6]. Nonstructured methods are those that do not have a formal procedure for eliciting preferences, and they do so in an ad hoc manner or they assume that the information is given a-priori by the DM. The second subcategory is about the interactivity of

Fig. 1 Framework for partial
information methods
(Adapted from [1])

Preference statements	Structured
	Non-structured
	All at once
	Interactive
	Flexible
	Fixed process
Forms of Partial Information	Ranking
	Bounds
	Holistic Judgments
	Arbitrary linear inequalities
Synthesis step	Surrogate weights
	Decision rules
	Linear programming models
	Simulations and/or sensitivity analysis

the procedure. Interactive procedures are those in which the DM interacts with a
decision support tool (e.g., a DSS) and therefore calculations are performed after
each interaction, in order to refine the results obtained. In methods which do not
have this interactivity feature, information is provided all at once by the DM. The
third subcategory is about the flexibility of the process. In general, methods are
considered to be flexible when they enable DMs to conduct the elicitation process
in different manners so that the method can be adapted according to the DM's needs.

The second classification in Fig. 1 concerns the forms of partial information
given by the DMs, which can be one or more of the following types of information:
ranking of criteria scaling constants; upper and lower bounds for criteria scaling
constants; holistic judgments from the comparison of alternatives; and also arbitrary
linear inequalities regarding the marginal value functions. The third classification in
Fig. 1 is about the synthesis step, i.e., given the partial information provided by the
DM, which mechanism is applied to compute a recommendation. Surrogate weights
are useful when the DMs do not want to provide too much information during the
process. Decision rules such as maximin, minimax regret, and central values are also
widely used. Linear programming problem models can be applied for computing
dominance relations and/or potential optimality of alternatives. Finally, simulation
and sensitivity analysis can also be performed to compute a recommendation.

Most of the partial information approaches found in the literature work based
on a nonstructured process (e.g., [4, 7–11]), but some of them use a structured
procedure to elicit preferences. The methods developed by Edwards and Barron
[12], Malakooti [13], Salo and Hamalainen [14], and Mustajoki et al. [15] have a
structured elicitation process based on the swing procedure, while de Almeida et
al. [1] and Frej et al. [16, 17] use the classical tradeoff procedure to structure the

elicitation process. It is important to emphasize that these two procedures work in distinct manners. The tradeoff procedure was developed first, with a robust axiomatic structure, but the elicitation procedure itself required high cognitive effort from DMs, which leads to a high rate of inconsistencies. The swing procedure simplifies the elicitation process, and this makes it easier for the DM to supply the information required since such simplification allows the DM to consider only linear value functions, which is a disadvantage of this procedure. Therefore, Edwards and Barron [12] claim that the classical tradeoff procedure leads to an elicitation error, while the swing procedure leads to a modeling error.

The second subcategory of preference statements is about the interaction with the DM. Some methods are operated by means of interactive DSSs, which are based on interaction steps with the DM to establish preferences and calculation steps, interactively (e.g., [1, 4, 11, 13, 18–20]). Other methods establish the DM's preferences directly, without this interactive process with the DM (e.g., [5, 8–10, 12, 21–23]).

The third subcategory is about the flexibility of the method. Some partial information methods conduct the elicitation process in a flexible way, giving different options to the DM during the process. Graphical visualization tools with the possibility of making a holistic evaluation is an example of such flexibility. Different ways of stating preferences is another example of flexibility that a DSS may give to the DM. Section 4 illustrates an example of a DSS that operates a partial information method with a variety of flexibility tools. The methods developed by Park and Kim [19], Malakooti [13], Dias and Clímaco [24], Salo and Hamalainen [14] Sarabando and Dias [25], Punkka and Salo [10], de Almeida et al. [1], and Frej et al. [16, 17] all contain examples of flexible processes.

The second category is about the forms of partial information given by the DM. Some of them work based on a ranking of the scaling constants of the criteria that the DM has established; others work based on bounds for the values of the weights; holistic judgments between alternatives are also used by some methods; and finally, there are methods that work with arbitrary linear inequalities with the value functions. Most of the methods use a combination of these forms of partial information. For example, Salo and Punkka [26], Danielson et al. [22], de Almeida et al. [1], and Frej et al. [16, 17] use ranking and bounds. Park and Kim [19], Park et al. [27], Kim and Han [23], Dias and Clímaco [24], Park [9], and Punkka and Salo [10] use ranking, bounds, and arbitrary linear inequalities. Salo and Hamalainen [14] use ranking, bounds, and holistic judgments. Malakooti [13] uses ranking, bounds, holistic judgments, and arbitrary linear inequalities. Other methods use only holistic judgments [20] and others use only arbitrary linear inequalities [18, 28].

Finally, the last classification is about how the methods conduct the synthesis of the partial information obtained in order to build a recommendation for the DM. Possible ways to conduct such synthesis steps are: to use surrogate weights (e.g., [7, 12, 22, 29]); to apply decision rules, such as maximin, minimax regret, etc. (e.g., [25, 27]); to run linear programming models (e.g., [1, 8–10, 13, 16, 17, 20, 30]) or even to perform simulations and/or sensitivity analysis [31]. Some methods also use more than one of these techniques in order to perform the synthesis step.

There are also group decision-making methods that work based on partial information about the DMs' preferences. These approaches embrace another synthesis step in order to aggregate the preferences of different DMs in order to build a recommendation for the group as a whole. One way to do this is using indicators and decision rules [24, 32–34]. Another way is to aggregate DMs' different results (e.g., [35–42]). But there is a challenge related to this procedure, which is how to establish weights for the different DMs. Consensus reaching is also approached by some group decision methods [37, 39]. Other methods try to build a common interval model for the group [33, 43–45]. Finally, voting procedures can also be used to aggregate DMs' results [35, 43].

The next section illustrates one of these partial information methods mentioned above; the one developed by de Almeida et al. [1], the Flexible and Interactive Tradeoff (FITradeoff) method. This method has a structured elicitation process based on the tradeoff procedure, and the elicitation is carried out interactively with the DM, in a flexible way. The forms of partial information used are ranking and bounds for the scaling constants of the criteria. Finally, the synthesis step is based on linear programming models. This method is also suitable for aiding group decision situations. The FITradeoff Decision Support System is described in detail in the following section.

3 DSS for the FITradeoff Method

The Flexible and Interactive Tradeoff method was originally developed by de Almeida et al. [1] to solve choice MCDM/A problems in situations in which only partial information about decision-makers' preferences is available. The method is operated by means of a DSS, which is available to readers for free by request at www.fitradeoff.org. The system is interactive and works by asking the DM questions regarding tradeoffs among different criteria of the MCDM problem.

Figure 2 shows the initial screen of the DSS. By clicking on the "open" button at the top left of the screen, an Excel file can be uploaded with the data of the problem, which basically consists of the consequences matrix with its criteria, alternatives, and the performance of the criteria in each alternative. The model of the Excel spreadsheet can be downloaded by clicking on the button "new."

Once the user imports the data of the problem into the DSS, the screen in Fig. 3 appears. The Table on the upper left side of Fig. 3 shows the information about the criteria of the problem, i.e., if they are defined on a discrete or continuous scale, and if they are to be minimized or maximized. The table on the lower left side of the screen shows the consequences matrix of the problem. On the right side of the screen, there is a box that shows the initial order in which criteria were input. This initial order can be changed by clicking on the "Step 1 (Ranking the criteria scaling constants)" button. If the DM agrees with the initial order, he/she can go directly to the step of eliciting the scaling constants of the criteria by clicking on the "Step 2 (Flexible Elicitation)" button. On the bottom right side of the screen, there

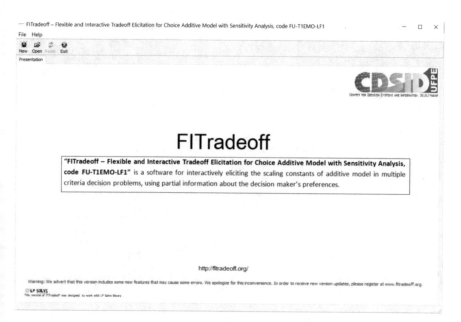

Fig. 2 Initial screen of the FITradeoff Decision Support System

is a box in which the DM can enter a value for the equivalence distance between alternatives, i.e., the value for the maximum difference between the global value of two alternatives below which they are considered indifferent (or equivalent).

The first step of the method consists of establishing the ranking of the criteria scaling constants, according to the DM's preferences. By clicking on the "Step 1 (Ranking the Criteria Scaling Constants)" button, the screen in Fig. 4 appears for the DM. The DM may rank criteria weights in two different ways: by holistic evaluation (Fig. 4) or by pairwise comparison (Fig. 5), by clicking on the "Change to Pairwise Comparison" button at the bottom of Fig. 4. Figures 4 and 5 show an example of a problem with seven criteria.

To rank the criteria scaling constants based on the holistic evaluation procedure, the DSS puts a hypothetical alternative with all criteria in the worst possible outcome to the DM and asks him/her which criterion would he/she choose to raise to the best outcome (maximum value), in order to improve that hypothetical alternative. The criterion that the DM chooses will become the first in the order of the criteria weights. Then, the DM is asked, again, which criterion would he/she choose to raise to the best outcome, now assuming that the first criterion has the maximum value. This criterion will be the second in the order of the criteria weights, and so on. As an output of this process, inequalities Eq. (2) are obtained.

$$k_1 > k_2 > \cdots > k_n \qquad (2)$$

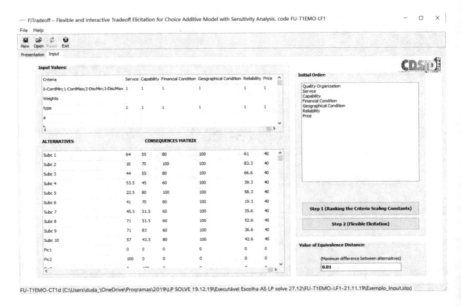

Fig. 3 Visualization of problem data in FITradeoff DSS

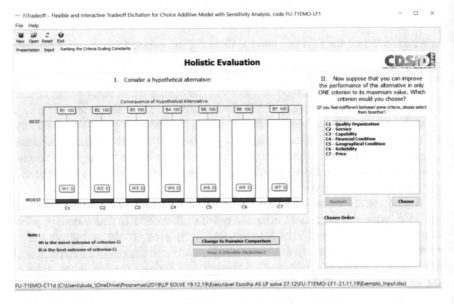

Fig. 4 Ranking of criteria scaling constants by holistic evaluation

Another way to order the scaling constants of the criteria is by pairwise comparisons between criteria. For instance, Fig. 5 shows a question put to the DM in which he/she has to choose between two hypothetical consequences: consequence

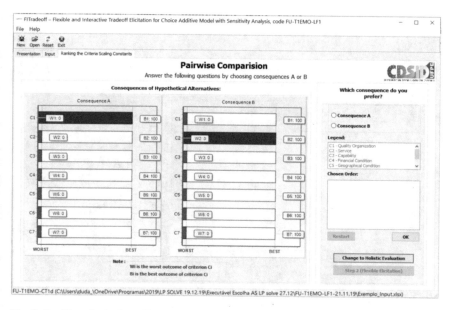

Fig. 5 Ranking of criteria scaling constants by pairwise comparison

A, with the best outcome in criterion C1 and the worst outcome in all other criteria, and consequence B, with the best outcome in criterion 2 and the worst outcome in all other criteria. Therefore, if the DM prefers consequence A, then the inequality $k_1 > k_2$ is obtained; otherwise, the reverse inequality is true. By asking the DM questions of this type, the order of the criteria weights in Eq. (2) can also be obtained.

The possibility of evaluating the order of criteria weights in two different ways is one of the features of the flexibility of this DSS. In general, a holistic evaluation is easier to conduct when the number of criteria is relatively small. Otherwise, when the set of criteria is wide, then pairwise comparisons can be a cognitively easier alternative way to do so.

The next step in FITradeoff is the flexible elicitation process itself. The process of flexible elicitation consists of eliciting preferences from DMs in a flexible way. Preference relations between consequences are declared by the DM in this step, which are easier compared to indifferent statements required by the classical tradeoff procedure. Partial results are available for visualization at any time during the process. Moreover, the DSS allows the DM to stop the elicitation process before the end if he/she thinks that the partial results are enough for his/her decision process.

During the flexible elicitation process, the DSS puts questions to the DM, asking him/her to compare different levels of the criteria, by considering tradeoffs between them. For instance, Fig. 6 illustrates a question the DSS puts to the DM in this phase. The comparison is between consequence A, with an intermediate outcome

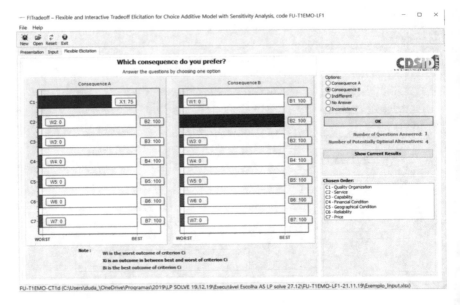

Fig. 6 Flexible elicitation step

for criterion C1 and the worst outcome for the others, and consequence B, with the best outcome for criterion C2 and the worst outcome for the others. For details on how these intermediate values for criteria are computed, see de Almeida et al. [1].

If the DM declares preference for consequence A, then according to the multiattribute value function, the inequality $k_1 v_1 (75) > k_2$ would be satisfied. On the other hand, if the DM declares preference for consequence B, the opposite inequality $(k_1 v_1 (75) < k_2)$ would be satisfied. In these inequalities, v_1 is the value function of criterion C1 normalized on a 0–1 scale. The DM may also state that he/she is indifferent between these two consequences; in this case, equation $k_1 v_1 (75) = k_2$ would be verified. If the DM thinks that this question is too hard to answer, then he/she could choose the option "No answer;" in this case, another question would be computed for the DM without any loss of information. Another possible answer is "Inconsistency," which can be chosen whenever the DM thinks that the current question made by the DSS is not consistent with his/her previous answers, and then he/she would have the possibility of revising these previous answers. Therefore, during this step, as more questions of this type are put to the DM, inequalities of type Eqs. (3) and (4) are obtained.

$$k_i v_i \left(x_i' \right) > k_{i+1} \tag{3}$$

$$k_i v_i \left(x_i'' \right) < k_{i+1} \tag{4}$$

The set of inequalities consisting of Eqs. (2), (3), and (4), together with the equation for normalizing weights, form a so-called weights space, which is the set of feasible values that criteria scaling constants can assume. The inequalities and equations of the weights space act as constraints for linear programming (LP) models, which run, at each interaction, in order to find a recommendation for the MCDM problem. Such models depend on the problematic that is being dealt with.

For the choice problematic, de Almeida et al. [1] developed LP models to test the potential optimality of the alternatives; as for the ranking problematic, Frej et al. [16, 17] developed LP models to find dominance relations between alternatives to build a ranking of them. Therefore, as an output for the choice problem, at each interaction, there is a subset of potentially optimal alternatives (POA), i.e., alternatives that can be better than all other alternatives in terms of global value within the current space of weights.

For the ranking problematic, the output is a partial (or complete) order of the alternatives, depending on the level of information that the DM provides. The system is interactive, so, at each interaction, the DM answers another question and the weights space is updated, and therefore the results are refined according to the new information provided.

At any time during the elicitation step, the DM is able to visualize partial results. By clicking on the "Show Current Results" button on the screen shown in Fig. 6, the DM will be able to visualize the set of POA (in choice problems) or the current ranking obtained (in ranking problems). Another feature of the flexibility of the FITradeoff DSS is the graphical visualization provided to analyze partial results. For instance, in the case of Fig. 6, it can be seen that the subset of POA consists of four alternatives. These alternatives can be visualized in a comparative manner, using graphics such as the bar graph in Fig. 7 and the spider graph in Fig. 8.

The bar graph in Fig. 7 shows the performance of the alternatives with respect to each criterion. Criteria are represented in the horizontal axis, ordered from left to right. Each potentially optimal alternative is represented by a different color and

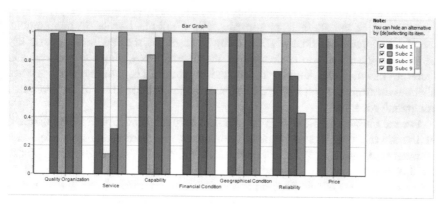

Fig. 7 Bar graph for visualization of partial results

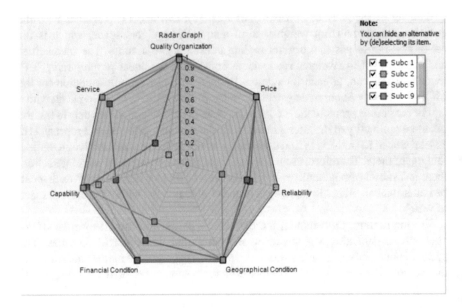

Fig. 8 Spider graph (also known as a radar graph) for visualization of partial results

their performance is reflected by the height of the bars, measured in a normalized ratio scale from 0 to 1. Alternatives can be analyzed in a comparative manner in each criterion. For instance, in criterion "quality organization," it can be seen that the four alternatives being compared have a very similar performance. As for criterion "service," alternatives "Subc 1" and "Subc 9" have a great advantage over the others. Moreover, the DM can choose to deselect alternatives from the graphic, in order to compare a subset of them, which is also a flexibility feature of the DSS.

Another type of visualization provided by the DSS is the spider (or radar) graph, illustrated in Fig. 8. The analysis here can be conducted similar to the bar graphic analysis; each color represents an alternative, and the tips of the stars represent the performance of the alternatives normalized in a ratio 0–1 scale. In this graphic, criteria are ordered anticlockwise. By using these graphs, the DM has the possibility of undertaking a holistic evaluation of the alternatives during the process, and therefore this may well shorten the elicitation process. The DM may also deselect alternatives from the graph, should he/she wish to evaluate fewer alternatives in a comparative manner.

For the ranking problematic, the graphical output is similar to a Hasse diagram of the alternatives. In this graphic, alternatives are represented by circles, and dominance relations between alternatives are indicated by directed arrows. Those dominance relations are achieved based on an LP model [16, 17]. The transitivity reduction property of this diagram avoids unnecessary arrows to be drawn, which could let the diagram polluted with too much information. Figure 9 shows an example of this graphic. The levels of the ranking are separated by dashed

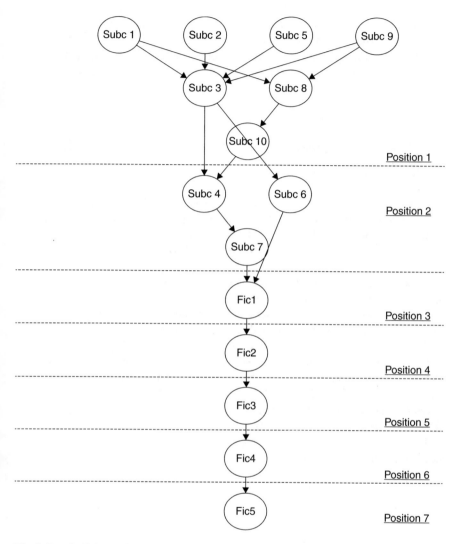

Fig. 9 Levels of the ranking

lines. When there is no arrow between two alternatives, this means that they are incomparable to each other, for the current level of information that the DM has provided. Since the information provided is partial, the recommendation is also a partial ranking; whenever the DM provides additional preference information, the ranking is refined and a complete order of the alternatives may be achieved.

The FITradeoff method was applied with a view to solving MCDM practical problems over a range of very diverse issues [46–49]. This method is also suitable for aiding group decision-making problems [16, 17]. DMs can engage in the elicitation process simultaneously with or separately from the process of applying the method, in accordance with their availability. The whole process needs to be guided by an analyst, whose role is to show DMs the graphical visualization during the process and to recommend whether or not it is appropriate to conduct a holistic evaluation at that point. The next section presents a further discussion of these issues.

4 Different Perspective for Preference Modeling: Holistic Evaluation

In Preference modeling, most studies are based on elicitation procedures considering a decomposition perspective, such as those previously described. A different perspective is based on Holistic Evaluation, which in many cases can be applied to disaggregation procedures, such as that in the UTA (UTilités Additives) method ([50–52]).

Figure 10 shows the connection between the action space and the consequence space. From the decomposition perspective, the preference modeling is conducted in the consequence space. On the other hand, from the holistic evaluation perspective, the preference modeling is conducted in the action space [53].

In the FITradeoff method, DMs can apply both perspectives. The holistic evaluation presented in the FITradeoff method used graphical visualizations to support the DM to reach a better understanding of MCDM/A problems. This phase encourages flexibility in the decision-making process since the DM can evaluate the alternatives and define the dominance relation between them, thereby reducing the time taken to solve the problem [53].

In other words, by using the graphical visualization presented in the FITradeoff DSS for the choice problematic, DMs can evaluate the POAs and if they desire, they

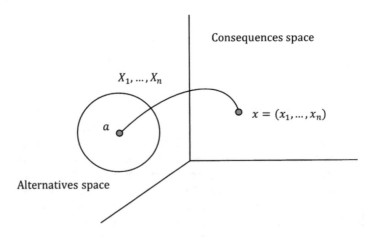

Fig. 10 Action and Consequence Space (Adapted from [2])

can define the final alternative for the problem before the decomposition process is completed. Currently, in the FITradeoff DSS for the choice problematic there are three types of graphics that are included, namely, the bar graph, the bubble graph, and the spider graph.

For the ranking problematic [16, 17], the holistic evaluation can be also used to support DMs to solve the problem. In this problematic, the DMs can use the graphics to compare alternatives which are incomparable in some positions of the ranking, and if they desire, they can define dominance relations between them, which should be implemented in the FITradeoff algorithm that is used to update the ranking.

Therefore, a holistic evaluation plays a special role in the FITradeoff decision-making process since DMs have the flexibility to proceed in the FITradeoff decision process considering the use of both perspectives (the decomposition process and the holistic evaluation).

Thus, in order to improve the holistic evaluation phase, behavior studies are performed with the graphics presented in FITradeoff DSS for the choice problematic in addition to using other visualizations. These studies are undertaken to investigate how DMs evaluate alternatives and select the best alternative in MCDM/A problems which are represented by graphical and tabular visualizations. Also, to conduct these studies, neuroscience tools are used to construct experiments and to collect DMs' physiological variables which are used to investigate DMs' behavior. These studies have two main objectives: to prompt the analyst to have insights that will assist him/her to discuss issues with and advise DMs and to generate suggestions for improving the design of the DSSs.

5   Modulating the Decision Process and the Design of a DSS with Decision Neuroscience

The term modulation with the meaning of transformation is presented in the study by Korhonen and Wallenius [54]. In this study, they emphasized that aspects of behavior should be included during the decision-making process in order to represent the DM's preferences coherently. Therefore, in this section, drawing on behavioral studies that were conducted using Neuroscience tools, the modulation (transformation) of the FITradeoff decision-making process, and the improvements in its DSSs, both for the choice and the ranking problematics, are discussed.

According to Wallenius and Wallenius [55], taking aspects of behavior into consideration is a trend that seeks to advance research into decision-making. However, few studies are presented in the literature concerning the use of the Neuroscience approach to investigate MCDM/A methods [56].

Therefore, in order to extend behavioral studies in MCDM/A methods, neuroscience experiments are conducted to investigate the holistic evaluation phase [57–70].

5.1 Neuroscience Experiments

Before describing the three experiments which are constructed, it is important to call attention to the Neuroscience approach. This approach is used in these experiments as a supplement to support the investigation of DMs' behavior when they undertake a holistic evaluation.

The Neuroscience approach has been used in connection with many areas of knowledge to investigate the behavior of users and improve the systems and methods applied [71]. An important field of study is *Neuroeconomics* and many papers have been published that take a *Neuroeconomics* approach.

In general, in *Neuroeconomics* studies, the behavior of the players is investigated during games in order to improve classical economic models and to include aspects of behavior which hitherto such models have not considered [72–75].

The *NeuroIS* approach is another area which investigates users' behavior when they are interacting with Information Systems (IS) [76, 77]. Also, *Consumer Neuroscience* and *Neuromarketing* are adjacent areas which investigate consumer behavior and use this information to construct desirable products [78–80].

Regarding the MCDM/A approach, some studies are presented in the literature to investigate DMs' behavior when they are solving problems using some specific methods [81–85]. However, according to Hunt et al. [56], the number of studies is insufficient and this lack of studies represents a gap about this theme in the literature.

Therefore, some studies are undertaken to extend research about MCDM/A. In these studies, experiments were constructed using two pieces of neuroscience equipment (Eye-Tracking and the Electroencephalogram—EEG). It is common to find in the literature that such equipment has been used. Eye-Tracking is used to collect DMs' eye movements, and the EEG is used to collect the frequencies of brain activity while DMs are evaluating the visualizations.

The experiments were constructed and applied in different years: the first experiment took place in 2017; the second in 2018; and the third in 2019. All three experiments are applied to Management Engineering students of the Federal University of Pernambuco—Universidade Federal de Pernambuco (UFPE). The students had been attending Multicriteria Decision-Making classes when the experiments were performed. These experiments are approved by the Committee for Ethics in Research at UFPE.

The first experiment was constructed using the graphics presented in the FITrade-off DSS for the choice problematic and two additional visualizations (a table and a bar graph with table). This experiment presented 24 visualizations with three, four, and five alternatives evaluated in three, four, and five criteria. These visualizations were generated from MCDM/A problems some of which had the same value for the criteria weights and others had different values for the criteria weights [60, 63, 67–70].

The second experiment was constructed to compare bar graphs and tables. These visualizations presented three, four, and five alternatives evaluated in four and five criteria [58, 65, 66].

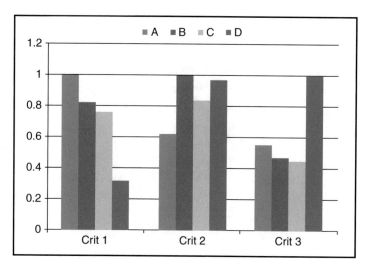

Fig. 11 Bar graphic with four alternatives and three criteria

Finally, the third experiment was constructed using, in most cases, visualizations with two alternatives. This experiment used bar graphs, spider graphs, and tables [57, 61, 62]. Both the second and third experiments presented 22 visualizations.

Therefore, in accordance with MAVT concepts [2], the students had to make tradeoffs between the alternatives and the criteria weights in order to select the best alternative in each visualization. This task was the only one required in all the experiments. Also, no time-limit was imposed on the experiments. Figures 11 and 12 presented two of the visualizations used in these experiments.

5.2 Behavioral Results from the Neuroscience Experiments

The main aims of the behavioral studies are to prompt the analyst to have insights and to generate improvements for the DSSs. Therefore, based on the Behavioral Results, important propositions were drawn up to achieve these goals.

One important proposition was to make use of the Success Region Based Decision Rule. Based on this rule, direct recommendations can be presented to the analyst. Also, the rule represents an improvement in the FITradeoff DSS, since the recommendations can be made available by including a button placed on each graphical or tabular visualization screen.

The Success Region Based Decision Rule makes recommendations about the level of confidence the DM can have when using the visualizations to select the best alternative. Therefore, to generate recommendations about this level of confidence, what is considered is the probability of success and the standard deviation [61, 62].

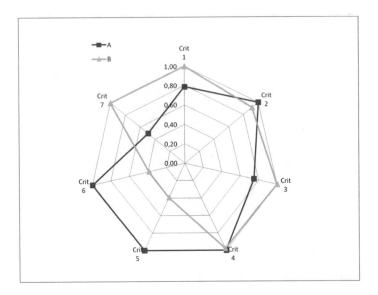

Fig. 12 Spider graphics with two alternatives and seven criteria

The probability of success is estimated from the Hit Rate variable [63, 67] since from the study of discrete distributions it is observed that the task of the experiment (to select the final alternative with only one chance) is similar to a Bernoulli event [86].

The Hit Rate (HR) variable is computed in the first experiment developed, and it is replicated in the other experiments [63, 67]. The HR value is the ratio of the correct answer (answers where the participant selected the correct alternative) times the total number of answers (which is equal to the total number of participants who participated in each experiment).

It is worth mentioning that the correct alternative was previously calculated using an MAVT context ([2]). Thus, after data were collected, the HR values were obtained for each visualization. Therefore, the HR values represent the performance of success that each visualization obtained in the required task.

Thus, by using general HR values (0–100%) the probabilities of success are obtained. Also, based on these probabilities of success, the values of standard deviations are computed according to the Bernoulli distribution [86]. Hence, based on the combination of the probability of success and the standard deviation, recommendations are provided considering regions in the Success Region Based Decision Rule, as illustrated in Table 1.

Region A presented probabilities of success between 0.2 and 0.8; and standard deviations between 0.4 and 0.5. Thus, for visualizations which present probabilities of success below 0.5, the recommendation is to not use these visualizations to define the dominance relation between alternatives. On the other hand, for visualizations which present probabilities of success between 0.5 and 0.8, the analyst should advise

Table 1 Recommendation Rule based on HR values

HR value (%)	Probability of success	Standard deviation	Region	Recommendation
$0 \leq HR \leq 10$	$0 \leq \pi \leq 0.1$	$0 \leq \sigma \leq 0.3$	C	Do not use
$10 < HR \leq 20$	$0.1 < \pi \leq 0.2$	$0.3 < \sigma \leq 0.4$	B	Do not use
$20 < HR \leq 50$	$0.2 < \pi \leq 0.5$	$0.4 < \sigma \leq 0.5$	A	Do not use
$50 \leq HR \leq 80$	$0.5 < \pi \leq 0.8$	$0.4 < \sigma \leq 0.5$	A	Risk in use
$80 < HR \leq 90$	$0.8 < \pi \leq 0.9$	$0.3 < \sigma \leq 0.4$	B	Possible use
$90 < HR \leq 100$	$0.9 < \pi \leq 1$	$0 \leq \sigma \leq 0.3$	C	Use

the DM that even with intermediate values of the probability of success, these visualizations presented higher values of standard deviation, and thus it is risky to use them to define dominance relations between alternatives.

Region B presented probabilities of success between 0.1 and 0.2 or 0.8 and 0.9; and standard deviations between 0.3 and 0.4. As for region A, for visualizations which present probabilities of success below 0.5, the recommendation is to not use them. On the other hand, for visualizations which present probabilities of success between 0.8 and 0.9, the analyst should advise the DM about the Confidence in using them. However, the analyst also should reinforce the intermediate variations of these visualizations. In this situation, the analyst and DMs should carefully evaluate if the visualizations can be used to define dominance relations between alternatives.

Region C presented probabilities of success between 0 and 0.1 or 0.9 and 1; and standard deviations between 0 and 0.3. Thus, for visualizations which present probabilities of success between 0 and 0.1, the recommendation is to not use these visualizations. On the other hand, for visualizations which present probabilities of success between 0.9 and 1, the recommendations are to use these visualizations to define dominance relations between alternatives.

Another suggestion for improving the DSSs is to include the tabular visualization. Since participants must have to select the best alternative in each visualization evaluated, it is suggested from behavioral results that these participants positively used the tabular visualization to select the best alternative [63, 67]. Thus, a direct recommendation from these studies is the inclusion of the tabular visualization, in an adequate way, in the FITradeoff DSS for the choice problematic. Moreover, in the FITradeoff DSS for the ranking order problematic, all the visualizations (bar graph, spider graph, and table) should be included, since the only one currently presented is the graphical output illustrated in Fig. 9.

In addition, given the graphical output illustrated in Fig. 9, another suggestion for improvement is the possibility of revealing in this graph the dominance relation generated by a holistic evaluation process. Figure 13 illustrates the dominance relation (in red) generated between the alternatives Supplier 2 and Supplier 4 based on the holistic evaluation process, which can be performed using a graphical or tabular visualization.

Finally, based on the EEG behavioral results, the analyst can be prompted to have additional insight. Thus, based on the frontal Theta (4–8 Hz) and parietal Alpha (8–13 Hz) activities, the Alpha-Theta Diagram is proposed. This diagram presented

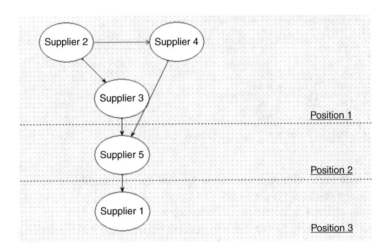

Fig. 13 Dominance relations defined from the holistic evaluation

four quadrants, which reveal specific patterns of behavior. These quadrants are generated considering the increase in Theta values, in frontal channels, and the decrease in Alpha values, in parietal channels, as an indication of cognitive effort and engagement (attention) when performing a required task [87–89].

Therefore, Relaxing behavior is presented in the upper left quadrant and shows negative values for Theta and Positive values for Alpha. Participants classified as relaxed presented low cognitive effort and engagement during the holistic evaluation process. Indefinition behavior is presented in the upper right quadrant and shows positive values for Theta and Alpha activities, participants considered indefined presented high cognitive effort and low engagement during the experiments. Involvement behavior is presented in the lower left quadrant and shows negative values for Theta and Alpha activities. Participants who were considered involved presented low cognitive effort and high engagement. Lastly, Diligence behavior is presented in the lower right quadrant and shows positive values for Theta and negative values for Alpha. Participants considered diligent presented a high cognitive effort and high engagement during the required task. Participants who did not present any of these patterns of behavior presented a disperse pattern during the experiment.

This diagram is a new proposition for classifying a participant's behavior. Also, it is observed that in most cases, a participant presents a unique behavior during the whole experiment. Therefore, what can be reinforced is the recommendation about the level of confidence in visualization when evaluating which of them were evaluated by participants who presented desirable patterns of behavior, such as Diligent and Involved behavior. For further details, see de Almeida and Roselli [57].

6 Conclusions

This chapter presented a discussion on how the decision process can be improved based on findings obtained from neuroscience experiments, and how neuroscience decision tools can cause users to have insights that aid the design of a DSS. The special case of the FITradeoff DSS was analyzed based on its decision process, which combines two paradigms in preference modeling: elicitation by decomposition and holistic evaluation.

Neuroscience experiments bring insights into how decision-makers act when making decisions and when they and/or an analyst are evaluating their preferences. Such investigation about how users behave when using a DSS can help to design and improve the decision support tool.

Concerning the behavioral studies, an interesting finding is related to the way in which DMs are most likely to view the results when making a holistic evaluation and taking into consideration the different kinds of visualization: visualizing a table, a bar graph, or even a spider graph. Holistically evaluating potentially optimal alternatives in the FITradeoff for the choice problematic, when used for finalizing the process, may help DMs to achieve a solution even before the elicitation ends, in which case the process can be shortened thus saving DMs time and effort.

Another way to exploit holistic evaluation is to use it to collect information for the elicitation process itself. For example, using the FITradeoff DSS for the ranking problematic, alternatives within the same group may be holistically compared and the DM can define a dominance relation, without needing to use the LP model to make calculations for the respective pair of alternatives.

Also, in these situations, the recommendations include using behavioral studies in order to support the analyst when advising DMs about the level of confidence they may have in visualization in order to define a dominance relation between alternatives.

The main contributions of the paper to the scientific community rely on the insights for the decision process and Decision Support Systems that can be gathered from the application of neuroscience experiments and its results. The design and modulation of DSSs can be strongly improved when considering behavioral aspects from DMs. This chapter has shown how these neuroscience tools could be applied for the FITradeoff method and its DSS, but other MCDM/A methods and support systems could be analyzed and redesigned considering such behavioral aspects.

Future studies should explore how the insights provided by neuroscience tools may help to improve the decision support systems of other MCDM partial information methods, in order to try to narrow the gap between theoretical methodological development and practical application in MCDM problems.

Acknowledgments This work had partial support from the Brazilian Research Council (CNPq).

References

1. de Almeida, A. T., Almeida, J. A., Costa, A. P. C. S., & Almeida-Filho, A. T. (2016). A new method for elicitation of criteria weights in additive models: flexible and interactive tradeoff. *European Journal of Operational Research, 250*(1), 179–191.
2. Keeney, R. L., & Raiffa, H. (1976). *Decision analysis with multiple conflicting objectives.* New York: Wiley & Sons.
3. Belton, V., & Stewart, T. (2002). *Multiple criteria decision analysis: an integrated approach.* New York: Springer Science & Business Media.
4. Salo, A. A., & Hämäläinen, R. P. (1992). Preference assessment by imprecise ratio statements. *Operations Research, 40*(6), 1053–1061.
5. Weber, M. (1987). Decision making with incomplete information. *European Journal of Operational Research, 28*(1), 44–57.
6. Von Winterfeldt, D., & Edwards, W. (1986) Decision analysis and behavioral research.
7. Danielson, M., & Ekenberg, L. (2017). A robustness study of state-of-the-art surrogate weights for MCDM. *Group Decision and Negotiation, 26*(4), 677–691.
8. Kirkwood, C. W., & Sarin, R. K. (1985). Ranking with partial information: A method and an application. *Operations Research, 33*(1), 38–48.
9. Park, K. S. (2004). Mathematical programming models for characterizing dominance and potential optimality when multicriteria alternative values and weights are simultaneously incomplete. *IEEE Trans Syst Man Cybernet Part A: Syst Hum, 34*(5), 601–614.
10. Punkka, A., & Salo, A. (2013). Preference programming with incomplete ordinal information. *European Journal of Operational Research, 231*(1), 141–150.
11. White, C. C., & Holloway, H. A. (2008). Resolvability for imprecise multiattribute alternative selection. *IEEE Transactions on Systems, Man, and Cybernetics-Part A: Systems and Humans, 38*(1), 162–169.
12. Edwards, W., & Barron, F. H. (1994). SMARTS and SMARTER: Improved simple methods for multiattribute utility measurement. *Organizational Behavior and Human Decision Processes, 60*(3), 306–325.
13. Malakooti, B. (2000). Ranking and screening multiple criteria alternatives with partial information and use of ordinal and cardinal strength of preferences. *IEEE Transactions on Systems, Man, and Cybernetics-Part A: Systems and Humans, 30*(3), 355–368.
14. Salo, A. A., & Hamalainen, R. P. (2001). Preference ratios in multiattribute evaluation (PRIME)-elicitation and decision procedures under incomplete information. IEEE Transactions on Systems. *Man, and Cybernetics-Part A: Systems and Humans, 31*(6), 533–545.
15. Mustajoki, J., Hämäläinen, R. P., & Salo, A. (2005). Decision support by interval SMART/SWING—incorporating imprecision in the SMART and SWING methods. *Decision Sciences, 36*(2), 317–339.
16. Frej, E. A., de Almeida, A. T., & Costa, A. P. C. S. (2019). Using data visualization for ranking alternatives with partial information and interactive tradeoff elicitation. *Operational Research, 19*, 909–931.
17. Frej, E. A., de Almeida, A. T., & Roselli, L. R. P. (2019). Solving Multicriteria Group Decision-Making (MCGDM) problems based on ranking with partial information. In *International conference on group decision and negotiation* (pp. 3–16). Cham: Springer.
18. Mármol, A. M., Puerto, J., & Fernández, F. R. (2002). Sequential incorporation of imprecise information in multiple criteria decision processes. *European Journal of Operational Research, 137*(1), 123–133.
19. Park, K. S., & Kim, S. H. (1997). Tools for interactive multiattribute decision-making with incompletely identified information. *European Journal of Operational Research, 98*(1), 111–123.
20. Salo, A. A., & Hämäläinen, R. P. (1995). Preference programming through approximate ratio comparisons. *European Journal of Operational Research, 82*(3), 458–475.

21. Athanassopoulos, A. D., & Podinovski, V. V. (1997). Dominance and potential optimality in multiple criteria decision analysis with imprecise information. *Journal of the Operational Research Society, 48*(2), 142–150.
22. Danielson, M., Ekenberg, L., Larsson, A., & Riabacke, M. (2014). Weighting under ambiguous preferences and imprecise differences in a cardinal rank ordering process. *International Journal of Computational Intelligence Systems, 7*(supp 1), 105–112.
23. Kim, S. H., & Han, C. H. (2000). Establishing dominance between alternatives with incomplete information in a hierarchically structured attribute tree. *European Journal of Operational Research, 122*(1), 79–90.
24. Dias, L. C., & Clímaco, J. N. (2000). Additive aggregation with variable interdependent parameters: the VIP analysis software. *Journal of the Operational Research Society, 51*(9), 1070–1082.
25. Sarabando, P., & Dias, L. C. (2010). Simple procedures of choice in multicriteria problems without precise information about the alternatives' values. *Computers & Operations Research, 37*(12), 2239–2247.
26. Salo, A., & Punkka, A. (2005). Rank inclusion in criteria hierarchies. *European Journal of Operational Research, 163*(2), 338–356.
27. Park, K. S., Kim, S. H., & Yoon, W. C. (1997). Establishing strict dominance between alternatives with special type of incomplete information. *European Journal of Operational Research, 96*(2), 398–406.
28. Ahn, B. S., Park, K. S., Han, C. H., & Kim, J. K. (2000). Multi-attribute decision aid under incomplete information and hierarchical structure. *European Journal of Operational Research, 125*(2), 431–439.
29. Stillwell, W. G., Seaver, D. A., & Edwards, W. (1981). A comparison of weight approximation techniques in multiattribute utility decision making. *Organizational Behavior and Human Performance, 28*(1), 62–77.
30. Ahn, B. S., & Park, K. S. (2008). Comparing methods for multiattribute decision making with ordinal weights. *Computers & Operations Research, 35*(5), 1660–1670.
31. Montiel, L. V., & Bickel, J. E. (2014). A generalized sampling approach for multilinear utility functions given partial preference information. *Decision Analysis, 11*(3), 147–170.
32. Chen, Y., Kilgour, D. M., & Hipel, K. W. (2012). A decision rule aggregation approach to multiple criteria-multiple participant sorting. *Group Decision and Negotiation, 21*(5), 727–745.
33. Contreras, I., & Mármol, A. M. (2007). A lexicographical compromise method for multiple criteria group decision problems with imprecise information. *European Journal of Operational Research, 181*(3), 1530–1539.
34. Hinojosa, M. A., & Mármol, A. M. (2011). Egalitarianism and utilitarianism in multiple criteria decision problems with partial information. *Group Decision and Negotiation, 20*(6), 707–724.
35. Ackerman, M., Choi, S. Y., Coughlin, P., Gottlieb, E., & Wood, J. (2013). Elections with partially ordered preferences. *Public Choice, 157*, 145–168.
36. Baucells, M., & Sarin, R. K. (2003). Group decisions with multiple criteria. *Management Science, 49*(8), 1105–1118.
37. Dias, L. C., & Clímaco, J. N. (2005). Dealing with imprecise information in group multicriteria decisions: a methodology and a GDSS architecture. *European Journal of Operational Research, 160*(2), 291–307.
38. Jiménez-Martín, A., Gallego, E., Mateos, A., & del Pozo, J. A. F. (2017). Restoring a radionuclide contaminated aquatic ecosystem: A group decision making problem with incomplete information within MAUT accounting for veto. *Group Decision and Negotiation, 26*(4), 653–675.
39. Keeney, R. L. (2009). The foundations of collaborative group decisions. *International Journal of Collaborative Engineering, 1*(1–2), 4–18.
40. Kim, S. H., & Ahn, B. S. (1997). Group decision making procedure considering preference strength under incomplete information. *Computers & Operations Research, 24*(12), 1101–1112.

41. Kim, S. H., & Ahn, B. S. (1999). Interactive group decision making procedure under incomplete information. *European Journal of Operational Research, 116*(3), 498–507.

42. Sarabando, P., Dias, L. C., & Vetschera, R. (2019). Group decision making with incomplete information: a dominance and quasi-optimality volume-based approach using Monte-Carlo simulation. *International Transactions in Operational Research, 26*(1), 318–339.

43. Adla, A., Zarate, P., & Soubie, J. L. (2011). A proposal of toolkit for GDSS facilitators. *Group Decision and Negotiation, 20,* 57–77. https://doi.org/10.1007/s10726-010-9204-8.

44. Hämäläinen, R. P., & Pöyhönen, M. (1996). On-line group decision support by preference programming in traffic planning. In *Negotiation processes: modeling frameworks and information technology* (pp. 185–200). Dordrecht: Springer.

45. Kim, S. H., Choi, S. H., & Ahn, B. S. (1998). Interactive group decision process with evolutionary database. *Decision Support Systems, 23*(4), 333–345.

46. Carrillo, P. A. A., Roselli, L. R. P., Frej, E. A., & de Almeida, A. T. (2018). Selecting an agricultural technology package based on the flexible and interactive tradeoff method. *Annals of Operations Research, 2018,* 1–16.

47. Fossile, D. K., Frej, E. A., da Costa, S. E. G., de Lima, E. P., & de Almeida, A. T. (2020). Selecting the most viable renewable energy source for Brazilian ports using the FITradeoff method. *Journal of Cleaner Production, 2020,* 121107.

48. Frej, E. A., Roselli, L. R. P., Araújo de Almeida, J., & de Almeida, A. T. (2017). A multicriteria decision model for supplier selection in a food industry based on FITradeoff method. *Mathematical Problems in Engineering, 2017,* 4541914.

49. Pergher, I., Frej, E. A., Roselli, L. R. P., & de Almeida, A. T. (2020). Integrating simulation and FITradeoff method for scheduling rules selection in job-shop production systems. *International Journal of Production Economics, 227,* 107669.

50. Jacquet-Lagreze, E., & Siskos, J. (1982). Assessing a set of additive utility functions for multicriteria decision-making, the UTA method. *European Journal of Operational Research, 10*(2), 151–164.

51. Siskos, Y., Grigoroudis, E., & Matsatsinis, N. F. (2016). UTA methods. In S. Greco, M. Ehrgott, & J. Figueira (Eds.), *Multiple criteria decision analysis. International Series in Operations Research & Management Science* (Vol. 233). New York, NY: Springer.

52. Siskos, E., Askounis, D., & Psarras, J. (2014). Multicriteria decision support for global e-government evaluation. *Omega, 46,* 51–63.

53. de Almeida, A. T., Frej, E. A., & Roselli, L. R. P. (2021). Combining holistic and decomposition paradigms in preference modeling with the flexibility of FITradeoff. *Central European Journal of Operations Research, 29,* 7–47. https://doi.org/10.1007/s10100-020-00728-z.

54. Korhonen, P., & Wallenius, J. (1997). *Behavioral issues in MCDM: Neglected research questions. Multicriteria analysis* (pp. 412–422). Heidelberg: Springer.

55. Wallenius, H., & Wallenius, J. (2020). Implications of World mega trends for MCDM research. In S. Ben Amor, A. de Almeida, J. de Miranda, & E. Aktas (Eds.), *Advanced studies in multicriteria decision making* (1st ed., pp. 1–10). New York: Chapman and Hall/CRC, Series in Operations Research.

56. Hunt, L. T., Dolan, R. J., & Behrens, T. E. (2014). Hierarchical competitions subserving multiattribute choice. *Nature Neuroscience, 17*(11), 1613.

57. de Almeida, A. T. & Roselli, L. R. P. (2020). NeuroIS to improve the FITradeoff decision-making process and decision support system. In: *Proceedings of the NeuroIS Retreat 2020.*

58. de Almeida, A. T., Roselli, L. R. P., Costa, A. P. C. S., Goncalves, J. M. S., & Andrade, A. L. (2018). *Decision process improvement based on behavioral experiments of multi-attribute choices with graphical visualization.* Philadelphia, US: Society of NeuroEconomics, 16th, Proceedings.

59. de Almeida, A. T., & Roselli, L. R. P. (2017). Visualization for decision support in FITradeoff method: exploring its evaluation with cognitive neuroscience. In *Lecture Notes in Business Information Processing. 282 edn* (pp. 61–73). New York: Springer International Publishing.

60. de Almeida, A. T., & Roselli, L. R. P. (2017). *Improving preference modeling for multi-criteria decision-making with cognitive mechanisms analysis.* Toronto, Canadá: Society for Neuroeconomics, 17, 2017.
61. Roselli, L. R. P., & de Almeida, A. T. (2020). Analysis of graphical visualizations for multi-criteria decision making in FITradeoff method using a decision neuroscience experiment. In *Lecture Notes in Business Information Processing. 384 edn* (pp. 42–54). New York: Springer International Publishing.
62. Roselli, L.R.P., & de Almeida, A.T. (2020). Improvements in the FITradeoff Decision Support System for ranking order problematic based in a behavioral study with NeuroIS tools. In: *Proceedings of the NeuroIS Retreat 2020.*
63. Roselli, L. R. P., de Almeida, A. T., & Frej, E. A. (2019). Decision neuroscience for improving data visualization of decision support in the FITradeoff method. *Oper Res Int J, 19,* 933–953.
64. Roselli, L. R. P., Pereira, L. S., Silva, A. L. C. L., de Almeida, A. T., Morais, D. C., & Costa, A. P. C. S. (2019). Neuroscience experiment applied to investigate decision-maker behavior in the tradeoff elicitation procedure. *Ann. Oper. Res., 289,* 67–84.
65. Roselli, L. R. P., & de Almeida, A. T. (2019) Investigating graphical visualization in FITradeoff method with neuroscience using EEG and eye-tracker. Local proceedings for Group Decision and Negotiation. In: 19th International Conference on Group Decision and Negotiation, Loughborough. *Proceedings of the 19th International Conference on Group Decision and Negotiation*
66. Roselli, L. R. P., & de Almeida, A. T. (2019). Analyzing graphical visualization for multi-attribute decision making using EEG and eye-tracker. In *NeuroPsychoEconomics Conference.* Rome: Poster Section.
67. Roselli, L. R. P., Frej, E. A., & de Almeida, A. T. (2018). Neuroscience experiment for graphical visualization in the FITradeoff decision support system. In Y. Chen, G. Kersten, R. Vetschera, & H. Xu (Eds.), *Group Decision and Negotiation in an Uncertain World. GDN 2018. Lecture Notes in Business Information Processing, vol 315.* New York: Springer International Publishing.
68. Roselli, L. R. P., Frej, E. A., & de Almeida, A. T. (2018). Improving graphical visualization in the FITradeoff DSS using neuroscience experiment. In *2018 INFORMS International Conference. Proceedings of the 2018.* Taipei: INFORMS International Conference.
69. Roselli LRP, Frej EA, de Almeida AT (2017) Designing preference modeling for FITradeoff method with decision neuroscience experiments. In: 17th International Conference on Group Decision and Negotiation, Stuttgart, Proceedings of the 17th International Conference on Group Decision and Negotiation
70. Roselli, L. R. P., & de Almeida, A. T. (2017). Cognitive analysis for improving preference elicitation confidence of scale constants in multi-attribute value theory. In *16th Society for Neuroeconomics.* Toronto: Poster Section.
71. Linkov, I., Cormier, S., Gold, J., Satterstrom, F. K., & Bridges, T. (2012). Using our brains to develop better policy. *Risk Analysis: An International Journal, 32*(3), 374–380.
72. Fehr, E., & Camerer, C. F. (2007). Social neuroeconomics: the neural circuitry of social preferences. *Trends in Cognitive Sciences, 11*(10), 419–427.
73. Glimcher, P. W., & Rustichini, A. (2004). Neuroeconomics: the consilience of brain and decision. *Science, 5695,* 447–452.
74. Kenning, P., & Plassmann, H. (2005). NeuroEconomics: An overview from an economic perspective. *Brain Research Bulletin, 67*(5), 343–354.
75. Loewenstein, G., Rick, S., & Cohen, J. D. (2008). *Neuroeconomics. Annual Review of Psychology, 59,* 647–672.
76. Dimoka, A., Pavlou, P. A., & Davis, F. D. (2007). Neuro-IS: the potential of cognitive neuroscience for information systems research. In: *Proceedings of the 28th International Conference on Information Systems,* pp. 1–20.
77. Riedl, R., Davis, F. D., & Hevner, A. R. (2014). Towards a NeuroIS research methodology: intensifying the discussion on methods, tools, and measurement. *Journal of the Association for Information Systems, 15*(10), 2014.

78. Goucher-Lambert, K., Moss, J., & Cagan, J. (2017). Inside the mind: using neuroimaging to understand moral product preference judgments involving sustainability. *Journal of Mechanical Design, 139*(4), 041–103.

79. Khushaba, R. N., Wise, C., Kodagoda, S., Louviere, J., Kahn, B. E., & Townsend, C. (2013). Consumer neuroscience: Assessing the brain response to marketing stimuli using electroencephalogram (EEG) and eye tracking. *Expert Systems with Applications, 40*(9), 3803–3812.

80. Morin, C. (2011). Neuromarketing: the new science of consumer behavior. *Society, 48*(2), 131–135.

81. Barberis, N., & Xiong, W. (2009). What drives the disposition effect? An analysis of a long-standing preference-based explanation. *The Journal of Finance, 64*(2), 751–784.

82. Chuang, H., Lin, C., & Chen, Y. (2015). Exploring the triple reciprocity nature of organizational value cocreation behavior using multicriteria decision making analysis. *Mathematical Problems in Engineering, 2015*, 1–15.

83. Nermend, K. (2014). The implementation of cognitive neuroscience techniques for fatigue evaluation in participants of the decision-making process. *Neuroeconomic and Behavioral Aspects of Decision Making, 2014*, 329–339.

84. Özerol, G., & Karasakal, E. (2008). A parallel between regret theory and outranking methods for multicriteria decision making under imprecise information. *Theory and Decision, 65*(1), 45–70.

85. Trepel, C., Fox, C. R., & Poldrack, R. A. (2005). Prospect theory on the brain? Toward a cognitive neuroscience of decision under risk. *Cognitive Brain Research, 23*(1), 34–50.

86. Hines, W. W., & Montgomery, D. C. (1990). *Probability and statistics in engineering and management science*. New York: Wiley.

87. de Loof, E., Vassena, E., Janssens, C., de Taeye, L., Meurs, A., Van Roost, D., & Verguts, T. (2019). Preparing for hard times: scalp and intracranial physiological signatures of proactive cognitive control. *Psychophysiology, 56*, 10.

88. Holm, A., Lukander, K., Korpela, J., Sallinen, M., & Müller, K. M. I. (2009). Estimating brain load from the EEG. *Scientific World Journal, 9*, 639–651.

89. Macdonald, J. S. P., Mathan, S., & Yeung, N. (2011). Trial-by-trial variations in subjective attentional state are reflected in ongoing prestimulus EEG alpha oscillations. *Frontiers in Psychology, 2*, 82.

From Radical Movement to Organizational Mainstream: A Behavioral Economics Perspective on DSS History

David Arnott and Shijia Gao

Abstract Decision support systems (DSS) began as a radical movement in opposition to the total management information systems (MIS) orthodoxy of the 1970s. MIS aimed to support all decisions for all managers in an organization while DSS were small-scale systems developed in an evolutionary, exploratory way to support a manager making an important decision. DSS has remained a significant part of managerial and executive work to this day. By 2020, large-scale business intelligence and analytics (BI&A) systems emerged as the major information technology (IT) expenditure in organizations—large-scale decision support had become mainstream. Using the dual process theory of decision cognition from behavioral economics as a theory lens, we analyze decision support history and identify which decisions in organizations can effectively be supported by different decision support approaches. Our analysis is at odds with IT vendors' and consultants' marketing narratives. We find that BI&A and data science are mainly appropriate for well-understood operational decisions, while DSS is the only approach that effectively supports strategic decision-making. We suggest that large-scale BI&A and small-scale DSS will continue to coexist into the future; the first controlled by IT departments, the second by business managers and executives.

Keywords DSS · Business intelligence and analytics · Data science · History · Behavioral economics

1 Introduction

Decision support systems (DSS) began as a radical movement in opposition to the total management information systems (MIS) orthodoxy of the 1970s. By 2020, large-scale DSS, in the form of business intelligence and analytics (BI&A)

D. Arnott (✉) · S. Gao
Faculty of Information Technology, Monash University, Melbourne, VIC, Australia
e-mail: david.arnott@monash.edu; caddie.gao@monash.edu

© Springer Nature Switzerland AG 2021
J. Papathanasiou et al. (eds.), *EURO Working Group on DSS*, Integrated Series in Information Systems, https://doi.org/10.1007/978-3-030-70377-6_13

systems, had become the largest spend on business IT worldwide [1]. This path from innovative small-scale systems to organizational mainstream IT has involved a number of decision support generations and approaches that emerged in parallel with innovations in hardware and software, and changes in the nature of business organizations and how they are managed. In this chapter, we focus on those types of decision support that have had significant commercial impact on organizations: small-scale DSS, executive information systems (EIS), and BI&A. This means that some of the decision support types we described in Arnott and Pervan [2] are not addressed in the chapter, namely, group support systems, intelligent DSS, negotiation support systems, and knowledge management-based DSS. We do include data science in our discussion.

A difficulty in viewing the history of DSS is the use of the term "DSS." Originally, DSS was a term to describe a class of small-scale information systems that supported a manager making a decision. It was also used to identify a particular development philosophy. It then became the term for the academic field that studies IT-based management support and the top journal of the field was titled *Decision Support Systems* and remains one of the highest rated journals in information systems (IS) research. The term has also been used to describe the broad class of systems that support decision-making, including the original small-scale DSS but also EIS and BI&A. In this chapter, we use "decision support" to generally describe IT-based management support in research and practice and "DSS" to describe small-scale bespoke systems that support a manager making an important decision.

In considering and analyzing the history of decision support, we have chosen behavioral economics as the theory lens through which the history will be viewed. Behavioral economics is the current orthodoxy for understanding and explaining the nature of human decision-making [3]. As the systems we are considering are devoted to supporting decision-making, behavioral economics is an obvious choice for a theory lens. Behavioral economics is a complex set of theories, models, and methods. We have chosen to use its overarching theory, the dual process theory of decision cognition, as our primary lens.

The chapter is organized as follows: first the behavioral economics of decision-making is summarized to support our review of decision support history. The next three sections follow the history of IT-based management support from total MIS of the 1960s and 1970s to DSS, BI&A, and data science of 2020. The organizational landscape of current decision support is then explored in more detail. This is followed by an analysis of what decisions the various decision support approaches are capable of addressing. Finally, some concluding comments are made as well as some observations about the possibilities of the field.

2   What Is to Be Supported

All generations and types of IT-based management support ultimately exist for one reason: supporting decision-making. The goal of the systems in this chapter is to make a human decision-maker more effective for one or more decision tasks. Over time, the decision support literature has utilized three fundamental ways of understanding decision-making: the rational model of economic decision-making; early behavioral economics, especially Simon's phase model of decision-making; and contemporary behavioral economics, which is the current orthodoxy in descriptive decision-making theory.

The rational economic model is a prescriptive approach that specifies how a perfect decision should be made. It is the basis of neoclassical economics and involves maximizing an economic construct subject to one or more constraints. An alternative to the rational economic theory is behavioral economics which relaxes many of the perfect assumptions of the rational model and is mainly descriptive in nature. Nobel Laureate Herbert Simon was the seminal figure of this field and his phase model has been extremely influential in decision support theory. The phase model holds that decision-making occurs in iterative and recursive sequences of processes involving intelligence, design, and choice. Unfortunately, the phase model has not withstood empirical testing despite its face validity. Contemporary behavioral economics offers an alternative to both rational economics and Simon's model and is firmly based on empirically validated theory derived mainly from cognitive and social psychology. In Arnott and Gao [4], we presented an overview or primer on behavioral economics for decision support researchers.

The main organizing theory of contemporary behavioral economics is the dual process theory of decision cognition which holds that decision-making occurs within and between two cognitive systems. Nobel Laureate Daniel Kahneman states: "System 1 operates automatically and quickly, with little or no effort and no sense of voluntary control. System 2 allocates attention to the effortful mental activities that demand it, including complex computations." ([5], pp. 20–21). System 1 is associated with expertise and expert judgment while System 2 is the realm of the calm rational advisor, but also the learner and novice. The essence of System 2 is the application of a set of rules or algorithms to a decision task. Over time, System 2 tasks can be converted to System 1 through exposure and experience, and from System 1 to 2 by education or in organizations by analysis and directed intervention. Table 1 shows the properties of the two cognitive systems.

While described as discrete systems, System 1 and 2 can operate at the same time and can interact. Evans [6] described the situation as "like two minds in the same body." Kahneman and Frederick [7] explain: "System 1 quickly proposes intuitive answers to judgment problems as they arise, and System 2 monitors the quality of these proposals, which it may endorse, correct, or override." Far from being ineffective or second rate, in management decision-making, the fast, intuitive processes of System 1 can lead to superior outcomes compared to System 2 dominated processes [8–10]. Difficult and strategic management tasks will likely be System 1 dominant and a decision-maker's conception of such a task is likely to be volatile. Knowing when to replace System 1 intuitions with System 2 rules and algorithms is a difficult decision for both managers and analysts. It is also a decision that depends on context, particularly the skills and experience of the decision-maker. Bazerman and Moore [11] argued that "a complete System 2 process is not required for every managerial decision, a key goal for managers should be

Table 1 The two cognitive systems of decision-making

System 1	System 2
Unconscious	Conscious
High capacity	Low capacity
Automatic	Controlled
Holistic	Analytic
Associative	Rule based
Effortless	Effortful
Fast	Slow
Skilled	Rule following
Highly contextualized	Decontextualized
Personalized	Depersonalized
Acquisition by biology, exposure, and experience	Acquisition by cultural and formal tuition

to identify situations in which they should move from the intuitively compelling System 1 thinking." System 2 managerial tasks are likely to be more stable in their internal representation and are easier to understand and explain.

Underlying the dual process theory of decision-making is the heuristics and bias stream of behavioral economics research. Tversky and Kahneman [12] identified three general and innate heuristics that guide decision-making. The action of these general heuristics means that decision-makers can quickly and effortlessly arrive at a decision. While general heuristics are a source of effectiveness in human decision-making, they are subject to cognitive biases that can lead to poor decisions and, in some rare cases, catastrophic failure. Cognitive biases are behaviors that prejudice decision quality in a significant number of decisions for a significant number of people; they are inherent in human reasoning. Biases can act on both System 1 general heuristics and specialized System 2 heuristics. In addition to dual process theory, general heuristics, and cognitive biases, behavioral economics includes prospect theory, an alternative to the expected utility model, and nudging and debiasing—methods for improving decision-making.

In summary, the current orthodoxy in understanding human decision-making is the set of theories, processes, and methods that comprises contemporary behavioral economics. The overarching theory that provides this understanding is the dual process theory of decision cognition, an empirically validated theory that has replaced the phase model. We will use dual process theory to help understand the history of decision support. The perfectly rational decision model of economics represents a prescriptive technical view of decision-making, while the early phase model and its replacement, the contemporary dual process theory, represent a behavioral view. These fundamental views of decision-making have been influential in the history of decision support.

3   Business IT in the 1960s and 1970s

Before discussing the history of the decision support field, it is informative to recall the nature of the business IT environment before its emergence. Business IT in the 1960s and 1970s was dominated by the idea of a total management information system (MIS), shown in Fig. 1. The developers of MIS saw managers in an organization matrix, often depicted as a pyramid as seen in Fig. 1. This matrix is defined by business functions and levels of decision-making. The essential idea was to support the information needs of all cells in the matrix from the newly created computerized data files of an organization. As Gallagher [13] stated "The ultimate goal of an effective management information system is to keep *all* levels of management *completely* informed on *all* developments in the business which affect them" (our emphasis). MIS academics and practitioners believed that, given sufficient time and resources, they could specify the information and decision-making requirements of each cell of the pyramid. Books such as Thierauf [14] provided generic designs for at least the operational cells of a manufacturing company. In a sense, MIS was a product of its socio-economic context. As Arnott and Pervan [2] observed "The world of MIS was that of the Cold War and the multi-national corporation. The focus of management in this environment was total integration, efficiency, and central control."

   MIS projects had strong support and advocacy from IT groups in organizations, as well as IT vendors, and IT and management consultants. This advocacy was based on untested and untestable claims of the benefits of total MIS. A general belief was that the provision of more, even real time, data to managers at all levels in all functions would lead to significantly improved decision-making. Normally, the conception of a decision process was based on rational economic and management

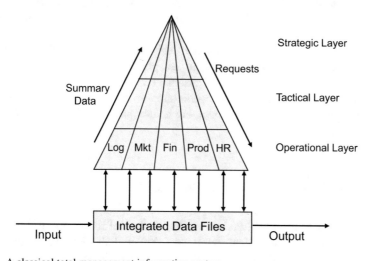

Fig. 1 A classical total management information system

science models. In essence, they believed that all System 1 decisions made by management were in some way deficient and should be transformed into computer-based System 2 decisions using the new techniques of system analysis and design. The most nuanced and reasoned expression of classical MIS was Davis [15] who stated, "MIS design should reflect not only rational approaches for optimization but also the behavioral theory of organizational decision making" (p. 15). His call for a behavioral consideration in MIS design went largely unheard.

There was some criticism of the MIS approach at the time. Ackoff [16] questioned the assumption that a lack of information was management's key problem and the assertion that if a manager had the information that MIS analysts thought they needed then their decision-making would improve. Harvard professor John Dearden was perhaps the most influential critic of MIS. In Dearden [17, 18], he was critical of the possibility of an expert system analyst understanding management tasks, especially strategic tasks, and building systems to support them. In his words, "... the notion that a company can and ought to have an expert (or a group of experts) create for it a single, completely integrated super-system—an MIS—to help it govern every aspect of its activity is absurd" ([18], p. 90). He also identified a key reason for the strong advocacy of the MIS approach: "... the early success of information technology in renovating logistics systems has been so great that there is a natural inclination to try the same methods on the company information systems as a whole." ([18], p. 96). The logistics systems of the 1960s and 1970s used batch processing of transactions and management science models to optimize stock control. The decisions were highly structured and well-understood System 2 decisions, the most amenable to computerization. Gorry and Scott Morton [19] argued that "Management Information Systems ... (is) an area that has almost nothing to do with real managers or information but has been largely routine data processing" (p. 61). One of this chapter's authors was involved with developing a total MIS in the early 1970s and their experience strongly supports Gorry and Scott Morton's assessment—MIS had virtually nothing to do with genuine decision support.

By the 1980s, MIS as a vehicle for decision support was discredited. The mainframe computers of the time could not physically support the aims of the MIS approach and the new cohort of systems analysts were unable to effectively design systems for management decision support. MIS were very successful in supporting the operations of a business, but no complete total large-scale MIS was ever achieved.

4   The Radical Movement of Early DSS

Gorry and Scott Morton [19] laid down the intellectual foundation of DSS based on early behavioral economics, but it was not until the late 1970s and early 1980s that the new approach gained traction. By 1980 many aspects of Western society had changed, and the emphasis was now on empowering individuals, the democratization of decision-making, and the flattening of management structures. The late 1970s saw a convergence of a number of factors that together enabled the birth of DSS:

1. The development of minicomputers with relational data base and financial modelling software, and personal computers (called microcomputers at the time) with spreadsheet software.
2. The 1978 Nobel Prize in Economics to Herbert Simon, the first in behavioral economics.
3. A generation of academics interested in supporting management decisions, notably Peter Keen, Michael Scott Morton, Andrew McCosh, Anthony Gorry, Ralph Sprague, and Stephen Alter.

The radical aspect of DSS was to support an individual user making an important decision rather than provide data processing related to a generic task specification. As Keen and Scott Morton [20] observed, the aim was to "support, rather than replace managerial judgment." Accordingly, the original DSS were small-scale systems that supported one manager for one decision, a fundamentally different proposition than the MIS philosophy of supporting all managers for all decisions in an organization. Another major difference between MIS and DSS was that DSS was widely successful. We assume that readers of this collection will be in some part familiar with the nature of early DSS. We have addressed this history in Arnott and Pervan [2, 21], as have Hosack, Hall, Paradice, and Courtney [22]. Here, we focus on one important differentiator between MIS and DSS—the approach to systems development and use.

Figure 2 shows the two most influential models of DSS development and use— the Keen and Sprague models. The contextual assumptions for DSS development and use were radically different to MIS [23]. First, the analyst and manager/user working together could not precisely define the decision task; second, users were not entirely sure what they needed from a DSS; third, the user's understanding of the decision task was shaped and changed by using the DSS; and fourth, and an important feature of DSS, its use is discretionary—managers can choose whether or not to use the system. These four characteristics of the development and use context are unique to DSS to this day and separate the field from other approaches to business IT. In DSS, development and use are not separate activities or processes, they are intricately interconnected.

Keen [23] argued that adaptive design is the key element of DSS: "... the label 'Support System' is meaningful only in situations where the 'final' system must emerge through an adaptive process of design and usage" (p. 15). Keen's model, the left-hand side of Fig. 2, explains the evolutionary nature of the relationship between the user, analyst, and system. The model is about understanding decisions

---

[1] At the time, a DSS analyst was termed a builder to emphasize difference to MIS personnel.

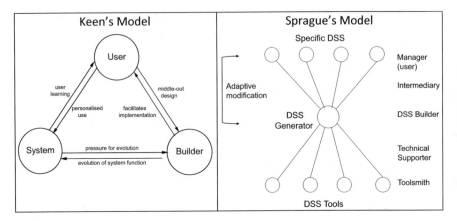

Fig. 2 Two models of DSS development and use

and the processes of supporting a manager; technology is a second-order issue. This development approach was, and probably remains, alien to corporate IT departments and is sometimes derisively called anarchy, shadow, or feral [24–26]. The other panel of Fig. 2, Sprague's model, also embraced the adaptive or evolutionary nature of DSS and the importance of the user being intimately involved with the system development [27]. Sprague took a more technical view of DSS and focused more on the role of specific and general DSS software and data management. He also saw some role for the corporate IT department in providing technical support and data curation but believed that most DSS should be developed in user departments. Sprague's model can be thought of as an organizational view of DSS development and use while Keen's is more idealized and represents an analyst's or consultant's view.

Both Keen's and Sprague's models are firmly based on early behavioral economics and, in particular, the phase model of decision-making and the idea of semi-structured decisions [28]. The system development and use scenario described above meant that the founders of DSS understood that managerial decision-making is complex and inherently volatile. They understood the dominance of System 1 decision processes for managers, especially senior executives. In a sense, the iterative development of small-scale systems with strong user involvement meant that DSS development and use was training System 2 processes in the manager's mind. Through cycles of system use, learning, and system modification, they were moving System 1 management decisions to analytic and rule-based System 2 processes or engendering a strong interaction between Systems 1 and 2 processes in the user.

5 Joining the Organizational Mainstream

The 1980s saw the co-existence of early DSS and MIS, the latter morphing into the support and automation of operational business processes. In the late 1980s, another approach to supporting management decision-making emerged—executive information systems (EIS). In the seminal EIS book, Rockart and DeLong [29] identified the nature and methods for EIS use in organizations. Corporate IT departments enthusiastically adopted EIS and they became pervasive in IT portfolios. Rockart and DeLong thought that DSS were middle management tools and that senior management needed more data reporting about their organizations using large-scale databases and graphical user interfaces. An important feature of EIS was the ability to drill-down a report hierarchy in order to investigate a business problem; they especially supported the intelligence part of the phase model. The drill-down features were enabled by the development of multidimensional databases [30].

The EIS philosophy had much in common with classical MIS. There were, however, important differences between EIS and MIS. First, EIS recognized that managers differ in cognitive style and abilities and that no EIS could support all managers in an organization; Second, EIS was not based solely on an organization's databases, it used external and special purpose data sets as well; and finally, EIS used a new approach to link the provision of information to important business objectives—the critical success factor approach, a similar approach to today's key performance indicators.

The bull market of the 1980s led to a concentration of capital in very large enterprises through a plethora of mergers and acquisitions. To support managers in the new mega-organizations the relational databases and data cubes of EIS were inadequate. The data environment that evolved to support these organizations was that of data warehouses [31] and divisional or functional data marts [32]. These were typically developed by the central IT department and were large-scale multidimensional databases, or collections of databases. By 2000, EIS and data warehousing morphed into business intelligence systems which were marketed as being able to support the decision-making of most managers in an organization; an echo of the ambitions of classical MIS. An important distinction between business intelligence and previous large-scale decision support systems is that although they support hierarchical reporting, they have a strong business analytics component [33]. These analytics include small-scale DSS modelling approaches and management science models. In business intelligence projects, the reporting and analytics components are so interrelated that they are known as business intelligence and analytics (BI&A) systems. Surveys by industry analysts show that BI&A has been the top, or near the top, of CIO technical priorities since 2005; Kappelman et al. [1] reported that BI&A is the largest organizational spend on business IT and has been since 2015. Large-scale decision support, both reporting and analytics, had entered the organizational mainstream.

Much like MIS, BI&A has been oversold by IT departments, vendors, and consultants. Our empirical research [34] found that in organizations BI&A systems have two major forms: enterprise BI&A that aims to address the whole organization and smaller functional BI&A systems that support a function or department. A third approach, self-service BI&A, is emerging in practice [35]. In a similar manner to early DSS, functional BI&A systems are often termed shadow or feral systems because they are not developed by the corporate IT department and are not included in the organization's formal IT project management and governance structures. Our research found that enterprise BI&A systems are mainly restricted to supporting operational decisions that are System 2 in nature. In addition to these decisions, functional BI&A systems support both operational and tactical decisions that have a strong interaction between System 1 and 2 processes. We did not find any BI&A support for System 1 decisions. Our study found that although BI reporting and analytics has been oversold, there are areas of organizational decision-making where they have had a significant positive impact.

In addition to mainstream BI&A, two further decision support approaches have emerged in organizations since 2010. The first is the much-hyped concept of big data and in particular, big data analytics [36]. The volume and variety of data sources that contemporary organizations can exploit had significantly increased. However, like previous approaches, the analysis of this "big" data to support management decision-making, especially senior management, was oversold by vendors and consultants, as well as in the professional and academic literatures. For example, McAfee and Brynjolfsson [37] proclaimed big data to be "The Management Revolution" in an influential *Harvard Business Review* article. Although they also cautioned "big data's power does not erase the need for vision or human insight" (p. 65), it was the "Revolution" headline that was marketed by vendors and consultants. In academe, two influential editorials Chen, Chiang, and Storey [38] in *MIS Quarterly* and Abbasi, Sarker, and Chiang [39], in the *Journal of the Association for Information S*ystems, argued for an expansion of big data analytics research in IS, largely based on rational decision-making. Despite these calls for action, the promise of big data analytics for decision support has not been delivered in practice; influential industry analyst Gartner Inc. dropped big data from its list of important business IT technologies in 2015.

The second recent addition to decision support has been data science. Originating in computer science, data science is firmly based on the philosophy of rational decision-making. It uses machine learning and other AI techniques in addition to statistical and other modelling approaches to suggest optimal solutions to a decision problem. These decisions are strongly System 2 in nature.

6   The 2020 Landscape of Decision Support

Figure 3 graphically shows the history described in the previous sections. The 2020 landscape of IT-based decision support in organizations is more complex than at any time of its history. Large-scale BI&A systems are a major, often the

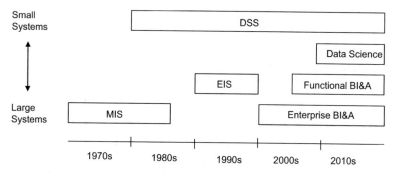

Fig. 3 A timeline of decision support approaches

largest, expenditure on IT in organizations. Functional BI&A systems have emerged across organizations as divisions, subsidiaries, and departments feel the need for tailored and specific decision support. Business analytics, as part of BI&A, and data science have returned modelling to the center of decision support attention. The variety and volume of data sources has increased and includes not only operational organizational data but external data sets, web-based data, and social media.

Despite the developments in large-scale and scientific decision support as shown in Fig. 3, the original version of DSS, small-scale bespoke systems that support a manager making an important decision, remains an important and integral part of contemporary managerial work. It may even form the majority of decision support in organizations, but no research has been undertaken on this issue. In our DSS/BI case study research, we have found that senior executive teams have access to small groups of DSS analysts who build bespoke, ad hoc systems for executives' decision support. These systems are usually ephemeral in nature. We have found that the analysts in these groups are well educated and high performing, many have PhDs in information systems and other business fields. They stand in stark contrast to the structured development teams of large-scale decision support in corporate IT departments and the often-lone data scientist. The decision tasks that these DSS analyst's support are not well understood, often difficult to analyze and communicate, and are often highly volatile. These decisions have the potential to change the nature of the organization; they are highly strategic. There is further discussion on this issue in the next section. We have found that the development and use environment for these DSS groups is most like Sprague's model of DSS in that the analysts mostly work through an intermediary, who in some cases, is themselves a senior executive or manager.

Table 2 provides further analysis of the types of decision support in today's organizations; much of the table is self-explanatory. The table illuminates important differences between the decision support approaches. Both BI&A approaches aim to address all decision-makers within their organizational scope. This scope can be flexible—for example, we have studied one functional BI&A system that was developed in one function but has users in a number of other functions. On the other

Table 2 Characteristics of decision support in 2020

	BI&A (enterprise)	BI&A (functional)	Data science	DSS
Organizational scope	All decision-makers in an organization	All decision-makers in a function	Any defined problem	Any decision-maker
Dominant decision-making approach	Early behavioral economics, Rational economics	Early behavioral economics, Rational economics	Rational economics, Computer science	Behavioral economics (some rational economics)
Decision tasks	System 2	System 2, S1/S2 interaction	System 2	S1 → S2, S1/S2 interaction
Dominant technology	Data warehouse, data marts, BI reporting and analytics	Data marts, BI reporting and analytics	Python, R, SQL, Hadoop	Spreadsheets, Data feeds from BI, Opportunistic
Governance archetype	Federal	Feudal	Anarchy	Anarchy
Dominant development method	Agile	Agile, Some evolutionary	Ad hoc	Evolutionary, Agile
Developers	IT department, Vendor, Consultants	Shadow developers	Data scientist	User and analyst, Consultant
Developers (quality, nature)	Standard IT project	High performing	High performing	High performing
Frequency of use	Regular	Regular	Ad hoc to regular	Ad hoc, Sometimes intense
Lifecycle	Very long	Medium to long	Varies greatly	Short
Cost/decision	Very low	Low to medium	Varies greatly	High

hand, DSS address one manager or a small group of managers, while data science is aimed at a problem rather than a person. Both types of BI&A share a technology base, but DSS is dominated by PC applications and feeds from larger databases, including BI&A. Data science uses a particular set of data and analytics languages and applications. BI&A is still dominated by an early behavioral economics theory base, the "intelligence" in its title even comes from Simon's phase model. We believe that Simon has been more influential than other Nobel Prize winners because he bridged the behavioral and the technical views of decision-making, being both a professor of psychology and computer science.

The governance structures of the various decision support approaches are shown in the table using the framework of Weill and Ross [26]. Enterprise BI&A falls under the normal, highly structured, governance processes of an organization's IT division. Their federal governance model involves policies, procedures, and committees that cross central IT and functional areas. Functional BI&A is part of a functional vice-president's domain or a senior manager's department and uses a feudal governance model. Data science and DSS use the appropriately named anarchy governance model; their operation and funding is at the whim of an executive sponsor.

Underlying the analysis in Table 2 is the role of corporate IT departments, IT vendors, and IT consultants in decision support projects. Over decision support history, from total MIS to BI&A systems, there has been a continual and determined push to develop and deploy large-scale systems to support management decision-making in organizations. One reason for this movement is that large-scale decision support is the type of information system and type of project management and systems development that corporate IT departments understand and are highly competent with. They are also the projects with the most financial return to vendors and consultants. CIOs who we have interviewed genuinely want to help managers throughout their organizations and senior executive teams have been willing to provide CIOs with budget for large-scale BI&A. To make the business case for BI&A projects attractive, the systems have to able to support as many users in as many parts of the organization as possible. This keeps the cost of supporting each decision low. It also leads to the continuous overselling of large-scale BI&A to organizations, both to sponsors and users.

The overselling of data science to organizations could be a case of what economists call a mutually assured delusion [40]. These situations arrive when actors in a market *ex ante* willfully ignore evidence of the limitations of their product or service and *ex post* act in collective denial about their product or services' use outcomes. For data science, the claims of strategic decision support, of optimal solutions that are preferable to any managerial judgment, and the desire to supplant managers in organizational decision-making, lie at the basis of the delusions. When all actors in a market, in this case IT departments, vendors, consultants, and academics, share delusions, a dangerous groupthink situation can also arise [41]. The reasons for the limitations of data science in practice are further discussed in the next section.

7   What Is Actually Supported, and What Can Be

While BI&A and data science have been seriously oversold to organizations, with claims of universal support and strategic impact, there are important areas of an organization's decision-making that can benefit from all approaches to IT-based decision support. Figure 4 shows the 2020 decision support landscape from the perspective of the decisions supported by the different system types. Decisions are defined in nine categories by the dual process theory of behavioral economics and the organizational nature of the decisions. The figure is based on our analysis in Arnott et al. [34] and is a reconceptualization of the Gorry and Scott Morton MIS framework from 1971. The allocation of BI&A systems and DSS to the various cells is based on our case study research, while the allocation of data science is based on

	Operational	Tactical	Strategic
System 2 Decisions	**1** Enterprise BI&A Functional BI&A DSS Data Science	**2** Enterprise BI&A Functional BI&A DSS Data Science	**3** *Functional BI&A* DSS
Decisions with a strong System 1/2 interaction	**4** Functional BI&A DSS	**5** Functional BI&A DSS	**6** DSS
System 1 Decisions	**7** *Intuition*	**8** *Intuition*	**9** *Intuition*

Fig. 4 Decisions supported by IT-based decision support

Power [42]. Pure System 1 decisions are intuitive and unconscious and are not yet amenable to IT-based decision support.

Figure 4 does not show the relative presence or importance of the various decision support approaches in each cell, only their existence. The vast majority of IT-based decision support applications actually occur in Cell 1 of Fig. 4; Cell 1 comprises almost all enterprise BI&A and data science applications. Functional BI&A and DSS are the most significant approaches in Cell 2. For decisions with a strong interaction between Systems 1 and 2, functional BI&A and DSS are effective in organizations. These decisions are not well understood by the manager and analyst and require continuous development and use cycles. We believe that DSS is the appropriate support for all types of tactical and strategic decisions. Figure 4 shows, in italics, some presence of BI&A strategic support in Cell 3. This identification is based on our research, but this case study was a large government organization that operates in a relatively stable environment and has a low turnover of executives. We believe that this successful strategic use of functional BI&A is the exception rather than the rule.

Who decides what conception of a decision is to be supported by IT-based decision support and how accurate is that conception? Can an analyst, data scientist, or developer be effective in understanding decisions other than highly structured System 2 decisions? One of the best insights into these questions, shown in Fig. 5, is the 3-Gap framework of Kayande et al. [43]. We believe the framework can be generalized to BI&A and data science and to the conceptualizations of decisions in any decision support project. The framework shows that there are three models at play in decision support: the model of the decision in the manager's mind, the "true" model in reality, and the model of the decision embodied in the system. The "DSS model" is essentially the model in the analyst's mind made explicit. Figure 5 shows that there are three gaps in the conceptualization of these models,

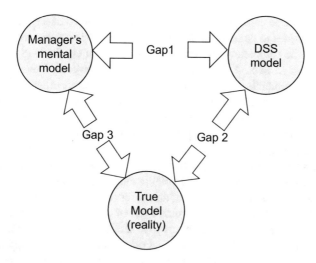

Fig. 5 Kayande et al.'s 3-Gap framework of DSS models (Reproduced from [43])

gaps that erode the effectiveness of any form of decision support. Gap1 adversely affects the use and acceptance of a DSS and arises when the manager has little understanding of the logic and processes embodied in the system. Gap 2 arises when the implemented system embodies an incomplete or unfaithful model of reality. Gap 3 is a consequence of a manager's lack of understanding of a decision.

Gaps 1 and 2 are increased when an analyst is unable to fully understand the nature of the decision. As discussed above, this is most likely for strategic and some tactical tasks and when a decision involves a strong interaction between System 1 and 2 thinking. The only decision support project that can work to close the gaps for strategic decisions is a DSS, as it is the only approach that can effectively use evolutionary development. As shown in Keen's model in Fig. 2, a small-scale DSS can be continuously modified and rebuilt, even discarded, as the manager and analyst gain deeper understanding of the decision and what support IT can provide. It is not possible to continuously evolve a BI&A system; the expense would be prohibitive, and no corporate IT project management office would permit it. Gap 3 is particularly problematic in large-scale BI&A systems where there are many users and accordingly many different mental models in managers' minds. This is one reason for the concentration of enterprise BI&A in Cell 1 of Fig. 5.

The most contentious of the current decision support approaches is data science. As mentioned above, data scientists have mainly come from a computer science background, and they have a fundamentally different view of the business world to BI&A and DSS analysts. The latter focus their system development on user decision-making, whereas data scientists have a worldview that is scientific and aims for the automation of System 2 decisions. As the name suggests, data science is focused on data and its analysis, not decision-making. Yet data scientists make strong claims for their ability to support, even replace, decisions in organizations.

In terms of the three gaps in Fig. 5, data scientists assume that the gaps do not exist for their techniques to be of value. Their system development process assumes that a problem can be completely specified, that is, they assume the DSS organizational context outlined in Sect. 4 does not exist for their problems. Data scientists have two common complaints about business; first, that managers often can't provide the problem specification and data sets they need. Second, they are often frustrated that managers fail to act on their data science insights—insights that they assume are optimal for the business. These common complaints show that data scientists have difficulty in understanding the business context of their work and don't understand that managers act on multiple competing, sometimes conflicting, priorities and goals and that managerial processes can be volatile and subject to individual differences. Power [42] when considering the use of data science for management support stated, "Analytic applications using the new data sources will most likely be focused at the day-to-day part of the organization hierarchy on operational control and operational performance decisions." All this means that data science can only support System 2 tasks that are well understood. Fortunately for data science, these tasks are important to organizations and represent a very large source of projects.

We now turn to the last aspect of Fig. 4, Cells 7, 8, and 9—the System 1 row. In business, considerable management attention is currently being devoted to ideas that improve System 1 decision-making, especially for strategic decisions. Nobel Laureate Thaler [44] stated "my hunch is that as the importance of a decision grows, the tendency to rely on quantitative analyses done by others tends to shrink. When the championship or the future of the company is on the line, managers tend to rely on their gut instincts." Further, Winter [45] argued "In many cases a decision based on emotion or intuition may be more efficient—and indeed better—than a decision arrived at after thorough and rigorous analysis of all the possible outcomes and implications." The desire to move from System 2 to System 1 decision-making by senior executives in order to improve their effectiveness was captured by Nordisk CEO Lars Rebien Sørensen who was rated the Number 1 CEO in the world by the *Harvard Business Review*. Sørensen related: "I'm gradually learning to be less rational and more emotional" ([46], p. 54). Amazon CEO Jeff Bezos regularly communicates his strategy to shareholders and managers. Amazon is one of the most data and analytics driven organizations in the world. However, Bezos' view on management decision-making follows a different and more nuanced strategy. He wrote to managers "... never use a one-size-fits-all decision-making process. Many decisions are reversible, two-way doors. Those decisions can use a light-weight process. For those, so what if you're wrong?" and "... most decisions should probably be made with somewhere around 70% of the information you wish you had. If you wait for 90%, in most cases, you're probably being slow ... you need to be good at quickly recognizing and correcting bad decisions." [47]. Bezos is articulating a decision-making portfolio within Amazon; operational tasks are automated or supported by both operational IS, BI&A, and data science projects, but managers need to develop a set of System 1 decision-making processes in order to be effective. This is a considerable distance from the marketing narrative of BI&A and data science systems. Developing DSS that supports a manager's transition from

System 2 to System 1 decision-making could be a productive territory for decision support research and practice, it represents a grand challenge for DSS researchers.

8 The Way Ahead

After all, the past is our only real guide to the future ...
— *Professor Michael Mandelbaum*

The organizational decision support landscape in 2020 has evolved to encompass four major approaches: DSS, enterprise BI&A, functional BI&A, and data science. Throughout decision support history there has been a tension between the desire of corporate IT to deploy large-scale decision support projects and the decision support needs of managers. The hyping and overselling of MIS, EIS, and BI&A have led to disappointment and delusion amongst important decision-makers in organizations and may have damaged the reputation of business IT. The relatively new approach of data science is currently in a strong hype stage. Alongside the large system hype, for around 40 years small-scale DSS have provided valuable support to managers and executives.

Behavioral economics provides our best understanding of human decision-making processes. It also provides insight into what decision support is possible for different types of decision. We know that BI&A and data science are only successful with supporting well understood, highly structured decisions that are mainly operational in nature. We know that DSS is the only approach that effectively supports strategic decision-making and that functional BI&A and DSS can effectively support tactical decisions. We know that this is the general decision support scenario that is successful in organizations. What we don't know is the future, but we believe that it will continue roughly in this form for a significant time.

It is important for the future of decision support that IT departments, IT vendors, consultants, and academics stop overselling BI&A and data science to organizations. There is nothing wrong with scientifically focused data science and large-scale BI&A *per se*. Problems arise with these approaches when:

1. The target decisions are not well understood
2. There are a number of different ways of conceptualizing the decisions
3. There is no consensus about the nature of the decision and how to make it effectively
4. When many decision-makers are intended to be supported
5. When there is time pressure on decisions
6. When the analysts believe they know best the decision and data needs of managers

We have used the dual process theory of decision cognition to identify the types of decisions that fit the six factors. Projects that tackle these decisions should be avoided or cautiously approached by BI&A and data science advocates and decision-makers in organizations. Operational System 2 decisions should be BI&A and data science's hunting ground.

Like Hosack et al. [22] we believe that the original form of DSS is alive and well. DSS is the only form of decision support that effectively addresses senior managers making important decisions by assisting with strongly interacting System 1 and System 2 decision processes. While senior managers continue to need decision support and they have the power to fund bespoke projects, DSS will long persist in organizations.

References

1. Kappelman, L., McLean, E., Johnson, V., Torres, R., Maurer, C., Synder, M., Guerra, K., & Kim, K. (2020). The 2019 SIM IT issues and trends study. *MIS Quarterly Executive, 19*(1), 69–104.
2. Arnott, D., & Pervan, G. (2005). A critical analysis of decision support systems research. *Journal of Information Technology, 20*(2), 67–87.
3. Fox, J. (2015). A short history of modern decision making: From "economic man" to behavioral economics. *Harvard Business Review, 5*, 79–85.
4. Arnott, D., & Gao, S. (2019). Behavioral economics for decision support systems. *Decision Support Systems, 122*, 113063.
5. Kahneman, D. (2011). *Thinking fast and slow*. New York: Farrar, Straus and Giroux.
6. Evans, J. S. B. T. (2003). In two minds: Dual-process accounts of reasoning. *Trends in Cognitive Sciences, 7*(10), 454–459.
7. Kahneman, D., & Frederick, S. (2002). Representativeness revisited: Attribute substitution in intuitive judgment. In T. Gilovich, D. Griffin, & D. Kahneman (Eds.), *Heuristics and Biases: The psychology of intuitive judgment* (pp. 49–81). New York: Cambridge University Press.
8. Dijksterhuis, A., Bos, M. W., Nordgren, L. F., & van Baaren, R. B. (2006). On making the right choice: The deliberation-without-attention effect. *Science, 311*, 1005–1007.
9. Klein, G. (2004). *The power of intuition: How to use your gut feelings to make better decisions at work*. New York: Currency-Doubleday.
10. Reyna, V. F. (2004). How people make decisions that involve risk: A dual-processes approach. *Current Directions in Psychological Science, 13*(2), 60–66.
11. Bazerman, M., & Moore, D. (2013). *Judgment in managerial decision making* (8th ed.). Hoboken, NJ: John Wiley & Sons.
12. Tversky, A., & Kahneman, D. (1974). Judgment under uncertainty: Heuristics and biases. *Science, 185*, 1124–1131.
13. Gallagher, J. (1961). *Management information systems and the computer*. New York: American Management Association INC.
14. Thierauf, R. J. (1975). *Systems analysis and design of real-time management information systems*. Englewood Cliffs, NJ: Prentice-Hall Inc.
15. Davis, G. B. (1974). *Management information systems: Conceptual foundations, structure, and development*. Tokyo: McGraw-Hill Kogakusha.
16. Ackoff, R. L. (1967). Management misinformation systems. *Management Science, 14*(4), B147–B156.
17. Dearden, J. (1966). The myth of real-time management information. *Harvard Business Review, 44*(3), 123–132.
18. Dearden, J. (1972). MIS is a mirage. *Harvard Business Review, 50*(1), 90–99.
19. Gorry, G. A., & Scott Morton, M. S. (1971). A framework for management information systems. *Sloan Management Review, 13*(1), 55–70.
20. Keen, P. G. W., & Scott Morton, M. S. (1978). *Decision support systems: An organizational perspective*. Reading, MA: Addison-Wesley.

21. Arnott, D., & Pervan, G. (2014). A critical analysis of decision support systems research revisited: The rise of design science. *Journal of Information Technology, 29*(4), 269–293.

22. Hosack, B., Hall, D., Paradice, D., & Courtney, J. F. (2012). A look toward the future: Decision support systems research is alive and well. *Journal of the Association for Information Systems, 13*(5), 315–340.

23. Keen, P. G. W. (1980). Adaptive design for decision support systems. *Data Base for Advances in Information Systems, 12*(1/2), 15–25.

24. Furstenau, D., Rothe, H., & Dander, M. (2017). Shadow systems, risk and shifting power relations in organizations. *Communications of the Association for Information Systems, 41*, 3.

25. Kerr, D. V., Houghton, L., & Burgess, K. (2007). Power relationships that lead to the development of feral systems. *Australian Journal of Information Systems, 14*(2), 141–152.

26. Weill, P., & Ross, J. W. (2004). *IT governance: How top-performers manage IT decision rights for superior results*. Watertown, MA: Harvard Business School Press.

27. Sprague, R. H. J. (1980). A framework for the development of DSS. *MIS Quarterly, 4*(4), 1–26.

28. Simon, H. A. (1960). *The new science of management decision*. New York: Harper.

29. Rockart, J. F., & Delong, D. W. (1988). *Executive support systems: The emergence of top management computer use*. Illinois: Dow Jones-Irwin.

30. Codd, E.F., Codd, S.B., & Salley, C.T. (1993). *Providing on-line analytical processing (OLAP) to user-analysts: An IT mandate* (Unpublished Manuscript). E.F. Codd and Associates.

31. Inmon, W., & Hackathorn, R. (1994). *Using the data warehouse*. New York: John Wiley and Sons.

32. Kimball, R. (1996). *The data warehousing toolkit*. New York: John Wiley and Sons.

33. Watson, H. J., & Wixom, B. H. (2007). The current state of BI. *IEEE Computer, 40*(9), 96–99.

34. Arnott, D., Lizama, F., & Song, Y. (2017). Patterns of business intelligence systems use in organizations. *Decision Support Systems, 97*, 58–68.

35. Bani-Hani, I., Tona, O., & Carlsson, S. (2018). From an information consumer to an information author: A new approach to business intelligence. *Journal of Organizational Computing and Electronic Commerce, 28*(2), 157–171.

36. Watson, H. J. (2019). Update tutorial: Big data analytics: Concepts, technology, and applications. *Communications of the Association for Information Systems, 44*(21), 364–379.

37. McAfee, A., & Brynjolfsson, E. (2012). Big data: The management revolution. *Harvard Business Review, 90*(10), 61–67.

38. Chen, H., Chiang, R. H. L., & Storey, V. C. (2014). Editorial: Business intelligence and analytics: From big data to big impact. *MIS Quarterly, 36*(4), 1165–1188.

39. Abbasi, A., Sarker, S., & Chiang, R. H. L. (2016). Editorial: Big data research in informantion systems: Toward an inclusive research agenda. *Journal of the Association for Information Systems, 17*(2), i–xxxii.

40. Benabou, R. (2013). Groupthink: Collective delusions in organizations and markets. *Review of Economic Studies, 80*, 429–462.

41. Baron, R. (2005). So right it's wrong: Groupthink and the ubiquitous nature of polarized group decision making. *Advances in Experimental Social Psychology, 37*(35), 219–293.

42. Power, D. J. (2016). Data science: Supporting decision making. *Journal of Decision Systems, 25*(4), 345–356.

43. Kayande, U., De Bruyn, A., Lilien, G. L., Rangaswamy, A., & Van Bruggen, G. H. (2009). How incorporating feedback mechanisms in a DSS affects DSS evaluations. *Information Systems Research, 20*(4), 527–546.

44. Thaler, R. H. (2015). *Misbehaving: The making of behavioral economics*. New York: W.W. Norton & Company.

45. Winter, E. (2014). *Feeling smart: Why our emotions are more rational than we think*. New York: Public Affairs.

46. Ignatius, A. (2016). What CEOs really worry about. *Harvard Business Review, 94*(11), 52–57.

47. Yoo, T. (2017). A sign outside Amazon's new Australian warehouse is a reminder of how Jeff Bezos crushes his rivals. *Business Insider Australia*, 20 November.

The History and Future of PROMETHEE

Bertrand Mareschal and Georgios Tsaples

Abstract Decision-making rarely involves the evaluation of a decision on a single criterion. On the contrary, decisions involve multiple criteria that very often may involve dimensions that are not easily quantified and moreover could include alternatives that have conflicting objectives. As a result, the field of Decision Support emerged with the purpose of assisting decision-makers to structure their problems and formalize the process on which the final decision will be based. The purpose of the chapter is to present one of the well-known decision aid methods: PROMETHEE. In the following pages, the method is presented starting from its mathematical foundation. Furthermore, the latest research trends and software applications are illustrated while finally, future research directions are explained and discussed.

Keywords Decision support · PROMETHEE · Multi-criteria decision aid

1 Introduction

Decision-making rarely involves a single evaluation criterion: indeed, most of our decisions have at least economic, social and environmental consequences, and can involve multiple stakeholders as well. As a result, the optimization of a single and most often economic objective function using classical Operational Research techniques (e.g., Linear Programming, Integer and Mixed Integer Programming) is not providing solid grounds to assist decision-makers. Decision aid emerged as an alternate approach to mathematical optimization by contributing to the analysis of

B. Mareschal
Solvay Brussels School of Economics and Management, Université Libre de Bruxelles, Bruxelles, Belgium
e-mail: bmaresc@ulb.ac.be

G. Tsaples (✉)
Department of Business Administration, University of Macedonia, Thessaloniki, Greece
e-mail: gtsaples@uom.edu.gr

© Springer Nature Switzerland AG 2021
J. Papathanasiou et al. (eds.), *EURO Working Group on DSS*, Integrated Series in Information Systems, https://doi.org/10.1007/978-3-030-70377-6_14

the entire process and of its structure, ensuring that coherent, formal procedures are used to propose solutions and to justify the rationale of the decision [1].

More precisely, decision aid methods can be used in four particular problematics of decision-making:

α: Choosing the best option among a set of potential alternatives.
β: Sorting a small set of alternatives into a number of predefined categories.
γ: Ranking a set of alternatives with the purpose of comparing them.
δ: Describing the consequences of the possible alternatives.

Within the field of decision aid, a set of formal, quantitative approaches deals specifically with the multicriteria nature of decision-making: it is called multi-criteria decision aid (MCDA) and its specific purpose is to assist decision-makers to structure a multi-criteria decision problem [2] and to reach an informed decision [3]. There are many different approaches in MCDA and they can be broadly categorized into the multi-attribute utility and value (MAUT) approach, the outranking methods and the non-classical methods [4].

One of the most known and widely used MCDA outranking methods is PROMETHEE (the acronym stands for **P**reference **R**anking **O**rganization **METH**od for **E**nrichment of **E**valuations). Two basic variants of the method (PROMETHEE I and II) were developed by J.P. Brans and were presented for the first time in 1982. Over the years, the core method was extended and enriched with the works of J.P. Brans and B. Mareschal.

The purpose of this chapter is to introduce the basic elements of PROMETHEE and to illustrate how it can be applied to various problem settings as a decision support methodology.

The rest of the chapter is organized as follows:

Section 2 introduces the methodological bases of the PROMETHEE and GAIA methods by introducing their mathematical foundations and explaining in a step-by-step fashion how they can be applied. Section 3 is focused on the available software solutions that can assist decision-makers to apply the PROMETHEE methods. Section 4 provides an overview of the applications of the methods in the literature, while finally, conclusions and future avenues for research are presented in the last section of the chapter.

2 Methodology

2.1 PROMETHEE I and II

Most MCDA methods share similar notations and structures. As such, an alternative can be regarded as the object of a decision or a representation of an action that can be put into operation.

A criterion is a tool that represents a perception of the decision-maker (or different perceptions by different decision-makers) on how an alternative can be evaluated or compared to other potential alternatives.

As a result, an MCDA problem can be mathematically defined as follows:

$$\text{Max } \{g_1(a), g_2(a), \ldots g_j(a), \ldots g_m(a) | a \in A\} \tag{1}$$

A is a finite set of possible alternatives $\{a_1, a_2, \ldots a_i, \ldots a_n\}$ and $\{g_1(*), g_2(*), \ldots g_j(*), \ldots g_m(*)\}$ a set of criteria on which the alternatives are evaluated upon. The criteria might require maximization or minimization without an effect on the process. The MCDA problem thus attempts to identify an alternative that optimizes all the criteria.

Nonetheless, the case where an ideal alternative optimizes all the criteria at once is a rare occurrence and MCDA attempts to find a compromise solution taking into account the preferences of the decision-maker(s). For that purpose, all the information and data is transformed to an evaluation table (Table 1).

The preferences of the decision-maker are translated into a set of natural relations. These are *preference, indifference, and incomparability* and they are analyzed in Table 2.

The notion of incomparability means that no decision can be made between two alternatives without additional information and/or data either from the decision-maker or the analysis of the problem under study. Consequently, at their core, MCDA methods attempt to reduce or eliminate the incomparabilities in any given problem [5].

The differentiation of the PROMETHEE methods relies on valued preferences, keeping some of the incomparabilities and allowing for a partial compensation among the criteria. These aspects of PROMETHEE are especially important for various classes of decision problems, since incomparabilities can occur naturally, thus making them desirable to be incorporated in the decision-making process because they can reveal more insights regarding the decisions. Furthermore, the

Table 1 Evaluation table for MCDA

a/g	$g_1(*)$	$g_2(*)$	....	$g_j(*),$	....	$g_m(*),$
a_1	$g_1(a_1)$	$g_2(a_1)$		$g_j(a_1)$		$g_m(a_1)$
a_2	$g_1(a_2)$	$g_2(a_2)$		$g_j(a_2)$		$g_m(a_2)$
...	...	...		...		...
a_i	$g_1(a_i)$	$g_2(a_i)$		$g_j(a_i)$		$g_m(a_i)$
...	...	...		...		...
a_n	$g_1(a_n)$	$g_2(a_n)$		$g_j(a_n)$		$g_m(a_n)$

Table 2 Relations in MCDA

$\forall j : g_j(a) \geq g_j(b)$	$\Longleftrightarrow$	aPb
$\exists k : g_k(a) > g_k(b)$		
$\forall j : g_j(a) = g_j(b)$	$\Longleftrightarrow$	aIb
$\exists s : g_s(a) > g_s(b)$	$\Longleftrightarrow$	aRb

partial compensation in the values of the criteria is particularly useful for problems that are unstructured or for those that include several dimensions and no dimension should be easily replaced by another (e.g., assessment of sustainability) ([6, 7].

Besides the evaluation table, the PROMETHEE methods require additional information from the decision-maker(s). The first piece concerns the relative importance of the criteria, which is expressed by their respective weights that must follow:

$$\sum_{j=1}^{m} w_j = 1 \tag{2}$$

Furthermore, the PROMETHEE methods take into account the level of deviations between the evaluation of the alternatives in each criterion. For small levels of deviation, there might be the option of indifference by the decision-maker, while on the other hand, the bigger the deviation, the larger the preference of one alternative compared to another. This is expressed with a set of functions:

$$P_j (a, b) = F_j \left[d_j (a, b) \right], \forall a, b \in A \tag{3}$$

Where

$$d_j (a, b) = g_j(a) - g_j(b) \tag{4}$$

And for which

$$0 \leq P_j (a, b) \leq 1 \tag{5}$$

As it was mentioned above, some of the criteria might require minimization instead of maximization. In that case, the preference function is changed to:

$$P_j (a, b) = F_j \left[-d_j (a, b) \right], \forall a, b \in A \tag{6}$$

Hence, the information about and on the criteria is accompanied by the preference function enriching the process. This expanded criterion is called *generalized criterion* and six types of preference functions have been proposed. They are illustrated in Fig. 1.

The preference functions introduce a new set of extra parameters that need to be defined. These are:

- q is the threshold of indifference: it is the largest deviation which is considered as negligible by the DM.
- p is the threshold of strict preference: it is the smallest deviation which is considered as sufficient to generate a full preference.
- s is an intermediate value between q and p. It only appears in the case of the Gaussian criterion (type 6).

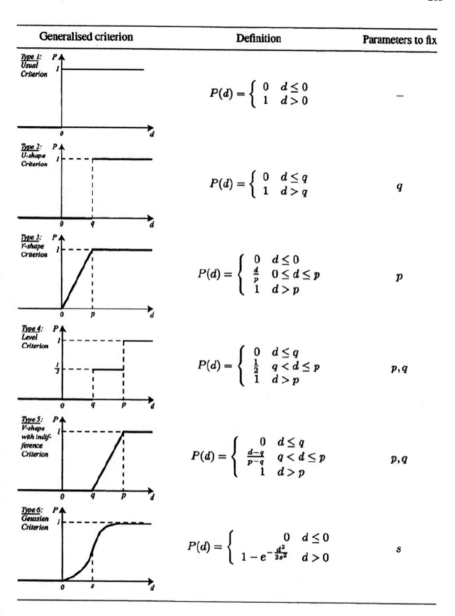

Fig. 1 Types of preference functions for the construction of the generalized criteria [5]

The PROMETHEE process continues with the aggregation of the preference indices.

Let a, b $\in A$ and

$$\pi\,(a,b) = \sum_{j=1}^{k} P_j\,(a,b)\,w_j \tag{7}$$

$$\pi\,(b,a) = \sum_{j=1}^{k} P_j\,(b,a)\,w_j \tag{8}$$

$\pi(a,b)$ is expressing the degree to which alternative a is preferred to alternative b over all the criteria and $\pi(b,a)$ the reverse (by how much b is preferred to a). In most cases, there is no alternative dominating any other on all criteria; for some criteria alternative a will be preferred to b and for other the reverse will apply. The following properties hold for all $(a,b) \in A$

$$\pi\,(a,a) = 0 \tag{9}$$

$$0 \le \pi\,(a,b) \le 1 \tag{10}$$

$$0 \le \pi\,(b,a) \le 1 \tag{11}$$

$$0 \le \pi\,(a,b) + \pi\,(b,a) \le 1 \tag{12}$$

It is clear that $\pi(a,b) \sim 0$ implies a weak global preference of alternative a over alternative b and $\pi(a,b) \sim 1$ implies a strong global preference of alternative a over alternative b. To gain clear insights on the strengths and weakness of each alternative, the outranking flows are defined.

- The positive outranking flow:

$$\varphi^+(a) = \frac{1}{n-1} \sum_{x \in A} \pi\,(a,x) \tag{13}$$

  – It expresses how an alternative a is outranking all the others. The higher the positive outflow the better the alternative

- The negative outranking flow:

$$\varphi^-(a) = \frac{1}{n-1} \sum_{x \in A} \pi\,(x,a) \tag{14}$$

  – It expresses how an alternative a is outranked by all the others. The lower the negative outranking flow the better the alternative.

Having all the information and calculation of the outranking flows, we are ready to construct the ranking of the alternatives.

2.1.1 PROMETHEE I Partial Ranking

The PROMETHEE I partial ranking is inferred by the positive and negative outranking flows

$$aP^Ib \quad \text{iff} \quad \begin{matrix} \varphi^+(a) > \varphi^+(b) \text{ and } \varphi^-(a) < \varphi^-(b) \\ \varphi^+(a) = \varphi^+(b) \text{ and } \varphi^-(a) < \varphi^-(b) \\ \varphi^+(a) > \varphi^+(b) \text{ and } \varphi^-(a) = \varphi^-(b) \end{matrix} \tag{15}$$

$$aI^Ib \quad \text{iff} \quad \varphi^+(a) = \varphi^+(b) \text{ and } \varphi^-(a) = \varphi^-(b) \tag{16}$$

$$aR^Ib \quad \text{iff} \quad \begin{matrix} \varphi^+(a) > \varphi^+(b) \text{ and } \varphi^-(a) < \varphi^-(b) \\ \varphi^+(a) < \varphi^+(b) \text{ and } \varphi^-(a) > \varphi^-(b) \end{matrix} \tag{17}$$

Where P^I, I^I, R^I stand for preference, indifference, and incomparability, respectively.

According to the definitions of the outranking flows:

$$\varphi(a) = \varphi^+(a) - \varphi^-(a) = \frac{1}{n-1} \sum_{j=1}^{k} \sum_{x} \left[P_j(a, x) - P_j(x, a) \right] w_j \tag{18}$$

Consequently,

$$\varphi(\alpha) = \sum_{j=1}^{m} \varphi_j(a) w_j \tag{19}$$

If

$$\varphi_j(a) = \frac{1}{n-1} \sum_{x} \left[P_j(a, x) - P_j(x, a) \right] w_j \tag{20}$$

$\varphi_j(a)$ is the single criterion net flow obtained when only criterion $g_j(*)$ is considered (100% of the total weight is allocated to the criterion). It expresses how an alternative a is outranking ($\varphi_j(a) > 0$) or outranked ($\varphi_j(a) < 0$) by all the other alternatives on criterion $g_j(*)$. The profile of an alternative consists of the set of all the single criterion net flows.

2.1.2 PROMETHEE II Complete Ranking

Often, a decision-maker might ask for a complete ranking. In that case we define
the net outranking flow:

$$\varphi(a) = \varphi^+(a) - \varphi^-(a) \tag{21}$$

The higher the net flow, the better the alternative:

$$aP^{II}b \text{ iff } \varphi(\alpha) > \varphi(b) \tag{22}$$

$$aI^{II}b \text{ iff } \varphi(\alpha) = \varphi(b) \tag{23}$$

The strength of PROMETHEE II is that the aggregation of the outranking
flows means that all alternatives can be compared among one another. This can
be easier for a decision-maker to understand and communicate; however, valuable
information is lost, especially concerning incomparabilities among alternatives.

A final remark concerning both the PROMETHEE approaches concerns the
weighting of the criteria. This process can be considered subjective since each
decision-maker may assign unique weight values to the criteria, which could
result in differentiations in the final ranking of the alternatives. As a result, both
PROMETHEE I and II could benefit greatly and increase the robustness of the
results by performing sensitivity analysis [8].

2.2 PROMETHEE Visualizations

One of the important aspects of the PROMETHEE methods is that it allows a
comprehensive visualization of the results that communicates the ranking in an
intuitive way, provides information about the positive and negative outranking flows,
and increases the transparency of the analysis.

In that aspect, several efforts have been performed in the previous years in that
direction. For example, Mareschal and De Smet [9] developed the "PROMETHEE
diamond," which can be used to represent the outranking flows along with the net
flow without losing information. However, the established visualization approach is
the GAIA plane. It is obtained from the unicriterion net flows and its purpose is to
analyze the impact of each individual criterion in the final results [5].

In particular, the GAIA plane can be considered complementary to the
PROMETHEE II complete ranking. This is an effort to visualize a decision-
making problem in a two-dimensional representation and to include all its aspects:
alternatives, criteria, weights, and preference parameters. Figure 2 below provides
an example of what the GAIA plane looks like.

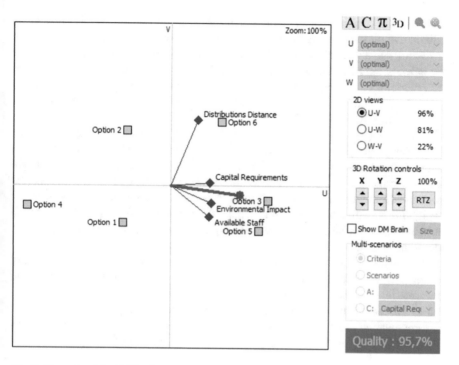

Fig. 2 Example of the GAIA plane

The alternatives are represented by bullets and the criteria with arrows. Already by representing these in a two-dimensional figure new insights can be gained. The position of the alternative provides the decision-maker with a first picture of existing similarities: the closer the actions, the more similar they are. Similarity and non-similarity are determined by the limit of indifference and preference. This means that the GAIA plane depends on the preference information provided by the decision-maker in the form of the parameters q, p, and/or s.

In a similar manner, the relative position of the criteria indicates the correlation and/or conflict among them. The closer the arrows are, the higher the contribution of the criteria to the decision problem. Information is provided also by the angle of the arrows: the greater the angle between the criteria, the greater the conflict.

As a result, the advantage of using the GAIA plane is that it allows the illustration of contradictory views. In addition, the length of a criterion measures its "discriminating" or "differentiating" power as a function of the data. The more different the actions in a criterion, the greater the arrow and, therefore, the more distinctive criterion. The discretionary power of a criterion depends on the selected limits and its corresponding weight.

Finally, the arrow represented by the letter D, known as the decision stick, illustrates the compromise chosen by the decision-maker as it corresponds to the weight adjustment. The visibility of the alternatives on this line is a clear way to show to the decision-maker their own priorities. The greater the visibility of an alternative on the stick, the better its ranking position. However, since it is only a two-dimensional representation, it can lead to a loss of information. The amount of information held, the so-called delta or D, depends on the data and the number of criteria. As a consequence of the loss of information, the classification resulting from the promotion of the decision stick does not necessarily have exactly the same results with PROMETHEE II. [10].

The research in visualizing PROMETHEE has not stalled in the later years. Schröder et al. [11] presented a new visualization tool which allows the joint representation of PROMETHEE I and II results. Furthermore, the new technique can perform in a group decision-making context by illustrating in a transparent way the differences of the decision-makers as they are represented by the different weighting schemes of the criteria. Finally, the technique offers a clustering of the alternatives under all these representations, thus increasing the transparency of the decision-making process.

In conclusion, PROMETHEE I and II do not only provide a structured way of ranking alternatives, but they also provide the decision-maker with enriched information that can assist her to better clarify their own preferences. Finally, powerful visualization techniques such as the GAIA plane, prove to be powerful communication tools that can further assist the decision-maker to fully understand how and why the particular ranking of the alternatives occurred.

3 PROMETHEE Software

The popularity and usability of the PROMETHEE methods, naturally led to the development of several software implementations over time. The most important are:

- PROMCALC was introduced at the end of 1980s. It was an interactive and graphical software running under MS-DOS.
- Ten years later, Decision Lab 2000 became the first MS-Windows implementation of PROMETHEE.
- Visual PROMETHEE is the currently available software.

Besides the PROMETHEE rankings and GAIA plane computation, Visual PROMETHEE includes many extensions and sensitivity analysis tools, including:

- Different graphical representations of the PROMETHEE rankings.
- PROMETHEE V for portfolio selection under constraints.
- GDSS-PROMETHEE extension for multiple decision-makers' analysis.
- Hierarchical organization of the criteria.
- Interactive weight sensitivity analysis tools.

The availability of interactive software and sensitivity ("what if") analysis tools is essential in the context of multicriteria decision aid: decision-makers should be able to easily check the impact of changes of their preference parameters on the results of the analysis. Visualization is also important, either through simple graphics or more elaborated analyses such as GAIA.

Visual PROMETHEE can be downloaded from the http://www.promethee-gaia.net web site. The site also includes additional information related to the PROMETHEE methods.

4   PROMETHEE Applications

The friendliness-of-use, the rich information provided, and the availability of the software have contributed to the increasing use of the PROMETHEE methods in a wide variety of areas. Searches in relevant scientific databases (ScienceDirect, Scopus, EBSCO, DOAJ, SpringerLink, etc.) are used to update the PROMETHEE Bibliographical Database (http://biblio.promethee-gaia.net). Figure 3 illustrates the areas of application as of February of 2020, [1] including over 2200 papers published by more than 4000 authors from 88 countries. The figure shows that the majority of the papers are related to societal issues. This is not unexpected since these types of problems are not easily quantified and involve multiple stakeholders. PROMETHEE is thus a natural candidate to structure such ill-defined problems.

Furthermore, Fig. 4 illustrates the number of papers that were published per year.

The figure reveals an upward trend for PROMETHEE, meaning that more and more authors are steadily using the methods to solve decision-making problems. Of these papers, real-life applications are also increasing, meaning that the method is considered an established one, thus suitable to be used. Finally, PROMETHEE covers problems that are not limited to industrial applications but concern wider societal issues [12].

5   Conclusions and Future Research

The focus of this chapter was to provide an overview of PROMETHEE as a multi-criteria decision aid method, how it can be used in supporting decisions, and where it can be applied. The chapter illustrated the structured way that the methodology proceeds in helping decision-makers, and how it can be used not only to rank alternatives but also to communicate and justify in an intuitive way any decision taken.

One of the constants of the method is that it evolves with new variations emerging to address problems. As a result, future directions for research could include the explicit incorporation of uncertainty in the evaluation of the decisions. Such an effort

---

[1] Some papers are related to more than one fields so the total percentage exceeds 100%

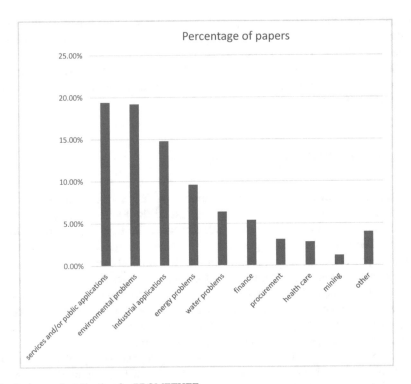

Fig. 3 Areas of application for PROMETHEE

has been attempted from the very first steps of PROMETHEE, when Mareschal [13] showed that insensitivity intervals can visualize the impact of varying weights on the rankings. Moreover, the existence of big data can stir the developments towards attempting to incorporate them in PROMETHEE analyses, maybe even changing the nature of what is considered a relevant criterion and what its values can be. In that regard, PROMETHEE can not only be combined with, but can also be adapted to act as an Artificial Intelligence (AI) algorithm.

As it was shown in the previous sections, visualization is an intrinsic part of PROMETHEE, with ongoing research efforts. Consequently, we believe that new attempts at more dynamic and interactive visualizations will continue to emerge in the field. Furthermore, decisions are rarely static: they need to be dynamic and constantly evaluated. Hence, the incorporation of the time dimension in the PROMETHEE framework is a promising and imperative research avenue.

Finally, the proliferation of mobile phones could signal a new surge of PROMETHEE applications, provided that software is developed that will be specifically designed for small screens and on-the-fly decision-making.

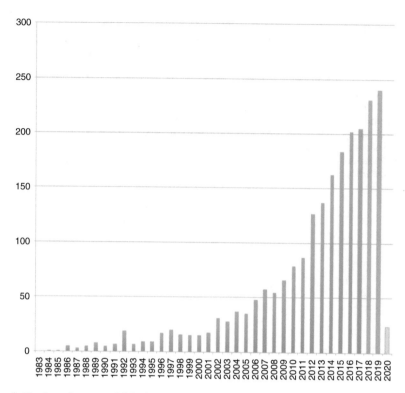

Fig. 4 Number of papers published per year (1982–2020)

References

1. Roy, B. (2005). Paradigms and challenges. In *Multiple criteria decision analysis: state of the art surveys* (pp. 3–24). New York: Springer.
2. Belton, V., & Stewart, T. (2002). *Multiple criteria decision analysis: An integrated approach.* New York: Springer Science & Business Media.
3. Tsaples, G., Papathanasiou, J., & Ploskas, N. (2017). Integrating system dynamics with exploratory MCDA for robust decision-making. *Lecture Notes in Business Information Processing, 282,* 179–192.
4. Greco, S., Ehrgott, M., & Figueira, J. R. (2016). *Multiple criteria decision analysis: State of the art surveys.* New York: Springer.
5. Brans, J.-P., & Mareschal, B. (2005). PROMETHEE Methods. In *Multiple criteria decision analysis: State of the art surveys* (pp. 163–196). New York: Springer.
6. Gervásio, H., & Da Silva, L. (2012). A probabilistic decision-making approach for the sustainable assessment. *Expert Systems with Applications, 39*(8), 7121–7131.
7. Munda, G. (2005). Measuring sustainability. A multi-criterion framework. *Environment, Development and Sustainability, 7*(1), 117–134.
8. Madias, E., Doulos, L., Kontaxis, P., & Topalis, F. (2019). A decision support system for techno-economic evaluation of indoor lighting systems with LED luminaires. *Operational Research, 2019,* 1–20.

9. Mareschal, B., & De Smet, Y. (2009). Visual PROMETHEE. developments of the PROMETHEE & GAIA multicriteria decision aid methods. In *2009 IEEE International conference on industrial engineering and engineering management* (pp. 1649–1649). New York: IEEE.

10. Ishizaka, A., & Nemery, P. (2013). *Multi-criteria decision analysis—Methods and software*. West Sussex: Wiley.

11. Schröder, T., Lauven, L., Beyer, B., Lerche, N., & Geldemann, J. (2019). Using PROMETHEE to assess bioenergy pathways. *Schröd, 27*(2), 287–309.

12. Mareschal, B. (2020). *PROMETHEE-GAIA Statistics*. Retrieved from http://www.promethee-gaia.net/assets/promethee-stats.pdf.

13. Mareschal, B. (1988). Weight stability intervals in multicriteria decision aid. *European Journal of Operational Research, 33*(1), 54–64.

On the Impact of Big Data Analytics in Decision-Making Processes

Fatima Dargam ⓘ, Shaofeng Liu ⓘ, and Rita A. Ribeiro ⓘ

Abstract We currently live in an era, in which data heavily, constantly, and globally flows into all areas of our activities. This mobile world is based on the concepts of the Internet of Things, which evolved by the digital transformation from Web 2.0 to 4.0, from a people-centric, participative, read-write web to a data-centered, semantic-oriented, and symbiotic web. It connects us at anytime with our conveniences and contacts, feeds our information needs, guides our shopping tendencies, and informs us about businesses and opportunities in a way that otherwise would be difficult to manage, due to the massive amount of data involved. Individuals and mainly organizations have to tackle the problem of how to process large amounts of data in support of their respective needs and operations, aiming at improving their handling and response efficiency. Big Data can be a strategic asset for organizations, but it is only valuable if used constructively and efficiently to deliver appropriate business insights. Moreover, we currently see special needs, like the one with the pandemic outbreak of COVID-19 that affected all the world, in which high-level technology and analytics tools for supporting decision-making have proven to be important allied components on the counter-attack and management of the overall crisis. Novel methods and technologies were required to be developed to enable decision-makers to understand and examine the massive, multidimensional, multi-source, time-varying information stream to make effective decisions, sometimes in time-critical situations. The current work evolves from the need and interest of board members of the EURO Working Group on Decision Support Systems EWG-DSS to tackle these emerging issues related

F. Dargam (✉)
SimTech Simulation Technology, Graz, Austria
e-mail: f.dargam@simtechnlogy.com

S. Liu
University of Plymouth, Plymouth, UK
e-mail: shaofeng.liu@plymouth.ac.uk

R. A. Ribeiro
UNINOVA, CA3, Caparica, Portugal
e-mail: rar@uninova.pt

© Springer Nature Switzerland AG 2021
J. Papathanasiou et al. (eds.), *EURO Working Group on DSS*, Integrated Series in Information Systems, https://doi.org/10.1007/978-3-030-70377-6_15

to Big Data and Decision-Making. The authors discuss the importance of having appropriate technologies for Decision-Making and Decision Support Systems to exploit the potentiality of Big Data analytics, so that we can treat crisis management in a more effective way; and organizations can improve their productivity to face increased competition in this new era. Our aim is to unveil the main impacts and challenges posed to decision-makers in organizations, in the new era of Big Data availability. An illustrative conceptual model is introduced to support the Big Data Analytics for Decision-Making in cross-domain applications.

Keywords DSS · Decision support systems · Decision-making · Big data · Analytics · Internet of things · DSS impact · Risk and crisis management

1 Introduction

The new knowledge era that we currently live in is based on a connected mobile-oriented world, in which data heavily and globally flows into all areas of our economy. Data are growing at an incredible rate and, as estimated in [1], in 2015 around 4.4 zettabytes were produced and by the year 2020 about 1.7 megabytes of new information will be created every second, for every person on the planet! This means that in every second on the internet the amount of data generated is more than the capacity of the entire internet of 20 years ago.

The world's current population (2020) is of approximately 7.8 billion people. In this connected world, Google searches are over 63,000 queries every second,[1] which makes around 2 trillion searches per year and the social media FaceBook generates on average four new petabytes of data per day and views 100 million h of daily videos.[2] Big Data (BD) is growing and moving fast from a variety of sources. Trillions of sensors are part of the Internet environments today, allowing monitoring, tracking and communication, populating the Internet of Things with real-time data. It is increasingly difficult to manage this flow, due to the exhaustive amount of data involved. Therefore, it is essential for businesses of all sizes— large and small— to have access to some form of data analytics in order to support more informed decisions to stay competitive in this new Big Data era.

The general aim of decision-making in the era of Big Data is to reduce large-scale problems to a scale that humans can comprehend and act upon. To this aim there are important challenges that must be addressed [2]: information scalability, visual scalability, display scalability, human scalability, and software scalability. Moreover, information noise filtering is another great challenge; data security and anonymity is also an important issue to be solved. To tackle Big Data in an effective way, advances and adaptation in technologies and in methodologies are urged. We

---

[1] https://seotribunal.com/blog/google-stats-and-facts/.

[2] https://www.brandwatch.com/blog/facebook-statistics/.

cannot count anymore with classical database and decision support tools to manage and analyze information data-sets.

What shall we do when modeling Decision Making to support the shift from available Data to available Big Data multiple sources? This question is not so simple to answer. Shall we preserve ourselves conservatives and ignore the new technological trends and behavior changes in our society? For sure not! If we want to technically survive within the next Information and Communication Technologies (ICT) generation, we also have to be open to accept and face the challenges of the new technological trends and services that influence Decision Making using Big Data. As for what technical needs concern, organizations have to tackle the problem of processing large data in support of their respective applications and operations, aiming at improving their handling and response efficiency. Moreover, we also have to tackle special needs, like with the pandemic outbreak of COVID-19 that affected all the world, in which high-level technology and analytics tools for supporting decision-making are proving to be important allied components on the counter-attack and management of the overall crisis, in an efficient and accurate way.

The main objective of this chapter is to discuss the impact and challenges of current research, trends and issues around the involved research areas of Big Data, decision support and decision-making. It is certainly not an exhaustive survey on any of the areas involved, but it reviews some relevant research work on the intersection between the areas of Decision Support and Big Data, in order to support the need to develop appropriate decision-making processes and tools for dealing with Big Data. The basic concept of the current work was already introduced in [3–5]. Concerning appropriate Decision-Making approaches to deal with Big Data Analytics, our work reviews Big Data decision-making literature and presents some insights on how to deal with Big Data for Decision-Making in some application areas.

The logical structure used to organize the remaining of the chapter is as follows. Section 2 focuses on the understanding of theoretical contribution from literature, from the background for "The Big Data Revolution" (Sect. 2.1); "Big Data Value Chain" (Sect. 2.2), through "Big Data Analysis and Decision Making Challenges" (Sect. 2.3) to Big Data tools and methodologies. Section 3 emphasizes on the practical aspect of Big Data for Decision Support, presenting decision-making as the logical next step after Big Data Analytics and detailing specific application areas. Namely: collaborative decision-making, dynamic-temporal-spatial decision-making, logistics and supply chain decisions, and crisis management, risky and critical decision-making. Based on the insights obtained from Sects. 2 and 3, Sect. 4 proposes a novel five-layer architecture which can be used to construct Big Data for Decision Support tools and systems. Finally, Sect. 5 draws some conclusions.

2 Background on Big Data for Decision-Making

2.1 The Big Data Revolution

Big Data can be understood as datasets from different sources that are too large to be treated by traditional data processing systems. Therefore, they require new processing Big Data technologies, which can handle essential tasks of data engineering, as well as data processing in support of data mining techniques and other data science activities.

There are three driving forces within the Big Data era, namely: Social; Mobile; and Cloud systems. These driving forces are based on some conceptual Big Data pillars, also known as the "Vs" of Big Data [6, 7]: Velocity; Variety; Volume; and Veracity of the Data. Considering those concepts, a Big Data platform should be able to help reliable store, access and analysis of any data, regardless of type, where it resides, or of how fast it is changing. It should also bring Value (another Big Data "V") to the application, by extracting business insights and revenue from data.

Big Data processing can also be compared to Business Intelligence (BI), when applied to very large datasets and processed in high speed in order to cater for the data explosion that is now happening in our daily routine. As verified in [8, 9], there is a shortage of data scientists and analytics professionals, who can evaluate business needs and impact, write the Big Data algorithms and program platforms, such as advanced learning algorithms, predictive analytics mechanisms, etc. The need for data scientists seems to be growing three times more than the one for statisticians and BI analysts. Data Scientists should have solid knowledge in statistical foundations and advanced data analysis methods combined with a thorough understanding of scalable data management, with the associated technical and implementation aspects. There is still a need to qualify those professionals within the academic sector. A solution in practice these days is that companies educate their current employees on data science because they already know the company's business. There is a need for training and educating employees and executives on interpreting data and understanding data analysis techniques. This is a clear consequence of the Big Data Revolution Era.

In order to understand better this "revolution", we discourse further about the Big Data Value Chain and Big Data Analysis and the Decision-Making Challenges that need to be considered, as well as the available systems.

2.2 Big Data Value Chain

According to recent European project's results published in [10], the Big Data Value Chain has identified several issues of their subtasks (e.g., data-level trust and permission management, privacy and security, models and methodologies for data curation activities, data storage open scalability, etc.) that need to be addressed

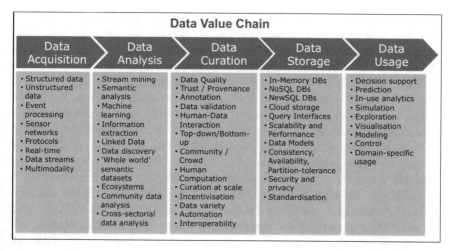

Fig. 1 Big Data value chain [10]

by standardization efforts within the areas involved. Figure 1 summarizes the main phases of the Data Value Chain, namely: Data Acquisition, Data Analysis, Data Curation, Data Storage, and Data Usage, as well as their respective tasks and characteristics.

As expected, Decision Support is the first and most important listed aim of Data Usage in the Big Data Value Chain. This enforces what many experts have been claiming about Big Data and Decision-Making, e.g., [11] "Big Data is useful, but if it does not primarily support us for making decision, then it is not valuable."

2.3 Big Data Analytics for Decision-Making

Within the era of Big Data, the analysis of overwhelming amounts of disparate, conflicting, and dynamic information is crucial to make effective and informed decisions in a timely fashion. The main challenges of Big Data analysis are to develop analytic tools and techniques enabling to synthesize information and derive insights from [2]: massive, dynamic, ambiguous, and often conflicting data; detect the expected and discover the unexpected; provide timely and understandable assessments; and to communicate effectively for supporting decision-making.

Big Data Analytics has been a key area of investment lately. It provides high value services across multiple markets, aiming at improving decision support. But what is now really different from Data Analytics? To answer this question, we look into a Big Data landscape, where we can identify some clear phases and processes, which compose the Big Data Ecosystem: Data Collection; Data Processing; Data Analysis and Data Execution. Data Collection implies the proper use of Networks, Infrastructure (e.g., IBM, Cloud era, Oracle, Cisco, Dell, Fujitsu, HP), and Data

Centers and Hardware (e.g., Dell, IBM, HP, Teradata, Oracle, EMC, Vmware, Equinix, etc.), in order to access and analyze a particular set of dynamic data. Data processing is directly influenced by the technologies used for the Storage and Database management. In this process, the available systems like in-memory (IMDS),[3]NoSQL,[4]Hadoop,[5]R,[6]MapReduce,[7]among others are usually considered. The Data Analysis process involves methods to deal with Analytics; Prediction; and as well as with Data Warehouses; cloud computing, as-a-service and mobile technologies. The Data Execution phase encapsulates the Services (e.g., KPMG, Deloitte, Accenture, IBM GS) that have to be placed available, their integration and specialized VARs (value-added-resellers), and Large Analytics (ISVs) Independent Software Vendors (e.g., SAP, SAS, Oracle, IBM MicroStrategy Quick View).

The aim of Big Data Analytics is to turn data into insights for better decision-making. According to the Gartner's Analytic Value Escalator,[8]considering value against difficulty, reproduced in Fig. 2, the way from hindsight, through insight into foresight is presented via an evolution from information to optimization through four types of Analytics: Descriptive; Diagnostic; Predictive; and Prescriptive. In Descriptive Analytics, we consider the question "What happened?", and we get in touch with reality in a report-oriented way. In Diagnostic Analytics, the aspect of discovering "Why did it happen?" is exploited as a matter of obtaining more insights of the situation. In Predictive Analytics, we consider the issue of "What will happen?", in order to understand the most likely future scenarios and their business implications. In Prescriptive Analytics, we consider the aspects of "How can we make it happen?" and "What should we do about it?" in order to optimize the scenario, as foresight, with collaboration for maximum business value by considering information via advanced analytics.

The development of data networks and the implementation of massive scale computing allowed the aggregation and modeling of data at a large scale, leading to the application of the resultant models to decision-making. Key issues, adapted from [2], to be addressed when developing methods, techniques, and tools for Big Data analytics are: (a) definition of intelligent reasoning techniques to support assessment, planning, and decision-making; (b) specialized data and visual representations, as well as interaction techniques, to help decision-makers to view, explore, and understand large amounts of information at once; (c) integration/fusion techniques that convert all types of conflicting, imprecise and dynamic data to support in-depth data analysis; (d) identify and select techniques to support production, presentation, and dissemination of the results of an analysis to communicate

---

[3]http://www.mcobject.com/in_memory_database.

[4]http://www.strozzi.it/cgi-bin/CSA/tw7/I/en_US/nosql/Home%20Page.

[5]https://hadoop.apache.org/.

[6]http://www.r-project.org/.

[7]http://en.wikipedia.org/wiki/MapReduce.

[8]https://www.gartner.com/smarterwithgartner/scale-the-value-of-analytics/.

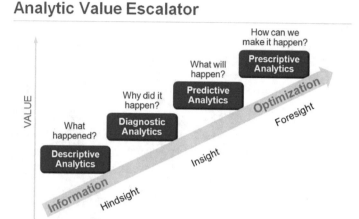

Fig. 2 Analytic value escalator (value × difficulty), Gartner (www.gartner.com)

information in the appropriate context to a variety of audiences. Attempting to address these issues, recent research and developments have reported various successful stories and lessons learnt in support decision-making. A comprehensive literature review on Big Data Analytics for felicitous decision-making is available from [12].

To illustrate significant potential applications of Big Data for public welfare, Fig. 3 (reproduced from [13]) shows the various impacts for which Data Science and Big Data Analytics can contribute to the Sustainable Development Goals established in 2015.

2.4 Big Data Tools and Approaches

This section presents some of the available tools used to tackle Big Data harvesting and analytics, as well as the methodologies and best practices. The illustration in Fig. 4 (reproduced from Znet[9]) summarizes the moving parts involved in the Big Data scenario with some citations of available platforms and methodologies for the processing of Big Data harvesting and analytics, envisaging the resulting insights to be applied in Decision-Making processes for different business objectives.

Big Data Harvest and Analysis intend to: (1) Collect information that reveals the plans, intentions, and capabilities of market competitors, so that the basis for decision-making and action taking is timely provided; (2) Produce timely

---

[9]www.blogs.zdnet.com/Hinchcliffe.

How data science
and analytics can
contribute to sustainable
development

❶ NO POVERTY
Spending patterns on
mobile phone services can
provide proxy indicators
of income levels

❷ ZERO HUNGER
Crowdsourcing or tracking
of food prices listed online
can help monitor food
security in near real-time

**❸ GOOD HEALTH AND
WELL-BEING**
Mapping the movement of
mobile phone users can
help predict the spread
of infectious diseases

❹ QUALITY EDUCATION
Citizen reporting can
reveal reasons for
student drop-out rates

❺ GENDER EQUALITY
Analysis of financial
transactions can reveal
the spending patterns
and different impacts
of economic shocks on
men and women

**❻ CLEAN WATER
AND SANITATION**
Sensors connected to
water pumps can track
access to clean water

**❼ AFFORDABLE AND
CLEAN ENERGY**
Smart metering allows
utility companies to
increase or restrict the
flow of electricity, gas
or water to reduce waste
and ensure adequate
supply at peak periods

**❽ DECENT WORK AND
ECONOMIC GROWTH**
Patterns in global postal
traffic can provide indicators
such as economic growth,
remittances, trade and GDP

**❾ INDUSTRY,
INNOVATION AND
INFRASTRUCTURE**
Data from GPS devices
can be used for traffic
control and to improve
public transport

❿ REDUCED INEQUALITY
Speech-to-text analytics
on local radio content
can reveal discrimination
concerns and support
policy response

**⓫ SUSTAINABLE CITIES
AND COMMUNITIES**
Satellite remote sensing
can track encroachment
on public land or spaces
such as parks and forests

**⓬ RESPONSIBLE
CONSUMPTION AND
PRODUCTION**
Online search patterns or
e-commerce transactions
can reveal the pace
of transition to energy
efficient products

⓭ CLIMATE ACTION
Combining satellite imagery,
crowd-sourced witness
accounts and open data can
help track deforestation

⓮ LIFE BELOW WATER
Maritime vessel tracking
data can reveal illegal,
unregulated and unreported
fishing activities

⓯ LIFE ON LAND
Social media monitoring
can support disaster
management with
real-time information
on victim location,
effects and strength
of forest fires or haze

**⓰ PEACE, JUSTICE
AND STRONG
INSTITUTIONS**
Sentiment analysis of
social media can reveal
public opinion on effective
governance, public service
delivery or human rights

**⓱ PARTNERSHIPS
FOR THE GOALS**
Partnerships to enable the
combining of statistics,
mobile and internet data can
provide a better and real-
time understanding of today's
hyper-connected world

www.unglobalpulse.org
@UNGlobalPulse 2017

Fig. 3 Big Data and the sustainable development goals [13]

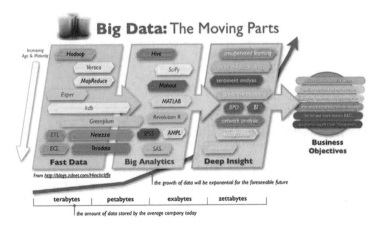

Fig. 4 Big Data scenario (www.blogs.zdnet.com/Hinchcliffe)

analysis that provides insight, warning, and opportunity to decision-makers in order
to guarantee an organization's protection of interests on the one hand, and the
forecasting of new investment trends on the other.

Existing Big Data commercial and non-commercial products are still not completely interoperable and most of the times can be complicated to be used, with high cost to end-users. Technologies for Big Data harvesting from multiple resources have been fast growing in the forms of data mining systems; search engines; query languages; filtering systems; cloud services, etc.

Examples of available Big Data Open-Source Tools can be found [14]. For data mining, some popular systems are supplied by: Orange; RapidMiner; Knime; Mahout; Keel; Weka; and Togaware. Within Data Analysis, the most popular platforms are supplied by: Hadoop, HPCC Systems; Dremel; HD; Amoa; Apache-Drill; and IKANOW. For Big Data Search, the most popular systems are supplied by: Lucene; Apache-Solr; and Elastic search.

Updated information about Big Data Analytics Tools for 2020 can be found in [15]. We list in Table 1 some popular frameworks used for Big Data available on the market, which are relevant references to the purpose of this work. A brief description of the tools is given for each item.

3   Decision-Making: A Consequence of Big Data Analytics

The main objective on Big Data Analytics is to extract knowledge from the data, which can be the next generation's breakthrough, driven by the demand of big volume, velocity, variability, and veracity of data. The extracted knowledge needs to be used into real decision-making process so that the value of Big Data Analytics becomes visible and explicit [12].

3.1   Decision-Making: Why Is It Different Nowadays?

It is a fact that, increasingly, business decisions are being supported by computer systems. However, this can also be a reason of great concern. Automatic decision-making can be adopted at different levels of organizations (e.g., finance and telecommunications industries), but not in all cases.

We are dealing now with a Big Data-Driven Decision-Making Era. As stated in [11], data analytics is gaining increasing attention in business and consequently also Data-Driven Decision-making (DDD). DDD refers to the practice of basing decisions on the analysis of data, rather than on intuition. DDD is a practice that different firms can engage into, in greater or lower degrees. Figure 5 illustrates this practice. In [11], they cite that the benefits of data-driven decision-making have been demonstrated conclusively, and a DDD measure was developed to rate organizations in how strongly they use data to make decisions across the company. It is shown that the more data-driven an organization is, the more productive it is. DDD is also correlated within a causal relationship with higher return on assets, equity, asset utilization, and market value.

Table 1 Big Data Tools and Technologies

Tools	Descriptions
ApacheHadoop/MapReduceTechnology	Hadoop is an open-source framework built on Java environment, which assists in the processing of large datasets in a distributed computing environment Hadoop uses MapReduce technology, which is responsible for processing jobs in distributed mode
ApacheCassandra	Cassandra is a free open-source distributed NoSQL DBMS that manages huge data volumes spread across numerous commodity servers, delivering high availability
ApacheSAMOA	SAMOA (Scalable Advanced Massive Online Analysis) is an open-source platform for big data stream mining and machine learning
ApacheSpark	Spark is an open-source framework for data analytics, machine learning algorithms, and fast cluster computing. Spark is written in Scala, Java, Python, and R
ApacheStorm	Storm is a free and open-source cross-platform distributed stream processing, and fault-tolerant real-time computational framework, by Backtype and Twitter.
BIRT iHub	This is a web-based embedded BI platform and data management system that handles data analytics within enterprises' infrastructures. It can transform complex data into advanced visualizations with embedded analytics and can deliver unparalleled Big Data management linked to cloud
CDH Cloudera	CDH (Cloudera Distribution for Hadoop) is a free open-source software version by Cloudera. It allows to collect, process, administer, manage, discover, model, and distribute unlimited data. CDH platform distribution encompasses Apache Hadoop, Spark, Impala, among others
Datawrapper	Datawrapper is an open-source platform for data visualization that aids its users to generate simple, precise, and embeddable charts very fast
Elastic search(Elastic stack)	Elastic search is a cross-platform, open-source, distributed, RESTful search engine based on Lucene. It comes as an integrated solution in conjunction with Logstash (data collection and log parsing engine) and Kibana (analytics and visualization platform) and the three products together are called as an Elastic stack
Flink	Apache Flink is an open-source, cross-platform distributed stream processing framework, written in Java and Scala, for data analytics and machine learning. It is fault tolerant, scalable, and high performing

(continued)

Table 1 (continued)

Tools	Descriptions
GoodData	A Big Data analytics tool for applications residing in clouds. Data can be loaded from any source, structured or not, to internal data sources. Clouds could be used as a hub of data supply chain. Interactive dashboards capitalize on critical business insights while promoting visual data discovery, exploration, and collaboration among teams
HPInformation infrastructure	This is used to capture, store, replicate, and scale data, as well as to manage, secure, govern, and leverage information seamlessly and across organization. HP Enterprise Services is a key implementer of the "Instant-On Enterprise," which is used to meet changing business models and the growing role of technology to drive business decisions and help organizations grow and improve their efficiency
IBMWatson	This IBM tool is a Big Data and analytics platform that provides real-time insights for real-world applications to support organizations decision-making power
IBMSPSS Modeler	SPSS Modeler is a proprietary software for data mining and predictive analytics, which provides a drag-and-drop interface to do everything from data exploration to Machine Learning
KNIME	KNIME (Konstanz Information Miner) is an open-source tool that supports Linux, OS X, and Windows OS, which is used for Enterprise reporting, integration, research, CRM, data mining, data analytics, text mining, and business intelligence
Lumify	Lumify is a free and open-source tool for big data fusion/integration, analytics, and visualization, which embeds features like: full-text search, 2D and 3D graph visualizations, automatic layouts, link analysis between graph entities, integration with mapping systems, geospatial analysis, multimedia analysis, real-time collaboration through a set of projects or workspaces
MongoDB	MongoDB is a free and open-source NoSQL document-oriented database written in C, C++ and JavaScript. It supports multiple operating systems including Windows Vista (and later versions), OS X (10.7 and later versions), Linux, Solaris, and FreeBSD
NetApp	NetApp data storage and management solutions help users to get control of their data, via cloud and virtualization services which include Dig Data analytics for decision support
OpenText	OpenText Big data analytics is a high-performing comprehensive solution designed for business users and analysts, which enables easy and fast access, blending, exploration, and analysis of data
OracleDataIntegrator	This tool is a comprehensive data integration platform, which covers from high-volume, high-performance batch loads, to event-driven, trickle-feed integration processes, to Service-Oriented-Architecture (SOA)-enabled data services
OracleData Mining	ODM is a proprietary tool for data mining and specialized analytics that allows you to create, manage, deploy, and leverage Oracle data and investment

(continued)

Table 1 (continued)

Tools	Descriptions
R	R is open-source, free, multi-paradigm and dynamic software environment, written in C, Fortran, and R programming languages, which is one of the most comprehensive statistical analysis packages broadly used by statisticians and data miners. Its use cases include data analysis and manipulation, calculation, and graphical display
Rapidminer	Rapidminer is an open-source JAVA cross-platform tool, which offers an integrated environment for data science, machine learning, and predictive analytics
SAPHANA	SAP HANA platform for Big Data combines database, data processing, and application platform capabilities and provides libraries for predictive, planning, text processing, spatial, and business analytics. This allows the analysis on massive quantities of real-time data for immediate answers without building pre-aggregates
SGIOmniStor	SGI storage solutions leverage an intelligent combination of leading storage technologies to produce tailored systems that meet both performance and budget goals. OmniStor is a flexible, scalable, and high-performance storage solution from SGI for Big Data environments
SplunkEnterprise	Splunk is a platform for real-time operational intelligence, which allows harvesting and exploiting data from different sources. A reduced version of Splunk can be used for free
1010data	1010data offers a complete suite of products for Big Data discovery and data sharing for business and technical users, providing direct access to the data and allowing for snapshots driven by the users' needs

There have been significant advancements in using Big Data Analytics to support decision-making in last few years. New architecture, tools and systems have been developed and tested, which can be used to support every single step of a decision-making process. In [16], an overview is presented mapping out a wide range of relevant approaches, tools, and systems to each of the four phases (intelligence, design, choice, implementation) of the decision-making process proposed by [17].

However, there are issues with this data-centrism. Our data-centered world interpretation as well as our data-centered decision-making open up many possibilities, but also involve risks. The main risk of data-centrism is that it encourages the false idea that "whatever the problem, the answer lies in data." In some cases, data analytics cannot deal with ambiguity or imprecision and most of the times it cannot compensate on subjectivity nor replace negotiations. It is our duty to try to combat the purely data-centrism tendency and avoid the dangerous consequences that it may bring. Some have also argued that, when decision-makers are surrounded by Big Data, it is not always easy to effectively connect decision-making tasks to the right data sources, hence more work is needed to ensure that only useful information and business insights are flowing to the right people at the right time [18]. In the work undertaken by Horita et al. [18], a framework is proposed to establish a seamless connection between decision-making and the right data sources to address the productivity issue.

Fig. 5 Data-related
processes and Data-Driven
Decisions DDD [11]

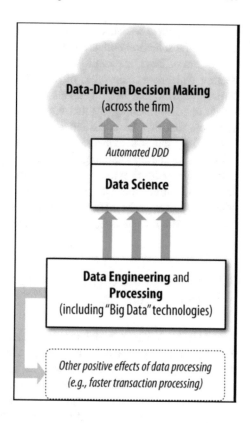

While organizations have to get ready to cope with high technology standards to face competition in this new Big Data-Driven Decision-Making Era, there is a clear and strong need to enforce the importance of Decision-Making and Decision Support Systems to exploit the potentiality of Big Data Analytics, using the appropriate technologies for their applications needs, including also the intelligence implied by decisions that does not always come as a by-product of data insights.

As stated in [6]: "Tapping into large-scale, fast-moving, complex streams of datasets has the potential to fundamentally transform the way organizations make their decisions." This view is echoed in [19], with a view that the appropriate use of Big Data Analytics should allow enterprises to take faster and more adequate decisions leading, e.g., to cost reduction, development of new products and creation of optimized tenders and emergence of market trends. Hence, the Big Data revolution must be able to develop competitive advantages to support more informed decisions. Decision-Making Processes in organizations have access to large collection of data and decision-makers must provide useful decisions using "good" data. For this purpose, Data Analytics is more and more useful. It is then a necessity to develop algorithms for selecting "good" data for decision support purposes. These algorithms must be developed as Decision Support Systems in order to support the decision-makers in an early step of the decisional processes, which is the selection/collection of "good" data.

The era of Big Data implies important challenges for decision-making to enable dealing with three main types of influencing factors for ensuring data quality [6]. Variety of available heterogeneous data: image, video, photos, voice, files, etc., which must be fused/aggregated into a single composite of comparable alternative solutions that can be classified and ranked, as shown in [20]. Other important influencing factors, also mentioned in [6, 7], were veracity (manipulation, noise) and velocity (constantly changing data sources). Therefore, the algorithms or systems that we aim to develop must be able to adapt the data during the process of problem solving. It implies that DSS will play a central role because they are developed as adaptable software for different users even during the solving problem process. The quality of data is then a big challenge in this Big Data era for decision-makers.

3.2 Decision-Making: Some Application Areas Affected by Big Data Revolution

Some application areas which require interactive and fast-time responsive Decision-Making support are heavily affected by the Big Data era. Mainly the ones using data coming from technical as well as social data-feeds. As examples of such areas, we can cite: Collaborative Decision-Making applications with web and social media input data; Dynamic-temporal spatial applications; Logistic and supply chain management applications; and Decision-Making in critical and crisis management applications. In the following four subsections, we discourse about those areas of applications and we try to identify the main technological challenges to handle Big Data—within each specific decision-making context—using the main quality data factors mentioned above: variety of heterogeneous data; veracity of data; and velocity [6].

3.2.1 Collaborative Decision-Making Applications

Tétard [21] showed that the introduction of ICTs into organizations inevitably leads to fragmentation of working time. He also showed that information overload is both a source and a consequence of this fragmentation. Given that human agents have limited cognitive capacities, we must attempt to reduce this excess workload, using appropriate tools. In addition, with the advent of ICTs, the classic DSS becomes partially usable only when the group of decision-makers comes together. We then witness a reinforcement of the collaborative work between different actors involved in the decision-making process.

Even when the organizational responsibility is singular, the decision is almost always prepared through a collaborative work (see [22–24]). Zaraté [25] has shown that the processes of decision-making in organizations have evolved from a cognitive point of view. We have gone from the context of a single decision-maker to an environment with multiple decision-makers, with access to huge and diverse information, who can work asynchronously or otherwise, and apart or together. Hence, she introduces new decision-making processes, called Collaborative Decision-making, in Big Data environments.

Businesses' necessity to be constantly reactive and the technological evolution lead to profound alterations in the organizational and cognitive processes. Organizational processes evolve and tend towards having more and more parties involved in the making of the decision: the responsibilities and the initiative tend to be more distributed. On the other hand, the necessity to often report and inform becomes a generalized imperative. A large proportion of a manager's activity consists of securing the participation of, involving and motivating as many of the actors concerned as possible. All these aspects invite us not only to review the classical model of decision-making, but to redesign the decision support which we offer, focusing on three essential elements: dealing with the massive amount of information available, the importance that must be attached to the processes of innovation and design, and finally a relativization of the choice stage and introduction of processes of negotiation and other collective processes [26, 27].

3.2.2 Dynamic-Temporal-Spatial Applications

In general, every decision is made within a decision environment and within a time frame. Classic decision-making models assume a static view where a decision is taken at a specific time t (single period) using a fixed set of criteria and alternatives. In dynamic decision-making (spatial-temporal), the selection process takes into account the temporal performance of alternatives during multi-periods (see [20, 28–30] for details). The reasoning for the dynamic (spatial-temporal) view is that as time passes, the decision environment may grow and expand, therefore, new information, criteria and new alternatives may appear or disappear (velocity factor of data quality) [6]. With the advent of "Big Data" and the profusion of information available in the Internet, the dynamic decision process is becoming ever more complex and nonlinear. There is a growing need for Large-Scale Spatial-Temporal Decision-Making (LSSTDM) tools capable of handling data and information which are: massive, multi-dimensional, multi-source, time-varying and include embedded uncertainties.

An interesting application of a large-scale dynamic decision method in the Space sector, as shown [31], is the development of autonomous hazard avoidance systems that allow safe landing on dangerous or insufficiently characterized areas on distant planets. Many other, examples and applications of dynamic decision problems (but mostly not yet in Big Data environments) in fields such as medicine, marketing, logistics, human resources, financial, political and aerospace, as well as, the challenges involved in those dynamic decision-making problems, can be found in [29, 30, 32, 33]. All these applications clearly demonstrate the emerging need for improved Large-Scale Spatial-Temporal Decision-Making (LSSTDM) models, techniques and tools, specifically when dealing with Big Data to support decision-makers.

3.2.3 Logistics and Supply Chain Management Applications

Modern logistics and supply chain management (SCM) are like the pulse and blood vessel of the business world which holds the key to economy growth. However, today's logistics and supply chain decision-makers have to effectively manage a massive flow of goods to achieve the best performance, at the same time create vast datasets. For example, big logistics companies have millions of shipments every day, their origin and destination, size, weight, content, and location need to be tracked across global delivery networks [34]. In short, decision-makers need to meet the challenge of structuring and linking various streams of data to create a coherent picture of logistics and supply chain problems, so that better insights into the whole logistics and supply chain network being analyzed can be gained [35].

In the current Digital Economy, the emergence of Big Data analytics has paved the way for developing new tools and techniques to support decision-making in logistics and SCM [36]. Even though there are a variety of Big Data analytics techniques available, the application of existing techniques in logistics and SCM are limited with many open questions. Future research should explore suitable Big Data analytical tools and techniques to support supply chains to generate useful insights from Big Data to drive SCM strategy, improve response time to customers, reduce time to market for new services, improve supply chain wide decision-making process, to enable a full supply chain visibility, ultimately to improve supply chain overall performance [37].

According to [38], a specific Big Data Architectural Framework should be considered for the area of Logistics and SCM, taking into account different layers like: Logistics Service Layer, Logistics Standards, Big Data Logistics Business Platform (BDLBP), Big Logistics Data and Resources Cloud Layer, and Consumption Channels.

3.2.4 Crisis Management, Risky, and Critical Applications

Decision-making approaches for applications concerning critical and natural crisis management using Big Data as input source, face some technological challenges in relation to scalable and reliable solutions that deal with large volumes of information, quasi-real-time responses and information visualization and distribution. A crisis decision-making situation derives from an unexpected change in the external or internal environment of a community, characterized by threats to basic values, urgency, and uncertainty [39].

Examples of this urgency-crisis kind may be applicable to situations of rapid contamination or nuclear accidents where timely interventions such as cleanups or evacuations may prevent or minimize the harmful disasters. Environmental crises often have to deal with uncertainties of various kinds regarding the nature of the processes involved (natural or technical); the effectiveness and side effects of potential interventions; as well as the severity of the threats and risks with relation to the health of the ecosystems and human beings involved. In this sense, risk assessment and data analytics over available data (Big Data) of past disasters, may contribute to anticipate potential hazards and better protect the life and health of the involved individuals and the public. A successful example of an EC project in this direction is the TRIDEC project,[10] which focused on new approaches and technologies for intelligent geo-information management in complex and critical decision-making processes in Earth sciences. Results of the project enabled multiple decision-makers to respond efficiently, within complex and critical Decision-Making situations, using a collaborative decision support environment.

Still in terms of crisis management, another need for Big Data Analytics and AI is in the combat of epidemic outbreaks. This can be exemplified with the situation we faced in 2020 with the outbreak of the corona virus. The COVID-19 pandemic scenario affected all the world and showed to us that, apart from the major importance of the front-end action and support from the healthcare and logistics sectors, the ICT sector and its high-level technology and analytic tools for supporting correct decision-making are important allied components for counter-attacking the virus infection process, as well as to deal with the management of the overall crisis in an efficient and accurate way. As application of Big Data analytics for supporting the corona virus crisis management, we can mention the approach of Location Data, which has played an important role in the contention of the infection in some countries, for instance in Israel. Although privacy concerns have limited the use of location data for anti-coronavirus efforts in some other countries, in Israel the citizens believed to have been exposed to the virus received alerts via their mobile phones, with the support of location data, ordering them to self-quarantine.[11] Another example was the use of Big Data Powered Maps to monitor the virus outbreak for guiding governments in taking more accurate and timely contention decisions. Such approach was early used by China, where tech-companies have integrated the coronavirus outbreak into Map Apps, making it easier for communities to avoid contaminated areas. The special 'epidemic maps' also showed the location of both confirmed and suspected coronavirus patients in real-time.[12]

From the exposed above, it is noticeable that Big Data approaches and analytic technologies can help a lot within natural crisis management decision-making situations, so that multiple source large-scale data can be fast and trustfully treated to provide emergency responses. Moreover, in those cases, intelligence and expertise

---

[10] http://www.tridec-online.eu/.

[11] https://www.theverge.com/interface/2020/3/25/21192629/coronavirus-surveillance-location-data-taiwan-israel-us-google.

[12] https://daxueconsulting.com/coronavirus-crisis-management/.

are needed within the decision-making process, in combination with data-driven insights. To complement, risk analyzer systems and resource management systems, combined with web and social media feedback and filtered information can help decision-makers provide efficient and time-optimal decisions, avoiding or highly mitigating hazardous consequences.

4 Conceptual Model for Big Data in Decision-Making

Based on extensive review on existing work in both Sects. 2 and 3, some clear gaps are identified:

- Existing work has made clear contribution to the understanding of Big Data topic, from data value chain through Big Data Analytics to Big Data tools and systems (see Sect. 2 for details). However, research on Big Data for decision support is under-researched.
- Existing work has recognized the importance of Big Data application in some areas (see Sect. 3 for details) such as in collaborative decision-making, dynamic-temporal-spatial decision-making, logistics and supply chain decision-making, and crisis management, risky and critical decision-making. But there is a lack of effective architecture that can be used to guide the construction of Big Data tools for decision support in wide application areas.

To fill the above identified research gaps, this chapter proposes a generic conceptual model for the development of Big Data tools for decision support. This Section starts with some background in Sect. 4.1, followed by the proposal of a conceptual architecture in Sect. 4.2, then the value and contribution of the proposed architecture are discussed in Sect. 4.3.

4.1 Background for the Proposed Model

Apart from the application areas considered in this chapter, there are many Decision-Making business opportunities already intelligently using collected Big Data from chains of Open Data. The new services and technological trends already absorbed from the market (e.g., Google glasses, RFID Radio-Frequency Identification cards, social media, social networks, web-based games, web-preferences in readings, traveling, hobbies, culture, fashion, e-commerce), currently supply much more data for analysis than we are ready to exploit in an intelligent and efficient way. The use of RFID cards is rather popular in healthcare applications [40]; in conferences, where they are used as badges to track participants' interest and interactions with other participants; and as client-cards for department stores, in order to track the visits and behaviors of their customers, so that they can better promote and sell products to them. Those trends of Big Data applications rely on robust and

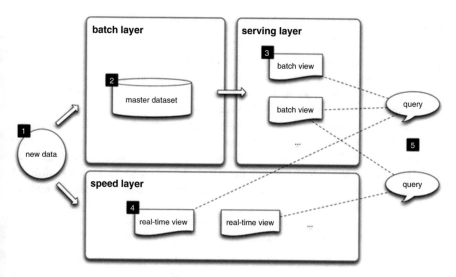

Fig. 6 Lambda architecture overview

appropriate platforms and architecture concepts. For the purpose of the work described in this chapter, we investigate Big Data architectures that are defined in layers, like for instance the Lambda Architecture39, which is a generic, scalable, and fault-tolerant data processing architecture being able to serve a wide range of workloads and use cases.

From a high-level perspective, the Lambda Architecture,[13] is defined as illustrated in Fig. 6, considering that: (1) Input data is dispatched to both the batch layer and the speed layer for processing; (2) The batch layer has the functions of managing the master dataset and pre-computing the batch views; (3) The serving layer indexes the batch views so that they can be queried in ad hoc way and in low latency; (4) The speed layer compensates for the high latency of updates to the serving layer and deals with recent data only; and (5) Queries can be answered by merging results from batch and real-time views.

The strengths of the Lambda Architecture lie in the definition of three clear layers: a batch layer, a serving layer, and a speed layer, for data processing, indexing, and querying. It is useful from data management point of view. However, this architecture does not go beyond data hence cannot offer links to decision-making to provide effective support for decision-makers who have specific business decision interest and preferences in mind. Hence, there is a need to propose a new architecture which integrates Big Data and Decision Support.

---

[13]http://lambda-architecture.net/.

4.2   Proposed High-Level Conceptual Model

Our proposed high-level model is shown in Fig. 7, which consists of five layers. In general, the proposed architecture considers the analytics for decision support embedded mainly in layers 3, 4, and 5. Layer 3 includes in its modules of: data policy; ontology; and templates, the domain-tailored information to facilitate the queries to be performed in the engine layer. Layer 4, among other tasks, caters for the performance of the Big Data Analytics meeting the requirements of application-specific Decision Support Systems to be interfaced via the post-processing layer. The last layer 5 takes into account the proper plug-ins to be used by different use-case applications, making direct link between analytics and decision-making support particularly evident.

The five layers of the conceptual model correspond to five phases in terms of information flow, as shown in Fig. 8. Each phase/layer deal with the following:

- Layer 1: The Big Data Input Layer has to be able to receive datasets from multiple sources, including open-data sources; industrial data; social media; real-time data; as well as data coming from sensors.
- Layer 2: The Big Data Collection and Treatment Layer, as the name suggests, is responsible for gathering as well as identifying, structuring, aggregating, semantically processing and making pre-contextual analysis of the data. This layer will also define the data protocols that will be used in further layers for processing the data.
- Layer 3: The Linked Big Data Layer contains the necessary databases (e.g., NoSQL/Hbase; RDBMS) for managing the acquired datasets, as well as relevant modules of ontology, data policy, privacy methodologies, data schemas, and templates, and a toolbox for data services. This layer encapsulates available tools of the Big Data ecosystem, like Hadoop for instance, and purpose-built modules.
- Layer 4: The Intelligence and Analytics Layer is responsible for: processing Big Data in both batch and real-time modes; managing queries in the different complexities and speeds needed; supplying the various types of data analytics as appropriate, considering high standards of visualization, data sharing as well as proper reporting techniques. This layer can also be seen as the Big Data engine layer. It may contain available Big Data ecosystem tools, connected with purpose-built modules and plug-ins. Sentiment analysis; business intelligence, social media; and predictive analytics, among other analytics modules find in this layer their operation place. As a consequence, this layer also includes a data storage component with processed data from layer 3 to be delivered in the next layer upon request.
- Layer 5: The Post-processing and Distribution Layer caters for the proper distribution of the data, in terms of format, contextualization, media, and business objectives, so that the information is delivered for further decision support in different domains and applications. Cross-sector examples to be considered in this layer as applications and end-users are: industries; public authorities; small

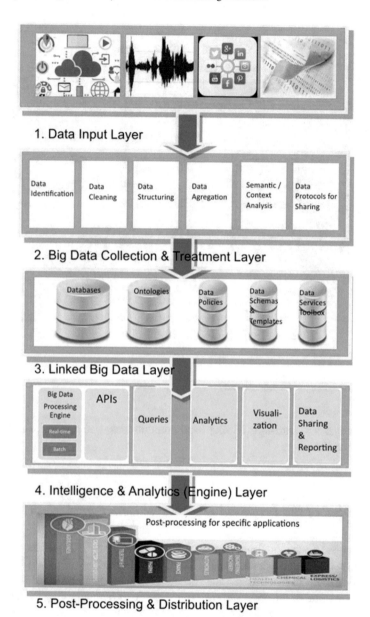

Fig. 7 Proposed Big Data for decision-making conceptual model

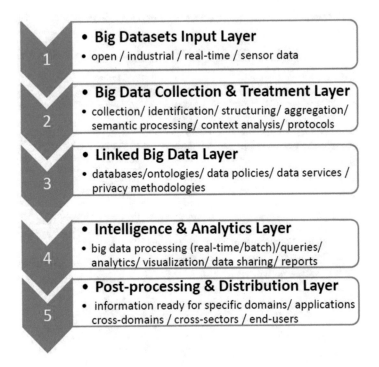

Fig. 8 Conceptual model process flow

enterprises and start-ups; NGOs; local communities; and research and scientific communities.

4.3 Value of the Proposed High-Level Conceptual Model

The proposed conceptual model provides a holistic view of Big Data support for decision-making, through the integration of key elements of Big Data and various application areas in practical world. This system thinking is illustrated in Fig. 9.

The key value of the proposed conceptual model is by integrating the key aspects of Big Data technology (including the Big Data value chain, Big Data Analytics, and Big Data tools and systems) and main decision support applications, it allows decision-makers to be able to understand the main phases of Big Data value chain from data acquisition to data usage, to draw business insights from the data, and to harvest and capitalize on the Big Data analysis results for effective decision support in practical application context, ultimately to allow the improvement on business performance.

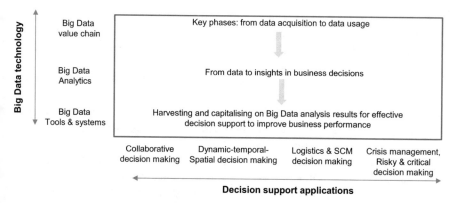

Fig. 9 Value of the proposed conceptual model

Compared with existing Big Data architecture, such as the Lambda Architecture, our proposed conceptual model has clear advantages. For example, the inclusion of Layer 5, post-processing and distribution layer allows the analytical results, such as the most relevant information and business insights, to be directed to the most relevant decision domains or cross-section end-users. This way, decision-makers can digest and use the information more effectively and make faster and better decisions according to their decision requirements and preferences.

5   General Remarks and Conclusions

This chapter presented a concise survey about Big Data and Decision-Making, which covered some decision-making application areas that can profit from proper analytics and post-processing approaches to support efficient Decision-Making. We are aware that some other important works on the related areas (Big Data, DSS, etc.) were not covered in this chapter. The chapter does not claim to be an exhaustive survey on any of the areas involved, but it reviews some relevant research work on the intersection between the areas of decision support and Big Data, supporting the need to develop appropriate decision-making processes for dealing with Big Data. References used in this work serve as a basis for supporting the emphasis we wished to give on the intersection of Big Data and decision support. Our main objective was to contribute to discussions and further careful developments in the involved research communities of Big Data and decision support.

Four application areas were emphasized, for having been heavily affected in their decision-making methodologies by the fact that their inputs now come from multiple Big Data sources. There is a tendency to treat these applications with DDD Data-Driven Decision-Making solutions. However, it is clear that those areas have to improve to cope with high technology standards to face competition in the Big

Data-Driven Decision-Making era. Further, there is a strong need to enforce the importance of Decision-Making and DSS to exploit the potentiality of Big Data Analytics, using the appropriate technologies for their applications needs, including the expertise and intelligence implied by some decisions.

This chapter also presented a high-level conceptual model layered architecture for a layered platform that fits the requirements of the motivated research work. It also enforced the need to build purpose-fit and appropriate DSS technology to be incorporated in decision-making procedures for big-data-affected applications. Furthermore, it unveils the need to build purpose-fit and appropriate DSS technology to be incorporated in decision-making procedures for big-data-affected applications. The European Commission programs for research and innovation projects, confirm the importance for the research line of this work to be established within the DSS communities.

There is much more still to be studied, tested, adapted, and newly developed, concerning appropriate Decision-Making approaches to deal with Big Data Analytics. Even though this chapter reviewed some current scenarios and presented insights on how to deal with Big Data for Decision-Making in some application areas, other application areas will also need to be the subject of study in future works.

Acknowledgments This chapter has evolved from other publications and white papers of the same authors, including also Pascale Zaraté. The researchers of collaborating in this work are long-term members of the Coordination and Advisory Boards of the EWG-DSS EURO Working Group on Decision Support Systems (www.ewgdss.wordpress.com). The EWG-DSS belongs to EURO, the Association of the European Operational Research Societies (www.euro-online.org). Parts of this research has been partially developed within the scope of COST Action no. TD1207, regarding methodological advances for DSS, in which Fatima Dargam collaborated in WG2; and also partially funded by FCT Strategic Program UID/EEA/00066/203 of UNINOVA, CTS with the participation of Rita Ribeiro.

References

1. Lyman, P., Varian, H. R. (2003). *How much information?* Retrieved from http://www.sims.berkeley.edu/how-much-info.
2. Thomas, J., & Cook, K. (2005). *Illuminating the path: Research and development agenda for visual analytics.* New York: IEEE.
3. Dargam, F. C. C. (2014). Decision making and the big data era. In *Proceedings of the IFORS 2014, The 20th Conference of the International Federation of Operational Research Societies, Stream: Decision Support Systems.* Barcelona: IFORS.
4. Dargam, F. C. C., Zaraté, P., Ribeiro, R., & Liu, S. (2015). *The Role of Decision Making in the Big Data Era. Proc. ICDSST-2015 International Conference on Decision Support System Technology on Big Data Analytics for Decision Making.* Belgrade: EWG-DSS.
5. Dargam, F. C. C., Zaraté, P., Ribeiro, R., & Liu, S. (2017). *The impact of big data on decision making processes. white paper.* Belgrade: EWG-DSS Report.
6. Janssen, M., Van der Voort, H., & Wahyudi, A. (2017). Factors influencing big data decision-making quality. *Journal of Business Research, 70,* 338–345.
7. Gandomi, A., & Haider, M. (2015). Beyond the hype: Big data concepts, methods, and analytics. *International Journal of Information Management, 35*(2), 137–144. https://doi.org/10.1016/j.ijinfomgt.2014.10.007.

8. Half, R. (2014). *Technology 2015 Salary Guide*. Retrieved from www.creativegroup.com/salary-center.
9. Nestler, S. (2015). *Data scientists: Data scientist shortage: Myth or reality?* Sunnyvale: LinkedIn Publication.
10. BIG Consortium (http://www.big-project.eu/). EC—FP7 Project: Big Data Public Private Forum (BIG), Deliverable D4.2.2: Final version of IPR: Standardisation & recommendations. Published online on 19/11/2014 (2014), Copyright © 2012, BIG Consortium. Retrieved from http://big-project.eu/sites/default/files/BIG_Deliverable_4.2.2_reviewed.pdf.
11. Provost, F., & Fawcett, T. (2013). *Data science for business*. CA, USA. ISBN: 978-1-449-36132-7: Published by O'Reilly Media, Inc..
12. Wang, H., Xu, Z., Fujita, H., & Liu, S. (2016). Towards felicitous decision making: An overview on challenges and trends in Big Data. *Information Sciences, 367–368*, 747–765.
13. United Nations Report on "Big Data for Sustainable Development", 2017, Retrieved from https://www.un.org/en/sections/issues-depth/big-data-sustainable-development.html.
14. Big Data Open Source Tools. (2015). Retrieved from http://www.bigdata-startups.com/open-source-tools/.
15. Software Testing Help Report on "Top 15 Big Data Tools (Big Data Analytics Tools) in 2020", Retrieved December 27, 2019, from https://www.softwaretestinghelp.com/big-data-tools/.
16. Elgendy, N., & Elragal, A. (2016). Big Data Analytics in support of the decision-making process. *Proc. Computer Science, 100*, 1071–1084.
17. Simon, H. (1977). *The New science of management decision*. Englewood-Cliffs: Prentice Hall.
18. Horita, F. E. A., de Albuquerque, J. P., Marchezini, V., & Mendiondo, E. M. (2017). Bridging the gap between decision making and emerging big data sources: An application of a model-based framework to disaster management in Brazil. *Decision Support Systems, 97*, 12–22. https://doi.org/10.1016/j.dss.2017.03.001.
19. Kościelniak, H., & Puto, A. (2015). Big Data in decision making process of enterprises. *Procedia Computer Sciences, 65*, 1052–1058.
20. Ribeiro, R. A., Falcao, A., Mora, A., & Fonseca, J. M. (2014). FIF: A fuzzy information fusion algorithm based on multi-criteria decision making. *Knowledge-Based Systems*, 58.
21. Tétard, F. (2002). *Managers, Fragmentation of Working Time, and Information Systems. PhD Thesis*. Turku, Finlande: University Abo Akademi.
22. Axelrod, R. (1992). *Donnant, donnant*. Paris: Odile Jacob.
23. Delahaye, J. P. (1995). *L'altruisme récompensé?* Paris: Pour la science.
24. Zachary, W. W., & Roberston, S. P. (1990). Introduction. In W. W. Zachary, S. P. Roberston, & J. B. Black (Eds.), *Cognition, computing and cooperation*. Norwood: Ablex Publishing Corporation.
25. Zaraté, P. (2013). *Tools for collaborative decision-making*. New York. ISBN: 978-1-84821-516-0: Wiley.
26. Lahlou, S. (2000). Les attracteurs cognitifs et le syndrome du débordement. *Intellectica, 30*, 75–115.
27. Sperber, D., & Wilson, D. (1990). *La Pertinence*. Paris: Odile Jacob.
28. Xu, Z. (2008). On multi-period multi-attribute decision making. *Knowledge-Based Systems, 21*(2), 164–171.
29. Campanella, G., & Ribeiro, R. (2011). A framework for dynamic multiple-criteria decision making. *Decision Support Systems, 52*(1), 52–60.
30. Javad, J., Ribeiro, R., & Dargam, F. C. C. (2014). *Dynamic MCDM for Multi Group Decision Making. Proc. of the Joint International Conference of Group Decision and Negotiation GDN-2014 (INFORMS GDN Section & the EURO Working Group on DSS) on Group Decision Making and Web 3.0, Toulouse, June 2014* (LNBIP) (Vol. 180, pp. 90–99). Switzerland: Springer Int. Publishing.
31. Ribeiro, R. A., Paris, T. C., & Simões, L. F. (2010). *Benefits of full-reinforcement operators for spacecraft target landing, volume 257 of Studies in Fuzziness and Soft Computing*. New York: Springer.

32. Yu, P.-L., & Chen, Y.-C. (2010). Dynamic multiple criteria decision making in changeable spaces: From habitual domains to innovation dynamics. *Annals of Operations Research.* https://doi.org/10.1007/s10479-010-0750-x.
33. Hsiao, N., & Richardson, G. P. (1999). In Search of theories of dynamic decision making: A literature review, *Proc. 17th International Conference of the System Dynamics Society, Systems Thinking for the Next Millennium*, eds R.Y. Cavana et al.
34. Addo-Tenkorang, R., & Helo, P. T. (2016). Big Data applications in operations/supply chain management: A literature view. *Computers and Industrial Engineering, 101*, 528–543.
35. Hazen, B. T., Boone, C. A., Ezell, J. D., & Jones-Farmer, L. A. (2014). Data quality for data science, predictive analytics, and big data in supply chain management: An introduction to the problem and suggestions for research and applications. *International Journal of Production Economics, 154*, 72–80.
36. Dubey, R., Gunasekaran, A., Childe, S. J., Wamba, S. F., Giannakis, M., & Foropon, C. (2019). Empirical investigation of data analytics capability and organizational flexibility as complements to supply chain resilience. *International Journal of Production Research.* https://doi.org/10.1080/00207543.2019.1582820.
37. Ferraris, A., Mazzoleni, A., Devalle, A., & Couturier, J. (2019). Big data analytics capabilities and knowledge management: Impact on firm performance. *Management Decision, 57*(8), 1923–1936.
38. Neaga, I., Liu, S., Xu, L., Chen, H., & Hao, Y. (2015). Cloud enabled big data business platform for logistics services: A Research and Development Agenda. In B. Delibasi, J. E. Hernández, J. Papathana-siou, F. Dargam, P. Zaraté, S. Liu, R. Ribeiro, & I. Linden (Eds.), *Proc. decision support systems V—Big Data analytics for decision making* (LNBIP) (Vol. 216). New York: Springer, ISBN: 978-3-319-18532-3.
39. Stern, E. (2000). Crisis Decision-making: A cognitive institutional approach. A Publication of the Baltic Sea Area Research Project- National Crisis Management from an International Perspective. Published by ÖCB - The Swedish Emergency Planning Agency ISBN: 91-7153-993-x, ISSN: 0346-6620.
40. Fosso, S., Wamba, S. F., Anand, A., & Carter, L. (2013). A literature review of RFID-enabled healthcare applications and issues. *International Journal of Information Management, 33*(5), 875–891.

The Evolution of DSS in the Pig Industry and Future Perspectives

Lluís M. Plà-Aragonès

Abstract The evolution of the pig industry over time has shown a concentration of production to maintain profit levels and the rise of new organisational structures like pig supply chains (PSC). At the same time, computers are becoming common tools at any level and little by little, sensors and electronic devices are invading the sector. In this context, there is a need of integration of data and information at different stages of PSC. Decision support systems (DSS) are the natural framework where decision models should be included in order to support farmers, advisers or management specialists in the decision-making process. The lack of adoption of past DSS tools may change in the near future were cloud computing-based DSS and Internet of Things (IoT) make integration, automation and data analysis easier. Data science methodologies and Artificial Intelligence (AI) enlarge the range of modelling techniques available to develop smart pig DSS at the service of the pig industry. There is a challenge of preparing the infrastructure capable of integrating old and new DSS and interconnect the number of new devices and sensors to deliver useful information not just on demand, but also in a preventive, either intelligent, manner anticipating decisions in a smart way.

Keywords Model-driven DSS · Smart farming · Pig management · Pig supply chain · Data analytics · Livestock precision farming

1 Introduction

The observed evolution of the pig industry is a result of the global economy, advances in technology, scientific developments and changes in social and cultural attitudes [1, 2]. Main pig producers in the world are China, the European Union

L. M. Plà-Aragonès (✉)
Department of Mathematics, University of Lleida, Lleida, Spain

AGROTECNIO-CERCA Center, Lleida, Spain
e-mail: lluismiquel@udl.cat

© Springer Nature Switzerland AG 2021
J. Papathanasiou et al. (eds.), *EURO Working Group on DSS*, Integrated Series in Information Systems, https://doi.org/10.1007/978-3-030-70377-6_16

(EU-28 members) and the USA [3]. Pig meat is the most consumed meat around the world and the prevalent source of animal protein for humans [3].

In the past, the farmer was the main decision-maker in the pig industry. However, during last decades, economies of scale have continued to accelerate changes in the pig production [4, 5]. And as consequence, pig supply chains are conformed coordinating pig producers with feedstuffs suppliers, abattoirs, meatpacking and processing plants and retailers among others limiting the past decision-making power of farmers. Past health problems with other species affecting humans like the Bovine Spongiform Encephalopathy (BSE) and aviary influenza have powering pig meat production. And consumer concerns about environment, animal welfare, food safety and food quality are new challenges [6, 7]. All in all, the resulting specialisation and technical improvement in the sector have complicated the way of making decisions as it requires more and more a whole chain vision [5, 7]. New Decision Support Systems (DSS) emanated from the Information and Communication Technologies (ICT) including the recent advances like the Internet of Things (IoT) are needed to coordinate and give sound decisional support to all the agents of the PSC. In parallel, the deployment of new DSS tools requires also the understanding of the context in which farmers, pig companies make decisions, and the consideration of the disruption new technologies may cause [8].

This chapter describe the old decision techniques based on periodical reports, the first information systems like DSS and how they have been evolving in the pig sector until now. Therefore, in Sect. 2 we present briefly the operation of the pig industry introducing in Sect. 3 the main decision problems they have. In the next section, past and present computer decision aid systems are described, before proceed in the next Sect. 5 with the review of the research contribution to DSS development. A critical view of current DSS is provided in Sect. 6 while Sect. 7 presents the role of emerging technologies and future prospects, pointing out the main challenges in the near future represented by the number of new devices, sensors and tools drawing what is called Agriculture 4.0, but limited to the pig industry. Finally, we end the chapter highlighting the main conclusions.

The content of the chapter and the approach to the pig industry is international in its scope. However, to contextualise several aspects and introduce some illustrative examples to better understand the real impact of the evolution and implications of DSS in this sector, we include a specific focus on the Spanish pig industry and the DSS tools they have been using and they actually use.

2 The Pig Supply Chain Structure

Pig production systems are organised differently according to country [1, 9–11], but the general trend is a concentration of production to maintain past profit levels, provoking a reduction in the number of farms while their sizes are increasing [12, 13]. There is also a general partition in two subsystems: the farming and meat processing subsystems, which hardly had collaborated in the past [11, 14]. So that,

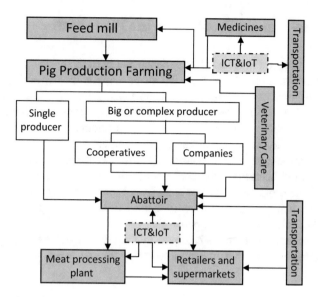

Fig. 1 Pig supply chain agents

PSC agents confront decision problems derived from the specialisation of farm units, diversification of products in meat processing plants and the coordination among them (see Fig. 1).

DSS is the natural framework where decision models should be included in order to support farmers, pig supply chain managers, advisers or pig industry specialists in the decision-making process [15]. Hence, the national structure of the sector has influence on the particular deployment of DSS tools and the adoption by the sector. For example, the prevalence of vertical integration in the Spanish and Polish sector facilitates a top-down adoption of new technologies and DSS tools by farmers and PSC agents forced by integrators companies and PSC managers [9, 11]. However, in France or Denmark, with a more horizontal structure [16] based on cooperatives and associations of producers tend to be more flexible and farmers have more decision power.

In spite of the interest PSC agents have in DSS tools, the problems farmers, advisers and PSC managers confront require the coordination with other agents or echelons in the chain [1, 11]. This is particularly true in the farming subsystem with decisions made at breeding level affecting downstream in the chain regarding, for example, the occupancy of fattening units. Fattening farms operate by all-in-all-out management (AIAO), i.e., pigs enter in a batch and a new batch does not enter in the farm until the last batch is emptied. It is recognised also a persistent lack of coordination between the farming and meat processing subsystem generating stress in the PSC [5] when offer and market demand do not match.

3 Decision-Making Problems in the Pig Industry

Traditionally, judgement based on experience had been the basis for pig production on traditional farm units. Nowadays, the increasing complexity of the pig industry make the adoption of more formal decision-making methods necessary [7]. The challenge of DSS application in the pig industry is to represent what is essential in the system in order to assist pig managers by finding relevant answers from a problematic situation that may initially seem chaotic.

There are three aspects to consider regarding the decision-making process: (1) the problem itself disturbing the performance of a PSC agent, (2) the interaction or impact of the problem over other activities of the same agent or different agents and (3) the human perception of the problem and the modelling approach to solve it. The latter includes a holistic perception of risk and decision criteria, but also reluctance to change and innovation. Note that the first aspect is the more appealing for researchers, but the others the more worrying for end-users.

3.1 Main Decision Problems

Under economic point of view, we have to consider the pull trait of the farming subsystem and the push trait of the meat processing subsystem. Within the farming subsystem, the rise of productivity, lower production cost components or both together are the driving criteria to identify main decision problems since market prices determining the income are beyond the control of decision-makers. Meat processors are concerned with customers likes and the problems they have are related with an unforeseen demand of a variety of products not always balanced with the number, size and quality of available pigs [1, 17]. They face to a very complex problem of cutting, packing and scheduling where the ideal pork generating zero stock does not exist.

In Table 1, there are several decision problems related with the pig industry and the agents involved. Then, the main cost component at any stage is feeding. Feeding is important either for assuring a good reproductive performance of sows and for the growing process of piglets to reach the marketing weight with a valued carcass composition. Different profiles of decision-maker can be identified such a feedmiller or a consulting nutritionist. There is the traditional problem of diet formulation enriched with new concerns about raw material purchase, greenhouse gas (GHG) emissions and feed delivery.

Farming units are specialised and traditional farrow-to-finish farm systems still exists but many have evolved to multi-site systems with breeding, rearing or fattening farms or a mix of them. Problems in these farm units are related with herd management and the biological nature of the animals. The replacement of unproductive sows is relevant in breeding farms and sow productivity involve both prolificity and reproductive rhythm [18]. While mortality, average daily gain, daily

Table 1 Main problems detected for different PSC agents

Main decision problem	Mill	Farm units: Sow Rearing Fattening	Abattoir Meat processor Retailer/Supermarket	Others: Medicines Consultants Providers
Feed and water	Purchase of raw material. Formulation of a minimum diet cost Scheduling milling activities	Control feed and water consumption. Marketing weight	Welfare regulations and pre-abattoir management	
Herd management		Replacement of sows Reproductive rhythm: piglets per sow per year Goal of number of farrowings per week Band management	Delivery to the abattoir Homogeneous marketing weight Lean percent	Medical care Disease control
Veterinary treatments	Additives and antibiotics	Prevention, protection, mitigation or curation measures.	Contamination: Salmonella, E. Coli	Selection of treatments
Variability	Future market prices	Homogeneity Batch management	Carcass homogeneity Grid payment Market diversification	Outsourcing
Environment	GHG emissions	GHG emissions Manure management. Temperature and humidity. Ventilation.	GHG emissions Waste management.	Unpleasant smells
Transportation and routing	Distribution to farmers. Procurement of raw material	Transfers from farm to farm Deliveries to the abattoir	Carcasses to meat packing plant Delivery to retailers/supermarkets	Deliver medicines and other services on time
Demand	Depends on farms	Push system Depends on abattoirs.	Pull system Depends on the market	
Information	Automatic operation Poor feedback from farms	Poor forecasts No relation with consumer demand	Poor feedback from farms Scheduling	

feed intake and feed conversion are the main Key Performance Indicators (KPI) in rearing and fattening farms. Monitoring animal growth and carcass or meat quality produced is very important to anticipate diseases or productivity disorders. Diseases are a permanent threat over performance and so, prevention and disease control besides feed management are important at this stage.

Abattoirs and meat processing plants have to make decisions regarding the payment grid to farmers to reward specific carcass conformation, transferring this way, costumer preferences to the farming subsystem. Market selection and product diversification are other kind of decisions affecting meat packing plant operation and retailers and supermarkets. Transportation, medicines and veterinary services are other agents taking a secondary role in the pig industry. However, the problems they have do not affect directly the pig sector itself like the routing problems for trucks.

A general concern embracing the pig industry and the entire primary sector is sustainability and the sensibility to mitigate environmental impact [19]. Policy makers may introduce additional constraints to pig production by regulations at local, national or international level forcing to consider additional decision criteria besides pure economic ones. Animal welfare, feeding additives, use of antibiotics, growth regulators and waste management are some examples.

3.2   Interactions or Impact Over Other Activities

The decision problems above mentioned were presented for single PSC agents. However, many of them concur in PSC networks, big companies, cooperatives or associations demanding global or integrated solutions beyond a single PSC agent's boundary. Competitive PSC implies coordination and collaboration under different contract agreements pursuing common goals and targets and exchange of information [20]. Integrators or executive committees of cooperatives when integrating vertically a PSC or coordinating a PSC network may have advantages solving decision conflicts between different agents of the chain. The inventory and flow of animal among farms, production-transportation-delivery of concentrates, carcass quality procuring meat products for targeted markets are some examples.

Coordination brings benefits for the whole PSC but sometimes puts also temporary problems within a specific PSC agent [1, 11]. For instance, feed mills have many formulae to produce and time to time they have to reformulate them according to changes in raw material prices, inventory or demand. Fattening stage can be divided in different feeding phases requiring an equilibrium between feed milling cost and growing performance. Solving the so-called multi-diet problem allows mills to save money instead of solving separate single diet problems. Breeding farms have also to synchronise reproductive rhythm of sows since farrowing rooms are limited and occupancy maximised. A goal of inseminations per week is normal to assure the fulfilment of farrowing rooms' capacity. In fattening farms, a buffer room can be considered to give flexibility to the batch management in fattening units.

The quality and homogeneity of carcasses in a meat processing plant is important to fulfil orders of specifics products efficiently like cured ham in Spain or alternative products reducing set up times.

3.3 Human Perception of the Decision Problems

Decision-makers are human and as consequence, not all the decisions made are rational based. An aspect to consider is the subjective perception of risk besides the available information and domain expertise at the moment to make a decision. Education, socio-cultural context and trending topics serve also to modulate problem perception and the need to react. Recall for instance, farmers attached to a specific sow and postponing the culling against rational evidences on their performances, simply because of emotional ties.

In agriculture, it is generally accepted that decision-makers are risk averse. Indeed, this fact show the reluctant attitude towards the introduction of changes like those related to innovation or DSS use. If changes are not mandatory, a lot of arguments tests and trials are required to convince decision-makers. A lot of research is devoted to investigate the value of information to measure the advantages of DSS [21, 22]. The value of information as expressed in the literature is eminently issued under an economic perspective. There are intangible or qualitative variables affecting decision-maker behaviour, making to ignore, relax or stress a specific problem. For instance, in Spain it is known that litter size records in some integrated farms tend to be contaminated by mistakes when integrator penalised farmers by pre-weaning mortality. The farmer discounts expected casualties beforehand and registers a lower litter size reducing pre-weaning mortality. This abnormal behaviour reduces the value of information regarding litter size records in these farms while the farm income is the same.

4 Computer-Based Systems for the Pig Industry Over Time

4.1 Situation Before the 1990s

The origin of present DSS tools can be found in the initial information systems existing in different countries by respective extension services around the 1980s. These primary information systems were centralised and oriented to collect data manually and register main events that occur on farm. In general, a public institution was behind them likewise an advisory or agricultural extension service with access to computer stations origin of the first management information systems (MIS) and posterior DSS. These public services guarantee and supervise the correctness of data collection, filtering and the elaboration of KPI based on statistics, rates and technical and economic indexes. Main outcomes were periodical reports to analyse results ex-post and performing benchmarking among producers and across countries lasting until nowadays as shown in Table 2. First comparisons served to improve production within herds and rise competitiveness by considering common technical KPI. For instance, in 2018 Danish sows were the most performant with 33.57 piglets weaned per sow per year while Italy produce more carcass meat per sow per year since average liveweight at slaughter is the highest, 170 kg (Table 2). During the eighties, the use of main computers by companies and public administration made easy to register data collected for benchmarking, gaining sectorial supports and being the origin of the first national and transnational databanks. This way GTT (technical herd management) and GTE (economic herd management) maintained by IFIP (www.ifip.asso.fr) the former ITP (Institut Technique du Porc) in France started the collection of data on paper, registering on main computers and issuing periodic benchmark reports.

Similarly, the idea was borrowed by the GTEP (technical and economic pig herd management), the French GTT system adapted to Spanish conditions. The GTEP was promoted by IRTA (Institut de Recerca Tecnico Agroalimentaries) in Catalonia an extended later over the rest of Spain. Then, in 2000 the current official record-keeping system in Spain, BDPorc (www.bdporc.irta.es) was created by the Ministry of Agriculture, with a database structure based in the GTEP.

In the research ground, the arrival of computers capable of solving more complex optimisation models stimulated the blooming of modelling approaches coping with decision problems. Thus, researchers achieved progress in understanding many biological and productive processes, as well as in genetic improvement, preparing the field for the next generation of DSS targeted for farmers.

4.2   The Arrival of Personal Computers on Farm

The irruption of personal computers (PC) on farm in the 1990s facilitated data collection, analysis and reporting by farmers themselves and made original cen-tralised MIS be transformed by a new wave of ICT and standalone software addressed to the sector. Many firms proposed different solutions for on farm use while corporations feed mills and meat processing plants adopted ad hoc solutions to run on workstations and with bridge applications to integrate data from different sources when possible. The use of modem, an epilogue of analogic communications, was common to transfer data when different production units belonged to the same company or cooperative and paved the way for the digital transformation.

An increasing interest in model-driven DSS tools appeared during this period. These DSS handled refined decision models and methods capable of dealing with livestock systems and intended for practical decision support. Piglet production and control diseases like classical swine fever and Aujeszky centred most modelling proposals. Sow farms were the first benefited of these advanced models given the complexity of the reproduction process and the number of variables to control as

Table 2 Comparison of some KPI for pig production in different countries: Australia (AUS), Brazil (BRA), Canada (CAN), Denmark (DEN), France (FRA), Germany (GER), the United Kingdom (UK), Italy (ITA), The Netherlands (NL); Spain (SPA) and the United States of America (USA)

	AUS	BRA	CAN	DEN	FRA	GER	UK	ITA	NL	SPA	USA
Pigs weaned/sow/year	24.79	28.71	24.66	33.57	28.49	30.10	27.35	25.08	30.55	27.45	26.80
Pigs reared/sow/year	24.19	27.85	24.17	32.49	27.69	29.22	26.24	23.93	29.76	26.18	25.70
Pigs sold/sow/year	23.72	27.15	23.32	31.42	26.62	28.49	25.41	23.33	29.01	25.19	24.54
Litters/sow/year	2.29	2.43	2.30	2.26	2.34	2.32	2.28	2.24	2.35	2.31	2.44
Rearing mortality (%)	2.40	3.00	2.00	3.20	2.81	2.90	4.06	4.60	2.60	4.63	4.10
Finishing mortality (%)	1.96	2.50	3.50	3.30	3.89	2.50	3.19	2.50	2.50	3.80	4.54
Finishing daily liveweight gain (g/day)	805	880	876	975	803	842	866	690	829	726	860
Finishing feed conversion ratio	2.87	2.50	3.00	2.63	2.75	2.79	2.79	3.74	2.56	2.48	2.68
Average liveweight at slaughter (kg)	121	110	128	113	120	122	110	170	121	112	127
Average carcase weight—cold (kg)	95.0	82.0	100.8	86.0	92.0	94.6	83.6	136.6	94.4	84.5	92.9
Carcase meat production/sow/year (kg)	2252	2226	2350	2704	2448	2695	2124	3187	2738	2129	2280

Source: https://projectblue.blob.core.windows.net/media/Default/Pork/Documents/CostofPigProduction2018_200302_WEB.pdf accessed 14-05-2020

well as the impact on final production [23]. Most of the DSS at this period were
developed as national research projects and did not reach the market. Reported
examples in the literature are: TACT in The Netherlands, supporting decisions on
replacement and insemination strategies [24]; EMISP in Greece, an integrated MIS
and DSS for specific daily management tasks in a pig breeding farm [25] and DSS-
IRTA in Spain, a DSS based on a Markov decision sow model [26].

4.3 Current Computer-Based Systems

Pig farming subsystem concentrates the interest on computer-based systems, either
in number of software products and in volume of customers. The functionality of
current software in pig farming is mainly based on important aspects like piglet
production, the provision of feedstuffs or concentrates, breeding, sow replacement
and waste disposal which may have a significant impact on system performance
[15]. Many current DSS proposals rely on herd management software since a
detailed record-keeping of individual events along animal's lifespan serve as raw
data susceptible of being used for decision aid systems. In this sense, different herd
management software of branded products present in Spain are shown in Table 3.
Some products like Bio Porcino, Aritmos granjas, Sistema Guals, IFR Pig control
Porcicontrol or Porcitec are from Spanish companies. Some Spanish companies
sell abroad like Agritec Software with more success than in Spain or seeking for
new markets like Guals. There are also foreign products marketed in Spain like
PigCHAMP, Isagri or PigFarm. PigCHAMP monitor sow productivity as other
record-keeping software, but it was developed in the late 1980s at the University
of Minnesota who transferred ownership to a group of PigCHAMP employees and
outside investors in 1999. Today, it is extended all around the world. The way

Table 3 Main farm management software available in Spain

Company	Product	Cloud	Other	Connect	web
Bio One	Bio Porcino	✗	✓	✗	https://www.bio-one.com/
ARITMOS	ARITMOS Granjas	✗	✓	✗	https://www.agriaritmos.com/
Big Dutchman	BigFarmNet	✓	✓	✓	https://www.bigfarmnet.com/
Guals	Sistema Guals	✗	✓	✗	http://www.guals.com/
Agrovision	Farm Gtep	✗	✗	✓	https://www.agrovision.com/
	PigManager	✗	✗	✓	
	PigVision	✓	✓	✓	
Skov	FarmOnline	✓	✓	✓	https://www.skov.com/es/pig/
FanCom	FarmManager	✗	✓	✓	https://www.fancom.es/
IFR	IFR PigControl	✓	✓	✓	https://www.ifr.es/
Software Products	InControl Porcino	✗	✗	✗	https://www.softpi.com/
Isagri	Isaporc	✓	✓	✓	https://www.isagri.es/
PC Pro Europa	Pigchamp	✓	✗	✓	https://www.pigchamp-pro.com/
Innovación Ganadera	PorciControl	✗	✓	✓	https://www.ganaderosonline.com/porcino
Agritec Software	Porcitec	✓	✓	✓	https://www.agritecsoft.com/porcitec/

foreign products land in the Spanish market varies from licensing to a Spanish-based company or other different partnership like contract agreements, re-sellers or sales representativeness. Agrovision for instance follow a similar policy to penetrate different national markets purchasing a dominant local product, e.g., GTEP in Spain or AgroSoft in the UK and Denmark, and new upgrades are adopt or converge to the matrix product PigVision.

Another interesting aspect to consider in the prevailing vertical integration of the Spanish sector is the incorporation of software companies as actors in the PSC procuring ICT services, e.g., IFR SA, to the holding of vertical integrators, e.g., Vall Companys SA. IFR SA is a local company who implemented the GTEP and GTEPWin software for IRTA and was in charge of the maintenance. Soon after the IRTA sold the product to Agrovision, Vall Companys took the control over IFR SA to cover their own ICT development department and to preserve all the expertise acquired besides IRTA in view of technological self-sufficiency. This relationship between both companies with a dominant position in respective sectors generates synergies since the software company, IFR, develops advanced ICT solutions for the integrator, Vall Companys, that they can test in field conditions. Depending on marketing plan or intended competitive advantage, developed products can be offered later to the rest of the sector. This way the development of particular solutions may be cost free for the integrator when shared with the rest of the market benefiting of the credibility of a tested product by a reputed company.

Products shown on Table 3 are not DSS since they do not include models. They have an operational scope and a track of daily and weekly operation while they support decision-makers reporting and updating KPI. Some of them include extensions presented as forecasting models where they only make simple previsions of future records based on actual ones. These products may change from country to country, for instance AHDB has published a list of recording and DSS in the UK.[1] From the thirteen products referred by AHDB, eight were classified as DSS because included a model. All of the DSS considered a growth model in view of improving the feed regime of animals or for analysing batch performance depending on the carcass information available from meat processing plants. Hence, the producer can see at a glance just how accurate the "draw" selection of fattened pigs has been.

At the moment, few more DSS tools are available as true commercial products intended for the sector. Maybe the oldest one is AUSPIG, a DSS for pig producers presented with four modules (http://www.porkcrc.com.au/What_is_AusPig.pdf). It is a deterministic, dynamic simulation model representing the biological connection between diet and reproduction [27], including an Expert System (ES) to analyse and interpret the model outputs. INRAPorc [28] similarly to AUSPIG is based in a growth model depending on how feed requirements are covered by the diet. Another French example dealing with strategic decisions is PORSIM (https://porsim.ifip.asso.fr) a DSS tool to evaluate investments on pig farming.

---

[1]https://pork.ahdb.org.uk/pig-production/recording/which-guide-recording-and-decision-support-systems/ accessed 14-05-2020

5   Research Questions Contributing to DSS Development in the Pig Sector

Research has played an important role in the pig industry. Much research has sought to increase the adoption of DSS tools in practice [8]. However, the development of DSS to this sector has shown similar drawbacks than other sectors in agriculture, i.e., lack of adoption.

First proposals had been promoted by national research projects like in The Netherlands, Greece, Spain, Denmark, France and Australia. Reported examples in the literature are AUSPIG [27], TACT-system [24]; EMISP [25]; DSS-IRTA [26] and INRAPorc [28].

The research on decision models suitable for decision support systems related to the farming subsystem produced many studies focused in five main aspects according to Cornou and Kristensen [21]: replacement decisions, production control, strategic planning and investment, optimisation of disease control and delivery policies while only one reference is found related to meat processing plants [17]. The central KPI for sow herd performance is the number of piglets weaned per sow per year, involving the length of reproductive cycle and litter size improvement [23] making sow replacement relevant to this end. Final performance is expressed in terms of kg of pig meat produced per sow per year involving growth models (e.g., [28]) being key indexes the average daily gain and feed conversion rate. Outcome of growth models depends on feed regime and diet formulation affecting manure composition and delivery policies to the abattoir. Production and disease control have been also of interest to prevent or mitigate problems affecting final performance on farm or food safety in meat processing plants. In 1990s, classical swine fever on farm and salmonella in meat plants and supermarkets provoked the investigation of preventive and control of disease outbreaks and infections starting the interest in the traceability of products. Other aspects related with environmental concerns started to deserve attention when farm size was increasing.

During the twenty-first century, economic performance, sustainability and pig supply chain coordination have gained more attention. The development of the sector reducing the number of farms but increasing the herd size move the interest in technical performance towards a sustainable economic performance, respecting the environment and sensitive with animal welfare [19]. In addition, globalisation forced to coordinate and organise the sector in pig supply chains [7] or supply chain networks [29]. Much of the research done during this period was funded by EU (see Table 4). All the proposals involved different EU countries in contrast with what had been seen before. Protein content of concentrates, waste management, nitrogen and phosphorus concentration in manure were studied to mitigate environmental problems. There were scarce proposals with a whole vision of the chain, tackling the vertical or horizontal interaction among PSC agents or connecting the farm and meat processing subsystems [4, 7].

Table 4 show most of the EU project funded under the Framework Program 6, 7 and Horizon 2020, reflecting very well the research topics of interest in last decades

Table 4 EU projects involving DSS tools for the pig sector

Project	Year	Program	Website	DSS
QPorkchains	2007–2011	FP6	www.wur.nl/en/show/QPorkchains-6.htm	N
Excelmeat	2011–2015	FP7 People	www.bdporc.irta.es/excelmeat	N
PigWise	2011–2015	FP7 Research	www.pigwise.eu	Y
EU-PLF	2012–2016	FP7 KBBE	www.eu-plf.eu	N
Foodie	2014–2017	CIP	www.foodie-project.eu	Y
EU PiG	2015–2020	Thematic network	www.eupig.eu	N
Feed-a-Gene	2016–2019	RI H2020	www.feed-a-gene.eu	Y
PigSys	2018–2020	ERANet SUSan	www.pigsys.eu	Y
IoF	2017–2020	RI H2020	www.iof2020.eu	Y
Cybele	2019–2021	IA H2020	www.cybele-project.eu	Y
SmartAgriHubs	2018–2022	IA H2020	www.smartagrihubs.eu	N

to date related to the pig industry. For instance, the QPorkChain was concerned with the pork supply chain and the quality of product and witnessed the evolution of a fatty product to a healthy and lean meat [20]. Genetics has reshaped the profile of traditional pigs and pig meat regarding litter size, fat content and meat quality. Excel meat project was in some way an extension of QPorkChain. Different kind of minor projects like PigWise, the PiG innovation group, Foodie and PigSys has been developed. PigWise developed an IT-based tool used to monitor performance, growth and welfare of pigs at the individual level, detecting problems in an early stage to prevent economical losses. The tangible result of the project is a mobile app for Android available to Production Managers and Veterinarians for real-time decision-making. Foodie project is not pig focused, it aims at deliver a cloud computing environment where spatial and non-spatial data related to agricultural sector are available for agrifood stakeholders groups and interoperable. The EU Pig innovation group is a thematic network of 19 partner organisations from 13 EU countries aimed to raise the competitiveness of the European pig industry by linking producers and sharing tried and tested best practice and innovations. The PigSys is an ERANet project, devoted to improving pig farming performance through whole system approach building a DSS but without including the meat processors subsystem. The EU-PLF project aimed to deliver a PLF-Blueprint for farmers on how to install and use particular tools based on image and sound analysis falling into PLF principles. It covered commercial farms for three different species in commercial farms: broilers, fattening pigs and dairy.

The rest of the projects on Table 4 are H2020 projects most of them declaring the intention of developing different DSS and abounding the use of new IC technologies. For instance, the Feed-a-gene project consider the development of a DSS for pig feeding making use of Livestock Precision Farming (LPF) by means of automatic feeding machines complemented with other sensor information: weight, temperature, humidity, ventilation. While the approach of the Internet of Farming

(IoF) is funding many showcases developing different decision support tools based on IoT platforms and Cloud computing solutions with four pilots for pig production considering the sensoring and control of pig farms, namely feed SC management, meat transparency and traceability, pig farm management and interoperable pig health tracking.

As IoF project, the project Cybele is not focused on pig production but contains a work package for image analysis devoted to pig live weight estimation. A part to generate innovation and create value by implementing PLF methods, the project intends to empower capacity building within the industrial and research communities. Finally, SmartAgriHubs involve 140 innovation hubs and 28 flag ships experiments in agriculture as benchmarks for other Innovation Experiments similar to the show cases of IoF. In particular four of 28 are relevant to the pig farming subsystem: adopting digital technology for farmers, prediction of early stage diseases, smart pig health and use of antibiotics and ammonia emissions monitoring. Although most of the research involving DSS tools has been done in EU-funded projects, other national initiatives are scarce but exist. For instance, worthy to mention the Danish PigIT project (https://pigit.ku.dk/) devoted to improve welfare and productivity in growing pigs using advanced ICT methods with significant results and international alliances.

6   Pitfalls and Lessons Learnt

6.1   Models or a Simplified Real World?

Model-driven DSS are important tools to better understand real farm behaviour and analyse different management strategies. Therefore, more of the pitfalls in DSS rely on the modelling approach not corresponded with the intended use of the tool. In addition, many assumptions implicit in mathematical models can lead to mistakes if ignored when using DSS in situations where basic assumptions fail. For instance, the clearest example is a deterministic model where we assume all parameters known. If some input parameter is subject to variability likely, the outcome will not correspond between the system and the model. Few models are prepared to offer support over time since input parameters may vary over time and should require updating procedures [30]. Most of the research questions contributing to DSS development have considered infinite time horizons, steady-state situations and general parameters. They are useful to compare different management policies or "What if . . . ?" situations. However, for effective decision support transient situations and finite time horizon have to be also considered. This can be particularly important in disease outbreaks, health emergencies or any other disturbing event affecting the PSC, as the impact and later recovery do not respond to steady-state assumptions.

Another problem with many existing decision models is the objective function, representing many times a sole economic criterion while there are other criteria concurring in the same problem. A single perspective in DSS with limited functionalities and task-specific force users to use additional DSS tools [31]. For instance, the least cost diet problem is affected by environmental constraints not considered in the past due to the rising concern on climate change, CO_2-eq emissions and excreta of N and P. Other variables representing animal health and welfare are also of interest in modern pig production and quite often in contradiction with strictly economic criteria abounding in the need of a better knowledge of decision criteria and how decisions are made.

The verification of models is important before proceed with the validation on field. Lack of precision or abuse of averages lead to ignore natural variability in many biological processes. For years, several sow replacement models had been verified using only general input averages, but not considered specific parameters of individual farms [23]. The resulting outcome could have interest for exploring strategic decisions, but it was less accurate to represent tactical or operational matters for a specific farm. Adapting DSS to uncertainty and be flexible for re-planning because of dynamic factors is necessary [31].

6.2 Standardisation and Integration

The relying question is how the different sources of information available to the PSC agents can supplement and support each other [32]. Both, standardisation and integration are necessary.

A problem met by the specialist and advisers when assisting farmers or pig companies is the analysis of pig performance. The heterogeneity of calculations, KPI and the misspelling of indexes and performance rates make them difficult to interpret or compare and can lead to confusion. For example, the calculation of the productivity index has different approaches and spellings according to current software (Table 3). This commercial policy contributes to diversify the market but goes against sharing data discouraging migration to the competitor. Hence, the existence in Spain of BDPorc as the official databank makes easier the comparison between producers with standardised performance measures. Almost all the record-keeping software referred in Table 3 allow users to export data by uploading the standard vector of information (VSI) to feed the BDPorc databank and take part in the national benchmark. In this sense, an important action launched by the main software companies in Spain and chaired by the University of Lleida was the creation of "Softporcino": a working group to set a core of basic calculations agreed by all pig software and BDporc defining a standard of KPI.

The integration from different sources of existing data and acquisition of new data is another problem for DSS adoption [32]. Farmers and managers do not want to waste time retyping data into a new software. In this sense, standardisation makes easier to share and integrate data already registered. Similarly, automatic

L. M. Plà-Aragonès

data gathering may save decision-maker time if the integration in existing DSS is automatic too.

Another beneficial dimension of integration is the ease coordination of processes and agents along the PSC. Many proposals deal with a sole problem for a sole PSC agent ignoring the relationship with other instances or problems like breeding farms with fattening farms, or fattening farms with the abattoir or the farming subsystem with the feed mill, or the meat packing plant with the fattening or breeding farms, or the meat packing plant with the retailer. There is a lack of proposals with a whole chain view [11] and the integration of different models and solutions [26]. For instance, the problem of carcass imbalance occurs when retailers make independent demands for individual pork chops resulting in surpluses of certain parts of the animal and shortages of others [1].

6.3   Research and Society

Research bodies are sometimes far from society problems. Research models tend to focus on academic aspects leaving aside practical ones. Many times, DSS have been based on what researchers and system analysts had considered necessary focusing in a specific problem and losing the holistic view a farmer must have [8]. For the same reason, researchers have blamed the pig industry for not adopting DSS rather than to criticise the poor design of the technology.

On the other hand, the timely use of DSS and the frequency are important aspects because if the frequency of use is low and the complexity of the tool big the future adoption is compromised. Otherwise, if the frequency of use is low and the complexity too, the added value is hardly appreciated. The increasing ability to represent complex systems and data acquisition have to be corresponded with a practical problem solving, involving end-users in every stage of DSS development. Recently, participatory research or multi-actor projects are promoted and funded by institutions around the world [29]. It is assumed that if end-user takes part in the research and development of practical solutions the time lasted in deployment, validation and adoption of a good solution will be shortened and of better quality. In this sense, there are academic institutions approaching to the sector. Different ways have been explored. Research institutes are supposed to be nearer to the society and to sectorial problems. In Wageningen, the blend of University and Research (WUR) offer the same umbrella to academics, researchers and project managers making easier the transfer of result to the society and vice versa. A similar organisation had concurred in the UdL-IRTA center in Lleida (Spain) where the GTEP, DSS-IRTA and the BDPorc were developed with a successful collaboration between researchers from the University of Lleida (UdL) and IRTA. However, the collaboration collapsed due to disputes between both institutions. In other countries, research institutes prevail strengthening the contact with companies of the sector and collaborating with academics. The blooming of start-ups sheltered by Universities has had an impact in the way academics transfer the knowledge to the general society and pig industry in particular [29].

6.4 How Decisions Are Made?

Many times, within the farming subsystem the farmer is who make decisions bridging the gap between theory and practice, balancing the desirable with the feasible, selecting a good enough alternative over the intended optimum. However, his/her viewpoint has not to be the same as the feedmiller, meat plant manager or any other farmer or PSC agent. Some authors claim that many DSS are developed to support real decision problems neglecting work practices and whether the solution proposed can be truly performed in practice [17, 22]. In other words, with a misleading idea of how decisions are made on field. For instance, the selection of fattened pigs by eye is feasible when the heaviest pigs are the first to be sent to the abattoir [17]. On the contrary, selecting pigs from one weight category not adjacent to another as other authors propose [12] would be difficult without individual measures of weight. In fact, little work has taken care and investigated how DSS are actually used [8].

Another aspect is the vertical integration or not. It is common in Spain, integrators own the pigs, provide feed and medical care, select the pigs to deliver to the abattoir and pay growers per animal or per pen. PSC manager pay attention to production cost and few KPI regardless operational decisions than farmers had been making. Not vertically integrated farmers produce fattened pigs and send them to the abattoir according to an expected live weight on their own risk.

Meat processors, including abattoirs, share the difficult task of matching the demand of customers with the production of farmers. Carcasses are classified and paid according to a reward system [17, 30] while supermarket demand is for individual primal cuts with different specifications which results in the requirement of slaughter a variety of pig sizes [1]. While the meat plant manager has the responsibility of paying according to carcass classification, the carcass value for the meat plant vary from pig to pig depending on the valuable cuts processed [17]. These problems emphasise the need to understand the context in which the decision-making takes place and the different profiles and approaches to the same problem.

7 Emerging Technologies and Future Prospects

7.1 The Forthcoming DSS, Swimming in (Big) Data Pool

The future of pig producers will rely on their ability to enhance their economic performance by improving productive efficiency rather than increasing farm size

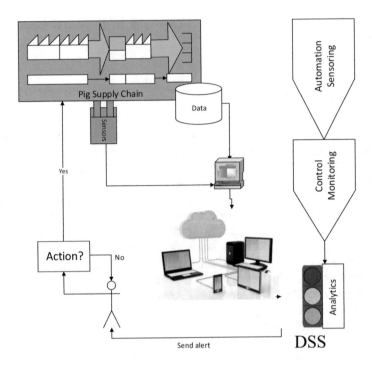

Fig. 2 Emerging DSS integrating new technologies

given actual constraints. DSS will be different than the current ones as they are evolving integrating progressively new ICT advances leading to reduce input cost and/or increase yield or sustainability values [33]. There are different drivers in the conformation of the forthcoming DSS like the massive volume of data with a wide variety and velocity (BigData) coming from the (1) **sensoring and automation**, used to (2) **monitoring and control** activities and processes to detect or anticipate problems by the use of (3) **analytic tools** in view of alerts emission (Fig. 2). The receiver of the alert, the decision-maker, can act or implement an action or not as response to the alert. Actions could be preventive, corrective or for verification. The capture of data will be at any level, any layer, of the PSC like in feed mills, on farm, within meat processors, supermarkets and retailers.

Other sources of data and information are internal like record-keeping systems, ERP or accounting programs. There will be more external data available, either public or private, available to complement the information processed by the DSS. Pieces of data can be processed before being supplied to the DSS by other technological elements like IoT platforms. The DSS could issue simple alerts linked to a single process (e.g., water consumption) or perform more complex analytics procedures, manage or combine smartly different alerts producing companion reports or dynamic dashboards. The hosting will be in the cloud, accessible from any device branched to internet. The DSS will be exploited as a Software as a

Service (SaaS) solution. The design of the DSS will be modular and capable of integrating different PSC agents. For this reason, they will be not only multi-data source but also multi-model, capable of fitting and providing integral solutions for specific PSC companies.

New digital technologies: There is a variety of new digital technologies to consider for improving the ability of existing DSS or developing new ones like new sensors for real-time monitoring, BigData, Artificial Intelligence (AI), the Internet of Things (IoT) and cloud computing [31]. The conceptualisation of DSS innovation offers a broad portfolio of research approaches depending on the complexity of the problem being addressed, stakeholders involved and existing institutional settings [33]. The evolving use of sensor technology makes available large amount and more precise data at farming and meat processing levels monitoring animals, carcasses and pork chops. The smart devices that will be incorporated into the pig industry will be connected to the Internet allowing for the formation of IoT networks. IoT technologies allow for communication between farm sensors, devices and equipment and will facilitate the automation of multiple procedures contributing to adaptable DSS for improving decisions on pig production and reproduction, animal health and welfare, meat processing and quality.

Sustainable DSS and standardisation: The development of DSS for the pig industry is expensive. New projects must consider not only the maintenance or upgrading of a DSS, but also the sustainability and connectivity with third-party products to avoid premature obsolescence. Open data, open source initiatives and open IoT platforms and repositories may help to this purpose and facilitate the establishment of standards. This policy may help the substitution, interchangeability and incorporation of new devices in existing platforms or the proposal of new ones.

Consultancy: Advisory services will benefit of new DSS generation and range from sole operator consultants through large agri-business companies and extension officers. Knowledge and advice networks besides private and public advisors can play a role in turning raw data and information into tacit knowledge and advice for later diffusing and transferring knowledge to farmers. They have a profile of end-users of DSS with different characteristics than farmers or PSC managers. Education will play a role preparing the PSC agents and pig industry businesses for the digital era. Perception of the value of advice services will be variable due to cultural legacy and expectations surrounding benefits of DSS adoption.

New benchmark interests: The amount of data registered besides the increasing competition facilitate the sharing of economic information like production cost components (Fig. 3) enriching the classic KPI of technical performance (Table 3). Today, financial analysis and profit projections complement production data to help control costs, manage risk and increase revenue.

As not all the farms are equally efficient, competition leads managers to try to identify best practice farm units and to improve the less efficient units by implementing best practices. Different farms tend to organise their operations in different ways, so consequently values for individual outputs will also tend to differ. This group of farms could then be used as benchmark or a point of reference for less efficient units and for benchmarking performance. Therefore, the

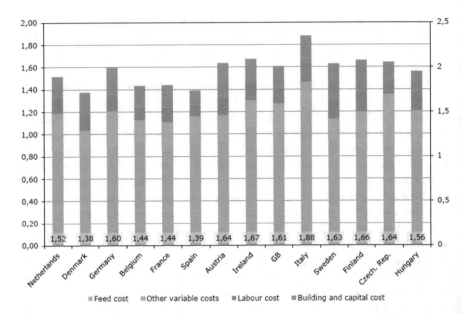

Fig. 3 Cost of production compared (€/kg hot carcass weight), split into cost categories in selected EU countries given a closed cycle pig farm Source: InterPIG/Wageningen Economic Research, year 2018

increasing capacity of analysis allow DSS to consider new benchmarking methods. For example, Data Envelopment Analysis (DEA) permit to identify the efficient production frontier and the measurement of technological change over time.

7.2 Whole Chain View and Digitalisation

At present, the information available for decision-making in the pig industry is considering a combination of observations of the animals, their environment and production results [21] reported rather disconnected from the information handled by abattoirs, meat processors, retailers and supermarkets in contact with the customers [1].

It is expected a tighter coordination of PSC agents vertically and horizontally remarking the need of DSS with a whole chain view (Fig. 4). A subsequent concentration will facilitate the creation of big firms or associations in the pig industry with more investment capacity in new ICT and DSS developments. The generation and management of more information is increasing. For instance, sensors and devices for automatic data acquisition are rising the need of data cloud storage and computing, accessible or integrated in existing decisional structures of pig companies.

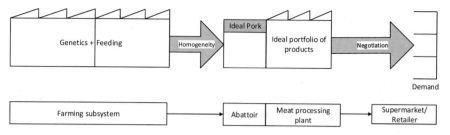

Fig. 4 Schematic representation of a PSC

Expected benefits for the pig industry of new ICT advances are precise automation and improved decision-making. However, as these technologies are disruptive in a way they change the traditional way of making decisions, the adoption will be progressive over time and among PSC agents. This novelty requires the acquisition of expertise selecting processes and actors candidates for innovation and proposing a sequence or road map for the transition towards digitalisation.

7.3 Externalities and Disturbing Shocks

Globalisation has brought a lot of advantages to the society, but at the same time in recent times we have observed some disadvantages as problems can be propagated everywhere and have a global impact.

The COVID-19 has been a pandemic disease with great economic effects all around the world. To date it is unpredictable the consequences of additional outbreaks. The primary sector in general and the pig production in particular have apparently suffered a low impact, but we need time to see the medium long-term effects.

Nowadays, China is the first pig producer. However, the African swine fever (ASF) affecting Chinese farms has stimulated pig production in the rest of the world with an increment of exports to cover China deficit. The threat of infectious diseases is always present for commercial farms. There have been outbreaks of ASF in some Central and Eastern European countries affecting domestic pigs and more in wild boars. The risk still exists but the situation seems under control. At least ASF is not progressing to prominent producer countries although it is always stalking. ASF reduce the trading of products of pig origin—including ham, sausages or pâté—or any equipment or other goods which could potentially be contaminated with ASF virus coming from countries with outbreaks. The recovery of the internal market in China will be slow, but once recovered a world crisis in the pig sector would be expected whether an ASF outbreak do not hit before in western countries.

In addition, the economic and technological rivalry between China and the USA may affect the development of new emerging technologies in view of new DSS developments. The battle for 5G communications and infrastructures, cloud hosting and services can draw different technological scenarios and opportunities of DSS for smart agriculture. Depending on the evolution of the commercial war China-USA and the position of EU, Japan and G8 new technological advances will be more accessible or not.

Finally, proprietary data is a controversial topic involving the property right and use of data collected by the pig industry, stored in the cloud managed by service providers. It also encompasses data privacy and security, which provokes in pig companies a lack of trust concerning ownership and third-party usage of their own data.

7.4 Advances in Other Fields Reverting in DSS

The DSS in the pig industry cover only a part of livestock production and the primary sector. Advances in other fields may also impact in future developments. Below we present some of them.

Artificial intelligence is one methodological source for BigData analytics. AI offers formal general algorithms for prediction and pattern classification methods. Machine learning, neural networks and automatic reasoning, are some examples. Recognition of natural language can be useful to develop new DSS interfaces. Sound and image analysis may allow scientist to study animal behaviour detecting welfare or disease in animals issuing alerts. Image analysis can be useful either for live pigs, carcasses or products. Live weight or counting of pigs can be estimated from image analysis. Temperature, fat and lean content or defaults in post-mortem inspection, carcasses or pork chops can be shown with thermographic cameras, ultrasounds, X-ray. AI can procure more data and information to develop dedicated DSS to solve a specific problem, e.g., estimate life weigh to deliver pigs to the abattoir, or contribute to more complex DSS devoted to a wider view of the business, integrating all the information available progressing to a total digitalisation of activities.

Virtual reality (VR) is being developed mainly for video games, but there are simulation tools based in VR to represent simulation models. VR may allow the farmer to visit the farm seeing the performance of each animal in a virtual walk. Also, a facility, either farm or meat processing plant, can be seen and visited before built, as there are engineering studios using already this technology. The exploration of new alternatives or the analysis of different decisions could reach to be observed with VR, not only calculated, summarised or reported on a sheet.

Biotechnology can contribute introducing new genes and shaping the different genotype of pigs for specific goals like ham production, fresh lean meat consumption or better feed conversion. New decisions regarding the introduction or selection of new genes or breeds will be more relevant in future. The creation of new farms producing pigs for medical use of components could complement the present use as meal. Biotechnology may produce also biosensors to provide data of body condition and health status of animals, helping to reveal hidden characteristics, making diagnosis of diseases or with particular interest in meat quality traits or animal growth capabilities.

Nanoscience can provide methods to simplify for instance animal identification or the traceability of products. As consequence the data available for safer PSC avoiding infections or human health problems by contaminations will improve and waste will be reduced. Another application is based on nanoLEDs to overcoming the limits of diffraction with superresolution lighting on a chip (https://cordis.europa.eu/project/id/737089). This way, image analysis would benefit of higher resolution and powering new applications.

8 Conclusions

DSS for the pig industry must adapt to enable decision-makers to make more informed decisions in view of satisfying demand, remaining sustainable and respectful with animal welfare while preserving the economic viability. The evolution of the pig industry over time has shown a concentration of production to maintain past profit levels and new organisational structures like PSC. Computers are common tools in the pig industry and little by little, the development of new IC technologies and sensors offers the potential to collect large volumes of data. DSS are the natural framework where decision models should be included in order to support farmers, advisers or management specialists in the decision-making process. Cloud computing-based DSS and agriculture 4.0 make data integration, automation and data analysis easier. Data science methodologies and AI enlarge the range of modelling techniques available to develop smart pig DSS with a whole chain view. There is a challenge of preparing a modular infrastructure capable of integrating old and new DSS and interconnect the number of new devices and sensors to provide useful information not just on demand, but also in a preventive, either intelligent, manner anticipating decisions in a smart way. There also exists issues pertaining to data governance and externalities related to globalisation that may have a positive or negative impact depending on future evolution. Other developments in biotechnology, nanotechnology and virtual reality may enlarge the frontiers of DSS tools for the pig industry.

Acknowledgements Lluís M. Plà wishes to acknowledge the financial support of the CYTED Program (516RT0513-Red Iberoamericana de Agro-Bigdata y DSS en Agricultura: BIGDSSAGRO).

References

1. Taylor, D. H. (2006). Strategic consideration in the development of lean agri-food supply chains: A case study of the UK pork sector. *Supply Chain Management: An International Journal, 11*(3), 271–280.

2. Trienekens, J., Petersen, B., Wognum, N., & Brinkmann, D. (2009). *European pork chains. Diversity and Quality Challenges in Consumer-oriented Production and Distribution.* Wageningen: Academic Publishers. ISBN 978-90-8686-103-3.
3. Faostat. (2020). *Statistics of livestock primary in the section of Production.* Retrieved May 23, 2020, from http://www.fao.org/faostat/en/#data/QA.
4. Nadal-Roig, E., Plà-Aragonès, L. M., & Alonso-Ayuso, A. (2019). Production planning of supply chains in the pig industry. *Computers and Electronics in Agriculture, 161,* 72–78.
5. Perez, C., de Castro, R., & Font i Furnols, M. (2009). The pork industry: A supply chain perspective. *British Food Journal, 111*(3), 257–274.
6. Backus, G., & Dijkhuizen, A. A. (2002). *Kernkamp lecture: The future of the European pork chain* (pp. 8–11). Minnesota, USA: Allen D. Leman Swine Conference.
7. Rodríguez, S. V., Faulin, J., & Plà, L. M. (2014). New opportunities of operations research to improve pork supply chain efficiency. *Annals of Operations Research, 219,* 5–23.
8. Rose, D. C., Morris, C., Lobley, M., Winter, M., Sutherland, W. J., & Dicks, L. V. (2018). Exploring the spatialities of technological and user re-scripting: The case of decision support tools in UK agriculture. *Geoforum, 89,* 11–18.
9. Boger, S., Hobbs, J. E., & Kerr, W. A. (2001). Supply chain relationships in the Polish pork sector. *Supply Chain Management, 6*(2), 74–83. https://doi.org/10.1108/13598540110387573.
10. Klein, K. K., Walburger, A. M., Faminow, Larue, B., Romain, R., & Foster, K. (1996). An evaluation of supply chain performance in the Canadian pork sector. *Supply Chain Management, 1*(3), 12–24. https://doi.org/10.1108/13598549610155288.
11. Perez, C., de Castro, R., Simons, D., & Gimenez, G. (2010). Development of lean supply chains: A case study of the Catalan pork sector. *Supply Chain Management, 15*(1), 55–68. https://doi.org/10.1108/13598541011018120.
12. Khamjan, S., Piewthongngam, K., & Pathumnakul, S. (2013). Pig procurement plan considering pig growth and size distribution. *Computers & Industrial Engineering, 64*(4), 886–889.
13. Nadal-roig, E., & Plà, L. M. (2014). Multiperiod planning tool for multisite pig production systems. *Journal of Animal Science, 92,* 4154–4160.
14. Trienekens, J., & Wognum, N. (2013). Requirements of supply chain management in differentiating European pork chains. *Meat Science, 95*(3), 719–726.
15. Plà-Aragonés, L. M. (2010). DSS in pig production systems. In B. Manos, N. Matsatsinis, K. Paparrizos, & J. Papathanasiou (Eds.), *Decision support systems in agriculture, food and the environment: Trends, applications and advances* (pp. 101–117). Hershey: IGI Global.
16. Hobbs, J. E., Kerr, W. A., & Klein, K. K. (1998). Creating international competitiveness through supply chain management: Danish pork. *Supply Chain Management, 3*(2), 68–78. https://doi.org/10.1108/13598549810215388.
17. Plà, L. M., Pages, A., Nadal, E., Mateo, J., Tarrafeta, P., Mendioroz, D., Perez, L., & López, S. (2018). Economic assessment of pig meat processing and cutting production by simulation. *International Journal of Food Processing Engineering.* https://doi.org/10.1515/ijfe-2018-0100.
18. Hindsborg, J., & Kristensen, A. R. (2019). From data to decision—Implementation of a sow replacement model. *Computers and Electronics in Agriculture, 165,* 104970.
19. Gray, J., Banhazi, T. M., & Kist, A. A. (2017). Wireless data management system for environmental monitoring in livestock buildings. *Information Processing in Agriculture, 4*(1), 1–17.
20. Lehmann, R. J., Hermansen, J. E., Fritz, M., Brinkmann, D., Trienekens, J., & Schiefer, G. (2011). Information services for European pork chains—Closing gaps in information infrastructures. *Computers and Electronics in Agriculture, 79*(2), 125–136.
21. Cornou, C., & Kristensen, A. R. (2013). Use of information from monitoring and decision support systems in pig production: Collection, applications and expected benefits. *Livestock Science, 157*(2–3), 552–567.
22. Fountas, S., Carli, G., Sørensen, C. G., Tsiropoulos, Z., Cavalaris, C., Vatsanidou, A., Liakos, B., Canavari, M., Wiebensohn, J., & Tisserye, B. (2015). Farmmanagement information systems: Current situation and future perspectives. *Computers and Electronics in Agriculture, 115,* 40–50.

23. Plà, L. M. (2007). Review of mathematical models for Sow Herd management. *Livestock Science, 106*, 107–119.

24. Jalvingh, A. W., Dijkhuizen, A. A., & van Arendonk, J. A. M. (1992). Dynamic probabilistic modelling of reproduction and replacement management in sow herds. General aspects and model description. *Agricultural Systems, 39*(2), 133–152.

25. Maliappis, M. T., Yialouris, C. P., Deligeorgis, S. G., & Sideridis, A. B. (1997). EMISP: An Expert Management Information System for Pigs. *Proc. of 1 European Conference for Information Technology in Agriculture, 1997*, 325–330.

26. Plà, L. M., Pomar, C., & Pomar, J. (2004). A sow herd decision support system based on an embedded Markov model. *Computers and Electronics in Agriculture, 45*(1-3), 51–69.

27. Thornley, J. H. M., & France, J. (2007). *Mathematical models in agriculture: Quantitative methods for the plant, animal and ecological sciences* (2nd ed.). Wallingford: CABI.

28. van Milgen, J., Valancogne, A., Dubois, S., Dourmad, J.-Y., Sève, B., & Noblet, J. (2008). InraPorc: A model and decision support tool for the nutrition of growing pigs. *Animal Feed Science and Technology, 143*(1–4), 387–405.

29. Wolfert, S., Ge, L., Verdouw, C., & Bogaardt, M.-J. (2017). Big data in smart farming—A review. *Agricultural Systems, 153*, 69–80.

30. Kristensen, A. R., Nielsen, L., & Hielsen, M. S. (2012). Optimal slaughter pig marketing with emphasis on information from on-line live weight assessment. *Livestock Science, 145*, 95–108.

31. Zhai, Z., Martínez, J. F., Beltran, V., & Martínez, N. L. (2020). Decision support systems for agriculture 4.0: Survey and challenges. *Computers and Electronics in Agriculture, 170*, 105256.

32. Lytos, A., Lagkas, T., Sarigiannidis, P., Zervakis, M., & Livanos, G. (2020). Towards smart farming: Systems, frameworks and exploitation of multiple sources. *Computer Networks, 172*, 107147.

33. Fielke, S., Taylor, B., & Jakku, E. (2020). Digitalisation of agricultural knowledge and advice networks: A state-of-the-art review. *Agricultural Systems, 180*, 102763.

Game-Based Learning and Decision-Making for Urban Sustainability: A Case of System Dynamics Simulations

Stefano Armenia, Federico Barnabè, and Alessandro Pompei

Abstract This chapter aims to contribute to the current debate on how to face the challenge of managing limited resources in a sustainable way, specifically addressing the issue of *urban sustainability*. In this context, and more in general about the broad field of sustainability, academic literature specifically emphasizes that *computer simulation* could provide a potentially useful tool. More in detail, several calls for more research point to the use of computer-based learning laboratories—the so-called Interactive Learning Environments (ILEs)—not only to enhance individual as well collective learning but also to facilitate decision-making with a forward-looking orientation in complex sustainability systems. Particularly, ILEs are seen as complementary tools to—if not even as an evolution of—existing Decisions Support Systems (DSSs), traditionally used to analyze available data and steer decision-making. Starting from these considerations, this study aims to: (1) outline the role that DSSs and ILEs may play in fostering learning acquisition and supporting decision-making in and about complex sustainability-related systems; (2) discuss the main results of an ILE-based project used to support learning and decision-making about an urban sustainability context. From a methodological and technical point of view, this study employs System Dynamics (SD) modeling principles and tools. Specifically, a System Dynamics computer model was used to portray the urban environment under analysis (i.e., the simulated city); the model was subsequently transformed into an ILE used to explore the effects of managerial decisions related to the concept of "urban metabolism."

S. Armenia (✉)
Link Campus University, Rome, Italy
e-mail: s.armenia@unilink.it

F. Barnabè
University of Siena, Siena, Italy
e-mail: federico.barnabe@unisi.it

A. Pompei
Sapienza University of Rome, Rome, Italy
e-mail: alessandro.pompei@uniroma1.it

© Springer Nature Switzerland AG 2021
J. Papathanasiou et al. (eds.), *EURO Working Group on DSS*, Integrated Series in Information Systems, https://doi.org/10.1007/978-3-030-70377-6_17

Keywords Interactive learning environments · Urban sustainability · Computer simulation · System dynamics · Decision support systems

1 Introduction[1]

This chapter aims to contribute to the current debate on how facing the challenge of managing limited resources in a sustainable way, specifically addressing the issue of *urban sustainability*.

As many authors, regulators, institutions, and agencies underline (e.g., [1, 2]), our urban environments are on the verge of a huge collapse and are increasingly difficult to manage; several causes are behind the problems affecting such environments (e.g., overcrowded population, mismanagement of available resources, myopic managerial behaviors) and a systemic approach to decision-making is advocated and at the center of a lively debate that engages both academics and practitioners (e.g., [3]).

In this context, and more in general about the broad field of sustainability, academic literature specifically emphasizes that *computer simulation* could provide a potentially useful tool for investigating urban environments' characteristics, and subsequently designing and testing sustainability management policies (e.g., [4]). More in detail calls for more research point to the use of computer-based learning laboratories—the so-called *Interactive Learning Environments* (hereafter ILEs)—not only to enhance individual as well collective learning but also to facilitate decision-making with a forward-looking orientation in complex sustainability systems [5–8]. Particularly, ILEs are seen as complementary tools to—if not even as an evolution of—existing Decisions Support Systems (DSSs) (e.g., see [9]), traditionally used to analyze available data and steer decision-making.

Starting from these considerations, this study aims to:

1. Outline the role that DSSs and ILEs may play in fostering learning acquisition and supporting decision-making in and about complex sustainability-related systems,
2. Discuss the main results of an ILE-based project used to support learning and decision-making about an urban sustainability context.

Two streams of research are used as the main theoretical and methodological references for this work.

---

[1] Although this study is the result of a joint collaboration, Stefano Armenia is to be considered the author of the Sect. 2—"Concept and Evolution of Decision Support Systems"; Federico Barnabè is to be considered the author of the Sects. 1 and 3—"Introduction" and "The Potentials of Interactive Learning Environments in Facilitating Learning and Decision-making"; Alessandro Pompei is to be considered the author of the Sect. 4—"Research Design". One-third of the other Sects. 5 and 6 is to be attributed to each of the three authors.

First, this study builds on the concept of "urban metabolism" [2, 10]. The concept of urban metabolism aims at identifying and analyzing the interactions between the natural and the human systems in a specific region (or environment); therefore, this approach not only allows describing how the human–environment interaction takes place but also explaining how this interaction entails and informs strategic decisions related to the management of the resources at disposal, subsequently generating an array of impacts and consequences (even in terms of harmful side-effects, such as increased pollution, CO_2 emissions, and traffic congestion).

Second, from a methodological and technical point of view, this work employs System Dynamics (hereafter SD) modeling principles and tools [11–15]. Specifically, a System Dynamics computer model was used to portray the urban environment (i.e., the simulated city) under analysis; the SD model was then transformed into an Interactive Learning Environment (see [5, 6, 16, 17]) subsequently used to explore the effects of managerial decisions related to the concept of urban metabolism as aforementioned.

In terms of expected findings, it is to emphasize that the focus of the SD-based ILE employed in this research is educational (see [18]): particularly, the simulations with the ILE are meant to explore the effects generated by the players' decisions about the simulated urban environment, with specific regard to the link that brings routinely human and business activities carried out in an urban environment to (positively and negatively) impact on the urban environment itself (e.g., in terms of new job opportunities which are offered, but also in terms of CO_2 emissions that are generated).

The structure of the chapter is as follows. The second and third sections briefly present the fundamental characteristics of Decision Support Systems and Interactive Learning Environments, emphasizing their main areas of application and opportunities for future research in the field of sustainability. The fourth section presents the research design, while Sect. 5 describes the ILE and some examples from an ILE-based simulation. Section 6 provides the discussion, as well as the limitations and some ideas for further research.

2 Concept and Evolution of Decision Support Systems

The task of management is that of bringing an effort to its ultimate good conclusion, by deciding the needed courses of action at certain turning points, where a decision from someone having a systemic perspective is needed. This is true in all fields of human knowledge including the security and safety assurance for people.

All managerial tasks have the latent need to be supported in their effort to do a better job, and a relevant, effective, and useful Decision Support System can play a crucial role in helping "self-confident professionals" to rely on the evidence provided by facts [19] and not on wrong mental models or beliefs that are backed only by expertise (which of course could be biased by past experiences). As reported in [19], most of the early authors refer to the Gorry and Scott Morton

[20] paper ("A Framework for Management Information Systems") published in Sloan Management Review in 1971 as the true starting point for DSS technology. Later on, the Sprague [21] paper ("Framework for the Development of Decision Support Systems") in MIS Quarterly in 1980 summarized all the essential elements for the design, development, implementation, and use of decision support systems. As still reported in [19], early case studies analyzed by Keen [22] showed a number of benefits identified by DSS users among which cost and time savings, thanks to faster and more effective responses.

These and similar general benefits still appear today in the literature, even if the underlying DSS technology has changed several times and even though the technology gets different labels than the core idea of DSS. In fact, DSS architecture builds on mainly three components:

1. A dialog manager/interface between the user and functional routines
2. A data manager
3. Functional routines

In Carlsson [19], the author also refers that Sprague [23] collected the following "DSS characteristics" from several authors:

1. DSSs aim at the less well-structured, underspecified problems of upper-level management
2. DSSs combine the use of models or analytic techniques with traditional data access and retrieval functions
3. DSSs focus on features which make them easy to use by non-computer people in an interactive mode
4. DSSs emphasize flexibility and adaptability to accommodate changes in the environment and the decision-making approach of the user

Thus, a distinctive feature of the early descriptions of a DSS is that it should support all phases of decision-making (hence "decision support").

From a wider perspective, we can see that modern DSSs are not only based on Information Technology (IT) but also on methodology. The engine of the decisional process can be represented by the diagram in Fig. 1. Here we did not represent explicitly the technological stack, which by the way can be quite complex in data representation and fruition because we wanted to provide a perspective on the fact that calculus methods are a key element in modern DSSs.

From this perspective, it is worth also mentioning that such methodologies rely on a number of underlying decision-making theories/models, whose evolution is captured in Table 1, which correlates various decision-making theories, modes, and attributes.

Whereas it is not the aim of this work to discuss in detail the information provided in Table 1, it is still to emphasize that, over the last 40 years, DSSs certainly have evolved from mere descriptive/diagnostic power in operational/tactical environments to the prescriptive/predictive power with a focus on strategic decision-making, capable of an effective response also to potential future environments (hence with an aim to resilience building for the system under analysis).

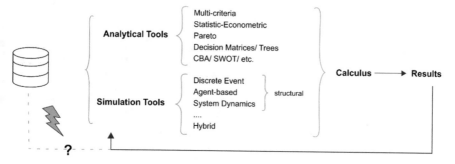

Fig. 1 A generic representation of the decisional process. Source: Armenia [24]

In this context, IT and computer simulation offer the potential for further development of DSSs, specifically when they are seen as (or embedded into) peculiar Interactive Learning Environments, presented subsequently.

3 The Potentials of Interactive Learning Environments in Facilitating Learning and Decision-Making

3.1 Defining an ILE

Over the last few years, we have been witnessing an increasing interest not only toward the use of computer simulation in management science but also toward the development of the so-called learning laboratories, usually referred to as *Interactive Learning Environments* (hereafter ILEs [16]). In this study, we specifically refer to computer-based ILEs where the interaction [35] between a user (sometimes referred to as the player or the learner) and the learning environment is primarily devoted to knowledge acquisition (i.e., learning [36]), specifically through an interactive process whereby knowledge is created through the transformation of experience (the so-called experiential learning, [37, 38]). Subsequently, the second goal of ILEs is to facilitate decision-making and gain policy insights [39, 40].

ILEs fundamentally consist of two main and interrelated components, i.e., an underlying computer simulation model, and a graphical interface. While the simulation model is at the heart of the simulator, the interface is the place where the interaction between the user and the model takes place. The users take on the role of decision-makers within the system and are called on to face complex issues in different scenarios. Notably, ILEs are often built on real-world cases and can use historical data as inputs to the model or to inform the decisions taken by the users.

Before presenting more detailed information about the main constituents of an ILE and its main goals, it is immediately to be emphasized that ILEs are also referred to with other labels and names, such as "Microworlds" (a term

Table 1 A general approach to decision-making

Decision-making models			
Analytic		Reflective thinking [25] Organizational Decision Making [26, 27] The Knowing organization [28]	Strategic, Informed Decision Making for the Future [29] Intelligent Organizations [30]
Rules-based		Organizational Decision Making [26, 27] The Knowing organization [28]	
Belief-driven		Behavioural Decision Theory [31]	
Cognitive	Naturalistic decision making [32] Rapid Processing decision theory [33]	Learning Organization [34] The Knowing Organization [28]	
Decision-making attributes			
Timing	Immediate	Short term	Long term
Type	Critical, Urgent	Operational, Tactical	Strategic
Environment	Dynamic	Recurring	Uncertain
Objective	React	Explain, optimize	Predict, Act
Technology	Mental simulation of options using leading practices and pattern matching	Applying logic or rules, plus computerized, probabilistic information processing	Simulation and decision tools with impact analysis
Knowledge	Tacit knowledge	Tacit and explicit knowledge	Convergence of explicit knowledge with tacit and cultural knowledge
Strategies	Heuristic	Algorithm	Convergent analytics

Source: Adapted from Podolak et al. [29]

that was used for the first time by Papert in the book titled *Mindstorms*—[41]—and, subsequently, employed by other authors—e.g., [42]), "Virtual Worlds" [43], "Learning Laboratories" [44], "Computer-Based Learning Environments" [45], and "Management Flight Simulators" [15]. Interestingly about the aims of this study, ILEs have also been used as a specific form of DSSs (e.g., see [3, 6]).

Overall, the three terms included in the acronym ILE well explain the fundamental rationale of this tool: as Isaacs and Senge [45] point out, the central purpose of an ILE "is to provide decision-makers with new opportunities for learning through conceptualization, experimentation and reflection that are not easily achieved in everyday management activities." Stated differently, ILEs provide virtual, low-cost, and safe laboratories where learning acquisition is sped up and decision-making skills are tested and developed [15].

With this said, the following sub-sections focus on the presentation of the main components of ILEs, on their key features, and, finally, on the main areas of application.

3.2 Main Components of an ILE

From a technical point of view, an ILE is made of two key constituents, i.e., a computer simulation model and a graphical interface that allows the interaction between the model and the users.

The simulation model is at the heart of the ILE. Notably, the issue under investigation is relevant for the choice of the modeling technique to use (e.g., a System Dynamics model or an Agent-Based Model).[2]Moreover, and depending on the ultimate purpose of the ILE, the models at the core of the simulator might not necessarily and exactly have to mirror the reality under investigation, especially when the ILE is designed with a learning objective. Stated differently, modeling and building the ILE often entails some degree of simplification, whether in terms of the variables included in the model, the boundaries being set, or the level of aggregation chosen [15, 46].

Overall, the model—and subsequently the ILE—should be oriented to support the users to make decisions and action about a specific underlying issue and within a specific context. As clearly emphasized by Sterman [47].

> every model is a representation of a system—a group of functionally interrelated elements forming a complex whole. But for the model to be useful, it must address a specific problem and must simplify rather than attempting to mirror in detail an entire system. (. . .) The usefulness of models lies in the fact that they simplify reality, putting it into a form that we can comprehend. But a truly comprehensive model of a complete system would be just as complex as that system and just as inscrutable.

Notably, one of the features allowed by modern modeling software and computers is that models can largely and thoroughly use available data, for example, provided by an organization's internal database (e.g., historical data about the organization, its sales, the workforce) or by an external source (e.g., a table providing data about market prices). The model can be therefore and quite easily linked to an organization's internal database and be used as a specific form of DSS.

On top of the model, an ILE displays a graphical interface.

The interface allows the interaction between the user and the computer model. Therefore, it must contain all the relevant features, leverages and information that

---

[2]As an example, computer models could be developed and simulated according to different paradigms such as the following ones [46]: (1) Discrete event simulations (DES) are process-oriented models simulated with discrete variables and calculations; (2) Agent-based simulations (ABS) are individual-centric, being focused on specific "agents" with their own thread of control and active objects. (3) SD simulations, based on the concept of feedback loops, focus on how system structures affect system behavior, and are simulated with continuous change.

the user will need to interact correctly and fruitfully with the model and to take a decision within the simulated environment.

Usually, the interface displays a control panel and a number of graphs, tables and figures reporting data. Additional elements can be included as well, such as further information for the users, multimedia objects, and pop-up windows useful to give the player cognitive feedback, for example, when specific critical values of key variables are reached during the simulation.

Notably, when deciding to develop an ILE, it is relevant to keep in mind who will be the users, what their needs, and which are the ultimate aims assigned to the simulator.

Concerning the users, ILEs provide computer laboratories where participants will have the opportunity to develop essential skills, improve decision-making, conduct experiments, and play. In this context, ILEs are open to any kind of user that might benefit from the interaction with the simulator, thereby including at the same time students and managers, less experienced people and professionals, novices, and experts in specific fields or about specific issues. Obviously, the ILE should provide the user with a simulation experience customized to his/her needs and expectations.

Indeed, ILEs can be designed and used to allow different kinds of interaction between the model and the user, with the following ones being the most relevant.

First of all, we make a distinction between *single-user vs. multi-user ILEs*, with the former being a simulator that allows one single player to interact with the ILE and the latter allowing multiples users to interact and take decisions simultaneously.

Subsequently focusing on multi-user ILEs, it is possible to distinguish between *symmetric and asymmetric ILEs*, where the first category allows the interaction of multiple players with the ILE, anyhow having at disposal the same decisions within the simulated environment, while the second one entails the participation of multiple users having different decisions at their disposal.

Additionally, ILEs can be either *cooperative* or *competitive* ones, with the former category including simulators where the users take decision and action to cooperatively reach a shared goal, and the latter category including simulators where the players compete to perform and succeed.

Also depending on the features aforementioned, an ILE could provide the users with additional information and data about the system under investigation and the task to accomplish, as well as additional multimedia objects useful to highlight specific situations/results/information, tutorials to be used to test and explore the behavior of the model, some indications and hints about how to play the simulator, however avoiding to overwhelm the users with irrelevant information or graphical features (e.g., [48, 49]).

3.3 Key Features of an ILE

To be effective learning tools and aid for decision-makers, ILEs should be designed taking into account some key features. Among the features highlighted by previous studies in the field (e.g., [50, 51]), the following ones are particularly relevant: transparency, realism, no-threatening and user-friendly environment. More details are provided hereafter.

3.3.1 Transparency

Transparency is often mentioned as a key feature of an ILE. Alessi [50], for instance, refers to the transparency of an ILE in terms of *designing the degree of model visibility*:

> some model parts may be visible and some hidden, and the degree of visibility may change or depend on learner progress. Visibility may be provided in different ways, for example, showing the stocks and flows in a flow diagram, showing the underlying equations, or showing a causal loop diagram. Parts of a model may be hidden at some times and made visible at others, depending on particular needs and objectives.

The idea underlying the concept of transparency is that if the relationships between structure and behavior are clearly shown and they are understandable and relatable to policymaking, it becomes possible to foster the learning process. It is obvious that the degree of transparency should be selected depending on the learning goals to be achieved.

3.3.2 Realism

One of the first tasks a researcher should satisfy in designing an ILE is to pursue reality. This means that the simulation environment should resemble as closely as possible a real-world environment although a delicate balance between realism and usability is to be ensured.

In principle, the ILE should be easily understandable, clear in its functioning and objectives, and recognizable by the users in its basic features. For instance, decision-makers could be accustomed to read and get information from accounting-oriented spreadsheets and they could consequently benefit from having the chance to consult such reports during the simulation ([52]: 324). In some cases, especially when dealing with professionals or operators, it could be also better to have interfaces reproducing as many features as possible of the original software used by their company (e.g., see [53]). However, the ILE does not necessarily need to be completely realistic, or at least "adding realism for realism's sake is misguided" ([48]: 336).

3.3.3 No-Threatening and Friendly-User Environment

An ILE proves its validity and usefulness when able to enrich managers' and users' mental models, make their ideas clear and explicit, challenge their beliefs, conduct many cycles of action and reflection. To do so, ILEs should provide a no-threatening environment for the user.

Overall, an ILE should represent an open and free-risk space where the users will have the opportunity to develop skills, test policies and strategies, shorten users' learning curve, and also develop forms of collaborative learning. However, this process has its risks, since within ILEs "managers' beliefs are called into question. Inconsistencies are revealed. If trust and openness are not well established, individuals may be threatened and react defensively" ([44]: 200). Interestingly, Isaacs and Senge [45] clarify this statement:

> at the individual level, recent research and theory suggest that confronting management problems that are complex, nonroutine, and counterintuitive, such as CBLEs [Computer-Based Learning Environments] pose, can create embarrassment and threat, and tend to trigger a set of self-fulfilling and self-sealing behaviors that diminish learning and the likelihood for change.

Last, specifically adopting a technical point of view, an ILE should be a friendly-user environment. In detail, within a well-designed and effective ILE, the computer is merely the tool through which the interaction takes place. In principle, participants should not think about the computer, while only focusing on their way of thinking, their strategies, and the issues they are facing.

If all the previous features are properly taken into account in designing an ILE, it will presumably become possible to correctly pursue and achieve the above mentioned key-goals.

3.4 Typical Applications of ILEs

In broad terms, computer-based ILEs are powerful tools for analyzing systems with significant dynamic complexity and certainly have several virtues, as well emphasized by Sterman [15]:

> they provide low-cost laboratories for learning. The virtual world allows time and space to be compressed or dilated. Actions can be repeated under the same or different conditions. (...) Virtual worlds provide high-quality feedback. (...) Formalizing qualitative models and testing them via simulation often leads to radical changes in the way we understand reality. (...) Most important, when experimentation in real systems is infeasible, simulation becomes the main, and perhaps the only, way you can discover for yourself how complex systems work.

The breadth and variety of applications witnessed by massive literature support the statement above. Yet, the field of application for ILEs is still expanding, due to at least two main reasons.

The first one is related to the continuous advancement of technology, ICT (Information and Communication Technology), and computer science (e.g., [54]), which are pushing the field and research ahead, for example, toward the use of ILEs in multiplayer online formats (e.g., [55]) or in combination with virtual reality and artificial intelligence (e.g., [56]).

The second one is related to the main aims that can be assigned to ILEs. In this specific regard, we share the position of Davidsen [16], who emphasizes that computer-based ILEs can be developed and used for two main purposes: learning and research validation.

As to the former, using ILEs to foster *learning* entails the ability to influence the formation of mental models [57] governing human decision-making and action in complex, dynamic, domains. In this regard, as examples, Machuca [58], as well as Größler et al. [59], discussed and demonstrated how it is possible to enhance learning with computer-based ILEs, and Qudrat-Ullah [60] demonstrated that the participants involved in computerized ILEs-based programs perceive important learning benefits and educational value.

When analyzing the latter, i.e., research validation, ILEs are used to pursue the goal of identifying and analyzing the mental models governing human decision-making in complex and dynamic domains. For instance, previous literature provides a number of studies where ILEs were used with the experimental design for the specific purpose to inform and analyze decision-making *during* the computer-based game or simulation. Examples include ILE-based experiments about the management of natural resources (e.g., [61–63]) and the negotiation of policies that ultimately will affect climate change [3], just to name a few.

Additionally, it is noteworthy that ILEs can also be used as research validation tools for an *ex post* analysis of policymakers' decisions in a simulated environment [64], with the famous Beer Distribution Game experiment and the subsequent model-based analysis (see [15, 65, 66]) being one well-known example.

With this said, the field of ILEs still presents many opportunities, and calls for more research are advocated within the academic community in several areas of application and for various purposes. Specifically, this study addresses the call for more research about the analysis of decision-making and performance measurement [5], focusing on urban collective policymaking through ILEs in the context of urban sustainability management.

Whereas a rich literature already provides evidence that computer modeling can be effectively used to model and analyze urban sustainability (e.g., [67–69]) and sustainable urban development (e.g., [70]), not many studies are to be found—to our knowledge—if oriented toward the analysis of ILE-facilitated policymaking and governance about urban sustainability, with rare and quite specific exceptions (e.g., [71]), thereby calling for more exploration and evidence (e.g., [72]).

4   Research Design

This study developed and subsequently tested a System Dynamics-based ILE with the ultimate goal of favoring learning and collective decision-making about an urban sustainability environment. Whereas we already highlighted some information about ILEs and their main strengths, this section provides more details about the research project (the "SUSTAIN" project) in which an ILE was developed by means of System Dynamics as the underlying modeling and simulation methodology.

SUSTAIN is an ERASMUS+ project with an innovative perspective on urban sustainability. Its target is to promote among higher education students—which are the policymakers of tomorrow—the importance of sustainability principles when facing the typical problems of an urban environment. In order to achieve its goals, the research team developed a course that is based on an interactive board game with an analytical style of education, allowing students to learn about transportation sustainability and societal metabolism while playing. The course and the board game are supported by an illustrative simulation model based on the System Dynamics methodology, which allows the students to experiment with their decisions in a consequence-free environment. As mentioned, the model was embedded into an Interactive Learning Environment [5, 6, 16] developed with the software Stella Architect.

System Dynamics [12–15] is an established modeling methodology particularly suitable to analyze complex and dynamic systems. Over 60 years of contributions about a variety of domains witness the breadth of scope and applications and also the enduring validity of SD. With specific regard to the aims of this study, SD—according to a wide scientific literature and several educational experiences—helps to improve the understanding of urban dynamics (e.g., [68]) raising awareness about the related complexities and the need of the systems thinking approach [73] to urban sustainability [15]. As mentioned, to introduce students to systems thinking, we have developed an illustrative simulation model that is described subsequently alongside with the main features of the ILE that embeds the computer model. Notably, the SD model and the SD-based ILE are to be considered as two of the main outputs of this research project.

5   Results: the SD Model and the ILE

The model is divided into several sections: Investment-general variables, Transport, Waste management, Water management, Environment, Energy, Urban planning. Each of them has its variables and internal dynamics, but, from a systemic point of view, they can be seen as a whole big system that represents a "city" [74]. As underlined by Davidsen [17] within a single ILE, the system under investigation is usually analyzed into sub-systems and various sub-models are consequently built. These sub-models are then integrated into a sort of super-model and are interrelated using chains that indicate the transfer of variable values from one model to variables in any of its co-models during the simulation.

The basic objective pursued with the simulation can be summarized in trying to increase simultaneously: the population (social aspect), the city's budget (economic aspect), and the environmental well-being (environmental aspect). Users' success (or failure) will be measured with the following parameters:

1. Population number—maximizing
2. City's budget—maximizing
3. NOx (oxides of nitrogen) and PM10 (particulate matter)—minimizing
4. Water availability—maximizing

The optimization goal can be reached by investing in specific sectors, but it is also necessary to pay attention to the side-effects of each investment.

From a technical point of view, in order to make the model easily accessible by the students and the public in general, it was transferred on a web application that allows building ILEs based on the System Dynamics methodology. Thanks to this tool, it was possible to structure the simulation environment with an introduction and the description of the problem that the students are going to face, and also with small "systemic examples" about the problem, a short tutorial of the environment, a dashboard with all the investment-related levers and decisions to make, control panels with graphs and plots of the dynamics of the relevant variables inside the model, and a performance board with the objectives' scores.

Two screenshots from the ILE are portrayed in Figs. 2 and 3. In detail, Fig. 2 displays the "Tutorial" placed as the first window of the simulator and meant to provide a brief training for the ILE's users, while Fig. 3 portrays the main Decision board of the ILE.

According to the classification already provided in Sect. 3, the ILE developed in this study is meant to provide the users with a "multiplayer," "asymmetric," and "cooperative" game.

Even though the ILE can be played only by a single user in its current version, the main goal of the project is to use the simulator for educational purposes and

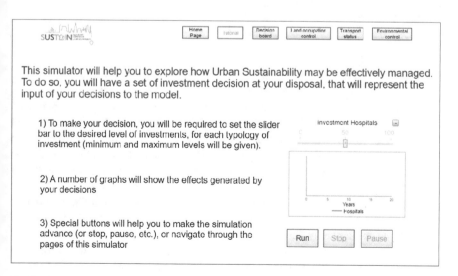

Fig. 2 Screenshot of the tutorial page within the ILE

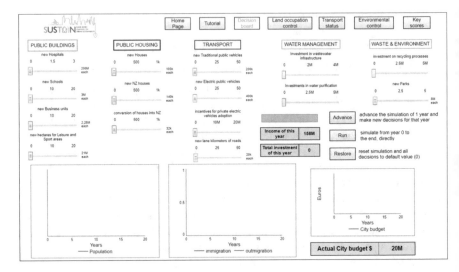

Fig. 3 Screenshot of the decision board within the ILE

Table 2 Investment options within the ILE

Investment decisions	
New Schools	New Traditional Public Vehicles
New Hospitals	Incentives for Private Electric Vehicle Adoption
New Houses	Conversion of Houses into Near Zero ones
New Near Zero Houses	New Lane Kilometers of Roads
New Leisure and Sport Areas	Wastewater Infrastructures
New Green Areas	Water Purification
New Business Units	Recycling Processes

to support collective decision-making processes, i.e., the ILE would be best used through the participation of the players in the form of a *multi-user game.*

Second, if played by more than one user, the ILE provides the participants with a *cooperative* decision-making game. Stated differently, the users will interact with the computer model within the ILE acting as Heads of the City Departments (the sectors we mentioned above). At the same time, the ILE also challenges the players providing a partially *competitive* game since each player will have to pursue his/her own goal, according to the Department placed under his/her control.

Moreover, the ILE has the features of a mainly *asymmetric* simulation. In detail, to manage the City in a sustainable way, the users have at their disposal a set of investments, as shown by Table 2.

Investments are carried out both individually (i.e., each Head of Department has his/her goals to achieve) and at the group-level (i.e., some investments can be funded by all of the players simultaneously). From a technical point of view, while interacting with the ILE, players define investment decisions that provide the inputs

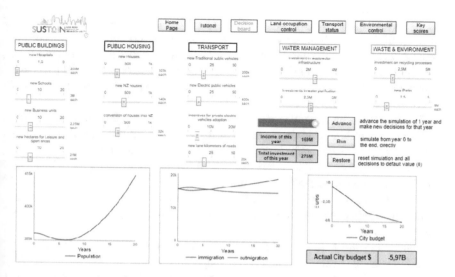

Fig. 4 Example of dynamics from one ILE-based simulation run

for the computer simulation, therefore testing and refining their ideas within this safe environment, and immediately checking the consequences of their policies and gaining valuable insights [40]. An example of a simulation run is displayed in Fig. 4.

In detail, the simulation model can also be used to develop and analyze scenario exemplars on how sustainable urban transportation and a balanced societal metabolism can be achieved while taking into account formal decision-making processes.

6 Discussion, Limitations, and Further Research

This study focused on the use of computer-based Interactive Learning Environments [5, 6, 16] in the context of urban sustainability [10]. In detail, the model at the heart of the ILE is a System Dynamics model [12–15].

The study had two main aims, i.e., first, to outline the role that DSSs and ILEs may play in fostering learning acquisition and supporting decision-making in and about complex sustainability-related systems, and second, to discuss the main results of an ILE-based project used to support learning and decision-making about an urban sustainability context.

DSSs and ILEs have a long tradition in the field of management and have already proved to effectively support understanding and learning at the individual as well as the collective level [36]. As mentioned in our study, DSSs and ILEs might be even seen as complementary tools, given the potentials of modern IT tools that allow integrating the two of them.

In more detail, this chapter discussed how an ILE can be developed and employed in a specific sustainability-related context—i.e., urban sustainability—to portray and analyze the complex hierarchy of interconnections between the physical (i.e., the simulated City with its infrastructures) and the human (in this case, the users that play the role of administrators in the City), thereby allowing exploring the concept of urban metabolism [10].

The ILE has been already tested in some experiments, and this allows providing both some general insights about the use of ILEs and some more specific reflections about the context under analysis and the ILE presented in this study.

About the former, we emphasize that there are a few "basic rules" that should be considered to design and effectively employ ILEs: (1) focus on conceptualization and abstraction; (2) incentive users' investigation; (3) create opportunities for participants' reflection; (4) stimulate the development and implementation of new theories/skills.

Concerning the latter, the ILE developed with the SUSTAIN project already provided valuable insights about urban sustainability issues.

First, the ILE demonstrates that a systemic approach to urban sustainability is necessary and that an "acting locally, thinking globally" approach to decision-making is recommended [44] when managing the resources available in such a context.

Second, the use of System Dynamics as the underlying modeling methodology and the development of a stimulating graphical interface for the ILE allowed examining—and representing—the "dynamic complexity" characterizing this specific system [15]; in detail, the model (and, subsequently, the ILE) takes into consideration systemic and dynamic features, such as multiple causal linkages among variables, the existence of feedback loops, the effect of time delays, and the presence of non-linearities. All these factors are entailed by the concept of dynamic complexity.

Third, the use of the ILE allowed not only a process of learning but also the exploration and a better and more complete understanding of the effects and the impacts which are generated by the policies carried out in this context (e.g., growth and limits to growth—[13]), as well as the emergence of side-effects, such as negative harmful consequences in terms of pollution and NOx emissions.

With this said, this study is not without limitations, that anyhow might open interesting avenues for further research.

First, it is to be emphasized that modeling and simulating an urban environment necessarily entail some choices in terms of the level of simplification, aggregation, exclusions, and boundaries [15]. Stated differently, the model and the ILE represent a typical city with its typical sustainability-related issues: when the ILE will be devoted primarily to learning acquisition and to facilitate discussion and knowledge sharing [75] in groups of students this will not be relevant. Contrariwise, if the ILE should be used to mirror a "real" underlying urban environment, the model and the ILE would need to be subsequently refined, better calibrated, and more extensively validated [76]. However, the opportunity to employ the approach outlined in this study to other urban contexts is an appealing one.

Second, the ILE has been already used and tested in in-class simulations but the data from those sessions and the feedback gathered are still to be analyzed in-depth. This may stimulate more research about the role that group dynamics and behavorial factors may play in affecting the users' performance within the simulated environment [5, 77–79]. With this perspective, the authors intend to gather more data and feedback through the organization of online simulation sessions, thereby expanding the amount of data at disposal.

Third, the ILE presented in this study is devoted to foster learning and has not been meant for research validation. This is something that the authors might explore in future research.

References

1. EEA—European Environment Agency. (2015). *Urban sustainability issues—Resource-efficient cities: Good practice*. Copenhagen: Denmark.
2. EU—European Union. (2018). IN-DEPTH REPORT: Indicators for sustainable cities environment, science for environment policy, November 2015 (revised March 2018) Issue 12.
3. Sterman, J. D., Franck, T., Fiddaman, T., Jones, A., McCauley, S., Rice, P., Sawin, E., Siegel, L., & Rooney-Varga, J. N. (2015). WORLD CLIMATE: A role-play simulation of climate negotiations. *Simulation & Gaming, 46*(3–4), 348–382.
4. Ford, A. (1999). *Modeling the environment. An introduction to system dynamics modeling of environmental systems*. Washington, DC: Island Press.
5. Alessi, S. M., & Kopainsky, B. (2015). System dynamics and simulation/gaming: Overview. *Simulation & Gaming, 46*(3–4), 223–229.
6. Davidsen, P. I., & Spector, J. M. (2015). Critical reflections: Symposium on system dynamics. *Simulation & Gaming, 46*(3-4), 430–444.
7. Kunc, M., Giorgino, M. C., & Barnabè, F. (2020). Developing forward-looking orientation in Integrated Reporting. *Meditari Accuntancy Research*. https://doi.org/10.1108/MEDAR-12-2019-0664.
8. Papathanasiou, J., Armenia, S., Pompei, A., Scolozzi, R., Barnabè, F., & Tsaples, G. (2019). Sustainability Literacy through game based learning. In *Proceedings of the 12th annual International Conference of Education*. Seville, Spain: Research and Innovation (ICERI 2019).
9. Beroggi, G. E., Waisel, L., & Wallace, W. A. (1995). Employing virtual reality to support decision making in emergency management. *Safety Science, 20*(1), 79–88.
10. Pincetl, S., Bunje, P., & Holmes, T. (2012). An expanded urban metabolism method: Toward a systems approach for assessing urban energy processes and causes. *Landscape and Urban Planning, 107*(3), 193–202.
11. Armenia, S. (2020). *The value of systems thinking and system dynamics in the management of complex organizations: A selection of case studies*. Napoli, Italia: Editoriale Scientifica, Collana punto org, ISBN: 978-88-9391-859-6.
12. Forrester, J. W. (1961). *Industrial dynamics*. Cambridge: The M.I.T. Press.
13. Forrester, J. W. (1968). *Principles of systems*. Cambridge: The M.I.T. Press.
14. Richardson, G. P., & Pugh, A. (1981). *Introduction to system dynamics modeling with dynamo*. Waltham: Pegasus Communications.
15. Sterman, J. D. (2000). Business dynamics. In *System thinking and modeling for a complex world*. Boston: McGraw-Hill.
16. Davidsen, P. I. (2000). Issues in the design and use of system-dynamics-based interactive learning environments. *Simulation & Gaming, 31*(2), 170–177.

17. Davidsen, P. I. (2000). The system dynamics approach to computer-based management learning environments. In J. D. W. Morecroft & J. D. Sterman (Eds.), *Modeling for learning organizations* (pp. 301–315). Portland, Oregon: Productivity Press. 1st Paperback edition.
18. Morecroft, J. D. W., & Sterman, J. D. (2000). *Modeling for learning organizations* (pp. 267–287). Portland, Oregon: Productivity Press. 1st Paperback edition.
19. Carlsson, C. (2018). Analytics mobilized with digital coaching. *Intelligent Systems in Accounting, Finance and Management, 25*(1), 3–17.
20. Gorry, G. A., & Scott Morton, M. S. (1971). A framework for management information systems. *Sloan Management Review, 13*(1), 55–70.
21. Sprague, R. H. (1980). Framework for the development of decision support systems. *MIS Quarterly, 4*(4), 1–26.
22. Keen, P. G. W. (1981). Information systems and organizational change. *Communications of the ACM, 24*(1), 24–33.
23. Sprague, R. H. (1981). Decision support systems: A tutorial. In D. Young & P. G. W. Keen (Eds.), *DSS-81 transactions* (pp. 193–203). Georgia: Atlanta.
24. Armenia, S. (2019). Smart model-based governance: Taking decision making to the next level by integrating data analytics with systems thinking and system dynamics. In *New challenges in corporate governance: Theory and practice*. Italy: Naples.
25. Dewey, J. (1910). *How we think*. Boston: Heath.
26. March, J. G. (1994). *A primer on decision making: How decisions happen*. New York: Free Press.
27. Simon, H. A. (1977). *The new science of management decision (revised edn)*. Englewood Cliffs, NJ: Prentice-Hall.
28. Choo, C. W. (1996). The knowing organization: How organizations use information to construct meaning, create knowledge and make decisions. *International Journal of Information Management, 16*(5), 329–340.
29. Podolak, I., Ayanso, A., Connolly, M., Law, M., & Cosby, J. (2017). Convergent analytics and informed decision-making: A retrospective multimethod case study project in Kenya. *Health Policy and Technology, 6*(2), 214–225.
30. Schwaninger, M. (2009). *Intelligent organizations: Powerful models for systemic management* (2nd ed.). Berlin: Springer.
31. Edwards, W. (1961). Behavioral decision theory. *Annual Review of Psychology, 12*(1), 473–498.
32. Tversky, A., & Kahneman, D. (1979). Prospect theory: An analysis of decision under risk. *Econometrica, 47*(2), 263–291.
33. Klein, G. (2008). Naturalistic decision making. *Human Factors, 50*(3), 456–460.
34. Argyris, C., & Schön, D. (1978). *Organizational learning: A theory of action perspective*. Reading, MA: Addison-Wesley.
35. Atkinson, R. K., & Renkl, A. (2007). Interactive example-based learning environments: Using interactive elements to encourage effective processing of worked examples. *Educational Psychology Review, 19*(3), 375–386.
36. Kim, D. H. (1993). The link between individual and organizational learning. *Sloan Management Review, 35*(1), 37–50.
37. Kolb, A. Y., & Kolb, D. A. (2012). Experiential learning theory. In N. M. Seel (Ed.), *Encyclopedia of the sciences of learning* (pp. 1215–1219). New York, US: Springer.
38. Kolb, D.A. 1984, Experiential learning: Experience as the source of learning and development. Englewood Cliffs, New Jersey: Prentice-Hall.
39. Lane, D. C. (1995). On a resurgence of management simulations and games. *Journal of the Operational Research Society, 46*(5), 604–625.
40. Lane, D. C. (2012). What is a 'policy insight'? *Systems Research and Behavioral Science, 29*(6), 590–595.
41. Papert, S. (1980). *Mindstorms*. New York: Basic Books.
42. Morecroft, J. D. W. (1988). System dynamics and microworlds for policymakers. *European Journal of Operational Research, 35*(3), 301–320.

43. Schön, D. (1983). *The reflective practitioner*. New York: Basic Books.
44. Senge, P. M., & Sterman, J. D. (2000). System thinking and organizational learning: Acting locally and thinking globally in the organization of the future. In J. D. W. Morecroft & J. D. Sterman (Eds.), *Modeling for learning organizations* (pp. 195–216). Portland, Oregon: Productivity Press. 1st Paperback edition.
45. Isaacs, W., & Senge, P. M. (2000). Overcoming limits to learning in computer-based learning environments. In J. D. W. Morecroft & J. D. Sterman (Eds.), *Modeling for learning organizations* (pp. 267–287). Portland, Oregon: Productivity Press. 1st Paperback edition.
46. Pidd, M. (2004). *Systems modelling: Theory and practice*. New York: John Wiley & Sons, Inc..
47. Sterman, J. D. (1991). *A Skeptic's guide to computer models (reprinted article)*. Cambridge: Massachusetts Institute of Technology.
48. Diehl, E. W. (2000). Managerial microworlds as learning support tools. In J. D. W. Morecroft & J. D. Sterman (Eds.), *Modeling for learning organizations* (pp. 327–337). Portland, Oregon: Productivity Press. 1st Paperback edition.
49. Winch, G. W., & Arthur, D. J. W. (2002). User-parameterised generic models: A solution to the conundrum of modelling access for SMEs? *System Dynamics Review, 18*(3), 339–357.
50. Alessi, S. M. (2000). Designing educational support in system-dynamics-based interactive learning environments. *Simulation & Gaming, 31*(2), 178–196.
51. Barnabè, F. (2009). Bridging the gap between knowledge and action using Interactive Learning Environments. In M. Ortiz & C. Rubio (Eds.), *Educational evaluation: 21st Century issues and challenges* (pp. 291–331). New York: Nova Science Publisher.
52. Bianchi, C. (2002). Introducing SD modelling into planning and control systems to manage SMEs' growth: A learning-oriented perspective. *System Dynamics Review, 18*(3), 315–338.
53. Fischer, M. M., & Barnabè, F. (2009). Microworld development: Transforming tacit knowledge into action. *Simulation & Gaming, 40*(1), 84–97.
54. Puustinen, M., & Rouet, J. F. (2009). Learning with new technologies: Help seeking and information searching revisited. *Computers & Education, 53*(4), 1014–1019.
55. Gold, S. (2017). Beat the market simulation: A self-study business economics game. *Developments in Business Simulation and Experiential Learning: Proceedings of the Annual ABSEL conference, 44*, 1.
56. Almousa, O., Prates, J., Yeslam, N., Mac Gregor, D., Zhang, J., Phan, V., Nielsen, M., Smith, R., & Qayumi, K. (2019). Virtual reality simulation technology for cardiopulmonary resuscitation training: An innovative hybrid system with haptic feedback. *Simulation & Gaming, 50*(1), 6–22.
57. Vennix, A. M. J. (1996). *Group model building. Facilitating team learning using system dynamics*. Chichester, UK: Wiley.
58. Machuca, J. A. D. (2000). Transparent-box business simulators: An aid to manage the complexity of organizations. *Simulation & Gaming, 31*(2), 230–239.
59. Größler, A., Rouwette, E., & Vennix, J. (2016). Non-conscious vs. deliberate dynamic decision-making—A pilot experiment. *System, 4*(1), 1–13.
60. Qudrat-Ullah, H. (2010). Perceptions of the effectiveness of system dynamics-based interactive learning environments: An empirical study. *Computers & Education, 55*(3), 1277–1286.
61. Kunc, M., & Morecroft, J. D. W. (2007). Competitive dynamics and gaming simulation: Lessons from a fishing industry simulator. *Journal of the Operational Research Society, 58*(9), 1146–1155.
62. Moxnes, E. (1998). Not only the tragedy of the commons: Misperception of bioeconomics. *Management Science, 44*(9), 1234–1248.
63. Moxnes, E. (2004). Misperception of basic dynamics: The case of renewable resource management. *System Dynamics Review, 20*(2), 139–162.
64. Sterman, J. D. (2018). System dynamics at sixty: The path forward. *System Dynamics Review, 34*(1-2), 5–47.
65. Sterman, J. D. (1989). Modeling managerial behavior: Misperceptions of feedback in a dynamic decision making experiment. *Management Science, 35*(3), 321–339.

66. Sterman, J. D. (1992). Teaching takes off. Flight simulators for management education. *OR/MS Today, 20*(5), 40–44.
67. Barredo, J. I., & Demicheli, L. (2003). Urban sustainability in developing countries' megacities: Modelling and predicting future urban growth in Lagos. *Cities, 20*(5), 297–310.
68. Forrester, J. W. (1969). *Urban dynamics*. Cambridge: The M.I.T. Press.
69. Tan, Y., Jiao, L., Shuai, C., & Shen, L. (2018). A system dynamics model for simulating urban sustainability performance: A China case study. *Journal of Cleaner Production, 199,* 1107–1115.
70. Bach, M. P., Tustanovski, E., Ip, A. W., Yung, K. L., & Roblek, V. (2019). System dynamics models for the simulation of sustainable urban development. *Kybernetes, 49*(2), 460–504.
71. Xing, Y., Lannon, S. C., & Eames, M. (2014). Exploring the use of systems dynamics in sustainable urban retrofit planning. *Urban Retrofitting for Sustainability: Mapping the Transition to, 2050,* 49–70.
72. Barnabé, F., & Perissi, I. (2019). Towards smart model-based governance by systems thinking. Guest editorial. *Kybernetes, 48*(1), 2–6.
73. Senge, P. M. (1990). The fifth discipline. In *The art and practice of the learning organization.* New York: Doubleday-Currency.
74. Armenia, S., Barnabé, F., Pompei, A., & Scolozzi, R. (2019). The challenge of managing resources for a sustainable urban environment: A System Dynamics-based ILE. In *61st Conference of the Operational Research Society*. Canterbury, UK: University of Kent.
75. Ford, D., & Sterman, J. D. (1998). Expert knowledge elicitation for improving mental and formal models. *System Dynamics Review, 14*(4), 309–340.
76. Barlas, Y. (1996). Formal aspects of model validity and validation in system dynamics. *System Dynamics Review, 12*(3), 183–210.
77. Barnabè, F., & Davidsen, P. I. (2020). Exploring the potentials of behavioral system dynamics: Insights from the field. *Journal of Modelling in Management, 15,* 339–364.
78. Kunc, M., Malpass, J., & White, L. (Eds.). (2016). *Behavioral operational research*. London: Palgrave Macmillan.
79. Lane, D. C. (2017). 'Behavioural system dynamics': A very tentative and slightly sceptical map of the territory. *Systems Research and Behavioral Science, 34*(4), 414–423.

Advanced Rule-Based Approaches in Customer Satisfaction Analysis: Recent Development and Future Prospects of fsQCA

Evangelia Krassadaki, Evangelos Grigoroudis, and Constantin Zopounidis

Abstract Customer satisfaction is assessed by various quantitative and qualitative methods. Several quantitative methods adopt a regression analysis procedure, including Multiple Criteria Decision Aid (MCDA) techniques. However, most of them are compensatory approaches, based on an additive model that assumes preference independence among customer satisfaction criteria. During the last years, several rule-based methods have been proposed in the customer satisfaction analysis problem. Such approaches do not assume an analytical aggregation formula, and thus they may offer an alternative in this problem. The fsQCA method focuses on linguistic summarization of "if-then" type rules. This method provides all necessary/sufficient combinations (rules) of satisfaction criteria, which lead to the output (overall satisfaction). In this context, the criteria (causal conditions) constitute the input variables, while the presence of overall satisfaction is the desired outcome. The main aim of this chapter is to present the current progress in advanced rule-based approaches applied in customer satisfaction analysis, as well as the future prospects of fsQCA. For this reason, the chapter presents the theoretical background of the alternative tool that can identify any non-linear and asymmetric relationship among attribute performance and overall satisfaction. The applicability is illustrated through a case study. The dataset is analyzed using the fsQCA method, and the results are compared with an additive value-based model (MUSA method). The results provide a more detailed and valid analysis of customer satisfaction data and indicate the complementary nature of the alternative approach. Finally, the chapter discusses the potential future research efforts,

E. Krassadaki (✉) · E. Grigoroudis
School of Production Engineering and Management, Technical University of Crete, Chania, Greece
e-mail: lia@ergasya.tuc.gr

C. Zopounidis
School of Production Engineering and Management, Technical University of Crete, Chania, Greece

Finance Department, Audencia Business School, Nantes, France

© Springer Nature Switzerland AG 2021
J. Papathanasiou et al. (eds.), *EURO Working Group on DSS*, Integrated Series in Information Systems, https://doi.org/10.1007/978-3-030-70377-6_18

345

given that rule-based approaches have gained increasing attention during the last years in analyzing customer satisfaction data.

Keywords fsQCA method · Rule-based methods · Customer satisfaction · MUSA method · Multicriteria decision aid

1 Introduction

Customer satisfaction analysis is one of the most important issues concerning business organizations of all types, which is justified by the customer-orientation philosophy of modern enterprises. Many different approaches exist in the customer satisfaction and service quality measurement literature, such as [1]:

- Quantitative methods and data analysis techniques: descriptive statistics, multiple regression analysis, factor analysis, probit-logit analysis, discriminant analysis, conjoint analysis, and other statistical quantitative methods (DEA, cluster analysis, probability-plotting methods) [1–4].
- Quality approaches: Malcolm Baldridge award, European quality model, ideal point approach, SERVQUAL [5–10].
- Consumer behavioral analysis: expectancy disconfirmation model, motivation theories, equity theory, regret theory [11–16].
- Other methodological approaches: customer loyalty, Kano's model, Fornell's model [17–21].

Each approach differs with regard to the method used, the assumptions made, the nature of the results, etc. In this regard, several studies have adopted a mixed-methods approach for analyzing customer satisfaction [22].

Customers' satisfaction evaluation has also been studied from a Multiple Criteria Decision Aid (MCDA) point of view. The MUSA (MUlticriteria Satisfaction Analysis) method is a characteristic example in this area [1, 3, 23]. MUSA is a well-known approach for measuring and analyzing customer satisfaction, which has been applied in many different fields (see for example [23–25]). The method is a preference disaggregation model, which follows the principles of ordinal regression analysis (inference procedure). It evaluates the satisfaction level of a set of individuals based on their values and expressed global preferences. Its main goal is the aggregation of individual opinions into collective value functions assuming that customers' global satisfaction depends on a set of independent variables called criteria or satisfaction dimensions. The main advantage of the MUSA method over the traditional customer satisfaction models is that it fully considers the qualitative form of customers' judgements and preferences, as usually expressed in real-world customer surveys.

Recently, fuzzy and rule-based methods are adopted in for analyzing customer satisfaction. Fuzzy-set theory and rule-based systems have traditionally been used in numerous scientific and engineering applications [26], being the core of thousands of patents for instruments used to control everything, from small appliances to subways and trains. The last two decades, these systems have also been used successfully in performance evaluation. Such applications concern numerous issues, as for example financial and capital management [27, 28].

It seems reasonable that tools that have been successfully used in the context of performance evaluation would also be suitable for evaluating customer satisfaction. Indeed, there is a great research discussion about the advantages of using fuzzy-set theory and rule-based systems for analyzing customers' satisfaction. The pioneers of the application of such approaches comment on synergies among specific features of a product or a service; therefore, they express concerns about the basic underlying principle that overall satisfaction is proportionally related to the satisfaction level of a single attribute. Such concerns are based on the fact that previous approaches fail to take into account the interaction between various attributes.

It can be argued that overall satisfaction is a distinct measurement that is not merely a combination of satisfaction of individual attributes [29] and that overall satisfaction and attribute satisfaction are separate but related concepts [30]. For example, the MUSA method considers an additive utility function and, consequently, it assumes preference independence, among satisfaction criteria, which is a rather strong assumption. This is an important issue because, based on real-world experience, some features could positively or negatively interact (see for example [31]).

In addition, as Woodside [32] notes, in any given dataset, not all cases support an exclusive positive or negative relationship between the independent and dependent variables X and Y, respectively. Hence, it seems more realistic to examine the combinatory conditions for which X is a positive influence on Y, as well as the combinatory conditions when X is a negative influence on Y. Furthermore, in real-world situations more than one combination of conditions may lead to high values in an outcome condition (i.e., dependent variable of overall satisfaction). Therefore, any insightful combination of conditions has an asymmetric, rather than a symmetric relation with an outcome condition.

For example, Angilella et al. [31] have proven that there are synergies among satisfaction criteria and for this reason they have proposed the MUSA-INT method, which considers such synergies between satisfaction levels on two criteria. The method takes into account positive and negative interactions among criteria by employing additive utility functions, augmented with components representing positive and relative interactions between two satisfaction levels of two criteria. By using MILP (Mixed Integer Linear Programming) techniques, the MUSA-INT method can identify all minimal pairs of sets of couples of interacting criteria.

Furthermore, various methodological approaches are based on fuzzy-set theory and rule-based systems. Ammar et al. [33] describe an innovative approach based on the use of fuzzy-rule-based systems and illustrate a fuzzy rule-based Decision Support System (DSS) for analyzing customer satisfaction in a corporate information division of a major US electric utility. Furthermore, Kwong et al. [34] have developed a methodology of generating customer satisfaction models for new product development using a neuro-fuzzy approach. As the authors claim, in contrast to previous research, non-linear and explicit customer satisfaction models can be developed using such approach. In this case, collected satisfaction data are the main input to an ANFIS (Adaptive Neuro-Fuzzy Inference System) for generating the fuzzy rules. Given that ANFIS-based models are considered as black boxes, the proposed methodology involve (a) data collection using market surveys; (b) generation of fuzzy rules based on market survey data using an ANFI model; (c) extraction of significant fuzzy rules and the corresponding internal models using a rule extraction method; and (d) formulation of customer satisfaction models by aggregating internal models of the most significant fuzzy rules. This approach has been compared with statistical regression analysis in order to validate its effectiveness and the experimental results suggested that the proposed approach outperformed the statistical regression method in terms of mean absolute error and variance of errors.

In this chapter, we present the fuzzy-set Qualitative Comparative Analysis (fsQCA) method proposed by Ragin [35], as a useful tool for customer satisfaction analysis. The method is based on a combination of two well-recognized methodologies: fuzzy-set theory and knowledge-based rule systems [36, 37]. In this regard, the next section presents the algorithmic steps of the method. This will be followed by a section presenting an illustrative case study, including the comparison of both MUSA and fsQCA results, as well as a section of open issues and robustness of fsQCA results. The final section presents concluding remarks and future prospects.

2   Fuzzy-Set Qualitative Comparative Analysis (fsQCA)

Fuzzy-set theory has provided researchers with a new perspective on many scientific problems. In particular, the fuzzy-set Qualitative Comparative Analysis (fsQCA) has gained in popularity across various disciplines. Recently, fsQCA has gained increasing attention in customer satisfaction analysis, too [22, 38, 39]. Using fsQCA, researcher may identify the sufficient or necessary criteria (or causal conditions herein), as well as on their combinations, which are linked to the outcome (overall satisfaction). Or, in other words, researchers can investigate all those configurations of causal conditions which lead to the presence (or absence) of the outcome. The essence of the method is the understanding of how different configurations of variables are linked to a certain outcome. This approach does not assume neither an additive formal model nor that satisfaction and dissatisfaction, in our case, are the flip sides of the same coin.

The fuzzy-set-based method, proposed by Ragin [35], differs from regression-based methods and other conventional statistical techniques in important ways. As Mahoney and Goertz [40] and Pajunen [41] emphasize, in contrast with correlational techniques, which attempt to estimate the net effect of an independent variable on an outcome variable, fsQCA attempts to identify the conditions that lead to a given outcome [42]. According to Woodside [32, 43], while multiple regression analysis focuses on net effects and statistical significance of one set of relationships, fsQCA examines several alternative causal paths, including system dynamics simulations and fuzzy-set qualitative comparative analysis. Thus, fsQCA is a tool that helps traditional correlational analyses in three main ways: (a) asymmetry (the relations between independent and dependent variables are treated as not symmetric), (b) equifinality (multiple pathways and solutions lead to the same outcome), and (c) causal complexity (combinations of causal conditions lead to the outcome). Thus, analysts do not focus on the estimation of independent net effects but on the estimation of combinatorial effects [44].

Initially, in the 1980s a crisp set-based approach, as a qualitative comparative case-oriented research technique based on Boolean algebra was proposed by Charles Ragin [45], using dichotomous variables. Qualitative Comparative Analysis (QCA)-based applications in various domains are presented in Marx's paper [46]. The QCA method compares cases by examining combinations of explanatory variables with the presence or absence of an outcome. Each explanatory variable is typically coded as either being present or absent. It is comparative in the sense that it explores similarities and differences across cases by comparing combinations. The goal is to explore how different combinations or causal paths (rules) are connected to different outcomes. In this way, it is a comparative exploration and examination of empirical diversity [46]. In addition, QCA allows for multiple conjunctural causation [35, 45, 47]. This means that the method explores the combinations that generate the same general outcome, addresses complex and seemingly contradictory patterns of causation—a condition can be important in both its presence and absence—and that it eliminates irrelevant causes (via logical minimization). An additional feature of the QCA method is that it aims to produce a model which explains all the cases present in a research population.

In the 1990s, a fuzzy-set approach was proposed by Ragin [35, 48], allowing the use of multi-value fuzzy scores, the so-called fsQCA. Thus, the integration of the basic fuzzy-set principles with the qualitative comparative analysis produced a family of methods that provide researchers with an alternative to conventional, correlational reasoning methods. The fsQCA analyzed a set of relations, where a set can be a group of values. The main aim of the method is to identify all necessary and sufficient conditions that lead to a specific outcome condition [48]. Necessary conditions are those that produce the outcome. All cases that display the outcome also display the necessary condition or, in set notation, the outcome set is a subset of the necessary condition set. Nevertheless, necessary conditions by themselves are not always enough to produce the outcome. Sufficient conditions are those that always lead to the outcome; however, they may not be the only conditions that lead to this outcome. Several alternative sufficient conditions may co-exist. The sufficient condition set is a subset of the outcome set [49].

Four major tasks are related to the application of the fsQCA method: (a) calibration of fuzzy sets of each condition and the outcome condition, (b) creation of a Truth Table and its minimization, (c) analysis of necessary and/or sufficient pathways (rules) which lead to the outcome by calculating three type of solutions: *Complex*, *Parsimonious*, and *Intermediate*, and (d) assessment of consistency and coverage solutions' scores. Nevertheless, the aforementioned four major tasks do not indicate a serial process; rather they show what a researcher has to elaborate with. Mendel and Korjani [50, 51] describe in detail the algorithmic steps of the method for establishing sufficient conditions. The authors explain that there are two kinds of fsQCA, one for establishing sufficient conditions and one for establishing necessary conditions. Since "if-then" rules concern sufficient conditions, they focus in the former fsQCA method (in the application example section, we present the necessary conditions results, too). Thus, they explain in a mathematical model that combinations of conditions (or combinations of satisfaction criteria in our case) in fsQCA are of three types (causal combinations, surviving causal combinations, and actual causal combinations) as follows:

The causal combinations S_F are equal to 2^k, where k is the number of conditions (satisfaction criteria in our case). These combinations are called in literature either as causal combinations or as the firing level fuzzy sets by Mendel and Korjani [50, 51], who follow a traditional type-1 fuzzy logic systems (T1 FLS) approach. In this chapter, the two terms are used interchangeably. These S_F combinations are described analytically in Step 5.

The surviving causal combinations S_{FS} are a subset of the initial causal combinations. These combinations express the survived rules, whose membership scores are higher than 0.50 for an adequate number of cases, given a frequency threshold (e.g., frequency threshold that covers at least 1 or 2 cases). Therefore, the subtraction of the surviving causal combinations from the initial causal combinations $S_F - S_{FS}$ gives the set of those combinations, called remainders by Ragin. These remainder-type combinations are not included in the revised Truth Table (in the initial Truth Table all combinations exist) and are taken into consideration for the calculation of solutions either as "absent" (Complex solution) or "don't care" (Parsimonious solution) for the presence (or absence) of the outcome condition. Noting, that Intermediate solution does not take into consideration the remainders. For more details, see Step 6 for the surviving causal combinations and Step 8 to Step 9 for the provided solutions.

The actual causal combinations S_{FA} are the survived combinations whose consistency is higher or equal a consistency threshold that should always be higher or equal to 0.75. Thus, there may exist a subset $S_{FS} - S_{FA}$ of causal combinations which pass the frequency threshold, but they do not pass the consistency threshold. This subset of causal combinations is included in the Truth Table and is taken into consideration as "absent" both in Complex and Parsimonious solutions. Therefore, the Truth Table contains the actual causal combinations (as "present") and the aforementioned subset of combinations as absent.

In this regard, Mendel and Korjani [50, 51] explain that the initial causal combinations of conditions are diminished in a lower number of combinations, firstly by examining the frequency threshold and secondly by examining the consistency threshold. Subsequently, the Truth Table which contains certain combinations is minimized for the exploration of either Complex or Parsimonious solutions. The Intermediate solution lies between these two solutions (Complex and Parsimonious) (see Step 7 below for further details on actual causal combinations and Steps 8 and 9 for further details on the provided solutions).

The main steps of the fsQCA method, according to Mendel and Korjani [50, 51], are the following:

2.1 Step 1

Choose a desired outcome O and its appropriate cases, $S_{cases} = \{1, 2, \ldots, N\}$. Let S_{cases} be the finite space of all appropriate cases (x) that have been labeled 1, 2, $\ldots$, N. It is assumed that cases have no natural ordering, each case is identified by an integer. In our application, each case corresponds to a reply in the satisfaction survey.

2.2 Step 2

Choose k causal conditions to the outcome, $S_C = \{C_i, i = 1, 2, \ldots, k\}$. In our specific application, each satisfaction criterion is considered as a causal condition to the outcome (overall satisfaction).

2.3 Step 3

Treat the desired outcome and causal conditions as fuzzy sets and calculate membership functions (MFs) for all of them, $\mu_O(\omega)$ and $\mu_{C_i}(\varphi_i)$, $i = 1, 2, \ldots, k$. For calibration purposes, the method uses the logistic function (a common "S" shape function), by means of at least three anchors of *inclusion, exclusion,* and *crossover* point or in other words for more in, or more out, or even the crossover point of *neither in nor out* (fuzziness) the fuzzy set, respectively.

2.4 Step 4

Evaluate these MFs for all available cases, the results being derived MFs, $\mu_O(\omega(x)) \equiv \mu_O^D(x)$ and $\mu_{C_i}(\varphi_i(x)) \equiv \mu_{C_i}^D(x)$, $x = 1, 2, \ldots, N$.

2.5 Step 5 (Causal Combinations)

This step refers to *causal combinations* according to Ragin (or the firing level fuzzy sets). Develop 2^k candidate causal combinations and view each as a possible corner in a 2^k-dimensional vector space.

Let S_F be the finite space of 2^k candidate causal combinations, called herein as firing level fuzzy sets, F_i with $i = 1, 2, \ldots, k$ and $j = 1, 2, \ldots, 2^k$, then

$$S_F = \{F_1, F_2, \ldots, F_{2^k}\} \ni F_j = A_1^j \wedge A_2^j \wedge \cdots \wedge A_k^j \text{ with } A_i^j = C_i \text{ or } c_i. \quad (1)$$

where c_i is the complement of C_i.

By this step, the method establishes one candidate rule for the desired outcome O that has the form: IF F_1 or F_2 or $\ldots$ or $F2^k$ THEN O, where the logical OR operation is implemented using the maximum. In the rest of the method, these candidate rules are either deleted or simplified.

2.6 Step 6 (Surviving Causal Combinations)

In this step, the 2^k candidate causal combinations are reduced to a much smaller subset of surviving causal combinations. Thus, MF of each of the 2^k candidate causal combinations in all the available cases are computed, and only the R_S surviving causal combinations (firing level surviving rules) are kept, whose MF values are greater than 0.50 for an adequate number of cases (this frequency threshold is set by the user, i.e., 1 or 2 for small number of cases).

$$\left. \begin{aligned} &\mu_{F_j} : (S_F, S_{cases}) \to [0, 1] \\ &x \mapsto \mu_{F_j}(x) = \min \left\{ \mu_{A_1^j}(x), \mu_{A_2^j}(x), \ldots, \mu_{A_k^j}(x) \right\} \end{aligned} \right\} \quad (2)$$

$$\mu_{A_i^j}(x) = \mu_{C_i}^D(x) \text{ or } \mu_{C_i}^D(x) = 1 - \mu_{C_i}^D(x) \text{ for } i = 1, 2, \ldots, k. \quad (3)$$

$$\left. \begin{aligned} &t_{F_j} : ([0, 1], S_{cases}) \to \{0, 1\} \\ &x \mapsto t_{F_j}(x) = \begin{cases} 1 & \text{if } \mu_{F_j}(x) > 0.5 \\ 0 & \text{if } \mu_{F_j}(x) \leq 0.5 \end{cases} \end{aligned} \right\} \quad (4)$$

$$\left. \begin{aligned} &N_{F_j} : \{0, 1\} \to 1 \\ &t_{F_j} \mapsto N_{F_j} = \sum_{x=1}^{N} t_{F_j}(x) \end{aligned} \right\} \quad (5)$$

$$\left. \begin{array}{l} F_l^S : (S_F, I) \to S_{F_S} \\ F_j \mapsto F_l^S \left\{ F_j (j \to l) \, | N_{F_j} \geq \text{freq}, \quad j = 1, 2, \ldots, 2^k \right\} \end{array} \right\} \tag{6}$$

where $\mu_{F_j}(x)$ in (4) is the firing level for the j-th rule and freq in (6) is an integer frequency threshold that must be set by the user. Ragin [49] observed that each case can have at most only a single membership score greater than 0.50 in the logical possible combinations from a given set of causal conditions. This is proven by Mendel and Korjani [50, 51] in the min-max theorem.

2.7 Step 7 (Actual Causal Combinations)

This step refers to the *actual causal combinations*, where the consistencies or the subsethood of the R_S surviving causal combinations are calculated, whose result is the actual causal combinations (actual rules). The method adopts Kosko's subsethood formula in order to compute the consistency [52] as given in (7) hence to examine if the causal combination (antecedents) is a subset of the outcome. According to the method, these combinations' consistencies must be greater than a predefined threshold, normally above 0.80 but certainly not less than 0.75. This is a mapping from $\{S_{FS}, O, S_{\text{cases}}\}$ into S_{FA}, S_{FA} is a subset of S_{FS} (the superscript A denotes "actual").

$$\left. \begin{array}{l} SS_K \left(F_l^S, O \right) : \left\{ S_{FS}, O, S_{\text{cases}} \right\} \to [0, 1] \\[2mm] \left\{ \mu_{F_l^S}(x), \mu_O^D(x) \right\}, x = 1, 2, \ldots, N \mapsto SS_K \left(F_l^S, O \right) = \dfrac{\sum\limits_{x=1}^{N} \min \left\{ \mu_{F_l^S}(x), \mu_O^D(x) \right\}}{\sum\limits_{x=1}^{N} \mu_{F_l^S}(x)} \end{array} \right\} \tag{7}$$

$$\left. \begin{array}{l} F_m^A : [0, 1] \to S_{FA} \\[2mm] SS_K \left(F_l^S, O \right) \mapsto F_m^A = \left\{ F_l^S (l \to m) \, | SS_K \left(F_l^S, O \right) \geq \text{cons}, l = 1, 2, \ldots, R_S \right\} \end{array} \right\} \tag{8}$$

where cons in (8) is the consistency threshold (higher than 0.75).

Steps 5 to 7 partition S_F into three mutually exclusive subspaces, as follows: (a) $S_F - S_{FS}$ whose elements are the causal combinations whose firing levels do not pass the frequency threshold (freq) and are called *remainders* by Ragin [49], (b) $S_{FS} - S_{FA}$, whose elements are the causal combinations whose firing levels pass the frequency threshold, but whose consistencies are lower than the defined consistency threshold *cons*, and (c) S_{FA}, whose elements are the causal combinations whose firing levels pass the frequency threshold and whose consistencies are larger than *cons* (consistency threshold).

2.8   Step 8 (Complex and Parsimonious Solutions)

The Quine-McCluskey (QM) algorithm [53, 54] is used two times to obtain the Complex solutions (prime implicants of a Boolean function-PI) R_C, or the Parsimonious solutions (minimal prime implicants-MPI) R_P. This is a mapping of actual causal combinations S_{FA}, remainder causal combinations $S_F - S_{FS}$ and $S_{FS} - S_{FA}$ into S_{FPI} and S_{FMPI}:

$$\left. \begin{array}{l} F^{\mathrm{PI}} : \left\{ S_{FA}, S_{FS} - S_{FA}, S_F - S_{FS} \right\} \to S_{FPI} \\[2mm] \{F_j\}_{j=1}^{2^k} \mapsto \{F_n^{PI}\}_{n=1}^{R_C}, F_n^{\mathrm{PI}} = QM_{\mathrm{PI}} \begin{pmatrix} S_{FA} & \text{Present} \\ S_F - S_{FS} & \text{Absent} \\ S_{FS} - S_{FA} & \text{Absent} \end{pmatrix} \end{array} \right\} \quad (9)$$

$$\left. \begin{array}{l} F^{\mathrm{MPI}} : \left\{ S_{FA}, S_{FS} - S_{FA}, S_F - S_{FS} \right\} \to S_{FMPI} \\[2mm] \{F_j\}_{j=1}^{2^k} \mapsto \left\{F_p^{\mathrm{MPI}}\right\}_{p=1}^{R_P}, F_p^{\mathrm{MPI}} = QM_{\mathrm{MPI}} \begin{pmatrix} S_{FA} & \text{Present} \\ S_F - S_{FS} & \text{Don't care} \\ S_{FS} - S_{FA} & \text{Absent} \end{pmatrix} \end{array} \right\} \quad (10)$$

Ragin [49] considers the prime implicants of Boolean logic as the *Complex solution* (linguistic summarization of R_C terms), the minimal prime implicants as the *Parsimonious solution* (linguistic summarization of R_P terms), where the intermediate solutions have to be explored using a methodology called counterfactual analysis. He believes that the most useful linguistic summarization is an intermediate summarization. Note that linguistic summarization, which is proposed by the method, is rather a descriptive model than a predictive one, as for example the Wang-Mendel method [55], meaning that predictive are those models whenever they allow us to predict the value of some target characteristic on the basis of observed values of other characteristics of an object.

2.9   Step 9 (Intermediate Solutions)

Counterfactual analysis concerns each term of the Complex solution (one at a time), but constrained by each term of the Parsimonious solution (one at a time) to obtain the Intermediate solutions, the most useful solutions. The procedure requires the knowledge of an expert because he/she has to declare the presence or the absence of each causal condition or its complement on the desired outcome. Mendel and Korjani [50, 51] distinguish the *intermediate solutions* from the *simplified intermediate solutions* and from the b*elievable simplified intermediate solutions*. In general, an Intermediate solution has a number of causal conditions between the number in the Complex and the Parsimonious solutions. The Intermediate solutions are further discussed in the application example.

2.10   Step 10 (Coverage)

A coverage score is computed for every kind of solutions, Complex, Parsimonious, and Intermediate. There are three types of coverage: a) the *solution coverage* C_S, which is the proportion of cases that are simultaneously covered by all of the terms combined by the union (OR), b) the *raw coverage* C_R, which is the proportion of cases that are covered by each term one at a time, and 3) the *unique coverage* C_U which is the proportion of cases that are uniquely covered by a specific term meaning that no other terms cover those cases. Coverage measures how much of the outcome is covered (explained) by each solution term and by the solution as a whole. It is computed by examining the original fuzzy dataset considering the solution, composed of one or more solution terms.

There is no threshold for coverage, as there is for consistency, because coverage is used descriptively. Thus, there are no guidelines for a "good coverage" threshold. The coverage score calculation is presented in the application example.

3   An Illustrative Case Study

3.1   Dataset

The application dataset is originated by Angilella et al. [31]. As presented in Table 1, the dataset concerns 24 customers who have expressed their overall satisfaction (O) and their satisfaction during a survey from a retail enterprise on three criteria: Product (C_1), Purchase procedure (C_2), and Services (C_3). A predefined three-level ordinal satisfaction scale is used, both for criteria and overall satisfaction: Dissatisfied (D), Satisfied (S), and Very Satisfied (VS). In the current application, each answer corresponds to a situation, whereas someone is either dissatisfied or satisfied or very satisfied, no other terms except satisfaction are used.

3.2   MUSA Results

Using the multicriteria method MUSA it seems that customers have an overall low satisfaction given that the average overall satisfaction index is 50.79% (see Table 1). Similarly, the average satisfaction indices for all criteria are relatively low: C_1 (47.96%), C_2 (51.35%), and C_3 (60.25%). Accordingly, the most important criterion

Table 1 Original dataset Angilella et al. [31][a]

Case	C_1	C_2	C_3	O
1	VS	S	D	S
2	D	D	D	D
3	VS	VS	VS	VS
4	VS	D	S	S
5	D	D	D	D
6	VS	VS	VS	VS
7	VS	D	VS	S
8	VS	D	VS	S
9	S	S	S	S
10	D	D	D	D
11	S	VS	D	S
12	D	D	D	D
13	VS	VS	VS	VS
14	S	VS	D	S
15	D	D	D	D
16	VS	VS	S	VS
17	VS	VS	VS	VS
18	VS	VS	S	VS
19	S	S	S	S
20	S	D	D	D
21	S	VS	S	VS
22	S	S	VS	S
23	D	VS	S	D
24	D	S	VS	S

[a]D dissatisfied, S satisfied, VS very satisfied

Table 2 MUSA results

Criteria	Weight (%)	Average satisfaction index (%)	Average demanding index (%)	Average impact index (%)
C_1	25.95	47.96	56.84	13.50
C_2	48.10	51.35	7.07	23.40
C_3	25.95	60.25	−84.59	10.32
O		50.79	−3.80	

is C_2, with a weight of 48.10%, while C_1 and C_3 are of lower importance, having a weight of 25.95%, each. Customers appear low satisfied on the most important criterion C_2, while they seem to be more satisfied on the less important criterion C_3. These results justify the low value of the average global satisfaction index (50.79%).

The average impact indices (last column of Table 2) show the influence on overall dissatisfaction of each criterion. As it can be observed, the C_2 criterion (Purchase) seems to have the larger impact on customer dissatisfaction (23.40%), while the influence of criteria C_1 and C_3 (Product and Services) is lower.

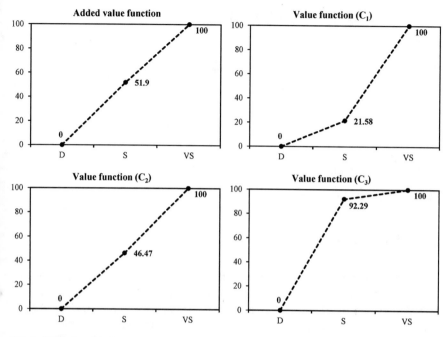

Fig. 1 Value functions

The added value function (overall satisfaction) appears to have a "linear" form, as shown in Fig. 1, indicating that customers have an overall neutral demanding level, since the average demanding index is -3.8% (neither demanding, nor non-demanding). On the other hand, customers seem to be demanding on C_1 (average demanding index 56.84%), which is shown from the convex form of the estimated value function, meaning that are not satisfied unless they receive the best quality level. On the contrary, customers are not demanding regarding C_3 (average demanding index -84.59%), as shown by the concave form of the estimated value function, indicating that customers express their satisfaction although only a small portion of their expectations is fulfilled. Finally, similar to overall satisfaction, the estimated value function of C_2 has a "linear" form, and thus customer appear to have a neutral demanding level for this particular criterion.

The relative action diagram shows that the C_2 criterion (Purchase) is a critical satisfaction dimension as it is located in the action opportunity quadrant, as shown in Fig. 2. This particular criterion requires immediate improvement, given its high importance and low performance (satisfaction). On the other hand, as the action diagram shows, the retail enterprise seems to pay unnecessary attention to C_3 (Services), as this criterion is located in the transfer resources quadrant (company's resources may be used to improve other critical satisfaction criteria). Finally, the C_1 criterion appears to have the lowest performance (satisfaction), but due to its relatively low importance it is located in the status quo quadrant, and it is considered as a potential threat. Figure 2 presents also the improvement diagram (right diagram) that may prioritize improvement actions.

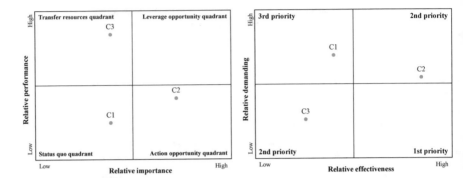

Fig. 2 Action and improvement diagrams

3.3 fsQCA Results

In the current case study, we present results following the algorithmic steps by Mendel and Korjani [50, 51], while an alternative way is the use of the free fsQCA software by Ragin [49]. According the framework of the previous section, the satisfaction criteria are considered as the causal conditions for the outcome (overall satisfaction). Thus, the causal conditions are: C_1 (Product), C_2 (Purchase), C_3 (Services). The outcome condition is the overall satisfaction, noted as O. The cases correspond to the customers participated in the survey, $S_{cases} = \{1, 2, \ldots, 24\}$.

The data, as well as the fuzzy-membership scores (MFs) are presented in Table 3. Numerical values were obtained for causal conditions C_1 to C_3 and the outcome condition for 24 responses (cases 1–24 in Table 3). The three-level ordinal scale used in the survey indicates that whenever customers reply, either overall or per criterion, VS (Very Satisfied) is considered as more in the fuzzy set of satisfied; therefore, a fuzzy score of 0.95 is assigned, following the proposed anchors by Ragin. On the contrary, when customers reply D (Dissatisfied), this indicates that they are more out the fuzzy set of satisfied; the fuzzy score is set equal to 0.05 (an alternative fuzzy score equal to 0 for full non-membership is discussed in the next section). Finally, when customers reply S (Satisfied), they express satisfaction of a lower degree than VS. In this sense, the value of 0.70 is assigned (an explanation for the specific fuzzy score, along with alternative membership scores are discussed in the next section, where it is shown that the crossover point may vary from 0.61 to 0.94).

Using the aforementioned qualitative breakpoints (0.05, 0.70, 0.95), four fuzzy sets are developed, one for the outcome (overall satisfaction), and three sets for each criterion—causal conditions (C_1, C_2, and C_3). As previously noted, the fsQCA method uses the logistic "S" shape function. Also, the method can handle the negation of fuzzy sets, absence of satisfaction, but this last opportunity is not applied herein, since customers in such surveys express their satisfaction, not dissatisfaction, assuming that satisfaction and dissatisfaction are not the flip sides of the same coin.

According Ragin [49], the first phase of the fsQCA analysis calculates the necessary conditions (see Table 4). The C_1 criterion (Product) exceeds the consistency

Table 3 Data and fuzzy-membership matrix

Case	Outcome		Causal conditions and derived MF scores					
	O	MF(O)	C_1	MF(C_1)	C_2	MF(C_2)	C_3	MF(C_3)
1	S	0.70	VS	0.95	S	0.70	D	0.05
2	D	0.05	D	0.05	D	0.05	D	0.05
3	VS	0.95	VS	0.95	VS	0.95	VS	0.95
4	S	0.70	VS	0.95	D	0.05	S	0.70
5	D	0.05	D	0.05	D	0.05	D	0.05
6	VS	0.95	VS	0.95	VS	0.95	VS	0.95
7	S	0.70	VS	0.95	D	0.05	VS	0.95
8	S	0.70	VS	0.95	D	0.05	VS	0.95
9	S	0.70	S	0.70	S	0.70	S	0.70
10	D	0.05	D	0.05	D	0.05	D	0.05
11	S	0.70	S	0.70	VS	0.95	D	0.05
12	D	0.05	D	0.05	D	0.05	D	0.05
13	VS	0.95	VS	0.95	VS	0.95	VS	0.95
14	S	0.70	S	0.70	VS	0.95	D	0.05
15	D	0.05	D	0.05	D	0.05	D	0.05
16	VS	0.95	VS	0.95	VS	0.95	S	0.70
17	VS	0.95	VS	0.95	VS	0.95	VS	0.95
18	VS	0.95	VS	0.95	VS	0.95	S	0.70
19	S	0.70	S	0.70	S	0.70	S	0.70
20	D	0.05	S	0.70	D	0.05	D	0.05
21	VS	0.95	S	0.70	VS	0.95	S	0.70
22	S	0.70	S	0.70	S	0.70	VS	0.95
23	D	0.05	D	0.05	VS	0.95	S	0.70
24	S	0.70	D	0.05	S	0.70	VS	0.95

Table 4 Necessary conditions analysis for the outcome (overall satisfaction)

Conditions	Consistency	Coverage
C_1	0.936	0.888
C_2	0.861	0.896
C_3	0.807	0.873

threshold of 0.9, which indicates that it produces the outcome (overall satisfaction). Therefore, C_1 is a necessary condition for the presence of the outcome (overall satisfaction). Appendix 1 presents the analytical calculations, while it should be noted that this first phase is somehow different from the algorithmic steps of Mendel and Korjani [50, 51] followed in this chapter.

Three causal conditions (satisfaction criteria) indicate $2^3 = 8$ causal combinations ($j = 1, 2, \ldots, 2^k$ and $i = 1, 2, \ldots, k$, with $k = 3$ in the current case study), whose MFs have to be evaluated for every case (respondent in the survey). These causal combinations, which constitute the set S_F in this application example, are the following:

1. $C_1 C_2 C_3$
2. $C_1 C_2 c_3$
3. $C_1 c_2 C_3$
4. $c_1 C_2 C_3$
5. $C_1 c_2 c_3$
6. $c_1 C_2 c_3$
7. $c_1 c_2 C_3$
8. $c_1 c_2 c_3$

where upper-case letters express presence and lower-case letters absence of a condition (complement fuzzy set). For example, combination $C_1 c_2 c_3$ indicates the presence of satisfaction for the first condition (Product), and the absence of satisfaction for the second (Purchase) and the third condition (Services), respectively.

By this step, the fsQCA method establishes one candidate rule (F) for the desired outcome O that has the form:

$$\text{IF } F_1 \text{ or } F_2 \text{ or} \ldots \text{or } F_8 \text{ THEN O}$$

where the logical OR operation is implemented using maximum. In the rest of the method, these candidate rules are either deleted or simplified.

In Step 6, we compute the MF of each of the causal combinations in the available cases in order to conclude on the surviving causal combinations S_{Fs}. Combinations of causal conditions are represented by the logical AND, which is accomplished by taking the minimum membership score of each case in the sets that are intersected. The results are presented in Table 5, which are calculated as it is analytically presented in Table 6.

For example, the first customer (case 1) expressed during the survey for each of the criteria the following satisfaction VS-S-D, which corresponds on the causal combination $C_1 C_2 c_3$ or $\min\{0.95, 0.70, 1 - 0.05\} = 0.70$. Similarly, the satisfaction levels of the second customer (case 2) for each of the criteria is D-D-D, which refers to the causal combination $c_1 c_2 c_3$ or

Table 5 Causal combinations whose MF values are higher than 0.50

Case (x_i)	$\mu F_{j*}(x_i)$	$F_{j*}(x_i)$	Case (x_i)	$\mu F_{j*}(x_i)$	$F_{j*}(x_i)$
1	0.70	$C_1 C_2 c_3$	13	0.95	$C_1 C_2 C_3$
2	0.95	$c_1 c_2 c_3$	14	0.70	$C_1 C_2 C_3$
3	0.95	$C_1 C_2 C_3$	15	0.95	$c_1 c_2 c_3$
4	0.70	$C_1 c_2 C_3$	16	0.70	$C_1 C_2 C_3$
5	0.95	$c_1 c_2 c_3$	17	0.95	$C_1 C_2 C_3$
6	0.95	$C_1 C_2 C_3$	18	0.70	$C_1 C_2 C_3$
7	0.95	$C_1 c_2 C_3$	19	0.70	$C_1 C_2 C_3$
8	0.95	$C_1 c_2 C_3$	20	0.70	$C_1 c_2 c_3$
9	0.70	$C_1 C_2 C_3$	21	0.70	$C_1 C_2 C_3$
10	0.95	$c_1 c_2 c_3$	22	0.70	$C_1 C_2 C_3$
11	0.70	$C_1 C_2 c_3$	23	0.70	$c_1 C_2 C_3$
12	0.95	$c_1 c_2 c_3$	24	0.70	$c_1 C_2 C_3$

Table 6 Firing levels for six surviving causal combinations and 24 cases[a]

Case	Memberships of surviving causal combinations (minimum of three causal conditions): firing levels					
	$C_1C_2C_3$	$c_1c_2c_3$	$C_1C_2c_3$[b]	$C_1c_2C_3$[b]	$c_1C_2C_3$	$C_1c_2c_3$
1	0.05	0.05	**0.70**	0.05	0.05	0.30
2	0.05	**0.95**	0.05	0.05	0.05	0.05
3	**0.95**	0.05	0.05	0.05	0.05	0.05
4	0.05	0.05	0.05	**0.70**	0.05	0.30
5	0.05	**0.95**	0.05	0.05	0.05	0.05
6	**0.95**	0.05	0.05	0.05	0.05	0.05
7	0.05	0.05	0.05	**0.95**	0.05	0.05
8	0.05	0.05	0.05	**0.95**	0.05	0.05
9	**0.70**	0.30	0.30	0.30	0.30	0.30
10	0.05	**0.95**	0.05	0.05	0.05	0.05
11	0.05	0.05	**0.70**	0.05	0.05	0.05
12	0.05	**0.95**	0.05	0.05	0.05	0.05
13	**0.95**	0.05	0.05	0.05	0.05	0.05
14	0.05	0.05	**0.70**	0.05	0.05	0.05
15	0.05	**0.95**	0.05	0.05	0.05	0.05
16	**0.70**	0.05	0.30	0.05	0.05	0.05
17	**0.95**	0.05	0.05	0.05	0.05	0.05
18	**0.70**	0.05	0.30	0.05	0.05	0.05
19	**0.70**	0.30	0.30	0.30	0.30	0.30
20	0.05	0.30	0.05	0.05	0.05	**0.70**
21	**0.70**	0.05	0.30	0.05	0.30	0.05
22	**0.70**	0.05	0.05	0.30	0.30	0.05
23	0.05	0.05	0.05	0.05	**0.70**	0.05
24	0.05	0.05	0.05	0.05	**0.70**	0.05

[a]Numbers in bold indicate the one causal condition for each case whose membership score is greater than 0.50
[b]For $C_1c_2C_3$ and $C_1C_2c_3$ the set-theoretic consistency calculations are presented analytically for each case in Appendix 2, see the second column from the right

$\min\{1 - 0.05, 1 - 0.05, 1 - 0.05\} = 0.95$. The responses of the fourth customer (case 4) in the satisfaction survey are VS-D-S, which corresponds on the causal combination $C_1c_2C_3$, or $\min\{0.95, 1 - 0.05, 0.70\} = 0.70$. These combinations are presented in Table 5, along with their corresponding membership scores $\mu_{F_{j*}}(x_i)$. In this table, we notice that all membership scores are higher than 0.50, as this is explained more analytically in the next Step 7 (see Table 6).

Table 7 summarizes the firing level[1] of causal combinations and shows that 6 out of 8 combinations initially survived, assuming that the frequency threshold set by

---

[1]Firing level is common in fuzzy set literature and is the same as in Ragin's terminology "fuzzy set membership of cases in the causal conditions."

Table 7 Distribution of cases across combinations and consistency of combinations[a]

Best instances	Causal combinations			Corresponding vector space corner	Number of cases with membership larger than 0.50	Set-theoretic consistency
	C_1	C_2	C_3			
3, 6, 9, 13, 16, 17, 18, 19, 21, 22	1	1	1	$C_1C_2C_3$	10	**1.000**
2, 5, 10, 12, 15	0	0	0	$c_1c_2c_3$	5	0.263
1, 11, 14	1	1	0	$C_1C_2c_3$	3	**1.000**
4, 7, 8	1	0	1	$C_1c_2C_3$	3	**0.886**
23, 24	0	1	1	$c_1C_2C_3$	2	0.814

[a] Actual causal combinations whose consistency scores are higher than 0.85 are written in bold

the researcher is 2. Although Ragin proposes for large datasets a frequency threshold of at least 10 cases, for small datasets such threshold is not clearly defined. The threshold selected in this case study is justified because it covers more than 90% of cases and the size of the dataset is quite small (24 cases).

The initial survived combinations are the following: $C_1C_2C_3$, $c_1c_2c_3$, $C_1C_2c_3$, $C_1c_2C_3$, $c_1C_2C_3$, and $C_1c_2c_3$. Or in other words, in the specific dataset, there are six initially survived causal combinations, as regard the answers expressed by customers. Thus, two combinations are missing because no customer has expressed such type of answer:

- $c_1C_2c_3$: the absence of satisfaction from the product and the presence of satisfaction from the purchase process and the absence of satisfaction from the offered services
- $c_1c_2C_3$: the absence of satisfaction from the product and the absence of satisfaction from the purchase process and the presence of satisfaction from the offered services

Table 7 presents the initial survived and the non-survived combinations. The first column of this table ("Best instances") presents the cases, and it has been created by matching up the first and last columns of Table 5.

As mentioned above, two combinations do not exist, while one more combination should be excluded if the threshold is 2: the combination $C_1c_2c_3$ with one case in the dataset. Therefore, these three configurations with a frequency lower than 2 (either 0 or 1) are the remainders $S_F - S_{FS} = 8 - 5 = 3$, while the final surviving causal combinations are finally five $S_{FS} = 5$. The remainders of the current case study are the following three:

- $c_1C_2c_3$ (zero instances)
- $c_1c_2C_3$ (zero instances)
- $C_1c_2c_3$ (one instance, case 20)

In general, the specific step tries to establish one candidate rule typology for the desired outcome O (overall satisfaction) that has the form:

IF *combination* 1 OR *combination* 2 OR ... OR *combination* 5, THEN O

where the logical OR operation is implemented using the maximum.

In Step 7, we compute the consistencies of the final surviving causal combinations and keep only those combinations (actual causal combinations) S_{FA} whose consistency is larger than a given threshold. For our case study, the consistency threshold is set equal to 0.85. Thus, three causal combinations ($C_1C_2C_3$, $C_1C_2c_3$ and $C_1c_2C_3$) are considered for further analyses (see combinations in bold in Table 7). Or in other words, from five final survived causal combinations, two of them ($c_1c_2c_3$ and $c_1C_2C_3$) although they have passed the frequency threshold test, they do not pass the consistency threshold test. Therefore, these two combinations are excluded $\left(S_{FS} - S_{FA} = 5 - 3 = 2\right)$. Moreover, the set-theoretic consistency in the last column of Table 7 is calculated following the subsethood Kosko's formula adopted by the fsQCA method [52] (see in Appendix 2 an example calculation for (O, $C_1c_2C_3$) and (O, $C_1C_2c_3$) which have a set-theoretic consistency of 0.886 and 1.000, respectively).

Therefore, from the eight (8) candidate causal combinations, six (6) of them exist in the dataset and finally five (5) survived. By examining these six combinations for each of the 24 cases, we noticed that there is only one for each case whose membership score is greater than 0.50 (see Table 6). These causal combinations are summarized in Table 7 (column "corresponding vector space corner"), and the final surviving causal combinations are those whose frequency threshold is at least two cases (five causal combinations). Subsequently, the actual causal combinations are taken into consideration, three (3) out of five (5) surviving, those which have a consistency value greater than or equal to 0.85 (threshold set by the authors), as written in bold in Table 7. Thus, from the eight possible configurations, we concluded with three of them (causal combinations = 8, surviving combinations = 5, actual combinations = 3). Thus, the three actual rules are: $C_1C_2C_3 + C_1C_2c_3 + C_1c_2C_2 \rightarrow O$, when the + denotes the union-OR-operation.

Therefore, the eight possible combinations (causal combinations) are included in the initial Truth Table (Table 8). Subsequently, the final Truth Table (Table 9) is constructed. This Truth Table shows the five surviving combinations, where in each row an outcome value (a score of 1 or 0 on the dependent variable O) is assigned, which is related to frequency and consistency chosen thresholds (see "Outcome" column in Table 9). There are three actual causal combinations, written in bold in Table 9; one combination is missing ($C_1c_2c_3$) because it represents one case (lower than the frequency threshold of at least two cases) and two combinations ($c_1C_2C_3$ and $c_1c_2c_3$) indicate the absence (value 0) of the outcome (overall satisfaction) since their consistency is lower than 0.85 (0.814 for $c_1C_2C_3$ and 0.263 for $c_1c_2c_3$,), as presented in Table 7. Lastly, it is worth noting that each row in the revised final Truth Table is not a single case, but a summary of all cases with a certain combination of input values, as the "number of instances" column presents in Table 8 or Table 9.

Table 8 The initial Truth Table (all possible combinations)

Condition			Outcome	Number of instances
C_1	C_2	C_3	O	
1	1	1		10 (41%)
0	0	0		5 (62%)
1	1	0		3 (75%)
1	0	1		3 (87%)
0	1	1		2 (95%)
1	0	0		1 (100%)
0	1	0		0
0	0	1		0

Table 9 The revised (final) Truth Table[a]

Condition			Outcome	Number of instances
C_1	C_2	C_3	O	
1	**1**	**1**	**1**	**10**
1	**1**	**0**	**1**	**3**
1	**0**	**1**	**1**	**3**
0	1	1	0	2
0	0	0	0	5

[a]The actual causal combinations are given in bold

In Step 8, the fuzzy Truth Table is minimized. Typically, the method applies the Queen and McClasky (QM) algorithm to minimize Boolean functions two times, one for the Complex and another one for the Parsimonious solutions, respectively. Ragin proposes QM algorithm for the logical simplification of the Truth Table. For the complex solution, actual causal combinations S_{FA} are set as present ("Outcome" column of Table 9), while all the rest combinations are set as absent. The Complex and Parsimonious solutions are as follows:

3.4 Complex Solution

Using the QM algorithm[2], the prime implicants for $C_1C_2C_3 + C_1C_2c_3 + C_1c_2C_3$ are $C_1C_2 + C_1C_3$. More specific:

$$C_1C_2C_3 + C_1C_2c_3 + C_1c_2C_3 = (C_1C_2c_3 + C_1C_2C_3) + (C_1C_2C_3 + C_1c_2C_3)$$
$$= C_1C_2 + C_1C_3$$

when "+" expresses the logical OR.

---

[2]Or the Carnaugh maps, as in our case the causal conditions are quite few (see Appendix 4 for the application of the Carnaugh maps).

The QM minimization algorithm is very effective whenever there are many causal conditions and combinations; therefore, it is very difficult to do this by hand. In the current application, it is not necessary.

The Complex solution (prime implicants) indicates that there are two pathways to overall satisfaction. These two combinations generate the same general outcome, the presence of overall satisfaction. In a rule-based syntax, these are as follows:

> IF simultaneously satisfied from "Products" (C_1) and "Purchase" (C_2) THEN "Overall satisfied" (O) OR

> IF simultaneously satisfied from "Products" (C_1) and "Services" (C_3) THEN "Overall satisfied" (O).

In a Boolean-based terminology, the Complex solution indicates for the desired outcome two sufficient causal combinations for overall satisfaction, either, the presence of satisfaction from the "Products" (C_1), along with the presence of satisfaction from the "Purchase" (C_2), or alternatively, the presence of satisfaction from the "Products" (C_1), along with the presence of satisfaction from the "Services" (C_3). In simple words, these two sufficient pathways for the outcome can be described as *"satisfied from product and purchase"* or *"satisfied from product and services."* These two pathways (rules) are exactly the same as the solution proposed from Angilella et al. [31] for the specific dataset. The consistency scores of the solution terms C_1C_2 or C_1C_3 and the solution as a whole, are equal with 1.000, 0.955, and 0.963, respectively, which are very high (for calculations see Appendix 3).

The other two solutions provided by the fsQCA are the Parsimonious and the Intermediate, although as Elliott [44] notes, the Complex solution is the most appropriate, especially when the number of causal conditions is not large. In that vein, for the current application of 24 cases and three conditions, the Complex solution is considered as the most appropriate although the Parsimonious and Intermediate are presented, too.

3.5   Parsimonious Solution (Minimal Prime Implicants)

For the Parsimonious solution, the three remainders are set as "don't cares" and QM algorithm is used once more. Thus, there is one pathway to overall satisfaction (C_1): the presence of satisfaction from the product (necessary condition). In a rule-based syntax, the solution is as follows:

> IF satisfied from "Products" (C_1) THEN "Overall satisfied" (O).

In Step 9, the Intermediate solutions (counterfactual analysis) are calculated using the QM algorithm. This procedure takes into consideration both the Complex and Parsimonious solutions and modifies the Complex solution subject to the constraint that a Parsimonious solution term must always be present in the final

Intermediate solutions. In this regard, the Intermediate solution in the current application when C_1 is present, and C_2, C_3 are either present or absent is exactly the same as the Complex solution. In a rule-based syntax, the Intermediate solutions are as follows:

IF simultaneously satisfied from "Products" (C_1) and "Purchase" (C_2) THEN "Overall satisfied" (O) OR

IF simultaneously satisfied from "Products" (C_1) and "Services" (C_3) THEN "Overall satisfied" (O).

In summary, the Complex, Parsimonious, and Intermediate solutions are as follows, where O expresses the outcome (overall satisfaction):

$$\begin{cases} \text{Complex} : (C_1C_2 + C_1C_3) \rightarrow O \\ \text{Parsimonious} : C_1 \rightarrow O \\ \text{Intermediate} : (C_1C_2 + C_1C_3) \rightarrow O \end{cases}$$

Step 10 refers to the calculation of coverage, which is a descriptive measure, showing how much of the outcome is covered by each solution term and by the solution as a whole.

Let us examine the raw coverage of the Complex solution. The solution is composed of two terms: C_1C_2 and C_1C_3. The raw coverages of C_1C_2 and C_1C_3 are 0.7964 and 0.7607, respectively, which are considered as high. In addition, the solution coverage (O, C_1C_2 or O, C_1C_3) is 0.9357, which is very high, too (see Appendix 3 for detailed calculations). Therefore, the high consistency score of C_1C_2 (1.000) along with its coverage score (0.7964) indicate that data are absolutely consistent with the argument that C_1C_2 is a subset of the outcome O (overall satisfaction), and its coverage of O is 79.64%. That is, C_1C_2 accounts for 79.64% of the sum of the membership in O. Similarly, the high consistency score of C_1C_3 (0.955) along with its coverage score (0.7607) indicate that the data are largely consistent with the argument that C_1C_3 is a subset of the outcome O (overall satisfaction), and its coverage of O is 76.07%. That is, C_1C_3 accounts for 76.07% of the sum of the membership in O.

4 Robustness Analysis

In order to discuss the robustness of the results of the current case study, we may examine some alternative MF values and cutoff thresholds. Initially, we consider the MF scores, especially for the midpoint of the three-level ordinal scale of "Satisfied." In this sense, by changing the MF score corresponding to "Satisfied" customers and leaving all required cutoff thresholds stable (frequency threshold = 2, consistency threshold = 0.85), we concluded that an MF score in the interval of 0.61 to 0.94 provide exactly the same solutions (Complex, Parsimonious, and Intermediate). Thus, the MF applied score for "Satisfied" of 0.70, as it has been presented in the previous section, belongs to the specific limited range of values [0.61, 0.94]. The specific result justifies why we have chosen for the specific 3-values ordinal scale the specific fuzzy-membership scores and especially for the crossover point of "Satisfied" as the distances between "Very satisfied" and "Satisfied" are close as the empirical facts indicate.

Subsequently, we examine the consequences if the two membership values of 0.05 and 0.95 change to 0 and 1 (full non-membership and full membership), respectively, assuming that crossover point is 0.70. The results indicate that the solutions are unchanged if the consistency cutoff threshold is equal to 0.80, instead of 0.85. In case that the consistency cutoff threshold is as previous (0.85), then both Complex and Parsimonious solutions become C_1C_2.

Similarly, we examine the consequences of the chosen fuzzy score 0.05 ("Dissatisfied") by changing it to 0, when the other fuzzy scores remain the same (the crossover point is 0.70 for "Satisfied" and the score of 0.95 for "Very satisfied" is the threshold for full membership). Using the same frequency and consistency thresholds (2 cases and 0.85 for consistency), the results indicate the same solutions (Complex, Parsimonious, Intermediate).

Another effort concerns the effect of the chosen consistency (subsethood) cutoff threshold on the solution. The applied cutoff of 0.85 could be considered as an arbitrary value. Thus, by examining the consistency cutoff values we conclude that if the consistency cutoff threshold ranges from 0.82 to 0.88, the provided solution is the same. More specifically, by observing the last column of Table 7, we observe that if the cutoff is smaller than 0.82, supposing that frequency cutoff threshold is unchanged (freq = 2), then another causal combination, $c_1C_2C_3$, is added in the actual causal combinations. Similarly, if the cutoff consistency threshold is higher than 0.88, then the combination $C_1c_2C_3$ is excluded from the analysis as it is considered as absent because its consistency is lower (0.886). Thus, the range of consistency values that provide exactly the same solution terms is [0.82, 0.88]. A higher consistency cutoff threshold provides a different Complex solution with one term (C_1C_2), while a lower one provides three terms in the Complex solution (C_1C_2, C_1C_3, C_2C_3).

In conclusion, we tried to examine the consequences in the provided solutions by applying multiple values for either the fuzzy scores or consistency (subsethood) threshold. The consistency cutoff ranging is small (0.82–0.88) but still exists. Regarding the calibration of fuzzy sets, as Ragin ([49], p. 93) notes "*the calibration of fuzzy sets is a key operation, to be performed with great care*," we emphasize that the solutions are affected by the membership values in the fuzzy sets, while a rather large range of values [0.61, 0.94] of the crossover point give always the same solutions. Thus, the value 0.70 (used in here) or even the value of 0.94 (not applied herein) could be used as the crossover point for the current fuzzy sets.

5 Conclusions and Future Research

The analysis of customer satisfaction data has gained increased attention during the last 20 years, and several alternative quantitative models have been applied in order to assess and analyze customer preferences and expectations. The customer satisfaction analysis problem has the following important distinguished characteristics [1]:

1. The data of the problem are based on the customers' judgments and are directly collected by surveys.
2. These customers' judgments usually have an ordinal form, and thus appropriate tools should be used in order to consider this qualitative nature of data.
3. It is a multivariate evaluation problem given that customer's overall satisfaction depends on a set of variables representing product/service characteristic dimensions.

Moreover, the aforementioned problem does not simply focus on assessing how satisfied customers are, but it is a problem of analyzing and understanding customer preferences (e.g., why customers are satisfied or dissatisfied, what product/service attribute affects mostly this satisfaction/dissatisfaction).

In this context, several MCDA (e.g., MUSA method) and regression-type approaches has been applied, using an additive formula in order to aggregate partial evaluations in an overall satisfaction measure. Such additive models have strong theoretical assumptions (e.g., mutual preferential independence), and they are compensatory models (they allow the poor performance of one criterion to be compensated by the strong performance of another criterion). However, these assumptions cannot be easily justified, while compensation is not always valid in customer satisfaction behavior (e.g., the poor performance on a single criterion may lead to a low overall satisfaction, regardless of the performance of the other criteria).

Rule-based approaches do not assume an analytical aggregation formula, and thus they may offer an alternative in the customer satisfaction analysis problem. During the last years, several such rule-based method have been applied, including rough sets theory [56–59], fsQCA [22, 38, 39], neuro-fuzzy approaches [34, 60], and other rule-based approaches [27, 33].

The main aim of this chapter is to present how the fsQCA method can be applied in the customer satisfaction analysis problem. The method focuses on linguistic summarization of "if-then" type rules and provides all necessary/sufficient combinations (rules) of satisfaction criteria, which lead to the output (overall satisfaction). The advantage of fsQCA over other methods is its ability to discover rules. Unlike quantitative methods which are based on correlations, fsQCA seeks to establish logical connections between combinations of causal conditions and an outcome, the result being rules that summarize the sufficiency between subsets of all of the possible combinations of the causal conditions or their complements and the outcome [50, 51]. The rules which are connected to the outcome by the logical OR are the possible paths from the causal conditions to the outcome, and they represent equifinal causation, i.e., different causal combinations leading to the same outcome. For example, in the presented case study satisfaction from product and purchase or from product and services lead to overall satisfaction. Through a step-by-step presentation of the fsQCA method, its major strengths and limitations can be identified.

As already emphasized, the major strength of the fsQCA method is its ability to analyze customer satisfaction data, without assuming an analytical aggregation formula (aggregation in fsQCA is implemented through the "if-then" rules). This way, the method may indirectly consider potential interactions among satisfaction criteria. In addition, the fuzzy nature of the method gives the ability to model customer behavior more realistically.

On the other hand, the fsQCA method requires a lot of effort to calibrate the model parameters (e.g., fuzzy sets and cutoff thresholds). Examining alternative values for the model parameters gives the ability to evaluate the robustness of results. However, as noted by Roy [61], robustness is a tool of resistance of decision analysts against the phenomena of approximations and ignorance zones or in other words robustness is a tool to analyze the gap between the "true" DM's model and the one resulting from a computational mechanism. In this context, robustness analysis should be distinguished from the sensitivity analysis, which is marginal and depends each time on the changes of one or more parameters. Therefore, future research efforts may focus on the development of a methodological framework for analyzing the robustness of fsQCA, including the development of alternative robustness measures.

An alternative future research approach is the adoption of an aggregation-disaggregation framework for estimating the model parameters. Contrary to the traditional aggregation paradigm, where the model parameters are known a priori and the results are unknown, the philosophy of disaggregation involves the inference of models (model parameters) from a given set of model results (see [62] for a detailed discussion).

Moreover, an interesting future research direction is the combination of the fsQCA method with other approaches in the customer satisfaction analysis problem. For example, the fsQCA method may consider and customer satisfaction and dissatisfaction differently, assuming that they are not flip sides of the same coin. This is consistent with the theory of attractive quality (or Kano's model), which assumes that different satisfaction criteria can cause satisfaction and dissatisfaction [20]. More specifically, the integration of the fsQCA with the Kano's model may help separate the factors that lead to satisfaction from those that lead to dissatisfaction.

Finally, it is important to note that, similarly to other customer satisfaction analysis models, the fsQCA method is a collective approach, given that provided results try to explain the whole customer satisfaction dataset. However, collective models assume a homogenous dataset, which is not always valid in real-world applications. Thus, future research efforts may focus in developing an fsQCA framework that can segment the customer datasets in smaller but more homogenous groups, according to specific customer profile characteristics.

In any case, it should be emphasized that the customer satisfaction analysis problem is not a technical or quantitative issue, but rather a problem of customer behavior. In this sense, it is enough to identify pathways or conditions that lead to customer satisfaction, but more importantly to explain why such results and develop potential improvement actions.

Appendix 1: Necessary Conditions Analysis

Case	(O)	C_1	C_2	C_3	O, C_1(min)	O, C_2(min)	O, C_3(min)	(O, C_1) OR (O, C_2) OR (O, C_3)(max)
1	0.70	0.95	0.70	0.05	0.70	0.70	0.05	0.70
2	0.05	0.05	0.05	0.05	0.05	0.05	0.05	0.05
3	0.95	0.95	0.95	0.95	0.95	0.95	0.95	0.95
4	0.70	0.95	0.05	0.70	0.70	0.05	0.70	0.70
5	0.05	0.05	0.05	0.05	0.05	0.05	0.05	0.05
6	0.95	0.95	0.95	0.95	0.95	0.95	0.95	0.95
7	0.70	0.95	0.05	0.95	0.70	0.05	0.70	0.70
8	0.70	0.95	0.05	0.95	0.70	0.05	0.70	0.70
9	0.70	0.70	0.70	0.70	0.70	0.70	0.70	0.70
10	0.05	0.05	0.05	0.05	0.05	0.05	0.05	0.05
11	0.70	0.70	0.95	0.05	0.70	0.70	0.05	0.70
12	0.05	0.05	0.05	0.05	0.05	0.05	0.05	0.05
13	0.95	0.95	0.95	0.95	0.95	0.95	0.95	0.95
14	0.70	0.70	0.95	0.05	0.70	0.70	0.05	0.70
15	0.05	0.05	0.05	0.05	0.05	0.05	0.05	0.05
16	0.95	0.95	0.95	0.70	0.95	0.95	0.70	0.95
17	0.95	0.95	0.95	0.95	0.95	0.95	0.95	0.95
18	0.95	0.95	0.95	0.70	0.95	0.95	0.70	0.95
19	0.70	0.70	0.70	0.70	0.70	0.70	0.70	0.70
20	0.05	0.70	0.05	0.05	0.05	0.05	0.05	0.05
21	0.95	0.70	0.95	0.70	0.70	0.95	0.70	0.95
22	0.70	0.70	0.70	0.95	0.70	0.70	0.70	0.70
23	0.05	0.05	0.95	0.70	0.05	0.05	0.05	0.05
24	0.70	0.05	0.70	0.95	0.05	0.70	0.70	0.70
Sum =		14.75	13.45	12.95	13.1	12.05	11.3	14
Consistency		$C_1 = 13.1/14 = 0.936$			$C_2 = 12.05/14 = 0.861$			$C_3 = 11.3/14 = 0.807$
Coverage		$C_1 = 13.1/14.75 = 0.888$			$C_2 = 12.05/13.45 = 0.896$			$C_3 = 11.3/12.95 = 0.873$

Appendix 2: Indicative Calculations for Consistency

Consistency calculations (based on MFs and intersection of sets) of $(O, C_1c_2C_3)$.

Cases	(O)	C_1	C_2	C_3	c_2	$C_1c_2C_3$ (min)	$O, C_1c_2C_3$ (min)
1	0.70	0.95	0.70	0.05	0.30	0.05	0.05
2	0.05	0.05	0.05	0.05	0.95	0.05	0.05
3	0.95	0.95	0.95	0.95	0.05	0.05	0.05
4	0.70	0.95	0.05	0.70	0.95	0.70	0.70
5	0.05	0.05	0.05	0.05	0.95	0.05	0.05
6	0.95	0.95	0.95	0.95	0.05	0.05	0.05
7	0.70	0.95	0.05	0.95	0.95	0.95	0.70
8	0.70	0.95	0.05	0.95	0.95	0.95	0.70
9	0.70	0.70	0.70	0.70	0.30	0.30	0.30
10	0.05	0.05	0.05	0.05	0.95	0.05	0.05
11	0.70	0.70	0.95	0.05	0.05	0.05	0.05
12	0.05	0.05	0.05	0.05	0.95	0.05	0.05
13	0.95	0.95	0.95	0.95	0.05	0.05	0.05
14	0.70	0.70	0.95	0.05	0.05	0.05	0.05
15	0.05	0.05	0.05	0.05	0.95	0.05	0.05
16	0.95	0.95	0.95	0.70	0.05	0.05	0.05
17	0.95	0.95	0.95	0.95	0.05	0.05	0.05
18	0.95	0.95	0.95	0.70	0.05	0.05	0.05
19	0.70	0.70	0.70	0.70	0.30	0.30	0.30
20	0.05	0.70	0.05	0.05	0.95	0.05	0.05
21	0.95	0.70	0.95	0.70	0.05	0.05	0.05
22	0.70	0.70	0.70	0.95	0.30	0.30	0.30
23	0.05	0.05	0.95	0.70	0.05	0.05	0.05
24	0.70	0.05	0.70	0.95	0.30	0.05	0.05
Sum =						4.4	3.9
Raw Consistency =						3.9/4.4 = 0.886	

Consistency calculations (based on MFs and intersection of sets) of $(O, C_1C_2c_3)$

Cases	(O)	C_1	C_2	C_3	c_3	$C_1C_2c_3$ (min)	$O, C_1C_2c_3$ (min)
1	0.70	0.95	0.70	0.05	0.95	0.70	0.70
2	0.05	0.05	0.05	0.05	0.95	0.05	0.05
3	0.95	0.95	0.95	0.95	0.05	0.05	0.05
4	0.70	0.95	0.05	0.70	0.30	0.05	0.05
5	0.05	0.05	0.05	0.05	0.95	0.05	0.05
6	0.95	0.95	0.95	0.95	0.05	0.05	0.05
7	0.70	0.95	0.05	0.95	0.05	0.05	0.05
8	0.70	0.95	0.05	0.95	0.05	0.05	0.05
9	0.70	0.70	0.70	0.70	0.30	0.30	0.30
10	0.05	0.05	0.05	0.05	0.95	0.05	0.05
11	0.70	0.70	0.95	0.05	0.95	0.70	0.70
12	0.05	0.05	0.05	0.05	0.95	0.05	0.05
13	0.95	0.95	0.95	0.95	0.05	0.05	0.05
14	0.70	0.70	0.95	0.05	0.95	0.70	0.70
15	0.05	0.05	0.05	0.05	0.95	0.05	0.05
16	0.95	0.95	0.95	0.70	0.30	0.30	0.30
17	0.95	0.95	0.95	0.95	0.05	0.05	0.05
18	0.95	0.95	0.95	0.70	0.30	0.30	0.30
19	0.70	0.70	0.70	0.70	0.30	0.30	0.30
20	0.05	0.70	0.05	0.05	0.95	0.05	0.05
21	0.95	0.70	0.95	0.70	0.30	0.30	0.30
22	0.70	0.70	0.70	0.95	0.05	0.05	0.05
23	0.05	0.05	0.95	0.70	0.30	0.05	0.05
24	0.70	0.05	0.70	0.95	0.05	0.05	0.05
Sum =						4.4	4.4
Raw Consistency =						4.4/4.4 = 1.000	

Appendix 3: Indicative Calculations for Coverage and Consistency of the Solution Terms

Coverage calculations (based on MFs and intersection/union of sets) of (O, C_1C_2), (O, C_1C_3)

Cases	(O)	C_1	C_3	C_1C_3 (min)	O, C_1C_3 (min)	C_2	C_1C_2 (min)	O, C_1C_2 (min)	(O, C_1C_2) OR (O, C_1C_3) (max)
1	0.70	0.95	0.05	0.05	0.05	0.70	0.70	0.70	0.70
2	0.05	0.05	0.05	0.05	0.05	0.05	0.05	0.05	0.05
3	0.95	0.95	0.95	0.95	0.95	0.95	0.95	0.95	0.95
4	0.70	0.95	0.70	0.70	0.7	0.05	0.05	0.05	0.70
5	0.05	0.05	0.05	0.05	0.05	0.05	0.05	0.05	0.05
6	0.95	0.95	0.95	0.95	0.95	0.95	0.95	0.95	0.95
7	0.70	0.95	0.95	0.95	0.70	0.05	0.05	0.05	0.70
8	0.70	0.95	0.95	0.95	0.70	0.05	0.05	0.05	0.70
9	0.70	0.70	0.70	0.70	0.70	0.70	0.70	0.70	0.70
10	0.05	0.05	0.05	0.05	0.05	0.05	0.05	0.05	0.05
11	0.70	0.70	0.05	0.05	0.05	0.95	0.70	0.70	0.70
12	0.05	0.05	0.05	0.05	0.05	0.05	0.05	0.05	0.05
13	0.95	0.95	0.95	0.95	0.95	0.95	0.95	0.95	0.95
14	0.70	0.70	0.05	0.05	0.05	0.95	0.70	0.70	0.70
15	0.05	0.05	0.05	0.05	0.05	0.05	0.05	0.05	0.05
16	0.95	0.95	0.70	0.70	0.70	0.95	0.95	0.95	0.95
17	0.95	0.95	0.95	0.95	0.95	0.95	0.95	0.95	0.95
18	0.95	0.95	0.70	0.70	0.70	0.95	0.95	0.95	0.95
19	0.70	0.70	0.70	0.70	0.70	0.70	0.70	0.70	0.70
20	0.05	0.70	0.05	0.05	0.05	0.05	0.05	0.05	0.05
21	0.95	0.70	0.70	0.70	0.70	0.95	0.70	0.70	0.70
22	0.70	0.70	0.95	0.70	0.70	0.70	0.70	0.70	0.70
23	0.05	0.05	0.70	0.05	0.05	0.95	0.05	0.05	0.05
24	0.70	0.05	0.95	0.05	0.05	0.70	0.05	0.05	0.05
Sum	14				10.65			11.15	13.10
	Raw coverage (O, C_1C_3) = 10.65/14 = 0.7607					Raw coverage (O, C_1C_2) = 11.15/14 = 0.7964			Solution coverage = 13.1/14 = 0.9357

Consistency calculations (based on MFs and intersection/union of sets) of (O, C_1C_2), (O, C_1C_3)

					Solution Membership			Solution Consistency		
Cases	(O)	C_1	C_2	C_3	C_1C_2 (min)	C_1C_3 (min)	(C_1C_2) OR $(C_1 C_3)$ (max)	$O, C_1 C_2$ (min)	$O, C_1 C_3$ (min)	(O, C_1C_2) OR (O, C_1C_3) (max)
1	0.70	0.95	0.70	0.05	0.70	0.05	0.70	0.70	0.05	0.70
2	0.05	0.05	0.05	0.05	0.05	0.05	0.05	0.05	0.05	0.05
3	0.95	0.95	0.95	0.95	0.95	0.95	0.95	0.95	0.95	0.95
4	0.70	0.95	0.05	0.70	0.05	0.70	0.70	0.05	0.70	0.70
5	0.05	0.05	0.05	0.05	0.05	0.05	0.05	0.05	0.05	0.05
6	0.95	0.95	0.95	0.95	0.95	0.95	0.95	0.95	0.95	0.95
7	0.70	0.95	0.05	0.95	0.05	0.95	0.95	0.05	0.70	0.70
8	0.70	0.95	0.05	0.95	0.05	0.95	0.95	0.05	0.70	0.70
9	0.70	0.70	0.70	0.70	0.70	0.70	0.70	0.70	0.70	0.70
10	0.05	0.05	0.05	0.05	0.05	0.05	0.05	0.05	0.05	0.05
11	0.70	0.70	0.95	0.05	0.70	0.05	0.70	0.70	0.05	0.70
12	0.05	0.05	0.05	0.05	0.05	0.05	0.05	0.05	0.05	0.05
13	0.95	0.95	0.95	0.95	0.95	0.95	0.95	0.95	0.95	0.95
14	0.70	0.70	0.95	0.05	0.70	0.05	0.70	0.70	0.05	0.70
15	0.05	0.05	0.05	0.05	0.05	0.05	0.05	0.05	0.05	0.05
16	0.95	0.95	0.95	0.70	0.95	0.70	0.95	0.95	0.70	0.95
17	0.95	0.95	0.95	0.95	0.95	0.95	0.95	0.95	0.95	0.95
18	0.95	0.95	0.95	0.70	0.95	0.70	0.95	0.95	0.70	0.95
19	0.70	0.70	0.70	0.70	0.70	0.70	0.70	0.70	0.70	0.70
20	0.05	0.70	0.05	0.05	0.05	0.05	0.05	0.05	0.05	0.05
21	0.95	0.70	0.95	0.70	0.70	0.70	0.70	0.70	0.70	0.70
22	0.70	0.70	0.70	0.95	0.70	0.70	0.70	0.70	0.70	0.70
23	0.05	0.05	0.95	0.70	0.05	0.05	0.05	0.05	0.05	0.05
24	0.70	0.05	0.70	0.95	0.05	0.05	0.05	0.05	0.05	0.05
Sum					11.15	11.15	13.60	11.15	10.65	13.10
	Consistency $C_1C_2 =$ 11.15/11.15 = 1.000					Consistency $C_1C_3 =$ 10.65/11.15 = 0.9552			Solution consistency = 13.10/13.60 = 0.9632	

Appendix 4: Minimization using the Carnaugh Maps (Complex Solution)

C_1	C_2	C_3	O
1	1	1	1
1	1	0	1
1	0	1	1
0	1	1	0
0	0	0	0
1	0	0	0
0	1	0	0
0	0	1	0

$O(C_1, C_2, C_3)$

C_1 \ C_2C_3	00	01	11	10
0	0	0	0	0
1	0	1	1	1

References

1. Grigoroudis, E., & Siskos, Y. (2010). *Customer satisfaction evaluation: Methods for measuring and implementing service quality.* New York: Springer.
2. Allen, D. R., & Rao, T. R. (2000). *Analysis of customer satisfaction data.* Milwaukee: ASQ Quality Press.
3. Grigoroudis, E., & Siskos, Y. (2002). Preference disaggregation for measuring and analyzing customer satisfaction: The MUSA method. *European Journal of Operational Research, 143*(1), 148–170.
4. Vavra, T. G. (1997). *Improving your measurement of customer satisfaction: A guide to creating, conducting, analyzing, and reporting customer satisfaction measurement programs.* Milwaukee: ASQC Quality Press.
5. EFQM. (2006). *The EFQM excellence model.* Brussels: European Foundation for Quality Management.
6. Ginter, J. L. (1974). An experimental investigation of attitude change and choice of a new brand. *Journal of Marketing Research, 11*(1), 30–40.
7. NIST. (2006). *Baldrige national quality program: Criteria for performance excellence.* Washington, DC: National Institute of Standards and Technology, US Department of Commerce.
8. Parasuraman, A., Zeithaml, V. A., & Berry, L. L. (1985). A conceptual model of service quality and its implications for future research. *Journal of Marketing, 49*(3), 41–50.

9. Parasuraman, A., Zeithaml, V. A., & Berry, L. L. (1988). SERVQUAL: A multiple item scale for measuring consumer perceptions of service quality. *Journal of Retailing, 64*(1), 14–40.
10. Parasuraman, A., Zeithaml, V. A., & Berry, L. L. (1991). Refinement and reassessment of the SERVQUAL scale. *Journal of Retailing, 67*(4), 420–450.
11. Homans, G. C. (1961). *Social behavior: Its elementary forms*. New York: Harcour, Brace and World.
12. Horton, R. L. (1974). The Edwards personal preference schedule and consumer personality research. *Journal of Marketing Research, 11*, 335–337.
13. Loomes, G., & Sugden, R. (1982). Regret theory: An alternative theory of rational choice under uncertainty. *The Economic Journal, 92*(368), 805–824.
14. Oliver, R. L. (1977). Effect of expectation and disconfirmation on postexposure product evaluations: An alternative interpretation. *Journal of Applied Psychology, 62*(4), 480–486.
15. Oliver, R. L. (1980). A cognitive model of the antecedents and consequences of satisfaction decisions. *Journal of Marketing Research, 17*(11), 460–469.
16. Oliver, R. L. (1997). *Satisfaction: A behavioral perspective on the customer*. New York: McGraw-Hill.
17. Bass, F. M. (1974). The theory of stochastic preference and brand switching. *Journal of Marketing Research, 11*(1), 1–20.
18. Fornell, C. (1995). The quality of economic output: Empirical generalizations about its distribution and relationship to market share. *Marketing Science, 14*(3), 203–211.
19. Johnson, M. D., & Fornell, C. (1991). A framework for comparing customer satisfaction across individuals and product categories. *Journal of Economic Psychology, 12*(2), 267–286.
20. Kano, N., Seraku, N., Takahashi, F., & Tsjui, S. (1984). Attractive quality and must-be quality. *Hinshitsu, 14*(2), 147–156.
21. Newman, J. W., & Werbel, R. A. (1973). Multivariate analysis of brand loyalty for major household appliances. *Journal of Marketing Research, 10*(4), 404–409.
22. Miranda, S., P. Tavares, and R. Queiro R. (2018). Perceived service quality and customer satisfaction: A fuzzy set QCA approach in the railway sector, Journal of Business Research, 89, 371-377.
23. Grigoroudis, E., & Siskos, Y. (2004). A survey of customer satisfaction barometers: Results from the transportation-communications sector. *European Journal of Operational Research, 152*(2), 334–353.
24. Grigoroudis, E., Politis, Y., & Siskos, Y. (2002). Satisfaction benchmarking and customer classification: An application to the branches of a banking organization. *International Transactions in Operational Research, 9*(5), 599–618.
25. Tsafarakis, S., Kokotas, T., & Pantouvakis, A. (2018). A multiple criteria approach for airline passenger satisfaction measurement and service quality improvement. *Journal of Air Transport Management, 68*, 61–75.
26. Bezdek, J. C. (1993). Fuzzy models: What are they, and why? *IEEE Transactions on Fuzzy Systems, 1*(1), 1–5.
27. Ammar, S., Wright, R., & Selden, S. (2000). Ranking state financial management: A multilevel fuzzy rule based system. *Decision Sciences, 31*(2), 449–481.
28. Ammar, S., Duncombe, W., & Wright, R. (2001). Evaluating capital management: A new approach. *Public Budgeting & Finance, 21*(4), 47–69.
29. Spreng, R., MacKenzie, S., & Olshavsky, R. (1996). A reexamination of the determinants of consumer satisfaction. *Journal of Marketing, 60*(3), 15–32.
30. Oliver, R. L. (1993). Cognitive, affective, and attribute bases of the satisfaction response. *Journal of Consumer Research, 20*(3), 418–430.
31. Angilella, S., Corrente, S., Greco, S., & Słowiński, R. (2014). MUSA-INT: Multicriteria customer satisfaction analysis with interacting criteria. *Omega, 42*(1), 189–200.
32. Woodside, A. (2013). Moving beyond multiple regression analysis to algorithms: Calling for adoption of a paradigm shift from symmetric to asymmetric thinking in data analysis and crafting theory. *Journal of Business Research, 66*(4), 463–472.

33. Ammar, S., Moore, D., & Wright, R. (2008). Analysing customer satisfaction surveys using a fuzzy rule-based decision support system: Enhancing customer relationship management. *Journal of Database Marketing & Customer Strategy Management, 15*, 91–105.

34. Kwong, C. K., Wong, T. C., & Chan, K. Y. (2009). A methodology of generating customer satisfaction models for new product development using a neuro-fuzzy approach. *Expert Systems with Applications, 36*(8), 11262–11270.

35. Ragin, C. C. (2000). *Fuzzy-set social science.* Chicago: University of Chicago Press.

36. Zadeh, L. A. (1973). Outline of a new approach to the analysis of complex systems and decision processes. *IEEE Transactions on Systems, Man, and Cybernetics, SMC, 3*(1), 28–44.

37. Zadeh, L. A. (1996). Fuzzy logic = computing with words. *IEEE Transactions on Fuzzy Systems, 4*(2), 103–111.

38. Almoraish, A., & Gounaris, S. (2018). How does past and present customer experience explain the satisfaction with the supplier? A fuzzy set qualitative comparative approach. In *Proceedings of the 2018 European Marketing Academy Annual Conference.* Strathclyde: University of Strathclyde. Retrieved from https://strathprints.strath.ac.uk/64364.

39. Baquero, A., Delgado, B., Escortell, R., & Sapena, J. (2019). Authentic leadership and job satisfaction: A fuzzy-set Qualitative Comparative Analysis (fsQCA). *Sustainability, 11*(8), 1–16.

40. Mahoney, J., & Goertz, G. (2006). A tale of two cultures: Contrasting quantitative and qualitative research. *Political Analysis, 14*(3), 227–249.

41. Pajunen, K. (2008). Institutions and inflows of foreign direct investment: A fuzzy-set analysis. *Journal of International Business Studies, 39*(4), 652–669.

42. Schneider, C., & Wagemann, C. (2010). Qualitative Comparative Analysis (QCA) and fuzzy-sets: Agenda for a research approach and a data analysis technique. *Comparative Sociology, 9*(3), 376–396.

43. Woodside, A. (2011). Responding to the severe limitations of cross-sectional surveys: Commenting on Rong and Wilkinson's perspectives. *Australasian Marketing Journal, 19*(3), 153–156.

44. Elliott, T. (2013). *Fuzzy set qualitative comparative analysis: An introduction.* Research Notes: Statistics Group, UCl.

45. Ragin, C. C. (1987). *The comparative method: Moving beyond qualitative and quantitative strategies.* Berkeley, LA: University of California Press.

46. Marx, A. (2006). Towards more robust model specification in QCA results from a methodological experiment, COMPASSS Working Paper. Retrieved from http://www.compasss.org/wpseries/Marx2006.pdf.

47. Rihoux, B. (2003). Bridging the gap between the qualitative and quantitative worlds? A retrospective and prospective view on Qualitative Comparative Analysis. *Field Methods, 15*(4), 351–365.

48. Ragin, C. C. (1999). Using qualitative comparative analysis to study causal complexity. *Health Services Research, 34*(5), 1225–1239.

49. Ragin, C. C. (2008). *Redesigning social inquiry: Fuzzy sets and beyond.* Chicago: Chicago University Press.

50. Mendel, J. M., & Korjani, M. M. (2012a). Charles Ragin's fuzzy set Qualitative Comparative Analysis (fsQCA) used for linguistic summarizations. *Information Sciences, 202*(20), 1–23.

51. Mendel, J. M., & Korjani, M. M. (2012b). Fast fuzzy set Qualitative Comparative Analysis (Fast fsQCA). In *Proceedings of the 2012 Annual Meeting of the North American Fuzzy Information Processing Society* (pp. 1–6). Berkeley, CA: NAFIPS.

52. Kosko, B. (1986). Fuzzy entropy and conditioning. *Information Sciences, 40*(2), 165–174.

53. McCluskey, E. J. (1966). *Introduction to the theory of switching circuits.* New York: McGraw-Hill.

54. Quine, W. V. (1952). The problem of simplifying truth functions. *American Mathematical Monthly, 59*(8), 521–531.

55. Wang, L. X., & Mendel, J. M. (1992). Generating fuzzy rules by learning from examples. *IEEE Transactions on Systems, Man, and Cybernetics, 22*(2), 1414–1427.

56. Chen, W. (2009). Analysis of a customer satisfaction survey using rough sets theory: A manufacturing case in Taiwan. *Asia Pacific Journal of Marketing and Logistics, 21*(1), 93–105.
57. Greco, S., Matarazzo, B., & Słowiński, R. (2006). Rough set approach to customer satisfaction analysis. In S. Greco, Y. Hata, S. Hirano, M. Inuiguchi, S. Miyamoto, H. S. Nguyen, & R. Słowiński (Eds.), *Rough sets and current trends in computing-RSCTC 2006* (Lecture Notes in Computer Science) (Vol. 4259). Berlin, Heidelberg: Springer.
58. Greco, S., Matarazzo, B., & Słowiński, R. (2007). Customer satisfaction analysis based on rough set approach. *Zeitschrift für Betriebswirtschaft, 77*, 325–339.
59. Salajegheh, S., Salehi, A., & Zakeri, V. (2016). Measuring levels of customer satisfaction using rough set theory. *International Journal of Humanities and Cultural Studies, 2016*, 279–295.
60. Zarandi, M. H. F., Turksen, I. B., & Maadani, B. (2004). Customer satisfaction assessment with fuzzy queries and ANFIS for an automotive industry. In *Proceedings of the 2004 IEEE Annual Meeting of the Fuzzy Information (NAFIPS 2004)* (Vol. 2, pp. 723–728). Alberta, Canada: NAFIPS.
61. Roy, B. (2010). Robustness in operational research and decision aiding: A multi-faceted issue. *European Journal of Operational Research, 200*(3), 629–638.
62. Siskos, Y., Grigoroudis, E., & Matsatsinis, N. F. (2005). UTA methods. In J. Figueira, S. Greco, & M. Ehrgott (Eds.), *Multiple criteria analysis: State of the art surveys* (pp. 297–344). New York: Springer.

Use of Multicriteria Analysis for Enchancing Sustainable Urban Mobility Planning and Decision-Making

Maria Morfoulaki and Jason Papathanasiou

Abstract The publication of the White and Green European Transport Paper in 2011 highlighted the need of shifting the urban mobility planning, towards more sustainable means of transport (public transport, bicycle, and pedestrian trips). The new urban mobility planning aims in giving space to the human (citizen) rather than to the motorized vehicles (cars).

Since 2013, the European cities were encouraged to support the policy mentioned above, by developing local Sustainable Urban Mobility Plans (SUMPs) based on the specific procedure that was launched by the DG Move. Towards the end of 2019, the updated specifications were published, giving more detailed instructions for the SUMPs development as there was a low number of local authorities who managed to follow the cooperative philosophy of SUMP.

One of the most critical steps in this 12-step procedure is the assessment—with specific criteria—of all the alternative measures and infrastructures, which will be optimally combined, in order to better respond to the problems and the vision of each area and also covering their specific criteria and particularities. That was even more difficult in the European countries, like Greece, where the citizens' attitude is not in favor of "green mobility" and the authorities are not familiar with co-planning and co-creative procedures.

The aim of the proposed article is to present a methodological framework based on the use of Multicriteria Analysis in order to enhance the implementation of the SUMP development as regards, mainly the evaluation of alternative measures and the selection of the most appropriate for each urban area according to their Sustainable Efficiency Index (SEI).

M. Morfoulaki (✉)
Centre for Research and Technology Hellas, Hellenic Institute of Transport, Thessaloniki, Greece
e-mail: marmor@certh.gr

J. Papathanasiou
Department of Business Administration, University of Macedonia, Thessaloniki, Greece
e-mail: jasonp@uom.edu.gr

© Springer Nature Switzerland AG 2021
J. Papathanasiou et al. (eds.), *EURO Working Group on DSS*, Integrated Series in Information Systems, https://doi.org/10.1007/978-3-030-70377-6_19

Keywords Sustainable mobility · Transport planning · Multicriteria decisions · Mobility measures · Impact

1 Introduction

The planning of urban transport in a more sustainable and human centric philosophy is an integral part of the overall urban planning processes that currently are taking place in modern cities [1]. The main idea is based on the minimization of the urban/network space, which is given to the private vehicles, construction of infrastructures for public transport, walking and biking, development of new transport schemes such as bike or car sharing systems. These new ways of urban trips are going to significantly influence many aspects of the quality of life in cities such as residents' health, safety, economic, and developmental opportunities, as well as conditions of work and leisure.

The first European strategy towards a more sustainable transport planning was launched in 1992, when the first version of the EU White Paper was released, which was mainly focused on coherence and fair modal competition (COM(1992) 0494) [2]. The second version was released in 2001 (COM(2001) 370 final), promoting regulated competition, modal integration, multimodality and bottleneck elimination, user and real cost-focused transport policy, alternative fuels and transport globalization, among other strategic and legislative documents [3].

In 2007, the Green Paper on Urban Mobility (COM(2007) 551 final) was adopted. It aimed at addressing challenges towards the achievement of free-flowing and green cities, as well as smart, accessible, safe, and secure public transport, with a shift in urban mobility culture being the overarching objective [4].

The 2009 Action Plan on Urban Mobility (COM(2009) 490 final) operationalized the Urban Mobility Policy through 20 actions in five thematic areas that cover policy integration, citizen-focused and environmentally oriented policies, funding, knowledge dissemination, capacity building and optimization through institutional, management, and technological innovation [5].

In 2010, the Europe 2020 strategy (COM(2010) 2020) was introduced, aiming at three priority areas for Europe, namely smart, sustainable, and inclusive growth, taking into consideration the economic and social impacts of the financial crisis. The strategy was translated into quantifiable targets that directly or indirectly relate to the areas of innovation, education, digital society, climate, energy, mobility, competitiveness, employment, skills, poverty reduction, and governance. Thus, one can understand that mobility is a crucial component for the success of Europe's transformative path, while urban mobility in particular, largely influences strategy implementation in the aforementioned areas [6].

The significance of transport and mobility and the future thereof in the European context is addressed more in a much detailed manner in the 2011 White Paper on Transport Policy (COM(2011) 144 final) [7]. It is focused on the realization of a European Transport future, structured upon a competitive, economically, socially, and environmentally sustainable, as well as integrated, safe, secure, and resource efficient Single European Transport Area, where innovation takes place in many levels, e.g., technology, regulation, governance, funding, infrastructure. This vision is expressed through a set of 40 relevant initiatives that constitute the backbone of EU Transport Policy and that set is the main policy instruments that materialize goals and strategies into actions, results, and impacts, throughout the years until 2050. Although urban mobility is addressed explicitly in the form of integrated urban mobility (Urban Mobility Plans, urban road user charging and near-zero emission urban logistics), the majority of the remainder initiatives interact physically and/or functionally with the urban environment and the urban mobility system.

The accompanying Impact Assessment (SEC(2011) 358 final) highlighted the unsustainability of the transportation system, primarily in terms of GHG emissions, oil dependency, congestion, internalization of social costs and correspondence to mobility needs and aspirations of people and businesses [8].

Thus, as far as urban mobility is concerned, the role of Sustainable Urban Mobility Plans, charging schemes and urban logistics are pivotal for the development of sustainable urban mobility systems throughout the EU, while the international dimension should also be taken into consideration.

The first version of Guidelines for Sustainable Urban Mobility Planning was published in late 2013 by DG Move. A number of 1168 planning practitioners and other experts from all over Europe had contributed to a comprehensive consultation for the definition of this new planning concept. In parallel, the European Commission had systematically developed its urban mobility policy and published its Urban Mobility Package that included a definition of the concept of "Sustainable Urban Mobility Plans" [9].

Six years later major new developments in many areas of urban mobility took place. New technologies, driverless electric vehicles, new business models provided "Mobility as a Service," shared mobility and cycling. As a result, an update of the original SUMP Guidelines was published in the end of 2019 [10].

The updated SUMP Guidelines offer concrete suggestions on how to apply the SUMP concept and prepare an urban mobility strategy that builds on a clear vision for the sustainable development of an urban area. This process of developing and implementing an SUMP is defined into 4 main phases and 12 main steps:

- **Phase 1: Preparation and Analysis**

  - Step 1: Set up working structures
  - Step 2: Determine the planning framework
  - Step 3: Analyze mobility situation

- **Phase 2: Strategy Development**

  - Step 4: Build and jointly assess scenarios
  - Step 5: Develop vision and strategy with stakeholders
  - Step 6: Set targets and indicators

- **Phase 3: Measure Planning**

  - Step 7: Select measure packages with stakeholders
  - Step 8: Agree on actions and responsibilities
  - Step 9: Prepare for adoption and financing

- **Phase 4: Implementation and monitoring**

  - Step 10: Manage implementation
  - Step 11: Monitor, adapt, and communicate
  - Step 12: Review and learn lessons

The current 12-step methodology of Sustainable Urban Mobility Planning, the so-called SUMP Cycle is presented in Fig. 1 below.

The concept of Sustainable Urban Mobility Planning, as defined in the Urban Mobility Package, is based on eight commonly accepted guiding principles. The planning addresses the needs of all urban functional areas and is based on the close cooperation across institutional boundaries, together with the active involvement of the citizens. The planning also assesses the current and future performance of the urban transportation system creating on the same time a clear vision for the future developing of all transport modes in an integrated manner. Finally, it arranges a very detailed monitoring and evaluation plan assuring also the quality of its implementation.

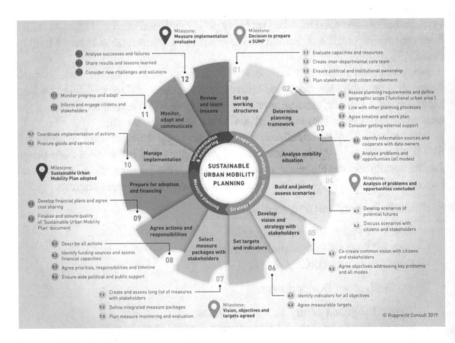

Fig. 1 SUMP planning cycle (source [10])

It becomes clear that the methodology of SUMP planning is based on an approach according to which, the future of the city problems and its solutions to those problems are considered from a greater number of aspects, so that experts from the field of transportation engineering are becoming a necessary part of a broader interdisciplinary team. In this team, a significant role in the decision-making process is given to professionals from other fields, but also to the public.

There are many decisions during the SUMP process, so different parameters should be taken into account. The selected strategy that will be followed in order to serve the vision of the city, the targets of the city future development plan, the selected measures and infrastructures that are going to achieve these targets but are also feasible to be realized in the specific time limits.

In these circumstances, the cost-benefit analysis (CBA) method, which is based on the calculation of the cost of infrastructure construction, operation, and maintenance on the one hand, and benefits on the other (social, environmental, etc.), has certain limitations. These are primarily related to how difficult it is to adequately valorize alternative solutions in urban areas in terms of their specific impact on the environment or community through calculation in monetary values [1].

The SUMP cycle methodology demands in many steps the ex ante evaluation of measures and infrastructures taking into account specific criteria such as the time for their implementation, their effect to the vision and targets that were originally set, the institutional and legal complexity for their implementation/operation as well as the overall cost and funding opportunities. This evaluation must take into account the opinion of the various stakeholders and relevant authorities but also the citizens as well.

In order to improve the decision-making process under such complex circumstances, it is important to apply new tools that target on raising the level of transparency and objectivity of the solution selection process. Multiple Criteria Decision Aid (MCDA) techniques are nowadays broadly used to find solutions to complex problems, such as those relating to the selection of mobility infrastructures and measures in urban areas.

The aim of this chapter is to analyze how the MCDA-selected methodology can be used in order to improve the quality of decision-making in the sustainable urban mobility planning process.

2 Use of MCDA Methods for Decision-Making In Mobility Planning of Urban Areas

Given that the transport infrastructure planning problems can be characterized as structured problems, they are suitable for the application of MCDA methods. An analysis on papers from relevant scientific bases (Fig. 2) that was presented in details in a relevant scientific literature review [1] shows that MCDA methods have been

Phase	Paper, year of publishing	Type of infrastructure/problem description	Applied methods in making decisions about transport infrastructure										
			AHP	ANP	ELECTRE	PROMETHEE	REGIME	MAVT	SAW	TOPSIS	MCA and GIS combination	MCA and CBA combination	DEX
PLANNING	[52], 2011	All infrastructure				+			+	+	+		
	[27], 2008	Transport infrastructure – in general	+										
	[28], 2003	Transport infrastructure – in general	+		+	+							
	[29], 2006	Transport infrastructure in urban areas / selection of a railway line	+										
	[33], 2008	Transport infrastructure in urban areas / selection of city bypass route /investment – project appraisal											+
	[34], 2009	Transport infrastructure in urban areas / selection of a new metro line route – EU funded project						+					
	[35], 2010	Transport infrastructure in urban areas / bicycle facility planning							+		+		
	[37], 2011	Transport infrastructure in urban areas / GPF location selection	+										
	[38], 2010	Transport infrastructure in urban areas / selection of a location for a port for nautical tourism					+						
	[42], 2003	Transport infrastructure in urban areas / selection of an (project) alternative for improvement of road infrastructure							+				
	[48], 2003	Transport infrastructure in urban areas / selection of an optimum transport system	+										
	[53], 2012	Transport infrastructure in urban areas / transport planning on neighbourhood level	+	+				+				+	
	[54], 2008	Transport infrastructure in urban areas / selection of a GPF location and definition of the GPF investment strategy	+				+						
	[55], 2011	Transport infrastructure in urban areas / selection of an urban railway transport project	+										
DESIGN	[28], 2003	Transport infrastructure design – in general	+		+	+							
	[39], 2003	Transport infrastructure in urban areas / selection of the GPF type on an already defined location	+										
MAINTENANCE/ RECONSTRUCTION	[12], 2006	Transport infrastructure in urban areas / selection of an alternative for road infrastructure and crossing with railway infrastructure – transport investment	+										
	[40], 2010	Transport infrastructure in urban areas /selection of an optimum pedestrian crossing on an already defined location	+										
	[44], 2009	Transport infrastructure in urban areas / road maintenance management	+				+						
	[50], 2011	Transport infrastructure in urban areas / rehabilitation and maintenance of roads	+										

Fig. 2 Application of MCA methods in different phases of transportation projects of urban areas (source [1])

used as a decision-making tool in the process of planning, design, maintenance, and reconstruction of transport infrastructures and measures in urban areas.

This review shows that, regardless of the type of issue considered, the AHP method is the most frequently used when compared to other MCDA methods. Less frequently used MCDA methods are PROMETHEE and SAW, and then ELECTRE, ANP, REGIME, MAUT, and finally TOPSIS.

The AHP (Analytic Hierarchy Process) method was developed by Thomas L. Saaty in 1970s [11]. The application of AHP has been intensified over the past decade in decision-making processes relating to transport infrastructure. The main advantage of the AHP method lies in the possibility of selecting the best solution by setting the hierarchy of goals, criteria, and alternative solutions and in enabling the decision-making process based on collaboration between different stakeholders (professionals and the public) [12].

The MCDA methods are also applied when environmental and social criteria are important because these criteria cannot always be quantified in monetary terms nor evaluated by using CBA, but they can be evaluated in relative pair-wise comparison of alternatives. In recent years, the combination of the MCDA and CBA is suggested, in order to ensure that advantages of both methods are applied, while minimizing their respective disadvantages. MCDA is commonly used ex ante on micro-scale and ex post on the urban or suburban scale, while CBA is much more used for infrastructure projects on a bigger scale as an ex ante approach. It is emphasized that the CBA is efficient, and the MCDA is an effective decision-making tool. The authors of the review suggest the combined use of the two methodologies because this can guarantee a more thorough analysis (and knowledge) of priorities and impacts of each alternative. They state that MCDA is a good tool for indirect actions where soft and indirect effects prevail, while the CBA works better for direct strategies where monetary costs and benefits are dominant.

MCDA is often incorporated in more complex decision-making systems that can help decision-makers in preparing inputs for the MCDA application (e.g., criteria weights). New methods have been developed on the basis of advantages and disadvantages of the existing MCDA, CBA, and other different methods as well that offer support to the multicriteria decision-making process.

At the design phase, MCDA has proven to be quite useful for selecting the type or form of transport facilities, at a given location. However, according to the review of other relevant papers, the authors suggest the use of the AHP, PROMETHEE, or ELECTRE methods, in the planning phase, for selecting appropriate solutions.

In accordance to the above-mentioned previous review, MCDA is the main methodology proposed by the authors of the SUMP specifications, as part of the measures selection during the third and most crucial phase of the planning procedure. During the seventh step of the cycle, an appraisal of all measures that were preselected takes place in order to identify the most suitable and effective ones for the SUMP. The new specification of SUMP proposes to:

- Consider the likely impact of measures on the performance of the transport system (by changing the demand of travel, changing the supply of transport facilities, or by changing the cost of provision and operation of the transport system).
- Assess for each measure the likely performance against each of the city's objectives (effectiveness), the likelihood of being approved (acceptability), and implications for the city's budget (value for money).

The MCDA methodology is considered as the most appropriate methodology used by many cities, during a series of workshops, to evaluate the different measures and select the most effective for each city. According to the SUMP specifications, a list of measures and infrastructures should be given to the selected group of experts (stakeholders or even citizens' groups) in order to allow each expert to rate individually each and every measure. The rating should be done with an eye to the final impact of each measure on the targets and the vision of the urban area as well as the feasibility of its implementation with the given resources (pre-feasibility check) ensuring that all costs and benefits—not just those that can be easily calculated or valued—are taken into account. The final scores that will be considered will compare and prioritize the measures. For a more qualified average, it can be useful to weight the ratings of experts depending on their field of expertise (e.g., environmental experts get a higher weighting in the air quality rating, financial experts in the cost rating).

The design of a methodological framework of an MCDA application in a group of Greek experts in order to evaluate specific sustainable mobility measures is presented in the next section.

3 Developing an MCDA-Based Methodological Framework for Evaluating Specific Sustainable Mobility Measures: A Greek Example

3.1 The Status of the Sustainable Urban Mobility Planning Implementation in Greek Municipalities

Even though Greek research teams participated in many projects since 2010 aiming to promote the sustainable urban mobility planning, and offering specific instructions for SUMPs implementation, there was no concluded SUMP in Greece until 2018. That was the result of a delay from the relevant central governmental bodies to give specific information, guidance, or even to enforce the local authorities for implementing sustainable urban mobility plans. During 2017, the Green Fund of the Ministry of Environment, provided funds to more than 150 Greek Municipalities for implementing their SUMPs according to the European specifications and at the same period, the Ministry of Transport started the implementation of a national guide on enhancing SUMP development. This work ended with the publication of the current national framework of SUMPs (Article 22 of Law 4599/2019) [13], where the definition of SUMPs and guidance for its implementation are provided; nonetheless, specifications that are more detailed are still expected.

Three years later, Greece is characterized by a relatively low percentage of SUMP implementation, as, only 20 (out of the 150 Municipalities that were funded) have concluded or started the development of an SUMP, and almost 30 are in the phase of public procurement, facing severe delays within the process. According to the results of a recent survey in the Municipal and Regional Staff of the Region of Central Macedonia in the framework of REFORM projects, there are many reasons responsible for this low percentage implementation of SUMP [14].

A sustainable mobility policy requires that cities, especially the ones belonging to a wider metropolitan area, abandon their "stand-alone culture" and participate into a constructive open dialogue with other local authorities, governments, stakeholders, and citizens. "Silo" approaches in the political level of local sustainable mobility planning are "transferred" in the technical departments who are eventually asked to implement or supervise the implementation of local SUMPs. The majority of Greek Municipalities suffer from limited resources and know-how for the SUMP definition and as they claimed, they need guidance in order to support this new co-planning philosophy of urban mobility planning. More specifically in a targeted survey which was conducted in the framework of REFORM Interreg Europe Project, the relevant Greek authorities declared that specific instructions should be given on how to select the measures that will better serve the local vision and will target and create the institutional and legal framework for implementing these measures [15].

Taking into account that specific need, a methodological framework was designed for guiding the evaluation and selection of specific mobility measures according to the targets and vision of each area, and taking into account the opinions of various stakeholders and interest groups. The framework is based on the application of PROMETHEE multicriteria analysis and is analytically presented in the next sections [16–20].

3.2   Selection of Sustainable Mobility Measures Using MCDA

The main target of the methodological framework is to use Multicriteria Analysis in order to easily rank and evaluate a list of measures that most of the cities use to adopt in their SUMPs, taking into account the opinions of different experts on sustainable mobility planning (stakeholders and relevant engineers).

The methodology is based on the calculation of the sustainable efficiency index (SEI) for each proposed measure. For this calculation, specific weight should be given as a first step to each policy objective that will be served by the SUMP implementation. For the proposed methodology these main objectives are:

- Accessibility and Operation of the Transport System
- Environment
- Society
- Economy
- Transportation system quality

However, apart from these objectives, a very crucial parameter for the successful implementation of the SUMP measures is the easiness of implementation as regards the institutional interactions, the authorization of the SUMP owner to implement these measures, legal barriers and difficulties for finding funding opportunities etc. For this reason, weight should be given also to the specific parameter called:

• Easiness of Implementation (Institutional Interactions/Funding opportunities)

For each one of the above objectives, specific result indicators have been determined. So, as a second step, the weight of each result indicator should be evaluated, answering to the question: "how much does each indicator contribute into bringing the city closer to its specific vision of sustainable mobility and development?" These indicators per objective are presented below.

Accessibility
• Increase in the number of kilometers carried out by bicycle.
• Increase in the number of kilometers carried out by Public Transport.
• Increase in pedestrian kilometers.
• Reduction of travel time between specific O-D pairs carried out on foot.
• Reduction of the travel time between specific O-D pairs carried out by bicycle.
• Reduction of the average walking distance to/from the bus stops for specific O-D pairs.

Society
• Reduction (%) of dead and seriously injured in road accidents within the urban network.
• Reduction of social exclusion due to low accessibility in transport services of people with mobility problems.

Environment
• Reduction (%) of CO_2 and NOx emissions caused by traffic.
• Reduction (%) of noise emissions caused by traffic.

Economy
• Increase of new jobs.
• Contribution of measures to the various economic sectors of the city (tourism, entrepreneurship, etc.)

Transportation System Quality
• Upgrading the quality of the Public Transport system.
• Upgrading the offered quality of bicycle infrastructures.
• Upgrading the quality of infrastructure offered for walking.

Easiness of Implementation/Interactions
• The institutional responsibility for the implementation of the measures exclusively belongs to the Municipality or there is a need for cooperation with other bodies.
• Interaction of the measure with other measures or infrastructures that need to be implemented before.
• Legal and institutional barriers that need to be solved for implementing the current measure.
• Total investment amount.

- Opportunities to include the project in European, national or regional funding schemes or capability to be financed by own resources.

The third step of the methodology regards the evaluation of the intensity with which each measure affects the result indicators of the policy objectives while the fourth step regards the evaluation of the intensity with which each measure affects the result indicators of the easiness of the implementation. For the pilot implementation of the methodology and based on the selection of measures that so far seems to be mainly proposed and adopted by the Greek Authorities who implement their SUMPs, specific measures were selected for evaluation as presented below:

1. Development of a shared system of Electric and Conventional Bicycles as well as small-capacity electric cars that will be used for transportation within the urban center and in the streets of light traffic and will ensure the reduced environmental nuisance. The system will be installed and managed by a private company in collaboration with the Municipality.
2. Redesign of the existing Public Transport system that works to serve the citizens more efficiently, using the existing infrastructure.
3. Introduction of a new bus line by the operator of the existing Public Transport System, which will use new technology (electric or hybrid) small bus and will serve the residents of areas with low existing service.
4. Development of a new high frequency municipal bus line, which will operate in addition to the existing Public Transport System using new technology (electric or hybrid) small buses and will serve the residence areas with low PT services.
5. Conversion of central commercial axis of the city to a 3 km long pedestrian walkway with open spaces for the citizens and infrastructures for biking and recreation areas.
6. Conversion of the main commercial axis into a light traffic road, with exclusive access to buses, taxi, electric vehicles, bicycles, and many open spaces for pedestrians.
7. Conversion of a municipal open space to a central bioclimatic park with recreation areas, cultivation, thematic parks, etc.
8. Development of a high technology traffic and parking monitoring, and management center offering real-time traffic information and routing services to the citizens (web or mobile app).
9. Implementation of infrastructures and creation of incentives to promote e-mobility. Installation of electric vehicle charging stations in several axis of the urban network and in off-road parking stations of the city center. Reduced cost of on-road parking.
10. Implementation of infrastructures for enhancing the mobility of people with disabilities. Crossing ramps, sound traffic lights, smart crossing infrastructure, placement of ramps in the public transport fleet and in all public buildings, dismantling of all the physical obstacles on sidewalks, ensuring the necessary width for pedestrians and wheelchairs on each sidewalk, strict policing of illegal parking that prevents the mobility of disabled people.

The fifth step of the methodology is about the application of the PROMETHEE multicriteria analysis and finally, the sixth step of the framework combines the outputs of the PROMETHEE (14–18) analysis with the weight given to each objective in order to calculate the sustainable efficiency index (SEI) for each proposed measure. That six-steps' methodological framework is presented in Fig. 3 below.

The current methodological framework was used to collect opinions of experts from the technical staff of Greek Municipalities and transportation planning engineers. The main characteristic of both of these groups is their experience in developing and implementing SUMPs. A specific questionnaire was used for collecting the experts' opinions. After the first round of analysis, an open call for more experts will be done in order to select the evaluation scores of at least 50–70 experts, coming from different types and sizes of cities with different characteristics. This will give robust results for the Sustainable Efficiency Index value according to the specific characteristics of each planning area. The specific weights and rankings could be then used as standard values by all the relevant experts who are dealing with sustainable urban mobility planning in Greece.

The results that address the first and the second steps of the framework aiming to calculate the weights of each objective and result parameter are presented in the next section.

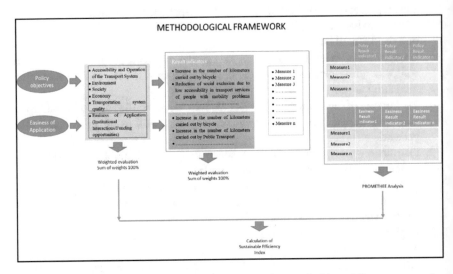

Fig. 3 Methodological Framework for evaluating alternative sustainable mobility measures using MCDA

4 Calculating the Weights and Ranking the Objectives and Result Indicators

4.1 Collecting the Relative Data

The methodological framework is based on the weights that the experts of sustainable mobility planning gave to specific parameters and their influence in the successful implementation of the mobility solutions/measures. The 10 experts who shared their experience are coming mainly from the technical departments of Municipalities (7/10) who have already worked for developing their SUMPs and are currently in the procedure of implementing the proposed infrastructures and measures (5/7). Two of them (2/7) are currently developing their SUMPs. The rest of the experts (3/10) are engineers who have worked as external consultants of the Municipalities during the SUMPs development in order to ensure the successful implementation of them and the achievement of their targets.

The questionnaire was formulated after many relevant discussions with the experts as regards to specific obstacles and difficulties that they faced during the SUMP development but also the knowledge that they earned during the monitoring phase and the real implementation of the proposed measures. After the first round of discussions, a first draft version of the questionnaire was developed and was sent to expert group for comments. Taking into account all the inputs and comments, the final version was set and sent back to the experts. A 3 months period was given to them in order to discuss their inputs with all the relevant personnel of the Municipalities who worked for the different stages of the SUMP implementation.

4.2 Ranking of the Objectives and Result Indicators

For the initial analysis of the questionnaire results, an excel data base was developed and all the replies of the questionnaires were imported there. The average weights (%) were used for ranking the importance of the different objectives, result indicators, and the parameters of the Easiness of Implementation criterion as it is presented in the tables below.

Initially, the average weights that were given by the experts as regards the six main objectives were analyzed and ranked. These results are presented in the following Table 1 and Fig. 4.

Table 1 Ranking of the sustainable mobility planning objectives according to their importance weight

Objectives	Average weights (%)
Accessibility	26
Environment	20
Easiness of **Implementation**/Interactions	15
Society	14
Transportation system quality	13
Economy	12

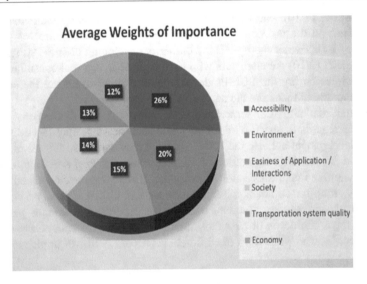

Fig. 4 Average weights of objectives according to their importance

Then the average weights that were given directly from the experts to the result indicators were also calculated. The results are presented in the Table 2 and Fig. 5 below. A correction factor was also calculated for each result indicator weight, in order to take into consideration the importance that the experts allocated to the respective objective of each result indicator. The two different weights (before and after the correction) are presented in the Table 2 below while the differences in the ranking of the indicators is presented in the Table 3.

Both the weights were taking into account for the implementation of the multicriteria analysis in order to see possible differentiations in the ranking of the measures.

Table 2 Ranking of the sustainable mobility planning result indicators according to their importance weight

Objectives	Result indicators	Average weight given by the experts group (1)	Average weights in relation to the objective importance (2)
Accessibility	Increase in the number of kilometers carried out by bicycle	5.91	6.28
	Increase in the number of kilometers carried out by Public Transport	10.09	10.72
	Increase in pedestrian kilometers	7.45	7.92
	Reduction of travel time between specific O-D pairs carried out on foot	8.09	8.60
	Reduction of the travel time between specific O-D pairs carried out by bicycle	4.18	4.44
	Reduction of the average walking distance to/from the bus stops for specific O-D pairs	6.36	6.76
Society	Reduction (%) of dead and seriously injured in road accidents within the urban network	8.36	8.41
	Reduction of social exclusion due to low accessibility in transport services of people with mobility problems	7.45	7.50
Environment	Reduction (%) of CO2 and NOx emissions caused by traffic	5.64	5.30
	Reduction (%) of noise emissions caused by traffic	5.09	4.79
Economy	Increase of new jobs	4.45	4.16
	Contribution of measures to the various economic sectors of the city (tourism, entrepreneurship, etc.)	5.36	5.00
Transportation system quality	Upgrading the quality of the Public Transport system	7.00	6.53
	Upgrading the offered quality of bicycle infrastructures	6.91	6.45
	Upgrading the quality of infrastructure offered for walking.	7.64	7.12

M. Morfoulaki and J. Papathanasiou

Table 3 Differentiations in the Ranking of the sustainable mobility planning result indicators according to the two alternative calculations of the importance weight

Result indicators	Ranking according to Weights 1	Ranking according to Weights 2	Difference in the final ranking
Increase in the number of kilometers carried out by bicycle	10	10	⟷
Increase in the number of kilometers carried out by Public Transport	1	1	⟷
Increase in pedestrian kilometers	5	4	⬆ +1
Reduction of travel time between specific O-D pairs carried out on foot.	3	2	⬆ +1
Reduction of the travel time between specific O-D pairs carried out by bicycle.	15	14	⬆ +1
Reduction of the average walking distance to/from the bus stops for specific O-D pairs.	9	7	⬆ +2
Reduction (%) of dead and seriously injured in road accidents within the urban network	2	3	⬇ -1
Reduction of social exclusion due to low accessibility in transport services of people with mobility problems	6	5	⬆ +1
Reduction (%) of CO_2 and NOx emissions caused by traffic	11	11	⟷
Reduction (%) of noise emissions caused by traffic	13	13	⟷
Increase of new jobs	14	15	⬇ -1
Contribution of measures to the various economic sectors of the city (tourism, entrepreneurship, etc.)	12	12	⟷
Upgrading the quality of the Public Transport system	7	8	⬇ -1
Upgrading the offered quality of bicycle infrastructures	8	9	⬇ -1
Upgrading the quality of infrastructure offered for walking	4	6	⬇ -2

4.3 Ranking of the Easiness of Implementation Parameters

After the ranking of the objectives and the result indicators, the average weights of the Easiness of Implementation parameters were also calculated. The weights were given by the expert group in each one of the parameters as it is presented in the next Table 4 and Fig. 5. The specific weights were also used in the next steps of the framework, during the multicriteria analysis.

Table 4 Ranking of the measures' easiness of implementation parameters according to their importance weight

Easiness of Implementation Parameters	Average weights (%)
Legal and institutional barriers that need to be solved for implementing the current measure	23.64
Interaction of the measure with other measures or infrastructures that need to be implemented before	20.91
Opportunities to include the project in European, national or regional funding schemes or capability to be financed by own resources	20.91
Total investment cost	17.73
The institutional responsibility for the implementation of the measure exclusively belongs to the Municipality or there is a need for cooperation with other bodies	16.82

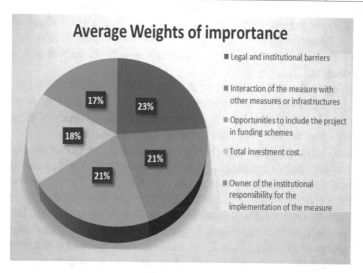

Fig. 5 Average weights of easiness of implementation parameters according to their importance

4.4 Main Conclusions of the Ranking Procedure

It becomes obvious from the above results that according to the specific expert group opinions, the Accessibility and the Society are the main objectives that an SUMP should serve in order to give positive result as regards the (%) increase in the number of kilometers carried out by Public Transport, the (%) reduction of dead and seriously injured in road accidents within the urban network and also the reduction of travel time between specific O-D pairs carried out on foot, which seem be the three more important result indicators (similar results for the two alternative rankings).

Additionally, very crucial parameters for the successful implementation of the SUMP's measures and the achievements of its targets are the legal and institutional barriers that need to be solved as well as the interaction with other measures, infrastructures, or policies.

5 Conclusions

Sustainable Urban Mobility Planning is a rather new concept with high potentialities of improving low carbon economy policies. Up to now, despite the existence of many studies, the availability of several reference documents and a series of European projects and initiatives, only a limited number of cities across Europe have adopted an SUMP [21]. This is due to competence, knowledge, technical and normative limits together with poor financing by the local administration. This problem is encountered even more in countries like Greece where the mobility attitude of the public in not in favor of environmentally friendly means in the area of transportation.

According to the technical staff of the Greek public authorities that are responsible of implementing the new planning philosophy, one of the main difficulties that they face is to evaluate the alternative measures that answer to their needs and visions and adopt the most effective and easy for implementation.

The classic transportation models and methodologies for evaluating the different scenarios of alternative measures and infrastructures are very demanding as they use a huge amount of data, simulation procedures, and complex assignment algorithms for calculating the effect on transport and environment. Nevertheless, social, financial, or institutional parameters are not taken into account. Due to their complexity, these models can mostly be used in calculating the effect on an already selected group of measures in order to evaluate their specific affect to the traffic and/or their performance within the already existing transportation network.

The development of a methodology that will be easily adjusted to the needs and capacity of each stakeholders' group, in order to highlight the preferable list of measures that will be included in the sustainable mobility plan of an urban area could give a proper answer to the specific need. The methodology should take into account the opinions of different scientific experts (e.g., urban planners, transportation engineers, environmental engineers, economists, sociologists, group of citizens) but also the legal and institutional barriers for each measure implementation.

As mentioned previously, that need led to the use of Multicriteria Analysis, for implementing the methodological framework, which is presented in the current work. The current framework, is based on the calculation of the sustainable efficiency index (SEI) for each proposed measure of an SUMP, using specific weights that a group of experts give to the main policy and easiness objectives as well as to the result indicators. After the evaluation of the intensity with which, each measure affects the result indicators and the final calculation of the SEI, a ranking of all the measures takes place.

The specific framework was developed upon the needs of the Greek authorities (staff of Municipalities and Regions) who are trying to follow the step-by-step procedure of SUMP cycle, facing a lot of difficulties and barriers especially in their cooperation with the involved parties and the opinions' exchange procedure. The challenge of the proposed framework is that when using the multicriteria analysis methodology, they will easily collect all the different and sometimes contradictory planning views of the involved parties and will create a final list of measures, which reflects their views and preferences and contributes to the development of a commonly accepted plan.

The application of the specific framework to a large number of relevant experts could lead to the creation of a final list of weights and a specific ranking of measures that could be used horizontal in each urban area according to its characteristics. A further analysis of differentiations between different planning areas characteristics or profile of experts will be of interest to be further explored.

References

1. Deluka-Tibljaš, A., Karleuša, B., & Dragičević, N. (2013). Review of multicriteria-analysis methods application in decision making about transport infrastructure. *GRADEVINAR 65, 7,* 619–631.
2. The Future Development of the Common Transport Policy: A global approach to the construction of a community framework for sustainable mobility—White paper. COM (92) 494, 2 1992.
3. European Transport Policy for 2010. Time to decide—White Paper. COM (2001) 370, 12 2001.
4. Green Paper from the Commission to the Council, the European Parliament, the European Economic and Social Committee and the Committee of the Regions—Adapting to climate change in Europe—options for EU action {SEC(2007) 849}, June 2007.
5. European Parliament, the European Economic and Social Committee and the Committee of the Regions—Action Plan on Urban Mobility, 30 September 2009.
6. European Parliament, the European Economic and Social Committee and the Committee of the Regions—A European Strategy for Low-Emission Mobility, 20 July 2016.
7. European Commission, White Paper "Roadmap to a Single European Transport Area— Towards a competitive and resource efficient transport system", 28 March 2011.
8. European Commission, White Paper, Impact Assesment, SEC 2011, Accompanying document to the Roadmap to a Single European Transport Area—Towards a competitive and resource efficient transport system, 28 March 2011.
9. European Commission, Guidelines-Developing and implementing a Sustainable urban mobility plan, 2013.
10. Guidelines for developing and implementing a Sustainable Urban Mobility Plan (2nd edition), 2019.
11. Saaty, T. L. (1996). *The analytic hierarchy process, drugo izdanje.* Pittsburg: RWS Publications.
12. Tudela, A., Akiki, N., & Cisternas, R. (2006). Comparing the output of cost benefit and multicriteria analysis: An application to urban transport investments. *Transportation Research Part A: Policy and Practice, Elsevier, 40*(5), 414–423.
13. Article 22, Greek Law 4599/209 "Sustainable Mobility Plans", Greek Parliament, 2019.
14. Reform Project-Integrated REgional Action Plan For Innovative, Sustainable and LOw CaRbon Mobility, "Action Plan of the Region of Central Macedonia", December 2018.

15. Maria Chatziathanasiou, Maria Morfoulaki, Konstantia Mpessa, Lambrini Tsoli "A Regional Competence Centre for SUMPs in Central Macedonia, responding to the identified local needs", CSUM 2020.
16. Brans, J. P., & Mareschal, B. (2005). PROMETHEE methods. In J. Figueira, S. Greco, & M. Ehrgott (Eds.), *Multiple criteria decision analysis: State of the art surveys* (pp. 163–196). New York: Springer Science + Business Media, Inc..
17. Brans, J. P., Mareschal, B., & Vincke, P. (1984). PROMETHEE: A new family of outranking methods in multicriteria analysis. In J. P. Brans (Ed.), *Operational Research '84* (pp. 477–490). North Holland: PROMETHEE.
18. Brans, J. P., & Vincke, P. (1985). A preference ranking organization method. *Management Science, 31*(6), 647–656.
19. Brans, J. P., Vincke, P., & Mareschal, B. (1986). How to select and how to rank projects: The PROMETHEE method. *European Journal of Operational Research, 24*(2), 228–238.
20. Brans, J. P., Macharis, C., & Mareschal, B. (1988). The GDSS PROMETHEE procedure (a PROMETHEE-GAIA based procedure for group decision support). *Journal of Decision Systems, 7*, 283–307. Special Issue "Decision support systems—Groupware, Multimedia, Electronic Commerce".
21. Reform Project, "EU good practices on sustainable mobility planning and SUMP Report" January 2019.

Index

A

Accountability, 155, 159, 160
Adaptive learning, 37
Adaptive Neuro-Fuzzy Inference System
(ANFIS), 348
Additive aggregation methods, 214
Advanced ICT technologies
BDA, 145
enterprise systems, 146
IoT, 145
KM and learning, 145
knowledge mobilisation, 145
role, 145
Affective NSS, 180
African swine fever (ASF), 319
Agriculture 4.0, 300, 321
Agriculture, DSS
author-keywords network, 109, 110
bibliometric network analysis, 100–101,
107–108
GIS technologies, 108
keyword clusters, 109
naïve Bayes text classification, 99–100,
103, 105
SCOPUS database, 101, 102
semi-automated method, 102
user-centered design, 111
AHP, *see* Analytic hierarchy process (AHP)
AI, *see* Artificial intelligence (AI)
Algorithms
accountability, 155
automated decision making, 153
ethics, 156
explicability, 155
fairness, 155

innovative, 157
social responsibility, 164
software implementation, 160
Analytical concession-advising technology
(AC-AT), 173
Analytic hierarchy process (AHP), 23, 25, 84,
85, 87, 88, 92, 172, 207, 384, 385
Analytics, 10, 11, 37–40, 154
See also Big Data Analytics (BDA)
ANFIS, *see* Adaptive Neuro-Fuzzy Inference
System (ANFIS)
API, *see* Application programming interfaces
(API)
Application-oriented models, 172
Application programming interfaces (API), 87,
89
Arbitrary linear inequalities, 217
Artificial intelligence (AI), 161, 193, 270, 320
adaptive learning, 37
AI-augmented loan application DSS, 40
collaborative AI, 37–39
DSS, 37, 38, 40
human–technology collaboration, 38
learning DSS, 39
organizations, 39
philosophical basis of DSS, 38
traditional DSS, 39, 40
Aspiration-based models, 174
Asynchronous communication, 175
Asynchronous medium, 176
Authorship evolution, 65–66
Automated decision-making, 153, 155
Automated decisions, 158, 159, 161
Automated recommendation, 158, 159, 161
Automatically controlled devices, 155

© Springer Nature Switzerland AG 2021
J. Papathanasiou et al. (eds.), *EURO Working Group on DSS*, Integrated Series in
Information Systems, https://doi.org/10.1007/978-3-030-70377-6

Automatically formulated recommendations,
    158
Automatic negotiations, 173
Automatic pricing, 162
Automatic vehicles, 153
Automation, 156, 157
Automatising decisions, 155
Autonomous artefacts
    challenges, 154
    decision capacity, 154, 155, 164
    decisions and recommendations, 158–159
    development, 155
    e-commerce platforms, 155
    fundamentals, 156–157
    implemetation, 160
    industrial production perspective, 156
    process, 159–160
    raw material, 157–158
    society impacts, 161

B
BAM, *see* Business Activity Monitoring
    (BAM)
Behavioral economics, 240–242, 244–246,
    250, 251, 255
Behavioral studies, neuroscience experiments
    aims, 229
    Alpha values, 232
    confidence, 231
    dominance relations, 230, 231
    DSSs, 231
    EEG, 231
    HR variable, 230
    indefinition behavior, 232
    MAVT context, 230
    participant's behavior, 232
    proposition, 229
    recommendations, 231
    relaxing behavior, 232
    success probability, 230, 231
    Success Region Based Decision Rule, 229
    Theta and Alpha activities, 232
    visualizations, 231
Bernoulli distribution, 230
BI, *see* Business intelligence (BI)
BI&A, *see* Business Intelligence and Analytics
    (BI&A)
Bibliographic analysis
    betweenness centrality, 21
    centrality measures, 21
    citation network, 20
    closeness centrality, 21

co-citation coupling, 20
CRExplorer software, 21
DCA, 20, 21
mathematical graphs, 19
social network, 19, 21
Vosviewer software, 20, 22
WOS dataset, 19
Bibliographic databases, 16
Bibliometric network analysis, 107, 109
    academic research, 100
    country co-authorship networks
        1999-2008, 110
        2009-2019, 111
    VOS technique, 101
Big Data (BD), 8, 10–12, 81, 145
    advanced learning algorithms, 276
    analytics for decision-making (*see* Big Data
        Analytics (BDA))
    challenges, 274
        data types and sources, 121
        variety, 122–123
        velocity, 122
        volume, 121–122
    DDD (*see* Data-Driven Decision-making
        (DDD))
    decision-making, 275, 281
    decision support, 275
    employment agencies, 124
    Google searches, 274
    job markets, 124
    Lambda Architecture, 291, 295
    predictive analytics mechanisms, 276
    proposed conceptual model, 294–295
    revolution, 276
    RFID cards, 290
    sensors, 274
    tools and technologies, 279–284
    value chain, 276–277
    "Vs", 276
Big Data Analytics (BDA), 145, 146, 248
    aim, 278
    analytic value escalator, 278, 279
    application areas, 275
    BI&A, 248
    challenges, 145–146, 277
    decision support, 277
    descriptive, 278
    developing methods, techniques and tools,
        278–279
    diagnostic, 278
    harvesting and analytics, 279–281
    multi-stage process, 145
    predictive, 278

prescriptive, 278
and sustainable development goals, 279, 280
Big social data, 81
Biotechnology, 320–321
Black-box learning procedure, 162
Black-box models, 205, 206, 208
Blockchains, 155
Boolean algebra, 349
Boundary-spanning mechanisms
    boundary objects, 143, 144
    boundary practice, 144
    boundary spanners, 143, 144
    complementary perspectives, 144
    knowledge mobilisation activities, 144
    motivation systems, 144
Bovine Spongiform Encephalopathy (BSE), 300
Business Activity Monitoring (BAM), 122–123
Business analytics, 10, 11, 247, 249, 284
Business decision-making, 145, 146
Business intelligence (BI), 276
    architecture, 116, 117
    big data challenges, 121–123
    challenges
        methodology, 123–124
        specific domain, 123
    data extraction planning, 117
    data mining/machine learning, 118
    data warehouses, 117–120
    decision-making process, 116
    employment agencies, 124
    engineering, 120–121
    job markets, 124
    managerial challenges, 124
    in 1980s and 1990s, 115
    transdisciplinary approach, 124
    V-shaped approach, 121
Business intelligence and analytics (BI&A), 116
    CIOs, 251
    and data science, 240
    decision support approaches, 251–252
    definition, 116
    and EIS, 240
    enterprise BI&A, 248, 250, 255
    functional BI&A, 248–251, 255
    large-scale DSS, 239–240, 247, 248
    self-service BI&A, 248
Business model, 161
Business organizations, 346
Buyer-seller negotiation, 181

C
Calendar application, 47
Candidate rules, 352, 360, 362
Career-oriented network, 91
CDSS, *see* Clinical decision support systems (CDSS)
Choice problematic, 227
Chronic diseases, 192
Citation network, 20
Classical DSS, 9
Clinical decision support systems (CDSS), 25, 27, 29, 30
Closeness centrality, 62
Co-citation network, 20, 21
Cognitive biases, 242
Collab-Net project
    application, 71
    data collection, 70
    DSS interface, 70
    EWG-DSS Coordination Board, 56
    ISMICK conference, 57
    MCDA scientific domain, 70–71
    network analysis (*see* Social network analysis)
    Version 1, 57–58
    Version 2, 58–59
    Version 3, 59, 60
    Version 5, 59–60
    Version 6, 69, 70
Collaborative AI, 37–39
Communication acts, 176, 177
Communication behavior analysis, 176
Communication component, 175
Communication dimension, negotiation
    automate checklists, 177
    communication media classification, 176
    comprehensive survey, 176
    electronic, 175
    empirical research, 177
    face-to-face, 175
    media richness theory, 176
    negotiators, 175
    NSS, 175
    relationship, 175
    schmoozing, 175
    semantic meaning, 177
    situational diagnosis, 177
    text mining, 177
Communication media, 176, 181
Communication patterns, 178
Communication research, 169
Communication variables, 182
Competition density, 162

Competitive positions (CP), 6, 7
Completeness
    data mining, 204
    definition, 203
    DEX models, 204
    machine learning, 203
    PD_manager, 203
    robustness, 203
Comprehensibility
    black-box model, 205
    challenges, 206
    data mining, 205
    definition, 205
    expert modeling, 205
    interpretability, 205
    machine learning, 205
    open-box model, 205
    trustworthy AI, 206
Computational intelligence, 12–13
Computer-based ILEs, 326, 329, 334, 335, 341
Computer simulation
    development of DSSs, 329
    and graphical interface, 329, 331
    ILEs (*see* Interactive learning environments
        (ILEs))
    in management science, 329
    sustainability management policies, 326
    urban environments' characteristics, 326
Concession-based negotiation
    AC-AT, 173
    alternatives, 170
    autonomous software agents, 172
    concession behavior, 171, 173
    confidential preference information, 174
    curves, 171
    face-to-face negotiations, 170
    issues, 169
    multi-issue negotiations, 171
    NSS, 171, 172
    post-settlement phase, 174
    preference models, 174
    SNT approach, 170
    trade-offs, 173
Concession making, 181
Consistency
    data mining, 205
    definition, 204
    dominance, 204, 205
    logical and preferential, 204
    MCDA, 204
Consumer Neuroscience, 228
Contemporary behavioral economics, 241, 242
Convenience
    data mining, 206

    definition, 206
    DSS modeling, 206
    expert modeling, 207
    MCDA, 207
    software libraries, 206
    XMCDA, 207
Co-occurrence analysis, 98
Corona virus
    crisis management, 289
    outbreak, 289
Correctness
    assessment, 203
    data mining, 202
    decision problem, 202
    decision task, 202
    DSS model, 203
    medication change, 203
    quantitative measures, 202
Cost-benefit analysis (CBA), 383, 385
Counterfactual analysis, 354, 365
COVID-19, 275, 289, 319
CP, *see* Competitive positions (CP)
CRExplorer software, 21
Critical success factors (CSF), 7
Crossing country borders, 142
CSF, *see* Critical success factors (CSF)
Cultural context, 42
Customer loyalty, 346
Customer satisfaction
    ANFIS, 348
    business organizations, 346
    complex solution, 364–365, 375
    consumer behavioral analysis, 346
    criteria/satisfaction dimensions, 346
    dataset, 355, 356
    fsQCA (*see* Fuzzy-set qualitative
        comparative analysis (fsQCA))
    fuzzy and rule-based DSS, 346, 347
    fuzzy-set theory, 347
    independent and dependent variables, 347
    MCDA, 346
    methodology, 348
    MILP techniques, 347
    MUSA, 346, 347, 355–358
    MUSA-INT method, 347
    neuro-fuzzy approach, 347
    parsimonious solution (minimal prime
        implicants), 365–366
    performance evaluation, 347
    quality approaches, 346
    quantitative methods and data analysis
        techniques, 346
    robustness analysis, 366–367
    rule-based systems, 347

and service quality measurement, 346
statistical regression method, 348
Cynefin concept, 43

D

Data analysis, 90, 122, 193, 194, 276, 278
Data analytics
    DSS in the pig industry, 320
    See also Big Data Analytics (BDA)
Data driven autonomous artefacts, 159
Data-Driven Decision-making (DDD), 281,
        285, 295
Data fusion, 13
Data manipulation, 158, 159
Data mining, 192, 194, 201, 206, 208
Data processing (DP), 2
Data warehouses
    BI infrastructure, 119
    definition, 118, 119
    design, 121
    ETL, 118, 120
    implementation, 118, 119
    OLAP querying tools, 119
    operational and analytical application, 119
    operational data bases, 117
DCA, *see* Document co-citation analysis
        (DCA)
Decision aid
    MCDA (*see* Multi-criteria decision aid
        (MCDA))
    quantitative approaches, 260
Decision Analysis models, 194
Decision autonomy, 158
Decision biases, 181
Decision context
    chaotic context, 44
    complex contexts, 44, 45
    complicated, 44, 45
    cultural, 42
    Cynefin concept, 43
    decision-making situations, 43
    decision support, 43
    descriptive and predictive analytics, 45
    disordered, 44
    DSS, 44
    machine learning techniques, 45
    natural language, 42
    philosophical basis of DSS, 44
    philosophy, 45
    physical, 42
    process, 45
    sentence, 42
    social-psychological, 42

technology, 45
temporal, 42
time, 43
traditional processing, 44
types, 42
Decision Deck initiative, 207, 208
Decision EXpert (DEX) model
    characteristics, 199
    classification accuracy, 201
    decision analyst, 200, 201
    decision table, 201
    digression, 201
    machine learning algorithms, 201
    medication change, 199, 200
    modeling process, 199, 200
    performance, 200
    PPMI data, 200
    qualitative MCDA, 199
    structure, 199
Decision makers (DMs), 181, 193
    criteria scaling constants, 219
    decision-making process, 214, 218
    decision rules, 216
    partial information, 214
    preference statements, 215, 218
    preference structure, 214, 215
    rationality, 214
    recommendation, 215
    scaling constants, 214
    traditional methods, 215
Decision-making
    using BD
        challenges, 286
        collaborative applications, 286–287
        critical and crisis management
            applications, 288–290
        data-centrism, 284
        DDD, 281, 284–285
        dynamic-temporal spatial applications,
            287–288
        Lambda Architecture, 291
        logistics and SCM applications, 288
        proposed high-level model, 292–294
        tools and technologies, 282–284
    characteristics, 250
    cognitive systems, 242
    democratization, 244–245
    dual process theory, 239–242, 255
    evaluation criterion, 259
    overarching theory, 242
    Simon's phase model, 241, 250
Decision-making processes, 37, 47, 79, 82
Decision neuroscience
    behavioral results, 229–232

Decision neuroscience (*cont.*)
  experiments, 228–229
  MCDM/A methods, 227
  modulation, 227
  tools, 227
Decision rules, 216
Decision support, 37, 154, 208
Decision support systems (DSSs)
  analytics, 37–40
  approaches and technologies, 193
  articles in 1990-1999
    centrality measures, 23, 24
    co-citation network, Vosviewer, 23, 24
    journals, 23
    management decision-making theory,
      24
    Vosviewer co-occurrence network, 22,
      23
  articles in 2000-2009
    CDSS, 25
    centrality measures, 26–27
    citing and cited articles, top ten journals,
      26–27
    Vosviewer co-occurrence network, 25,
      26
  articles in 2010-2019
    CDSS, 27, 29
    centrality measures, 28–29
    journals cited, 27–28
    Vosviewer co-occurrence network,
      27–28
  artificial intelligence, 37–40
  benefits, 2
  BI&A system (*see* Business intelligence
    and analytics (BI&A))
  big data, 8
  "black box" approach, 3
  categories, 15
  characteristics, 3, 328
  classical contribution, 9
  community, 52
  components, 3, 328
  computational intelligence, 12–13
  conference, 2
  cost-effectiveness, 2
  data processing (DP), 2
  decisional process, 329
  decision-making theories/models,
    328, 330
  definition, 193
  development and use, 245, 246
  DEX (*see* Decision EXpert (DEX) model)
  digital economy, 8
  DSS-81, 2

  DSS articles, 17, 18
  economics, 2
  and EIS, 36, 240, 247, 253, 255
  ESI VI—EURO Summer Institute, 52
  EURO Working Group, 53
  evolution (*see* DSS evolution)
  feature, 3
  future development, 9
  GIS, 29
  grand challenges, 34, 46–47
  history, 1, 8, 33
  human–computer systems, 97
  humans, 39
  human–technology collaboration, 38
  IFPS-based DSS projects, 1
  and ILEs, 341–342 (*see also* Interactive
    learning environments (ILEs))
  information systems development process,
    3
  innovations, 1
  IS journals, 29
  knowledge-driven, 193
  MIS, 33
  model-based approach, 192
  model-driven, 193
  modelling approaches, 29
  models, 192
  naïve Bayes, 98
  for pig industry (*see* Pig industry)
  probability estimates, 9
  productivity, 2
  professionals, 9
  projects, 192
  as radical movement, 239, 244–246
  research literature, 192
  scientometric techniques, 15–16
  self-confident professionals, 9, 327
  semi-structured and unstructured decisions,
    15
  small-scale bespoke systems, 249
  strategic management (*see* Strategic
    management, DSS)
  technological tools, 34, 47
  technologies, 34
  the 2020s, 9–13
  users' priorities, 2
  using BD (*see* Decision-making)
  Web of Science Categories (SC), 17
  Woodstrat, 9
  WOS (*see* Web of Science (WOS))
Decision tasks, 202, 240, 241, 245, 249, 250
Decision trees, 194, 195, 197, 198, 202–206
Deep learning algorithms, 155
Degree centrality, 61

DFM, *see* Dimensional Fact Model (DFM);
    Document feature matrix (DFM)
Dichotomous variables, 349
Digital coaching systems, 13
Digital economy, 8, 12
Digital fusion, 13
Digitalization, 9, 10, 12, 13
The digital disruption, 10
The digital revolution, 10
D2I joint industry, 13
Diligent and Involved behavior, 232
Dimensional Fact Model (DFM), 121
Distributive action, 176
Document co-citation analysis (DCA), 20, 21
Document feature matrix (DFM), 100
Dominance, 205
Dominance-Based Rough Set Analysis
    (DRSA), 205
Dominance relations, 224, 231, 233
DSS, *see* Decision support systems (DSSs)
DSS capabilities, 182
DSS design, 40–42, 46
DSS evolution
    artificial intelligence, 36
    computer science, 36
    concepts, 36
    database management, 36
    decision-making processes, 37, 47
    decision support, 37
    GDSS, 35
    general managerial problem formulation,
        37
    IBM-PCs, 35
    local area network technology, 36
    nonspecialized environments, 35
    OLAP, 36
    personal computers, 35
    programming languages, 36
    research, 36
    in 1970s, 34
    in 1980s, 35, 36
    technology tool development, 37
    word processing software, 35
DSS projects, 192
Dual process theory of decision cognition,
    239–242, 255

E
E-commerce platforms, 155
E-commerce software, 82, 87
Economic models, 162
Eigenvector centrality, 62
Electroencephalogram (EEG), 228

Electronic communication, 175
Electronic media, 175, 182
Elicitation procedure, 217
Embedding, 195
Emotional contagion, 178
Emotional dimension, negotiation
    analysis, 179
    dimensional classification, 180
    economic outcomes, 178
    emotional patterns, 179
    empirical research, 179
    experimental systems, 180
    face-to-face negotiations, 178
    inferential processing, 178
    intra-and interpersonal effects, 178
    NSS, 178
    peaceful solution, 180
    psychophysical indicators, 180
    research, 178
    self-monitoring devices, 180
    short-term/long-term emotions, 180
    situational factors, 178, 179
    text mining, 179
    transition probabilities, 180
    two/three-dimensional coordinate systems,
        179
Emotions as social information (EASI), 178
Empirical research, 177, 183
Enterprise systems, 145, 146
ERP systems, 146
EURO Working Group on Decision Support
    Systems (EWG-DSS), 73–75
    Collab-Net (*see* Collab-Net project)
    events, 53–56, 73–74
    history, 52–53
    publications, 53–56, 73–74
Executive information systems (EIS), 36, 240,
    247, 253, 255
Experimental systems, 180
Expert modeling, 194, 195, 201, 208
Explanation methods, 206
Extract-Transform-Load (ETL), 118–120

F
Face-to-face negotiations, 175
Fairness, 155, 159
Financial decision-making (FIRST), 192
FITradeoff DSS
    choice MCDM/A problems, 218
    consequences matrix, 218
    criteria scaling constants, 218, 220, 221
    criteria weights evaluation, 219
    criterion "quality organization", 224

FITradeoff DSS (*cont.*)
  DM preference, 222
  dominance relations, 224
  elicitation process, 224
  equivalence distance, 219
  flexible elicitation process, 221
  graphical visualization, 223–225
  hypothetical alternative, 219
  hypothetical consequences, 220, 221
  inequalities, 222, 223
  LP, 223
  MAVT, 222
  MCDM practical problems, 225
  paradigms, 233
  POA, 223
  preference information, 225
  preference relations, 221
  problem data visualization, 220
  ranking problematic, 223
"5C requirements", DSS models
  completeness, 203–204
  comprehensibility, 205–206
  consistency, 204–205
  convenience, 206–207
  correctness, 202–203
Flexible and Interactive Tradeoff (FITradeoff),
    214, 218
Flexible elicitation process, 221, 222
Formal bargaining models, 172
Formal verification, 160
Fornell's model, 346
Framing biases, 181
Fuzzy rule-based DSS, 347
Fuzzy-set qualitative comparative analysis
    (fsQCA)
  actual causal combinations, 350, 353
  application, 349–350
  asymmetry, 349
  Boolean algebra, 349
  candidate rules, 360
  causal combinations, 350, 352
    actual causal combinations, 363
    and consistency of combinations,
        361–362
    firing levels, 360–362
    initial survived and non-survived
        combinations, 362
    MF values, 360
  causal complexity, 349
  causal conditions (satisfaction criteria),
        358–360
  complex and parsimonious solutions,
        354
  coverage score, 355
  in customer satisfaction analysis, 348
  data and fuzzy-membership matrix, 358,
        359
  equifinality, 349
  free software, 358
  fuzzy-membership scores (MFs), 358, 359
  fuzzy-set principles, 349
  initial Truth Table, 363, 364
  intermediate solutions, 354–355
  Kosko's formula, 363
  MFs, 351
  min-max theorem, 353
  multiple regression analysis, 348–349
  necessary conditions analysis, 349, 350,
        358–359, 370
  overall satisfaction, 362–363
  QCA-based applications, 349
  QM algorithm, 364
  regression-based methods, 348
  remainders, 350
  revised (final) Truth Table, 363, 364
  set-theoretic consistency, 363, 371–372
  steps, 351
  sufficient conditions, 349, 350
  surviving causal combinations, 350,
        352–353
  T1 FLS approach, 350
  variable configurations, 348
Fuzzy-set theory, 346–348

G
GAIA plane, 266–269
Geographic Information Systems (GIS), 23,
    29, 108, 110
Graphical visualization, 217, 226
Group decision support systems (GDSS),
    23–25, 35
Group support systems, 240

H
History of DSS
  behavioral economics, 240
  IT-based management support, 243–244
  small-scale information systems, 240
  3-gap framework, DSS models, 248, 253
Hit Rate (HR) variable, 230
Holistic evaluation, 219, 224, 227
Human agency, 206
Human agents, 144
Human decision-making, 193

I

ICDSST, *see* International Conference
  on Decision Support System
  Technology (ICDSST)
ICE framework, 181
Ideal negotiation process, 183
Inconsistency, 222
Indefinition behavior, 232
Inferential processing, 178, 179
Information and Communication Technologies
  (ICT) generation, 275
Information systems, 80
Information technology (IT), 15
Integrative/distributive communication
  behavior, 183
Intelligent DSS, 240
Interactive learning environments (ILEs)
  applications
    learning, 335
    multiplayer online formats, 334
    research validation, 335
    urban sustainability, 335
    virtual reality and AI, 334
  "basic rules", 340
  as complementary tools, 326
  components, 331–332
  computer-based, 326, 329
  decision-making theories/models, 328, 330
  definition, 329–330
  DSS architecture and characteristics,
    327–329
  graphical interface, 329
  key features
    no-threatening environment, 333–334
    realism, 333
    transparency, 333
    user-friendly environment, 334
  limitations and research, 340–341
  SD-based ILE, 327, 337 (*see also* System
    dynamics (SD))
  simulation model, 329, 331, 336
  SUSTAIN project, 336, 340
  urban metabolism, 327, 340
International Conference on Decision Support
  System Technology (ICDSST), 53,
  56
International political negotiations, 174
Internet of things (IoT), 145, 274, 300
Interpersonal effects, 178
Interpretability, 205
Intrapersonal effects, 178
IoT orientations, 145

Issues-communication-emotions (ICE), 169
IT-based management support, 240
  decision support approaches, 250–253
  history, 243
  large-scale BI&A systems, 248–251
  MIS, 243–244 (*see also* Management
    information systems (MIS))
  supporting decision-making, 240–241

K

Kano's model, 346
KM approaches, 131
KM frameworks, 131
KM life cycles, 131
KM measurement, 131
Knowledge-based rule systems, 348
Knowledge-based view (KBV), 130
Knowledge boundary, 131, 142–143
Knowledge building, 130
Knowledge-driven DSS, 194
Knowledge economy, 130
Knowledge fusion, 13
Knowledge holding, 130, 131
Knowledge management (KM)
  cognitive gaps, 131
  conferences, 130
  disciplinary guidance, 130
  international journals, 130
  process frameworks, 130
  reviews, 131
Knowledge management-based DSS, 240
Knowledge mobilisation
  barriers, 142
  business decision-making, 146
  cognitive gaps, 131
  conditions, 131
  enterprise systems, 146
  ICT technologies, 145
  KM process model, 131
  networks, 144
  project management, 146
  publications, 146
  SLR approach (*see* Systematic literature
    review (SLR))
Knowledge motivation systems, 144
Knowledge networks, 143, 146
Knowledge spanners, 143
Knowledge taxonomy and ontology, 143
Knowledge transfer, 143, 146
Knowledge translation, 143
Knowledge utilisation, 130, 131
Kosko's formula, 353, 363

L

Large-scale BI&A systems, 248–249, 251, 253, 255

Large-Scale Spatial-Temporal Decision-Making (LSSTDM) tools, 287

Learning DSS, 39

Liability issue, 157

Linear programming (LP), 216, 218, 223

Livestock precision farming (LPF), 311

LNBIP books, 53

Logrolling, 182

Louvain method, 63

M

Machine decision-making, 193

Machine learning, 184

Macro-level analysis, 179

Management information systems (MIS), 33, 146, 154, 305

   classical total MIS, 243

   criticism, 244

   developers, 243

   and EIS, 247, 253, 255

   goal, 243

   IT-based management support, 243–244

   orthodoxy, 239

   socio-economic context, 243

Manufacturing, 146

Market positions (MP), 6

MCDA, *see* Multiple Criteria Decision Aid (MCDA)

MCDM partial information methods

   aggregation function, 215

   arbitrary linear inequalities, 217

   combination, 217

   decision-making methods, 218

   DMs, 215

   FITradeoff, 218

   flexibility, 217

   interactive procedures, 216

   linear programming models, 217

   literature work, 216

   nonstructured elicitation processes, 215

   parameters, 215

   preference statements, 217

   robust axiomatic structure, 217

   scaling constant of criterion, 215, 217

   structured elicitation process, 216

   synthesis, 217

Mean absolute error, 348

Meat processing plants, 301–306, 309, 310, 315, 320

Mechanism design theory, 158

Media richness theory, 176

Membership functions (MFs), 351, 352, 358–360, 366, 367, 371–374

"Microworlds", 329–330

Min-max theorem, 353

MIS, *see* Management Information Systems (MIS)

Mixed Integer Linear Programming (MILP) techniques, 347

Mobile devices, 123

Model-based DSS development

   data, 194, 195

   Decision Analysis, 194

   developing, 192

   DEX, 192

   embedding, 192, 195

   expert modeling, 194, 195

   "5C requirements" (*see* "5C requirements", DSS models)

   implementing, 192

   models, 192

   PD_manager (*see* PD_manager healthcare project)

   user types, 207

Model-driven DSS, 193–194, 306, 312

Modern DSS, 328

Modern software, 16

MP, *see* Market positions (MP)

Multi-agent systems, 155

Multi-attribute utility and value (MAUT), 260, 384

Multiattribute value theory (MAVT), 215, 229, 230

Multi-criteria decision aid (MCDA)

   evaluation table, 261, 262

   non-classical methods, 260

   outranking methods, 260 (*see also* PROMETHEE (MCDA outranking methods))

   problem, defined, 261

   quantitative approaches, 260

   relations, 261

Multi-criteria decision analysis (MCDA), 204, 207

Multi-criteria decision-making, 80

Multicriteria Decision-Making/Aiding (MCDM/A)

   behavioral studies, 227

   DMs' behavior, 228

   DM's rationality, 214

   Neuroscience approach, 227

   partial information methods (*see* MCDM partial information methods)

preference modeling, 214
theoretical research, 214
Multicriteria preference modeling
decision neuroscience, 227–232
DMs (*see* Decision makers (DMs))
FITradeoff (*see* FITradeoff DSS)
MAVT, 215
partial information methods, 214–218
MUlticriteria satisfaction analysis (MUSA)
method
action and improvement diagrams, 357–358
added value function, 357
advantages, 346
average impact indices, 356
characteristics, 346
and fsQCA results, 348
MUSA-INT method, 347
original dataset, 355, 356
value functions, 357
Multi-issue negotiations, 173
Multiple Criteria Decision Aid (MCDA), 346, 368
and CBA, 385
environmental and social criteria, 385
methods for decision-making, 383–386
scientific domain, 70–71
SUMPs in Greek Municipalities, 386–387
sustainable mobility planning, 387–390
transport facilities, 385
Multiple regression analysis, 348–349
MUSA-INT method, 347

N

Naïve Bayes text classification
agriculture domain-related documents, 99
DFM, 100
document, 99
machine learning technique, 99
non-agriculture domain-related documents, 99
publications, 1990-2019, 105
results, 103, 104
word cloud per 5-year period, 105, 106
"Naïve" Data Mining, 208
Nanoscience, 321
Nanotechnology, 38
Natural language processing (NLP), 91
Negative emotions, 182
Negotiation agents, 180
Negotiation problem, 181

Negotiation processes
collective decision, 168
communication, 169
communication component (*see* Communication dimension, negotiation)
complex phenomena, 168
economic effects, 183
economic outcome, 168
efficiency and fairness, 168
emotional level (*see* Emotional dimension, negotiation)
empirical research, 168
ICE framework, 169, 170
implementation phase, 168
NSS (*see* Negotiation support systems (NSS))
prescriptive model, 183
Negotiation research, 183
Negotiation support systems (NSS), 240
additive utility model, 172
affective, 180
comprehensive, 183
conceptual issues, 184
decision support component, 169
design, 168
development, 167
early systems, 171
literature, 172
multi-issue negotiations, 171
substantive behavior, 181
supports, 168, 171
text-based communication channels, 179
Negotiator preferences, 172
Negotiators' decision making, 181
Neuroeconomics, 228
Neuro-fuzzy approach, 347
NeuroIS approach, 228
Neuromarketing, 228
Neuroscience experiments
application, 233
bar graphs and tables, 228
choice problematic, 228
experiments, 228
knowledge areas, 228
MAVT concepts, 229
MCDM/A, 228
neuroeconomics, 228
NeuroIS approach, 228
visualizations, 228
Neuroscience tools, 220, 227, 719

NLP, *see* Natural language processing (NLP)
Non-digitals, 10
NSS Negoisst, 177

O

Online analytical processing (OLAP), 25, 36,
    89, 116, 119, 123
Open-box/white-box/glassbox models, 205
Open source software (OSS), 83–85
Optimal negotiation processes, 177
Ordinal regression analysis, 346
Organisational culture, 142
Organisational studies, 161
Organisation structure, 142
OSS, *see* Open source software (OSS)

P

Pandemic outbreak, COVID-19, 275, 289, 319
Pareto efficiency, 168
Pareto improvement, 174
PD_manager healthcare project
    aim, 196
    a-priori accuracy, 197, 198
    data mining, 196
    decision models, 199
    decision trees, 197, 198
    DEX (*see* Decision EXpert (DEX) model)
    machine learning algorithms, 197
    medication change, 196
    patients monitoring, 196
    problematic issues, 198
    requirements, 196
    single verbal value, 197
Philosophical basis, DSS, 37, 38
Physical context, 42
Pig industry
    computer-based systems
        GTEP, 306
        IFR SA company, 309
        KPI comparisons for pig production,
            306, 307
        management software in Spain,
            308–309
        MIS and posterior DSS., 305
        origin of DSS tools, 305
        personal computers (PC) on farm, 306,
            308
        pig farming subsystem, 308
    decision-making problems
        farming units, 302
        feeding, 302
        human perception, 305
        interactions/impact, 304–305
        main decision problems, 302–304
    DSS development, 310–314 (*see also* Pig
        supply chain (PSC))
    evolution, 299
    model-driven DSS, 306, 312
    pig meat, 300, 310, 311
    research and society, 314–315
    research on decision models, 310–312
Pig management, 302, 303, 308
Pig supply chain (PSC)
    agents, 301
    competitive, 304
    coordination, 304
    development of DSS
        AI, 320
        benchmarking performance, 317–318
        biotechnology, 320–321
        consultancy, 317
        nanoscience, 321
        new digital technologies, 317
        sustainable DSS and standardisation,
            317
        virtual reality (VR), 320
        whole chain view and digitalisation,
            318–319
    farming and meat processing subsystems,
        300–301
    fattening farms, 301
    pig production systems, 300
    standardisation and integration, 313–314
Positive emotions, 182
Potentially optimal alternatives (POA), 223
Power/political/pragmatic boundary, 142
Predictive analytics, 37
Preference disaggregation model, 346
Preference modeling
    alternatives, 227
    choice problematic, 227
    decomposition perspective, 226
    elicitation procedures, 226
    FITradeoff, 226, 227
    graphical and tabular visualizations, 227
    graphical visualization, 226
    holistic evaluation, 226
Preference-modeling model, 204
Preference relations, 221
Preference statements, 215, 217
Prelude projects, 46
Prescriptive analytics, 37
Principal component analysis, 12
Principle of dominance, 204
Production position (PRO), 7
Productivity, 7

PROMETHEE (MCDA outranking methods)
AI algorithm, 270
applications, 269, 270
decision support methodology, 260
complete ranking, 265
differentiation, 261
GAIA plane, 266–269
MCDA problem, 261
negative outranking flow, 264
notations and structures, 260
notion of incomparability, 261
partial ranking, 265
positive outranking flow, 264
preference functions, 262, 263
visualizations, 262, 270
extensions and sensitivity analysis tools,
268
outranking methods, 172
popularity and usability, 268
software, 268–269
Public Transport system, 388, 389, 393

Q

Quality organization criterion, 224
Quantitative measures, 202
Quine-McCluskey (QM) algorithm, 354, 364,
365

R

Radio-Frequency Identification (RFID) cards,
290
RAs, *see* Research Areas (RAs)
Rational economic model, 241
Raw material, 157–158
Reciprocity, 173
Recommender systems, 155
Regression-based methods, 348
Research Areas (RAs), 17–19
Research collaboration
DSS community, 52
Resource-dependent concession, 172
Responsibility, 157
Return on net assets (RONA), 7, 12
Reverse engineer, 174
Reverse inequality, 221
Risk and crisis management, 288–290
Robotics, 38
RONA, *see* Return on net assets (RONA)
Rule-based methods, 346, 368
Rule-based syntax, 365, 366
Rule-based systems, 346, 347

S

SBU, *see* Strategic business units (SBU)
Schmoozing, 175
Scientometrics, 15, 16
SDSS, *see* Spatial Decision Support Systems
(SDSS)
Security, 160
Self-monitoring devices, 180
Self-service BI, 124
Set-theoretic consistency, 363, 371–372
Single negotiation text (SNT), 174
Single Vertex Connected Components, 67
SIPA model, 182
SLR descriptive analysis
findings, 135
geographic distribution, 135, 141
JKM, 135
journals, 135
Learning Organisation, 135
papers collection, 135, 136
publications, 135, 141
research methods, 135
SLR thematic analysis
advanced ICT technologies, 145–146
boundary-crossing mechanisms, 143–144
business decision-making, 146
knowledge boundaries, 142–143
SMAC Advisor, 203
Smart farming, 312, 321
Social choice theory, 162
Social learning, 144
Socially unconstrained behavior, 175
Social media
big data, 80, 81
data, 80
data analytics, 81
data-based decision-making, 80
decision-making, 80
multi-criteria decision-making, 80
social big data, 81
user-generated content, 92
Social media data, decision-making process
AHP, 84, 85, 90
consumers' decision-making, 80
costs, 83
criteria, 85, 86
e-commerce software, 82, 87
emergency cases, 81
fuzzy criteria, 83
indicators, 85, 86
knowledge base/community support
indicators
Udemy, 88
YouTube, 88

Social media data, decision-making process
 (*cont.*)
  knowledge sources, 85, 86
  online forum Stackoverflow, 85
  open source products, 83
  OSS, 83–85
  Search, Google search engine, 85, 86
  social media marketing, 80
  software alternatives, 83
  software products, 82
  Stackoverflow, 87, 88
  TCO, 83–85
  WooCommerce system, 86, 87
Social network analysis, 19, 21
  authorship evolution, 65–66
  centrality measures, 61–62
  co-authorship network
    in 1989–2019, 67–69
    in 2019, 66–69
    in EWG-DSS events, 61, 63
  component, 61
  co-topic relationship, 62, 64
  data collection and preparation, 64–65
  data sets, 61
  graph metric, 61, 62
  Louvain method, 63
  work done, 62
Social-psychological context, 42
Social psychology, 169, 241
Social responsibility, 157, 164
Spatial decision support systems (SDSS), 21,
    25–27, 30
Statistical analysis, 177
Statistical regression method, 348
Strategic business units (SBU), 4–7
Strategic management, DSS
  competitive positions, 6, 7
  computer technology, 5
  CSF, 7
  emerging strategy, 5
  market positions, 6
  Memo module, 8
  production position, 7
  production sold, 7
  profitability and capacity limits, 7
  RONA, 7
  SBU, 4–7
  vs. strategic planning, 4
  Woodstrat, 5–8
Substantive behavior, 181, 182
Substantive decision support, 179
Success Region Based Decision Rule, 229, 230

Supply chain management (SCM), 288, 295
Sustainable efficiency index (SEI), 387, 390,
    396
Sustainable mobility, 386–390
Sustainable transport planning, 380
Sustainable Urban Mobility Plannings
    (SUMPs)
  CBA method, 383
  classic transportation models, 396
  cycle methodology, 383
  guidelines, 381
  implementation, 387–391
  phases and steps, 381–382
  planning cycle, 382
  ranking, 391–396
  specification, 385
  urban mobility, 381
  in Urban Mobility Package, 382
Symbolic models, 205
Syntactic and semantic boundaries, 143
Systematic literature review (SLR)
  advantage, 132
  Boolean operators, 133
  cross-referencing, 133
  database searching, 133
  descriptive analysis (*see* SLR descriptive
    analysis)
  features, 131
  five-stage methodology, 132
  inclusion and exclusion criteria, 133, 134
  literature search, 133
  quality assessment criteria, 134
  research method, 131
  scientific databases, 133
  subjective bias, 134
  thematic analysis (*see* SLR thematic
    analysis)
  topic areas, 132
  two-stage paper selection, 134
System dynamics (SD)
  modeling methodology, 336
  modeling principles and tools, 327
  SD-based ILE, 327
    cooperative decision-making game, 338
    decision board, 337, 338
    investment options, 338
    parameters, users' success, 336–337
    simulation run, 339
    SUSTAIN project, 336
    systems thinking, 336
    tutorial page, 337
    urban sustainability environment, 335

T
Tabular visualization, 227, 229, 231
TCO, *see* Total cost of ownership (TCO) approach
Temporal context, 42
Text messages, 176
Text mining, 177, 179, 184
Theta and Alpha activities, 232
Time-dependent concessions, 172
Total cost of ownership (TCO) approach, 83–85
Transparency, 206
Travel industry, 162
True concessions, 173
Type-1 fuzzy logic systems (T1 FLS) approach, 350
Typical model representations, 194

U
University research program, 13
Unsupervised learning, 90
Urban environments, 326, 327, 336, 340
Urban metabolism, 327, 340
Urban sustainability, 326, 335, 336, 339, 340
Urban transportation, 380, 382
User-generated content, 92
UTilités Additives (UTA) method, 226

V
Value creation, 173
Variance of errors, 348
Veracity of big social media data
    API, 89
    data analysis, social network, 89–90
    disadvantages, 89
    guidelines, 92
    HTML, 89
    OLAP, 89
    social media services, 89

    structuredness-veracity matrix, social media sources, 90
    traditional HTML web pages, 89
    veracity challenges, 91–92
    Web 2.0, 89
    web crawlers, 89
    Web scraping process, 89
Virtual reality (VR), 320, 321, 334
Visualization of similarities (VOS), 101
VOS, *see* Visualization of similarities (VOS)
Vosviewer software, 20, 22, 98
Voting, 163
"Vs" of Big Data, 145, 276

W
Weather application, 47
Web of Knowledge, 16
Web of Science (WOS)
    citation structure, 16
    Clarivate Analytics, 16
    DSS journal articles (1990-2019), 17–19
    environmental and medical areas, 18
    ISI Subject Categories, 17, 18
    journals, 16
    Research Areas (RAs), 17–19
    search parameters, 16
    search terms, 16
Web of Science Categories (SC), 17
Word processing software, 35
World Wide Web, 89
WOS, *see* Web of Science (WOS)

X
XMCDA standard, 207

Y
Yield management models, 162

Printed in the United States
by Baker & Taylor Publisher Services